Biological Psychology

Eugene H. Galluscio *Clemson University*

Biological
Psychology

MACMILLAN PUBLISHING COMPANY *New York*

Editor: Christine Cardone
Production Supervisor: Charlotte V. Hyland
Production Manager: Nicholas Sklitsis
Text Designer: Leon Bolognese
Cover Designer: Robert Freese
Cover Photograph: Magnetic resonance image of a brain, sagittal section. From
Custom Medical Stock Photo.
Photo Researcher: John Schultz
Illustrations: FineLine Illustrations, Inc. and Cecile Duray-Bito

This book was set in Baskerville by Polyglot,
printed and bound by R. R. Donnelley & Sons Company.
The cover was printed by Phoenix Color Corp.

Macmillan Publishing Company
866 Third Avenue, New York, New York 10022

Collier Macmillan Canada, Inc.

LIBRARY OF CONGRESS CATALOGING-IN-PUBLICATION DATA

Galluscio, Eugene H.
    Biological psychology/Eugene H. Galluscio.
        p.   cm.
        Bibliography: p.
        Includes index.
        ISBN 0-02-340472-8
        1. Psychobiology.   2. Human evolution.   I. Title.
    QP360.G337   1990
    152–dc20   89-12384
                                                                                CIP

Printing: 1 2 3 4 5 6 7   Year: 0 1 2 3 4 5 6

To My Wife Carolyn

Preface

This book was written to be used as the primary text for college-level courses in biological psychology, physiological psychology, psychobiology, neuroscience, and other courses that are primarily concerned with the biological mechanisms underlying human behavior. Much of the book is based on lectures from the junior and senior level courses in biological psychology and the physiology of sensory information processing that I teach at Clemson University. This book will also be of interest to anyone who wishes to have a better understanding of the biological bases and the evolutionary origins of contemporary human behavior. The content is unique from other texts now available because it presents biological psychology within an evolutionary framework. You will find that the evolution of behavior is integrated within every chapter, unlike other texts in biological psychology that briefly address evolution in one chapter.

Orientation of the Text

Why write a book like this? I pose this question to myself as much as I address it to you. There are, I suppose, two reasons. First, as I already noted, existing texts in this area do not present the material as I do in my courses—from an evolutionary perspective. It is my firm belief that understanding the origins of behavior, how it evolved over time, is essential for the complete understanding of contemporary human behavior.

The second reason is a bit more complex. Biological psychology is a complex, difficult, and technical area of study. Consequently, most books on this topic are jammed with specific facts, difficult concepts, complex figures, anatomical drawings, and hundreds of references to specific research findings (which is also true with this book). Frequently, my students have complained to me that the texts I have assigned for my courses are either "too difficult," "hard to follow," "awkwardly written," just plain "boring," or they suffer from some combination of these problems.

I have been teaching undergraduate and graduate level courses in this field for almost 20 years. In that time I have thoroughly enjoyed introducing my students to the excitement, wonder, and joy that I have experienced from the study of the biological mechanisms that underlie animal and human behavior. Teaching is one of the great pleasures of my life. Teaching biological psychology has been most gratifying for me not only when I am able to communicate my own fascination with this material, but also when I can transmit that same sense of awe and excitement to my students. And this was my goal in writing this book.

Writing Style

From the outset I have made every effort to make this book as readable and enjoyable as it is informative. Reviewers have characterized my writing style as "clear," "precise," "flowing," "comfortable," "exciting," and "engaging." If they are correct in their assessment, I have accomplished exactly what I set out to do: I have presented this difficult material in an enjoyable and meaningful package.

Throughout the book, I have attempted to include many of the examples and life experiences that I use in my lectures. Doing so helps to bring the material to life. Wherever possible, I have tried to demonstrate how this area of science is important and relevant to our daily lives. Additionally, I have attempted to convey something about the lives and characteristics of the wonderful and interesting people whose research efforts have contributed to the wealth of information that we share in the text. Finally, where it seemed appropriate, I have tried to sprinkle the text with humor. A little sugar coating on the pill helps to make the reading more enjoyable.

Organization of the Book

The sixteen chapters of the text may be conveniently divided into four parts. The first part, comprised of Chapters 1 through 4, is basic to the remainder of the text and should be read before the other chapters. The remaining three parts of the book are relatively independent from each other and may be assigned in an order that suits the particular needs of the user.

Part 1   The first four chapters introduce the fundamental concepts of biological psychology. Chapter 1 provides a historical perspective to the study of brain and behavior and introduces the reader to the major concepts of modern evolutionary theory, including the most recent thinking concerning the path to the evolution of humans. Chapter 2 provides the reader with an understanding of the building blocks of the central nervous system, the neurons. This chapter introduces cell theory; discusses the evolution, anatomy, and physiology of the neuron; and provides a thorough review of intraneuronal and interneuronal communication. Chapter 3 presents the physical and functional anatomy of the central and peripheral nervous systems and discusses the dynamic interaction between the neuronal and hormonal (endocrine gland) control systems. Much emphasis is placed on understanding the anatomy of the nervous system from an evolutionary perspective. Chapter 4 introduces the evolution of sexual reproduction strategies and relates sexual reproduction to species generation. The dynamic roles of genetic coding, sex hormones, and brain organization are discussed as they relate to gender differentiation and sexual behavior.

Part 2   Chapters 5 through 9 are concerned with the biological mechanisms for sensing, integrating, and responding to environmental events. Chapter 5 provides some basic principles concerning the evolution, structure, and function of sensory systems. These basic principles are discussed more specifically and in greater detail in Chapters 6 through 9. Chapter 5 also provides a thorough review of the sensory coding theory and introduces the "real world simulation" model of sensory processing. Purposefully, the visual system is covered (Chapters 6 and 7) in greater detail than the other sensory systems. The anatomy, physiology, and peripheral and central sensory neural coding strategies are discussed for each sense modality, with some emphasis placed on the evolution of the sensory systems from earlier, more simple forms. The integration of body senses and motor behavior is addressed in Chapter 9.

Part 3   Brain mechanisms associated with basic consummatory behaviors (eating and drinking), arousal and sleep, and behavioral plasticity (learning) are addressed in Chapters 10, 11, and 12. Central brain systems and the peripheral mechanisms for the control of eating and drinking behavior are covered in Chapter 10. Additionally, the theories of hunger and satiety are addressed in this chapter. Chapter 11 deals with the nature and evolutionary significance of biological rhythms. The latter part of the chapter addresses the neural and biochemical models for sleep, dreaming, and arousal. Chapter 12, which covers the plasticity of neural systems (learning), is by far the largest chapter in the text and may be divided into two parts. The first part outlines various forms of learning and provides the reader with an understanding of learning at the subcellular and cellular levels in simple (invertebrate) organisms. The second part of the chapter is concerned with brain mechanisms associated with learning in complex organisms, including humans.

Part 4   The final four chapters of the book discuss the most complex forms of human behavior: emotions, language, abnormal behavior, and higher cognitive functions. The neuronal, neurochemical, and hormonal factors underlying emotional behaviors in animals and humans are addressed in Chapter 13. The latter part of this chapter concentrates on the neural systems for aggressiveness and reward (pleasure) in the mammalian brain. In Chapter 14 we look at the malfunctioning brain and the associated "abnormal" behaviors. Abnormal behaviors are defined and classified in terms of their symptoms and etiology. Consistent with the nature of the text, the emphasis is placed on the genetic, neuronal, and biochemical correlates of schizophrenia and the major affective disorders.

The first part of Chapter 15 addresses communication in a variety of animals, emphasizing the evolution of complex language in humans. The latter half of the chapter deals with the brain mechanisms for the control of language and speech, including the evidence for lateralization of language function in humans. Chapter 16 is unique for books of this type. It is an attempt to bridge the gap between the philosophy of mind and biological psychology. After reviewing several philosophical theories concerning the nature of the mind and the relationship between the mind and brain, a tentative brain model for consciousness is presented. Finally, we examine correlations between lesions to the brain and conscious mental experience.

Features

It may be helpful to become familiar with some of the features of the book before reading the first chapter. Each of the chapters opens with a **chapter outline** of the topics that are to follow. This is followed by a list of **learning objectives**. These brief statements identify skills or behavioral outcomes that should result from reading and studying the material in the chapter. Additionally, the learning objective statements should alert and guide the reader to the major concepts and principles covered in the chapter. The learning objectives are written in a way that should allude to the depth of understanding expected of the reader. For example, statements such as "know," "understand," or "be able to" are asking for a greater depth of understanding than statements such as "recognize" or "be familiar with." Reviewing the learning objectives after studying the chapter may serve as a "self-test" of how well the reader assimilated the major concepts in the chapter.

The end of each chapter contains a **chapter summary**, a short list of **recommended readings**, and a list of the **key terms** that have been introduced in the chapter. The chapter summary is intended to be used as a concise review of the major issues and concepts covered in the chapter. The chapter summary and the learning objectives (given in the beginning of the chapter) are useful pedagogical tools that provide feedback about the completeness of understanding of the chapter material. The list of recommended readings provides additional sources that deal in greater depth with the material covered in the chapter. As the term suggests, the key terms list is comprised of the definitions of important terms introduced in each chapter. Each new term is clearly identified in **boldface** type within the text.

Spotlights and Observation Boxes

Integrated throughout the book are blocks of text identified as "Spotlights" and "Observations." These features serve two important purposes. First, they are strategically placed to provide breaks in the text—a change of pace that will add diversity and interest to the reading. More important, the Spotlights and Observations are designed to supplement the body of the text with additional information.

Generally, the **Spotlights** contain material that amplifies, clarifies, or in some way adds to major points within the text. The **Observations** tend to be shorter points of interest that are related to the issues being discussed in that portion of the chapter.

Biological Art and Figures

Much thought and energy has gone into the selection and quality of the illustrations and figures for this book. Each figure was selected for sound pedagogical reasons and not to fill up space.

There is a full color insert containing photomicrographs and other illustrations that benefit from the use of color. Careful consideration was given to the selection of each of the color plates. In each case the plate was chosen because the use of color added to the *instructional value* of the figure; that is, besides being attractive and interesting to look at, the color plates are used in places where it would have been difficult or impossible to communicate the same information without the use of color. References to the color plates are made throughout the text.

Color is also used in many of the figures and anatomical drawings found in the body of the text. Again, our goal was to use color intelligently to enhance the informative value of the figure. Color is used to delimit the boundaries of critical structures, differentiate one structure from another, identify structures having similar function, highlight important features within a figure, identify the structures and pathways of neural systems, and color is used in other ways that make the figures more meaningful.

Acknowledgments

Like most authors, I would like to consider this to be my book. That, however, is far from the truth. This book is, in reality, the product of many minds in addition to my own. First, I must acknowledge the hard work of hundreds of talented and creative scientists whose research data represent the building blocks of this text. I also owe a great deal to the reviewers whose constructive criticism of the original versions of the manuscript has helped improve this text in many ways:

Tony Bourgeois, Texas A&M University
Michael Crabtree, Washington and Jefferson College
Stephen F. Davis, Emporia State University
Jon H. Kaas, Vanderbilt University
George F. Michel, DePaul University
Jack R. Nation, Texas A&M University

Donald Novin, University of California, Los Angeles
Elizabeth Adkins Regan, Cornell University
Earl L. Simson, Rhode Island College
Roger K. Thomas, Texas Christian University
R.C. Wilcott, Case Western Reserve University

Additionally, I want to acknowledge the talented staff at Macmillan, including Charlotte Hyland, the production supervisor, and a host of copyeditors, artists, photoresearchers, proofreaders, and the like who have all contributed immeasurably to the "look" and "feel" of the book. I am particularly thankful to Christine Cardone, the Psychology Editor at Macmillan, for her support, encouragement, and technical assistance on countless aspects of the production of the book.

Finally, I must acknowledge the contribution of my wife, Carolyn, to whom I dedicate this book. This project would not have been completed without her gentle support, infinite patience, and understanding.

Eugene H. Galluscio

Brief Contents

Contents

Chapter 12
**Learning and
Remembering
page 452**

Introduction

It is early morning. The dew still lies heavily on the trees. A male empis fly has been busily making a large silken ball from small secreting organs located in the tarsi of his front legs. The ball, nearing completion, now nearly equals his size. As he finishes his labor, the fly deftly attaches a silken thread to the ball to be used as a handle during his nuptual flight.

Within a few minutes after he carries the ball aloft the male fly locates the female. She is larger than the male, thicker in the abdomen, and full of eggs. The male approaches her from the front, presenting the ball as an apparent gift to induce receptivity. After the female has accepted the ball, holding it with her legs, the male circles behind her to complete the copulatory act. As soon as the union is completed the male departs in search of his next meal and the female promptly discards the ball.

The sexual behavior of the empis fly may seem strange to you. It is clear that the male fly exerts a great deal of energy, first making and then transporting the silk ball, only to have it unceremoniously discarded by his mate! Most observers of nature know that, perhaps with the exception of humans, animals are very efficient in the conservation and use of energy. Why then do we see this apparent waste of energy? The silken ball is what ethologists call a **releaser,** a stimulus that is designed to trigger some form of behavior; in this case, sexual receptivity.

The question remains: Why does the empis fly need this elaborate, and apparently uneconomical, mechanism to ensure mating? A more interesting question may be: How did this unusual sexual behavior come to be?

Figure 1.1
a. The male empis fly carrying a silk ball.
b. The male presents the ball to the female as part of their mating courtship. The ball serves as a releaser for copulation and in some species may protect the male from being eaten by the voracious female.

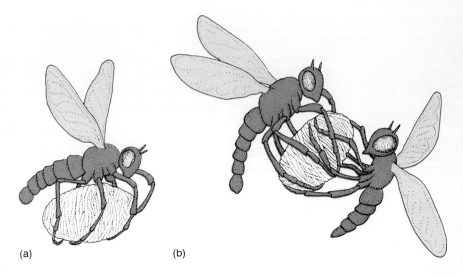

(a)   (b)

I have selected this example from the family Empididae for two reasons. First, because one of the main themes of this book is concerned with the *evolution* of behavior. The contemporary sexual behavior of this little fly is difficult, if not impossible, to understand fully unless we know something about how it evolved. Second, the Empididae provide a unique insight into the evolution of behavior because there are several contemporary species of the family that evidence the intermediate stages that led to the evolution of this unusual form of sexual behavior.

Most species of empis flies feed almost exclusively on other insects. In the mating behavior of the most ancient forms, the male first kills an insect and presents it to the female prior to mating. This behavior seems to have the adaptive advantage of providing the female with a food source so she will not need to hunt following mating and, therefore, she will be able to remain with the eggs for a longer period after they are deposited. Additionally, these empis females are voracious insectivores, and the prize kill may serve to protect the male against being her next meal!

In more modern forms, the male wraps the freshly killed insect in a thin layer of silk before presenting it to his mate. The silken wrap apparently helps to prolong the consumption of the gift, further protecting the male and increasing the time that the female will remain to protect the fertilized eggs. Still more modern species capture smaller prey and thicken the wrapping until it approximates the shape of a silk ball. In the most advanced forms, the ball alone serves as the releaser eliciting receptive sexual behavior from the female. Some species of empis have evolved to feed only on plant matter. It is interesting to note that the silk ball releaser is still required before the females of these vegetarian species will accept a mate.

When viewed from a historical, evolutionary perspective, the mysterious sexual behavior of the more advanced forms of empis flies is no longer so mysterious. Behavior evolves just as physical attributes evolve, by building on earlier forms. Without some understanding of the past, we cannot hope to understand fully the present. This is no less true for human behavior than it is for the behavior of empis flies. Here then is one of the primary themes of this book. Contemporary behavior can be understood fully only when we understand how and from what it evolved.

Human behavior is distinctly human because it has a history that is unique from that of all other contemporary species. In the following chapters, I will attempt to explore this history with you and from that evolutionary perspective explain the biological bases of human behavior.

Biological Psychology

Chapter 1

Evolving

Psychology as a Field of Science

The Heart or the Head?
Localization or Unity of Function?
Nature or Nurture?
What Is the Nature of Mind?

The Theory of Evolution

Genes and Evolution
Natural Selection
The Development of New Species

The Evolution of Humans

The Mammals
The Primates
The First Hominids
Early Humans
Review

Contemporary Humans

The Importance of Language
Parallel Evolution

Chapter Learning Objectives

After completing the study of this chapter, you should have achieved the following learning objectives.

1. Be able to discuss the historical development of psychology as an academic discipline.

2. Understand how early beliefs concerning the nature of humans continue to influence modern thought.

3. Be familiar with the essential issues of concern to the physiological psychologist.

4. Be able to compare and contrast Darwinian and Lamarckian theories of evolution.

5. Be able to discuss how genes influence both the physical and behavioral characteristics of organisms.

6. Know how the theory of natural selection accounts for the generation of new species.

7. Be able to trace the major evolutionary developments that led to humanlike primates, starting from the evolution of the mammals.

Psychology as a Field of Science

Individuals have always had an interest in the factors that arouse, direct, and sustain their behavior as well as the behavior of the other people and the animals that share their environment. The *scientific* study of behavior is, however, relatively new. Psychology is a little over 100 years old. That may seem old to you, but compared to other academic disciplines, such as mathematics and astronomy, psychology is quite new.

Like other emerging disciplines, psychology drew heavily upon the knowledge base of other, well-established fields of study. Psychology, as an academic discipline, has its roots in philosophy—the study of knowledge and knowing—and biology—the study of life. Philosophers also devised what is known today to be the scientific method. This is a complex set of rules that allows us to ask questions about the world around us and to be relatively assured that we will arrive at reliable conclusions. A review of some of the basic questions that faced early philosophers and biologists is instructive, because these questions continue to color our thinking today, and many of the questions are still hotly debated by modern psychologists.

The Heart or the Head?

The Egyptians believed that the heart was the source of life. This may seem rather silly to us today, but on reflection, we should not be too surprised at their thinking. The Egyptian physicians and anatomists noted that the heart had connections to all parts of the body (the arteries and veins). They also noted that when a person was under stress or emotionally aroused, the heart became noticeably more active, and when the heart stopped, death followed. The Egyptian belief that the heart was the site of life's forces is reflected rather clearly in the practice of the embalmers who carefully preserved the heart but quite unceremoniously discarded the brain before burial.

The Mesopotamians, the Hebrews, and even some of the Greeks believed that the heart, and not the brain, was the source of intelligence and feelings. Of the Greeks, Homer and Aristotle were among the more notable who came down strongly on the side of the heart. It was Aristotle who observed that he could not find the equivalent of the human brain in many of the invertebrate animals that he studied, but all animals seemed to have a heart and circulatory system. Because all of the animals he observed evidenced behavior and possessed a circulatory system, he concluded that the heart must be the source of emotions and intelligent behavior.

In our culture the heart is still closely associated with emotions (although, doubtlessly, few would seriously consider it to be the *physical source* of feelings). If you doubt this, simply insert the word *heart* or *brain* in the following sentences.

1. When I heard her sad story, my _____ went out to her.
2. I love you with all of my _____ .
3. She practiced until she was able to recite it by _____ .
4. He has a _____ as cold as ice.

Wouldn't we all feel a little odd singing "I left my *brain* in San Francisco" or listening to a rendition of "*Brain* and Soul"?

Democritus was among the first to propose that the brain was the seat of intelligence and the soul, although he also believed that anger was in the heart and desire was to be found in the liver! It was Hippocrates, however, and his colleagues who were the first to use empirical methods to demonstrate that the brain was indeed the source of behavior. Hippocrates noted that injury to the brain could produce various deficits in behavior, including impaired intelligence, speech and motor defects, and irrational thought. Hippocrates also noted that "irritation" to one side of the brain produced its effect on the other side of the body (Clark & O'Malley, 1968).

In the third century B.C., knowledge concerning the anatomy of the body increased rapidly. In Alexandria, Herophilus and Erasistratus performed systematic dissections of the human nervous system. They identified the ventricles in the brain, differentiated between the cortex and the underlying white matter, observed that nerves were different from the blood vessels originating in the heart, and even distinguished between nerves associated with "movement" and nerves associated with "feeling." Some 500 years later, Galen put to rest the heart-versus-brain debate. In carefully controlled experiments, he examined the behavioral effects of lesions made to the brains of laboratory animals. Galen demonstrated beyond doubt that the brain was the control center for physical and mental activity.

Once the brain was clearly identified as the organ that was the source of behavior, attention was directed at understanding how the brain was organized and how it functioned. The advent of the microscope led to the discovery of cells in nervous tissue. In 1885, exactly 200 years after Robert Hooke discovered the existence of cells in plants and blood, O. F. C. Deiters described in very accurate detail the anatomy of the neuron. At about the same time, the brilliant German physicist and physiologist Hermann von Helmholtz was attempting to study the speed of conduction through nerves. Using techniques that he developed to measure the velocity of a bullet as it exited the barrel of a gun, von Helmholtz found that nerve transmission was only about 30 meters per second. Previously it was thought that nerve transmission, like electrical conduction through wire, was close to the speed of light. To his credit, von Helmholtz related nerve transmission time to delays in our ability to react to events in the environment. Perhaps for the first time, human performance was related to measurable physiological events in the nervous system.

As scientists gathered more information concerning the nature of nerve transmission, a perplexing question arose. It became apparent that all nerves send essentially the same type of message. How, then, is it true that what we experience from nerve signals varies from one nerve to another? How can it be that optic nerves, auditory nerves, and tactile nerves all carry essentially the same type of signal, yet we *perceive* the signals so differently? The answer can be found in Johannes Müller's **doctrine of specific nerve energies**.

Müller, one of the most important figures in nineteenth-century physiology, proposed that what we perceive from a given neuron depends as much on where the neuron's signal is sent as on the type of signal being sent by the neuron. Müller suggested that each sensory nerve was *specific* for the *quality* and the *location* of its information. For example, a touch receptor in the tip of the finger could only report information about touch in that specific location. If the cell were stimulated by other means, electrically for example, the signal sent by the cell would still be perceived as touch. Taking this one step further, if the same neuron was stimulated by any means anywhere along its path to the brain, it would still report touch at the tip of the finger! Apparently, the quality and location of sensation for a given neuron are determined by the place in the brain that receives the information. Consequently, if Müller's doctrine was correct, it must also be true that the brain can be divided into functionally different areas. This notion was once hotly debated.

Localization or Unity of Function?

Is the brain organized like a kidney or the liver in that all parts of the organ do essentially the same thing? Or is the brain organized in a more complex way? Can the brain be divided into smaller structures, each having a somewhat unique function? These would seem to be relatively straightforward questions.

For early philosophers, however, these questions seemed rather tricky. If the brain is the locus of intelligent behavior, the rational soul, then it must not be reducible to smaller parts. (Here the word *soul* has a complex meaning grounded in religious dogma. It connotes, among other things, the special gift of reason given exclusively to humans by a divine being, the key to immortality, the place where metaphysical animal spirits interact with the physical body.) It was unthinkable that a metaphysical and immortal life force, especially one given to us by God, could be divided into parts like an orange. This belief in an indivisible soul was so strong that the great French philosopher, mathematician, and anatomist, René Descartes, pronounced that the soul could only be located in one place within the brain, the pineal gland. The only logic leading to this decision was that all other structures in the brain are doubled. There are identical structures in the left and right halves of the brain. Only the pineal gland, located on the midline of the brain, is a signal structure (see Figure 1-1). Even Marie-Jean-Pierre Flourens, one of the greatest nineteenth-century anatomists and the man who successfully demonstrated that lesions to the cerebellum and medulla produced predictably different behaviors, fell victim to this type of thinking. When Flourens found that large lesions to the cortex failed to produce any loss in function, he concluded that the cortex must be the locus of the indivisible soul.

The first real challenge to the idea of an indivisible brain came at the beginning of the nineteenth century from a rather unusual source, the phrenologists (Young, 1970). Franz Joseph Gall's **phrenology** was based on a clever and unique, but fundamentally incorrect, notion that the mental character of men and women could be divided into a number of moral and intellectual faculties which were reflected in the conformation of the skull. Gall assumed that each mental faculty was located in a well-defined area of the brain. He proposed that individuals who evidenced a greater-than-average amount of a given faculty would concurrently have an enlarged brain for the area that represented that faculty. He took this line of reasoning one fanciful step further by suggesting that the enlarged brain area would produce a measurable enlargement of the skull above it. The idea was as captivating as it was incorrect. Gall attracted many loyal followers, and **cranioscopy** (reading the faculties by palpating bumps on the skull) became quite popular (Figure 1-2).

Although phrenology was based more on fiction than fact, it nonetheless stimulated a useful controversy, and much effort was generated in search of brain regions that could be localized by function. In 1825, Jean Baptiste Bouillaud, studying brain-injured patients, showed that focal lesions could produce paralysis of a small group of muscles without affecting other muscles in the body. In 1861, Paul Broca received instant recognition when he reported a case of aphasia (loss of speech) resulting from a small tumor in the left anterior, frontal lobe. A few years later, Carl Wernicke reported that a lesion to the left posterior temporal lobe produced a qualitatively different form of aphasia. In 1870, two German physicians, Gustav Fritsch and Edward Hitzig, demonstrated that direct electrical stimulation to the cortex of the brain produced muscle action on the opposite side of the body. They showed that increasing the electric current increased the number of muscles that were affected and that moving the stimulating probe to different locations affected different muscle groups. Localization of function was proven beyond a reasonable doubt.

Figure 1-1
a. René Descartes at the court of Queen Christina of Sweden. *b.* Descartes believed that the body was controlled by the soul, which he placed in the pineal gland. He believed that the pineal gland was the only possible location for the soul because it was centrally located in the brain and was the only structure that did not have a homologous structure in each side of the brain. (Courtesy of the Granger Collection.)

(a)

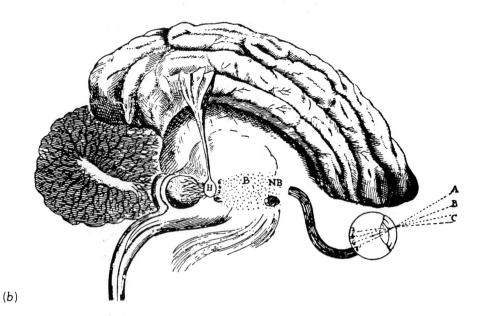

(b)

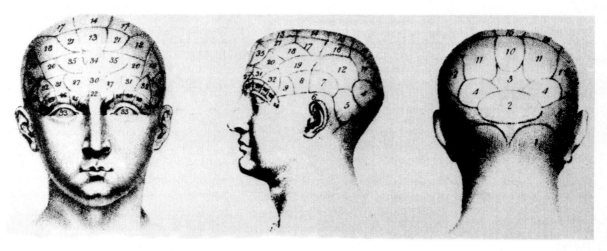

Figure 1-2
Three views of a map of a skull used by phrenologists to measure the faculties of the brain. Gall, the founder of phrenology, believed that the brain could be divided by function into 27 faculties. Further, he maintained that the local area of the brain representing a given faculty would vary in size depending on the degree to which that particular faculty was evident in the individual. Gall maintained that the portion of the skull situated over the brain area for a given faculty would also vary in size. Consequently, the phrenologist incorrectly believed that measuring the contours of the skull (cranioscopy) provided an indirect measure of the person's faculties. (From the National Library of Medicine.)

Nature or Nurture?   A question that intrigued early philosophers and one that has greatly influenced modern psychology was concerned with the origins of knowledge. Specifically, philosophers were interested in knowing whether knowledge was determined at birth (inherited) or whether it was the product of experience. It is interesting to note that originally the question was posed as a dichotomy. That is, early philosophers were prone to believe that all behavior was either innately determined or acquired through experience. This dichotomy of philosophical thought has come to be known as the **nature–nurture controversy**.

Plato, a proponent of the nativist school of thought, believed that all knowledge was determined at birth. He delighted in making public demonstrations to support his views. It was reported that, with his students close in tow, he would have an uneducated beggar or slave state the Pythagorean theorum simply by asking him a few, somewhat leading, questions. Thus he demonstrated, at least to his own satisfaction, that the knowledge of the theorum had always been there and only needed to be drawn out.

At the other end of the nature–nurture continuum, the English philosopher John Locke proposed that humans were born in a "tabula rasa," or blank slate. Locke, using this analogy, suggested that all knowledge could be attributed directly to the individual's personal experiences. Locke maintained that we come into the world knowing nothing, ready to have our living experiences recorded in our brain, as if on a blank slate.

These opposing views concerning the origins of knowledge created great debates among the early psychologists. Proponents of the nativist (nature) side of the controversy held to the deterministic belief that behavior was primarily (if not totally) determined by our genetic inheritance. Supporters of the empiricist (nurture) position attempted to explain all behavior in terms of experience and learning. One ardent supporter of the empiricist school of thought went so far as to try and demonstrate how an unhatched chick *learns* to peck its way out of the shell!

These views of the origins of knowledge seem too narrow and rigid to us today. Modern psychologists are likely to pose the nature-versus-nurture question quite differently. We are more likely to accept the notion that both biology and experience play important roles in what we know and, therefore, in how we behave. The more appropriate question would be, How do our genetic potential for experience and our life experiences interact to produce what we know, and in what ways do they determine how we behave?

We know, for example, that monozygotic twins (twins that developed from a single fertilized egg that split apart after the first cell division) have the identical genetic makeup. They should have the same genetic potential, and therefore, we would expect them to have very similar patterns of behavior. If the twins are separated soon after birth and raised in very different family environments, they will behave much more differently than they would if they were raised together. Their behavior, however, may still be more similar than that of two unrelated and genetically disparate individuals who were raised together. Children who have **chromosome 21 trisomy (Down's syndrome)** will have greatly impaired intellectual capability. They are, however, trainable, and with very special care they can be taught a variety of useful behaviors. However, no environmental conditions, not even those most conducive to intellectual development, will allow a child with Down's syndrome to have the verbal and quantitative skills of nonhandicapped individuals.

Clearly, genetics and the environment both influence behavior. It is our task to understand how these two factors interact in a dynamic way throughout the life span of the individual and produce the behaviors we observe. To this we must add—how did the behavior evolve over evolutionary time to its present form?

What Is the Nature of Mind?

Now we turn to the most difficult, and in some ways, the most fundamental question in the field of psychology: What is *mind*? The word itself can mean many different things to us, and this fact may make the question more perplexing. Unfortunately, mind is sometimes associated with the concept of the soul. Often it is equated with the ability to reason, and because of these two associations, mind is thought (perhaps erroneously) to be unique to human beings.

Socrates argued that only humans possess the ability to reason and that this unique mental ability distinguishes us from all other living creatures. This Socratic "man/beast" dichotomy has had a profound influence on many subsequent philosophies concerning the nature of mind. As was mentioned earlier, Descartes, the very influential French philosopher, proposed that mind was a special gift from God and that it was unique to human beings. Descartes reasoned that, coming from God, mind must have a metaphysical nature, and therefore, it cannot be subjected to direct analyses and measurement, as can the various parts of the body. This is the crux of the mind/body controversy that is still with us today. The Cartesian philosophy of mind and body—that is, Descartes' conception—presents us with several interesting problems.

1. Mind and body are qualitatively different; mind is metaphysical, and body is physical (this kind of philosophical thought is called **dualism**). The metaphysical mind, located in the pineal gland, according to Descartes, cannot be subjected to empirical study.

2. Because mind and body are qualitatively different, there must also be two kinds of energy or life forces: one force that drives the physical part of the being and another form of energy, the mental force of the mind. This idea requires us to accept the notion that there must be a mechanism by which the metaphysical mind interacts with the physical body (this notion is called **interactionism**). This raises another difficult question: How does a nonphysical force interact with and control a physical force?

Opposing the concepts of dualism and interactionism are the monist philosophies of mind and body. As the name would suggest, the monist philosophies accept the presence of only one kind of existence. Two extreme monist views are those held by the mentalists and the materialists. **Mentalism** proposes that only mind exists. The physical world is viewed as nothing more than a product of the mind. That is, the physical world (including me and the book you hold in your hands) exists only in your mind, similar to a dream. It is difficult to argue against the mentalist point of view, and it is impossible to disprove. Of course, it is also impossible to prove! **Materialism**, as you may have guessed by now, proposes that there is only a physical world and that the mind does not exist. If we define mind not as an ethereal soul but as conscious experiences, such as the ability to reason and to reflect on our thoughts, or simply as mental activity, it is difficult to take materialism very seriously. In fact, critics of this philosophy are apt to point out that materialists have not only lost their souls, they have also lost their minds!

More contemporary and rational monist philosophies attempt to accommodate both mind and body within their view of existence. That is, they attempt to integrate mental and biological attributes of mind. The two monist positions that seem to be most consistent with the empirical data on brain and behavior are the **identity** and **emergent property** views (Sperry, 1970a).

The identity position asserts that mind and brain activity are the same thing—they are simply two ways of describing the same physical state. This view is analogous to two levels of description of a newspaper cartoon. The cartoon could be described in terms of the individual dots of print that compose the picture or in terms of the overall impression made by all of the dots. In either case, we would be describing the same thing, but the descriptions would sound very different indeed. One problem with the identity position is that it fails to identify just how consciousness is a physical property of the brain. Why do some brain activities equal conscious experiences, whereas others—for example, cerebellar and spinal activities—do not?

The emergent property view is closely related to the identity position. It equates the property of mind with the organization and interaction of the nerve cells in the brain. The quality of mind is thought to be the outcome of the organization and the dynamic interaction of the many neurons in the brain, not of the neurons themselves. The analogy frequently used to describe emergent properties is the qualitative changes in matter that we see in many chemical reactions. For example, think of what happens when we take molecules of oxygen (O_2) and hydrogen (H) and join them chemically to form water (H_2O). Two clear gases join to produce a liquid having very different physical qualities than the gases of the component molecules. The mind, then, can be thought of as an emergent physical property of many neurons in dynamic interaction. The quality of mind changes as the combination of neurons and their patterns of interactions change.

In the last chapter of this book we deal with this issue in much greater detail. When we do, I defend my position that the term *mind* is, in many ways, counterproductive to our understanding of behavior, and I offer an alternative terminology.

The Theory of Evolution

The primary theme of this book is the *evolution* of behavior. Consequently, it is important for us to have a basic understanding of the theory of evolution and the process of evolutionary change.

In the middle of the nineteenth century two amateur naturalists, quite independently, developed the modern theory of evolution. **Charles Darwin**, the son and grandson of famous scientists in their own right, and **Alfred R. Wallace**, who had a less advantaged background, were both fascinated by the wide variety of life forms that populated the planet. Each began, in his own way, to speculate on what mechanisms were at work in nature to produce the wide number and diversity of species.

The theory of evolution they were to formulate was not the first to be widely accepted. Their best-known predecessor, **Jean-Baptiste de Lamarck**, had posited a theory that was based on the notion that species evolved through the transmission of **acquired characteristics**. Lamarck proposed that organisms, when confronted with varying environmental conditions, were somehow able to register these environmental pressures and change in order to meet them. Lamarck believed that organisms change through life experiences, and then subsequently, pass these changes on to their progeny. This is simply not so. Modern genetics has demonstrated that the organism is determined almost entirely at the moment of conception. Furthermore, the potential characteristics the organism will be able to transmit to future generations are also fixed at conception. How, then, do organisms change over time, and how are new species generated?

Genes and Evolution **Evolution** is the process by which succeeding generations or organisms change in both their physical appearance and their behavior. At one level this change can be viewed as the long-term adaptations of species to environmental pressures. At a more basic level, evolution is seen to be what it actually is—changes in the molecular organization of the organism. Specifically, the evolutionary process is determined by changes in the genes.

The gene is a complex molecule of **deoxyribonucleic acid (DNA)**. The DNA molecules, which are found in the nucleus of the cell, carry the blueprints for all of the biochemical activity that sustains and duplicates life. Each DNA molecule is made up of components called **nucleotides**, which are, in turn, composed of four different bases that are anchored to a lattice of sugar-phosphates. The complete DNA molecule is actually two long twisted strands that form a double helix. I discuss the DNA molecule and its function in reproduction in detail in Chapter 4.

Small segments of the DNA molecule serve as the code or template for the production of specific proteins, including enzymes and hormones, that are essential for normal life. For our purposes, it is important to understand that the exact sequence of the bases on the DNA molecule govern the chemical composition of the proteins they produce. Because proteins determine the structure and function of the individual cells of the body, it follows that the specific morphology, physiology, and behavior of the organism are determined to a great degree by its unique genetic composition.

Each species has a typical chromosomal complement that may be characterized by the number, size, and shape of the chromosomes. I have already noted, with the example of Down's syndrome, that anomalies and deviations to chromosomes, although rare, do occur. Polysomy, the presence of an additional chromosome from a pair (e.g., Down's syndrome), is just one of several possible chromosome aberrations. Segments of a chromosome may be absent (deletion), repeated (duplication), or inverted. Such aberrations start a chain of events as the molecular level of organization that eventually influence the morphology and function of cells, tissues, organs, and the whole organism. Most chromosomal aberrations have profound effects. In fact, it is thought that the majority of these mutations go undetected, because they are lethal and the organism is incapable of surviving to birth.

The duplication of genes, which occurs as cells divide, is a very precise process. On occasion, minor errors may occur that lead to a difference in just one or more base pairs out of the hundreds of pairs that compose a gene. These relatively slight "errors" in the genetic blueprint may then be replicated and passed on to the next generation. The effect of most chance alterations to genes is likely to be detrimental or neutral. Sometimes, these genetic errors prove to be advantageous, providing some physical or behavioral characteristic that better suits the organism for survival. These random errors in the replication of genes increase the genetic variation of the species. As you will see later, genetic variance is an important factor in the development of new species.

Natural Selection   Although Darwin and Wallace developed similar theories of evolution quite independently, and they both presented papers on this subject at the same meeting of the Linnaean Society in London, it was Darwin's book *On the Origin of Species* (1859) that popularized the theory. Darwin also was the subject of much criticism because he included human beings as part of the biological continuum proposed in his theory, something that Wallace was unable to accept. For these reasons, Darwin, rather than Wallace, is best remembered as the originator of the theory. Darwin's theory proposed a process of **natural selection** that differed

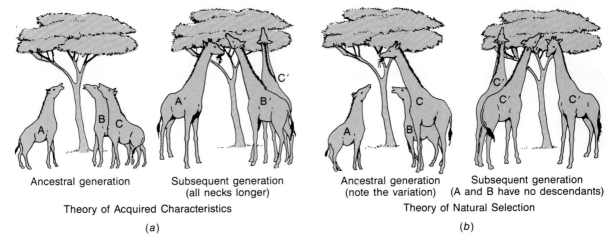

Ancestral generation | Subsequent generation (all necks longer)

Theory of Acquired Characteristics

(a)

Ancestral generation (note the variation) | Subsequent generation (A and B have no descendants)

Theory of Natural Selection

(b)

Figure 1-3.
a. Depiction of the Lamarkian theory of the inheritance of acquired characteristics, which assumes that the ancestral generation is modified by experience and that all members—A, B, and C—contribute equally to the subsequent generation. *b.* Depiction of the natural selection model of evolution. Here only animal C is well adapted to environmental pressures and is the only member to survive, have descendents, and contribute to the gene pool of subsequent generations. (From Downs & Bleibtreu, 1972.)

markedly from Lamarck's theory in that it recognized the importance of individual differences within species. Natural selection proposes that the competition for food, space, and available mates determines which organisms within a given species will be successful. By virtue of their edge in competitiveness or their ability to attract mates, these individuals increase the probability that they will pass their characteristics on to the next generation (Appleman, 1970).

Figure 1-3 depicts the difference between Lamarck's theory, based on the transmission of acquired characteristics and the Darwinian process of natural selection. As can be seen, the Lamarckian view does not allow for individual differences in the ancestral generation, and it presumes that the organism changes as a result of environmental conditions and then passes these changes on to subsequent generations. The natural selection model shows that the individuals in the ancestral generation who are most suited to meet environmental challenges survive and have the opportunity to pass on their more adaptive characteristics.

If the process of natural selection determines the evolution of morphological changes in organisms, how are separate and distinct species determined? Before we can address this question, we need to review some of the factors and mechanisms that influence the process of natural selection.

The Power of Genetic Influences on Behavior

The definition of any species, including human beings, depends on the form and organization of the brain just as much as it does on the shape of the body. The genetic makeup of the individual controls the structure and function of the brain, and therefore, the genes are critical for the expression of behavior.

Genetic material (the gene) is resistant to change. It is that relative invariance that accounts for the stability of most characteristics of a species over time. Mutations of the genetic material, although rare, do occur. The number of different genetic mutations in humans is greater than you might imagine. Over 2,000 mutations have been described in humans, and at least 300 of them are known to have an effect on the central nervous system. Most of these "local" mutations produce subtle effects that are not readily detected (Gullotta, Rehder, & Gropp, 1982).

In addition to localized mutations, more drastic changes can occur on the chromosomes. Their number and length can change. A fragment of a chromosome may be lost or translocated to another chromosome. We have already noted the far-reaching effects of Down's syndrome, which occurs when an extra chromosome of the 21st pair is present.

Mutations are not the only indicators of the power of the gene on behavior. The genetic influence on behavior can be demonstrated quite well using selective-breeding techniques. I should point out that controlled genetic studies are not done with humans for several reasons. First, it obviously is not ethical to breed humans selectively. Second, you typically

need large numbers of subjects, making the cost of housing and maintenance an important consideration. Additionally, the animals need to reach sexual maturity quickly. Otherwise, the researcher might not live long enough to see the results of his or her selective breeding on several generations. Finally, it is helpful to use simple animals with less complex genetics and more simple nervous systems. For these reasons, geneticists are likely to use insects like the fruit fly and small mammals like mice as their subjects.

Now consider the following examples. The first example demonstrates the effect of crossbreeding two closely related species of crickets, *Teleogryllus commodus* and *Teleogryllus oceanicus*. The males of each of these species have their own distinctive song that is clearly innately determined. If the larvae, are raised in isolation (and thus never hear the song) or are made deaf, the song they produce remains unchanged. When the two types are crossed, the hybrids of the first generation produce a song that is different from either parent's. If the hybrids are mated back to a parent, the progeny of this pairing produce yet another song. See Spotlight Figure 1-1a. As was true of the songs of the parent species, the songs of the hybrids are totally independent of experience. Clearly, these differences in behavior reflect the genetic makeup of the individual (Bentley, 1971).

You may feel a bit uncomfortable with an example using invertebrates. Now consider Tryon's well-known selective breeding for maze-learning ability in rats (Tryon, 1940). Tryon tested a group of

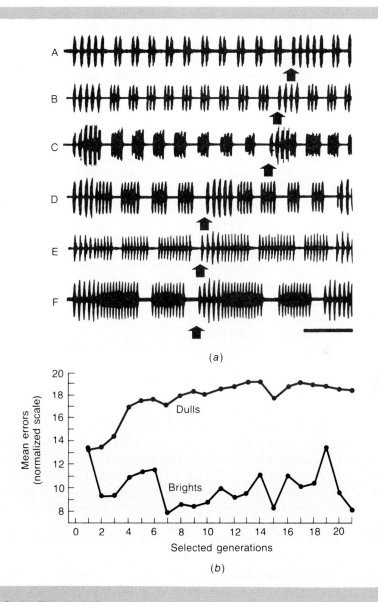

(a)

(b)

Spotlight Figure 1-1
a. The heredity of song in the cricket. A and F are the songs of the male
T. oceanus and *T. commodus*. From B to E are the songs of various hybrids.
Each song is composed of a chirp, indicated by the arrow, followed by a series
of trills. The bar at the bottom left represents 100 msec. (From Bentley, 1971.)
b. The distribution of maze errors for successive generations of rats that were
selectively bred for high and low errors. (From Tryon, 1940.)

rats on their ability to travel through a complex maze for a food reward. Following the testing, he selected the animals with the best performance and mated them. Similarly, he selected the rats that had the highest number of errors and mated them. In the next stage of his research, Tryon tested the progeny of the first group of rats. The offspring of the good performers were tested, and only the best performers of that group were retained for mating. In a like manner, the offspring of the poor performers were tested, and only those with the worst performance were retained for mating. This same procedure was repeated for the next 20 generations.

As you can readily see from the data in Spotlight Figure 1-1b, the performance of the selectively bred rats became very different in just a few generations. By the seventh generation there was practically no overlap between the "maze bright" and the "maze dull" animals. Clearly, intelligent behavior (at least as intelligence can be measured by the rat's ability to navigate through a maze for a food reinforcement) can be modified through selective breeding.

1. **Relative adaptive fitness:** This is the combination of physical and behavioral characteristics of a given species that permits it to compete and survive in one or more environments. Fitness is mediated at all levels—at the level of the individual, the group, and the entire species population. The term **multiple causality** refers to the notion that changes in adaptive fitness may, and probably do, occur simultaneously at all levels of genetic potential—the individual, the group, and the species population.

2. **Gametic potential:** Gametes are the sex cells of organisms that have sexual reproduction. Each parent provides half of the genetic material for the offspring; that is, the male sperm and the female ovum each contain half of the genetic material required to produce a genetically complete egg. In most species the male produces a greater number of gametes, and therefore, has a greater gametic potential for producing young. Additionally, males must compete with other males for the relatively scarce female gametes.

3. **Kinship genetics:** Closely related individuals within a species have genes in common with each other. The more closely related the individuals are, the greater the commonality of their genetic material. Siblings share 50% of their genetic material, as do parents and their young. Half siblings share 25% of their genes, and so on. In a very real way, behavior that is protective of close relatives is protective of one's own genetic potential. Therefore, there is a tendency for developing and retaining individual and group behaviors that aid the survival of closest relatives.

4. **Sexual selection:** Individuals who are most successful in mating are most likely to have their physical and behavioral characteristics passed on to future generations. There are positive selective pressures for those characteristics that most successfully ward off competitors for mates and for those characteristics that are the most effective attractors of mates. These same characteristics are the ones that are most likely to be found in future generations.

5. **Population homozygosity:** *Homozygosity* implies having the same genetic material at the same loci of two genes. When applied to population genetics, the term refers to the genetic commonality of a given species. Population homozygosity gives a species its uniqueness, and it is what differentiates the species from all others. It is what makes robins, robins; dung beetles, dung beetles; and leopard frogs, leopard frogs.

6. **Population heterozygosity:** In a similar fashion, population heterozygosity refers to the variance of genetic material to be found in a species. This variance accounts for individual differences within a species. It is what accounts for variations in size, skin color, hair patterns, and a host of other discernible physical and behavioral characteristics. Population heterozygosity helps ensure that there will be individuals possessing different potentials for adapting to changing environments.

7. **Radiation:** There is a natural tendency for organisms to disperse into all parts of the environment in which they are suited for survival. As population density increases and as competition from other species puts pressure on the limited environmental resources that are available to support the group, members of the group will disperse into adjacent environmental spaces that are capable of supporting the species.

8. **Isolation:** This occurs when physical barriers develop between groups of individuals within a species, preventing contact between the groups. The isolation may be due to great distances separating the groups or to other physical barriers such as mountain ranges, bodies of water, or the presence of hostile environments that will not support the species.

9. **Genetic drift:** The physical separation that results from isolation prevents opportunities for the sharing of genetic materials between the isolated groups. As the processes of adaptive fitness and sexual selection continue to operate in each of the groups, and as chance mutational changes occur in one group but not the other, the separated pools of genetic materials begin to differ from each other. If there are concurrent changes in the environments of the isolated groups, the rate of the genetic drift will increase.

The Development of New Species

Now let us return to the question of the origin of new species. The sequence of events for the process is depicted in Figure 1-4. Through the natural process of radiation, members of the species attempt to enter into

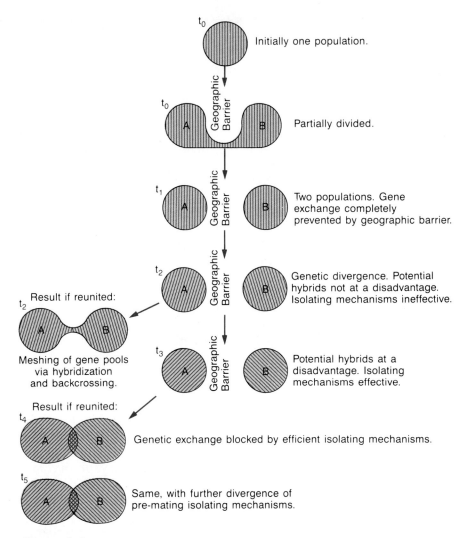

t_0 — Initially one population.

Geographic Barrier

t_0 — Partially divided.

Geographic Barrier

t_1 — Two populations. Gene exchange completely prevented by geographic barrier.

Geographic Barrier

t_2 — Genetic divergence. Potential hybrids not at a disadvantage. Isolating mechanisms ineffective.

Result if reunited:

t_2 — Meshing of gene pools via hybridization and backcrossing.

Geographic Barrier

t_3 — Potential hybrids at a disadvantage. Isolating mechanisms effective.

Result if reunited:

t_4 — Genetic exchange blocked by efficient isolating mechanisms.

t_5 — Same, with further divergence of pre-mating isolating mechanisms.

Figure 1-4
Schematic representation of the effect of isolation and genetic drift on population genetics and the generation of new species. At level t_1, two subgroups from the same population are physically isolated. At level t_2 the two groups may be reunited without disadvantage to the hybrids produced by mixing the gene pools. At level t_3 the gene pool of groups A and B are sufficiently different that breeding is not possible, or hybrids are disadvantaged for survival. (From J. L. Brown, 1975.)

all available niches. Because of great distances or physical barriers, two groups from within the species become isolated. The processes of adaptive fitness and sexual selection continue to function independently in each group. Those individuals in each group who are the most fit and those who are most successful in mating have the greatest genetic influence on their respective groups. In some species, such as the lion and walrus, this is particularly true for the few males who are the most successful breeders. Also, there would be behaviors evidenced by the most successful males that favor the survival of their closest relatives.

At this point, if the two groups were reunited, the population genetics would remain largely unchanged. However, continued isolation would produce further genetic drift, increasing the population heterozygosity of the species. Changes in the environments influencing the two groups would hasten the genetic drift. Changes in weather, flora, and fauna experienced by one group, but not the other, would exert selective pressures on that group. Individuals possessing characteristics that were best suited to the changed conditions would be more likely to survive and more likely to pass their characteristics on to new generations.

As the process of genetic drift continues, a point will eventually be reached when individuals representing each group are sufficiently different that they are *physically* or *behaviorally* incapable of mating. That is, if the two groups were reunited, they would not or could not mate. By definition they would now be two distinct species. Organisms that are genetically incapable of producing viable offspring and/or ones that have physical or behavioral characteristics that prevent mating belong to different species.

At this juncture it is important to reemphasize two points. First, natural selection operates in a manner that influences the evolution of *both* the morphology and the behavior of organisms. The physical characteristics of the organism, both internal and external, evolve in parallel with the evolving patterns of behavior. Second, natural selection emphasizes the **biological continuity** between species. All contemporary species can be viewed as being related to some degree in that, at some point in time, they had a common ancestor. It was the concept of biological continuity that was so controversial when Darwin published *On the Origin of Species*. The notion that all organisms, including humans, had a common inheritance was not in concert with the religious dogma of the time, which preferred to view human beings as a special creation. The scientific community's eventual acceptance of the notion that men and women were inexorably linked to all other species opened up human morphology and human behavior to the more rigorous study previously reserved for "lower" species.

A final point concerning the process of natural selection should be considered before we turn, more specifically, to the evolution of humans. The process of evolution is sometimes misperceived as being focused or directed toward a given end. There is an egocentric view that all animals are evolving so as to become more humanlike. This view attempts to place all organisms on a continuum, from the simplest to the most complex, with men and women at the top of the ladder. It is simply incorrect.

Jerison (1985) accurately points out that evolution is not the result of some inherent urge towards a better life. Rather, organisms are continuously changing so as to be better suited to survive in the environment that confronts them. Spiders are becoming more efficient spiders; lizards are more efficient lizards. Evolution occurs in a framework in which species maintain their status relative to other species. Each species evolving in a way that will make it more competitive and more likely to survive while competing with other species for life's resources (Van Valen, 1973). Just how changes in their environmental niches will control their evolu-

Figure 1-5
The fallacious chain of life model of evolution. This model of evolution makes the erroneous assumption that all forms of life are evolving to be more humanlike. (From Downs & Bleibtreu, 1972.)

tion in the future is difficult to predict. There is, however, no reason to suppose that they are becoming more like human beings. Figure 1-5 demonstrates the inappropriate "chain of life" view and the more generally accepted view of the generation of species (Salthe, 1972; Stini, 1975).

An Observation: Changing the Odds

Some years ago when I was serving as a judge at a regional science fair, I observed an excellent project that was designed to demonstrate, in miniature, the process of evolution through natural selection. The student used a mutant form of fruit fly that has very shriveled wings and cannot fly. This mutation is not seen very often in the normal population of fruit flies, because this characteristic is based on a recessive gene and because the flightless insect does not have much of a chance to survive in its natural setting.

The student took two populations of fruit flies; one was normal, and the second consisted entirely of the mutant, flightless variety. She then placed the two groups of flies in a large cage (their ecological niche) that contained all of the necessary sources of food and water to support the flies. However, she modified their niche to shift the odds in favor of the flightless insects by suspending flypaper from the ceiling of the cage. Then she "let nature take its course." Under these conditions, being flightless had an adaptive advantage. Within several months all traces of the "normal" flies were gone, as only the progeny of the flightless variety survived.

Normally, environments do not change so drastically or suddenly as was true in this science fair project. Rather, more subtle changes occur over long periods of time. There is some evidence that evolution did not progress at a smooth and steady pace. For example, Gould (1980a) has proposed that evolution occurs in cycles of rapid change alternating with longer periods of relative stasis ("punctuated equilibria"). The rate of the evolutionary process is thought to be driven by alternating patterns in the rate of change in the world's environments. When climatic conditions change rapidly, the rate of extinction for existing life forms also increases. Independent of whether evolution occurs smoothly or in a punctuated fashion, it is clear that environmental influences direct the course of evolutionary change just as surely as the introduction of fly paper did in the science fair project.

The Evolution of Humans

To reconstruct the stages in the evolution of contemporary humans, we will go back in time to the late Triassic period, about 200 million years ago. This sounds like an enormous span of time; but in terms of the more than 4.5 thousand million–year geological history of our planet, it is indeed modern history.

The Mammals   In the late Triassic period we find the earliest fossil evidence of mammals. These amazing animals were small, rodentlike creatures that, surprisingly, came on the scene during the latter stage of the age of dinosaurs. Most were the size of the contemporary mouse, but some were as large as domestic cats. It is interesting to speculate on how these early mammals were able to compete successfully with their much larger reptilian neighbors. The answer, of course, lies in how they differed from their larger reptilian ancestors.

1. Mammals developed a new and more protective method of reproduction in that they bore live young rather than laying eggs. Additionally, following birth, the young were nurtured by the parent with food (milk) produced within the parent. This very successful reproductive strategy greatly enhanced the survival of mammalian young, and it is dealt with in greater detail in Chapter 4.

2. Mammals developed the ability to regulate body temperature. There is evidence to suggest that some dinosaurs had a limited ability to control body temperature, although not by the same mechanism and not with the efficiency found in mammals. The high metabolic activity and the effective insulating hair of mammals allowed them to maintain body heat without depending on the warming rays of the sun. Mammals could be, and probably were, nocturnal foragers and hunters. Thus, they were able to be active at night in a niche for which reptiles were not normally well adapted. In daylight the relatively defenseless mammals probably lay dormant in underground burrows, rock crevices, or other protected locations.

3. Unlike the reptiles, mammals developed specialized teeth for both cutting and grinding. This development allowed the mammals to become **omnivorous**, that is, to have a diversified animal and plant diet.

4. Finally, compared to the reptiles, mammals developed significantly larger brains for their body weight. Increases in the brain–to–body weight ratio are relatively well correlated with increases in intelligent behavior (Radinsky, 1975). **Biological intelligence** is directly related to brain mass and brain complexity. This will be discussed in greater detail in Chapter 3.

The Primates   Approximately 65 million years ago the number and variety of dinosaurs decreased suddenly. The cause of this phenomenon is not well understood; however, most paleontologists attribute this massive extinction to rapidly changing climatic conditions. What is important here is that the mammals were apparently better able to adapt to these changing conditions, and they rapidly radiated into the niches formerly held by the dinosaurs. Predating this event about 75 million years ago—a separate line of mammals, the **prosimians,** had begun to adapt to an **arboreal** habitat, living and feeding in the trees. Their number increased greatly with the extinction of the large reptiles, and they were the precursors of the very successful primates, who differed from the early mammals in several significant ways (Tuttle, 1972).

1. The hands and feet of the arboreal primates were modified for mobility and feeding in the trees, not for terrestrial environments. Nails replaced claws, and both the hands and feet developed an opposable toe or thumb, thus permitting a **prehensile** grasp. Although some primates developed some form of **brachiation** (locomotion by swinging, using the forelimbs), most retained a quadrapedal posture and walked on the top surface of limbs.

2. The eyes rotated forward on the head, improving depth perception—a clear advantage when moving from limb to limb and tree to tree. No longer on the ground, where scent marking had an important function, olfaction in arboreal primates became less important and vision became the preeminent sense modality. Color vision to enhance discrimination between edible and nonedible fruits and flowers developed.

3. The number of infants produced from each conception was greatly reduced, with one being the modal number. The arboreal environment required close and constant contact between mother and infant. Parental nurturing was thus enhanced.

4. The ratio of brain to body mass increased significantly over that of the earlier mammals, with clear implications for increased biological intelligence. Figure 1-6, adapted from Jerison, shows the range of brain–to–body weight ratios for several groups of contemporary species, including the primates.

The First Hominids

The first **hominid** (humanlike) primate was probably *Ramapithecus.* (There are some researchers who would disagree and place *Ramapithecus* in a divergent line separate from humans [see Fisher, 1988a, for a review].) The somewhat limited fossil evidence shows that this small hominid was widely dispersed in Africa, Europe, and the Middle East some 10 to 12 million years ago. *Ramapithecus,* being small yet having a brain the size of the gorilla (approximately 400 cc), is generally considered to have been a transitional form of primate. *Ramapithecus* had a semierect, bipedal posture and probably spent most of his time in the trees, but fed on the ground in a fashion similar to the contemporary baboon. The hominid line of primates differed from the other primates in several important ways (Tattersall, 1975).

1. The canine teeth grew progressively smaller as did the back molars. The loss of large canines for defense and social displays was evidently a necessary adjustment for an omnivorous diet of seeds, nuts,

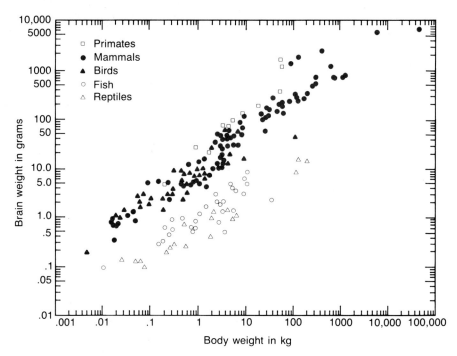

Figure 1-6
Brain–to–body weight ratios of 198 vertebrate species graphed on log–log coordinates. Ratios falling toward the top and right of the graph represent the highest brain–to–body weight ratios. (Adapted from Jerison, 1969.)

roots, insects, and possibly carrion. Small canines and flat molars are essential adaptations for the grinding action needed to accommodate such a diversified diet. The evidence also indicates that meat became an increasingly important factor in the diet as the hominid line became a more efficient hunter.

2. There was a rapid adaptation to a terrestrial, rather than an arboreal, environment. The reason for this is not well understood. Changes in climate may have reduced the size of forests, which were replaced by grasslands, thus producing population pressures on some arboreal species. There is, however, some evidence to suggest that the hominids became terrestrial *before* moving out of the forest habitat.

3. Skeletal adaptations to facilitate an upright posture and bipedal locomotion became more evident. These included modifications to the foot, leg, and pelvis. Additionally, the **foramen magnum**, the opening where the spinal column meets the skull, rotated almost 90° so that the face was parallel to the spine and perpendicular to the ground when in the upright posture. The quadrapedal skeletal features and several stages of bipedal development are shown in Figure 1-7.

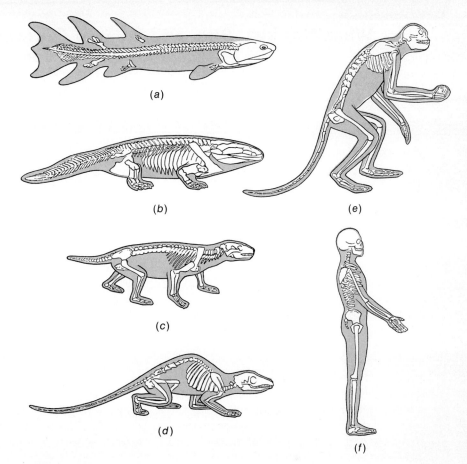

Figure 1-7
The evolution of the skeleton from early bony fish to humans. *a.* The undifferentiated spinal column of the bony fish. Similarly shaped vertebrae joined to short ribs facilitate side-to-side swimming movements. *b.* The terrestrial amphibian required a more sturdy spine to compensate for the lack of buoyancy provided by water. Specially shaped vertebrae accomodate the attachment of the limbs to the spine. *c.* The spine of a mammal-like reptile shows still more specialized vertebrae. Vertebrae near the limbs are larger and specially shaped to modulate the limbs. *d.* Early arboreal mammals developed a curved spine that allows for arching and extending the backbone. This form of spine, like that of the modern squirrel, accomodates movement in the trees and on the ground. *e. Mesopithecus,* an early primate, was able to stand on its hind legs for brief periods. The backbone is more rigid and the vertebrae have a variety of shapes. The large vertebrae in the lumbar region and the massive pelvis help to support the weight of the body. *f.* The vertebrae in man are very rigid and strongly locked together. This limits flexibility but permits a bipedal posture. The vertebrae become increasingly large from the neck down to the pelvic area, where the weight is transmitted to the legs. The foramen magnum has rotated to accommodate a forward-looking position for the skull. Also, the ribs are flattened to help center the weight over the pelvis when in the upright position.

What Monkey, Ape, and Human Chromosomes Can Tell Us about Evolution

Normally, chromosomes are not readily observable in the nucleus of the cell, because the genetic material is unraveled in very long strings of DNA. During cell division, the genetic material coils upon itself and forms the visible genes that make up the rodlike chromosomes. Therefore, it is necessary to find cells that are in the process of cell division if we wish to see the genes that form the chromosomes. Typically, this is done by taking a sample of blood and making a culture of the white blood cells. (The red platelets do not have a nucleus and therefore cannot form chromosomes.) The dividing white cells are treated in a way that causes them to rupture, thus allowing the chromosomes to disperse on a microscope slide. The material is then stained with a dye that is specific for nucleic acids. In some cases, a dye that phosphoresces under ultraviolet light is used. This technique is particularly useful for highlighting the individual genes.

The size and number of chromosomes vary widely from one species to another. *Drosophila*, the fruit fly, has only four pairs of chromosomes, which are very large and relatively easy to map. In New World monkeys the number of chromosome pairs varies from 20 to 62. The number of chromosomes in Old World monkeys is much more consistent. Among the great apes that are most closely related to humans—the orangutans, gorillas, and chimpanzees—the number of chromosomes is 24 pairs. Humans have 23 chromosome pairs.

As you might expect, the similarity between the number and structure of the chromosomes is directly related to the closeness between two species. Examination of the chromosomes under high power reveals distinctive light and dark bands. An early discovery showed that the pattern of these bands was remarkably constant between the orangutan, the gorilla, the chimpanzee, and humans (Yunis & Prakash, 1982). But what of the fact that humans have one less pair of chromosomes than the great apes? Does this indicate a large difference in our genetic makeup? Not at all. Careful examination shows that one of the human chromosomes is actually two of the chromosomes of the apes that appear to be fused end to end. See Spotlight Figure 1-2. Five chromosomes appear to be identical across all four species. The others differ slightly, mainly due to the inversion of certain segments. In some cases small fragments that are present in one species are absent in the others.

Of the three apes, the chimpanzee appears to be the most closely related to humans. The remarkable similarities between the chromosomes of human beings and the chimpanzee are reflected in the biochemistry of the two species. For example, the well-known A, B, and O blood types used by anthropologists to study human variation are identical to those of the chimpanzee. Also, DNA molecules from humans and chimpanzees can be made to unite in the laboratory. A strand of human DNA combines with a strand of chimpanzee DNA, forming a hybrid molecule. This "human-ape" molecule differs by only 1% of the length of either natural parent molecule (King & Wilson, 1975)!

We can only speculate about the genetic makeup of the hominids that were the precursors to humans. However, because these extinct forms were more closely related to us than any of the contemporary great apes are, it is a relatively safe bet that their chromosomes would be even more similar to our own.

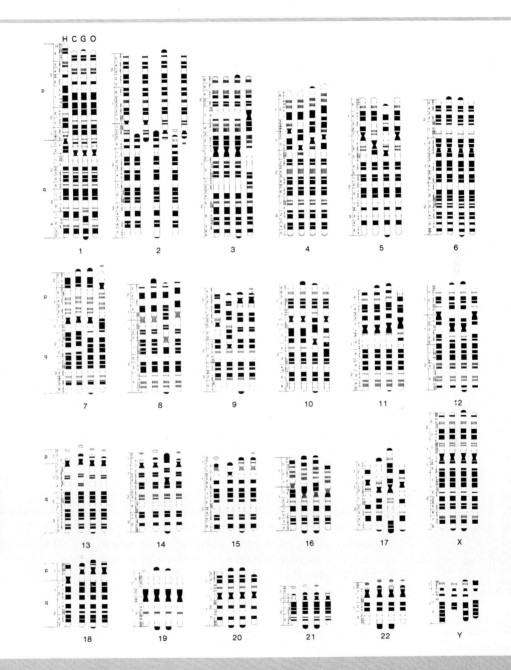

Spotlight Figure 1-2
A comparison of selected chromosomes—numbers 1 to 22 in humans (H), chimpanzees (C), gorillas (G), and orangutans (O). The chromosomes were stained to show banding. In humans, chromosome 2 results from the fusion of two chromosomes (2p and 2q) present in the three great apes. (From Yunis & Prakash, 1982.)

Bipedalism is mechanically less efficient than the quadrapedal form of locomotion. This point is particularly compelling in view of the relatively awkward bipedal movement of the early hominids. What factors, then, led to this relatively inefficient means of locomotion? The hands and feet that had once adapted for grasping in an arboreal environment did not adapt easily to a quadrapedal terrestrial environment. Witness the relatively awkward quadrapedal movements of contemporary apes such as the chimpanzee and gorilla. Also, the power grasp of the hands and feet was probably retained to allow the young to cling to the mother, an adaptation that had been essential for survival in the trees. Another contributing factor may have been the rigidity of the spinal column developed in arboreal primates, particularly the brachiators. A relatively stiff spine, which helps maintain balance in the trees, does not lend itself to efficient quadrapedal movement, as seen, for example, in the fluid movement of members of the cat family.

Surely the bipedal form of locomotion and the upright posture did have some adaptive advantages. They freed the front limbs for communication and the use of tools. The upright stance placed the head at the top of an extended body, providing for better visual defense in the tall grasses of the savanna. The eyes of a 5-ft-tall, 130-lb hominid would have been considerably higher than those of a 1,000-lb carnivorous cat. These advantages were, however, the by-products of a bipedal form of locomotion that was necessitated by the arboreal heritage of the terrestrial hominids.

4. The hominids had a tendency toward **sexual dimorphism**. Males tended to be larger than females and probably had other differentiating physical characteristics. Sexual dimorphism is very evident in some contemporary primates such as the orangutan, the baboon, and the gorilla, and it is evident to a somewhat lesser degree in humans. Typically, sexually dimorphic species have a division of labor that is sexually related as well. This is particularly true in those species that have a complex social structure, as is seen with baboons. In the hunter-gatherer social system of the hominids there surely was a division of responsibility that was to some degree determined by sexual dimorphism.

5. The hominids evidence a truly remarkable increase in the ratio of brain to body mass. In less than 4 million years—a very brief moment in terms of evolutionary time—the size of the hominid brain grew from around 500 cc in *Australopithecus* to 1000 cc in *Homo erectus*. The average-sized brain of humans is approximately 1,500 cc. Figure 1-8 shows the relative brain size and the time separating several representative species of hominids.

6. Finally, the period of infant dependency was increasing. A combination of factors made this both necessary and possible. First, the increasingly large head necessary to accommodate larger brains meant that the young had to be born more **altricial** (less well developed and there-

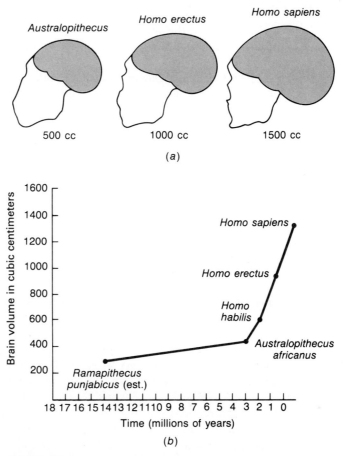

Figure 1-8
Schematic showing the relative brain size and the time separating several hominids and humans. *a*. The brain size compared to the size of the face. *b*. Graph of the rapid increase in brain size, in a relatively short time, from *Australopithecus africanus* to *Homo sapiens sapiens*. (Adapted from Poirier, 1977.)

fore more dependent). To make this point clear, you need only think of the head and body proportions of a newborn horse, for example, compared to that of a human infant. The relative size of the head and body of the young horse is not much different from that of the adult animal. The head of a newborn infant, however, is quite large compared to the body. (The characters in the "Peanuts" cartoons are only an exaggeration of reality!) Now think of the physical capabilities of a horse and those of a human just a few hours after birth. How do they compare a year after birth? Second, the division in labor associated with sexual dimorphism and social cooperation left the females free to provide extended care for the young. This extended period of parenting also provided a greater opportunity for the young to learn and to develop more complex patterns of communication.

The sequence of events in the evolution of the hominids that led to contemporary human beings is confusing and somewhat tenuous. The fossil evidence is preciously small, and dating techniques for relatively recent events lack the precision necessary for unequivocal judgments. The evidence suggests, however, that the evolutionary path of the hominids is probably not a simple and unbroken line. The fossil record from southern and northeastern Africa indicates that there were at least three hominids that shared the planet between 2.5 and 4 million years ago: **Australopithecus africanus**, the more robust **Australopithecus boisei**, and the most recently discovered and most humanlike **Homohabilis**. All three probably shared a common ancestor in *Ramapithecus*. There is some evidence that another African hominid, **Australopithecus afarensis** (named after the Afar Depression in Ethiopia) may be in line between *Ramapithecus* and the other hominids. However, some anthropologists believe that *afarensis* is a modern form of *Ramapithecus*.

Of the three coexisting hominids, *habilis* had the largest brain size (about 680 cc); a rounded, rather than flattened, forehead; a very modern looking foot structure; and the most humanlike dentition. There is considerable evidence that *Homo habilis* was a tool maker and may have built very primitive shelters. These characteristics warranted the name *Homo*, and *Homo habilis* is considered by some authorities to be the most likely candidate of the three hominids to be in direct lineage to contemporary humans. What factors led to evolutionary oblivion for the two australopithecines is not known. It is possible that they were unable to compete successfully with *Homo habilis* or simply could not adapt to changing environmental conditions (Leakey, 1966; Tobias, 1965).

Early Humans   *Homo habilis* was the likely predecessor to **Homo erectus**, who came on the scene between 700,000 and 750,000 years ago. The skeletal structure of *erectus* is quite similar to that seen in humans, and therefore, this small hominid has been included in the genus *Homo* by many researchers. There are, however, significant morphological differences between *erectus* and human beings. Specifically, the *erectus* skull had a heavier jaw, marked flattening of the forehead (**platycephaly**), the remnant of a midsagittal crest (which served as an anchor for large masticating muscles), and a cranial capacity of approximately 1,000 cc. Fossil evidence, tools, and shelter artifacts show that *erectus* probably radiated from Africa to Europe, Asia, and the Indonesian archipelago, possibly by crossing the land bridge between Africa and the Middle East. *Erectus* were clearly tool makers and tool users, and it is likely that they used fire to herd animals when hunting and to cook food. The evidence suggests that *Homo* *erectus* had a complex social structure requiring coordinated hunting and gathering activities, the division of work between males and females, food sharing, and other cooperative social behaviors (Howells, 1966).

The first true humans, **Homo sapiens neanderthalis**, appeared between 150,000 and 300,000 years ago. There has been much debate concerning the relationship between Neanderthal man and **Homo sapiens sapiens** (contemporary humans), and the controversy is likely to continue for some time because of the inaccuracy of dating methods. (*Sapiens* means "*intelligent*" "*knowing*" humans. It is interesting to note, as an aside, that we chose to call ourselves *Homo sapiens sapiens*, thus placing greater emphasis on our intelligence. Supposedly, this further distinguished us from "infrahuman" species.)

There appear to be at least three possible scenarios concerning the relationship of *neanderthal* and contemporary humans. The first holds that *neanderthal* is in a direct line between *Homo erectus* and human beings, and is the precurser to contemporary humans. The second suggests that *neanderthal* is a direct descendant of *Homo erectus*, predated humans, and coexisted with contemporary humans for some time, but is not in direct lineage with humans. The third theory posits that *neanderthal* predated humans and was a contemporary of *Homo sapiens sapiens*, but had a totally separate lineage, sometimes referred to as "presapiens." Figure 1-9 represents the probable path to the evolution of human beings.

No matter which theory is eventually proven accurate, *neanderthal* clearly had a brain-to-body ratio equal to or greater than that of humans. The fossil evidence indicates that the brain of *neanderthal* averaged 1,500 cc or more—significantly larger than that of *erectus*. *Neanderthal* was far ranging. Evidence of his tools, shelters, and ceremonial burial sites have been found in Africa, the Middle East, Europe, and Asia. The fact that later *neanderthals* practiced the ceremonial burial of animal bones, buried their dead, and had a relatively stable stone tool industry clearly points to a sophisticated social structure indicative of a primitive culture. By comparison, it has been proposed that humans probably differed from *neanderthal* by having a more complex and sophisticated language, a more stable tool industry, cognitively meaningful pictorial symbols, and a sense of time that related past, present, and future events (Kennedy, 1975).

Review In a few pages we have traced evolution from mammals to primates to hominids, and finally, to humans. Let us now review the significant patterns and trends of evolution leading to humans.

1. Self-regulation of body temperature opened up the nocturnal niches to which the reptiles were not well suited. This adaptation allowed mammals (including early human beings) to enter into colder climates that were not available to cold-blooded terrestrial species.

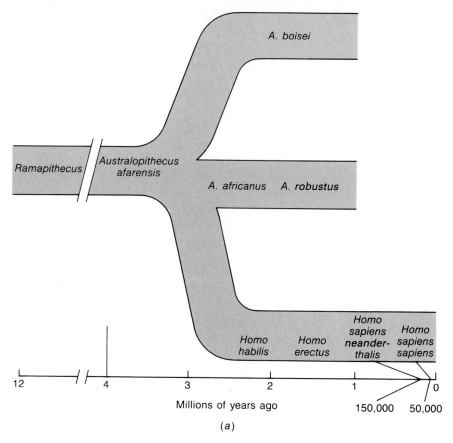

Figure 1·9
a. This schematic shows one of several theories representing a probable path to *Homo sapiens sapiens. b.* Hominid skulls and facial reconstructions drawn to scale. Note the trend for an increase in cranial size and a decrease in jaw size.

    2. The shift from an egg-laying to a live-born reproduction strategy decreased significantly the number of young that could be produced by a single conception and increased greatly the need for more efficient post-natal parenting. The radiation of primates to an arboreal environment placed even greater pressures on effective parenting and producing fewer offspring with each pregnancy. Additionally, there was a trend toward infants becoming more altricial, thus increasing the period of infant dependency on the parent.
    3. Specialized dentition for cutting and grinding accommodated a diversified plant and animal diet. This was to be a particularly important adaptive advantage for the early terrestrial hominids. The omnivorous

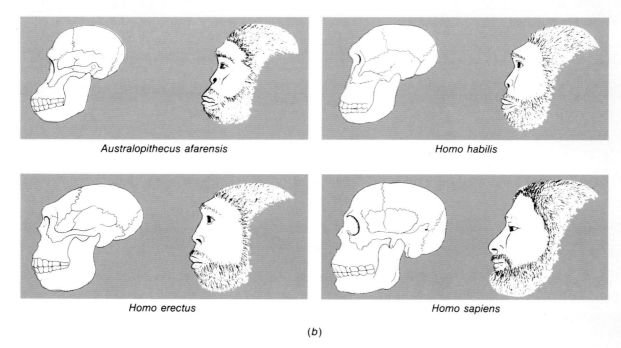

Australopithecus afarensis   Homo habilis

Homo erectus   Homo sapiens

(b)

Figure 1-9 (Continued)

diet made several levels of the food chain available to the terrestrial hominids.

4. The shift from a terrestrial to an arboreal environment placed increased importance on vision, rather than olfaction, as the primary sense modality. Color vision and good depth perception were necessary for survival. These visual capabilities were retained as effective adaptations when the hominids moved back to the ground.

5. The arboreal niche of the early primates mandated significant modifications to the hand and foot. The power grasp and flat nails needed for locomotion in the trees profoundly influenced the subsequent adaptations to a terrestrial environment. The bipedal form of locomotion, the power grasp for subsequent tool use, and the fine manual dexterity for tool making may all be linked directly, or indirectly, to the arboreal niche.

Contemporary Humans

Jerison (1973) has proposed that the remarkable increase in brain growth evidenced between *Homo erectus* and *Homo sapiens sapiens* was likely attributable to the early radiation of humans from the warm environment of Africa into less hospitable climates. He reasoned that colder climates and associated glaciation forced the various *Homo* species to establish relatively fixed homesites from which small hunting and gathering bands operated in a relatively restricted range. Fixed homesites stimulated social interaction between group members (particularly between adults and young), increased the usefulness of divided labor within the group, and served as a catalyst for the development of increasingly complex forms of communication.

The Importance of Language

Communication was, doubtlessly, the driving force behind the truly remarkable expansion of human intellect that has taken place in the past 50,000 to 75,000 years. The enormous knowledge base we currently possess has little to do with the continued evolution of the brain or increases in biological intelligence. Rather, it is attributable to a cultural revolution—a revolution that was fueled by language. The brain of the earliest *Homo sapiens sapiens* who lived in caves and traveled in hunter-gatherer groups of probably no more than 50 individuals has changed very little. It pleases me to think that if we could resurrect one of them today and raise him or her in our complex society, he or she would have the same intellectual potential as any of us!

Language, then, is the key to understanding many of the complex behaviors that are distinctly human. In every other species, contemporary or extinct, each new generation benefits little, if at all, from the life experiences of their parents and their parents' parents. What oyster, sparrow, or zebra is better able to survive because of the life experiences of its parents? Oral and symbolic language allowed each new generation to build on the experience base of previous generations. It is due to language—not any recent developments in the brain—that knowledge has increased at an exponential rate (e.g., Fisher, 1988b).

Parallel Evolution

The human brain is the end product of many evolutionary steps; each step, an adaptation to specific environmental pressures. Language, as well as all other forms of complex behavior, evolved along with the evolution of an increasingly large and complex brain. This is the central theme of this book: brain and behavior have undergone **parallel evolution**. The fine motor ability that we have with our fingers, but not with our toes, is directly related to the size, complexity, and evolutionary history of the parts of the brain that control those appendages.

To help clarify this point, I direct your attention to Figure 1-10. The figure shows four animals and the amount of brain (more specifically, the amount of thalamus, a structure within the brain that is associated with processing body senses) dedicated to various parts of the body. The point is that the amount of brain dedicated to a given body area is more closely related to the *importance* of that area for the behavior of the animal than it is to its size. Those parts of the brain that represent the tactile hairs on the nose of the rat, the prehensile tail of the spider mon-

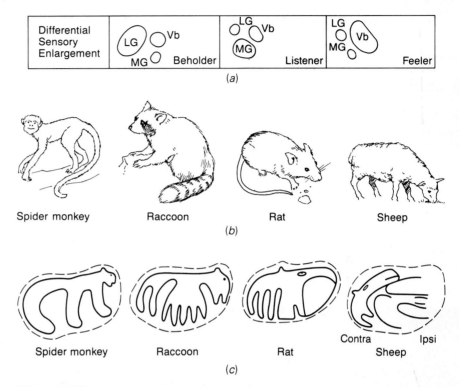

(a)

(b)

(c)

Figure 1-10
a. The relative size of various thalamic nuclei for a "beholder," a "listener,"
and a "feeler." The lateral geniculate nucleus (LG) is for vision, the medial
geniculate (MG) processes audition, and the ventrobasal nuclei (Vb) represents
body sense information. *b.* Behavioral specialization in four mammals. *c.* The
relative areas of enlargement of the ventrobasal nuclei in the thalamus. Note
that the more important a particular form of behavior is to the animal, the
more brain mass for that behavior is found. (From Welker, 1973.)

key, the front paws of the raccoon, and the lips and tongue of the sheep
are all exaggerated in size relative to the brain area for other parts of
the body. The complexity of these portions of the brain have evolved
in parallel with the importance and complexity of the parts of the body
they innervate.

When examining the structure and function of the brain, we are in a
very real sense examining the underlying mechanisms of behavior. Anal-
ogously, studying the evolution of the brain will provide insight into the
evolution of behavior. This was the point of the empid fly example made
in the preface of this book. Contemporary behavior is more fully understandable when viewed in an evolutionary context. In Chapter 3 we
review the structure, function, organization, and evolution of the human
brain and the other structures that comprise the central nervous system.

Having a basic understanding of the anatomy and physiology of the central nervous system is a necessary first step to understanding the biological bases of behavior.

CHAPTER SUMMARY

1. Psychology, as a science, is relatively young. The roots of psychology are found in philosophy, medicine, and the natural sciences. Physiological psychology is concerned primarily with the study of the physical factors that arouse, sustain, and direct the behavior of humans and animals.

2. There are three primary concerns in the study of the physiological bases of behavior: (a) how the brain and central nervous system may be divided by function (localization versus unity of function), (b) what the relationships between the biological potential of the organism and the influence of environmental pressures on behavior (the nature–nurture controversy) are, and (c) what the physical correlates of consciousness (the nature of mind) are.

3. To understand contemporary human behavior, it is important to know how that behavior evolved over time. The evolution of species through the process of natural selection accounts for both the physical and behavioral attributes of the various species.

4. The ultimate source of evolutionary change rests at the molecular level of living matter. The genes that make up the chromosomes of every cell direct the production of the essential proteins required to sustain and reproduce life. Random changes to genes are the source of genetic variation within a species.

5. Contrary to Lamarck's theory of the inheritance of acquired characteristics, evolution is thought to take place through the process of natural selection, as first proposed by Darwin and Wallace. The key factors involved with the generation of new species include (a) the radiation of individuals into all available niches, (b) the isolation of subpopulations of a given species, and (c) the genetic drift that occurs during long periods of isolation.

6. Mammals evidence several major adaptive advantages over reptiles, amphibians, and birds. These include the regulation of body temperature; live birth and greater maternal care; a more diverse diet; and, most important, a larger brain relative to body weight. A special group of mammals, the primates, evolved in an arboreal (tree) environment. Their major adaptations to an arboreal niche included grasping hands and feet, improved depth perception and color vision, and increased brain size.

7. Although there is still considerable debate concerning the evolution of humans, the first hominids (humanlike primates) are thought to have evolved in southern Africa. The key features of these ground-dwelling prehumans included modification of the pelvis and legs to permit walking on two legs, rotation of the foramen magnum (the place where the spine joins the skull), flattening of the chest, changes in the teeth that reflect a varied diet, the tendency to produce altricial (more dependent) young, and the rapid increase in the size of the brain.

8. Although dating techniques lack precision, humans are thought to have appeared within the last 50,000 to 150,000 years. The evolution of language and a complex social structure are the key factors that define *Homo sapiens sapiens*. The rapid development of humans from a primitive hunter-gatherer society to our current condition can be attributed to a symbolic language.

SUGGESTED READINGS

Ardrey, R. (1966). *African genesis*. New York: Dell.

Brown, J. L. (1975). *The evolution of behavior*. New York: Norton

Jerison, H. J. (1973). *Evolution of the brain and intelligence*. New York: Academic Press.

Leakey, R. E., & Lewin, R. (1977). *Origins*. New York: Dutton.

Milner, P. M., & White, N. M. (1987). What is physiological psychology? *Psychobiology, 15,* 2–6.

Poirier, F. E. (1977). *In search of ourselves: An introduction to physical anthropology*. Minneapolis: Burgess.

KEY TERMS

Acquired characteristics Relating to the Lamarckian notion that physical characteristics acquired through the life experiences of an individual can be passed on to future generations.

Adaptive fitness The combined physical and behavioral characteristics of a species that make it well adapted to a particular environment.

Altricial The tendency for the young of a species to be very dependent on their parents for nurturance (opposite of *precocial*).

Arboreal Living entirely or most of the time in the trees.

Australopithecus afarensis Early form of hominid, similar to *Ramapithecus*.

Australopithecus africanus One of three hominid descendants of *Ramapithecus* that lived in Africa 2.5 to 4 million years ago.

Australopithecus boisei The more robust of the three hominid descendants of *Ramapithecus*.

Biological continuity The Darwinian notion that due to the process of natural selection, there is a common inheritance for all existing species.

Biological intelligence The potential for intelligent behavior related to the size of the brain, particularly as brain size increases in proportion to body mass.

Brachiation Locomotion by swinging, commonly seen in arboreal primates such as the gibbon.

Chromosome 21 trisomy A birth defect resulting from the presence of an extra chromosome of the twenty-first pair. (See Down's syndrome.)

Cranioscopy The process of skull measurement used by phrenologists to determine personality characteristics.

Darwin, Charles Naturalist and author of *On the Origin of Species*, which popularized the theory of natural selection.

Doctrine of specific nerve energies Proposed by Johannes Müller, the doctrine states that the quality and location of sensory information are determined by the location in the brain that receives the nerve signal and not by the nature of the nerve signal itself.

Down's syndrome A birth anomaly caused by an extra chromosome of the twenty-first pair of chromosomes. (See chromosome 21 trisomy.)

Dualism One of several philosophical views of mind and body maintaining that mind and body possess different qualities.

Emergent property Monist philosophy that views the mind to be a special property of the action and organization of the neurons in the brain.

Evolution The changes in species that occur over time.

Foramen magnum The opening at the base of the skull where the skull and spinal column meet.

Gametic potential The potential to influence the gene pool of a species through sexual selection.

Genetic drift Tendency of the population genetics of a species to change based on the influence of the most successful individuals in the population.

Hominid Term used to refer to all humanlike precursors to humans.

Homo erectus Descendant of *Homo habilis*; radiated through much of Africa, Europe, and Asia between 700,000 and 750,000 years ago.

Homo habilis The most humanlike of the three descendants of *Ramapithecus*.

Homo sapiens neanderthalis Early form of human beings; was a probable contemporary of *Homo sapiens sapiens*.

Homo sapiens sapiens Species name for humans.

Identity Philosophical position that brain and mind are exactly the same, and apparent differences are due to differences in the manner in which we describe them.

Interactionism A view of mind and body that proposes that the metaphysical mind and the physical body interact in the behavior of the individual.

Isolation The physical separation of groups of individuals from the same species—one factor influencing the development of new species through natural selection.

Kinship genetics The notion that closely related individuals share a more common pool of genes. In terms of natural selection, behaviors that protect close relatives also protect the individual's genetic potential.

Lamarck, Jean-Baptiste de Advanced the first comprehensive theory of evolution based on the inheritance of acquired characteristics.

Materialism Monist philosophy holding that only the material (physical) world exists.

Mentalism Monist philosophy holding that only the mind exists; the physical world is viewed as a production of the mind.

Monism Any philosophy that views mind and body as being one. (See mentalism, materialism, and emergent property.)

Multiple causality The neo-Darwinian idea that natural selection takes place on all levels including the individual, the group, and the population.

Natural selection A process fundamental to evolution as proposed by Charles Darwin. Species change and new species arise as a result of environmental pressures on living organisms. Characteristics of individuals that make them better adapted to survive in a given environment are more likely to be evident in their offspring.

Nature—nurture controversy The continuing philosophical debate over the relative importance of heredity and environmental experience on observable behavior.

Omnivorous A mixed diet of animal and plant materials.

Parallel evolution The simultaneous evolution of brain and behavior.

Phrenology Study of the shape of the skull, based on the erroneous belief that various behavioral characteristics are reflected in the contours of the skull.

Platycephaly Flattening of the forehead.

Population heterozygosity The variation in the population gene pool that accounts for individual differences.

Population homozygosity The similarity within the gene pool that defines the species.

Prehensile   Grasping ability, as in the prehensile tail of the spider monkey.

Prosimian   The most primitive and earliest group of primates.

Punctuated equilibria   Notion that evolution proceeds in periods of rapid change alternating with periods of stasis.

Radiation   The tendency for individuals within a species to migrate into all available niches.

Ramapithecus   Considered to be the first of the hominid (human-like), primates.

Relative adaptive fitness   The combined physical and behavioral characteristics of a species that make the species successful in one or more environments.

Sexual dimorphism   Physical differences between males and females of the same species.

Sexual selection   Darwinian principle that those individuals that are more successful at mating will have a greater influence on the evolution of the species.

Wallace, Alfred R.   Naturalist who, independently from Darwin, discovered the principle of natural selection.

Chapter 2

Organizing: Part 1: The Building Blocks

The Cell
> *Anatomy of the Cell*
> *The Evolution of the Neuron*
> *The Anatomy of the Neuron*

Intraneuronal Communication
> *The Resting Potential*
> *The Sodium–Potassium Pump*
> *The Action Potential*
> *Ion Channels*
> *Propagated Action Potentials*
> *Saltatory Conduction*

Interneuronal Communication
> *Synaptic Function*
> *Presynaptic Events*
> *Postsynaptic Events*
> *Neural Integration*

Neurotransmitters
> *Acetylcholine*
> *Amino Acid Transmitters*
> *Catecholamines*
> *Serotonin*

Chapter Learning Objectives

After reading this chapter, you should

1. Be able to define cell theory and discuss the similarities between single-celled organisms and the cells of multicellular organisms.

2. Know and be able to discuss the function of the major organelles in the cell.

3. Be familiar with the evolution of the neuron.

4. Be able to compare and contrast the structure and function of neurons with those of other cells.

5. Understand the physical events that contribute to the resting potential of the neuron.

6. Be able to discuss how the sodium–potassium pump and ion channels function to restore the resting potential of the neuron.

7. Understand the physical and chemical events that contribute to the propagated action potential.

8. Be able to discuss the evolutionary advantage provided by saltatory conduction.

9. Be able to discuss interneuronal communication in terms of presynaptic and postsynaptic events.

10. Know what is meant by the term *neural integration* and be able to discuss neural integration in terms of the spatial and temporal summation of synaptic events.

11. Be familiar with the major classes of neurotransmitters.

12. Be able to discuss how various drug effects are related to the action of neurotransmitters and their associated enzymes.

The Cell

All living organisms, either plant or animal, are composed of cells. This principle is known as cell theory. Stated somewhat differently, the cell is the simplest and most fundamental unit of all living organisms.

The earliest forms of plant and animal life were simple, single-celled organisms. In time, plant cells began to aggregate into colonies of cells. The earliest forms of colonial plants were composed of cells that had essentially the same form and function. A major step in the evolution of complex organisms, both plant and animal, was the development of multicellular forms having cells that were specialized in shape and function. This allowed for a greater complexity and diversity of life. This is not to say that single-celled organisms lack complexity.

Look at the **protozoan** shown in Figure 2-1. It is a fresh-water, single-celled animal known as **Stylonychia mytilus.** Although it is able to swim freely, it spends most of the time walking on the bottom of ponds searching for food. When observed moving, through the microscope, it is obvious that this protozoan has a front, back, top, and bottom. There are tentaclelike structures called **cirri** for locomotion and food detection, tactile hairs on the upper surface and sides for navigation, an oral opening for the ingestion of food, and many internal organelles that control various physiological functions as well as the protozoan's behavior—all of this in a microscopic organism having but one cell.

When compared to multicellular animals (**metazoans**), single-celled animals are limited in size and relatively simple. Using cells as building blocks and organizing them to form specialized organs were

Figure 2-1
Ventral (a) and side (b) view of *Stylonychia mytilus,* a free-swimming protozoan. (Adapted from Borradaile & Potts, 1961.)

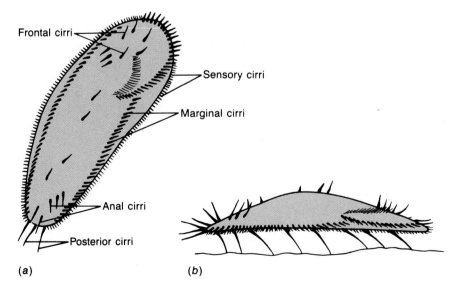

Frontal cirri

Sensory cirri

Marginal cirri

Anal cirri

Posterior cirri

(a)   (b)

truly significant steps in the evolution of new species. How this process began is not known. What is clear, however, is that it did happen and that this was the catalyst for the evolution of a wide diversity of multicellular organisms.

Anatomy of the Cell

The thousands and millions of cells that make up complex organs share many of the same structures and characteristics of the cells found in the protozoans. This should not be surprising, given that all cells had a common origin. Let us now review some of these structures found in animal cells and identify their specific functions.

CELL MEMBRANE

Every living cell is completely enclosed by a complex membrane that determines the cell's shape. The complexity of the membrane varies across cell types, which in turn determines the cell's physical properties. Generally, cell membranes are selectively permeable in that they allow some substances in solution to enter and exit the cell but restrict the passage of others. Some cell membranes are able to detect the presence of specific substances outside the cell (hormones, for example) and to pass that information to organelles within the cell.

The array of structures within the cell are suspended in a viscous substance, the **cytoplasm**. The cytoplasm is chemically quite complex, and it is constantly in motion. It has an important role in transporting substances from one part of the cell to another.

ENDOPLASMIC RETICULUM

Dispersed throughout the cytoplasm is a convoluted membrane, the **endoplasmic reticulum**. The convoluted surface is a way of putting a very large surface area in a small space. This strategy for increasing surface area is commonly found in nature. Think of trying to place a whole sheet of a newspaper in your pocket or purse. If the newspaper is crumpled or folded many times, it can be made to fit. The highly convoluted endoplasmic reticulum packs a large surface area inside the cell.

Two kinds of endoplasmic reticulum have been identified—smooth and rough—and they seem to have different functions. It is thought that the smooth type is primarily concerned with transporting cytoplasm throughout the cell. It may also serve to isolate substances in specified areas of the cell. The rough endoplasmic reticulum has many **ribosomes** dotting its surface. The ribosomes are known to synthesize complex protein molecules. Having a large surface area, the rough endoplasmic reticulum is capable of supporting many ribosomes, thus increasing the cell's ability to produce the needed proteins.

MITOCHONDRIA

The sausage-shaped **mitochondria** are responsible for supplying much of the energy that supports the metabolic activity of the cell. The interior of the mitochondria contains a very convoluted double membrane, the **cristae**. Biochemical action on the large surface area of the cristae breaks down blood sugar, the primary source of cell energy. Mitochondria are particularly numerous in cells that have high levels of metabolic activity.

GOLGI BODIES

These structures look like discs perforated with many holes. Pieces of the disc separate to form small **vesicles**, which are used as containers for substances manufactured in the cell. The mechanism by which the Golgi bodies enfold these substances between two layers of membrane is not known. The vesicles transport the substances produced by the ribosomes to the site of action. As might be expected, Golgi bodies are found in large numbers in cells that produce secreting chemicals.

NUCLEUS

The genetic material that directs the activity of the cell is found in the nucleus. The nucleus is typically shaped like a round or oblong ball and is enclosed in a porous membrane. The nucleus contains the **nucleolus** that manufactures ribosomes. The nucleus also has the **chromosomes**, which are constructed of enormous molecules of **deoxyribonucleic acid** (**DNA**). Specific segments of DNA on the chromosomes form the **genes**, which serve as templates for the production of **messenger ribonucleic acid** (**mRNA**). Messenger RNA exits the nucleus through pores in the nuclear membrane and subsequently attaches to ribosomes. In this way mRNA directs the production of specific proteins.

The Evolution of the Neuron

With the increasing complexity of metazoans, the need arose for cells that were capable of transmitting information from one part of the organism to another. Additionally, there was a need for cells to coordinate the activities of various systems within the organism. The **neuron** evolved to serve this function. One view of the evolution of neurons maintains that sensory-like cells on the surface of simple multicellular organisms produced electrical signals, which were transmitted to motor cells that abutted with them. These primordial neurons simply became more elaborate in shape and function over time. Generally, then, neurons are cells that have been greatly modified to transmit information, and they share many features in common with other cells found throughout the body (see Figure 2-2).

The Anatomy of the Neuron

Neurons have many shapes and come in various sizes, depending on their specific function (Palay & Chan-Palay, 1977). Most neurons can be divided into four distinct parts: the **soma**, or cell body; the **dendrites**; the **axon**; and the **terminal buttons**, or **end brush** (sometimes referred to as the terminal axon arbor). Figure 2-3 shows the principal regions of the neuron.

Figure 2-2
a. Schematic of the a typical body cell and a neuron depicting some of the structures that they have in common. Schematic (*right*) and electron micrographs (*left*) of selected organelles. *b.* The mitochondria consist of a pair of membranes enclosing two fluid-filled compartments. Mitochondria are the source of aerobic metabolism. *c.* The Golgi complex is a stack of membranous sacks. Vesicles that transport substances throughout the cell constantly bud off and fuse with the complex. *d.* There are two types of endoplasmic reticulum: rough, which is studded with ribosomes, and smooth, which is without ribosomes. The ribosomes are small bits of RNA that serve as templates for the production of essential proteins.

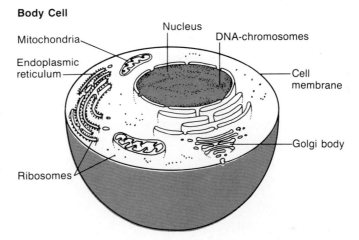

Body Cell

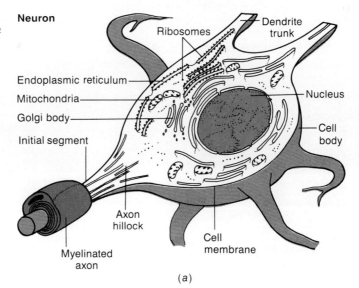

Neuron

(a)

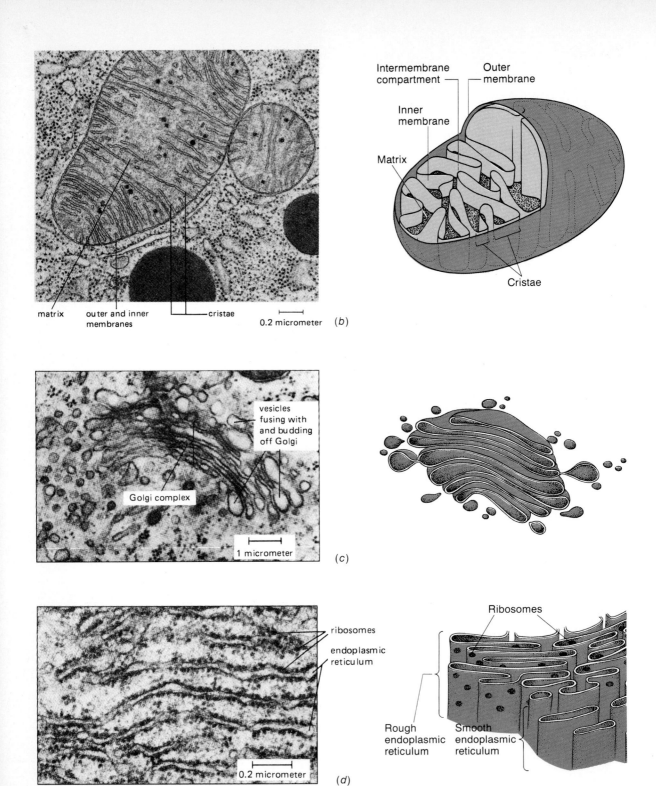

Intermembrane compartment

Outer membrane

Inner membrane

Matrix

Cristae

matrix   outer and inner   cristae
          membranes

0.2 micrometer   (b)

vesicles fusing with and budding off Golgi

Golgi complex

1 micrometer   (c)

ribosomes

endoplasmic reticulum

Ribosomes

Rough endoplasmic reticulum

Smooth endoplasmic reticulum

0.2 micrometer   (d)

Figure 2-2 (Continued)

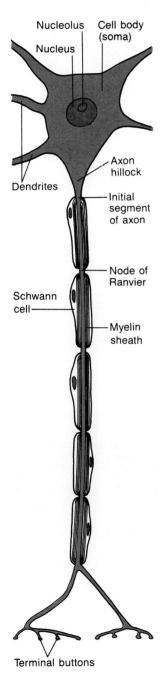

Nucleolus
Cell body (soma)
Nucleus

Dendrites

Axon hillock

Initial segment of axon

Node of Ranvier

Schwann cell

Myelin sheath

Terminal buttons

SOMA

The soma is enclosed in a membrane, as is the entire neuron. The shape of the soma varies widely in different types of neurons. Many organelles typically found in other cells, such as the nucleus, mitochondria, ribosomes, Golgi bodies, and the complex endoplasmic reticulum, are also found in the soma of the neuron. Mitochondria and Golgi bodies are particularly numerous, because neurons have a very high metabolic level and produce chemicals called **transmitter substances**, or **neurotransmitters.**

DENDRITES

Typically, the soma has many structures that branch repeatedly like the branches of a tree. These dendrites (the name is derived from the Greek word for "tree") take many forms and radiate out to receive information from other neurons. The membrane on the dendrites forms many knoblike structures, the dendritic spines, which have receptor sites for sensing neurotransmitters released by other neurons. Thus, information is passed biochemically between neurons across a **synapse**, a gap separating the two cells by approximately 200 angstroms. Synapses take place on the soma as well. In all, a neuron may have as many as 10,000 points of synaptic communication and may receive information from upwards of a thousand other neurons. We cover interneuronal transmission in much greater detail later in this chapter.

AXON

Most neurons have a long process extending from the soma to the site or sites where the neuron communicates with another neuron, a muscle, or a gland. The axon originates at a narrow portion of the soma, the **hillock**. Information is passed in one direction (the **orthodromic** direction), from the hillock away from the soma.

Axons are physically separated from other axons by special cells. In this way the activity of one axon cannot affect others that are in close proximity to it. Inside the central nervous system (CNS) this is done by a type of **glial** cell called **oligodendroglia**. Each oligodendroglion forms a sheath around several axons. This covering, called the **myelin sheath**, is made of fatty material (**lipoprotein**) and is similar in function to the insulation on a wire. In the peripheral nervous system (PNS; that portion of the nervous system found outside the skull and spinal cord) this same function is accomplished by **Schwann cells** that form tightly

Figure 2-3
Schematic of a typical neuron showing the soma with its associated dendrites, the myelinated axon, and the end brush with the terminal buttons.

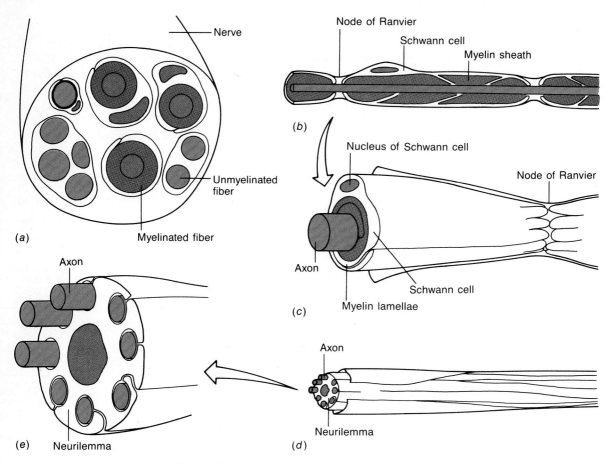

Figure 2-4
a. Myelinated and unmyelinated nerve fibers in a nerve bundle. *b.* The myelin-ated nerve fiber as seen with the light microscope. *c.* Reconstruction of the myelinated axon from electron micrographs. *d.* Several unmyelinated axons encased by a single neurilemma cell. *e.* Several unmyelinated axons as recon-structed from an electron micrograph. (From Noback, 1967.)

wrapped sleeves around the axon. Often the myelin sheath is interrupted every millimeter or so, forming short segments of unwrapped axon called the **nodes of Ranvier**. Figure 2-4 shows several types of myelination found in the mammalian nervous system.

END BRUSH
Axons typically terminate in a branching structure similar to the roots of a plant. At the terminus (end) of each filament there is a small

bulb called the terminal button. The neurilemma of the terminal button is thickened, and it is at this point that neurotransmitters are released into the synapse. The buttons contain **synaptic vesicles**, each of which holds several thousand molecules of neurotransmitter. In addition to making synapses on dendrites, the buttons also terminate on the soma and axons of other neurons, and on muscles and glands in the body. Each of these various types of synapses have a different purpose, and each is covered on more depth in subsequent sections of this chapter.

Intraneuronal Communication

So far we have examined the parts of the cell and looked at the neuron as a highly modified cell—a cell that has evolved specifically to communicate with other cells. Indeed, the neuron has become so specialized for its function that it has lost some of the capabilities possessed by most other body cells. For example, neurons within the mammalian brain have become dependent on specialized glial cells to provide their nutritional needs and remove their waste. It is interesting to note that neurons in the brain and spinal cord, once formed, have very limited ability to repair themselves, and they are unable to replicate new neurons if they become damaged. Unlike the neurons, the glial cells do replicate themselves. For this reason, all cancerous neoplasms (new growths) in the brain are associated with glia, never neurons (Allt, 1979). More is said about this in later chapters.

In examining the parts of the neuron, we saw that the cell is designed to send information in one direction from the soma, down the axon to the terminal buttons, and finally through the release of a neurotransmitter across the synapse; the neuron communicates with other cells. Now we examine how this process is accomplished.

The Resting Potential If you had a very sensitive voltmeter, and if you could place an electrode inside a neuron and a second electrode outside the membrane of the same neuron, you would measure a very small difference in voltage. The inside of the cell would have a -70 millivolt (mV) charge relative to the charge found in the extracellular fluid. This difference in voltage is the neuron's **resting potential**. (One millivolt is equal to one thousandth of a volt.)

The physical measurement of the resting potential as just described has actually been done using a giant axon found in the squid. This axon, which controls rapid motor action, can be seen without the aid of a microscope. It is almost .5 mm in diameter, hundreds of times larger than the axons found in mammals.

Techniques for the Microscopic Examination of Cells

If you were to examine a very thin slice of tissue, even under a very powerful microscope, you would not be able to differentiate between the parts of the cells or between the individual cells. The problem is that, in the natural state, there is very little contrast between the cells and the space around them and between the various structures in the cells.

In 1685, Marcello Malpighi observed the surface of the brain under a magnifying lens after first boiling the tissue and then flooding it with ink. The ink served to increase the contrast of the tissue components, leading Malpighi to observe the presence of "minute glands." Was Malpighi the first to observe neurons? No—it is more likely that the "glands" he

(a)

Spotlight Figure 2-1
a. Golgi stain of a few neurons in the cortex of human brain. *b.* Wisl-Wigert stain of the coronal section of rat brain. This complex stain highlights the nucleic acids found in the cell bodies pink (light structures) and the lipoproteins of the myelinated axons blue (dark structures). *c.* Myelin stain of the same coronal section of rat brain as seen in *b.* that only highlights the myelinated axon fiber tracts. *d.* Horseradish peroxidase stain of cells in the hindbrain using dark-field illumination. *e.* Scanning election micrograph of a nerve axon terminating on muscle fibers.

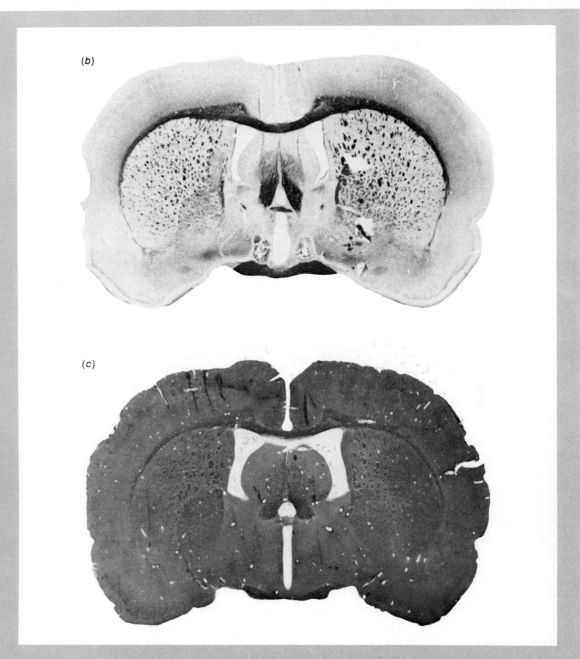

(b)

(c)

Spotlight Figure 2-1 (Continued)

(d)

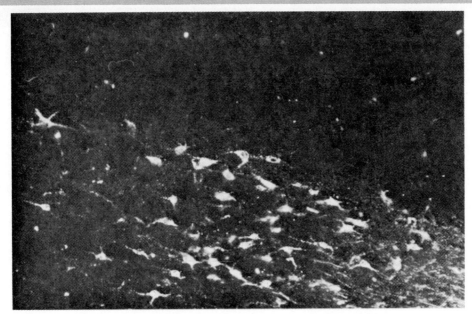

(e)

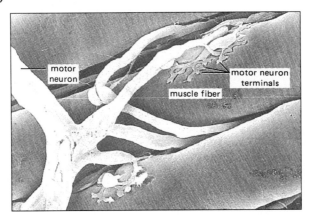

Spotlight Figure 2-1 (Continued)

observed were artifacts of the primitive optical system available to him. It was to be many years before concurrent advances in the optics of microscopes and new staining techniques were to provide us with the tools to examine cells in detail.

Many staining techniques are now available that allow us to view different characteristics of cells with the light microscope. The Golgi (silver) stain is unusual in that the stain completely covers the outside of the cell membrane. For reasons that are still unclear, this technique only stains a small number of cells. (This is characteristic of several salts of heavy metals.) For this reason they stand out in stark contrast against the surrounding unstained cells (Spotlight Figure 2-1a). Other staining chemicals, such as methylene blue and cresyl violet, are specific for nucleic acids and highlight the nucleus, nucleolus, and ribosomes found in the cell bodies (Spotlight Figure 2-1b). Still other stains are only taken up by the fatty myelin that surrounds neuron axons. These stains make it possible to identify

fiber bundles within the brain (Spotlight Figure 2-1c).

Some stains and tracer chemicals may be introduced into living tissue with interesting results. Horseradish peroxidase (HRP), a protein enzyme, when injected into a small area of the brain is taken up by living neurons and transported through the axons back to the cell bodies. Subsequently, when the tissue is thinly sliced and treated, the cell bodies containing the HRP can be highlighted under dark-field illumination. Using this technique, it is possible to identify the origin of neurons that terminate in the area of brain treated with the HRP (Spotlight Figure 2-1d).

Light microscopy has a limited ability to view organelles within cells and small parts of cells. The advent of the electron microscope allowed for levels of magnification more than 100 times greater than that provided by the most powerful light microscopes. To this the scanning electron microscope added the dimension of depth (Spotlight Figure 2-1e).

The resting potential is due to an unequal distribution of ions inside and outside the cell. Fortunately, this too can be demonstrated using the very large axon found in the squid. If the **axoplasm** (that part of the neuron's cytoplasm found inside the axon) is extruded from the axon and the ion content is analyzed, it is found to differ from the ion content of the extracellular fluid. Specifically, the axoplasm has a higher concentration of potassium ions (K^+) and a lower concentration of sodium (Na^+) and chloride (Cl^-) ions. Additionally, there are large protein anions in the axoplasm that are not found outside the cell. The relative concentrations of ions on either side of the neuron membrane are shown in Figure 2-5a and Figure 2-5b.

The Sodium–Potassium Pump

The question still to be addressed is: What causes the unequal distribution of ions across the membrane of the neuron? The physical mechanisms of **diffusion** (the tendency of ions to disperse equally to all areas of a solvent) and **osmosis** (the tendency for the solvent to move through a semipermeable membrane toward higher concentrations of solute) would both work to equalize the distribution of the various ions on either side of the membrane. Something must be at work to cause this disequilibrium.

The resting potential must be due to the selective movement of ions across the membrane. The protein anion is not a likely candidate. Although its negative charge may influence ions that are in close proximity to it, the anion has a very large molecular structure that will not permit it to cross the membrane. That is why the protein is found only inside the axoplasm where it is produced. One or more of the other ions must be responsible for the resting potential. A clue to this problem can be found in still another study making use of the squid axon.

If a segment of the squid axon is placed in seawater, it will continue to function for a short period of time. If the seawater contains sodium ions that are radioactive, thus allowing us to trace their movement, the radioactive ions are noted to enter the cell. This demonstrates that the membrane is permeable to sodium. More important, the concentration of sodium inside the cell does not change during the process. This proves that an equal number of sodium ions were forced out of the cell against the higher concentration of sodium ions in the seawater! This could only occur if there was an active, energy-driven mechanism at work. That mechanism is the **sodium–potassium pump**.

The membrane of the neuron, like other cell membranes, is constructed of two layers of lipid molecules. The membrane is only about 5 nanometers (nm) thick and has various protein molecules on its surface and embedded in the lipid layers. The specific proteins associated with a cell membrane do much to control its function. For example, the flow of various ions in and out of the cell is controlled by the specific proteins in the cell membrane. The proteins may be divided into five types that

Figure 2-5
a. By taking advantage of the giant axon of the squid, researchers are able to measure the electrical potential produced by the distribution of ions on either side of the cell membrane. *b.* Schematic representation of the significant ions found on either side of the neuron membrane. The relative concentrations (also shown in parentheses) are indicated by the size of the circles representing each ion species.

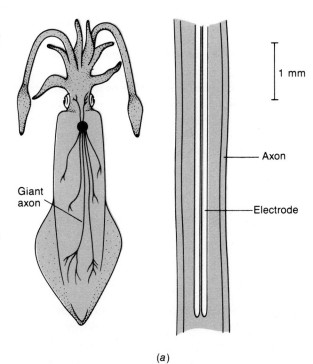

Giant axon

Axon

Electrode

1 mm

(a)

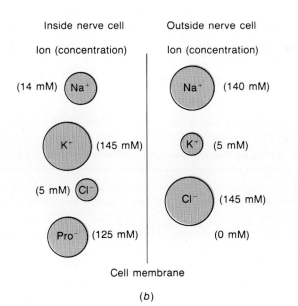

Inside nerve cell

Ion (concentration)

Outside nerve cell

Ion (concentration)

(14 mM) Na⁺

Na⁺ (140 mM)

K⁺ (145 mM)

K⁺ (5 mM)

(5 mM) Cl⁻

Cl⁻ (145 mM)

Pro⁻ (125 mM)

(0 mM)

Cell membrane

(b)

SPOTLIGHT 2-2

The Movement of Ions

There are several physical forces that influence the distribution and movement of molecules in solution. When a substance (the *solute*) dissolves in water, or in some other *solvent*, the molecules tend to disperse throughout the liquid. If you were to place a cube of sugar at the bottom of a beaker of water, the sugar molecules would eventually become distributed throughout the water, even without agitating the fluid. At first, the molecules of sugar would be more concentrated around the bottom of the beaker; however, they naturally tend to move from areas of high solute concentration to areas of low solute concentration. That is, *substances in solution tend to diffuse down the gradient of concentration to areas of lower concentration.*

Now assume that a membrane barrier is placed between two areas of solvent that have different concentrations of solute. If the barrier is freely *permeable* to both the solute and the solvent (i.e., allows molecules of both to pass through unimpeded), the molecules of both substances will move through the membrane and establish an equal distribution of the solute and the solvent on either side (Spotlight Figure 2-2a).

Now assume that the membrane is *semipermeable*, allowing the solvent to pass through freely but blocking the solute because its molecules are too large. The solvent will move across the membrane in the direction from the area of higher concentration to the area of lower concen-

tration. In ideal conditions, and in the absence of gravitational forces, the solvent would become distributed so as to equalize the concentration of solute on both sides of the membrane. The movement of solvent through a semipermeable membrane is known as **osmosis** (Spotlight Figure 2-2b). (In the presence of gravity a perfect balance in concentration levels could not be achieved. The force of gravity would produce *hydrostatic pressure* that works in opposition to osmosis and tends to equalize the amount of water on either side of the membrane.)

Some substances (electrolytes) form charged particles (ions) when they enter into solution. Common table salt, sodium chloride (NaCl), is a good example of an electrolyte. In solution, the sodium and chlorine atoms split apart, forming positively charged sodium ions and negatively charged chloride ions. Ions that carry a positive charge are called *cations*, and negatively charged ions are called *anions*.

Ions that have the same kind of charge tend to be repelled, whereas ions of different charges are attracted. When anions and cations are not equally distributed in solution, *electostatic pressure* moves the ions in a way that will balance the distribution. Anions move away from areas that have higher concentrations of negative ions toward areas that have higher concentrations of cations. Electrostatic pressure is largely responsible for the equal distribution of ions inside and outside of living cells.

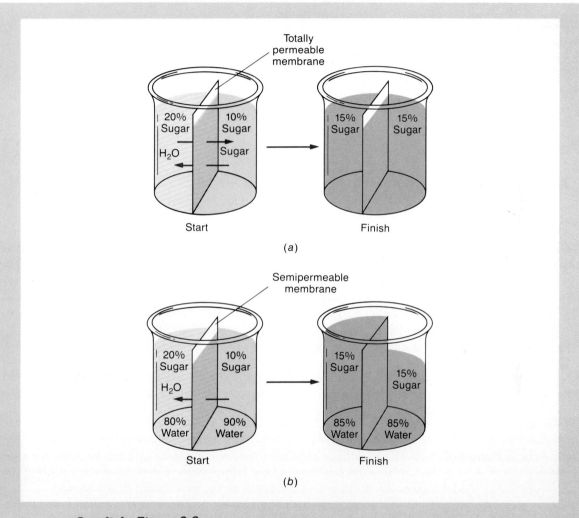

(a)

(b)

Spotlight Figure 2-2
a. With a completely permeable membrane both the solvent and solute are
able to cross over and equalize the concentration of solute on both sides.
b. With a semipermeable membrane only the solvent can pass through the
membrane. The solvent molecules move from the area of higher concentration
across the membrane (osmosis) to the area of lower concentration.

Figure 2-6
Schematic of the
sodium–potassium ion
pump. Note that for every
three Na$^+$ ions moved
out of the cell, two K$^+$
ions enter the cell. The
net result is a negative ion
charge between the
cytoplasm and the
extracellular fluid.

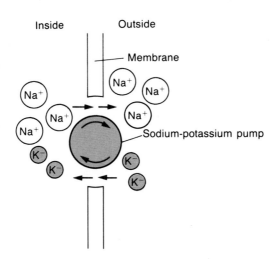

describe their function: pumps, channels, receptors, enzymes, and structural. The first four are of importance to us in this chapter.

Pumps differ from channels in that they actively move the ions through the membrane. Channels are passive and do not expend energy. Pumps and channels are usually named after the specific ions they control. The sodium–potassium pump controls the flow of sodium and potassium, pushing out approximately three sodium ions for every two potassium ions they allow to enter (see Figure 2-6). Because the remaining channels are not very permeable to Na$^+$, the net result is that the interior of the cell is negatively charged relative to the extracellular fluid. It has been estimated that 40% of the neuron's energy resources are used to drive the pump. This energy is provided by the mitochondria, and this accounts for the large number of mitochondria found in neurons.

The Action Potential

Now that we have seen how the resting potential is established, we need to address the problem of how information is sent down the length of the axon. To do this we turn again to the giant axon of the squid.

As noted earlier, using two electrodes and a voltmeter, we found that the resting potential of the cell was −70 mV. If the voltmeter is replaced by an oscilloscope, it is possible to make the same measurement and produce a record of the voltage over time. Now if small electric pulses are applied to the axon, we note that the charge inside of the axon changes for a short period of time and then it returns to −70 mV. Postive pulses increase the resting potential, whereas negative pulses decrease it. Small changes such as these are called **graded potentials**. Graded potentials that move in the more negative direction (more negative than −70 mV) are **hyperpolarizing**. When they move in a less negative direction, they are **hypopolarizing**.

Figure 2-7
Graphic representation showing the flow of Na^+ and K^+ ions across the cell membrane that produces the voltage changes associated with the propagated action potential. At the excitation threshold Na^+ voltage–driven channels open, allowing Na^+ in the extracellular fluid to enter the cell. The resulting positive charge inside the cell opens K^+ voltage–driven channels, causing K^+ ions to exit the cell. The sodium–potassium pump then returns the cell to the -70 mV resting potential.

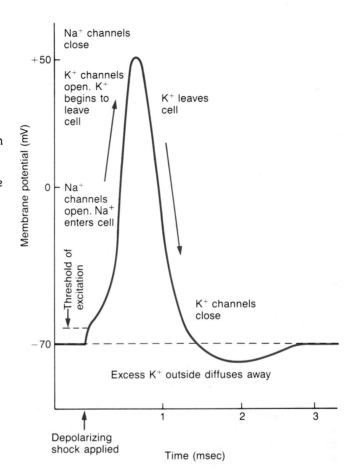

If several electric pulses are applied to the axon in rapid succession, the graded potential summates over time, producing larger graded potentials. When the graded potentials are in the hypopolarizing direction (becoming less negative), a point is reached when the polarity of the axon makes a sudden reversal and in less than 3 msec returns to its normal resting potential (see Figure 2-7). The reversal in polarity is termed the **action potential**, and the level of polarity where this reversal is triggered is called the **excitation threshold**. The threshold is usually in the range of -65 mV to -60 mV.

You may have guessed by now that the action potential is due to the movement of ions across the cell membrane. Experiments have shown that when the excitation threshold is reached, the membrane of the neuron suddenly becomes permeable to sodium ions, causing them to rush into the cell. This large influx of positively charged ions causes a drastic change in the potential inside the cell, making it positively charged. The presence of so many positively charged sodium ions causes a transient outflow of the positively charged potassium ions. Finally, the sodium–potassium pump pushes the sodium back out of the cell, and potassium enters, returning the cell to its original resting potential. But how is this orchestrated?

Ion Channels   As noted earlier, the neuron membrane has proteins embedded within the two lipid layers that serve as channels for the movement of ions through the membrane. The channels are specific in that they tend to be most permeable for only one type of ion. The channels act like valves, sometimes allowing their specific ions to flow freely and at other times shutting down the flow. The actual control of the valve is apparently accomplished by changing the shape of the protein molecule. Changes in the shape of complex molecules are called **conformation changes**. Many movements made by structures in single-celled organisms are accomplished using this mechanism. The proteins of some channels change shape in the presence of specific chemicals, whereas others (as in the case of the action potential) are sensitive to electrical charges. The latter are **voltage-dependent** channels.

When the membrane is depolarized and the excitation threshold is reached, sodium voltage-dependent channels open, allowing the influx of positively charged sodium ions. This in turn makes the inside of the cell more depolarized (positively charged), activating the potassium channels and allowing potassium ions to flow freely out through the cell membrane. The sodium channel is then closed, sodium is pumped out of the cell, and potassium is brought back into the cell. This sequence of channel action, combined with the operation of the sodium–potassium ion pump, determines the action potential wave form depicted in Figure 2-7. The exact mechanism that causes the protein molecules to return to the closed state is not known. The open state of the molecule is apparently unstable and can only be maintained for very brief periods. A schematic interpretation of the channel mechanisms is depicted in Figure 2-8.

Propagated Action   It was mentioned earlier that subthreshold graded potentials produced
Potentials   by stimulating the axon have a very short duration. That is, the small polarizing or depolarizing shifts away from the resting potential are actively eliminated by the cell's natural tendency to maintain its normal resting potential. What may also be noted is that the graded potential moves very rapidly in both directions (dromic and antidromic) away from the point of stimulation. The subthreshold electrical properties of the axon are said, therefore, to have **cable properties** in that the graded potential travels very rapidly and decreases in strength as it travels down the axon.

One is tempted to make the analogy with an electric current moving down a cable. The analogy is not totally accurate, because the progres-

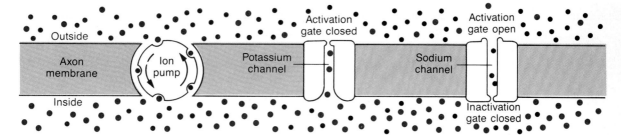

Figure 2-8

Schematic representation of the neuron cell membrane showing the sodium–potassium ion pump and the voltage-driven sodium and potassium ion channels. The fluid outside the membrane is 10 times richer in sodium ions than potassium ions. In the resting state (when there are no action potentials) the sodium and potassium channels are closed, and the sodium–potassium pump maintains the ion disequilibrium and the resultant −70 mV resting potential. When the excitation threshold is reached, the sodium ion channel opens, allowing sodium to enter. An instant later the sodium ion channel closes and the potassium channel opens, allowing the outflow of potassium ions. An instant later the potassium channel closes. The sequential opening and closing of the two voltage-driven channels produces the voltage shift observed in the propagated action. (From Stevens, 1979.)

sive decrement in strength of electric current in wire is due, primarily, to the resistance of the wire. In the axon the decrement is attributable mostly to capacitance (the different electric charge) between the axoplasm and the extracellular fluid. This capacitance effect interferes with the insulating properties of the cell membrane.

When a suprathreshold action potential occurs, the shift in polarity moves down the axon at a relatively slow rate compared to electrical conductance, and the size of the action potential does not diminish, as was noted with graded potentials. The propagated action potential is **nondecremental**. It is self-sustaining from the point of origin to the end brush. Note also that unlike graded potentials, which may vary over a range of values, the propagated action potential either occurs or it doesn't occur. This is often referred to as the **all-or-nothing response** of the neuron.

To visualize the propagated action potential, it may be helpful to compare it to a ripple moving across the surface of water. When the excitation threshold is reached, normally at the point of the hillock, the action potential occurs at that point and then moves in a smooth fashion down the axon. Stated in another way, the sequence of channel and pump events that produce an action potential at a given point occur in a continuous fashion down the length of the axon. This means, of course, that the energy required to maintain the resting potential at each point along the axon is expended as well. This explains why the propagated action potential is nondecremental; it is supported by energy stored by the action of the sodium–potassium pump and released by channel actions at successive points on the axon.

Consider the fact that neurons are capable of producing propagated action potentials many times each second, and that there are between 10^{10} to 10^{11} neurons in the human CNS. Is it any wonder that the CNS accounts for a large portion of the total metabolic energy expended by the entire body?

Saltatory Conduction   The movement of the propagated action potentials just described is accurate for unmyelinated neurons. Most neurons in the CNS, however, are myelinated by oligodendroglia, or Schwann cells. Myelination of axons was a significant evolutionary development, and it is most prevalent in the CNS of mammals. The adaptive advantage of myelination is that it increases the speed of conductance of neurons and produces a significant economy of energy.

There are actually two ways to increase the speed of axonal conductance. One is to increase the diameter of the axon. This is exactly why the giant axon of the squid is so large. Most mollusks have shells on their exterior and are relatively sedentary animals. The squid, however, evolved a very light internal shell and became a free swimmer. The rapid muscular movements required of this free-swimming form of mollusk could only be accomplished by the innervation of a rapid-acting nervous system. Because myelination of axons had not developed in the *Mollusca*, the squid evolved an enormous axon for this purpose.

The evolution of the myelin sheath made possible a new and more efficient means of increasing axon speed, **saltatory conduction** (*saltatory* comes from a Latin word meaning "to jump or dance"). Saltatory conduction takes advantage of the high speed of the cable qualities of the axon. This is how it works. The sheath has two effects: (1) it insulates the membrane of the axon from the extracellular fluid, thus reducing the capacitance effect; and (2) it eliminates any flow of ions in the segments of the axon under the sheath. Because myelinated axons have interruptions in the myelin sheath at approximately 1-mm intervals, the nodes of Ranvier, it is only at these points that the axon comes in contact with the extracellular fluid.

Try to visualize this sequence of events. The propagated action potential begins at the hillock. When the first myelinated segment is reached, the signal shifts into high gear by using the cable properties of the axon. Remember, however, that the cable qualities include the decremental loss of signal strength (this is moderated to some degree by the insulating properties of the sheath). The depolarized signal weakens until it reaches the first node of Ranvier, where it is slowed but strengthened by another propagated action potential and sent on using cable properties to the next node and so on. Each node of Ranvier acts like a booster on a high-power line. The net result is a nondecremental signal with a speed that can be in excess of 200 miles per hour (mph)! Also, this method of producing the propagated action potential conserves energy because the resting potential need only be depleted and regenerated at the nodes. The adaptive advantage in speed and energy conservation is quite apparent. See Figure 2-9 for a pictorial comparison of myelinated and unmyelinated propagated action potentials.

Figure 2-9
Comparison between the smooth action potential of unmyelinated axons (a) and the faster, saltatory propagated action potential seen in myelinated axons (b). Note the decremental cable transmission between the nodes in the myelinated axon.

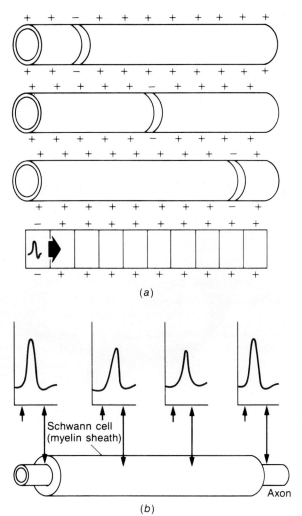

Interneuronal Communication

Thus far we have seen how a resting potential is established in the neuron and how this then permits the neuron to send a propagated action potential down the length of its axon. Under normal conditions the action potential starts at the point of the hillock and terminates at the end brush. Next we need to turn to interneuronal communication, that is, we need to understand how one neuron affects the behavior of another neuron. As was true with intraneuronal transmission, interneuronal transmission takes place in only one direction. The direction of communication is controlled by the synapse.

Synaptic Function   In the mammalian nervous system neurons rarely come into direct contact with each other. In most instances the cells interact biochemically across a small gap, the synapse (Bennett, 1973). The evolution of synaptic transmission introduced a new level of complexity and sophistication to interneuronal communication. Unlike direct electrical coupling, commonly found in many of the invertebrates, synaptic transmission ensures that communication between any two neurons is always unidirectional. Cell A can influence cell B without the action of cell B having an effect on cell A (see Figure 2-10).

Figure 2-10
Cell A is able to affect the resting potential of cell B across the synapse, shown in higher magnification at right. The synaptic action is unidirectional from A to B and does not affect the subsequent action of cell A.

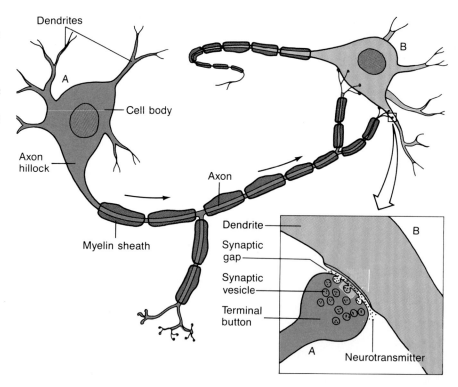

Each neuron synthesizes, stores, and transmits only one neurotransmitter at all the branches of its axon. This is known as **Dale's law**. There are some possible exceptions to this law, but none have been proven unequivocally (Osborne, 1979). Also, as we discuss later in this section, synaptic transmission makes use of special transmitter substances to effect communication between the neurons. Many different transmitter substances have been identified, and each one can be found to be active in one or more neural circuits in the CNS. In this way subsystems within the CNS may be isolated from other subsystems biochemically.

Presynaptic Events

Information at the synapse is passed in one direction, from the end brush of one neuron to the soma or axon of another. Events that take place at the end brush are termed **presynaptic**, whereas actions that take place on the other side of the synapse are called **postsynaptic**. The same terminology is used to refer to the cell structures associated with the synapse. Thus, the cell membrane where the buttons form one side of the synapse is called the **presynaptic membrane**, and the membrane forming the receiving side of the synapse is called the **postsynaptic membrane**.

The buttons found at the terminus of the end brush contain synaptic vesicles filled with thousands of neurotransmitter molecules. The walls of the vesicles are composed of membrane that is identical to the outside membrane of the neuron. The vesicles are produced in one of two places; by the Golgi bodies in the soma, and in some instances in the buttons themselves. The vesicles that are produced in the soma are transported to the end brush by the rhythmic constriction of delicate fibers and microtubules in the axon.

When a propagated action potential reaches the buttons, it causes voltage-driven calcium ion channels to open, allowing Ca^{2+} ions to enter the cell. This, in turn, causes vesicles that are in contact with the presynaptic membrane to join with the membrane, and in so doing, release their contents into the space of the synapse. The neurotransmitter molecules diffuse across the synapse and come in contact with the surface of the postsynaptic membrane. Figure 2-11 depicts the electrical and chemical events that occur at the synapse.

Postsynaptic Events

Upon reaching the postsynaptic membrane, neurotransmitters interact with protein molecules in the membrane called **postsynaptic receptors**. The result of this interaction is the production of small, momentary changes in the membrane potential of the postsynaptic cell. These graded potentials may be either hyperpolarizing or hypopolarizing. When the graded potential is hypopolarizing, it brings the postsynaptic cell closer to the excitation threshold; therefore, this type of synaptic action is called an **excitatory postsynaptic potential** (**EPSP**). Conversely, when the

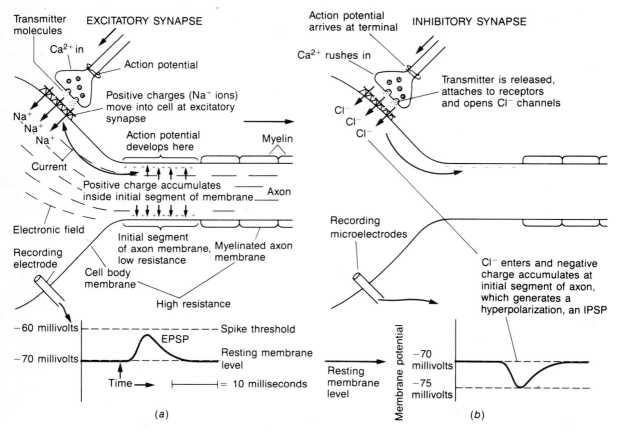

Figure 2-11
Schematic illustration of the postsynaptic effect of an excitatory synapse (a) and an inhibitory synapse (b). The EPSP is the result of the infusion of Na^+ ions, and the IPSP is due to the passage of Cl^- ions into the cell (or in some synapses, the passage of K^+ ions out of the cell). (From Thompson, 1985.)

graded potential is hyperpolarizing (made more negative relative to the extracellular fluid), the membrane potential is driven away from the excitation threshold. This is termed an **inhibitory postsynaptic potential (IPSP)**.

As you may have guessed, EPSPs and IPSPs are the result of the movement of ions in the area of the postsynaptic receptor sites. It has been shown that neurotransmitters that produce an excitatory effect cause the cell membrane to become momentarily more permeable to both Na^+ and K^+ ions. This causes Na^+ to enter the cell and K^+ to leave the cell. Because many more Na^+ ions enter than K^+ ones leave, the net change in potential is positive, hypopolarizing the cell. When neurotransmitters are inhibitory, they open K^+ or Cl^- channels, allowing K^+ to leave the cell, or allowing Cl^- to enter the cell. The result is that the cell becomes more negatively charged relative to the extracellular fluid and is, therefore, farther from the excitatory threshold and less likely to produce a propagated action potential.

The momentary nature of the postsynaptic potentials is attributable to several factors. The duration of the neurotransmitter's ability to hold ion channels open is limited. In some cases the transmitters are deactivated by enzymes that break down the transmitter molecule. For example, the very common neurotransmitter **acetylcholine (ACh)** is broken into two smaller components, choline and acetate, by its specific enzyme **acetylcholinesterase (AChE)**. More commonly, the transmitters are simply removed from the synaptic cleft by the presynaptic membrane of the button. This process, called **re-uptake**, is very rapid and gives the postsynaptic membrane a very brief exposure to the transmitter.

Figure 2-12 depicts the three most common types of synapses: **axodendritic**, **axosomatic**, and **axoaxonic**. The first two produce EPSPs and IPSPs, as just described. As can be seen in Figure 2-12, the axoaxonic synapse produces its effect in an indirect way by reducing the level of excitation of another synapse. Because the end result of axoaxonic transmission is reduced excitation, this type of transmission is called **presynaptic inhibition**. One example of presynaptic inhibition is found in the **Renshaw cells** in the spinal reflex arc. Here presynaptic inhibition is a means of regulating the frequency and magnitude of reflexive action (see Chapter 3).

Neural Integration   Keep in mind that the action of the sodium–potassium pump is not affected by postsynaptic potentials. It continues to operate and constantly works to maintain the resting potential of the cell at a -70 mV. Now try to visualize not just one but dozens of postsynaptic potentials acting on the cell. Many of the synapses produce EPSPs and move the graded potential toward the excitation threshold, whereas others produce IPSPs that hyperpolarize the cell.

The combined effect of the EPSPs and IPSPs summate in an algebraic fashion. This summation may be temporal and/or spatial. Several EPSPs that take place at the same time on different parts of the cell membrane sum to produce a shift in the graded potential that is greater than that produced by a single EPSP; this is called **spatial summation**. In a similar fashion, several EPSPs occurring in rapid succession produce a shift in the graded potential that is greater than that produced by a single EPSP; this is called **temporal summation**. Obviously, the same is true for the combined effect of IPSPs (see Figure 2-13).

Movement of the graded potential in response to the temporal and spatial summation of EPSPs and IPSPs is termed **neural integration**.

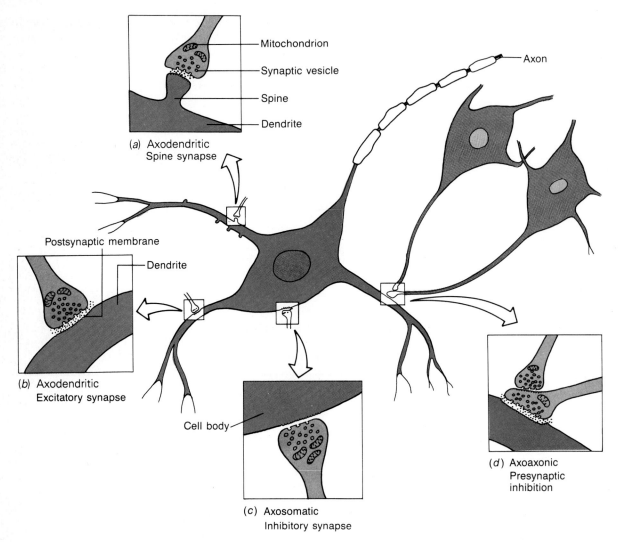

Figure 2-12
Schematic of the different types of synapses on a neuron. Both the spine (a)
and lower dendrite synapse (b) are thought to be excitatory. The axosomatic
synapse (c) is inhibitory. The axoaxonic synapse (d) produces presynaptic
inhibition. (Adapted from Iversen, 1979.)

When the graded potential reaches the excitation threshold, the all-or-
none propagated action potential is produced and the cell process begins
again. It is tempting to make the analogy between neural integration and
the way a hybrid analog-to-digital computer functions.

A digital computer processes sequences of yes/no, one/zero, or on/off
signals to make complex messages. Although it is very rapid, it only deals

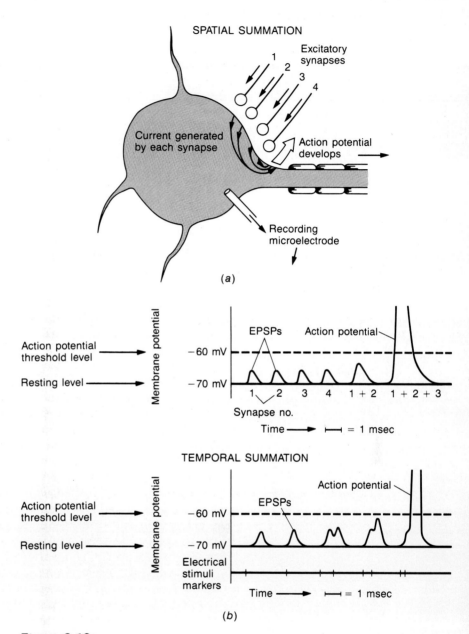

Figure 2-13
Schematic showing the effect of spatial summation of EPSPs (*a*) and temporal summation of EPSPs (*b*). Both types of summation may take place at the same time on the same cell. Summation of IPSPs occurs in the same fashion. (From Thompson, 1985.)

Degeneration and Regeneration of Neurons

Unlike the cells in other tissues, neurons have a limited ability to repair themselves. This is particularly true for neurons in mammals. There are, in fact, two general trends concerning the ability of neurons to regenerate: (1) regeneration is much more limited in warm-blooded animals (**homotherms**) compared to cold-blooded animals (**endotherms**) and (2) regeneration is more limited in the brain than in peripheral areas.

When a nerve cell axon is injured, several forms of regrowth can occur. Typically, if the injury occurs close to the cell body of the neuron, **retrograde degeneration** begins, resulting in destruction of the cell. If, however, the axon is transected at some distance from the cell body, degeneration takes place in the direction away from the soma. This is called **Wallerian**, or **anterograde, degeneration**. In nerve cells outside of the brain regeneration of the axon can occur. Sprouts emerge from the part of the axon that is still connected to the cell body and grow away from the cell body toward the original termination point of the axon. (see Spotlight Figure 2-3).

It is interesting to note that trans-neuronal atrophy may also occur. It seems that the loss of input resulting from degenerating neurons can cause otherwise healthy neurons to dysfunction and degenerate. Apparently, for some nerve cells, survival is dependent on continued input from other neurons.

The study of nerve cell degeneration and regeneration is important for several reasons. As you will see later, it is possible (using special staining techniques) to trace degenerating axons. By lesioning axons, waiting for them to degenerate, and then staining the degenerating tissue, it is possible to study the origin and termination points of nerve circuits in the brain. The regeneration of axons involves processes that are very similar to the ontological development of neurons in the fetus. Studying the regeneration process in mature cells may provide valuable data about the growth and organization of nerve cells in the developing fetus.

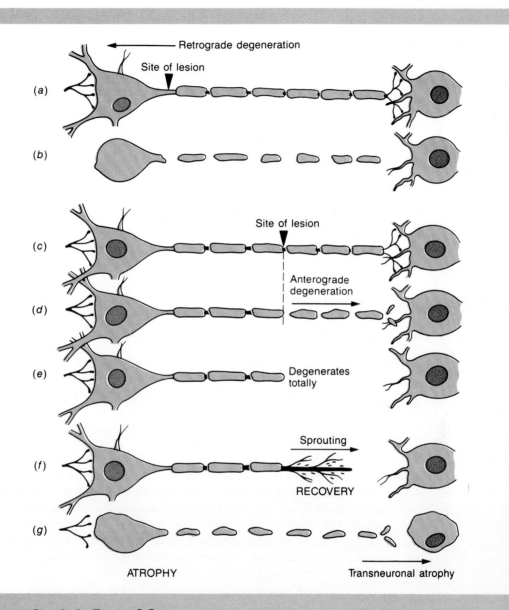

Spotlight Figure 2-3
The types of degeneration and regeneration. *a.* Lesion to the axon near the soma. *b.* Retrograde degeneration following transection of axon causing the cell to die. *c.* Lesion to the peripheral portion of the axon. *d.* Anterograde degeneration following transection of the axon. *e.* Atrophy of the nerve cell following anterograde degeneration. *f.* Regeneration of transected axon by sprouting of new nerve endings. *g.* Transneuronal degeneration. The loss of input may induce degeneration of other neurons in the pathway.

with one bit of information at a time, not unlike the all-or-none response of the neuron. An analog computer is able to sample voltage levels from several sources at the same time, integrate them, and make decisions about their combined effect, a process that is similar to neural integration. A hybrid analog-to-digital computer senses continuous analog data from one or more sources, integrates the analog data over periods of time, makes decisions about the combined level of the analog data, and converts the data to a digital output signal—quite like a neuron.

It strains one's imagination to think of 10^{10} analog-to-digital computers packaged into the brain. It is more awesome to imagine the number of possible combinations and permutations of potential interactions that could take place between them. It has been estimated that the number of interconnections that are possible between the neurons in the human brain is greater than the number of particles in the universe! (This is a figure I would rather not try to contemplate, much less try to document.)

Neurotransmitters

The study of the chemistry of the brain—specifically, the study of neurotransmitters—holds great promise for solutions to many fundamental questions about the brain and behavior. Clearly, the action of neurotransmitters is basic for normal brain activity. Anything that contributes to or detracts from the normal biological activity of these substances will consequently affect behavior.

The following conditions may all influence the normal action of neurotransmitters:

1. The chemical transmitter must first be synthesized. Most transmitter substances that have been identified to date are relatively simple compounds. Some are synthesized as the product of normal metabolism; others are parts of the proteins that we consume in our food.

2. Once transmitters have been synthesized or consumed, they must be transported to the axon terminal and stored in the vesicles. In some cases the synthesis may actually take place in the axon terminal.

3. The amount of transmitter substance available in the brain is regulated or limited. Usually, one step in the synthesis or storage process serves as the **rate-limiting factor**. Knowledge about the rate-limiting factor can be extremely important to us. Many brain disorders, such as major depression, are thought to result from abnormal levels of transmitter substance.

4. There must be a mechanism by which neurotransmitters are deactivated. If this were not true and the transmitter continued to act on the postsynaptic cells, the brain would go out of control. The deactivation of transmitter substances can take place in several ways. The substance

Figure 2-14
The process of pinocytosis. The neurotransmitter substance or its component parts move away from the synaptic cleft and are taken up by small pockets in the cell membrane that form the synaptic vesicles.

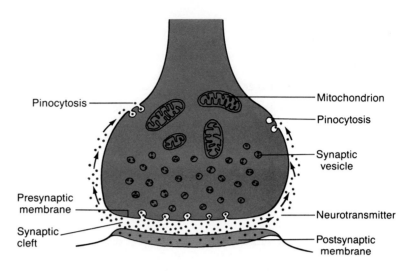

may be broken down into component parts by an enzyme that is specific for that neurotransmitter. The transmitter may attach to the postsynaptic membrane only briefly, and then it may be released and carried away. The rate of deactivation may vary widely. This may account for some of the variance in the effective time of different neurotransmitters.

5. Once deactivated, the transmitter must be dealt with in some way. It is thought that the transmitter substance or its component parts are taken back up by the terminals and reused. This may occur through a process called **pinocytosis**, in which a small pocket forms on the cell membrane and fills with the transmitter substance. The pocket then pinches off to form a synaptic vesicle (see Figure 2-14). Although this is an efficient mechanism, it is not perfect, and some of the transmitter is lost and ultimately metabolized. For this reason transmitter chemicals must be replaced constantly.

We have seen that neurotransmitters produce one of two effects, excitation or inhibition. There are, however, considerably more than two neurotransmitters. Some neurotransmitters appear to have only an excitatory function, whereas others are solely inhibitory. Others appear to be excitatory in some parts of the CNS and inhibitory in other parts.

Additionally, some neurotransmitters seem to produce their effect for a longer period of time. These transmitters, called **neuromodulators** appear to have their action at sites some distance from the synapse and they act more like hormones in that they enter the cell and then regulate the cell's activity for some time. (We discuss the way hormones affect the body and behavior in some detail in Chapter 4.) Table 2-1 lists those substances that are known to be neuro-transmitters and others whose role as a transmitter is suspected, but not yet proven. The table also shows the location in the CNS where the transmitters are believed to be active and their hypothesized effect.

Table 2-1. Probable Transmitter Substances

Probable Transmitter Substance	Location in CNS	Hypothesized Effect
Acetylcholine (ACh)	Brain, spinal cord, autonomic ganglia, target organs of the parasympathetic nervous system	Excitation in brain and autonomic ganglia, excitation or inhibition in target organs
Norepinephrine (NE)	Brain, spinal cord, target organs of sympathetic nervous system	Inhibition in brain, excitation or inhibition in target organs
Dopamine (DA)	Brain	Inhibition
Serotonin (5-hydroxytryptamine, or 5-HT)	Brain, spinal cord	Inhibition
Gamma-aminobutyric acid (GABA)	Brain (especially cerebral and cerebellar cortex), spinal cord	Inhibition
Glycine	Spinal cord interneurons	Inhibition
Glutamic acid	Brain, spinal sensory neurons	Excitation
Aspartic acid	Spinal cord interneurons, brain (?)	Excitation
Substance P	Brain, spinal sensory neurons (pain)	Excitation (and inhibition?)
Histamine, taurine, other amino acids; peptides such as oxytocin and endogenous opiates; many others	Various regions of brain, spinal cord, and peripheral nervous system	(?)

The number of substances that have been identified as candidate neurotransmitters has increased in recent years. However, the general trend in the evolution of species has been to increase in the diversity of uses for a given neurotransmitter rather than to increase in the number of transmitter substances (Venter et al., 1988). This is consistent with the conservative nature of the evolutionary process, which tends to build on existing mechanisms that have stood the test of time.

There is much that we do not know about the neurotransmitters in the CNS. The evidence that implicates various substances as neurotransmitters varies from strong to very weak. This is due to the extraordinary technical difficulties associated with "proving" that a given chemical is a neurotransmitter. Many substances at this point in time can only be characterized as potential candidates. In this introduction I am concentrating only on those neurotransmitters that have been studied extensively and that we can now claim with some degree of confidence to be neurotransmitters.

Acetylcholine

Acetylcholine (ACh) is the transmitter that operates in the peripheral nervous system at the junction of the nerves and muscles. Because of this we know more about acetylcholine than any other transmitter substance. There is now strong evidence to suggest that ACh functions as a transmitter in the central nervous system as well.

Acetylcholine is synthesized in one step from choline and acetyl coenzyme A (acetyl CoA). Choline cannot be manufactured in the body and must be obtained from food (eggs and many vegetables are rich sources of choline). The amount of available choline appears to be the rate-limiting factor for the production of ACh (Figure 2-15).

ACh may be synthesized in the terminal end of the neuron or in the cell body and transported to the synaptic terminal. When an action potential reaches the terminal, Ca^{2+}-specific channels open and Ca^{2+} enters the presynaptic cell. This causes ACh to be released into the

Figure 2-15
The acetylcholine synapse. ACh is synthesized from choline and acetyl CoA. After the ACh is released into the synapse, it is inactivated by AChE and broken down into choline and acetate. The choline is taken back into the presynaptic cell and reused to synthesize more ACh. (Adapted from Cooper, Bloom, & Roth, 1978.)

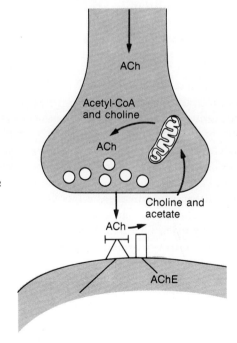

synapse. As we noted earlier in this chapter, ACh is inactivated by acetylcholinesterase (AChE), which breaks the ACh down into choline and acetate. Much of the choline is taken back into the axon terminal to be reused in the synthesis of ACh. The acetate is used by all cells for other metabolic processes.

ACh excites the skeletal muscles, but it inhibits heart muscle. This fact clearly demonstrates that a given neurotransmitter may produce different effects in different receptor targets. Evidently, the excitatory or inhibitory effect of the transmitter is determined by the nature of the receptor site. This explains why curare, a drug that blocks the effect of ACh in skeletal muscles, does not produce an effect on the heart. In a similar fashion, atropine blocks the effect of ACh in heart muscle but has no effect on skeletal muscle. In the same vein, nicotine mimics the effect of ACh, but only in skeletal muscle; and muscarine mimics ACh in heart muscle, but not in skeletal muscle.

Cholinergic activity can also be influenced by drugs that moderate the action of the enzyme AChE. For example, physostigmine blocks AChE. The net result of this is to prolong ACh action, which may lead to convulsions and even death. Some of the most deadly nerve gases developed for use in World War I produce their effect by blocking AChE. Fortunately, the use of these gases has been banned by international treaty.

Amino Acid Transmitters

Several amino acids are thought to be neurotransmitters. Some of these substances, such as **glutamic acid** and **aspartic acid**, appear to be only excitatory; others such as **gamma-aminobutyric acid** (**GABA**) are thought to be exclusively inhibitory. The evidence for most amino acid transmitters is still somewhat weak. However, there is good evidence to support GABA as a neurotransmitter. (See Cooper, Bloom, & Roth [1978] for a review.)

Gamma-aminobutyric acid is synthesized from L-glutamic acid by the enzyme glutamic acid decarboxylase (GAD). The glutamic acid is thought to be transported to the axon terminal by axoplasmic flow. There it is converted by GAD into GABA and stored in vesicles. As was true with ACh, the GABA is released into the synaptic cleft when action potentials open Ca^{2+} ion channels on the presynaptic membrane.

The postsynaptic membrane has GABA receptors, onto which the GABA molecules attach. When these receptor molecules are activated by the GABA, they open Cl^- ion channels on the postsynaptic membrane. Because the concentration of Cl^- is greater outside of the cell, Cl^- rushes in, increasing the cell's negative charge. This action produces an IPSP (Figure 2-16).

The importance of the inhibitory function of GABA can be demonstrated pharmacologically. A drug called bicuculline is a particularly potent blocker of GABA. Injected into the blood, even in minute quanti-

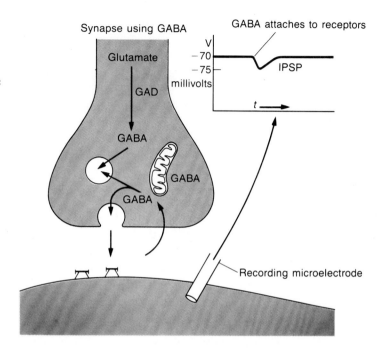

Figure 2-16
The formation of GABA from glutamate by the action of GAD. The GABA is released into the synaptic cleft by action potentials. The GABA attaches to receptor sites on the postsynaptic membrane. This causes Cl^- ions to enter the postsynaptic cell, producing an IPSP. (Adapted from Cooper, Bloom, & Roth, 1978.)

ties, it crosses the blood–brain barrier, freely causing convulsions and death. It is thought that the convulsions occur because the inhibitory action of the GABA circuits is lost. In the absence of this essential inhibition the excitatory neurons in the brain are unbridled.

Recently, GABA has been implicated in anxiety in humans. The tranquilizers Valium and Librium appear to act on specific receptor sites associated with the GABA synapses in the brain (Costa, 1983).

Catecholamines
The catecholamines are a diverse group of chemical substances widely distributed in the brain and peripheral nervous system. Two of the catecholamines, **dopamine (DA)** and **norepinephrine (NE)**, are of importance to us here.

Both neurotransmitters are synthesized from tyrosine, an amino acid that naturally occurs in many foods. In the first two steps of the synthesis, tyrosine is converted to L-dopa by the enzyme tyrosine hydroxylase, which is then converted into DA by a second enzyme, aromatic amino acid decarboxylase. Cells that use NE contain a third enzyme, dopamine-ß-hydroxylase, which converts the dopamine into norepinephrine. Tyrosine hydroxylase appears to be the rate-limiting substance for both neurotransmitters; therefore, the amount of tyrosine hydroxylase available in the cell determines the amount of neurotransmitter that can be synthesized (see Figure 2-17).

DA and NE are released into the synapse when an action potential causes Ca^{2+} to enter the axon terminal. The molecules of DA or NE diffuse across the synapse and attach to receptor sites on the postsynaptic membrane. It is thought that the DA and NE receptor sites do not control ion channels on the postsynaptic membrane directly. Rather, they influence the flow of ions indirectly through activation of a second-messenger system. (There is reason to believe that ACh synapses in the brain may operate in a similar fashion.)

Some of the DA and NE molecules are released by the receptor sites and diffuse back across the synapse, where they are taken up by the presynaptic membrane. Excess amounts of DA and NE are metabolized in the synapse by two important enzymes, **monoamine oxidase** (**MAO**) and **catechol methyltransferase** (**COMT**). MAO is also found in the mitochondria within the axon terminal where it metabolizes excess amounts of the neurotransmitters.

Dopaminergic and noradrenergic (norepinephrine) synapses in the brain may be either inhibitory or excitatory, depending on the nature of the target neuron. There are three major DA circuits in the brain, and all three start in the lower parts of the brain (in what is called the brain stem and midbrain) and send their fibers to higher brain centers. Dopaminergic circuits play an important role in motor behavior, and they are thought to be involved in some important way in schizophrenia, the most severe mental disorder. Degeneration of specific DA-containing neurons is the cause of Parkinson's disease, which is characterized by motor tremors, repetitive movements, "pill-rolling" movements of the fingers, and difficulty in standing and walking. Once treated surgically, Parkinson's disease is now controlled quite effectively with the administration of L-dopa, the precursor to dopamine.

The role of DA in schizophrenia was discovered serendipitously. Researchers noted that several drugs that are quite different chemically have antipsychotic properties. These drugs, including chlorpromazine and haloperidol, all have one common characteristic: they interfere with the DA synapse. The so-called **dopamine hypothesis of schizophrenia** proposes that schizophrenia is the result of overactive dopaminergic circuits in specific parts of the brain. It is interesting to note that the same drugs used to treat schizophrenia by depleting DA induce Parkinson-like symptoms. Conversely, the administration of L-dopa to treat Parkinson's disease produces schizophrenialike symptoms in some patients.

There are few noradrenergic circuits in the brain. Most of the NE circuits originate in the lower part of the brain and project their fibers to many widely distributed areas in the brain. Noradrenergic circuits have been implicated in wake and sleep cycles, attention levels, and learning. Powerful stimulants such as the amphetamines and cocaine are thought to produce their effect by increasing the activity of NE circuits.

Figure 2-17

a. The dopaminergic synapse. Tyrosine is converted into L-dopa, which is then synthesized into dopamine. Dopamine is released into the synapse when Ca^{2+} enters the axon terminal and diffuses to the postsynaptic membrane, where it attaches to receptor sites. Excess dopamine is broken down by MAO and COMT in the synapse and by MAO within the axon terminal. The metabolic products are further metabolized elsewhere and excreted from the body. *b.* The noradrenergic synapse. The processes of the adrenergic synapse are quite similar to that seen in the dopaminergic synapse. The presence of an additional enzyme; dopamine-β-oxidase converts the dopamine to norepinephrine. (Both figures adapted from Cooper, Bloom, & Roth, 1978.)

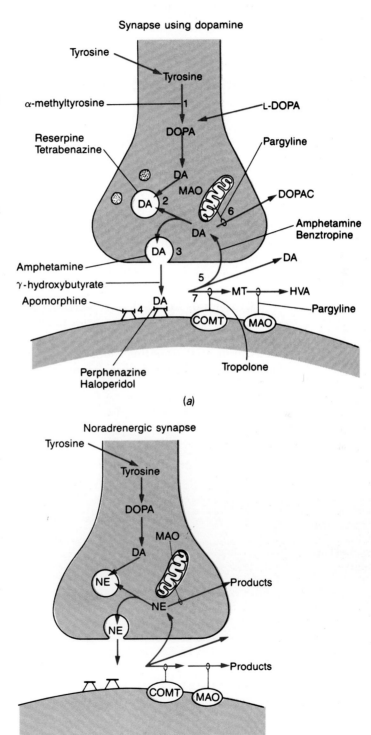

Synapse using dopamine

(a)

Noradrenergic synapse

(b)

Additionally, drugs that are used therapeutically to treat severe depression appear to act primarily on the NE system.

Serotonin

Serotonin (**5-hydroxytryptamine**, or **5-HT**), the last neurotransmitter we will discuss, is known to be an important factor in the regulation of body temperature and sleep. Serotonin is synthesized in two steps from the naturally occurring amino acid tryptophan. Tryptophan is transported down the axon to the terminal, where it is converted by the enzyme tryptophan hydroxylase into 5-OH-tryptophan, which is then converted into 5-HT (Figure 2-18).

Serotonin is released into the synapse by the presynaptic action potential and diffuses to the postsynaptic membrane, where it attaches to specific receptor sites. The action of 5-HT on the postsynaptic cell is not well understood, but it is thought to act primarily as an inhibitor. Serotonin is released and reabsorbed by the presynaptic cell. Excess levels of serotonin are metabolized in the synapse and the axon terminal by MAO.

Serotonin is found in large amounts in the pineal gland. (You will recall from Chapter 1 that Descartes placed the soul in the pineal gland because it is centrally located and it is the only structure in the brain that is not duplicated on either side.) Serotonin is converted in the pineal gland to a substance called melatonin. You will see in Chapter 11 that

Figure 2-18
The serotonergic synapse: Tryptophan is converted in two steps to 5-hydroxytryptamine, which is released into the synapse and becomes attached to receptor sites on the postsynaptic membrane. The 5-HT is then released and reabsorbed by the presynaptic membrane. Excess 5-HT is metabolized by MAO. (Adapted from Cooper, Bloom, & Roth, 1978.)

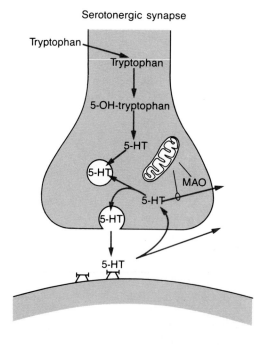

serotonin and melatonin function in rhythmic activities including the migratory behavior of birds and the 24-hour wake and sleep cycle.

Serotonin has been the object of much study because it has been linked with lysergic acid diethylamide (LSD), the powerful hallucinogenic drug. The shape of the LSD molecule is very similar to serotonin. Because of this, the receptor sites for serotonin accept the LSD molecule and in so doing block the effect of serotonin. The vivid hallucinogenic experiences produced by LSD may be due, at least in part, to the loss of inhibition in the serotoninergic circuits of the brain.

In this chapter we have reviewed the structures of the cell and discussed their specific functions. The neuron was described as a highly modified cell that has evolved very specifically to communicate and coordinate between the other neurons, muscles, and glands. Finally, the mechanisms that control intra- and interneuronal communication were reviewed. In Chapter 3 we consider how the neuron is used as a building block in the central and peripheral nervous systems. Also, we discuss the functional anatomy of the brain with particular attention to how the current structure and function of the human brain evolved.

CHAPTER SUMMARY

1. The earliest forms of plants and animals were single-celled organisms. Complex animals are groups of cells that have become specialized to perform different functions.

2. Each cell contains organelles that have their unique function. Neurons are thought to have evolved from special sensory cells in the outer layer of simple organisms. Neurons are specially modified cells that have many organelles in common with other body cells.

3. The typical neuron is comprised of a cell body, or soma, as well as dendrites, axons, and terminal buttons. Neurons come in many different shapes, and the shape of a neuron is closely related to its function.

4. Neurons have evolved to be so specialized for their unique function that they have lost some capabilities that are normally found in other cells. Glial cells, which outnumber the neurons by a factor of 10, provide much of the metabolic support required of the neurons.

5. Different techniques for staining brain tissue highlight various parts of cells. Modern staining techniques have been very useful in providing information about the organization of cells in the brain.

6. Neurons maintain a resting potential, with the inside of the cell being negative (-70 mV) compared to the outside. The resting potential is the result of the distribution of ions on either side of the cell membrane. Specific ion channels in the cell membrane and the action of the sodium–potassium pump maintain the resting potential.

7. Neurons send signals down the length of the axon in waves called propagated action potentials. This occurs when the membrane is depolarized, causing sodium ions to enter rapidly. Action potentials of a given neuron have approximately the same amplitude. This is the all-or-none response.

8. Immediately after an action potential, the cell enters a refractory period during which it is incapable of producing another propagated action potential.

9. Action potentials of unmyelinated axons move down the length of the axon rather slowly. Highly myelinated axons have saltatory conduction which greatly increases the speed of the action potential. This occurs because the action potential "jumps" between the nodes of Ranvier, using the cable properties of the myelinated segments.

10. Neurons do not come into direct contact; they communicate across a small gap called the synapse. The membrane of the sending neuron is called the presynaptic membrane. The membrane of the receiving neuron is called the postsynaptic membrane. There are two possible results of synaptic action: (1) the postsynaptic cell can be excited (EPSP), and (2) the postsynaptic cell can be inhibited (IPSP).

11. Action potentials cause neurons to release neurotransmitters into the synapse. The transmitter substances attach to receptor sites on the postsynaptic membrane. The bonding of the neurotransmitter to the receptor sites causes excitation or inhibition of the postsynaptic cell. The EPSPs and IPSPs produce small changes on the postsynaptic membrane called graded potentials. Graded potentials can be added in an algebraic fashion temporally and/or spatially.

12. Each neuron produces only one kind of transmitter substance. This is known as Dale's law. Different transmitters seem to be important for different aspects of behavior. In some instances the effect of a given transmitter substance is determined by the nature of the receiving cell.

13. Many drugs that are psychoactive produce their effect by acting on various aspects of the production, storage, transmission, and deactivation of neurotransmitters.

14. Some mental abnormalities, including depression and schizophrenia, are thought to be attributable to abnormal levels of neurotransmitters in various circuits of the brain.

SUGGESTED READINGS

Edelman, G. M., Gall, W. E., & Cowan, W. M. Eds. (1987). *New insights into synaptic function.* New York: Wiley.

Iversen, L. L. (1979). The chemistry of the brain. In *The brain* [a *Scientific American* book]. San Francisco: Freeman.

Kandel, E. R., & Schwartz, J. H. Eds. (1981). *Principles of neural science.* New York: Elsevier/North Holland.

Kuffler, S. W., Nicholls, J. G., & Martin, R. (1984). *From neuron to brain: A cellular approach to the function of the nervous system.* Sunderland, ME: Sinauer Associates.

KEY TERMS

Acetylcholine (ACH) Neurotransmitter commonly found in the central and peripheral nervous systems.

Acetylcholinesterase (AChE) Enzyme found in postsynaptic cells that breaks acetylcholine into choline and acetate.

Action potential Rapid shift in the polarity of the neuron which typically takes place at the point of the hillock.

All-or-nothing response Term used to describe the nature of intraneuronal communication. Once an action potential is triggered, it is propagated without decrement to the end of the axon.

Anterograde degeneration Axonal degeneration in the direction away from the cell body.

Aspartic acid An amino acid thought to be a central nervous system transmitter substance.

Axoaxonic The synapse of a button on another axon. This type of synapse results in presynaptic inhibition.

Axodendritic The synapse of a button on the dendrite.

Axon An elongated process that transmits action potentials from the soma to the end brush of the neuron.

Axoplasm Cytoplasm located in the axon.

Axosomatic The synapse of a button on the soma.

Cable properties The passive, decremental conductance of electrical energy down the length of the axon.

Catechol methyltransferase (COMT) An enzyme found in the synapse that breaks down dopamine and norepinephrine.

Cirri Tentaclelike structures found on some protozoa; used for locomotion and touch.

Chromosomes Segments of DNA material found in the nucleus of the cell; carry genetic information.

Conformation changes Changes in the shape of complex protein molecules in response to electrical charges or the presence of specific chemical substances.

Cristae A highly convoluted membrane inside the mitochondria. The breakdown of nutrients and production of energy occur on the cristae.

Cytoplasm Viscous fluid found inside all living cells.

Dale's law Each neuron synthesizes only one neurotransmitter.

Dendrites Branching structures extending from the soma of the nucleus that receive synaptic messages from other neurons.

Deoxyribonucleic acid (DNA) Complex molecule in the form of a double helix; strands of DNA make up the chromosomes that carry the genetic information of the cell.

Diffusion Tendency for molecules in solution to move from areas of high concentration to areas of low concentration.

Dopamine (DA) A catecholamine neurotransmitter substance.

Dopamine hypothesis of schizophrenia The theory that schizophrenia is related to overactive dopaminergic circuits in the brain.

End brush Rootlike structure at the end of the axon that contains synaptic buttons at the end of each filament.

Endoplasmic reticulum Highly convoluted membrane in the cell that directs the flow of cytoplasm and isolates substances is various areas of the cell.

Endotherm Animals that are not able to control body temperature internally.

Excitatory postsynaptic potential (EPSP) Hypopolarizing change in the membrane potential of the postsynaptic cell.

Excitation threshold Trigger point in the membrane potential of a neuron; excitation level that triggers an action potential.

Gamma-aminobutyric acid (GABA) An amino acid believed to be a neurotransmitter in the central nervous system.

Genes Segments of DNA on the chromosome that act as templates for the production of one or more proteins.

Glia (glial cells) Supportive cells in the central nervous system.

Glutamic acid One of several amino acids thought to be neurotransmitters.

Golgi bodies Organelles in the cell; package substances produced in the cell into small vesicles.

Graded potential Small (subthreshold) changes in the membrane potential produced by synaptic action.

Hillock Point where the soma and axon join. Propagated action potentials start at the hillock.

Homotherm Animals that possess the ability to regulate body temperature internally; mammals.

Hyperpolarize Increasing the negative membrane potential of the cell, making the neuron less likely to produce an action potential, and inhibiting the neuron.

Hypopolarize Decreasing the negative membrane potential of the cell, making the neuron more likely to produce an action potential, and exciting the neuron.

Inhibitory postsynaptic potential (IPSP) Hyperpolarizing the membrane potential of the postsynaptic cell.

Ion channel Proteins in the cell wall that allow ions to enter or exit the cell. Most ion channels are specific for a given species of ion.

Lipoprotein Fatty substances that make up the cell membrane.

Messenger RNA (mRNA) A complex macromolecule that exits the nucleus and acts as a template on ribosomes to direct the production of specific substances in the cell.

Metazoa All animals having more than one cell.

Mitochondria Organelles responsible for the metabolism of nutrients and the production of energy in the cell.

Monoamine oxidase (MAO) An enzyme found in the synapse and the axon terminal that breaks down dopamine and norepinephrine.

Myelin sheath Covering of fatty material on the axon similar to the insulation on a wire.

Neural integration The process of summing, spatially and temporally, the excitatory and inhibitory synapses on the neuron.

Neuromodulator A neurotransmitter that acts like a hormone by entering the cell and producing a relatively long change in the cell's activity.

Neuron A cell specially modified to transmit information.

Neurotransmitter Substance produced in the neuron and subsequently released into the synaptic cleft that causes postsynaptic changes in the membrane potential.

Nodes of Ranvier Gaps in the myelin sheath that are responsible for saltatory conduction.

Nondecremental transmission Transmission of the propagated action potential which is sustained in strength by the energy stored in the resting potential of the cell.

Norepinephrine (NE) A catecholamine neurotransmitter substance.

Nucleolus Organelle found in the nucleus. It is the site where ribosomes are produced.

Oligodendroglia Special glial cells found in the central nervous system that form the myelin sheath on axons.

Orthodromic The normal direction of neural transmission from the cell body to the end brush.

Osmosis The tendency of a solvent to flow across a membrane from areas of low concentration to areas of high concentration of ions in solution.

Pinocytosis The process by which a neurotransmitter is taken back into the presynaptic cell and packaged into vesicles.

Postsynaptic membrane The cell membrane across the synaptic cleft from the terminal button.

Postsynaptic receptors A protein molecule on the postsynaptic membrane that detects the presence of a neurotransmitter and controls the flow of ions across the postsynaptic membrane.

Presynaptic inhibition The action of an axoaxonic synapse. It produces inhibition by reducing the excitatory effect of the axon it innervates.

Presynaptic membrane Part of the membrane of the terminal button that forms the presynaptic side of the synaptic cleft.

Propagated action potential The movement of the action potential down the length of the axon.

Protozoa Single-celled animals.

Rate-limiting factor An element in the production of storage of neurotransmitter substances that controls the level of the transmitter in the brain.

Renshaw cell A cell that forms axoaxonic connections that self-regulate the frequency activation.

Resting potential The membrane potential of a neuron that is maintained by the sodium–potassium pump.

Retrograde degeneration Axonal degeneration in the direction toward the cell body.

Reuptake The process of removing transmitter substances by the presynaptic cell, thus limiting the time that the transmitter may affect the postsynaptic membrane.

Ribosomes Complex proteins found on the surface of the rough endoplasmic reticulum. They are the sites for the production of other proteins.

Saltatory conduction The rapid and efficient form of propagated action potentials found on myelinated axons. The action potential "jumps" from one node of Ranvier to the next.

Schwann cells Cells that produce the myelin sheath on axons in the peripheral nervous system.

Serotonin (5-hydroxytryptamine, or 5-HT) A neurotransmitter in the brain that is thought to influence temperature and sleep.

Sodium–potassium pump A metabolically active system that moves sodium ions out of and potassium ions into the neuron.

Soma The cell body of the neuron.

Spatial summation The additive effect of postsynaptic potentials occurring at many locations on the soma and dendrites.

Stylonychia mytilus A free-swimming freshwater protozoan.

Synapse The small space that separates neurons. Interneuronal transmission takes place across the synapse.

Synaptic vesicles Minute sacs that act as packages for intracellular substances.

Temporal summation The additive effect of rapidly occurring synapses.

Terminal buttons Knoblike structures at the end of each filament of the end brush.

Transmitter substance *See* Neurotransmitter.

Vesicles *See* Synaptic vesicles.

Voltage-dependent channel Ion channel that is controlled by the membrane potential.

Wallerian degeneration See Anterograde degeneration.

Chapter 3

Organizing: Part 2: The Nervous System

Evolution of the Nervous System

The Nerve Net
The Ganglion
The Segmented Nervous System
The Vertebrate Nervous System

Anatomy of the Spine and the Peripheral Nervous System

Spinal Cord and Peripheral Nerves
Autonomic Nervous System
Spinal Cord Reflex Arc

Anatomy of the Brain

The Hindbrain
The Cerebellum
The Midbrain
The Forebrain
Encephalization Revisited

The Endocrine System

Hormone Action
Hormone Regulation
Endocrine Glands and Hormones Important to Behavior

Chapter Learning Objectives

After reading this chapter, you should

1. Be able to discuss how the central nervous system evolved and be able to compare and contrast the adaptive advantage evident in each stage.

2. Understand and be able to recognize the conventional planes of view for depicting the central nervous system (coronal, horizontal, and sagittal). Know the standardized terms used to convey information about direction in the central nervous system.

3. Be familiar with the anatomy of the peripheral nervous system.

4. Be able to describe the spinal reflex arc and discuss the relationship between afferent neurons, efferent neurons, and interneurons.

5. Be able to compare the anatomy and function of the sympathetic and parasympathetic divisions of the autonomic nervous system.

6. Be able to identify the major anatomical features of the cross-sectional view of the spinal cord.

7. Be familiar with the ontological development of the mammalian central nervous system.

8. Be able to name the major ventricles in the brain.

9. Know the major structures that comprise the hindbrain, midbrain, and forebrain.

10. Be able to discuss the various physical and behavioral correlates of the encephalization process.

11. Know the two major classes of hormones and be able to compare and contrast their modes of action.

12. Be familiar with the major endocrine glands and the hormones that are important to behavior.

Evolution of the Nervous System

The earliest forms of metazoans were really not much more than colonies of slightly differentiated cells. These animals, like the contemporary sponges, were sedentary, and therefore, completely dependent on food that was in the water around them. These filter feeders were only able to survive if the water surrounding them contained sufficient nutrients; if not, they were unable to seek it out actively. These organisms do evidence some irritability. For example, if you poke the sponge rather vigorously in one spot, there is limited movement of the tissue in the immediate vicinity around the point of irritation. This movement is thought to be under the control of direct electrochemical communication between the membranes of the cells.

The key point is that these very primitive animals are at the mercy of their immediate environment because their behavior is very limited. They are unable to move in search of food or escape a noxious stimulus because they lack a sufficient nervous system to coordinate these behaviors.

The Nerve Net The first step in the evolution of a system of specialized cells to coordinate behavior was a nerve network similar to that seen in some species of the coelenterates. Figure 3-1 shows two examples of this primitive type of nervous system: the diffuse nerve network of the hydra (Fig. 3-1a), and the more highly developed nervous network of the medusa (Fig. 3-1b). Simple nervous systems such as these represent a major evolutionary advance and provide these organisms behavioral capabilities that exceed, by far, that evidenced in the sedentary sponges. Jellyfish, for example, are able to make coordinated movements of muscles that allow them to seek out and capture food and to escape from noxious stimulation.

In addition to coordinated movement, the more complex forms of coelenterates have evolved specialized sensory neurons that are sensitive to touch, chemicals in solution, and light (see Figure 3-1c). Therefore, in addition to simple movement, these organisms are able to detect changes in their environment and react to those changes. We have, then, in these primitive organisms, a complete nervous system for detecting and reacting to events in the environment.

The neurons found in simple nerve nets appear to be very similar in shape and function to neurons found in humans. The neurons produce propagated action potentials and interact with other neurons across a chemically mediated synapse (see Figure 3-1d). It appears that the basic model for intra- and interneuronal communication is well established in the nerve network. Furthermore, as we note in the remainder of this chapter, this basic model is so effective and complete that the course of evolution taken to produce more complex and varied behaviors was

Figure 3-1
Schematic of the neuron network of the hydra (*a*), and the medusa (*b*). Sensory cells in a representative coelenterate (*c*). The typical synaptic junction between neurons in a nerve network is shown in (*d*). (Adapted from Borradaile & Potts, 1961.)

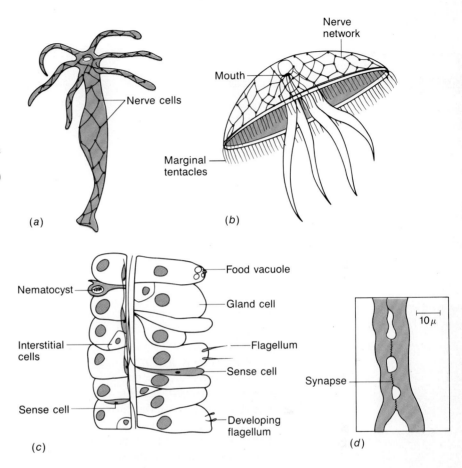

simply to add more neurons and interconnect them in more complex ways. The nervous systems of the cockroach, the clam, the eagle, and humans vary as greatly as do their behaviors. However, the basic building blocks (the neurons), their biochemistry, and the methods by which they operate remain remarkably the same.

The Ganglion   When the cell bodies of several neurons are grouped together, the mass of somas formed is called a **ganglion**. The ganglion first appears in **Platyhelminthes**, the phylum of flatworms. The nervous system of these free-swimming animals is essentially a nerve network, similar to that found in the jellyfish, with one very important difference. There is an aggregation of neurons in the anterior (head) end that forms a pair of **cerebral ganglia** connected by a bridge of fibers. (There are parasitic

Figure 3-2
Representative nervous
systems of planaria. The
head ganglia of *Dugesia*
(a) and *Planaria* (b).
c. The schematic of a
representative
platyhelminth, showing
the ladderlike crossing
fibers in the body.
(Adapted from Borradaile &
Potts, 1961.)

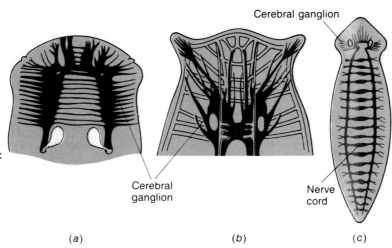

(a)   (b)   (c)

forms of Platyhelminthes that do not conform to this description.) Extending posteriorly from the cerebral ganglia to the tail end, there are two bands of fibers that have connecting bridges at intervals down the length of the body (Figure 3-2).

It is interesting to note that the very first structure representing the initial step in the evolution of the brain has *two* ganglia connected by a bridge of fibers. No doubt, this was necessary to accommodate the bilateral symmetry of the flatworm. What is important to note here is that each ganglion receives and sends information to one side of the body, and therefore, each side of the body can be controlled somewhat independently. The communication necessary to coordinate activity between both sides of the body takes place across the bridge of fibers connecting the cerebral ganglia and through the crossing fibers forming the ladderlike structure down the length of the body. This basic plan was retained in the evolution of all subsequent nervous systems. This is an important point, and it is fundamental to understanding the evolution of the human nervous system. In the process of evolution, all new structures evolve by building upon and elaborating on existing structures. As we will see, the human nervous system is the end product of many small evolutionary steps that have built upon the basic plan set down in the flatworm.

The Segmented Nervous System

The steps in the evolution of the invertebrate nervous system seem to be quite clear. Two representative examples, the earthworm and an insect, are depicted in Figure 3-3. Let us look at the earthworm first and see how this nervous system compares to that of the less well developed flatworm.

Unlike the flatworm, the body of the earthworm is segmented, and this is clearly reflected in the nervous system. On the **ventral** (under)

Figure 3-3
a. The nervous system of the roundworm, showing the supraesophageal ganglion (brain) and the suboesophageal ganglion.
b. Local segment and between-segment neural tracts in the earthworm.
c. The central nervous system of an insect. Note the recruitment of ganglia, particularly in the head. (Adapted from Borradaile & Potts, 1961.)

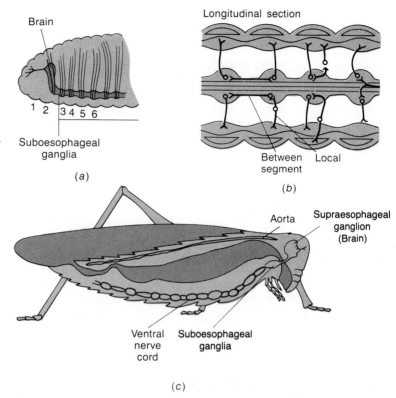

surface of the body there is a chain of paired ganglia. Each pair of ganglia control the activity in the local segment. Sensory (**afferent**) neurons bring information from the skin of a segment to the ganglion in that segment, where it is processed by other neurons (**interneurons**) and sent on to the motor (**efferent**) neurons that control the muscles in the same segment. The ganglia also communicate information between the segments via two strands of fibers that run the length of the body. At the anterior end, several segments have fused; and their ganglia are joined to form a much larger pair of ganglia, the **supraesophageal ganglia** (meaning, the ganglia above the esophagus). Note that each pair of ganglia is still connected by a bridge of fibers, as are the supraesophageal ganglia. In this way communication can take place between both sides of the segment as well as between segments.

Now compare the nervous system of the insect in Figure 3-3b with that of the segmented worm. Obviously, the two nervous systems are based on the same plan. What is notably different is that some segments in the abdomen and thorax of the insect have fused, as have the paired ganglia that innervate them. Additionally, many segments have fused to form the insect's head, and the ganglia representing these segments have joined to form two very large ganglion pairs, the supraesophageal and the **subesophageal ganglia**. The process of migration and fusion of neurons in the head is called **encephalization**, and it is a continuing theme in the evolution of the brain.

The Vertebrate Nervous System

The nervous system of the vertebrates is built on the same plan as that seen in the flatworm, segmented worm, and the insect. The similarities, however, are rather well masked by some significant structural differences in the vertebrates. The ganglia in the segmented nervous system are solid masses of cells. The vertebrate system, however, is based on a hollow tube that is filled with fluid. As we discuss later in this chapter, this allows the vertebrate brain to develop into a much more complex structure. Unlike the exoskeleton of the insect, the vertebrates, by definition, developed an internal bony structure, the skull and spinal column, that surrounds and protects the central nervous system. The central nervous system has migrated to the dorsal surface of the body, and for reasons that are not understood, the control for each side of the body has shifted to the **contralateral** (opposite) side of the central nervous system. The left side of the brain both controls and receives most of its sensory information from, the right side of the body. The converse is true for the right side of the brain, which controls the left side of the body. Also, the encephalization process has continued in the vertebrate CNS to the point that only remnants of the ganglia remain in the body, and almost all behavior is now controlled by the two enormous "aggregate ganglia" that form the brain.

Anatomy of the Spine and the Peripheral Nervous System

The anatomy of the human nervous system is extremely complex and frankly, it is not easy to learn. The purpose of the following sections of this chapter is to provide a brief introduction to the various structures that comprise the human nervous system so the reader will have a general understanding of their organization and function. In subsequent chapters, these structures are discussed in greater detail when we examine their specific role in overt behavior.

Spinal Cord and Peripheral Nerves

Traditionally, the central nervous system is divided into two parts, the central and peripheral nervous systems, which we have referred to already. The CNS is comprised of the brain and spinal cord, which are both enclosed in the bony mass of the skull and vertebral column. The PNS, then, is comprised of all the nervous tissue outside the protection of the bony mass. For convenience, we deal with the PNS and the spinal cord together.

SOMATIC NERVES

Bundles of axons that course together from one part of the body to another are called **nerves**. For the greater portion of their length, the somatic nerves are comprised of a mixture of incoming and outgoing fibers. The afferent somatic fibers carry information from the sensory organs to the spinal cord, and the efferent fibers take information from the spinal cord to the effector organs, the muscles and glands. Near the spine the afferent and efferent fibers become segregated. The afferent (incoming) fibers enter the spine on the dorsal (top) side, and the efferent (outgoing) fibers exit the spine on the ventral (under) side (Figure 3-4).

CRANIAL NERVES

The cranial nerves are essentially the same as the somatic nerves. However, they are different in that they enter and leave the CNS at the level of the brain. Table 3-1 lists the names of the 12 cranial nerves and identifies their function as afferent, efferent, or mixed.

Autonomic Nervous System

The autonomic nerves are intimately associated with emotional behavior, and they regulate many body functions that do not require conscious control. The term *autonomic* means "self-regulating," and it is a little misleading. It was once thought that the autonomic system operated automatically, without control from the CNS. We now know that the autonomic nervous system (ANS) is regulated in two ways: (1) by direct neuronal communication with the CNS and (2) through the production

Figure 3-4
Cross section of spinal cord showing afferent (sensory) fibers entering on the dorsal side and efferent (motor) fibers leaving on the ventral side. (See also Color Plate 2.)

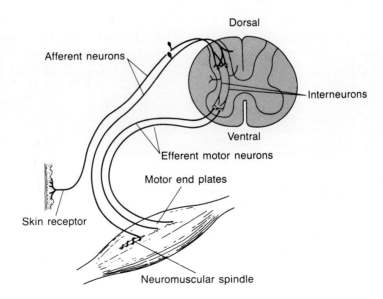

Orientation in the Central Nervous System

The CNS is a three-dimensional structure; therefore, it is very difficult to describe using two-dimensional figures. To help us find our way around the various structures in the brain and spinal cord and to avoid confusion, anatomists have adopted standardized terminology for communicating direction and adopted standardized ways of dissecting the CNS to expose internal structures.

Typically, the body and the CNS can be dissected in one of three cardinal planes. The plane that divides the left and right sides is called the **sagittal plane**; the plane dividing the front and back is called the **coronal plane**; and the plane that divides the upper and lower portions is called the **horizontal plane**. To avoid confusion, there are rules that govern the perspective or direction used to view these planes. For sagittal sections the **medial** (middle or central) portion is retained, and the tissue is viewed from the **lateral** (side) perspective. When the coronal plane is viewed, the **anterior** (front) portion is removed, leaving the **posterior** (back) portion to be viewed from the anterior, or frontal, perspective. When horizontal sections are made, the **dorsal** (top) portion is removed, and the **ventral** portion is viewed from the dorsal perspective.

Standardized terms are used to communicate the various directions in which the three planes are moved. The sagittal plane is moved in the medial or lateral direction. When the sagittal plane is made in the very center of the brain, it is called a midsagittal section. The coronal plane can be moved in the anterior or posterior direction, and the horizontal plane is moved in the dorsal and ventral directions. In addition to the directional terms used to communicate the position of the three cardinal planes, other terms have been adopted to provide directional information. The terms **cephalic** and **rostral** refer to the head end and can be used to mean "in the direction of the head." Similarly, the term **caudal** means the tail end and can be used to indicate a direction away from the head. Finally, the terms **proximal** and **distal** mean, respectively, near to and away from the trunk or center.

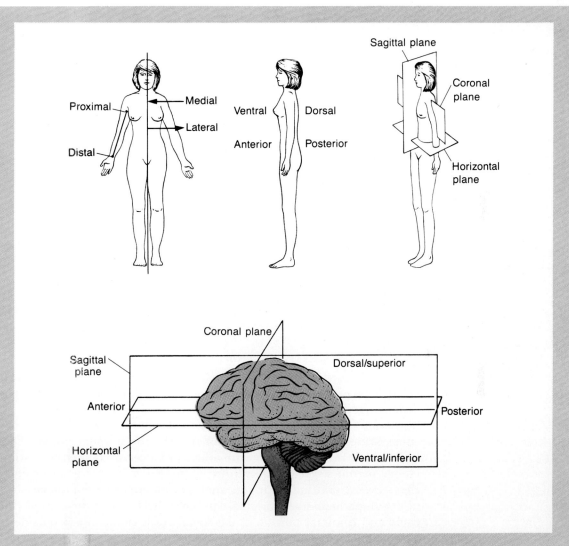

Spotlight Figure 3-1
Four drawings of the body and the brain showing the three cardinal planes and the terminology for the directional movement of the planes.

Table 3-1. The Cranial Nerves

Number	Name	Function(s)*
I	Olfactory	Smell (*a*)
II	Optic	Vision (*a*)
III	Oculomotor	Eye movement (*e*)
IV	Trochlear	Eye movement (*e*)
V	Trigeminal	Masticatory movement (*e*), Sensation of face and tongue (*a*)
VI	Abducens	Eye movement (*e*)
VII	Facial	Muscles of face (*e*)
VIII	Auditory/ vestibular	Hearing (*a*) Balance (*a*)
IX	Glossopharyngeal	Tongue (*a*), pharynx (*e*)
X	Vagus	Heart (*a*), blood vessels (*e*)
XI	Spinal accessory	Neck and visceral muscles (*e*)
XII	Hypoglossal	Tongue muscles (*e*)

* *a* = afferent; *e* = efferent

of hormones that are also under the influence of the CNS. The autonomic nerves may be divided by function into two subdivisions, the **sympathetic** and **parasympathetic** systems.

THE SYMPATHETIC DIVISION

The sympathetic subdivision activates **catabolic** processes that involve the expenditure of energy and prepare the organism for emergency actions. Activation of the sympathetic system increases the following: heart rate, blood pressure, perspiration, respiration, and the release of epinephrine (a stimulating hormone) from the adrenal gland. These sympathetic reactions, along with others produced by sympathetic stimulation, permit a great expenditure of energy in response to emergencies—events that induce fright, anger, or other strong emotions.

Sympathetic fibers originate in the ventral side of the central (**thoracic** and **lumbar**) portion of the spinal cord. Immediately outside the vertebrae they form strands of interconnected ganglia that run parallel to either side of the spinal cord (see Figure 3-5). Inside the sympathetic ganglia the fibers synapse onto **postganglionic** fibers that project to a target organ such as the heart, adrenal medulla, or the lungs. Norepinephrine is the neurotransmitter at the site between the postganglionic fiber and the target organ. (For the remainder of this book the term *ganglion* will be reserved for groups of nerve cell bodies found in the peripheral nervous system. **Nucleus** will be used to refer to aggregates of nerve cell bodies within the CNS.)

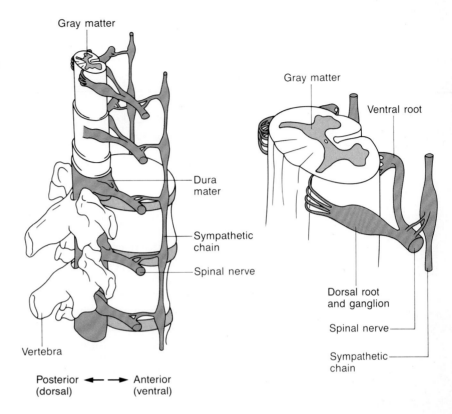

Figure 3-5
Spinal cord and associated structures including the sympathetic ganglia.

Gray matter

Gray matter

Ventral root

Dura mater

Sympathetic chain

Spinal nerve

Dorsal root and ganglion

Spinal nerve

Sympathetic chain

Vertebra

Posterior ←——→ Anterior
(dorsal)   (ventral)

THE PARASYMPATHETIC DIVISION

Activation of the parasympathetic subdivision produces **anabolic** effects that oppose the sympathetic subdivision. *Parasympathetic* means "against the sympathetic." The outcome of parasympathetic activation is the conservation of energy. It is best to think of the two autonomic systems working in concert. In the absence of emergency conditions, the two subdivisions work together to maintain **homeostatic** (normal or optimal) levels of activation. For example, sympathetic activation increases heart rate, and parasympathetic activation decreases heart rate. Just as a thermostat controls the temperature in a room by alternately turning the heater on and off, the ANS regulates heart rate, blood pressure, and other body functions by alternately activating the two subdivisions of the autonomic nervous system.

Parasympathetic fibers originate in the upper (**cervical**) and lower (lumbar and **sacral**) levels of the spinal cord. The fibers course to the parasympathetic ganglia, which, unlike the sympathetic ganglia, are located near the target organs. In the parasympathetic ganglia the fibers synapse on the somas of the postganglionic fibers, whose axons travel the short distance to the effector organ. Acetylcholine is the neurotransmitter at the site between the postganglionic fiber and the effector organ.

Spinal Cord   Figure 3-6 shows a cross section through the spine. Generally, the spinal
Reflex Arc   cord has two functions. First, information traveling to and from the brain
                  is channeled through the spinal cord. Second, the spinal cord is capable
                  of reflexive action, independent of the brain. Before dealing with these
                  two functions, we need to look at some features of the anatomy of the
                  spinal cord.

Looking at the cross section of the spinal cord, in tissue that has not been specially stained, we can see an inner core of gray matter and an outer section that is bright white. The outer section is comprised mostly of myelinated axons that travel to and from the brain. Generally, the fibers on the dorsal side are afferent, and those in the lateral and ventral portions are efferent. Fibers entering and exiting the spinal cord synapse on cell bodies in the gray matter. The gray areas in the dorsal half are called the **dorsal horns** and are composed of the somas of afferent neurons. Similarly, the gray areas on the ventral side are called **ventral horns** and contain the somas for efferent neurons. The small hole in the center is called the **central canal** (or Sylvian aquaduct), and it is filled with **cerebrospinal fluid**, a complex fluid that surrounds the CNS and fills several internal CNS cavities. The clear cerebrospinal fluid serves as a shock absorber between the CNS and the bony skull and vertebrae, and it also helps to transmit nutrients and other substances throughout the CNS.

Now let us look at the simple spinal **reflex arc** shown in Figure 3-6. Information from a sensory (afferent) neuron—in this case a touch receptor—travels from the skin surface along a nerve track of mixed sensory and motor neurons. As the fiber approaches the spinal column, it splits off with other sensory fibers and enters the **dorsal root ganglion**, where its cell body and the cell somas of other sensory neurons are

Figure 3-6
Cross section of the spinal cord showing the three-cell reflex arc. Also shown are the fiber connections that transmit information, related to the reflex, to higher centers in the brain and to neurons on the contralateral side of the spinal cord.

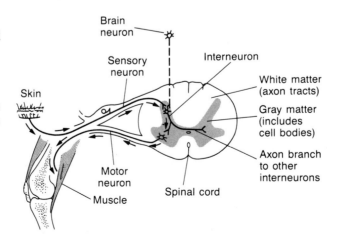

Figure 3-7
Schematics of
dermatomes in humans.
Each dermatome sends all
somatosensory
information through one
dorsal root ganglion.
a. The dermatome
pattern in the
normal bipedal
position. *b.* The
alignment of the
dermatomes in the
quadrapedal position,
giving a clearer segmental
pattern.

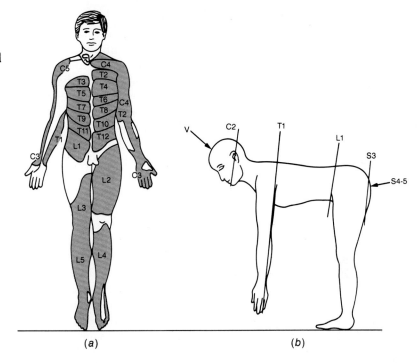

located. A short fiber from the soma continues through the **dorsal root**, enters the spine, and terminates in the dorsal horn. Here the cell synapses with an interneuron that sends a short axon to synapse with an efferent (motor) neuron in the ventral horn. The efferent neuron sends an axon through the **ventral root** to a mixed nerve track. The motor neuron finally terminates on a muscle, completing the three-cell reflex arc.

The reflex arc just described should seem familiar to you. It can be compared with the simple reflex circuit found in each segment of the earthworm. In fact, it can be shown that the surface of the body can be divided into separate patches called **dermatomes**. All the sensory information from a dermatome is processed at one vertebral level, through a single dorsal root ganglion. The pattern of human dermatomes is illustrated in Figure 3-7a. Note that the pattern on the skin surface for the various dermatomes does not appear to be particularly systematic. However, if the body is placed in the quadrapedal position, as is shown in Figure 3-7b, the segmented organization becomes very apparent, a clear reflection of our segmented and our quadrapedal history.

Anatomy of the Brain

As noted earlier, the brain and the spinal cord constitute the CNS. For convenience, we dealt with the spinal cord when we reviewed the PNS.

This was done because the spinal cord and the PNS are physically close to each other and because they interact functionally.

The structure and organization of the brain are difficult to comprehend. To help understand the complex relationships between the various brain structures, it is useful to consider the stages of its evolution. As the brain evolved, new structures developed and overshadowed existing structures. The old structures, however, did not disappear. They remained, and typically, they developed modified functions. This is consistent with the generally conservative nature of evolution—elaborating and building on existing structures. This evolutionary process is reflected, to some degree, in the developmental stages of the brain within the fetus.

If you could speed up the process and observe the developing brain in the fetus, it would be seen literally to fold on itself, the large cerebral hemispheres enveloping the **phylogenetically** (involving the developmental history of the species) older parts of the brain inside newer and larger structures. Figure 3-8a shows several stages in the **ontogeny** (developmental history of the individual) of the human infant brain. (The first five stages have been enlarged to show detail. A more accurate representation of their actual size, relative to the other developmental stages, is shown directly below each of the first five figures.) Note that the three major subdivisions of the brain—the **forebrain, midbrain,** and **hindbrain**—begin as small, inconspicuous swellings at the most anterior end of a hollow neural tube. The neural tube expands and forms the complex ventricles (cavities) that are filled with fluid (see Spotlight 3-2). The tube develops two folds; and the large **cerebral hemispheres** of the forebrain overgrow the midbrain and the hindbrain, and they partially obscure the **cerebellum**.

Figure 3-8 depicts the developing vertebrate brain and the brains of several representative vertebrate species, drawn to scale. As was evident in the developing fetal brain, the forebrain structures of the phylogenetically newer species can be seen to increase in size and complexity relative to the midbrain and hindbrain structures. The growth of the forebrain structures is most striking in the mammalian species represented in the figure (the horse and human). This represents a continuation of the encephalization process, with the recruitment of a greater portion of the neural mass in the most anterior part of the CNS. With this evolutionary perspective, let us turn to the more conspicuous and behaviorally important anatomical structures of the human brain.

As noted, neuroanatomists have divided the brain into three major areas: the hindbrain, midbrain, and forebrain. These major areas are further subdivided into five general divisions. Moving up from the base of the brain, they are the *myelencephalon, metencephalon, mesencephalon, diencephalon,* and *telencephalon* (see Table 3-2). These terms are a bit awkward, and frankly, they are not used as often as are the names of the

Figure 3-8
a. Stages in the development of the human brain from 25 days until birth. (The 25- to 100-day figures are much enlarged to show detail. The size relative to that of the other figures is shown directly below each stage.) The rapid growth of the cerebral hemispheres, compared to the midbrain and hindbrain structures, can be seen. (From Cowan, 1979) *b.* The developing vertebrate central nervous system, showing the three major subdivisions of the brain. *c.* The brains of five representative vertebrate species. The progressive increase in the size of the cerebrum is quite clear. Note the rapid increase in forebrain structures in the horse and human. *d.* The sagittal section shows the location of the hindbrain and midbrain structures in man. (From Hubel, 1979; see also Color Plate 4.)

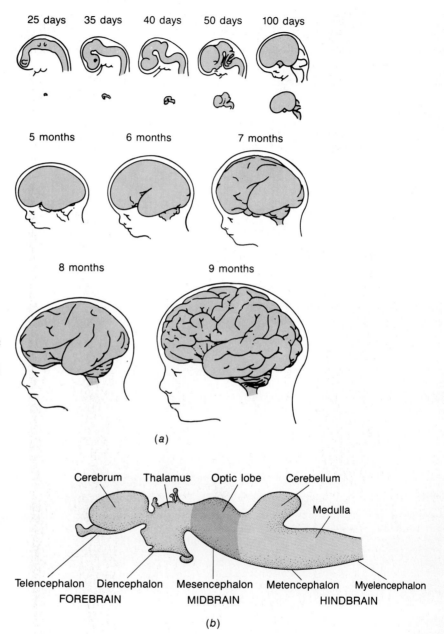

25 days 35 days 40 days 50 days 100 days

5 months   6 months   7 months

8 months   9 months

(a)

Cerebrum Thalamus Optic lobe Cerebellum

Medulla

Telencephalon Diencephalon Mesencephalon Metencephalon Myelencephalon
FOREBRAIN   MIDBRAIN   HINDBRAIN

(b)

(continued)

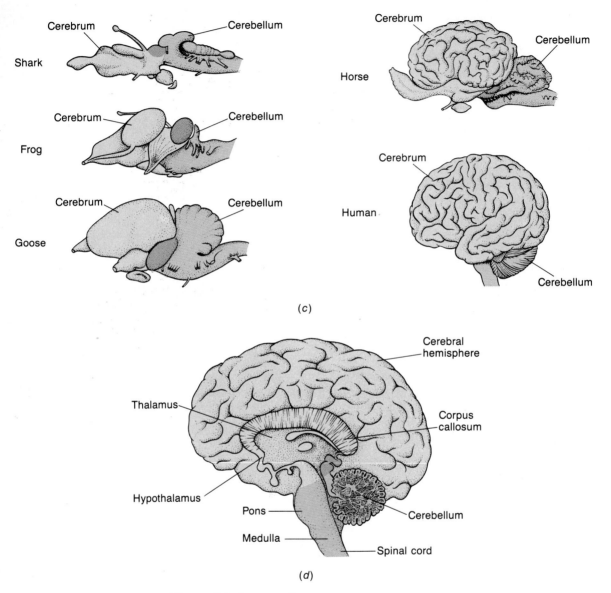

Figure 3-8 (continued)

specific structures within each level. They do serve a useful purpose, however, in that all vertebrate brains can be subdivided in the same way, and they help us understand the relationship of specific brain structures across different vertebrate species. We begin with the hindbrain, cerebellum, midbrain, and forebrain structures and then discuss the cerebral hemispheres.

Table 3-2. **Subdivisions of the Brain**

Major Division	General Division	Major Structures
Hindbrain	Myelencephalon	Medulla
	Metencephalon	Pons
		Cerebellum
Midbrain	Mesencephalon	Superior colliculi
		Inferior colliculi
		Tectum
Forebrain	Diencephalon	Hypothalamus
		Thalamus
	Telencephalon	Limbic system
		Basal ganglia
		Cerebral cortex

The Hindbrain The hindbrain is comprised of the **medulla** and the **pons**. Large bundles of fiber tracks that pass information to and from the upper levels of the brain course through these structures. The medulla is, quite literally, an extension of the spinal cord. This structure contains several important cell nuclei that are central to the control of vital body functions, including respiration, heart rate, and gastrointestinal activity. Additionally, many of the sensory and motor **cranial nerves** enter and exit the CNS at the level of the medulla (Figure 3-9).

The pons is the uppermost level of the hindbrain. It is broadened and rounded on the ventral side. The name *pons* comes from the Latin word for "bridge." When viewed in cross section, with the liberal application of imagination, the ventral surface of the pons has the appearance of a small footbridge. There is a very large bundle of fibers on the dorsal side of the pons that connects the pons to the cerebellum. The pons contains centers that have a role in feeding behavior and facial expression.

Portions of the **reticular activating system** (**RAS**) are located in the hindbrain. The nuclei in the RAS are very important in that they activate or excite higher structures in the brain. Some of these nuclei are also involved in the control of waking and sleeping, and they control the various stages of sleep that are evident in most mammals.

The Cerebellum The cerebellum is a phylogenetically old, highly convoluted structure. (The rounded part of each convolution is called a **gyrus**, and the folded portion is called a **sulcus**.) As previously noted, the cerebellum is attached to the pons by a broad band of crossing fibers (the **peduncle**). Other peduncles connect the cerebellum to the medulla and the midbrain. In humans the cerebellum functions primarily in the control of

The Ventricles of the Brain and Spinal Cord

Inside the brain and spinal cord is a complex system of cavities filled with cerebrospinal fluid. On close examination, the intricately shaped ventricles and the central canal that runs the length of the spinal cord can be seen to be one very complex structure. Each hemisphere of the brain has a large and oddly shaped **lateral ventrical**, as shown in Spotlight Figure 3-2. The lateral ventricles contains the **choroid plexus**, which is the primary source of the cerebrospinal fluid that fills the ventricles and surrounds the brain. Cerebrospinal fluid has two functions.

1. That part of the fluid that fills the space between the brain and the inside of the skull serves like a shock absorber for the brain. The brain is suspended in the fluid and normally does not come in direct contact with the bony interior of the skull. When subjected to very sudden movement, as may occur with a severe blow to the head, the brain can come into contact with the skull, resulting in a concussion or a contusion.

2. Cerebrospinal fluid percolates through the ventricles and mediates between blood vessels and brain tissue. The fluid aids in the transfer of materials from the blood to the brain tissues and vice versa.

The **third ventricle** lies on the midline of the brain and is bordered on both sides by the medial walls of the thalamus. The cerebrospinal fluid flows through the third ventricle and down a narrow opening to the **fourth ventricle**. The fluid leaves the ventricle system to bathe the brain and spinal cord through an aperture in the fourth ventricle.

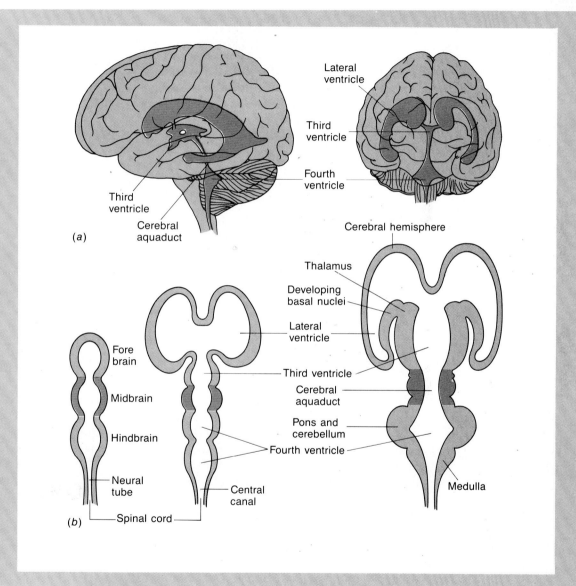

Spotlight Figure 3-2
a. Two shadow drawings of the brain showing the ventricles. *b.* Schematic showing the origin of the lateral, third, and fourth ventricles and the Sylvian aqueduct.

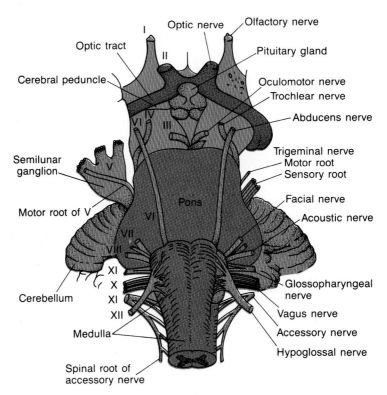

unconscious motor activity, balance, and muscle tone. The outer layer of
the cerebellum is just 2 to 3 mm thick and contains the neuron cell
bodies. The inner portion is bright white and is comprised of myelinated
axons. Being highly convoluted, the surface area of the cerebellum can
support an enormous number of cell bodies in a compact space.

It is possible to divide the cerebellum into three parts that provide
insight into the stages of its evolutionary development. The oldest part of
the cerebellum, the **archicerebellum**, developed in the first aquatic
vertebrates. It receives information from the balance organ (the vestibular organ in higher vertebrates) and controls motor tonus. The **paleocerebellum** evolved with the amphibians as they moved from the totally
aquatic environment of the fishes to a mixed aquatic–terrestrial niche.
Information from the muscles and joints in the limbs courses through the
spinal cord to this area of the cerebellum. Most skeletal muscles are
organized into opposable pairs. The *extensor* muscle of a muscle pair
opens the joint between two bones, and the *flexor* muscle causes the angle
between the two bones to become more acute. The paleocerebellum
provides the efferent control that coordinates the action of the extensor
and flexor muscles, and it provides for unconscious balance movements
necessitated by the force of gravity. The **neocerebellum** is found only in

mammals, and it is the newest addition to the cerebellum. It receives information from the motor cortex of the cereberal hemispheres and provides the unconscious, background muscle tone associated with the very fine, voluntary motor actions initiated in the motor cortex. In the evolution of the cerebellum we see another example of how newer structures develop from older structures. The older structures either retain their original function, or their functions are altered.

The Midbrain   The **mesencephalon**, or midbrain, is a continuation of the medulla and pons. This structure is still basically tubular, and it contains many fiber tracts that course to and from the higher centers of the brain. As is true for the pons and medulla, the midbrain is a phylogenetically old structure, and it has remained remarkably unchanged in structure and function.

In mammals there are several rather distinct nuclei in the midbrain, including several nuclei that control movement. The **oculomotor nucleus** serves the cranial nerve that controls eye movement. Two others, the **red nucleus** and the **substantia nigra** (dark substance), have a role in body movement. The unusual gate and motor tremors associated with Parkinson's disease are due to degeneration of the cell bodies in the substantia nigra.

At the most anterior portion of the midbrain, the **tectum**, there are four very prominent structures, the **corpora quadrigemina** (literally, the body having four twins). The uppermost pair, the **superior colliculi**, have an important function in vision. The lower pair, the **inferior colliculi**, are associated with audition. These structures are discussed in greater detail in the chapters dealing with sensation.

The Forebrain   The forebrain is, in phylogenetic terms, the part of the brain that has evidenced the most recent elaboration. In humans, its size and complexity cause it to dominate the lower brain centers. Like the cerebellum, the two cerebral hemispheres of the forebrain are highly convoluted; they have an outer cortex of cell bodies and an inner core of white myelinated fibers. The cerebrum also has several large subcortical nuclei, and we will deal with some of them first.

THE THALAMUS

Within each cerebral hemisphere there is a rounded mass of cell bodies called the **thalamus**, which may be divided into several smaller nuclei, each having clearly different functions. It is helpful to think of the thalamus as a relay station. The vast majority of fiber tracts bringing information to the cerebral cortex synapse in the thalamus. Within the thalamus there are nuclei that are specific in function for vision (lateral geniculate nucleus), audition (medial geniculate nucleus), and the body senses (the ventrobasal complex). There are also nuclei that project to

SPOTLIGHT 3-3

The Meninges and the Blood Supply for the Brain

The brain is extremely active, and for its size it uses up enormous amounts of energy. The brain, however, is unable to store the oxygen and glucose necessary to produce the large amount of energy needed. To sustain its normal high level of activity, the brain is critically dependent upon a rich supply of blood. Oxygen-rich blood is carried to the brain through the carotid and the vertebral arteries. The vertebral arteries fuse to form the basilar artery soon after they enter the skull. The basilar artery supplies blood to the brain stem and the lower posterior portion of the hemispheres. The remainder of the brain is supplied with blood from the carotids. The carotid and basilar arteries join to form a large sinus called the circle of Willis. As a result, each arterial system may provide some backup to the area served by the other.

The brain and the spinal cord are covered by a continuous sheath of membranous material called the **meninges**. The meninges, in addition to protecting the soft and delicate surface of the brain, support the veins and arteries. The meninges have three layers: (1) a tough and leath-ery outer layer, the **dura mater**; (2) a middle layer called the **subarachnoid space**; and (3) a very delicate inner layer, the **pia mater**. Blood vessels that serve the brain are physically supported by the dura mater. They penetrate the dura at various points and course parallel to the surface of the brain in the subarachnoid space. Blood vessels that enter the brain tissues are sheathed by pia mater.

The actual exchange of nutrients and waste products takes place in very fine capillaries. Unlike the exchange that is common in all other body tissues, the passage of materials into the brain is under the control of a highly selective mechanism called the **blood–brain barrier**. Many substances that may enter body tissues with relative ease are restricted from entering the brain. Undoubtedly, the purpose of the blood–brain barrier is to protect the brain from potentially harmful substances. It is thought that the barrier is formed by the tight-fitting endothelial cells that make up the capillary walls.

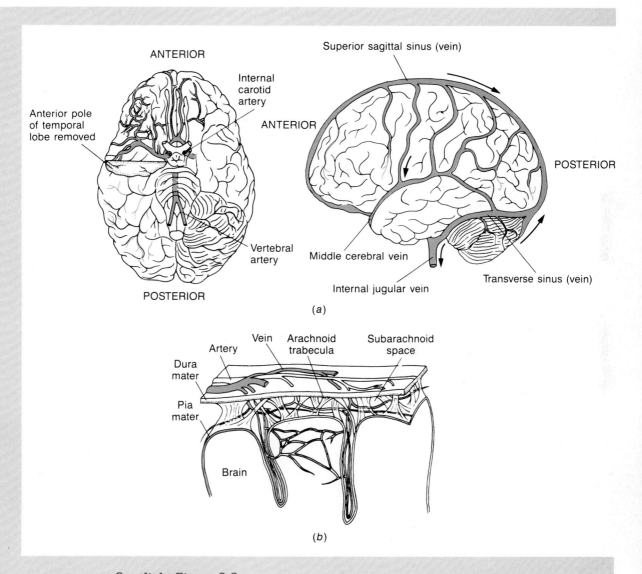

Spotlight Figure 3-3
a. The major veins supplying blood to the brain. *b.* Schematic drawing of the meninges showing the penetration of veins and arteries.

nonsensory areas of the cortex, and there are nuclei that receive information from the cortex.

The thalamus can be instructive in understanding the changing role of brain structures over evolutionary time. For example, in all mammals the **lateral geniculate nucleus** of the thalamus receives information from the eyes, where it synapses with the neurons that send information on to the visual centers in the cortex. As we discuss later, the final processing of visual information that results in the conscious awareness of sight takes place in the cortex. If the visual cortex of a primate is lesioned, the result is almost total blindness. If, however, the visual cortex of a less developed mammalian brain is destroyed, the result is quite different. A rodent deprived of its visual cortex loses some visual-processing capability, but it can still see. More important, the rodent will still be able to use the remaining vision intelligently. For example, it can perform a brightness discrimination task—choosing a bright or dark positive stimulus to receive a food reinforcement. The point to be made here is that, in the evolution of the mammalian brain, the thalamus has taken on a more peripheral sensory function as the cortex has developed the more dominant sensory role.

THE HYPOTHALAMUS

As its name suggests, the **hypothalamus** is a group of cell nuclei found ventral to the thalamus. The hypothalamus is located at the base of the brain just above the point where the nerves from the eyes meet and partially cross. The **pituitary gland** (**hypophysis**) is directly below and is attached to the hypothalamus by a short stalk. In the brain of humans the hypothalamus is no larger than the last digit of the small finger. It accounts for less than 1% of the total mass of the forebrain, yet it plays a central role in much of our most important behaviors.

The pituitary gland is under control of the hypothalamus, and together they regulate the action of the endocrine system. The endocrine glands secrete hormones directly into the bloodstream. The word *endocrine* comes from two Greek words: *endon*, meaning "within," and *krinein*, meaning "to secrete or separate." The hypothalamus activates the endocrine glands directly through neuronal transmission or indirectly with **releasing hormones** that stimulate the pituitary, which in turn activates other endocrine glands to release their hormones.

The term *hormone* means "to set into action." The hormones act like transmitter substances that influence the activity of neurons and cells in various body tissues. It is helpful to think of the CNS and the endocrine system as the two action systems, the two *executors* that control behavior. Together, the hypothalamus and the pituitary control functions as diverse as physical growth and the metabolism of calcium to eating, drinking, aggressiveness, and sexual behavior.

The hypothalamus is closely linked with other brain centers such as the limbic cortex, hippocampus, and amygdala, which are all related to emotional behaviors. As we discuss in greater detail later, these structures are part of the **limbic system**. Direct electrical stimulation of various regions of the limbic system, including the hypothalamus, can produce sexual behavior, a full-blown rage response, or the feeling of intense pleasure.

BASAL GANGLIA

The basal ganglia are comprised of the **caudate nucleus**, the **globus pallidus**, the **putamen**, and the **amygdala**. The first three nuclei are primarily concerned with motor behavior. The amygdala is in close proximity to the hippocampus and other limbic structures (see the following discussion) and is known to have a role in emotional behavior. Typically, the amygdala is included as part of the limbic system.

PALEOCORTEX

The cerebral hemispheres are covered with a thin mantle comprised primarily of cell bodies. The cell bodies in this cortex are organized into layers (the organization of cells within the tissues is termed the **cyto-architechtonics**). The portion of the cortex that is at the base of the cerebral hemispheres and that borders on the midbrain structures is distinctive in that, unlike the remainder of the cortex, it has four, rather than six, layers of cells. This more primitive cortex is called the **paleocortex**. In the evolution of the cerebral hemispheres the amount of paleocortex relative to **neocortex** (new cortex) has changed markedly. Figure 3-10 depicts this relationship. From the figure the progression is

Figure 3-10
Illustration of the expansion of neocortex from reptiles (a) through a primitive marsupial (b) to humans (c). The most primitive cortex (p) is specialized for olfaction, the slightly less primitive cortex (a) is folded under to form the hippocampus. The neocortex (n), which is very small or absent in reptiles, invades the cerebral hemispheres of mammals, particularly in primates and humans. Also shown are the basal ganglia (b), the ventricle (v) and the corpus callosum (cc). (From Romer, 1955.)

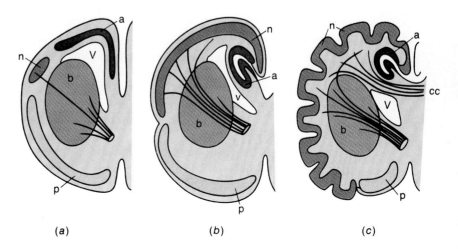

(a)   (b)   (c)

quite clear. As the brain evolved, the ratio of paleocortex to neocortex decreases markedly. Part of the primitive cortex folds on itself, is overgrown by the neocortex, and forms the **hippocampus**. The remaining portion shrinks in relative size and functions primarily in olfaction.

The hippocampus has been linked with memory and seems to be particularly important in solving spatially oriented memory tasks (Kesner & Novak, 1982; Thompson, 1981). As indicated earlier, the hippocampus is also closely linked with the hypothalamus and other brain centers that are related to emotional behavior. The same relationship is true for the olfactory cortex; therefore, it is included as part of the limbic system. It should not be surprising that the brain centers for the sense of smell are linked to centers controlling emotional behaviors. The importance of olfaction in the behavior of terrestrial mammals is quite evident. If you have owned a cat or a dog, you are already well aware of this. Olfaction is central to many key behaviors such as eating, mating, identification of young, and establishment of territories. One example should help to reinforce this point. If the olfactory epithelium is removed from an adult male dog, it will not mate, even if it was previously experienced in mating. Clearly, the sense of smell is critical in the survival of this species.

NEOCORTEX

In the evolution of the brain, the paleocortex and the other limbic areas were the first structures to comprise the forebrain. At the level of the amphibians and the reptiles, the limbic structures are, essentially, the entire forebrain. These animals are complete and surviving quite well. Their behavior, however, lacks the complexity and richness of the higher vertebrates. Many of the behaviors that we think of as being distinctly human—reasoning, language, altruism, and the like—are attributable to the evolution of the enormous, highly convoluted neocortex.

A histological examination of the cortex reveals a remarkably uniform outer layer of cell bodies approximately 3 mm thick. Close examination of the cytoarchitectonics, however, shows that the neocortex has six identifiable layers (Figure 3-11). The relative thickness of the layers varies from one area of cortex to another, suggesting that the cortex is not uniform in function. For example, sensory information projecting to the cortex from subcortical structures terminates in layer 4. This layer is much enlarged in those parts of the cortex that are the primary receptor areas for vision, audition, and **somesthesis** (body senses). Neurons that send information from the cortex to lower regions of the brain and to the spinal cord are found primarily in layers 4 and 5. It is not surprising that these layers, particularly layer 5, are thickest in the motor cortex.

The left side of Figure 3-11 shows a few representative neurons from each layer of the cortex; the center section depicts the distribution of the cell bodies, and the right section indicates the organization of the axons.

Figure 3-11
The six layers of the cortex are shown as seen under the light microscope. Each section of the figure shows how the cortex appears with various staining techniques. Note that the Nissl stain (*center*) and Weigert stain (*right*) reveal the columnar organization of the cortex.

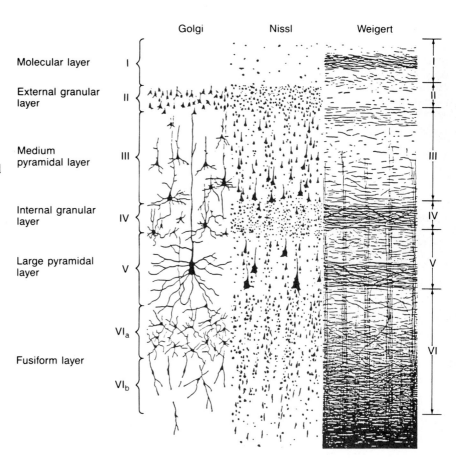

Careful examination of the center and right sections reveals that the cortex is organized into columns of cells. The somas are organized perpendicular to the surface of the cortex, and there are perpendicular tracts of axons. Recent studies have shown that these columns represent the basic functional units of the cortex. We have more to say about this in Chapters 5 and 6.

As the neocortex evolved, it became increasingly convoluted. (The term **gyrencephalic** is used to describe the convoluted cortex; and the term **lissencephalic** is used for smooth cortices, as seen in rodents, for example.) Most anatomists divide the cerebral hemispheres into five lobes, using conspicuous landmarks formed by the most prominent folds in the cortex (Figure 3-12, a & b). Viewed from the side, the **central sulcus** separates the **frontal** and **parietal lobes**. The **Sylvian**, or **lateral, fissure** marks the boundary between the frontal and parietal lobes and the **temporal lobe**. The **occipitoparietal fissure**, which is just barely visible from the lateral (side) aspect, defines the border of

Figure 3-12
The lateral view (*a*) and
midsagittal view (*b*) of the
cerebral hemispheres. The
major sulci that separate
the five lobes of the brain
are shown. (See also
Color Plate 3.)

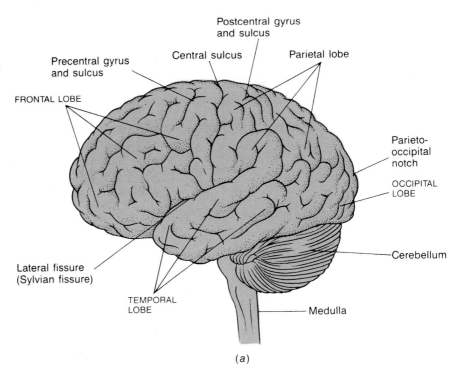

(*a*)

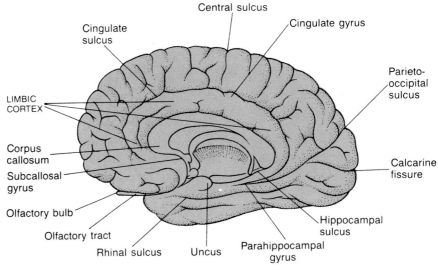

(*b*)

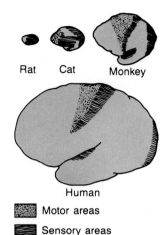

Rat   Cat   Monkey

Human

▨ Motor areas

▧ Sensory areas

▥ Association areas

Figure 3-13
Four representative
mammal brains showing
the proportion of cortex
dedicated to primary
sensory and motor
processing versus the
amount of association
cortex.

the parietal and **occipital** lobes. The fifth, or **limbic, lobe** can only be seen if the brain is cut anterior to posterior down the **longitudinal fissure** (this is called a **midsagittal section**), exposing the internal surface (Figure 3-12b). The limbic cortex is the narrow arc of cortex bordered by the **cingulate gyrus** and the **corpus collosum**, the large band of myelinated axons that connects **homotopic** (same location) areas of the two hemispheres.

The division of each hemisphere into five lobes has functional and geographic significance. Generally, the frontal lobes are specialized for more executive functions—the inhibition of behavior, planning, and decision making—and the control of fine motor action. The occipital lobe's primary function is vision. The primary function of the temporal lobe is audition. The anterior portion of the parietal lobe is concerned with somesthesis; the remainder is involved with the integration of visual and auditory information, and language.

Cortex that is not involved with the primary processing of sensory information is called (for the lack of a better term) **association cortex**. Since the turn of the century we have known that, in animals, the direct electrical stimulation to certain areas of the cortex would produce movements on the opposite side of the body. In the late 1940s studies of individuals undergoing neurosurgery showed conclusively that stimulation of motor cortex produces *involuntary* movement and that direct stimulation of sensory cortex produces the conscious experience of sensory stimulation. Stimulation of much of the cortex, however, fails to produce either effect. In fact, this is true for most of the cortex. Originally, these unresponsive cortical areas were called "quiet areas." It must have been awkward to think of so much of the brain doing nothing, so the more respectable and satisfying term "association cortex" was adopted.

We know now that association cortex has many different functions, including the inhibition of behavior, the integration of information, concept formation, and other "higher" mental processes that we associate with human and humanlike capabilities. If we look at several representative mammalian brains (see Figure 3-13), the relationship between sensory–motor cortex and association cortex becomes quite instructive. Moving from the less developed to the more complex mammals, the proportion of cortex available for primary processing of sensory information and for the control of motor action becomes progressively smaller. Said another way, the amount of association cortex becomes increasingly larger, and we must assume, increasingly important.

Encephalization *Revisited*

In the beginning of this chapter we noted that even in the most rudimentary nervous systems, the process of encephalization was evident. The tendency for nervous tissues to aggregate toward the head and form increasingly complex cephalic structures has been a continuing theme in the evolution of more complex brains. Encephalization and the related

SPOTLIGHT 3-4

The Triune Brain—Three Brains in One?

Some years ago Paul MacLean proposed that the human brain was actually three brains in one. At the core of this "triune brain" is the "reptile brain," which is comprised of those structures that are well developed in the brains of reptiles. According to MacLean, the reptilian brain within the human brain is comprised of the hindbrain, the midbrain, and some parts of the forebrain. It is primarily concerned with basic body functions such as respiration, blood pressure, and locomotion. Additionally, the reptile brain controls those behaviors that are essential for the survival of the species. MacLean proposed that most stereotypic and ritualistic behaviors, including sexual behavior, fighting, territorial defense, and so on, were all attributable to the reptilian brain (see Spotlight Figure 3-4).

Surrounding the reptilian brain is the "old mammalian brain," which is composed of some of the older forebrain structures. MacLean believes that the old mammalian brain is essentially the same in all mammals, but it is far less developed in reptiles. Like the reptilian brain, the old mammalian brain is involved in many behaviors that are critical for survival. Additionally, this division of the

brain has an important role in emotional behaviors such as fear, anger, and affectional love.

The most recent development in the brain is the "new mammalian brain," which consists of the cerebral cortex. This part of the brain is at least partially developed in all mammals; however, we see it most clearly in forms such as dolphins, primates, and humans, which have a significant amount of neocortex. This division of the brain is responsible for the most complex processing of sensory information and the control of very fine conscious motor activity. Furthermore, in humans, the new mammalian brain is responsible for consciousness, rational thought, and the other "higher-level" mental abilities. The three parts of the brain must work together. However, MacLean notes that integration between the three divisions of the brain is incomplete or imperfect. Psychological problems in humans may be attributed to "conflict" between the three systems (MacLean, 1970, 1977). MacLean's theory is not without its critics. The theory does, however, provide an interesting perspective of the functional evolution of brain structures.

increases in brain–to–body weight ratio are two telling indices of the evolving CNS. It may be helpful to summarize some of the more important steps in the encephalization process.

1. Paired cerebral ganglia form in the flatworm.
2. Segmental ganglia aggregate to form larger and more complex cerebral ganglia.
3. The nervous system develops from a hollow tube rather than solid ganglia.

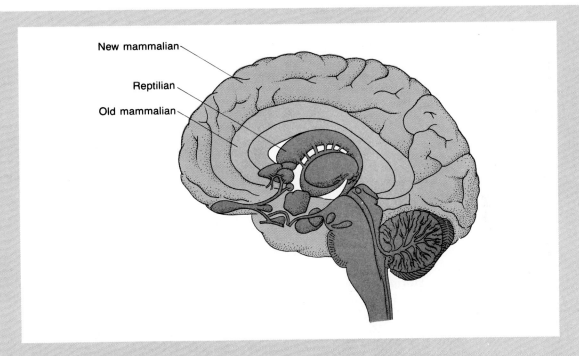

New mammalian
Reptilian
Old mammalian

Spotlight Figure 3-4
The triune brain. The "new mammalian brain," "old mammalian brain," and "reptilian brain," according to MacLean.

4. Nuclei, having specialized functions, form within cerebral ganglia, and the vertebrate CNS becomes divisible into a brain and spinal cord.

5. The forebrain develops out of midbrain structures, which, in turn, take on modified or new functions. Midbrain structures lose their independent capacity to support behavior.

6. Paleocortex becomes reduced, forming the hippocampus and olfactory projection areas.

7. The cortex becomes increasingly gyrencephalic, enlarging its surface area.
8. Primary sensory and motor cortical areas decrease relative to association cortical areas.
9. Association cortex acquires a prominent and dominant role in the overt behavior of the organism.

The Endocrine System

Earlier in this chapter it was noted that there are really two interrelated executor systems, the CNS and the endocrine system. Although each is sensitive to the action of the other because of various feedback mechanisms, each system exerts control in its own unique way. The CNS controls muscles and glands through the direct and precise action of the neurons. The endocrine glands produce their effects in a more general way by regulating the levels of hormones in the blood. In the remainder of this chapter we examine the main endocrine glands and their hormones, and we review how and where they produce their effects.

Hormone Action

Hormones have a profound effect on the metabolic activity of cells throughout the body. Through the action of hormones, the growth and differentiation of cells are regulated, and hormones modulate the activity of fully developed cells as well.

Hormones produce their varied effects on cells in two very different ways. Therefore, hormones are typically divided into two main groups based on their mode of action: (1) the **peptides** and **amine** hormones and (2) the **steroid** hormones. (Steroids are lipids that are synthesized from cholesterol.)

1. The peptides and amine hormones bind to receptor sites located on the surface of the membranes of the target cells. Contact by the hormone on the receptors causes the release of another substance inside the cell. (It was noted in Chapter 2 that some neural transmitters operate this way.) The intracellular substance released by the hormone is called a **second messenger**. The surfaces of many body cells are covered with receptor sites for one or more hormones. Typically, the peptide and amine hormones produce their effect rapidly, within a few seconds or minutes. This is not particularly fast compared to neuronal action, but it is quite rapid when compared to the action of steroids.

2. The steroid hormones enter the cell and bind to specific proteins in the cytoplasm. The united protein and steroid molecules then enter the nucleus of the cell, where they influence the transcription of genes. The genes, in turn, control the production of specific proteins. The steroid hormones tend to act more slowly and generally produce a longer-lasting effect.

Hormone Regulation   The production of hormones by the endocrine glands varies widely. Some endocrine glands produce hormones at a rather steady rate; others may have wide fluctuations in hormone production, depending on environmental influences and changing bodily activity and needs. All endocrine glands, however, are sensitive to the blood serum level of their specific hormone(s). High levels of a given hormone in blood serum inhibit the production and release of more of that hormone. Just as the thermostat on a hot water heater turns off the source of heat when the water reaches the prescribed temperature, this homeostatic mechanism is based on a negative-feedback loop.

The negative-feedback loops for the control of hormones can become quite complex. This is particularly true when one or more hormones influence the production of still another hormone. For example, the release of steroids produced by the cortex of the adrenal glands is controlled by a **tropic hormone** produced in the pituitary (**adrenocorticotropic hormone [ACTH]**). The ACTH is in turn controlled by a **releasing hormone (ACTHrf)** produced in the hypothalamus. Each of the three hormones involved is influenced by its own negative-feedback mechanism. To complicate the matter further, the hypothalamus is influenced by nonhormonal factors affecting the higher centers of the CNS.

A general model of the neuronal and hormonal feedback system is given in Figure 3-14. The figure shows how the neuronal and hormonal systems interact, in concert, to regulate metabolic activity and produce integrated behavioral responses. A brief example of the interaction between the neuronal and hormonal systems may be helpful at this point.

The steroid hormones produced by the adrenal cortex have varied and complex functions that protect the organism in times of physical and emotional stress. Now, suppose that as you are reading this book (enthralled with the lyrical beauty of the prose), someone comes up behind you without your knowledge and fires a starting pistol. At higher levels in the brain there may be an immediate, conscious experience of fear. The

Figure 3-14
General model of the control of the endocrine system. Note the interaction between the endocrine glands, the central nervous system, and the outside world.

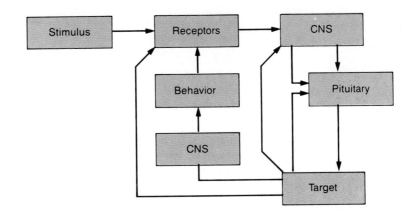

conscious awareness of the sound and the potential for danger that it represents results in the release of ACTHrf from the hypothalamus. The ACTHrf activates the pituitary to release ACTH, and simultaneously, feedback about the levels of ACTHrf and ACTH in the blood serum begins to regulate the flow of each hormone through inhibitory mechanisms. The ACTH acts on the cortex of the adrenal gland to release the steroids, which in turn act to heighten your body's defenses to stress. The blood serum levels of the steroids provide a negative-feedback loop to the pituitary and the hypothalamus, and in this way the steroid level is modulated.

Now suppose that, after emerging from under your desk, you are relieved to find several of your "good" friends who are laughing at your response to their "clever and sophisticated" attempt at humor. As you become conscious of the real nature of the situation and recognize that you are no longer in danger, the inhibitory effects of the high level of hormones in your blood on the hypothalamus and pituitary will cause the levels of ACTHrf, ACTH, and the adrenal steroids to return to their normal (nonstressed) level. (In the situation, as I described it, justifiable anger on your part may delay the return to the nonstressed level!)

Endocrine Glands and Hormones Important to Behavior

The purpose of this section is to introduce the reader to those endocrine glands and their secretions that are most important in understanding behavior. Some hormones not mentioned here have important functions in body growth, cell physiology, immunological defenses, and a variety of regulatory functions. (For a more comprehensive treatment of these hormones, see Turner and Bagnara, 1976, or Frieden and Lipner, 1971.) This is an abbreviated account, and many of the hormones outlined here are discussed in greater detail in other sections of this book. For example, the sex hormones produced in the testes and ovaries and other hormones produced in the pituitary gland that relate to sexual differentiation and sexual behavior are discussed in some detail in Chapter 4. Table 3-3 lists the main endocrine glands, the hormone(s) produced by the gland, the target or major function of the hormone, and the regulatory mechanism for the hormone.

PITUITARY HORMONES

The pituitary gland is situated in a small depression at the base of the skull. The gland has two distinct parts that are derived from different embryological sources. The anterior lobe of the pituitary, or the **adenohypophysis**, produces a number of secretions called "tropic hormones." Tropic hormones are given that name because they control endocrine glands situated in various parts of the body. The fact that the pituitary secretions affect the output of other endocrine glands is the reason that the pituitary has been called the "master gland." The posterior lobe of the pituitary, also known as the **neurohypophysis**, stores

---

Table 3-3. **Endocrine Glands, Hormones, Their Functions and Control Mechanisms**

Gland & Hormone	Target or Function	Control Mechanism
Anterior pituitary		
ACTH	Stimulates adrenal cortex	Hypothalamic ACTHrf* and cortisol
Thyroid stimulating hormone	Stimulates thyroid	Hypothalamic TSHrf and thyroxine
Follicle-stimulating hormone	Stimulates growth of ovarian follicles	Hypothalamic FSHrf, estrogen, and progesterone
Luteinizing hormone	Conversion of follicle to corpora lutea, secretion of sex hormones in testes and ovaries	LHrf, estrogen, progesterone, testosterone
Prolactin	Milk secretion in mammary glands	Hypothalamic prolactin inhibiting factor
Growth hormone	Stimulates growth	Hypothalamic GHrf
Posterior pituitary (hypothalamus)		
Vasopressin (ADH)	Kidney, blood pressure	Water balance feedback to the hypothalamus
Oxytocin	Contraction of uterine muscles, milk release	Mechanical stimulation of the breast
Thyroid adrenal cortex		
Thyroxine	Growth, metabolic rate	TSH
Glucocorticoids	Metabolism of carbohydrates, protein, and fats	ACTH
Mineralocoricoids	Electrolyte and water balance	Plasma ion concentrations (K^+, Na^+), angiotensin
Adrenal medulla		
Epinephrine and norepinephrine	Sympathetic arousal, emergency mobilization	Sympathetic preganglionic neurons
Pancreas		
Insulin	Glucose utilization	Plasma glucose levels
Glucagon	Glucose release	Plasma glucose levels

* rf = release factor

(continued)

Table 3-3. (Continued)

Gland & Hormone	Target or Function	Control Mechanism
Testes		
Testosterone	Sexual differentiation, maintenance of sexual anatomy and behavior	LH
Ovaries		
Estrogen	Sexual differentiation, maintenance of sexual behavior	LH, FSH
Progesterone	Maintenance of uterine wall, maintenance of sexual behavior	LH, FSH

hormones produced by hypothalamic nuclei and does not produce any hormones itself. The hormones are actually produced in the supra-optic nucleus and the paraventricular nucleus. The hormones are transported to the pituitary via axons and released by nerve impulses (see Figure 3-15).

1. *Adenohypophysis hormones:* Growth hormone, which is also known as somatotropin or **somatotropic hormone (STH)**, is produced in the adenohypophysis and acts in many parts of the body to stimulate the growth of cells and tissues. The production of growth hormone is cyclical, with the maximum rate of production taking place during the early stages of sleep.

Adrenocorticotropic hormone (ACTH) controls the production and release of hormones from the surface (cortex) of the adrenal glands. The release of ACTH is regulated by a hormone produced in the hypothalamus, ACTH release factor, as noted earlier. **Thyroid-stimulating hormone (TSH)**, as its name suggests, stimulates the thyroid gland to produce and release thyroxine. TSH also affects the size and development of the thyroid gland.

Two hormones produced in the anterior pituitary influence the gonads: (1) **luteinizing hormone (LH)** and (2) **follicle-stimulating hormone (FSH)**. LH stimulates the development and maintenance of the corpus luteum in the ovaries. It also stimulates the production of progesterone, which, in turn, maintains the uterine wall so that it may support the fertilized egg. In males, LH stimulates the production of

Figure 3-15
The anterior and posterior portions of the pituitary gland. Tropic hormones are produced in the anterior pituitary and released into the blood through the portal vessels. Hormones produced in the hypothalamus are transported to the posterior pituitary via hypothalamic axons and released by nerve impulses.

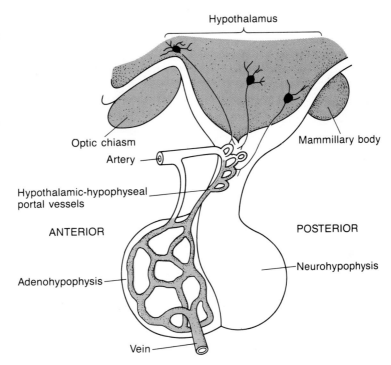

testosterone in the testes. FSH modulates the production of estrogen in females and testosterone in males. FSH also influences the production of eggs and sperm. (LH and FSH are covered in more detail in Chapter 4.)

2. *Neurohypophysis hormones:* The posterior portion of the pituitary stores two hormones that are produced in the hypothalamus: (1) the **antidiuretic hormone** (**ADH**), or **vasopressin**, and (2) **oxytocin**. ADH inhibits the production of urine and in so doing conserves water. ADH also increases vascular pressure by constricting the smooth muscle in the walls of veins and arteries. Oxytocin controls "milk letdown." Oxytocin is released when the nipple is stimulated by the suckling infant (see Figure 3-16). In the uterus, oxytocin causes the contraction of smooth muscle and may have a role in the uterine constrictions during birth. In males, oxytocin induces the muscle contractions associated with the ejaculation of sperm.

ADRENAL GLAND HORMONES

The adrenal gland, which is located adjacent to each kidney, is a complex structure. The outer portion, called the cortex, has three distinct layers of cells, each producing different hormones. The central core of the gland is called the medulla, and unlike the cortex, it is closely related to the ANS and is richly inervated with neurons from the ANS.

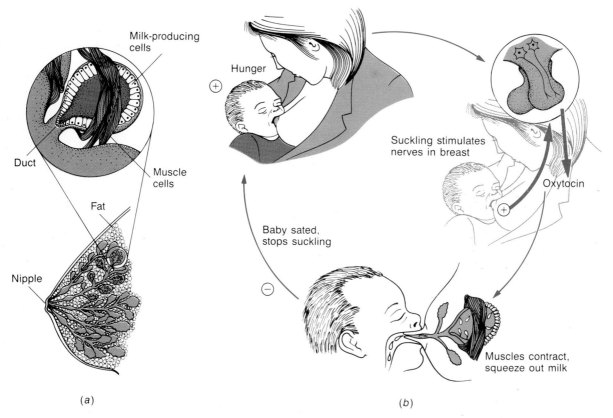

(a)   (b)

Figure 3-16

Oxytocin and breast-feeding. *a.* The human breast is a ducted, or exocrine, gland. The breast contains many clusters of milk-producing cells that surround hollow, bulbous structures. Each of the bulbs empties into a duct, and the numerous ducts lead to the nipple. In lactating women, milk is secreted into the bulbs, where it is stored. Mechanical stimulation of the nipple by the sucking action of the infant initiates a complex cycle of events that results in the release of the milk. *b.* Milk release is controlled by a complex negative-feedback loop. The mechanical stimulation produced by the sucking action of the infant excites receptors in the nipple, which send signals to the neurosecretory cells in the posterior half of the hypothalamus. This causes the release of oxytocin into the mother's bloodstream. When the oxytocin reaches the breast, it stimulates contractions of the muscles that surround the milk-containing bulbs, forcing milk into the ducts. The sucking action of the infant then draws the milk out of the nipple. The process continues until the infant stops feeding. With the nipple no longer being stimulated, oxytocin release stops, the muscles relax, and the milk flow ceases.

The cortex of the adrenal gland produces a variety of steroid hormones. Typically, these hormones are divided into two subgroups, the **glucocorticoids** and the **mineralocorticoids**. The glucocorticoids, as their name suggests, affect the metabolism of carbohydrates. They control glucose and protein metabolism, and they have a powerful anti-inflammatory effect that protects body tissues following injury. Mineralocorticoids affect the concentrations of ions in body tissues, and they maintain the distribution of ions in the blood and extracellular fluids. As mentioned earlier, the action of the adrenal cortex is controlled by ACTH produced in the anterior pituitary.

THYROID HORMONES

The thyroid gland is situated in the neck just below the larynx. The principal hormones produced by the thyroid are **thyroxine** and **calcitonin**, and both influence important metabolic processes, including carbohydrate metabolism. Thyroid activity is under the control of thyroid-stimulating hormone (TSH) produced in the adenohypophysis. TSH production is controlled by levels of thyroxine in the blood and by a releasing hormone (thyrotropin-releasing hormone) produced by the hypothalamus. Normal functioning of the thyroid is essential for growth. Thyroid deficiencies, particularly in early life, may result in stunted growth, facial anomalies, and mental retardation resulting from a marked reduction in brain size (cretinism).

GONADAL HORMONES

The male testes and female ovaries produce and secrete several hormones that influence the production of sperm and ova, regulate sexual differentiation and the development of secondary sexual characteristics, and control sexual behavior. We deal with the sex hormones in detail in Chapter 4. Our purpose here is simply to identify the sex glands and their related hormones and to review briefly the mechanisms that regulate the hormone levels.

The male testes produce **testosterone** (one of a class of hormones called androgens), which develops and maintains masculine characteristics. Testosterone production is controlled by luteinizing hormone (LH) that is produced in the anterior portion of the pituitary gland. LH, in turn, is influenced by a hypothalamic releasing factor called **gonadotropin-releasing hormone (GnRH)**.

The female gonads, the ovaries, produce two groups of hormones, the **estrogens** and the **progestogens**. The production of ovarian hormones is cyclical and varies widely between species. The estrous cycle (menstruation in women) is regulated by the cyclical variations in ovarian hormones. The ovaries are regulated by two hormones produced in the adenohypophyis, follicle stimulating hormone (FSH) and LH, which are in turn under the control of GnRH.

CHAPTER SUMMARY

1. The first step in the evolution of specialized cells that coordinate behavior is seen in the *nerve net*. The first "true brain" evolved as a mass of interactive nerve cells called a *ganglion*. The two head ganglia as seen in flatworms can be viewed as the basic bilateral plan from which more complex nervous systems evolved. The *segmented nervous system* in annelids and the *hollow core* nervous system in vertebrates represent significant evolutionary steps toward more sophisticated and complex nervous systems.

2. The vertebrate nervous system is divided into the central and peripheral nervous systems. Standardized directional terms are used to describe the relationship between structures in the central nervous system. The brain is typically shown in three cardinal planes: *coronal*, *horizontal*, and *sagittal*. The primary directional terms are *medial* (middle), *lateral* (side), *anterior* (front), *posterior* (back), *dorsal* (top), *ventral* (bottom), *cephalic* or *rostral* (toward the head), *caudal* (away from the head), *proximal* (near), and *distal* (far).

3. Somatic nerves are classified into *afferent* (sensory) and *efferent* (motor) nerves. The 12 cranial nerves are those nerves that enter and exit at the level of the brain. Some of the cranial nerves are afferent, some are efferent, and some are both afferent and efferent.

4. The *autonomic nervous system* is controlled neuronally and hormonally by the CNS, and it is associated with emotional behavior. The ANS can be divided into two subdivisions: the *sympathetic* and the *parasympathetic* nervous systems. Activation of the sympathetic nervous system produces the fight-or-flight reaction. Activation of the parasympathetic system produces anabolic effects that oppose the sympathetic subdivision. The two subdivisions of the ANS work together to maintain *homeostatic* levels of activation.

5. Each segment of the spinal cord receives information from a single *dermatome* of the body. All sensory neurons enter the spinal cord from the dorsal side; motor neurons exit the spinal cord on the ventral side. A *spinal reflex arc* consists of afferent neurons, interneurons, and efferent neurons.

6. The brain can be subdivided into the *hindbrain, midbrain* and *forebrain*. The hindbrain consists of the *medulla, pons,* and *cerebellum*. The midbrain includes the *tectum*, the *superior* and *inferior colliculi*, and several important nuclei, including the *substantia nigra, red nucleus,* and *oculomotor nucleus*. The forebrain is by far the largest portion of the brain in humans. The forebrain includes the *thalamus, basal ganglia,* and *cerebral cortex*, plus the various structures of the *limbic system*.

7. The cerebral cortex can be divided into five lobes: *frontal, temporal, occipital, parietal,* and *limbic*. *Paleocortex* is older cortex, and it is associated with the structures of the limbic lobe. *Neocortex*, the most recently developed structure in the brain, increases markedly in more complex mammals.

8. *Encephalization* is the evolutionary process by which the distal brain structures migrate toward the head, making the brain increasingly complex. Additionally, new brain structures overgrow and cover older brain structures. The new brain structures become increasingly important in overt behavior.

9. The endocrine system and the CNS make up the two executor systems of the body. Endocrine glands secrete hormones directly into the blood.

10. Hormones have a profound effect on the metabolic activity of cells throughout the body. Hormones can be divided into two groups based on their mode of action: *peptide/amine hormones* and *steroid hormones*. Hormones are regulated by negative-feedback, homeostatic mechanisms.

11. The secretions of many endocrine glands are regulated by secretions from the *pituitary gland*, which in turn is regulated by the hypothalamus. Both the pituitary gland and the hypothalamus are sensitive to feedback from hormones in the blood.

SUGGESTED READINGS

Barr, M. L., & Kiernan, J. A. (1983). *The human nervous system: An anatomical viewpoint* (4th ed.). Philadelphia: Harper & Row.

Carpenter, A., & Sutin, J. (1983). *Human neuroanatomy* (8th ed.). Baltimore, MD: Williams & Wilkins.

Frieden, E., & Lipner, H. (1971). *Biochemical endocrinology of the vertebrates.* Englewood Cliffs, NJ: Prentice-Hall.

Matzke, H. A., & Foltz, F. M. (1972). *Synopsis of neuroanatomy* (2nd ed.) New York: Oxford University Press.

Shepherd, G. M. (1983). *Neurobiology.* New York: Oxford University Press.

Turner, C. D., & Bagnara, J. T. (1976). *General endocrinology* (6th ed.). Philadelphia: Saunders.

KEY TERMS

Adenohypophysis Anterior, glandular portion of the pituitary gland.

Adrenocorticotropic hormone (ACTH) Hormone produced in the anterior portion of the pituitary gland; stimulates the cortex of the adrenal gland.

Afferent neuron Sensory neuron; brings information to the CNS.

Amygdala Part of the basal ganglia; involved with emotional behavior; included as part of the limbic system.

Anabolic Metabolic activity that conserves energy; parasympathetic action.

Anterior Anatomical term for front.

Antidiuretic hormone (ADH) Hormone produced in the hypothalamus and stored in the posterior portion of the pituitary; stimulates reabsorption of water from the kidneys.

Archicerebellum   *See* Cerebellum.

Association cortex   Areas of cortex not directly associated with sensory or motor function.

Autonomic nerves   Nerves that comprise the autonomic nervous system.

Basal ganglia   A group of forebrain nuclei including the globus pallidum, caudate nucleus, putamen, and amygdala. The first three have motor functions, and the amygdala is part of the limbic system.

Calcitonin   Hormone produced by the thyroid gland; regulates the level of calcium in the blood.

Catabolic   Energy-releasing metabolic activity; sympathetic action.

Caudal   Anatomical direction away from the head.

Caudate   *See* Basal ganglia.

Central canal   Tubular structure within the spinal cord; contains cerebrospinal fluid.

Central sulcus   Sulcus dividing the frontal and parietal lobes.

Cephalic   Anatomical direction toward the head.

Cerebellum   Highly convoluted hindbrain structure; controls unconscious motor activity; comprised of the archicerebellum, paleocerebellum, and neocerebellum.

Cerebral ganglion   Aggregate of cell bodies found in the head end of flatworms.

Cerebral hemispheres   Large forebrain structures including the cortex, basal ganglia, thalamus, hypothalamus, and limbic system.

Cerebrospinal fluid   Clear fluid that fills the ventricular system and the central canal.

Cervical   Most anterior portion of the spinal column.

Choroid plexus   Structure inside the ventricles that produces the cerebrospinal fluid.

Cingulate gyrus   Cortex between the corpus callosum and the cingulate sulcus.

Contralateral   Anatomical term for the opposite side.

Coronal plane   Plane through the central nervous system that divides the anterior and posterior sections.

Corpora quadrigemina   Tectum of midbrain; contains the superior colliculi, which function in vision, and inferior colliculi, which function in audition.

Corpus callosum   Large band of myelinated fibers connecting homotropic areas of the two hemispheres.

Cranial nerves   Afferent and efferent nerves for the face; most enter the CNS at the level of the medulla.

Cytoarchitectonics   Organization of cells in tissues.

Dermatome   Area of skin surface; has all sensory information channeled through one dorsal root ganglion.

Distal   Direction away from center.

Dorsal   Anatomical term for top or above.

Dorsal horns   Gray matter on dorsal side of spinal cord; contains afferent cell nuclei.

Dorsal root   Afferent nerve between the dorsal root ganglion on the dorsal horn.

Dorsal root ganglion   Group of afferent cell nuclei; found outside the vertebral column.

Dura mater   Leathery outer layer of the meninges.

Efferent neuron   Motor neuron; brings information from the CNS to muscles and glands.

Encephalization   Process in the evolution of the CNS marked by the migration of cells to the head end of the nervous system.

Endocrine glands   A number of glands that secrete directly into the bloodstream.

Estrogens   Hormones produced in the ovaries; develop and maintain female sexual characteristics and behavior.

Exocrine gland   Ducted glands; unlike endocrine glands, do not excrete directly into the bloodstream.

Follicle-stimulating hormone (FSH)   Hormone produced in the anterior portion of the pituitary; stimulates growth of ovarian follicles.

Forebrain   Phylogenetically newest portion of the brain, comprised of the cerebral cortex, basal ganglia, limbic system, thalamus, and hypothalamus.

Fourth ventricle   Fluid-filled space in the brain.

Frontal lobe   *See* Lobe.

Ganglion   Aggregate of neuron cell bodies; in vertebrate CNS used to describe aggregate of cell bodies found outside the skull and spinal column.

Globus pallidus   *See* Basal ganglia.

Glucocorticoids   Hormones produced in the cortex of the adrenal gland; regulate the metabolism of carbohydrates.

Gonadotropin-releasing hormone (GnRH)
Hormone produced in the hypothalamus; regulates the production of tropic hormones in the pituitary.

Gyrencephalic Having a convoluted cortex.

Gyrus The outside (rounded) parts of the convolutions in the brain.

Hindbrain Oldest portion of brain, comprised of the pons and medulla.

Hippocampus Forebrain structure derived from paleocortex; has significant role in memory.

Homeostasis Active process to maintain a normal or optimal level of activity.

Homotopic The same or equivalent place.

Horizontal plane Plane that divides the dorsal and the ventral portions.

Hypophysis *See* Pituitary.

Hypothalamus Forebrain nucleus; part of the limbic system; has control centers for vital body functions and emotional expression.

Inferior colliculi *See* Corpora quadrigemina.

Interneuron Neuron found within the CNS; passes information between afferent and efferent neurons.

Lateral Direction away from the medial (center).

Lateral fissure *See* Sylvian fissure.

Lateral geniculate nucleus Thalamic nucleus; specific for vision.

Lateral ventricle Large space found in each cerebral hemisphere; filled with cerebrospinal fluid.

Limbic lobe *See* Lobe.

Limbic system Forebrain structures associated with the expression of emotional behaviors.

Lissencephalic Having a smooth cortex.

Lobe Term used to divide the surface of the cerebrum geographically and by function. The five lobes are named the frontal, parietal, temporal, occipital, and limbic lobes.

Longitudinal fissure Midline fissure separating the two cerebral hemispheres.

Lumbar Lower portion of the spinal column, located between the thoracic and sacral regions.

Luteinizing hormone (LH) Hormone produced in the anterior pituitary; stimulates the conversion of ovarian follicles into corpora lutea.

Medial Anatomical direction of movement of the sagittal plane.

Medulla Hindbrain structure and extension of the spinal cord; has centers for vital body functions.

Meninges Complex membrane that completely encases the brain and the spinal cord; composed of the dura mater, pia mater, and subarachnoid space.

Mesencephalon *See* Midbrain.

Midbrain The mesencephalon, comprised of the corpora quadrigemina, red nucleus, and substantia nigra.

Midsagittal section A cut down the midline from anterior to posterior dividing the brain in half.

Mineralocorticoids Hormones produced in the cortex of the adrenal gland; regulate ion metabolism.

Neocerebellum *See* Cerebellum.

Neocortex Phylogenetically newer cortex; comprises major portion of cortex in higher mammals.

Nerve Groups of neuron axons in the peripheral nervous system.

Nerve network A rudimentary nervous system commonly seen in the coelenterates.

Neurohypophysis Posterior portion of the pituitary; stores and releases hormones produced in the hypothalamus.

Nucleus Anatomical term for aggregates of nuclei within the CNS.

Occipital lobe *See* Lobe.

Occipitoparietal fissure Sulcus separating the occipital and parietal lobes.

Oculomotor nucleus Hindbrain nucleus; controls eye movement.

Ontogeny The developmental history of the individual organism.

Oxytocin Hormone released by the posterior portion of the pituitary; produces contraction of smooth muscles in the uterus and initiates milk letdown.

Paleocerebellum *See* Cerebellum.

Paleocortex Phylogenetically older cortex; forms the hippocampus and olfactory projection areas in humans.

Parasympathetic nerves Part of the ANS; acts to conserve energy.

Parietal lobe *See* Lobe.

Peduncle Band of fibers connecting the cerebellum to the mid- and hindbrain.

Pia mater   Delicate inner membrane of the meninges.

Pituitary   Endocrine gland; produces tropic hormones that control the function of other endocrine glands.

Posterior   Anatomical term for back or rear.

Postganglionic   Autonomic fiber transmitting information from the ganglion to the target organ.

Progestogens   Hormones produced by the ovaries.

Proximal   Direction toward the center.

Putamen   *See* Basal ganglia.

Red nucleus   Hindbrain nucleus; has motor function.

Reflex arc   Found at the level of the spinal cord, comprised of an afferent neuron, interneuron, and efferent neuron.

Releasing hormone   Several hormones produced in the hypothalamus; activate the pituitary.

Rostral   Direction toward the head.

Sacral   Lowest, most posterior portion of the spinal column.

Sagittal plane   Plane that divides the left and right sides.

Second messenger   Substance produced inside the cell by peptide hormone action on cell membrane.

Somatotropic hormone (**SH**)   Produced in the anterior pituitary; stimulates growth; also called growth hormone.

Somesthesis   Body senses.

Spinal cord   Portion of the CNS below the hindbrain and encased in the vertebral column.

Subesophageal ganglion   Aggregate of nuclei located below the esophagus.

Subarachnoid space   Middle layer of the meninges.

Substantia nigra   Hindbrain nucleus; has motor function.

Sulcus   The inside (folded) part of the convolutions of the brain.

Superior colliculi   *See* Corpora quadrigemina.

Supraesophageal ganglion   Aggregate of nuclei located above the esophagus.

Sylvian fissure   Large sulcus between the temporal and the frontal and parietal lobes.

Sympathetic nerves   Part of the ANS; activate the organism for the release of energy.

Tectum   The roof of the midbrain; contains the superior and inferior colliculli.

Temporal lobe   *See* Lobe.

Testosterone   Sex hormone produced in the male testes.

Thalamus   Forebrain nuclei; relay station for sensory information.

Thoracic   Middle portion of the spinal column, between the cervical and lumbar regions.

Thyroid-stimulating hormone (**TSH**)   Hormone produced in the posterior portion of the pituitary; stimulates the thyroid gland.

Thyroxine   Hormone produced in thyroid gland; stimulates carbohydrate metabolism.

Triune brain   According to MacLean, the human brain can be divided into three divisions: the "reptilian brain," the "old mammalian brain," and the "new mammalian brain."

Tropic hormones   Hormones produced in the pituitary gland; regulate the production of hormones in other endocrine glands.

Vasopressin   *See* Antidiuretic hormone.

Ventral   Anatomical direction for bottom or under.

Ventral horns   Gray matter in ventral side of the spinal cord, contains cell nuclei for efferent neurons.

Ventral root   Efferent nerve; carries motor information from the ventral horns.

Chapter 4

Reproducing

Evolution of Sexual Reproduction

Biochemical Reproduction
Asexual Reproduction
Sexual Reproduction
Adaptive Advantages of Sexual Reproduction
Reproductive Strategies

Human Sexual Differentiation

Levels of Sexual Differentiation
Genotypic Determination
Gonadal Determination
Hormonal Determination
Internal Reproductive System Differentiation
External Genital Differentiation

Gender Identification

Secondary Sexual Determination
Anomalies of Gender Determination

Hormones and Sex

Organizing and Activating Role of Hormones on Sexual Behavior
Hormone Control of the Estrous and Menstrual Cycles
Hormone Influence on Sexual Behavior
Pheromones and Sexual Behavior

Neural Control of Sexual Behavior

Spinal Cord Mechanisms
Hypothalamic Mechanisms
Amygdala and Limbic Structures

Patterns of Human Sexual Behavior

Chapter Learning Objectives

After reading this chapter, you should

1. Understand the importance of biochemical duplication as the foundation of the reproduction of organisms.

2. Know and be able to discuss the adaptive advantages of sexual reproduction.

3. Be able to compare and contrast the r-selection and K-selection reproductive strategies. Be able to give examples of varying degrees of caregiving across species.

4. Be able to describe sexual differentiation at both the biological and psychological levels.

5. Be able to describe the effect of male and female hormones on the development of the internal sex organs, the external genitalia, and the development of secondary sexual characteristics.

6. Be familiar with the various gender differentiation anomalies and be able to relate them to the action of the sex hormones.

7. Be familiar with the organizing and activating effects of the sex hormones on sexual behavior.

8. Be able to differentiate between estrous and menstrual cycles and know how these cyclic patterns are influenced by hormone levels.

9. Understand and be able to give examples of the influence of chemical pheromones on overt sexual behavior.

10. Be able to discuss the role of the spinal cord, hypothalamus, and limbic system in sexual behavior.

11. Understand the importance of learning and social experience on the expression of sexual behavior in humans.

Evolution of Sexual Reproduction

An essential characteristic of all living things is their ability to reproduce. Whether through predation, disease, aging, or any of a number of environmental pressures, all individuals must die. The species, however, survives far beyond the life span of the individual. This, of course, is accomplished through the generation of new individuals. As we discuss later in this chapter, the reproduction of new individuals is accomplished by one of two methods: (1) via the replication of a single parent or (2) through the union of two parents.

Biochemical Reproduction

Before cells can replicate, molecules must be able to replicate. This is fundamental to life even before sex. Within every living cell is the biochemical information necessary to form new cells. In fact, every body cell has the genetic information necessary to form a completely new individual. The key element in this genetic code is the very large macromolecule deoxyribonucleic acid (DNA).

DNA is an extremely complex chain of sugars and phosphates bound together by four small bases: **thymine, cytosine, guanine**, and **adenine**. Various combinations of these sugars, phosphates, and bases form **nucleotides**. The sequence of the nucleotides within the DNA of a given species completely determines the sequence of the amino acids and proteins found in the organism. This is accomplished through an intermediary molecule, **ribonucleic acid** (**RNA**), which is transcribed from segments of the DNA molecule and in turn serves as the template for the production of amino acids and proteins. Therefore, DNA is in a very real sense the "fundamental biological invariant" that defines each species (Monod, Wyman, & Changeux, 1965).

The architecture of the DNA molecule is what determines its unique ability to replicate itself. Each DNA molecule is comprised of two identical spirals that are bound by the four bases to form a double helix. When DNA replicates itself, as it does in cell division, the two strands of the helix separate, and each serves as a template for the construction of another strand that is identical to itself. In this manner one molecule is able to make two molecules that are the same as the original. Here, then, is the secret of reproduction: (1) to divide and (2) to rebuild on the same model (see Figure 4-1).

Asexual Reproduction

The most primitive, single-celled forms of animals and plants multiply through **asexual** reproduction. When environmental conditions are favorable for supporting increased numbers of individuals, these simple organisms divide into two or more identical offspring. A key element in the process of asexual reproduction is the organization and division of the genetic material so that each new individual receives the same amount of genetic information. The process can be seen in many species of protozoans such as members of the genus *Amoeba*.

Figure 4-1
Replication of DNA. Individual nucleotides of all four types are produced and available within the nucleus of the cell before replication begins. The two strands of the DNA molecule separate at the juncture of the bases. Each parent strand then serves as a template for the assembly of a complementary strand. In this way two DNA molecules are synthesized that are chemically identical to the original molecule.

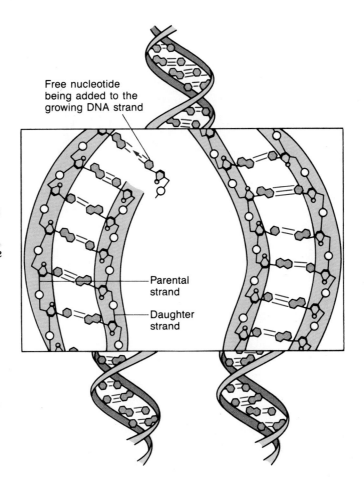

Free nucleotide being added to the growing DNA strand

Parental strand

Daughter strand

In the most primitive forms of protozoans the genetic material replicates and aggregates to the center of the cell nucleus. The genetic material of the nucleus and the nucleolus then divide in two, and the identical, newly formed nuclei migrate apart. The cell membrane then forms around the separated nuclei, forming two identical individuals (see Figure 4-2a).

In more complex forms of protozoans **mitotic** division occurs. In mitotic division the genetic material forms identifiable strands. These **chromosomes** may be seen to replicate themselves and divide into pairs of identical chromosomes. Each member of the pair then separates and migrates into one half of the nucleus before the nucleus divides, thus insuring that each new individual has identical genetic information. This process is identical to the cell division that occurs in the various tissues of the body.

A major limitation of asexual reproduction is that there is essentially no opportunity to share genetic material between individuals. With

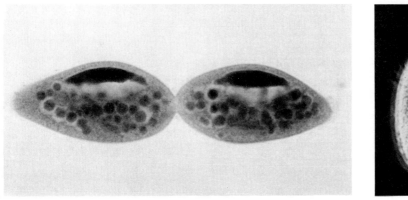

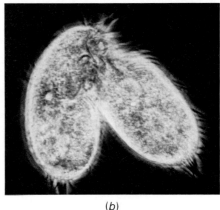

(a)   (b)

Figure 4-2
Reproduction in single-celled organisms. *a.* The simple asexual cell division in
the paramecium. Half of the nuclear material migrates to either end of the
cell and division follows, producing two genetically identical daugther cells.
b. Conjugation in *Euplotes*. One or more chromosomes are passed between
the individuals across a cytoplasmic bridge before cell division. After cell
division each individual will have gene combinations different from either
parent cell, thus increasing genetic variation.

the exception of some minor changes in the sequences of genes on the
chromosomes, each individual produces genetically identical offspring.
Because of this, the variance in the population genetics of the species is
greatly restricted. As we saw in Chapter 1, population heterozygosity
(the variance in the population genetics within a species) is an important
factor in both the adaptive fitness of a species and the generation of new
species.

The first step that was taken to increase population heterozygosity
was probably a process similar to **conjugation**. This can be seen in some
contemporary ciliates. Conjugation takes place as follows. During the
process of mitotic division, two individuals come together and exchange
one or more chromosomes *before* asexual division takes place (Figure
4-2b). In this way genetic information is shared between individuals,
providing a limited opportunity to increase genetic variance.

Sexual Reproduction   True sexual reproduction requires a special kind of cell division, **meiotic**,
or **reduction**, **division**. In meiotic division the chromosomes of a **germ
cell** form into **homologous** pairs. Each chromosome pair then separates,
and two daughter cells are formed, each having one chromosome from
each pair of chromosomes. These daughter cells, having one half of the
genetic material, are said to be in the **haploid** state. The daughter cells
then replicate their chromosomes and undergo a mitotic form of cell
division.

The final product of reduction division is four **gametes**, each having one half of the normal complement of chromosomes for the species. When the gametes (**sperm** for males and **ova**, or **eggs**, for females) are combined into a fertilized **zygote**, each chromosome joins with its homolog, and the full complement of chromosomes for the species (the **diploid** state) is reestablished. In some primitive animals the gametes are quite similar in size and form. In others, like humans, the sperm is not much more than a nucleus, made mobile by a flagellum. The egg is considerably larger and is immobile, and it contains a substantial food supply. The egg is formed in the following manner. In the first cell division in the formation of the ovum, most of the cell mass remains with one nucleus, and a **polar body** containing the other nucleus is formed. In the second cell division, the reduction division, the polar body divides, producing two polar bodies; and the egg divides, producing a third polar body and the large ovum. The polar bodies do not function in reproduction (see Figure 4-3).

It is interesting to note that the most primitive form of sexual reproduction takes place in animals that have both male and female organs. Animals that possess sex organs of both sexes are called **hermaphrodites** after the mythological son of Hermes and Aphrodite who was half man and half woman. There is evidence that hermaphroditic sexual reproduction takes place in some of the Coelenterata, specifically the *Ctenophora*, but these free-swimming relatives of the sponges seem to be capable of only self-fertilization (Borradaile et al., 1961). The flatworms are the first hermaphroditic animals to have a physical mechanism in place that ensures fertilization between individuals, thus increasing genetic vigor. Figure 4-4 shows hermaphroditic sexual reproduction in the common earthworm. The two bisexual individuals, facing opposite directions, set their bodies so that the male and female organs align. A mucous sheath is then formed to insure that the sperm from the male organ of one individual is passed to the female organ of the other. (In some species of annilids individuals may be differentiated by sex, each animal having only male or female sex organs and producing only one type of sex cell, either sperm or eggs.) We will have more to say about the bisexual origins of sexual reproduction later in this chapter.

Adaptive Advantages of Sexual Reproduction

The significance of meiotic division is that it provides a mechanism by which the traits of two parents can be combined. This, in turn, greatly increases the opportunity to diversify the gene pool of the species. As Bronowski (1973) put it, "Sex produces diversity, and diversity is the propeller of evolution."

For some 3 billion years, life on earth remained essentially unchanged. During this period the planet was populated only by a primitive form of algae that reproduced asexually. Suddenly, a great diversity of life emerged. The so-called Cambrian explosion took place about 600

Figure 4-3
a. The process of oogenesis. The formation of the ovum occurs in two stages. In the first meiotic division a small polar body is formed, leaving most of the cell mass for the developing egg. The second meiotic division produces two additional polar bodies and the ovum. (In some instances the polar body produced in the first cell division does not undergo the second meiotic division.) All four cells have the haploid number of chromosomes. The polar bodies have no function and die. For clarity, only four chromosomes are shown.
b. The process of spermatogenesis. As with oogenesis, spermatogenesis requires two stages. In the first stage the primary spermatocyte divides into two secondary spermatids. In the second stage four spermatocytes having the haploid number of chromosomes are formed. All four spermatids undergo differentiation to form sperm.

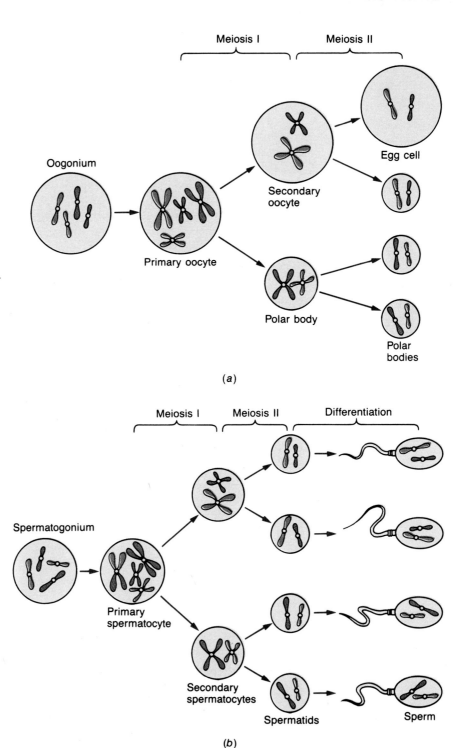

Figure 4-4
An example of hermaphroditic sexual reproduction. Each earthworm contains
male and female sex organs. The worms position themselves head to tail, thus
aligning the male organ of one of the worms with the female organ of the
other. This physical mechanism ensures that the sperm from one animal can
only enter the female organ of the other, thereby increasing genetic variance in
the species.

million years ago. In a very short time (in terms of phylogeny) all of the
major forms of life appeared in the fossil record (Gould, 1980b).

The physical events that triggered the sudden diversity of life are
not known, and they are not really of consequence to the point being
made here. The point is, without sexual reproduction, life forms have
limited variance within the species gene pool; and therefore, they are
resistant to change. Once sexually mediated reproduction evolved some-
time in the early Cambrian period, the mechanism for increasing the
variance of the species gene pool was in place. What followed is the great
diversity of life we know today.

Reproductive Strategies

The purpose of reproduction is the purpose of life—to replicate itself
and, in so doing, to insure the survival of the species. The reproductive
strategy best suited to serve this purpose is not the same in all species.
Some animals, like the fishes and amphibians, tend to produce many
young with each mating and usually provide little parental care after the
young are born. Evidently, large numbers of young are sufficient to
insure the survival of a few, even in the absence of parental protection
and nurturing. Other species, like birds and mammals, tend to produce
few young with each mating; however, they tend to provide the young
with sufficient parental care to help insure their survival.

The continuum from high production and low care to low production and high care is related to two reproductive strategies called **r-
selection** and **K-selection**. The r-selection strategy is typically associated with species having high reproductive rates, short life spans, rapid
development to sexual maturity, less organized social behaviors, and
poor survival rates. Species having a K-selection strategy typically have
opposite patterns (Pianka, 1970). In terms of reproductive effort, r-
selection places the emphasis on producing large numbers of offspring,
whereas K-selection places most reproductive energy resources on providing nurturance for a few young.

Let us compare four levels of caregiving as evidenced in representative species of fish, reptiles, birds, and mammals.

1. The female salmon lays many hundreds of eggs that are fertilized by the male *after* they are released into the water. Within days both parents die, and each egg is left protected only by a thin membrane. The developing embryo obtains oxygen directly from the water and is fed by a large **yolk sac**, a source of energy contributed by the female. (Typical of most species, the biological reproductive energy contributed by the female is greater than that of the male.)

2. The green sea turtle mates at sea, where the eggs are fertilized *within* the female. The eggs are protected by a hard outer shell. In addition to the yolk sac for nutrition, there is an **amnion** filled with fluid to protect the embryo; the **chorion**, which aides in the transfer of carbon dioxide and oxygen; and an **allantois**, which serves as a reservoir for metabolic wastes. The female comes to shore, buries the eggs in the sand, and returns to the sea. Upon hatching, the self-sufficient young scuttle to the sea, having never been in contact with either parent.

3. Nurturing patterns in birds are very diverse. The roles of males and females in nest building, incubating, and feeding vary widely. I will use a shorebird, the herring gull (*Larus argentatus*), as being somewhat representative. As is true in all birds, the eggs are fertilized inside the female, and the eggs are similar in structure to reptile eggs. Unlike the reptile, however, birds produce only a few eggs with each mating, and the eggs require incubation. In the herring gull, nest building and the incubation of the eggs are cooperative exercises. When the young hatch, they are blind, featherless, and totally dependent on *both* parents for food and protection from the weather and predators. Most birds are **monogamous** (have only one mate in a breeding season). This is probably due to the fact that, both as eggs and as chicks, the young require nurturing from both parents if they are to survive.

4. In mammals, such as humans, we see a very large shift toward the K-selection strategy. The egg is not only fertilized inside the female, but it remains inside until birth. This, of course, greatly limits the number of young that can be produced with each mating. To permit live birth, mammals have developed a *placenta* that is in contact with the wall of the uterus, and it is connected to the fetus via an umbilical cord. The placenta removes metabolic wastes and carries nutrition from the mother to the embryo. Because the embryo depends on food supplied by the mother, the yolk sac is less important and greatly reduced in size. The amniotic sac, however, retains the same function, protecting the embryo in fluid suspension. Following birth, the infant continues to be dependent on food (milk) supplied from the mother's body (see Figure 4-5).

Before we turn to a review of human sexual reproduction, one other variant of reproductive strategy deserves our attention. The amount of

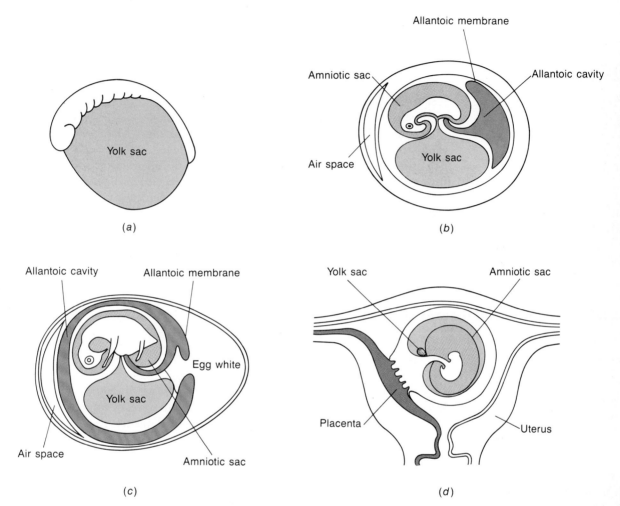

Figure 4-5
This figure shows four stages of protection in the developing embryo: *a.* The unprotected amphibious egg of a salamander lies totally unprotected in water. A yolk sac provides food for the developing embryo. *b.* The soft amniotic shell of the reptile. The amniotic sac cushions the embryo. The allantois absorbs the waste produced by the developing embryo. *c.* The eggs of birds are very similar to reptile eggs. The shell is more rigid, and the allantoic sac is supplied with blood vessels and serves as an embryonic lung. *d.* In the live-bearing embryo of the mammal the embryo is surrounded by tissue that contacts the uterine wall. The placenta removes waste and brings nutrients from the mother's body.

nurturance required by the young is not only determined by the number produced by each mating; it is also related to the level of maturation of the young at birth. The green sea turtle hatches from the egg and is completely self-sufficient, a little replica of the adult sea turtle. A robin is born blind, without feathers, and is dependent on its parents for several weeks before it can fend for itself. Now think of a human infant. What is he or she able to do after birth? How long will the infant be dependent on nurturing before he or she is capable of surviving without direct assistance from adults? Clearly, the maturation level at birth, ranging from very precocial to very altricial, determines the degree and duration of nurturing that is required by a given species. As we saw in Chapter 1, the trend in primates, hominids, and humans has been toward a K-selection strategy, with one being the modal number of infants per conception in humans. Additionally, the trend has been to produce increasingly altricial young, and thus the period of dependence on nurturing is lengthened.

Human Sexual Differentiation

To this point we have discussed the evolution of sex as a reproductive strategy. The adaptive advantage of sexual reproduction and the profound influence it has had on the proliferation of new species were reviewed. Finally, we discussed r-selection (high production/low nurturance) and K-selection (low production/high nurturance) as a continuum of reproductive strategies that have evolved to insure the survival of species. Now we turn to an examination of the human reproductive system.

Levels of Sexual Differentiation

Most people tend to think of gender in dichotomous terms. People are categorized as being either males or females. You probably remember being taught that gender is purely a genetic phenomenon. That is, if you received a Y chromosome from your father and an X chromosome from your mother, you are a male. If both the ovum and the sperm contained an X chromosome, you are a female. (Keep in mind that only the male parent has both X and Y chromosomes; therefore, he determines gender.) Actually, gender differences are much more complex than that. As we discuss in the following pages, it may be more accurate to think of gender as a continuum between maleness and femaleness than it is to dichotomize individuals by sex.

Genotypic Determination

Males and females begin life as a fertilized egg. Even with the aid of a microscope, male and female eggs appear to be identical. To differentiate the sex of a zygote, it would be necessary to examine its **karyotype**. That is, we would need to examine the chromosomes in the nucleus. More specifically, we would need to examine the two **sex chromosomes**, which are the only pair of chromosomes, among the 23 pairs that differ in males and females. (Actually, this could only be done by culturing the cell in a special medium that inhibits the separation of the double chromosomes, and then, by using a special stain that is specific for the nucleic acids in the chromosomes.) The male karyotype has the XY, and the female karyotype has the XX sex chromosome configurations.

Gonadal Determination

For the first 5 weeks human embryos are unisex in appearance. Within the developing fetus there are primitive structures, sometimes called primordial gonads, that will eventually develop into the gonads—the **testes** in males and the **ovaries** in females. These structures appear to be identical in the embryos of both sexes. They have a medullary core that has the potential to develop into a testis and an outer cortex that may develop into an ovary. The differentiation of the gonadal tissue is determined by the genotype of the embryo. If a Y chromosome is present, a specific (H-Y antigen) protein is produced that stimulates the medullary core to develop into testicular tissue while the cortex atrophies (Haseltine & Ohno, 1981; Ohno, 1979). In the absence of the protein, the gonadal core loses its capacity to become testicular tissue, and the alternative path of ovary development will take place.

Hormonal Determination

Both the testes and ovaries are capable of producing three types of sex hormones; androgens, estrogens, and progestins. The gonads differ, however, in the relative amounts of the hormones they produce. Androgens are produced in greater amounts by the testes, and the ovaries produce more estrogens. At about the eighth week of gestation the testes begin to produce large amounts of **testosterone** (an androgen), and the ovaries begin producing **estradiol** (an estrogen). Of the two hormones, the presence of testosterone appears to be more critical in the ensuing development of the fetus. Testosterone controls the masculinization process in the fetus. However, estradiol is not necessary for normal female development. Normal female development will ensue in the absence of both hormones. In fact, it is the *absence* of the male hormone that is the necessary condition for the development of female characteristics.

Internal Reproductive System Differentiation

The action of hormonal activity begins the differentiation process of the reproductive anatomy within the embryo. As can be seen in Figure 4-6, the 8-week-old embryo has both male (**Wolffian**) and female (**Müllerian**) reproductive structures. The Wolffian structure has the potential to develop into the male reproductive structures: the **epididymis**, the **vas deferens**, and the **seminal vesicles**. The **fallopian tubes**, the **uterus**, and the upper portion of the vagina develop from the Müllerian structure.

Figure 4-6
Differentiation of the internal sex organs. During fetal development the 8-week-old fetus is sexually undifferentiated. Genetic males and females possess primitive sex organs of both sexes. Under the influence of testosterone and Müllerian inhibiting substance (MIS), the female Müllerian structures degenerate, and the male Wolffian structures develop into the epididymis, vas deferens, and seminal vesicle. In the absence of testosterone the Müllerian structures develop into the fallopian tube, uterus, and upper portion of the vagina.

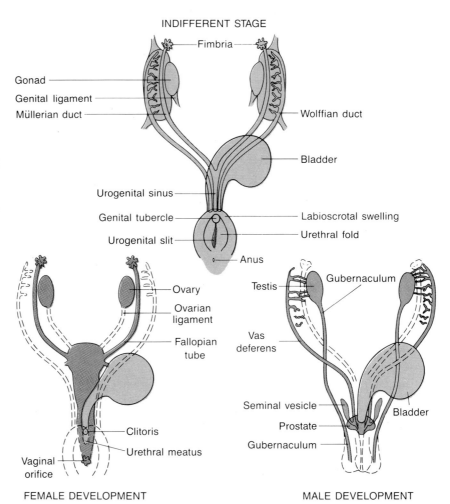

INDIFFERENT STAGE

Fimbria
Gonad
Genital ligament
Müllerian duct
Wolffian duct
Bladder
Urogenital sinus
Genital tubercle
Labioscrotal swelling
Urogenital slit
Urethral fold
Anus

Ovary
Ovarian ligament
Fallopian tube
Testis
Gubernaculum
Vas deferens
Seminal vesicle
Prostate
Bladder
Gubernaculum
Clitoris
Urethral meatus
Vaginal orifice

FEMALE DEVELOPMENT   MALE DEVELOPMENT

In order for the embryo to develop into a normal male or female, one set of primitive reproductive structures must be eliminated. This process appears to be somewhat more simple for female development than it is for males. In the absence of testosterone, the Müllerian structures begin to differentiate into female reproductive structures, and the Wolffian structures automatically degenerate. Two hormones are involved in the differentiation of male reproductive structures. Testosterone must be present to initiate growth and differentiation of the Wolffian tubes into male reproductive organs. Also, a second hormone, produced by the primitive testes, inhibits the development of the Müllerian structures. The biochemical structure of this hormone has not been identified; therefore, it has been named the **Müllerian inhibiting substance (MIS)**.

Evidence for the existence of MIS comes from individuals who develop abnormally with a full complement of both male and female internal sex organs. These individuals are genotypically male (XY), and externally they typically appear to be males. Their developing testes produce testosterone, which stimulates the production of the male reproductive structures. However, they fail to produce MIS, or their Müllerian structures are insensitive to its presence. The resulting condition, known as **persistent Müllerian duct syndrome**, could only occur if two hormones were involved, one to stimulate the differentiation of male structures and one to inhibit the growth of female structures (Sloan & Walsh, 1976).

External Genital Differentiation

Unlike the development of the internal reproductive structures, the external genitalia develop from structures that are common to both males and females. These structures—called the **genital tubercle**, **genital fold**, and **genital swelling**—develop into the penis and scrotum in males and the clitoris and labia in females (see Figure 4-7). The presence or

Figure 4-7

Differentiation of the external sex organs. Under the influence of androgens the genital tubercle, urethral folds, and labioscrotal (genital) swelling develop into the glans, penis, and scrotum in males. Alternatively, these same primitive structures develop into the clitoris and the minor and major folds of the female external genitalia.

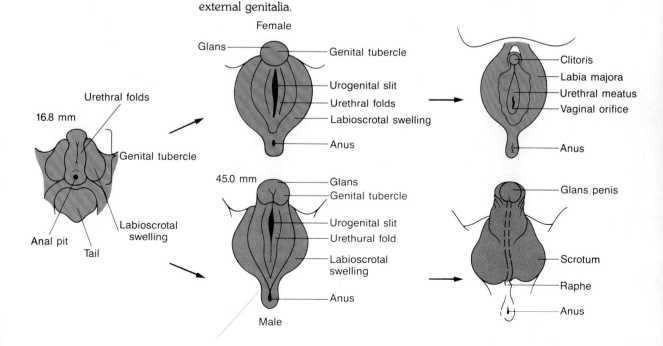

absence of androgens determines the direction of development. In the absence of androgens, female external genitalia develop. When androgens are present, development takes place in the direction of male genitalia.

As was true with the internal reproductive structures, anomalies can occur in the development of the genitals. Genotypic males may, due to a partial insensitivity to androgens, develop an undersized penis having the urinary opening at the base instead of the tip. Without karyotyping, these individuals may be mistakenly identified as females. Similarly, genotypic females may be born with complete Müllerian development but with an enlarged clitoris and fused labia, resulting in gender misidentification (Conte & Grumbach, 1978).

Gender Identification

The appearance of the external genitalia is of great importance in the development of the **psychosexual** differentiation of the individual. When an infant is born, the question uppermost in the minds of everyone concerned is, What is it? Of course, by that *what* we mean to ask, Is it a boy or a girl? Even before we do the "numbers check"—how many fingers and toes—we are likely to look between the legs to perform the "gender check." It is now possible to determine the sex of the developing fetus before birth by karyotyping cells that have been extracted from the amniotic fluid. This process, called **amniocentesis**, was originally developed to facilitate the early detection of genetic anomalies. That it is now becoming a common practice for determining fetal gender is a clear indication of the importance placed on the sex of children in our society.

The instant that the sex of the child is determined, the psychosexual development of the infant is under the influence of *both* biological and environmental determinants. Once a gender label has been assigned, the individual will be exposed, differentially, to experiences that are greatly determined by what gender he or she has been assigned. Therefore, external genitalia and gender label have a pervasive effect on gender-role identity (Money, 1987).

Secondary Sexual Determination

Sexual differentiation obviously does not stop at birth. After birth, males and females experience similar growth patterns. With the exception of the genitalia, young boys and girls remain remarkably similar until they reach puberty, when secondary sexual characteristics develop. The onset of pubescence occurs when glandlike cells in the hypothalamus secrete gonadotropin-releasing hormones (GnRH). The GnRH stimulates the production of two gonadotropic hormones, follicle-stimulating hormone (FSH) and luteinizing hormone (LH), in the anterior portion of the pituitary gland. The presence of the gonadotropic hormones in the blood induces the gonads to increase the production and secretion of sex hormones. Primarily, the testes produce testosterone, and the ovaries produce estradiol; however, small amounts of "opposite sex" hormone are produced by both glands.

During this period there are rapid body changes common to both men and women. These include skeletal growth in the legs, arms, and trunk; enlargement and further development of the genitals to make reproduction possible; changes in skin and sweat glands; and the production of pubic and axillary (underarm) hair. In women, the development of pubic and underarm hair is determined by an androgen (androstenedione) that is produced by the cortex of the adrenal gland.

During pubescence there are also gender-specific changes that produce sexually dimorphic characteristics. For females these include breast development, broadening of the hips, and an increase in subcutaneous fat. For males, the larynx enlarges, the vocal cords lengthen, shoulders broaden, and there are variations to the pattern of hair distribution that may include a receding hairline, facial hair, and increased hair on the upper torso. Additionally, males tend to develop greater muscle mass and body height (see Figure 4-8).

Figure 4-8
The development of secondary sexual characteristics in men and women.

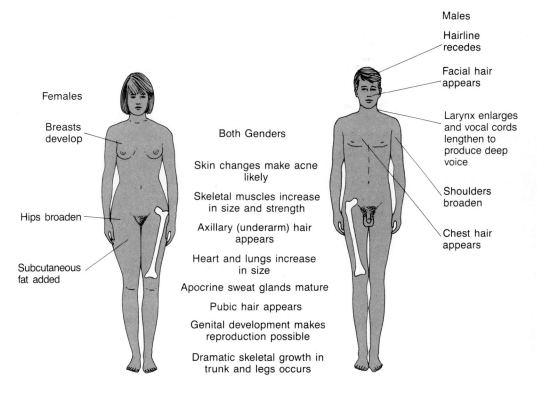

Males
Hairline recedes
Facial hair appears
Larynx enlarges and vocal cords lengthen to produce deep voice
Shoulders broaden
Chest hair appears

Females
Breasts develop
Hips broaden
Subcutaneous fat added

Both Genders
Skin changes make acne likely
Skeletal muscles increase in size and strength
Axillary (underarm) hair appears
Heart and lungs increase in size
Apocrine sweat glands mature
Pubic hair appears
Genital development makes reproduction possible
Dramatic skeletal growth in trunk and legs occurs

Table 4-1   **The Sex Hormones, Their Site of Origin in the
Body, and Their Primary Effects**

Class	Principal Hormone in Humans (Where Produced)	Examples of Effects
Androgens	Testosterone (testes)	Maturation of male genitalia: production of sperms, growth of facial, pubic, and axillary hair; muscular development; enlargement of larynx; inhibition of bone growth
	Androstenedione (adrenal glands)	In females, growth of pubic and axillary hair; less important than testosterone in males
Estrogens	Estradiol (ovaries)	Maturation of female genitalia; growth of breasts; alterations in fat deposits; growth of uterine lining; inhibition of bone growth
Gestagens	Progesterone (ovaries)	Maintenance of uterine lining

It should be noted that the bipotentiality for secondary sexual characteristics remains throughout the individual's life. If adult males are given estrogen (either therapeutically or to induce opposite-sex characteristics) breasts will develop, and facial hair will become thinner. Women who receive higher than normal levels of androgens (as will sometimes occur with a tumor on the adrenal cortex) will show increased facial hair and their voice may deepen. Table 4-1 presents the classification of sex hormones, their origin, and the effects they produce.

Sexual dimorphism in humans, though significant, is not as great as that seen in many other species, as for example, the peacock. In primates there is a great range of dimorphism. In some monkeys and apes, males and females appear to be almost identical. In others, like the gorilla and the baboon, males and females differ greatly. One need only think of the mandrill baboon. The male of this species is more than twice the size of the female, with enormous canine teeth, white markings on the upper eyelids, and colorful red and blue patches on his face. Generally, these gender differences reflect gender-role differences as well. The coloration on the face of the mandrill baboon serves as a sexual attractant for the female, and probably, along with his body size and large canines, it serves as a threat to other males who would compete for access to the females. As is true with other species of baboon, the males also play a dominant role in the defense of the troop against predators.

The lesser degree of sexual dimorphism in humans suggests that gender-role differences were likely to have been less important in our

Figure 4-9
Examples of sexual dimorphism in three primate species: the baboon, the lowland gorilla, and humans. Typically, large differences in body size and contour between males and females, as seen in the male baboon, may be linked to sexual attractiveness, competition with other males for access to the females, and gender differences in social behavior.

evolutionary history. It is likely, however, that male-pattern hair distribution and a relatively large and prominent penis may have served both as a sexual attractant and as a threat display for other males. Also, the larger body size and muscle mass probably reflect differences in social roles that placed greater importance on males as hunters and protectors of the group. The large and prominent female breasts may have evolved as a sexual attractant for males (Freedman, 1979). See Figure 4-9 for comparisons of sexual dimorphism between several representative species of great apes and humans.

Anomalies of Gender Determination

As we have seen, each developing fetus has primitive sex organs of both sexes and has the potential to develop male or female characteristics. Although the genotype of the fetus initiates the gender differentiation process, it is the level of intrafetal hormones that effects the final gender determination. Pioneering animal research on this question reported by Phoenix, Goy, Gerald, and Young (1959) and Young, Goy, and Phoenix (1965) demonstrated that the presence of inappropriate levels of sex hormones during critical periods of development can either masculinize a genotypic female or feminize a genotypic male. The researchers produced **pseudohermaphroditic** young by introducing male hormones into the mother during pregnancy. To illustrate this point, two examples of naturally occurring anomalous hermaphroditic differentiation in humans follow.

   1. **Androgen-insensitivity syndrome (AIS).** AIS is specific for genotypic males. It is a genetically transmitted, X-chromosome-linked error that causes all of the cells in the body to be insensitive to testosterone produced by the testes. Because the cells are unable to use testoster-

Figure 4-10
a. Genotypic male having androgen-insensitivity syndrome, an X-chromosome anomaly. Because the body cells are unable to use testosterone in both prenatal and postnatal life, the body fails to masculinize. *b.* Two genetic females with adrenogenital syndrome. The condition results from the overproduction of androgens by the adrenal glands that masculinizes the developing fetus. The individual on the left has had corrective surgery and hormone therapy to enhance female features. The individual on the right has had surgical repair and hormone therapy consistent with male psychosexual identity. (From Money & Ehrhardt, 1972.)

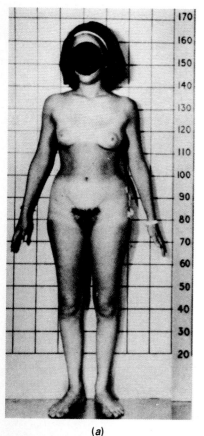

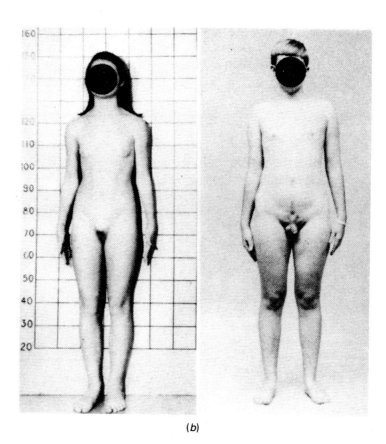

(a)   (b)

one in both prenatal and postnatal life, the body fails to masculinize. Initially, the fetus develops as a normal male. Testes form and the anti-Müllerian hormone blocks the development of the uterus and fallopian tubes. Thereafter, no further masculinization occurs, and the infant is born with female external genitalia. Later in life, female secondary sexual characteristics develop (Figure 4-10a). Typically, these individuals do not come to medical attention until pubescent age when they fail to menstruate or when their shallow vagina interferes with penile intromission (Lewis & Money, 1983). Because of the feminine appearance of their external genitalia and because they have been socialized as females, these individuals typically have a female gender identity and are sexually attracted to males.

2. **Adrenogenital syndrome.** Money (1974) reported a rather unique case of a genotypic female (XX) suffering from adrenogenital syndrome. This condition, resulting from the overproduction of androgens by the adrenal glands, causes masculinization of the fetus. The child was born with a fully formed penis; an empty scrotum; a uterus; and fully developed, but nonfunctioning, ovaries. He was originally diagnosed as a male with undescended testes, and the true problem was not determined until the child was 10 years old. By this time, having been raised as a male, he had developed a strong gender identity as a male. The child was then treated, without his knowledge or consent, with hormones to activate the ovaries and thus produce feminizing secondary sexual characteristics. This therapy was undertaken by a local physician who was operating under the erroneous assumption that the estrogens produced by the ovaries would feminize the *mind* as well as the *body*. When the boy's breasts began to develop and he started his first menstruation (through the penis), he was horrified! See Figure 4-10b for an example of androgenital syndrome.

Hormones and Sex

To this point we have reviewed the origins of sexual reproduction, various reproductive strategies, and the processes that control the sexual differentiation of internal and external sex structures. Now we examine the biological factors that determine sexual behavior. Specifically, we discuss the effects of hormones and the brain mechanisms that control sexual behavior.

Much of the data to be reviewed in this section are based on the study of animals. Perhaps a few words about the use of animals to study behavior would be appropriate here. You may wonder why we would study animals when our primary interest is human behavior.

Generally, animals are used to study behavior for two reasons. First, as we have already discussed, human behavior, like the behavior of other contemporary species, has evolved from the behaviors of common ancestors. Because of this, there is some degree of commonality between the biochemistry and brain mechanisms that control similar behaviors in rodents, monkeys, and humans. Therefore, it is possible to generalize between species. Also, some animals are considerably less complex than humans and are easier to study. The data obtained from these simple animal models provide insights on the more complex mechanisms in humans.

The second reason for using animals for research purposes concerns research ethics. Obviously, some experimental interventions could not be done on human subjects for ethical reasons. Therefore, we must turn to the use of animals as subjects to address these important questions. There are, of course, professional guidelines to ensure that research animals are protected against unnecessary discomfort.

Organizing and Activating Role of Hormones on Sexual Behavior

Sex hormones can influence sexual behavior in two ways. First, they have an *organizational* effect. As we have just seen, sex hormones influence the developmental organization of the sex organs. As we discuss in the next section, sex hormones also exert an influence on the organization of the brain. The morphology and organization of men's and women's brains are not exactly the same. These gender differences are the result of different levels of sex hormones that are present during the development of the brain. Sex hormones also produce an *activating* effect. They initiate the production of sperm in the testes and ova in the ovaries, and they make penile erection and ejaculation possible. Additionally, hormones appear to influence overt sexual behavior, particularly in nonhuman species.

Hormone Control of the Estrous and Menstrual Cycles

In most mammals the females progress through periods of time when their bodies are ready and able to become impregnated. These reproductive cycles are called estrous cycles, and we say that the female is in estrus during those periods when she is fertile and mating is likely to occur. For many mammals the estrous cycle is driven by a yearly, seasonal calendar that is timed so that the young will be born when food is abundant. The term *menstrual cycle* is reserved for those mammals, like the primates (including human beings), that have monthly reproductive cycles.

Both menstrual and estrous cycles are under the control of hormones produced in the anterior portion of the pituitary gland (the adenohypophysis) and in the ovaries. The sequence of events is begun by the pituitary, which secretes follicle-stimulating hormone to initiate the growth of **ovarian follicles**. The follicles are small globular structures comprised of epithelial cells. As the follicles grow, they begin to produce estradiol, which stimulates growth of the uterine lining. This is necessary for the uterus to implant and nurture the fertilized egg.

With continued growth of the follicles, estrogen levels also increase, triggering the release of luteinizing hormone from the adenohypophysis.

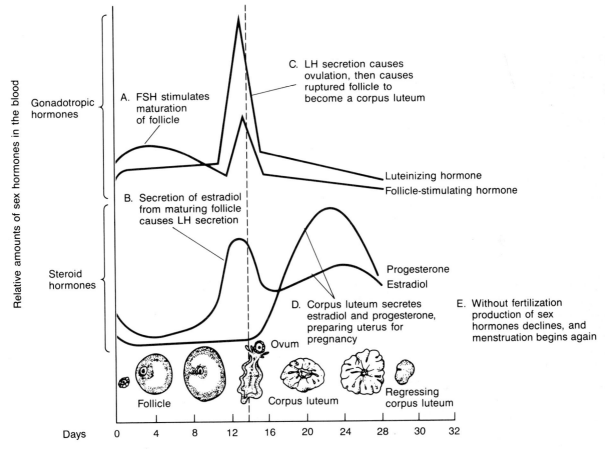

Relative amounts of sex hormones in the blood

Gonadotropic hormones

Steroid hormones

A. FSH stimulates maturation of follicle

C. LH secretion causes ovulation, then causes ruptured follicle to become a corpus luteum

B. Secretion of estradiol from maturing follicle causes LH secretion

Luteinizing hormone
Follicle-stimulating hormone

Progesterone
Estradiol

D. Corpus luteum secretes estradiol and progesterone, preparing uterus for pregnancy

E. Without fertilization production of sex hormones declines, and menstruation begins again

Ovum

Follicle

Corpus luteum

Regressing corpus luteum

Days   0   4   8   12   16   20   24   28   30   32

Figure 4-11
Blood serum levels of sex hormones and the life cycle of the ovarian follicle.

The LH induces the follicle to rupture, releasing the ovum into the peritoneal cavity. Following ovulation, and under the continued influence of LH, the follicle forms the **corpus luteum** (literally, the "yellow body"). The corpus luteum then secretes estradiol and **progesterone**, which maintains the lining of the uterus throughout the pregnancy (see Figure 4-11).

If fertilization does not occur, the corpus luteum degenerates and the cycle may begin again. In women it takes approximately 14 days for the corpus luteum to degenerate. During this process progesterone levels fall, causing the lining of the uterus to slough off, resulting in the menstrual discharge. If fertilization does occur, the corpus luteum continues to produce progesterone, which prevents further ovulation until the pregnancy is completed or terminated. Progesterone accomplishes this by blocking the effect of the GnRH that is continuously produced

Sexual Behavior in the Ring Dove

The ring dove is a small bird that is closely related to the domestic pigeon. The male and female are almost identical in appearance, and each has a distinctive black ring on the back of the neck that is the source of their name. These birds breed readily in the laboratory, and their sexual behavior has been described in great detail.

When a male and female ring dove are placed in the same cage, and appropriate nesting material is made available, the male will initiate his courtship behavior. The male's courtship consists of ritualistic bowing movements and cooing, and he pursues the female as she moves around the cage. After a period of time the male and female both emit characteristic "nest calls," which, in the natural setting, are used to indicate the selection of a suitable nesting site. For the next 7 or more days the male and female work together to build a nest. Copulation follows, and the female lays her eggs. The adults take turns incubating the eggs, which hatch in about two weeks. The young squabs are fed a special secretion called crop milk until they are able to peck grain. Between 2 and 3 weeks after the squabs hatch the adults begin to ignore them, and the cycle may begin again.

Hormone levels in the male and female ring dove vary widely during the various stages of courtship, nest building, mating, and caregiving (see Spotlight Figure 4-1a). For the male, testosterone levels increase dramatically during courtship, remain high during the nest-building stage, and drop precipitously following copulation. Estrogen levels increase in the female as she responds to the male's courtship display. As nest building begins, the estrogen decreases, and progesterone levels increase, peak during egg laying, and then drop rapidly. Prolactin levels rise in both the male and female during incubation and return to normal as the young squabs begin to feed themselves. Spotlight Figure 4-1b shows the reciprocal relationships between the birds' behavior, the environment, and hormone levels.

Spotlight Figure 4-1
a. The reproductive behavior of the ring dove: (1) Introduction of the male, (2) bowing and cooing courtship of the male, (3) male and female nest call to indicate the selection of the nest site, (4) cooperative nest building, (5) egg laying, (6) cooperative incubating, (7) eggs begin to hatch, (8) chicks fed with crop milk, (9) increasing reluctance to feed chicks, (10) adults ignore chicks and the cycle begins again. *b.* The reciprocal relationships between ring dove behavior, environmental conditions, and hormone levels. (Adapted from Lehrman, 1964.)

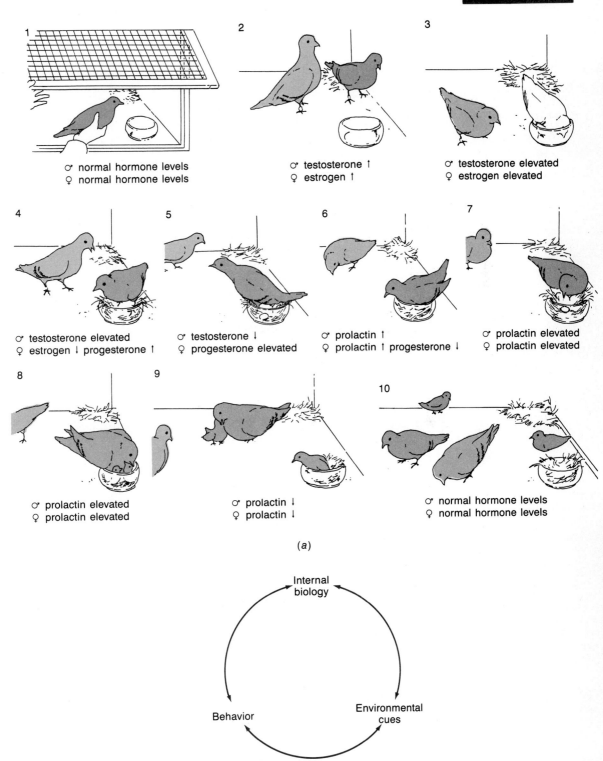

1 ♂ normal hormone levels
   ♀ normal hormone levels

2 ♂ testosterone ↑
   ♀ estrogen ↑

3 ♂ testosterone elevated
   ♀ estrogen elevated

4 ♂ testosterone elevated
   ♀ estrogen ↓ progesterone ↑

5 ♂ testosterone ↓
   ♀ progesterone elevated

6 ♂ prolactin ↑
   ♀ prolactin ↑ progesterone ↓

7 ♂ prolactin elevated
   ♀ prolactin elevated

8 ♂ prolactin elevated
   ♀ prolactin elevated

9 ♂ prolactin ↓
   ♀ prolactin ↓

10 ♂ normal hormone levels
   ♀ normal hormone levels

(a)

Internal
biology

Behavior

Environmental
cues

(b)

and released by the hypothalamus. While the GnRH is blocked, FSH will not be generated by the anterior pituitary, and new follicles will not form. Because it takes about 14 days to form a follicle and 14 days for the follicle to degenerate, the entire menstrual cycle takes about 28 days.

Hormone Influence on Sexual Behavior

Much of the data that we have concerning the control of overt sexual behavior by hormones comes from animal experiments. Before we deal with this data, a word of caution is appropriate here. Sexual behavior in nonhuman species is generally more stereotypic, less influenced by CNS inhibition, and less dependent on learning than is human sexual behavior. Although there are striking parallels between the biochemistry and brain mechanisms associated with sexual behavior of all vertebrates, it is risky, at best, to assume that the linkage between biology and behavior across species is homologous.

One example should be sufficient to make this point. As you know, humans are physically capable of having sex throughout the year, and they do not restrict their sexual activity to only those periods when the female is fertile. Animals who have annual estrous cycles become sexually active only for a short period when the females are in estrus. Additionally, females will not accept males, and the males show little or no sexual interest in females, at other times of the year. In some species, such as the elk and deer, the males' testes decrease in size, sperm production diminishes, and androgen secretion drops to levels where penile erection, intromission, and ejaculation are not possible. The point being made here is that the sex hormones, sex organs, and brain mechanisms to control sexual behavior are very similar across all mammals. Nonetheless, overt patterns of sexual behavior vary greatly across species.

If a male rat is castrated, his sexual activity will diminish and eventually cease. The same rat will become sexually active, however, if he is given testosterone replacement therapy (Bermant & Davidson, 1974). Similarly, male rats that have not reached sexual maturity will evidence adult mounting behaviors if treated with testosterone. Together these data suggest rather clearly that, at least in the rat, androgens are essential to initiate and sustain male sexual behavior.

Let us take this one step further. What do you suppose happens when an immature male rat is castrated to remove the influence of testosterone and given injections of estradiol? The overt behavior at maturity is feminized. He now shows sexual interest in other males, presents himself to be mounted (this behavior in rats is called **lordosis**), and even retrieves pups to a nest (behavior that is never seen in male rats). And what happens when testosterone is administered to an immature female? You guessed it: the testosterone masculinizes the brain. She develops sexual interest in estrous females, mounts them, evidences normal intromission movements, and even performs ritualistic cleaning of the penis (that is, licks where a penis would be if she were a male) following mounting! These data lead to two conclusions. First, the development of gender-specific behaviors is under the control of male and female sex hormones. Specifically, testosterone masculinizes the brain. In the absence of testosterone, estrogen feminizes the brain. Second, the potential for both male and female behaviors is available in the brain of each individual. The overt sexual behavior apparently is determined by the level of sex hormones during maturation.

Is it reasonable to generalize these data to human sexual behavior? The answer is a qualified no. You must keep two factors in mind. First, gender identity is greatly influenced by years of socialization to think of oneself as male or female. Second, as we discuss later in this chapter, human sexual behavior is *not* automatic and stereotypically triggered by biochemical events in the brain. Overt human sexual behavior is governed significantly by socialization and learning.

Pheromones and Sexual Behavior

We have seen how sex hormones play a central role in animal sexual behavior. This, however, is not a complete picture. For example, male rats show little or no interest in females that have had their ovaries removed. If the females are subsequently given injections of estradiol, the males show renewed sexual interest (and vice versa). The estrogen apparently modifies the female's odor and her behavior. Sexually experienced dogs that have had their olfactory areas lesioned show little or no sexual interest. In some species the females have swelling or coloration of the genital tissue when they are in estrus. This serves as an attractant for males who only show sexual interest in the estrus females. Adult male chimpanzees spend a great deal of time smelling, licking, and touching the swollen genital area of females nearing ovulation, but they ignore other females. If vaginal fluid from an estrous guinea pig is rubbed onto a nonestrous female or another male, males will attempt to mount the treated animal (and will, of course, be rebuffed, or worse). Clearly, olfactory, visual, and behavioral cues all seem to operate in arousing and directing sexual behavior.

Unlike hormones that produce their effect within the body, **pheromones** are chemicals that communicate information between organisms. We have already seen that olfaction is important to sexual behavior. Pheromones may act to influence the selection of a sexual partner, timing of the estrous cycle, regulation of pregnancy, and frequency of sexual activity. As was true with the study of hormones, much of the research on pheromones and their effect on sexual behavior has been done with animals.

1. *Pheromones and the estrous cycle.* Female mammals, when in groups, can influence each other's estrous cycle. When female mice are housed together in small groups of four or more, in the absence of males, they

tend to develop pseudopregnancies. Corpora lutea in their ovaries remain active for extended periods, thus inhibiting ovulation. This is known as the **Lee–Boot effect** after the researchers who first reported it (van der Lee & Boot, 1955). If female mice are housed in large numbers and in relatively crowded conditions, their estrous cycles lengthen and eventually stop. This effect, known as the **Whitten effect**, and the Lee–Boot effect are both produced by pheromones in the urine. Introducing the scent of urine from a normal male mouse will cause the estrous cycles to resume (Bronson & Whitten, 1968). It is interesting to note that the urine of a castrated mouse does not produce this effect.

2. *Pheromone effects on pregnancy.* If a recently impregnated mouse is placed in the same cage with a normal male other than the one that induced the pregnancy, the pregnancy is likely to be aborted. Known as the **Bruce effect**, this mechanism evidently allows the new male to eliminate the offspring of a potential competitor and subsequently impregnate the female with his own genes (Bruce, 1960). The aborted pregnancy is induced by a pheromone in the urine of the male.

3. *Pheromones as sexual attractants.* Anyone who has owned a female dog in season knows of the profound effect this condition has on male dogs in the local area. A pheromone in her vaginal discharge apparently telegraphs her fertile state and readiness to copulate. Bilateral destruction of the olfactory bulbs decreases androgen binding in the amygdala and hypothalamus of male dogs and eliminates their sexual activity (Lumia, Zebrowski, & McGinnis, 1987). Similar mechanisms are likely to be found in many mammals. A more striking example of pheromones as a sexual attractant is seen in some species of insects. The male **tussock silk moth**, for example, has enormous antennae that detect a pheromone produced by the female. The sense organ seems to be exclusively sensitive to the female attractant and allows the male to detect the presence of the female, without competition from other substances, at a range of several miles downwind. The tussock moth spends most of its life in immature larval stages and is a sexually active adult for only a few days in its life cycle. This remarkable mechanism has evolved to ensure that adult males find and mate with females so the females can lay their eggs before they die.

4. *Pheromone effects on the frequency of sexual activity.* Mammals have a refractory period between sexual encounters that is typically controlled by the male. If the same estrous female mouse is removed and reintroduced to a cage after each ejaculation by the male, the time between her reintroduction and the next intromission will increase with successive trials. If, however, a different estrous female is introduced on each trial, the male's refractory period remains relatively brief. This phenomenon, sometimes referred to as the **Coolidge effect,** is due to the unique odor of each female.

Figure 4-12
An example of the Coolidge effect. (From Beamer, Bermant, & Clegg, 1969.)

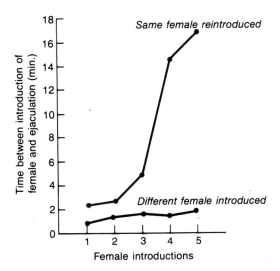

The Coolidge effect is particularly pronounced in species having harems that are controlled by the most dominant male or a few dominant males. In one study using sheep as subjects, the ram maintained a refractory period of less than 2 minutes between ejaculations when different ewes were sequentially introduced to the pen. When the same ewe was reintroduced, the refractory period lengthened to almost 18 minutes after only five trials (Beamer, Bermant, & Clegg, 1969). In part of this study the experimenters attempted to conceal the identity of a ewe by changing her physical appearance. They accomplished this by putting different coats and Halloween-like masks on her each time they reintroduced her to the pen. They thought that the ram would thus be fooled and would, consequently, have a decrease in his refractory period; he was not and did not. The masquerade did not "mask" the ewe's distinctive odor, which was the salient cue to her identity (see Figure 4-12). If, by the way, you conjure up mental images of sheep wearing coats and masks and think that they must have appeared rather humorous, they did

Another example of olfactory pheromones affecting copulatory frequency is seen in baboons. A male baboon is far more likely to mate with a female that has just mated with another male than he is to mate with a female that he has mated with last. This behavior evidently increases his chances of impregnating more females and in so doing increasing the survival of his gene pool. This behavior is likely controlled by the distinctive odor of each male's semen.

Neural Control of Sexual Behavior

We have seen that hormones influence sexual behavior in several important ways. Within the individual, male and female hormones control or
initiate gender-specific behaviors. As pheromones, they produce their
effect between individuals and operate to influence the choice of mate
and intromission frequency, and they can affect estrous cycle timing and
the success of a pregnancy. From Chapter 3 we know that behavior is
controlled both hormonally and neuronally, with the two systems working in concert. We now turn to neuronal mechanisms that control sexual
behavior.

Spinal Cord   Penile erection and ejaculation are controlled at the spinal level. It has
Mechanisms   been shown in several species of mammals that lesions to the spine at the
cervical level (where the spinal cord meets the hindbrain) do not prevent
penile erection or ejaculation. Because this surgical lesion isolates the
spinal cord from the brain, it is clear that these sexual behaviors are
mediated at the level of the spine.

If mechanical stimulation is applied to a dog's penis after the spine
has been transected, the dog will have a normal erection followed by
ejaculation. Also, the animal will be able to achieve subsequent erections
and ejaculations much more rapidly than an intact animal. This may be
attributed to the loss of inhibitory signals from the brain (Hart, 1967).
The fact that in normal dogs mechanical stimulation will only induce an
erection when an estrous female is present lends support to this notion.

Humans who have had an accidental transection of the spine are
also able to achieve erection and ejaculation with mechanical stimulation. Because all ascending pathways are severed, they have no conscious
awareness of the sexual arousal, unless they observe it visually.

Hypothalamic   The hypothalamus is actually a complex group of diencephalic nuclei.
Mechanisms   Each identifiable nucleus of cell bodies can be differentiated morphologi-
cally and by function. The important function that specific hypothalamic
nuclei have for the control of sexual behavior has been known for some
time. Most of this data has come from studies of animals, specifically,
studies of animals that have had very small electrodes placed precisely
into known locations in the brain. The stereotaxic surgical techniques
and the brain atlases necessary to place electrodes precisely in deep brain
structures were refined in the 1940s and 1950s (see Spotlight 4-2).

Much of the data to be reviewed in the next section is based on the
behavioral effects resulting from precise lesions made to small structures
in the brain. A word of caution is appropriate before we proceed. It is
often difficult to interpret the behavioral outcomes of lesions to the brain.
This research paradigm attempts to relate specific deficits or changes in
behavior to small lesions of specific brain structures. There is an inherent

problem in the interpretation of data using this research technique. The normal functioning of various brain loci is, to some degree, dependent on the normal functioning of other structures in the brain that either send information to them or receive information from them. Therefore, when one part of the brain is physically lesioned, it is difficult to know what other parts of the brain have been *functionally* lesioned because of their dependency on the lesioned structure. The point here is that the behavior deficit or change resulting from a precise lesion in a known location may be attributable, in part, to other brain structures that were in intimate communication with the lesioned structure and therefore dependent upon that structure for normal functioning. The loss of functional continuity between brain structures is known as **diaschisis**. Now let us examine the various brain structures known to control sexual behavior.

There are considerable data showing that the anterior area of the hypothalamus is functional in sexual behavior. Some of the earliest studies done on female guinea pigs showed that small lesions made in the most anterior nucleus of the hypothalamus will eliminate all sexual behavior. Additionally, it was shown that injections of estrogens following lesions of the anterior nucleus failed to initiate sexual behavior. Together, these data strongly suggest that an intact anterior hypothalamus is necessary for sexual arousal and normal behavior (Brookhart, Dey, & Ranson, 1940). See Figure 4-13 for a schematic diagram of the hypothalamus.

More recent studies have shown that the anterior hypothalamus — more specifically, the **medial preoptic area** (**MPOA**) — influences sexual behavior in males differently than in females. Lesions to the preoptic area eliminate all sexual behavior in male rats, and subsequent treatment with androgens fails to reestablish the sexual behavior. Conversely, electrical stimulation of the preoptic nucleus in male rats increases all aspects of sexual behavior (Malsbury, 1971). The direct application of testosterone to the preoptic nucleus greatly increases sexual behavior and will produce indiscriminate mounting behaviors. Males so treated will attempt to mount nonestrous females, other males, and inanimate objects. Injections of testosterone into the anterior hypothalamic area will also reinitiate sexual behavior in castrated rats.

Lesions to the preoptic area in female rats produce a very different effect, actually increasing the frequency of lordosis responses. Recent data (Numan, 1988) have shown that the MPOA plays a very central role in the maternal behavior of rats. Bilateral lesions made just posterior to the preoptic nucleus in the **ventromedial nucleus** completely eliminate sexual behavior in female rats. This effect is not reversed by treatment with estradiol and progesterone. As you might predict, electrical stimulation of the ventromedial nucleus increases female sexual behavior (Pfaff & Sakuma, 1979). Pleim and Barfield (1988) examined how the direct injection of various hormones into the brain affects the sexual

Stereotaxic Techniques

Stereotaxic surgery was developed as a research tool to provide access to brain structures deep within the brain while leaving surrounding structures relatively intact. Using two reference points, such as the ear canals and the chin, the stereo-taxic instrument is used to place the head (and the brain within it) in a known position. Knowing the position of the brain within the skull, it is possible to locate with some precision subcortical structures by solving a simple triangulation problem.

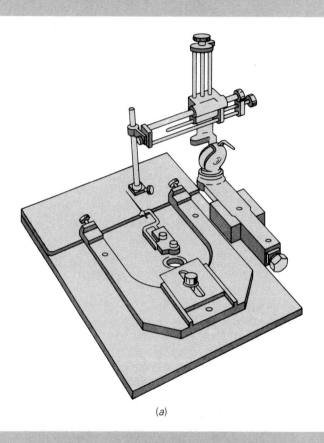

(a)

Spotlight Figure 4-2

a. A stereotaxic instrument for brain surgery in the rat. After being anesthe-tized, the rat's head is placed in a fixed position. The electrode carrier may be adjusted in three planes: anterior–posterior, dosal–ventral, and medial-lateral. In this manner a stimulating or lesioning electrode may be positioned in a desired location with great precision. b. A page from a stereotaxic atlas of the rat brain. The atlas provides the coordinates for various brain structures rela-tive to reference points on the skull. This specific coronal section is 0.6 mm anterior to the bregma landmark on the dorsal surface of the skull. The arrows designate the fornix (F), which is 7 mm below bregma and 1 mm lateral of the midline of the skull.

Atlases that relate the position of various brain structures to reference coordinates have been developed for many laboratory animals including pigeons, rats, cats, dogs, and monkeys. Stereotaxic surgical instruments and brain atlases have also been developed for humans. These instruments, of course, are not used for research purposes. They give neurosurgeons a valuable tool for gaining access to structures deep within the brain without causing excessive damage to surrounding structures (see Spotlight Figure 4-2).

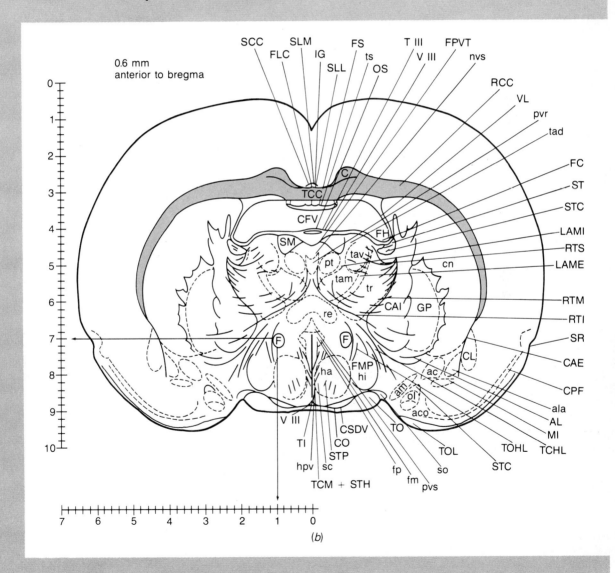

(b)

Figure 4-13
Schematic depicting the
hypothalamic nuclei.
Several of the
hypothalamic nuclei,
including the preoptic
nucleus, paraventricular
nucleus, ventromedial
nucleus, and lateral
hypothalamic area, have
been shown to influence
sexual behavior.

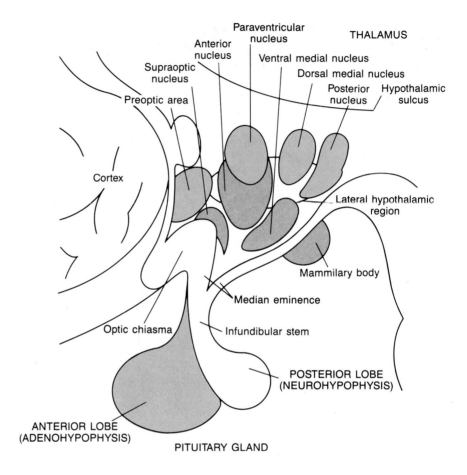

behavior of female rats. They showed that progesterone and estradiol
facilitate sexual receptivity when the hormones were injected into the
ventromedial nucleus of the hypothalamus. Progesterone appears to be
the more effective facilitator.

Gorski, Gordon, Shryne, and Southam (1978) identified a nucleus
within the preoptic area that is three to seven times larger in males than
in females. It is interesting to note that in castrated males this nucleus
developed to only half the size of that observed in normal males. Treating
the castrated males with testosterone reversed this effect. These data
support the notion that the preoptic area is functional in sexual behavior
(perhaps more so in males than in females). These data are also instructive in that they provide insight regarding the organizational effects that
hormones such as testosterone have on the brain (Arendash & Gorski,
1983).

The posterior portion of the hypothalamus is also involved in the
control of sexual behavior. Electrical stimulation of the posterior nucleus

will induce sexual behaviors in male rats. Unlike the indiscriminate sexual behavior induced by stimulation to the anterior hypothalamus, stimulation of the posterior nucleus is *stimulus specific* in that the sexual behavior is only observed when a receptive female is present. Lesions to the posterior nucleus of the hypothalamus affect sexual behavior in two ways. The posterior portion of the pituitary gland is dependent on posterior hypothalamic input for the production of gonadotropins. Therefore, posterior hypothalamic lesions eliminate gonadotropin production and cause gonadal atrophy. Additionally, the loss of neuronal output from the posterior hypothalamus reduces the level of sexual activity.

In females, lesions to the ventromedial nucleus terminate all signs of sexual receptivity. This effect cannot be reversed by the introduction of exogenous estrogens. Electrical stimulation in the same area facilitates female sexual behavior. Autoradiographic studies have shown that both males and females have estrogen and progesterone receptors in the ventromedial nucleus and the medial portion of the preoptic area (estradiol and progesterone influence female sexual behaviors). Males, however, have fewer than half of the receptors found in females (Rainbow, Parsons, & McEwen, 1982). This may be attributed, in part, to the defeminizing effects of androgens on the developing brain.

Amygdala and Limbic Structures

The amygdala is a large nucleus found in the temporal lobe. You may remember from the discussion of this structure in Chapter 3 that the amygdala is part of the limbic system, and as such, it influences emotional behaviors. In a seminal study done in 1937, Klüver and Bucy found that bilateral lesions to the anterior pole of the temporal lobe (including the amygdala) produced a complex pattern of behavioral changes. Specifically, these animals lost outward signs of fear, became docile, ate indiscriminately, failed to recognize familiar objects, and evidenced hypersexuality. Not only did the frequency of sexual behavior increase, but the animals also attempted to mate with sexually inappropriate objects.

Schreiner and Kling (1953) demonstrated that cats with lesions of the amygdala and a portion of the limbic cortex (the piriform cortex) were remarkably hypersexual. Male cats attempted to mate with other males as well as animals of different species. The hypersexual behavior was reduced by castration and could be reinstated with injections of testosterone, indicating that the presence of male sex hormones was a factor contributing to the hypersexual behavior. (See Figure 4-14). Subsequently, it has been shown that the hypersexual behavior is due largely to lesions of the limbic cortex (Green, Clement, & deGroot, 1957). The amygdala and limbic cortex, therefore, appear to have an inhibitory role in sexual behavior, and their mechanisms of action are less straightforward and less well understood than those observed in the hypothalamic nuclei.

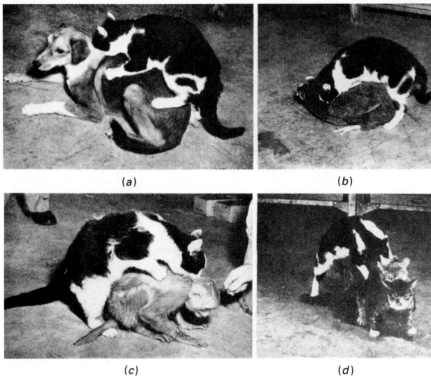

(a)   (b)

(c)   (d)

Figure 4-14
Hypersexuality of male cats with lesions of the amygdala and the surrounding
region of the temporal lobe. Respectively, *a*, *b*, and *c* show a cat attempting to
mount a dog, a chicken, and a monkey; *d* shows several treated cats attempting to mount in tandem. (From Schreiner & Kling, 1963.)

Patterns of Human Sexual Behavior

The sexual behavior of humans is influenced by the same hormonal and
neuronal mechanisms found in other mammals. Women who live in close
proximity, as in all-female dormitories, or in women's prisons, and who
also have very limited contact with men, tend to develop synchronized
menstrual cycles (McClintock, 1971). Recent studies (Preti, Cutler, Garcia, & Huggins, 1986; Russel, Switz, & Thompson, 1977) suggest that
the menstrual synchrony may be due to olfactory cues that are related to
the menstrual cycle. Women are more likely to engage in masturbation
or to initiate sexual activity with their partners actively at the time of
ovulation, the time when fertilization is most likely. However, women
who are taking birth control pills that block ovulation do not experience
similar peaks of sexual activity. These data suggest that the increased
sexual behavior noted during ovulation is attributable to hormone levels
in blood serum (Adams, Gold & Burt, 1978).

Sexual activity and blood serum levels of testosterone appear to be correlated in men. Men who have been castrated report continuing to have "sexual interest," but they lose their ability to attain an erection without therapeutic treatment with testosterone. Davidson, Camargo, and Smith (1979), working with men whose testes produced inadequate levels of testosterone, showed rather conclusively that the sexual behavior of their subjects was directly correlated with treatment levels of testosterone. In their study, the frequency of occurrence of penile erections, attempts at intercourse, masturbation, and orgasm increased as levels of testosterone increased in the blood serum. Hypersexuality similar to that reported in animals having Klüver–Bucy syndrome has been observed in men who have had an injury to the temporal lobe, thus implicating the temporal lobe and the amygdala in human sexual behavior (Terzian & Dalle Ore, 1955).

Irrespective of the data just described, overt sexual behavior in humans is clearly less mechanical and automatic, and it is influenced more by inhibitory brain centers and learned patterns of behavior than it is in other species. The fact that men and women may choose to remain celibate for religious or other reasons tells us a great deal about cultural influences on sexual behavior. We need only make a few other observations to make this point clear.

No other species, not even our closest primate relatives, practice the diversity of sexual stimulation methods known in humans. Manual and oral stimulation and the wide variety of coital postures practiced by humans are rarely observed in other species. I am reminded here of the story of a Frenchman who was boasting to his companion about knowing and having practiced 100 different coital positions. His companion (presumably not French) meekly admitted that he only knew of one, the position having the male and female facing each other, head to head, with the male above the female. At this the Frenchman bolted from his chair in apparent astonishment and responded, "Mon Dieu, 101!"

An Observation:

A Virus Gives Clues to Early Sexual Behavior?

New information about the earliest forms of human sexual behavior is being obtained from viruses that cause cold sores and venereal disease. By studying the amino acid composition of the herpes viruses, researchers have estimated that distinctly humanlike sexual behavior, including kissing and face-to-face mating, began approximately 8 million years ago.

Their conclusions are based on the fact that one of the two most common herpes viruses is specific for the mouth, and the other primarily infects the genitals. Both forms of the virus evolved from a single virus that infected both areas. That precursor virus was similar to the simian virus found in nonhuman primates today.

Contemporary primates have a great deal of oral–genital contact in their sexual exploration, grooming, and courting behaviors. These behaviors presumedly allow the same virus to populate both the oral and genital regions. For the two contemporary human strains to develop, the amount of oral–genital contact would have to be drastically reduced and the amount of oral–oral contact increased. These conditions would be more likely to occur with face-to-face copulatory postures. Researchers estimate that the divergence of the two viral forms occurred about 8 miilion years ago—about the same time that hominids diverged from the great apes.

Homosexual and bisexual behaviors also appear to be more commonly observed in humans than other species. The males in many primate species exhibit ritualistic mounting of other males as a sign of social dominance; and males and females of some mammal species frequently examine, smell, and lick the genital region of same-sex individuals. However, homosexual contact leading to orgasm is rarely seen in species other than humans, and exclusive homosexuality appears to be unique with humans (Ehrhardt & Meyer-Bahlburg, 1981). Homosexual behaviors (mounting in females and lordosis in males) may be produced under laboratory conditions where animals are neutered and given large doses of opposite-sex hormones. This, however, is not the same as homosexual or bisexual orientation in humans. There are some data to suggest that there may be biological factors underlying male homosexual behavior (e.g., Gladue, Green, & Hellman, 1984; Zuger, 1976), but the evidence to date is far too limited to be conclusive.

Finally, in the vast majority of species, sexual physiology and behavior have evolved to insure that mating only occurs when the female is in peak reproductive condition. Human sexual behavior is unique inasmuch as we mate at all times, irrespective of whether the female is able or likely to conceive. This is particularly difficult to understand from a purely biological perspective. By definition, the biological purpose of sexual behavior is to reproduce. Obviously, sexual behavior in humans serves a wider function.

It has been proposed that in humans sex has evolved a secondary function, that of strengthening the pair-bond over the long period of human infant dependency. Copulatory behavior has hedonistic (pleasurable) qualities for both men and women. Women may be the only females among the mammals to experience sexual orgasm as we know it. This may function to heighten their sexual interest and to increase their readiness for sexual activity, even during periods when they are not likely to reproduce young. Also, women do not have obvious physical changes to their sex tissues, nor do they produce readily detectable olfactory cues to signal periods of receptivity, as do many other species. Therefore, it has been suggested by some that frequent sexual activity, distributed across the menstrual cycle, evolved as a mechanism to enhance reproduction (Halliday, 1982).

CHAPTER SUMMARY

1. An essential characteristic of all living things is their ability to reproduce. The most basic, yet essential, form of reproduction is the duplication of organic molecules. Every cell in the body contains the biochemical information needed to form a new organism. This information is encoded in *deoxyribonucleic acid* (*DNA*). The unique architecture of the DNA molecule is what determines its unique ability to replicate itself.

2. Primitive, single-celled forms of plants and animals multiply through *asexual reproduction*. Sexual reproduction is made possible through the process of *meiotic*, or *reduction, division*. This process produces *gametes*, which have one half of the full complement of *chromosomes*. In this way two gametes (sex cells) join to produce a fertilized egg (*zygote*) that has the full number of chromosomes.

3. Sexual reproduction greatly increases the diversity of the genetic pool of the species. This in turn stimulates the evolution of new species. The explosion of new species that occurred in the *Cambrian* period is attributed to the evolution of sexual reproduction.

4. The number of offspring and the amount of caregiving provided to the young are major factors in the reproductive strategies of different species. Some species, like some species of fishes, produce many offspring but provide little or no maternal care. Other species, like humans, have few offspring with each mating but provide prolonged nurturance to assure survival.

5. Sexual differentiation takes place on several levels. The *genotype* of the fertilized egg is the most basic level of sexual differentiation. The genotype of the developing fetus determines the presence of specific proteins that in turn control the development of male or female *gonads*. The gonads determine the levels of three types of sex hormones: *androgens*, *estrogens*, and *progestins*, which influence the development of the internal reproductive organs and the external genitalia.

6. Secondary sexual characteristics are determined at puberty. The onset of puberty occurs when *gonadotropin releasing hormone* (*GnRH*) produced in the *hypothalamus* induces the secretion of *follicle-stimulating hormone* (*FSH*) and *luteinizing hormone* (*LH*) from the anterior pituitary. These gonadotropic hormones induce the gonads to increase the production of gender-specific sex hormones.

7. *Androgen-insensitivity syndrome* (*AIS*) and *andrenogenital syndrome* are examples of gender differentiation anomalies. AIS results in feminized males whose body cells do not respond to the male sex hormones.

Adrenogenital syndrome causes the masculinization of the female due to the overproduction of androgens by the adrenal glands.

8. Hormones have *organizing* and *activating* effects on sexual behavior. Sex hormones literally exert influence on the morphology and organization of the developing brain. Hormones also activate sexual arousal, initiate sperm and egg production, and make penile erection and ejaculation possible. Estrous and menstrual cycles are under the control of hormones that are produced in the anterior portion of the pituitary gland and in the ovaries.

9. Unlike hormones that produce their effect within the body, *pheromones* are chemicals that communicate information between organisms. Pheromones may influence the selection of a sexual partner, timing of the estrous cycle, regulation of pregnancy, and frequency of sexual activity.

10. The anterior area of the hypothalamus is functional in sexual behavior. The *medial preoptic area* and the *ventromedial nucleus* of the hypothalamus appear to be particularly important in the control of sexual behavior. The amygdala and various structures of the limbic system are known to influence sexual behavior.

11. Human sexual behavior is influenced by hormonal and neuronal factors similar to those observed in laboratory animals. However, human sexual behavior is clearly less mechanical and automatic than the sexual behavior of other species. Learning and social factors have a very important role in the overt sexual behaviors of men and women.

SUGGESTED READINGS

Feder, H. H. (1984). Hormones and sexual behavior. *Annual Review of Psychology, 35,* 165–200.

Greer, J. H., O'Donohue, W. T., & Shorman, R. H. (1986) Sexuality. In Coles, M. G. H., Donchin, E., & Porges, S. W. (Eds.) Psychophysiology: Systems, processes, and applications. New York: Guilford.

Halliday, T. (1980). *Survival in the wild: Sexual strategy.* Chicago: University of Chicago Press.

Keller, D. K. (1972). *Sex and single cell.* New York: Pegasus.

Money, J. (1987). Sin, sickness, or status? Homosexual gender identity and psychoneuroendocrinology. *American Psychologist, 42,* 384–399.

KEY TERMS

Adenine One of four small bases that form the central structure of the DNA helix; *see* Guanine, Cytosine, and Thymine.

Adrenogenital syndrome Masculinization of the genetically female fetus due to overproduction of androgens by the adrenal gland.

Androgen-insensitivity syndrome (AIS) A genetically transmitted, X-chromosome-linked error that causes all of the cells in the body to be insensitive to testosterone produced in the testes.

Allantois Structure in the egg that serves as a reservoir for metabolic wastes.

Amniocentesis Puncture of the amniotic sac to extract amniotic fluid, typically done to extract cells from the amniotic sac for karyotyping.

Amnion Fluid-filled structure in the egg that protects the developing embryo.

Asexual reproduction Form of reproduction common in many simple animals and plants; produces genetically identical offspring.

Bruce effect Aborted pregnancy resulting from the introduction of a new male animal. The effect is due to a pheromone in the urine of the newly introduced male.

Chorion Structure in the egg that aids the transfer of oxygen and carbon dioxide.

Chromosomes Strand of DNA material found in the nucleus; carries genetic information.

Conjugation Reproductive process in which chromosomes are passed between individuals before cell division takes place.

Coolidge effect Increased male sexual activity resulting from the introduction of new females.

Corpus luteum A yellowish structure that produces estradiol and progesterone; formed from the developing ovarian follicle following ovulation.

Cytosine One of four small bases that form the central structure between the DNA helix; *see* Guanine, Adenine, and Thymine.

Diaschisis The functional continuity between centers of the brain. When one structure of the brain is lesioned, others become functionally lesioned as well.

Diploid The complete complement of chromosomes.

Egg *See* Ovum.

Epididymis The elongated tube attached to the testes where sperm is stored.

Estradiol Female hormone produced in most mammals, including humans.

Fallopian tubes Females structure emanating from the uterus; channel for the passage of the ovum from the ovary to the uterus.

Gametes A mature haploid reproductive cell; the sperm or the ovum.

Genital fold Primitive tissue that differentiates into the labia minora in females and the base of the penis in males.

Genital swelling Primitive tissue that differentiates into the labia majora in females and the scrotum in males.

Genital tubercle Primitive tissue that differentiates into the clitoris in females and the glans in males.

Germ cells Cells produced in the ovaries and testes that mature into ova and sperm.

Gonadotropic hormones Hormones produced in the anterior portion of the pituitary that have a stimulating effect on the gonads. Follicle-stimulating hormone and luteinizing hormone are gonadotropic hormones.

Guanine One of four small bases that form the central structure of the DNA helix; *see* Cytosine, Thymine, and Adenine.

Haploid Genetic state having half of the full complement of chromosomes. The sex cells (sperm and ova) are haploid.

Hermaphroditic The state of having both male and female sex organs in the same individual. Planaria are hermaphroditic.

Homologous Corresponding in structure, as in chromosomes from the same pair, or homologous chromosomes.

H-Y antigen Protein that determines the differentiation of the primordial gonads.

K-selection Reproductive strategy having few offspring produced from each mating and placing emphasis on the nurturance of the young.

Karyotype The chromosomal configuration of the nucleus of the cell; the photomicrograph of the chromosomes.

Lee–Boot effect False pregnancies induced by the presence of a pheromone in the urine of females.

Lordosis The characteristic arching of the back and deflection of the tail by sexually receptive female rodents.

Medial preoptic area (MPOA) Cluster of cell bodies in the hypothalamus; influences sexual behavior.

Meiotic division Reduction division in the formation of sex cells that results in the haploid number of chromosomes.

Mitotic division Replication of a somatic cell into two daughter cells, each having the diploid number of chromosomes.

Monogamous Sexual pattern where males and females maintain only one sex partner.

Müllerian inhibiting substance A peptide, as yet unidentified, that inhibits the development of the Müllerian structures in the fetus.

Müllerian structures The embryonic primitive tissues of the female internal sex organs.

Nucleotides One of several complex compounds that form the building blocks of ribonucleic acid and deoxyribonucleic acid.

Ovarian follicles A small cavity of epithelial cells surrounding the ovum.

Ovary Female sex organ; site for the production of ova.

Ovum (Ova) The female sex cell, the egg.

Persistent Müllerian duct syndrome Sexual differentiation anomaly where the internal female sex organs develop in a genetic male.

Pheromone A chemical produced by an animal that affects the behavior or physiology of another animal. Pheromones usually produce their effect through olfaction or gustation.

Polar body Small, nonfunctioning cell produced during the development of the ovum.

Progesterone Hormone produced by the ovary; maintains the lining of the uterus during pregnancy

Pseudohermaphrodite Hermaphroditic individual produced by the introduction of opposite-sex hormones into the developing fetus.

Psychosexual Term used to refer to the gender identification of the individual.

r-selection Reproductive strategy having many young produced with each mating and requiring little parental nurturing.

Reduction division *See* Meiotic division.

Ribonucleic acid (RNA) A complex macromolecule composed of sugars and phosphates connected by nucleotide bases. RNA serves as a template for the production of specific amino acids and peptides in the cell.

Semenal vesicle Bulbous structure located near the prostate and bladder; stores spermatic fluid and releases sperm into the urethra during ejaculation.

Sex chromosome One of two chromosomes involved in sex determination; represented by the letters X and Y. The XX configuration determines females, and the XY configuration determines males.

Testes The male internal sex organs.

Testosterone Androgen hormone produced in the testes.

Thymine One of four small bases that form the central structure of the DNA helix; *see* Adenine, Guanine, and Cytosine.

Uterus Internal female sex organ; develops from Müllerian structures.

Vas deferens Tube connecting the epididymis and the seminal vesicle.

Whitten effect Synchronization of the menstrual or estrous cycle in groups of females.

Wolffian structures Primitive embryonic tissues of the internal male sex organs.

Yolk sac Structure in the egg that provides nutrients to the developing embryo.

Zygote The fertilized egg; has the diploid chromosome configuration.

Chapter 5

Simulating the Real World

The Origin of Sensory Cells
Sensitivity in Single-Celled Organisms
Specialized Receptor Cells

Sensory Processing
Accessory Structures
Transduction
Adaptation

Sensory Coding
The Doctrine of Specific Nerve Energies
Pattern Theory
A Combined View

The Simulation Hypothesis
Species-Specific Sensory Systems
Simulating the Real World

Central Regulation of Sensory Processes
Centrifugal Processes
Sensation versus Perception
Looking Ahead

Chapter Learning Objectives

After reading this chapter, you should

1. Be able to discuss the evolution of specialized sensory cells, beginning with sensitivity in single-celled organisms.

2. Be able to define and give examples of several accessory structures and understand how these structures function to alter energy in the environment.

3. Understand how environmental energy is transformed into neuronal events through the process of transduction.

4. Be able to give examples of adaptation in several sense modalities.

5. Be familiar with various ways that sensory information could be coded by the nervous system.

6. Be able to compare and contrast labelled line and pattern theories of sensory coding.

7. Understand the major points of the law of specific nerve energies and be able to relate the law to species-specific sensory capabilities.

The Origin of Sensory Cells

All animals are able to detect and react to physical events in their environment. In this chapter and the following chapters, which are concerned with the way that we and other animals sense the world around us, we examine how animals are able to transform physical events that occur in the environment into usable biological information. We trace the origin and evolution of specialized sensory cells that have been modified to detect changes in one type of physical energy, but not others. Finally, we look at how these sensory cells have become integrated over time with other cells in the CNS.

In addition to discussing the evolution of sensory cells and sensory systems in complex organisms, we also examine how humans and other animals process and act on sensory information. First, we examine the origin of sensory cells.

Sensitivity in Single-Celled Organisms

The origin of the various senses is closely associated with the evolution of movement. Clearly, there is little reason for organisms to be sensitive to the physical changes around them if they are not able to act on that information. We know from the discussion of the single-celled organism *Stylonichia* in Chapter 2 that protozoans are capable of some rather complex behaviors. It was obvious from the description of these simple organisms that they are quite capable of detecting changes in the environment and reacting to them.

The physical mechanisms by which single-celled organisms are able to detect environmental events and respond to them are becoming known to us. The physical events that control the reaction of ciliates to mechanical stimulation are particularly well known and serve nicely as an introduction to the evolution of sensory cells in complex organisms.

The paramecia, like the *Stylonichia mytilis* mentioned earlier, have an identifiable head end with an oral groove for ingesting particles of food, and they tend to move forward and backward in a line that is parallel with the length of the cell. You may recall that the *Stylonichia* moves along the bottom of its aquatic environment using cirri that line the ventral surface of the cell. Unlike *Stylonichia*, the paramecia swim through the water using a rhythmic beating of the cilia that cover the outside of the cell.

Now let us examine the physical events that cause paramecia to move in a given direction. When the back end of the cell membrane is deformed by mechanical means, the permeability of the membrane to potassium ions (K^+) changes. Specifically, the membrane becomes more permeable to K^+ ions. Because the concentration of K^+ is greater inside the cell, the K^+ ions move down the electrochemical gradient and pass out of the cell to the surrounding fluid. As the cell becomes hyperpolarized (more negative compared to the fluid outside the cell), the cilia beat to produce forward locomotion. Increasing the negative polarity increases the frequency at which the cilia beat, resulting in faster movement. Deforming the head end of the cell causes the cell to be more permeable to calcium ions (Ca^{2+}). Because the concentration of calcium ions is greater outside the cell, they move down the electrochemical gradient by entering into the cell. Increasing the concentration of Ca^{2+} causes the cell to depolarize (become more positive), and as you may have guessed by now, this causes the cilia to reverse the direction of their beating action, moving the cell backwards (Naitoh & Eckert, 1969).

As you can see from this example of protozoan behavior, the electrical properties of the cell membrane in single-celled organisms show remarkable similarities to the electrical properties of the neuron membrane. The flow of ions across the membrane in paramecia is regulated by ion channels that are specific for a given species of ion, just as it is in the neuron membrane. By regulating the flow of ions and consequently regulating the polarity of the intracellular fluid, the paramecium can effect an avoidance reaction or control the speed of forward motion. Lacking a nervous system, the paramecium provides impressive testimony to the capacity of intracellular specialization to achieve rapid, coordinated, locomotor responses to external stimulation.

The mechanism controlling motor behavior in paramecia is only one example of many that illustrates the interaction of protozoans with the environment. Single-celled organisms have the ability to detect and react to a wide variety of external stimuli including a number of chemicals in solution, the presence or absence of light, changes in temperature, and mechanical stimulation (Figure 5-1). It is likely that all of these stimuli produce their effect by inducing changes in the permeability of the cell membrane to specific ions (Bullock, Orkand, & Grinnell, 1977).

The electrochemical mechanisms that produce movement and other responses in single-celled organisms serve as the model for the evolution of more sophisticated sensory cells of the metazoans, cells that have developed to detect specific classes of physical stimuli. As noted in the remainder of this chapter and the subsequent chapters on sensory systems, all sensory cells function in essentially the same way. They react to physical stimuli by changing the permeability of their membrane and in so doing changing the polarity of cell relative to the extracellular fluid. This is typical of how the evolution process works by simply building onto and improving existing mechanisms.

The fossil record, unfortunately, can tell us very little about the origin of sensory neurons. Typically, only hard tissues, such as bones in the vertebrates, exoskeletons in the arthropods, and shells in the mollusks, fossilize well. Soft tissues like muscles, internal organs, and surface

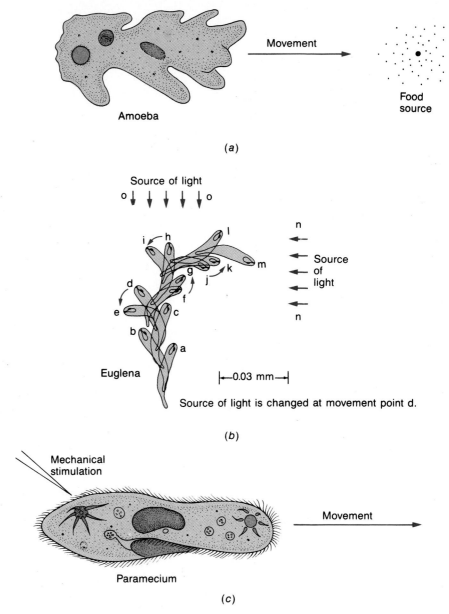

Figure 5-1
Various species of protozoans evidence sensitivity to a variety of physical stimuli. *a.* The amoeba goes toward a food source by moving its psuedopod. *b.* The euglena, which is attracted to light, changes direction of movement in response to the source of light. *c.* The paramecium changes direction of movement in response to mechanical stimulation.

tissues leave little or no fossil record. Therefore, our best guesses concerning the evolution of sensory neurons come from comparisons made between animals of various contemporary phyla and by observations of the ontogeny of cells in the developing organism. It is generally believed that the first sensory neurons developed from intracellular effector organelles such as cilia and flagella, which evolved into **independent effector cells** found in some forms of multicellular animals. The nematocysts that protect the hydra are an example of independent effector cells (see Figure 5-2). Because all neurons develop from the epithelial (outer) layer of the developing embryo, there is good reason to believe that the nervous system, including the sensory neurons, evolved from surface sensory-motor cells (Bullock & Horridge, 1965).

Specialized Receptor Cells

As metazoan organisms evolved, the independent effector cells located in the epithelial layer also evolved to serve more specialized sensory functions, and they became integrated with other neurons to form networks of interactive cells. There is a clear adaptive advantage for animals to have a variety of sensory cells that are specialized to detect specific classes of physical stimuli such as light energy, chemicals in solution, temperature, and mechanical stimulation.

The kind of physical energy that a sensory cell is specifically designed to detect (most sensitive to) is referred to as the cell's **adequate stimulus**. (Do not be confused by the word *adequate*. In this context it does not refer to intensity. Rather, it refers to the nature of the physical energy—light, mechanical stimulation, etc.) The unique sensitivity of a sensory cell to a specific form of energy is accomplished in one of several ways. In some of the more primitive sensory cells, the cell membrane may have a special process on the distal end that reacts to intensity changes in the adequate stimulus. In most cases a specially modified **receptor cell** is present that detects the adequate stimulus and subsequently interacts with the sensory cell. (The receptor cell may or may not be a true neuron.) In the most highly developed sensory systems, **accessory structures** are present around the receptor cells. The accessory structures modify the adequate stimulus in ways that enhance its effect on the receptor membrane. Figure 5-3 shows several sensory and receptor cells from a variety of vertebrate and invertebrate animals. Each cell is specially modified to detect a different adequate stimulus.

Figure 5-2
The hydra has sensory-motor cells called nematocysts that operate independent of a central nervous system. The nematocysts are sensitive to mechanical stimulation. When touched, the coiled barb within the cell (a) is fired (b) to defend the hydra from predators.

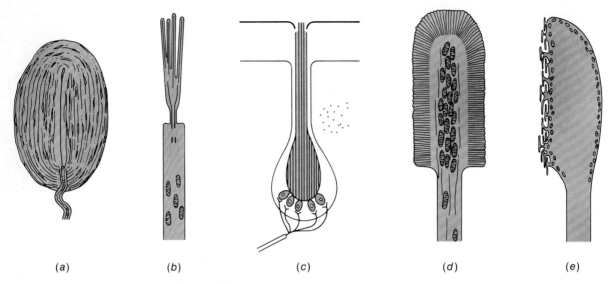

(a) (b) (c) (d) (e)

Figure 5-3
The cells shown have developed in a way to make each of them most
sensitive to a specific kind of physical energy. Some sensory cells, like the
stretch receptor (*e*), have highly modified dendrites that interact directly with
physical forces. Others, like the photoreceptor in *d*, are specialized receptor
cells that may not be true neurons. This type of receptor cell does not produce
action potentials; rather, it modulates the generator potential of its associated
sensory cell. *a*. The Pacinian corpuscle is a touch receptor found in mammals.
It is sensitive to distortions of the onionlike covering around the nerve ending.
b. A vertebrate olfactory receptor cell. This cell is sensitive to specific chemicals
that enter the mucus layer and come into contact with receptor sites on the
membrane of the cell. *c*. This cell is an electroreceptor like those found in
sharks and rays. It is sensitive to low-frequency electric fields. *d*. The photoreceptor from the eye of a planarian. This cell has light-sensitive chemicals
on the surface of the convoluted outer membrane that cause the cell to react
to changes in light intensity. *e*. A stretch cell from the muscle of the crayfish.

Sensory Processing

We have seen how single-celled organisms are able to detect and react to
events in the environment, and we have traced the evolutionary development of independent effector cells and specialized receptor cells in more
complex animals. We now examine a generalized model of complex
sensory systems and identify the events that occur at various stages of
processing sensory information.

Figure 5-4 represents a schematic model of a generalized sensory
system. The processing of sensory events occurs from the top to the
bottom on the model. Physical energy from the environment is modified
by accessory structures and focused on the receptor cell. The receptor cell

Figure 5-4
Schematic of a general model of a sensory system. Information flows from top to bottom. All of the features depicted are not present in all sense organs. (From Flock, 1970.)

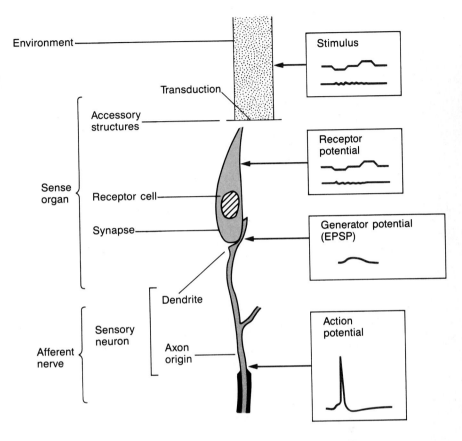

reacts to changes in the energy by producing a **receptor potential**. This, in turn, is transmitted to the sensory cell, producing a **generator potential**, which causes changes in the frequency or the pattern of action potentials in the sensory neuron. In this manner the sensory information is coded and transmitted to other sensory cells and eventually reaches structures in the brain where the conscious experience of the event takes place. Let us look at these steps in sensory processing in some detail.

Accessory Structures   Some sensory cells do not interact directly with their source of stimulation. Rather, there may be one or more structures between the sensory cell and the physical environment that modify the physical energy before it reaches the sensory cell. As noted earlier, these structures are called accessory structures. In some cases the accessory structures may be just a few cells that encapsulate the end of the sensory cell. In other instances the accessory structures may constitute a complex organ that radically modifies the energy source before it reaches the sensory cells.

Transduction   To be of any use to the neurons that make up the peripheral and central nervous systems, physical energy in the environment must be transformed into some other physical event namely, nerve impulses that may be transmitted to other neurons and eventually reach areas in the brain where they are analyzed and attain conscious experience. Receptor cells are **biological transducers** that convert physical energy into electrochemical events inside the cell. The process by which changes in physical states induce changes in nerve impulses is called **transduction**.

Actually, the term *transducer* is an engineering term used to describe any device that transforms one kind of physical energy into another form of physical energy. The speaker on your radio is a good example of a transducer. It converts electrical energy into the air movements that we detect as sound. Typically, the biological transducers are divided into four main categories based on the type of physical energy they transduce: those that respond (1) to radiant energy, (2) to mechanical motion, (3) to chemicals, and (4) to electrical fields. (Some researchers would disagree with this taxonomy and would prefer to subdivide these categories further. As an example, radiant energy could very logically be divided into photic and thermal energy.) The first three types of receptors are common to all mammals. Electroreceptors, receptors that detect electric fields, are less common, and they are found mostly in a few species of fishes.

To examine the transduction process in some detail we will look at a special type of touch or vibration receptor found in the dermis layer of mammals called the **Pacinian corpuscle**. This example was selected for two reasons. First, the example of touch was used in the beginning of the chapter to explain movement in paramecia, and it will be instructive to demonstrate the similarities between these two touch-sensitive cells. Second, the Pacinian corpuscle has been studied extensively, and we know a good deal about how this receptor cell works (Hubbard, 1958; Loewenstein & Rathkamp, 1958; Loewenstein & Skalak, 1966).

The distal end of the sensory nerve of the Pacinian corpuscle is encased in a nonnervous, egg-shaped capsule. The capsule is actually made of many concentric layers of cells that look like the rings of an onion. These cells are quite elastic, and their membranes are bathed with a lubricating liquid that allows the surfaces of the cells to slide across one another in a shearing action. The capsule is translucent in appearance and is quite large; large enough to be detected without the aid of a microscope.

When the shape of the capsule is distorted, as happens when the surface of the skin is compressed, the membrane of the nerve ending is also distorted. Changing the shape of the core receptor cell membrane causes the membrane to be more permeable to positive ions. This produces a flow of ions across the cell membrane that decreases the negative polarity of the cell (see Figure 5-5). This depolarizing shift away from

Figure 5-5
A. A schematic cross section through the encapsulated end organ of a Pacinian corpuscle.
B. Distortion of the capsule produces a distortion of the receptor cell membrane. This produces depolarization of the cell. The greater the distortion, the greater will be the depolarizing effect. C. With constant pressure the center axon returns to its normal cylindrical shape, and the cell returns to the resting potential. D. When the pressure is withdrawn, the axon is again distorted, producing a brief depolarizing effect. E. If sufficiently strong, the generator potential will produce an action potential at the point of the first node of Ranvier. (From Somjen, 1972.)

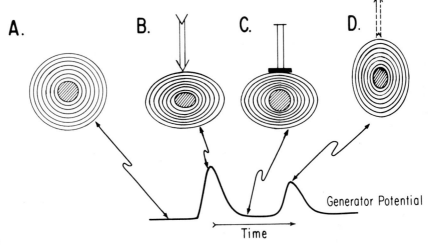

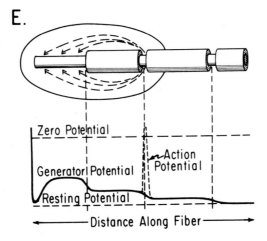

the resting potential is called a **receptor**, or **generator, potential**. The amplitude of the receptor potential is determined by the degree of distortion produced on the core cell membrane (Figure 5-5).

The similarities between the physical and biochemical events that control movement in the paramecium and the detection of touch in the Pacinian corpuscle are quite apparent. Mechanical distortion of the cell membrane changes the permeability of the cell to specific ions, which in turn causes a change in the polarity of the cell relative to the surrounding fluid. The degree to which the polarity is changed is directly related to the amount of distortion of the cell membrane. Once again we have an example of the conservative nature of the evolutionary process—find something that works, and build on that model.

If pressure on the capsule is held steady for a period of time, the shape of the pliable cells that make up the capsule conforms to the pressure allowing the membrane of the receptor cell nerve ending to return to its normal spherical shape. This, in turn, reverses the flow of ions and allows the electrochemical potential of the receptor cell to return to the resting potential (Figure 5-5C). When the pressure is subsequently removed, the capsule reverts to its round shape, in so doing causing a temporary distortion of the receptor cell membrane and producing another depolarizing effect (Figure 5-5D).

Figure 5-5B shows that the depolarization level of the receptor cell is directly related to the amount of force placed on the capsule. The depolarization that occurs on the unmyelinated, distal end of the receptor also induces a depolarizing effect at the first node of Ranvier, which is also encased in the capsule. If the threshold is reached, an action potential is generated at the first node and propagated down the length of the receptor cell axon. In this way, the information about pressure changes at the point of the Pacinian corpuscle may be communicated to the next sensory neuron.

Adaptation

It is important to understand that the receptor cell is sensitive only to *changes* in the intensity of the adequate stimulus. We saw, in the Pacinian corpuscle, that transduction takes place when pressure is applied, and it recurs when the pressure is removed from the capsule. When the adequate stimulus is held steady, the polarity of the cell returns to the level of the resting potential. It is important to note that the cell does nothing in response to pressure if the level of the pressure remains constant. This tells us something that is essential for understanding how we sense events in the world around us. Biologically, we are designed to detect changes in our physical environment. Our sensory systems are also designed so they will adapt to unchanging, steady states.

If you touch the tip of your finger very lightly with the eraser end of a pencil and then hold the pencil very steadily, you will at first experience the sensation of touch. After a brief period the sensation of touch will diminish. If the pencil is then withdrawn, the sensation of touch will return and then quickly disappear. The progressive decrease in receptor cell sensitivity to constant stimulation is called **adaptation**, and it is commonly found in most sense modalities. Adaptation is a clear reflection of the receptor cell's inability to report steady states. You have already experienced adaptation many times, although you may not be aware of that fact. When you walk into a delicatessen or a perfume store the experience is, at first, an intense sense of odor. This, however, decreases after a few minutes as the olfactory receptors adapt to the constant presence of the odor-producing substances. This form of adaptation is, presumably, somewhat of a blessing to people who work in sewers or other environments that have the continuous presence of intense and unpleasant odors.

Adaptation is produced and experienced somewhat differently in each sense modality. Some senses, like touch, adapt rather quickly, whereas others, like pain and olfaction, adapt much more slowly. (The relatively slow adaptation to pain has a clear advantage for the survival of the species.) When taking a hot bath, have you ever been dissappointed by how quickly the water in the tub cools? Actually, what you are experiencing are two processes taking place simultaneously. The water is in fact cooling, but very slowly, and your temperature receptors are adapting to the water temperature. Let's suppose that after soaking in the tub for 10 minutes you get out to answer the untimely ringing of the telephone. After 5 minutes of trying to convince the caller that you do not need another credit card, you return to the tub. You might be surprised to find the water feels much hotter than when you got out of the tub! How can this be?

The temperature receptors are sensitive to the difference between the temperature of the skin, called **physiological zero**, and the temperature of the environment. While you are soaking in the tub, your skin is warmed, decreasing the temperature differential between the skin and the water and, in turn, decreasing the generator potential being produced by the receptor cells. The perceived effect of this is that the water is cooling. After you leave the tub, your skin surface begins to cool (and the room air would feel much more cool than when you first entered the tub). When you return to the tub, the differential between skin temperature and the temperature of the water is increased, and the water *seems* hotter than it did before.

Sensory Coding

What causes optic fibers to produce the sensation of vision, auditory neurons the perception of sound, and olfactory neurons the sense of smell? These are more difficult and complex questions than you might think. We have known for some time that all neurons produce essentially the same kind of signal, an action potential. How is it, then, that action potentials, which are so much alike, can cause conscious experiences that differ so greatly?

The Doctrine of Specific Nerve Energies

In 1826, Johannes Müller, who knew nothing of propagated action potentials, proposed that the quality of perception was an inherent characteristic of specific nerves. That is, he believed that the nerves of each sense modality could provide information about that specific quality of sensation (e.g., audition or vision) and nothing else. Visual nerves could only report information about sight, the auditory nerves could only report information about sound, and the same was thought to be true for each identifiable sensory modality. You may recall from Chapter 1 that

Methods for Studying the Senses

There are two primary research methods for studying the sense organs and sensory experience: (1) the *physiological* approach and (2) the *psychophysical* approach. The physiological approach emphasizes the question, *How?* It tends to be *reductionistic* in that the physiological psychologists are more likely to study sensory experience in terms of the actions of organs, cells, and events at the subcellular level. Much of the work of physiological psychologists requires invasive techniques such as surgical lesions, injection of hormones, and electrical recording from centers deep in the brain. Therefore, much of their research is restricted to animals for ethical reasons. The studies of the morphology and biochemistry of the Pacinian corpuscle are representative of the physiological approach to the "how" question. Some of the questions might be, How is the Pacinian corpuscle organized? How do the cells in the capsule react to distortions of the surface of the skin? How is the generator potential produced?

The psychophysical approach is much older, and it attempts to examine perceptual experience, without much regard to physiology or the evolution of sense organs. Psychophysics relies on **introspection**—looking in and examining conscious experience. It is **phenomeno-** **logical** in that it attempts to describe the phenomena or appearances of mental experience. Because of this, the psychophysical studies are very dependent on the self-report of their subjects and deal almost exclusively with humans.

Psychophysics was quite important at the turn of the century, and many of the basic questions addressed by physiological psychologists have their roots in the early studies of the psychophysicists. Spotlight Figure 5-1 is representative of the psychophysical approach. This study, by Kenshalo and Scott (1966), showed the temporal course for adaptation to warm and cool over a 40-minute period for four subjects. The subjects reported the *conscious* experience of adaptation by indicating when the stimulus, produced by a thermal stimulator applied to the forearm, could no longer be detected as warm or cool. The graph shows that the time required for complete adaptation became greater as the temperature differential between the stimulus and the surface temperature of the skin (physiological zero) increased. The graph also shows that the self-report of the subjects, although similar in pattern, was not the same. This study is typical in that the subjective report of each subject is somewhat unique.

Müller's theory concerning specific nerve energies played a pivotal role in the debate over the functional division of the brain.

Throughout much of the latter part of the nineteenth century and the early part of this century researchers in the field of sensory physiology were divided into two camps in a great and lively debate over the underlying mechanism for coding sensory information. Proponents of

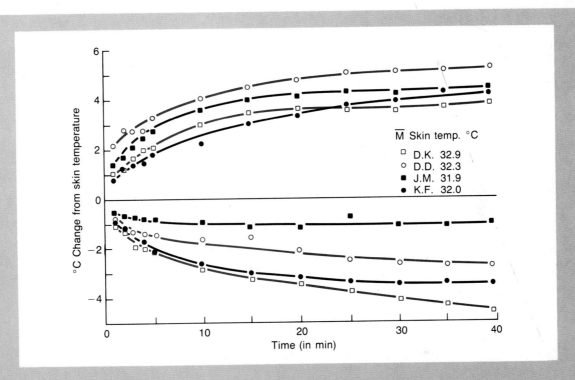

Spotlight Figure 5-1
The subjective report of four subjects to warm and cool stimuli. Each curve represents the adaptation over time to stimuli of varying intensity relative to skin temperature. (From Kenshalo & Scott, 1966.)

Müller's doctrine of specific nerve energies maintained that each sense modality was designed or tuned to detect its particular form of "adequate" stimulus. Further, they maintained that the nerves of each sense modality remained segregated within the central nervous system, and in this way, the quality of the stimulus was preserved until it reached the brain (e.g., Sherrington, 1906). Bullock (1965) and Mountcastle (1967) have referred to this as the principle of "**labelled lines**," suggesting that specific tracks of nerve fibers are labelled for only one quality of sensation. Because sensory fibers tend to be grouped according to their quality of sensation, Somjen (1972) has proposed that it may be more accurate to speak of a doctrine of "specific sense modalities" rather than specific nerve energies. Finally, supporters of the Müllerian doctrine proposed that the enormously complex organization of the neurons that project onto the brain accounts for the almost infinite gradations of perception within each sense modality.

Pattern Theory   The opposing view, known as the "**pattern theory**," maintained that the quality of sensation was attributable to the frequency and/or pattern of neuronal activity rather than to some inherent quality of the neurons that were activated. It was apparent to the pattern theorists that the activity of a single neuron could not account for the enormous variations and subtleties of sensation. Rather, the pattern theorists proposed that subtle variations in sensation were due to the combined activity of many neurons. Nafe (1968), for example, likened the information from a single neuron to that provided by a single light in an illuminated advertising sign composed of a matrix of many flashing lights. (A more modern analogy might be that of a single pixel on the screen of a computer or television cathode ray tube.) The information value of each light or pixel is determined by its own activity and the configuration of activity of its neighbors. Pattern theorists maintained that the quality of each sense modality was determined by the specific pattern of neuronal activity produced by large groups of neurons. These patterns of neuronal activity were seen to be unique for each sense modality.

A Combined View   As is true with many major theoretical debates in science, there is now evidence that supports both theories. Today, no one would seriously suggest that there could be any pattern of neuronal activity within the visual system that would cause the sensation of taste, smell, or touch. Nor is it likely that the activity of a single sensory neuron can specify the quality of sensation in any sense modality. The accumulation of evidence now suggests that the quality of sensation results from the relative activity of several sensory neurons. Furthermore, some central coding system is necessary to compare the activity of these sensory cells before the final sensory experience can occur (Uttal, 1973, pp. 24–26).

The distinguishing qualities of the major sense modalities are determined by *the location in the brain that receives the sensory information.* We know, for example, that direct electrical stimulation of sensory pathways at any point from the receptor cell to the primary projection area of the cortex of the brain produces the same quality of sensation. If the visual cortex is stimulated directly, by any physical means, visual experiences are elicited. If the auditory cortex is stimulated, the resulting experience will be some sense of sound.

If it were possible to graft the receptor end of touch receptors to the sensory nerves that exit the eye, would mechanical stimulation of the receptors produce the sensation of sight? Would we, in fact, see touch? Unequivocally, the answer is yes. How can I be so sure? Because the sensory signal, independent of how it was begun, will still end up in visual cortex, and it is this destination that determines the quality of sensation. Now let us look at other coding strategies within a given sense modality.

It is interesting to note that, with a few exceptions, neurons, including sensory neurons, constantly produce action potentials, even in the absence of innervation from other neurons or receptor cells (see Figure 5-6.) The output from receptor cells and other neurons seems only to

Figure 5-6

a. The sea slug *Aplysia california* is a convenient animal for studying the activity of single neurons. The animal has a very simple nervous system, and many of the individual neurons have been identified because they are gigantic compared to the neurons found in mammals. (From Kandel, 1976) *b.* The trace at the top represents the spontaneous activity of a giant neuron in the sea slug. The lower trace represents the spontaneous activity of the same cell after it has been isolated from all other cells. Spontaneous activity persists after isolation. (Adapted from Alving, 1968.)

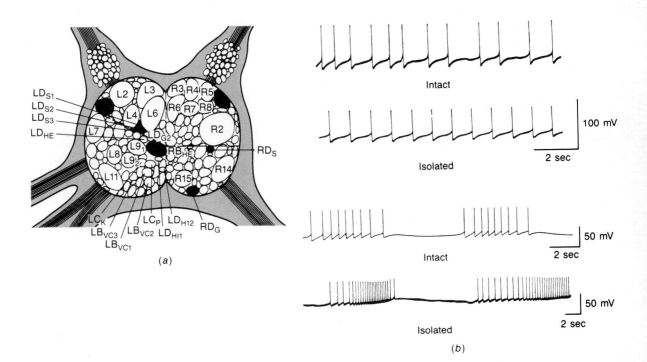

modify the spontaneous, or **base rate**, activity of the sensory neurons they innervate. The base rate activity may be increased, decreased, or altered into different temporal patterns. (Keep in mind that the size and wave form of the propagated action potential are invariant.) In the final analysis, changes in the base rate activity of sensory cells are the neural events that produce sensory experience within a given sense modality.

Changing the frequency and pattern of activity of neurons within the same neural circuit will alter the dimensions of sensation within the same sense modality. In a similar fashion, changing the number or sequence of neuronal activation will change the sensory experience. For example, the quantity and extent of stimulation may be coded by the rate at which action potentials are produced by the sensory cells and by the number of sensory cells involved. Stimulus duration may be encoded by bursts of activity that occur at the onset and termination of stimulation. The sequence of cell activation may code the direction of stimulation. We discuss stimulus coding in more detail in the subsequent chapters dealing with sensory systems.

The Simulation Hypothesis

Have you ever wondered if other people experience the world in exactly the same way that you do? When you stop to smell the roses (and I hope that you do), do they smell exactly the same to you as they do to me, or do we somewhow experience them differently? What about other species? Do they sense the world in the way that humans do? Clearly, they do not (see Figure 5-7).

Species-Specific Sensory Systems   These questions tug at a very central issue in understanding sensory processes. Our brain, and the brains of other animals, interact with the real world through a variety of biological sensors. The range of experiences available to each of us is limited in a very real way by the nature of our receptors. Quite literally, we are only able to experience a small subset of the physical events that take place around us. Specifically, we experience only what our biologically unique sensory systems allow us to experience.

We are all familiar with the fact that dogs are able to hear sound frequencies above the upper level of the human audible range. The so-called silent dog whistles take advantage of this fact. As I sit here at my word processor, my West Highland terrier is periodically nudged from a peaceful sleep by sounds that I am unable to detect—not because the sounds are too weak for me to hear; they are above the range of my transducers. But dogs, like my Westie, *are* able to hear quite well in the same frequency range as humans do. But do they hear the sounds in the frequencies that we share in common in the same way that we do? When I say, "Genie—wanna go out girl?" does she process and experience the

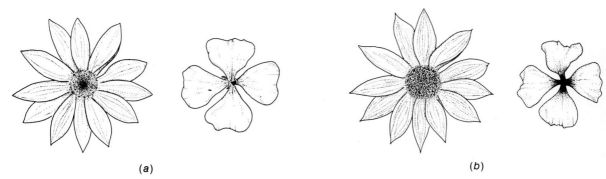

(a)   (b)

Figure 5-7
Many insects, including the honey bee, are sensitive to light in the ultraviolet range. The human visual system is totally insensitive to light in the ultraviolet range. *a.* Flowers as seen by humans. *b.* The same flowers as they would appear to an eye that is sensitive to ultraviolet light. The striking ultraviolet pattern, which is observable in the most sensitive spectrum for bees but is unseen by humans, probably serves as a visual map to the source of pollen.

sounds as I do? Probably not. (By the way, irrespective of how she detects the sounds, I have never known Genie not to want to go out!)

We can gain some insight to what other species sense by observing the physiological events that occur in the brain during the processing of sensory information. By examining how neurons in the brain respond to various forms of external stimulation and by measuring what forms of stimuli the brain seems to process most readily, we can make some informed guesses about what other species experience. By doing this, we can also gain some insights about how we experience the world as we do.

Studies have been done that have asked what a frog's visual system tells a frog. You may find the answer to be somewhat surprising. To do this sort of work, researchers use very fine electrodes that are capable of recording the electrical activity of individual sensory neurons. (See Spotlight 5-2 for a description of single-unit recording techniques.) In 1960, Maturana, Lettvin, McCulloch, and Pitts recorded the response of cells in the optic nerve of frogs (*Rana pipiens*) to various stimuli in a naturalistic visual display. The researchers identified one type of cell that responded very actively to small, dark moving shapes. The same cell, however, was totally unresponsive to a variety of other forms of visual stimulation (see Figure 5-8). Let us examine the behavior of this cell in some detail.

First, the cell does not respond to changes in illumination. Turning the room lights on and off produced no response other than the cell's normal base rate of activity. If a high-contrast bar was moved across the visual field of the cell, it still showed no response. If a complex, natural-looking scene was projected onto the visual field, the cell still remained

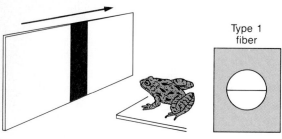

No spikes in response to room light ON
or OFF or to a large moving bar

or to illuminating or moving a natural-looking image.

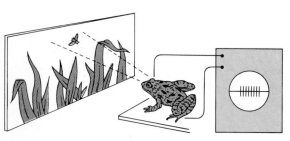

Good response to small, dark moving object in a 3° field,

even if the illumination is very faint, but

not if the edges are too fuzzy,

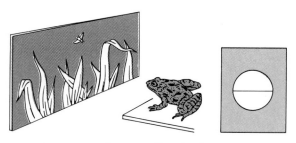

or to reversed contrast.

Figure 5-8
The response of a single cell in the optic track of the frog (*Rana pipiens*). See
the text for details. (Adapted from Maturana et al., 1960.)

quiet. Now, if a small, dark shape was moved in the field, the cell became quite active. Notice from Figure 5-8 that the cell completely ignored the spot if the spot was stationary. The cell only reacted to spots when they were moving. The cell was also active if the contrast between the moving spot and the background was decreased. However, if the border of the moving spot was made fuzzy or if reverse contrast was used (a white spot against a dark field), the cell did not respond. Grüsser and Grüsser-Cornehls (1972) have reported the existence of cells that behave similarly in the optic tectum of the frog. (The optic tectum would be roughly the equivalent of the visual cortex in the mammalian brain.) These cells are selectively responsive to small, dark spots that move in a restricted area of the visual field.

What do these data mean? Do frogs only see moving dots? No. There are other types of cells in the frog's visual system that respond to various kinds of visual stimuli, including edges, curves, and varying levels of illumination. So frogs must be able to see other types of visual stimuli in addition to moving dark spots. What these data do tell us is that the frog's visual system is particularly well designed to detect moving dark spots. Does this make sense for a frog? Well, put yourself in a frog's shoes (or more correctly, on a frog's lily pad). *Rana pipiens*, like many species of frogs, feeds on flying insects, which it captures in flight using the sticky tip of its tongue. To survive, these species of frogs have evolved to be particularly sensitive to moving dark spots, even when they are imbedded in a complex visual background. Apparently, these frogs have "bug detectors" in their visual systems, and for a frog that definitely makes sense.

An Observation:
If It Doesn't
Move, It
Isn't Food

When I was a boy, I caught a frog and tried to raise it at home in an aquarium. Much to my surprise, the frog refused to eat even the most tempting insects that I captured for it. After a few days, I had the bottom of that aquarium carpeted with delicious insects of every description, but still no success.

I thought at first that the frog wouldn't eat the insects because they were dead. After a week or so, I became very concerned, and in desperation, I tried an experiment to get my frog to eat. Tying a fly to a very fine length of monofilament line, I passed the dead fly in front of the frog. Wham! Out shot the tongue and in went the fly, monofilament line and all! Obviously, the frog did not recognize the insects on the floor of its aquarium as something to eat because they were not moving—moving dark spots.

I liked that frog, but not enough to spend a significant part of my day swinging insects in front of its nose just to get it to eat. So, I reluctantly let the frog go. My mother, however, was pleased.

Recording the Activity of Single Cells

The electrical events that occur within and between neurons may now be measured at the cellular level. Although the technology to accomplish this is quite new and sophisticated, it is readily available, and **single-unit recording** is now done routinely in many laboratories. As you might imagine, a major problem facing neuroscientists was how to develop recording electrodes small enough to record selectively the electrical activity of individual neurons.

There are two types of microelectrodes that can either be made by the researchers themselves or acquired commercially. Wire microelectrodes are made from tungsten or stainless steel, using a special process that etches the tip of fine wire into an extremely sharp point. The wire, with the exception of the tip, is then covered with an insulating varnish. In this way only the tip, which is smaller than the soma of the neuron, can record electrical events.

The second type of microelectrode can be made from very thin glass tubes.

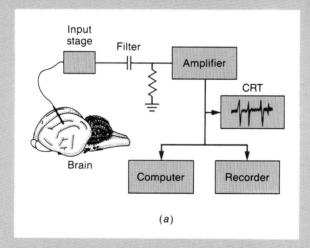

(a)

Spotlight Figure 5-2
a. A typical laboratory configuration for recording with microelectrodes on an oscilloscope display. *b.* Different electrical events can be detected by the position of the recording electrode. The uppermost electrode is positioned adjacent to the cell membrane of the soma. The trace to the right shows the effect of many afferent impulses arriving at the same time. (This is usually done by stimulating the afferent nerve track.) The tip of the middle electrode is in the soma of the cell. The trace on the right shows the large positive-going spike of an action potential. The lower electrode is placed near the axon of the cell. The electrode records the passing of the action potential as a positive–negative–positive triphasic sequence. *c.* Microelectrode positioned near the soma of a neuron. (Adapted from Somjen, 1972.)

The tubes are heated until the glass is soft and then stretched rapidly by a special device, a **micropipette puller**, producing two very fine hollow filaments. Because glass is not a conductor of electricity, a conducting fluid such as potassium chloride solution is forced into the electrode. Only the hollow tip of the electrode, where the electrolyte is exposed to the tissue, is able to record electrical events.

As you might expect, the electrical sig-nals detected by microelectrodes must be electrically filtered and amplified many times. The amplified signals may then be viewed on the cathode ray tube of an oscilloscope and/or processed by some other type of recording device. Spotlight Figure 5-2a shows the typical laboratory setup for microelectrode recording using an oscilloscope display.

The strongest single-unit recordings are made by microelectrodes that pene-trate the cell wall and record the electrical

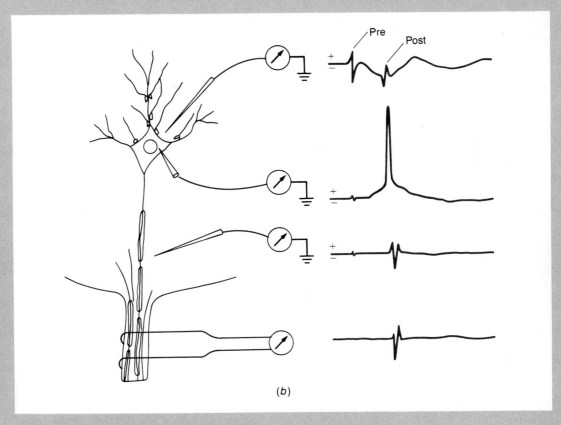

(b)

Spotlight Figure 5-2 *(Continued)*

SPOTLIGHT 5-2

activity from inside the cell. One might question whether neurons, penetrated thus even by such a fine probe, will still behave normally. The evidence suggests that they do. It is also possible to record neural activity by placing the tip of the microelectrode in close proximity to the soma or the axon of the neuron. The electrical events recorded this way, although considerably weaker, have a unique signature and may be recorded very reliably. Spotlight Figure 5-2b shows the various placements of microelectrodes and the recordings they produce.

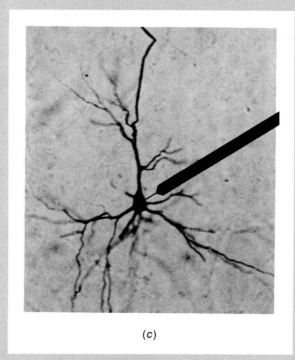

(c)

Spotlight Figure 5-2 (Continued)

Simulating the Real World   Each species, and to a lesser degree, each individual within a species, experiences the world in a unique way. The physical characteristics of the accessory structures, the biology and physiology of the transducers, the frequency and pattern of neuronal activity, and the complex organization and interaction of the sensory neurons in the peripheral and central nervous systems all combine to determine how the individual experiences the world. In a very real sense each individual creates a unique *simulation* of the physical world—unique insofar as its sensory biology is unique. To extend this concept a bit further, Gerbrandt (1980) suggests that the operating brain is in reality an "experience generator." That is, our experience of the world is the direct result of the brain in action, and the world that is experienced is determined by the nature of that action. I have more to say about this in the last chapter of this book, where I attempt to provide a coherent biological explanation of conscious experience.

Central Regulation of Sensory Processes

As organisms evolved, became more complex, and developed a variety of separate sensory systems, it was necessary to establish central regulatory mechanisms that could control, monitor, and maintain an orderly flow of information to the CNS. How is it possible that complex organisms, like humans, are able to make sense of the bewildering number of simultaneous sensory inputs that are directed towards the brain? The answer seems to be that they cannot; at least it appears that they are not able to process all of the available information at the same level at the same time. Some subset of the available sensory information seems to receive more or primary attention at the conscious level. Central neural mechanisms must exist that influence the flow of sensory information from the multiplicity of signals entering the brain.

I would like you to do a little experiential experiment here to help me get this idea across. As you read the next line of this text you are probably not conscious of the pressure on your buttocks—but now you are. Before I bring it to your attention, you are probably not aware of the pressure of your tongue against your teeth, or the sound of your breathing or the touch of your clothes on your body or the sense of warm or cool on the palms of your hands. If you were paying attention to these many and varied sources of stimulation, you probably were missing some of the finer points of what I am trying to say here. Notice that you are not (and in fact cannot be) processing all the sensory information that is available to your brain at the same level of attention.

Centrifugal Processes   It is important to understand that the brain is not a passive and indiscriminant receiver. Rather, the brain is an active processor that directly and selectively influences sensory input. The shifts in attention and conscious awareness that we experience reflect biological events within the brain, as do all other forms of behavior.

Many years ago the famous neuroanatomist Ramon y Cajal described **centrifugal** (efferent) **fibers** that travel from the brain down the optic nerve and enter the eye. The function of those nerve fibers was a mystery for some time. Subsequently, it has been demonstrated that central neural structures may actually regulate (inhibit or increase) the frequency of firing of output cells from the retina (e.g., Granit, 1955). Similar central control mechanisms have been identified for the body senses (e.g., Hagbarth & Kerr, 1954), the auditory system (e.g., Desmedt, 1960), and olfaction (Kerr & Hagbarth, 1955). Apparently, the brain can exert influence on sensory cells in the periphery, and in so doing, it has a *self-regulating* capability. (See Grüsser, 1986, for a review.)

Sensation versus Perception

As a physiological psychology text, this book is concerned primarily with the biological mechanisms of behavior. Therefore, the emphasis in the next few chapters is on the biological mechanisms that underly the process of sensation. The term *sensation* is typically understood to mean the biological events that bring sensory information from the receptor cells through the various intermediary peripheral and central nervous system structures to the brain. The term *perception* relates more to the conscious experiences that the sensation processes produce. Perception is the final step in the transduction → neuronal coding → sensing process.

What we perceive is not necessarily a totally accurate representation of the real world. In some instances our brain makes simulations of the world that appear to be correct but are actually quite wrong. Direct your attention to Figure 5-9 for a moment. If you get some distance from the figure, you will note that the colored portion appears to fill in the white spaces on the white side of the sine wave form, and the white portion fills in the colored spaces on the colored side of the figure. How can this be explained?

The answer seems to be related to the way our visual system is organized. The part of our visual cortex that processes color and the part of the cortex that processes features, like the line that makes up the sine wave form in Figure 5-9, are not located in the same place. In fact, some anatomists believe that the neural mechanism for detecting and interpreting features like lines and edges evolved independently from the

Figure 5-9

neural mechanism for encoding and interpreting color. (See Livingstone & Hubel, 1988, for a review). As you may know, many animals such as the ungulates and canines have the feature-coding system, but they do not have the ability to encode color.

Primates, including humans, possess both systems, and the illusory effect may be due to incompatible messages from each system. The color system is telling you that the surface of one side of the figure is colored whereas the surface of the other side is white. The edge-detection system is telling you that the sine wave pattern is determining the boundary between the two surfaces. Therefore, we perceive that the color "must" extend to the boundary. What is perceived as true is true in its consequences. I have more to say about the segregation of various visual capabilities in Chapter 7.

Mountcastle (1975), a noted neuroscientist, described perception as the "logical inferences" we make of the sensory data our brain receives. In effect, Mountcastle is telling us that perception is something more than simply the sum of neuronal impulses reaching the brain. As we saw in the illusion in Figure 9-5, the organization of our sensory systems can cause illusory perceptions. Perception may also represent what we bring to the sensory experience. Perceptions reflect who we are and what we have experienced in our lives.

Look carefully at Figure 5-10. What do you see? Can you make out the word FACE? Obviously, the letters that make up the word are incomplete. To see the word you must do some interpolating and filling in to make the final perception. Additionally, to accomplish the final conscious perception of the word, you must draw your experience with and memory of the alphabet. Suppose, for a moment, that you were Thai, Chinese, or Russian, and you were not familiar with the English alphabet. Could you have made the same interpretation of the stimulus? Suppose the stimulus in Figure 5-10 had been incomplete Chinese characters. Could you have drawn from your experience, filled in the gaps, and made the stimulus more meaningful? Probably not, unless you were experienced with Chinese characters.

It would be naïve to think that complex perceptions such as recognizing a word (written or spoken), identifying a melody, or recognizing a familiar voice can be explained only in terms of incoming sensory signals.

Figure 5-10

In the final analysis, these sensory experiences must be dealt with in the context of previous experiences. This, of course, requires resources drawn from many parts of the brain.

Looking Ahead   We are now going to examine the various sense modalities in detail. You will note that much more space in this book is dedicated to vision and audition than to the other senses. There are two reasons for this. First, vision and audition have been more widely studied than the other senses, and because of this we know more about them. More important, as a species, we have evolved to be much more dependent on these two senses than any of the others.

Over the years in my classes on physiological psychology, I have proposed to my students that they make a very difficult, hypothetical decision. I ask them to think about what sense modality they would choose to lose if they were forced to make that choice. I then ask them to rank order their senses, with the sense modality they would least want to lose on the top. I'll ask you the same tough question. If you are like the vast majority of my students, you have selected vision and audition, in that order. The other senses—olfaction, gustation, touch, and so on—usually show no clear order of preference but are invariably a poor third to the first two. Now let us turn to a more extensive examination of the visual system.

CHAPTER SUMMARY

1. The origin of the various senses is closely associated with the evolution of movement. The close relationship between sensation and movement can be seen in the mechanisms that control movement in single-celled organisms.

2. There is an adaptive advantage for animals to evolve specialized receptor cells that can detect specific classes of physical energy.

3. Receptor cells have evolved that are particularly sensitive to one type of physical energy. The *adequate stimulus* for a given receptor is the type of energy that produces the greatest effect on the receptor.

4. Structures like the lens of the eye that modify environmental energy before the energy reaches the sensory cells are known as *accessory structures*.

5. Receptor cells are actually biological transducers that convert physical energy into electrochemical events inside the sensory cells. The process by which environmental energy is changed into neuronal activity is called *transduction*.

6. The activity of receptor cells decreases when they are exposed to constant stimulation. This progressive decrease in activity is called *adaptation*. Some senses such as touch adapt rapidly, whereas others such as pain and smell adapt more slowly.

7. Johannes Müller introduced the *doctrine of specific nerve energies*. The doctrine maintains that each sensory nerve is specific for one quality of sensation. This view is consistent with the modern *"labelled line"* theories of sensory coding, which propose that sensory fibers are grouped according to their specific quality of sensation. Unlike the labelled line theories, *pattern theories* attribute the quality of sensation to the frequency or pattern of neuronal activity. There is good evidence to suggest that both theories have some validity, but neither theory alone can account for the many qualities of sensation.

8. Each species, and to a lesser extent, each individual within a species, experiences the world in a unique way. In a very real sense each individual creates a simulation of the external world. The characteristics of that simulation are determined by the biology and physiology of the receptors and the complex organization of the central nervous system.

9. Sensory experience is controlled by central processes. The brain can influence sensory cells in the periphery and, in so doing, demonstrates a self-regulating capability.

SUGGESTED READINGS

Goldstein, B. E. (1984). *Sensation and perception* (2nd ed.). Belmont, CA: Wadsworth.

Grüsser, O. J. (1986). Interaction of efferent and afferent signals in visual perception: A history of ideas and experimental paradigms. *Acta Psychologica, 63*, 3–21.

Wolfe, J. M. (Ed.) (1986). *The mind's eye: Readings from Scientific American.* New York: Freeman.

KEY TERMS

Accessory structure   Any structure, like the capsule of the Pacinian corpuscle, that modifies or transmits the adequate stimulus to the receptor cell.

Adaptation   The progressive decrease of receptor sensitivity to constant stimulation.

Adequate stimulus   The type of physical energy to which a given sensory cell is most sensitive.

Base rate   The spontaneous activity of neurons.

Centrifugal fibers   Neural fibers that bring information away from the CNS.

Generator potential   Local changes in the resting potential of sensory cells resulting from intensity changes of the adequate stimulus.

Independent effector cell   Cells like the nematocyst in hydra that are able to detect and react to stimuli independently from a CNS.

Introspection   Research methodology that requires the self-report of conscious experience.

Labelled lines   A concept proposed by Mountcastle and Bullock. It states that nerve fibers in the CNS are segregated by the quality of sensation. Each neuron is specific for one sensory quality such as touch, warmth, and light.

Pacinian corpuscle   Pressure or vibration receptor cell found in the dermis.

Pattern theory   Theory of sensory coding that

attributes the quality of sensation to the pattern of neuronal activity.

Phenomenology   Examination of the phenomena or appearances of mental experience.

Physiological zero   The temperature of the surface of the skin.

Receptor potential   Changes in the electrochemical activity of receptor cells when reacting to the adequate stimulus.

Single-unit recording   Recording the activity of a single neuron using microelectrode techniques.

Transduction   The process of changing one kind of physical energy to another; in the context of receptor cells, refers to the biochemical response of the cell to changes in the adequate stimulus.

Seeing: Part 1 The Eye

Chapter Learning Objectives

After reading this chapter, you should

1. Be able to trace the evolution of light-sensitive organs of animals.

2. Be able to compare and contrast the anatomy and function of simple, compound, and complex eyes.

3. Be very familiar with the various accessory structures of the vertebrate eye and know how they modify light energy before it reaches the retina.

4. Know how the rods and cones of the eye differ in their shape, distribution, biochemistry, and neural organization.

5. Understand how photolabile chemicals in the rods and cones of the eye react to changes in light.

6. Be able to compare and contrast the cellular organization of the retina in the simple compared to the more complex vertebrate eye.

7. Be familiar with the function of each type of cell in the retina of the vertebrate eye.

8. Understand what is meant by a duplistic eye and be able to cite evidence that supports the duplicity theory of primate vision.

Sensitivity to light may be almost as old as life itself. It is interesting to note that, with few exceptions, even the most simple plants and animals have evolved to have some mechanism for detecting light. Even animals like the earthworms that leave their tunnels only at night to mate and the cave-dwelling fish that live in total darkness have simple light-sensitive mechanisms that help them *avoid* contact with light.

Generally, visual systems have evolved to become ever more complex and more important to the life-style of the various species. It is important to remember, however, that evolution does not have predetermined goals. In some animals, such as the cave salamander, the eyes have atrophied and no longer function. The "quality" of vision is often an accurate reflection of the life-style of the organism. For example, free-swimming planaria may have relatively complex eyes, whereas the parasitic forms, which are equally or more specialized in terms of evolutionary development, have no eyes at all.

In this chapter we trace the evolution of light-sensitive organs in animals, with particular emphasis on understanding the relationship between the structure and organization of the visual apparatus with the life-style of the organism. We also examine the nature of light energy and the organic chemicals that are sensitive to the radiant energy. Next we examine the anatomy of the vertebrate eye in some detail. The last part of the chapter deals with the organization of the neural network of the eye, the retina.

The Evolution of the Eye

The simplest of single-celled organisms are able to detect the presence of light. The *Amoeba proteus* possesses a light-sensitive organelle that detects the presence or absence of light. Evidently, the amoeba is unable to determine the source of light and moves in random patterns until it stumbles on a lighted area. As we saw in the previous chapter (Figure 5-1b), the euglena is able not only to detect light but to determine the source of light, and it will actively move toward the light source. The mechanism that controls this positive photo **tropism** is elegantly simple, yet effective. (A tropism is any form of movement in response to physical energy that is natural for the species and is not dependent on previous experience. In this case, a positive photo tropism is the natural tendency for euglena to move toward the source of light. Other animals may evidence positive [move toward] or negative [move from] tropisms to a variety of physical stimuli including, for example, light, vibration, gravity, heat, and infrared radiation. I say more about tropisms in the chapter on learning and memory.)

Let's see how a single-celled organism can accomplish such a complex task as detecting the source of light and then appropriately responding to it. Similar to the amoeba, the euglena has a simple organelle that is sensitive to light. In addition, the euglena has evolved a small pigmented spot that covers half of the organelle. The spot casts a shadow over the light-sensitive organelle when the euglena moves away from the source of light. The shadow is eliminated when the animal is moving toward the source of light. Thus, the euglena is able not only to detect the presence or absence of light but also to detect the source of light.

Receptors for Light   Unicellular receptor cells that are sensitive to light are found in a wide range of metazoans. The simplest of these are found dispersed in the body walls of sea anenomes, earthworms, clams, and a variety of other life forms. These simple, primary sensory cells are typically nothing more than a sensory neuron containing a packet of photosensitive material. More complex photoreceptors developed along two evolutionary lines. One group is called the **ciliary type** because it contains a ciliary apparatus that aids the transmission of information between the two segments of the cell. This type of receptor cell is found in the vertebrate eye, which, of course, includes the human eye. The second type, found most commonly in arthropod and mollusk eyes, is called the **microvillous**, or **rhabdomeric**, type (Eakin, 1968). The microvillous type of photoreceptor typically contains a tightly packed stack of tubules or villi. Typically, the more complex forms of photoreceptors are found in visual organs that are composed of several types of tissues.

An Observation:

A Word About Some Terms

There is some confusion in the sensory literature concerning the terminology used to identify the various types of sensory cells and to the potentials that they generate. The term **primary sensory cell** is typically used to refer to true neurons that have a sensory function. The term **secondary sensory cell** is used to refer to highly modified receptor cells that may or may not be true neurons. These cells, like the receptors for taste and hearing, may originate from nonnervous tissues and synapse with sensory cells that are true neurons. The photoreceptors are sometimes included in this latter group, the secondary sensory cells. Frequently, the terms *receptor cell* and *sensory cell* are used interchangeably in the literature. In this book I use the term *receptor cell* to refer to the cell in which the initial transduction of the adequate stimulus takes place, independent of whether it is in a primary or secondary sensory cell. The term *sensory cell* is used to refer to all other cells in the nervous system that have a sensory function.

This problem in terminology extends to the terms *receptor potential* and *generator potential*. In this book the term *receptor potential* is used exclusively to refer to the voltage change that results from transduction in the receptor cell. The term *generator potential* is used to refer to the voltage change that initiates nerve impulses. In the case of primary sensory cells, the two potentials are in fact the same; thus, confusion in terminology may occur.

The two basic forms of photoreceptors may have had independent origins (Bullock, Orkland, & Grinnell, 1977); however, both have evolved a similar mechanism to enhance the efficient transduction of light energy (Figure 6-1). Both types of photoreceptors have developed highly convoluted membranes that are coated with the photosensitive pigment. This evolutionary invention has two significant outcomes. First, it increases the surface area on which the photosensitive chemical activity can take place. Second, it causes light to pass through many layers of photosensitive pigment, which greatly increases the probability that the

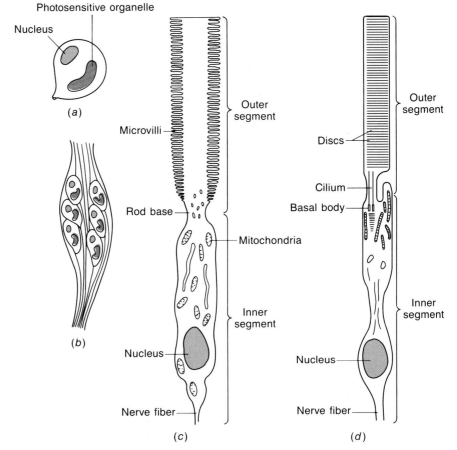

Figure 6-1
a. & b. Simple primary photoreceptors as found in the leech (a) and the earthworm (b). These receptors are little more than modified neurons having packets of photo-sensitive chemicals.
c. Microvillous or rhab-domeric type that is commonly found in molluscs and arthropods. d. Ciliary photoreceptor typical of the receptors found in the vertebrate eye. The outer segment of each receptor has the convoluted membrane that contains the photosensitive pigment. The inner segment contains the cell nucleus. Other organelles that are found in most animal cells are also found in the receptor cells. Most notably, receptor cells contain many mitochondria, which suggests that they have a high level of metabolic activity.

photons of light will impact with a photosensitive molecule. I have much more to say about the nature of light energy and the chemical events that cause transduction in the receptor cells later in this chapter.

Simple and Compound Eyes

Among the most simple eyes are the tiny **ocelli** that are common in many species of arthropods, such as insects, spiders, crabs, and scorpions. Usually the ocelli have just a few receptor cells under a single lens. The number of ocelli ranges from just one to eight, and they are very directional, each eye having a field of view of just a few degrees of arc. For this reason, ocelli have very limited, if any, feature detection capabilities. Their visual system does, however, provide limited information about light intensity and movement.

The compound eye is thought to have evolved from groups of ocelli. The individual **ommatidium** usually has several receptor cells at its base, and the ommatidium has a field of view that is even more directional than that found in the ocelli. It has been reported that an ommatidium of a worker honey bee responds only half as much to light that is one degree off center than it does to direct light (Synder, 1974). Although some insects have compound eyes containing hundreds or thousands of ommatidia (the eye of the dragonfly has more than 30,000 ommatidia), the compound eye is still primarily a motion detection visual system and provides its owner with very poor acuity when compared to the vertebrate eye. See Figure 6-2 for examples of simple (6-2a) and compound (6-2b–c) eyes.

There are two other characteristics of the compound eye that deserve mention before we move on. Many compound eyes, especially those found in insects, are able to discriminate between different wavelengths (colors) of light. We tend to think that color vision is a recent development because it is absent in so many vertebrates, particularly the mammals. To the contrary, color vision evolved quite early and seems to be scattered throughout the animal kingdom. Its presence or absence seems to be more closely related to its usefulness to the life-style of the species than to the evolving complexity of visual systems (Walls, 1942). In Chapter 5 it was noted that honey bees are sensitive to ultraviolet wavelengths and that many flowers present striking patterns under ultraviolet light that serve as maps to their source of pollen.

The second interesting characteristic of compound eyes is their ability to detect polarized light. As light from the sun passes through the earth's atmosphere, it becomes polarized so that some of the light wave movement is in parallel. Some insects, like the honey bee, are able not only to detect this polarized characteristic of sunlight but also to use it as a navigational aid. Under overcast conditions, when the sun cannot be viewed directly, honeybees that have located a particularly good source of food are able to communicate the direction of the food source to other bees using the information from polarized light (Frisch, 1967).

The Jumping Spider Eye—An Unusual Adaptation

Most web spiders, although they are predators, have very poor vision. These spiders have a few simple eyes that detect the presence of light and report motion, but they can do little else. Web spiders, as their name would suggest, rely on their web and a very acute sense of touch to capture their prey.

Unlike the web spiders, the jumping spider has two very large eyes in addition to several smaller eyes. Each of these large eyes has a single lens. Light passes through the lens down a long, narrow tubular structure. At the base of the tube are a relatively large number of receptor cells that can provide much greater detail than can the simple eyes of other spiders. The long, narrow tube greatly restricts the field of view for each of the large eyes; however, each eye is controlled by six muscles, and the spider can shift the direction of view by as much as 60° (Land, 1969). (See Spotlight Figure 6.1).

The ocelli of the jumping spider have a wider field of view and serve as motion detectors. They communicate information about movement, which, in turn, allows the spider to direct the large eyes toward the stimulus. Once the main eyes are directed at the object in question, they may track the object or move to other objects that are detected by the ocelli. The jumping spider does not build a nest that serves as a passive trap for capturing prey. Rather, the jumping spider is an active hunter that seeks out, visually identifies, and attacks its prey. The large, highly modified eyes are a unique adaptation for the life-style of this interesting spider.

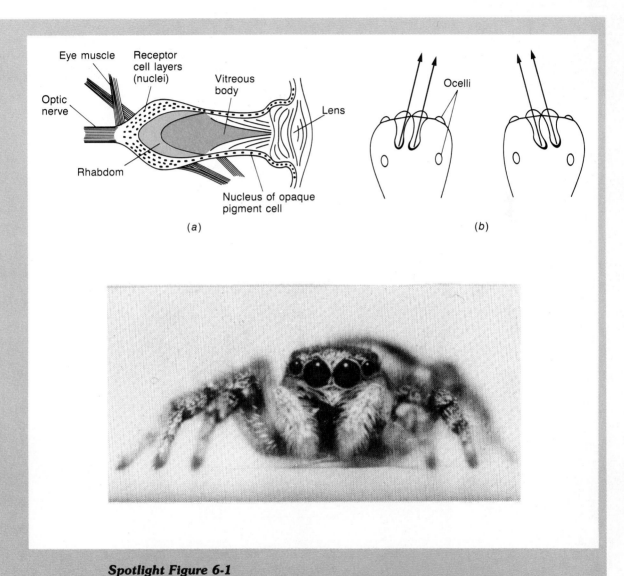

Spotlight Figure 6-1
a. The large eye of the jumping spider. (Only three of the six muscles that control the eye are shown.) *b.* Top view of the head of the jumping spider showing the position of the large eyes and the ocelli and demonstrating the movement of the large eyes to change the direction of gaze. (Parts *a.* and *b.* adapted from Brown & Deffenbacher, 1979.)

Figure 6-2
a. The simple ocellus found in many arthropods. *b.* A segment of the compound eye that is typical of many insects. *c.* Scanning electron migrograph of the compound eye of the fruit fly.

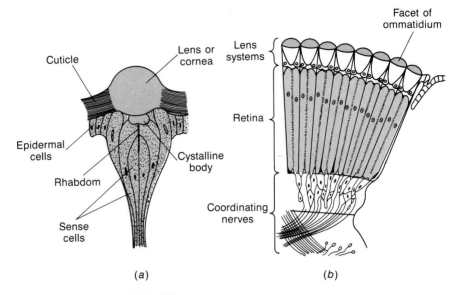

(a)   (b)

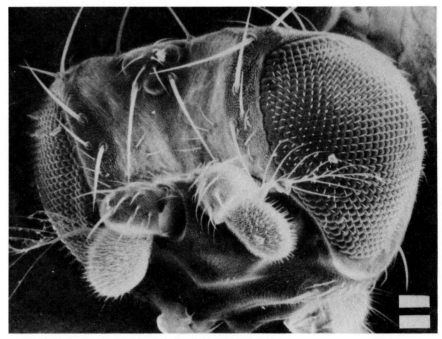

(c)

The Vertebrate Eye

Like the large eye of the jumping spider (see Spotlight 6-1), the vertebrate eye places many receptor cells under a single lens. There are several adaptive advantages to this strategy. One rather significant advantage is that this configuration allows for *good motion detection* and *good pattern vision* in the same eye. Let's see why this is true.

To examine the motion detection capabilities of this arrangment, let us look first at a less complicated eye—the pinhole eye of an invertebrate, the nautilus. The pinhole eye has the same general plan of the vertebrate eye, but the accessory structures are much less complicated (Figure 6-3). You may recall that euglena made effective use of a shadow to detect the source of light. The pinhole eye makes more effective use of a similar principle. The covering over the receptors now blocks all light except for the light that passes through the pinhole. This is the same principle of the lensless pinhole camera.

Because light must pass through the small opening of the pinhole eye, objects in the visual field are projected onto a few of the receptor cells. When objects subsequently move to different parts of the visual field, their images are projected onto other receptors, providing information about movement.

Now let's turn briefly to the question of pattern vision. Unlike the compound eye or the large eye of the jumping spider, the pinhole eye places many more receptor cells under a single lens that provides a wide

Figure 6-3
The pinhole eye of the nautilus. Note that as an object in the visual field moves from point A to point B in the figure, the projected image of the object moves over the receptor cells from point A′ to point B′.

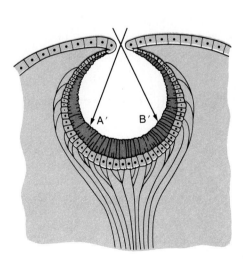

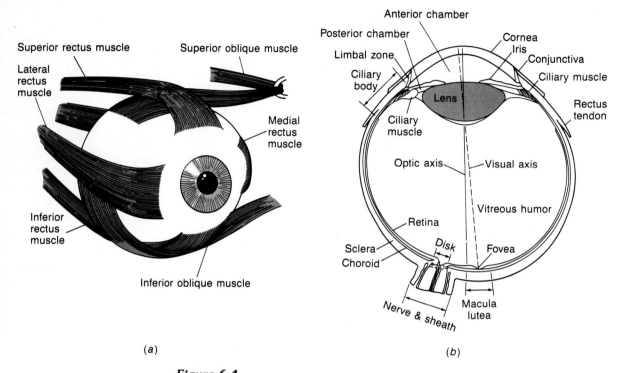

(a)   (b)

Figure 6-4
a. The extrinsic muscles of the eye. These muscles control the various types of eye movement, including rapid saccadic movements, smooth tracking movements, and the convergence of the eyes to focus on close objects.
b. Schematic of the sagittal section of the human eye showing the major structures. (See also Color Plate 7a.)

field of view. The complex pattern of the visual scene is projected onto a contiguous matrix of receptor cells. This is the necessary prerequisite for effective pattern vision. Now let us examine the vertebrate eye in some detail.

Anatomy of the Human Eye   The human eye, like all other vertebrate eyes, has evolved into a very complex organ (Figure 6-4). Most of the organ is comprised of nonnervous tissues that serve as accessory structures to modify the adequate stimulus before it reaches the receptor cells. Each eye rests in a bony orbit and is controlled by six **extrinsic** (meaning outside of the eye) **muscles**: the superior and inferior rectus muscles, the medial and lateral rectus muscles, and the superior and inferior oblique muscles (Figure 6-4a). The extrinsic muscles allow for horizontal and vertical movement of the eye in the orbit. These muscles are under conscious motor control and are used to produce both the jerky **saccadic** movements of the eyes, as well as the smooth tracking ones. Also, the extrinsic muscles cause the eyes to **converge** when focusing on objects that are close to the observer.

The ball of the eye is made up of three distinct layers of tissue (Figure 6-4b). The outermost layer consists of the **sclera**, or **sclerotic (hard) coat**. This tough, leathery material helps hold the shape of the eye and also serves to protect the more delicate interior structures. With the exception of the most anterior portion of its surface, the sclera is totally opaque. The anterior third of the sclera is crystal clear and has a greater curvature than the remainder. This structure is called the **cornea**. You can feel the margin and increased curvature of the cornea by closing your eyelid and *gently* moving your finger over its surface. The cornea bends the light that enters the eye. I have more to say about the cornea later in this chapter.

The middle layer of the eye is the **choroid coat**. In humans this layer is intensely dark black. When dissected from the eye, the choroid has the appearance of a dense, flat black, velvety material. Its purpose is to absorb light, and in so doing, to prevent the light from scattering inside the eye. In nocturnal animals the choroid may be lighter in color, and it may have a reflective surface. When this is true, the choroid reflects light back onto the receptor cells and increases the sensitivity of the eye to low levels of light energy. This is why the eyes of cats, dogs, and other primarily nocturnal mammals appear to "glow" when illuminated by a searchlight at night.

The innermost layer of the eye is the **retina** (meaning "net" or "network"). The retina is a complex network of nervous tissue that contains the receptor cells. The retina is, quite literally, an extension of the brain. If you could see a time-lapse film of the developing fetus, you would note a small dark spot forming on the brain very early in the fetal development. The spot would then enlarge into a disc and migrate on a stalk of fibers to the place on the head where the eyes are to form. You would then see the outer layers of the eye form around the disc (primitive retina) to form the eye. Later, I discuss the retina extensively.

Now let us move from anterior to posterior (the path of light) and examine the internal structures of the eye. Directly behind the cornea is a small chamber filled with a clear fluid, the **aqueous humor** (meaning "watery fluid"). The aqueous humor is chemically similar to blood plasma, and like blood it brings nutrients to the chamber and removes metabolic wastes. The fluid in the anterior chamber is replenished by fluid in the larger, posterior chamber, and it drains into the veinous system of the sclerotic coat. Poor drainage can result in **glaucoma**, a serious increase in the pressure inside the eye. If not corrected, glaucoma can lead to blindness.

On the posterior end of the small chamber is a complex muscle, the **iris**. The iris is actually two smooth muscles—the outer, radiating muscle and the inner sphincter. These **intrinsic** (meaning "inside the eye") muscles are controlled by the autonomic nervous system and work in concert to regulate the size of the pupil (the opening formed by the central edge of the sphincter). Sympathetic action causes the radiating muscle to constrict and the sphincter to relax, causing the pupil to enlarge (dilate). Parasympathetic action produces the opposite constricting effect. The autonomic system is sensitive to light levels and works, without conscious control, to adjust the level of light entering the posterior chamber.

I have heard it said that in years past skillful merchants were able to use the pupil size of their customers as a metric in bartering for price. When the right price was reached, they could detect an increase in pupil size, reflecting the customer's pleasure. This may or may not be true; however, Hess (1965) has shown that pupil dilation correlates closely with the sexual attractiveness of subjects in opposite-sex photographs, which apparently reflects sympathetic activation.

The color of the iris is determined by the pigment **melanin**. Blue eyes occur when the melanin is restricted to the posterior surface of the iris. The other colors—hazel, green, and brown—result from additional layers of melanin, with brown having the greatest amount of melanin.

Directly posterior to the iris is the **crystalline lens**. The lens is composed of several lamina (layers) of clear tissue like the layers of an onion. When dissected from fresh tissue, the lens feels like very pliable rubber. If you apply pressure to the lens, it will mold under the pressure but return to its original shape when the pressure is removed. The lens is suspended by many so called zonule fibers from a circular muscle, the **ciliary** muscle. The ciliary muscle is attached to the sclera, and like the iris, it is controlled by the ANS.

Unlike the lens of a camera, which focuses by moving closer or further from the film plate, the lens of the eye focuses light on the retina by changing its shape. The lens becomes more convex to focus on close objects and less convex to focus on distant objects. The lens begins this adjustment when objects are about 6 m from the eye (see Figure 6-5). This reflexive action is called **accommodation**, and it is under the control of the ciliary muscle. We consider the optical qualities of the lens and its control by the autonomic nervous system in the next section of this chapter.

Posterior to the lens is the large chamber of the eye. This chamber is filled with **vitreous humor** (glassy fluid). As you might expect, the vitreous humor is clear like the lens, aqueous humor, and cornea that precede it. A slight overpressure created by the vitreous humor helps to maintain the shape of the eye. The vitreous humor also helps to hold the retina in place against the choroid coat.

The Optical Properties of the Eye

To understand the optical properties of the eye, we must first have some understanding of the physical properties of light. Visible light represents only a small portion of the electromagnetic spectrum, which ranges from

Figure 6-5
a. The eye on the left is focused on a distant object, and the lens is in its relaxed (less convex) shape. On the right, the lens accomodates to focus on a close object by becoming more convex. This occurs when the ciliary muscle constricts and releases the natural tension on the zonule fibers connected to the lens.
b. Nearsighted individuals have elongated eyes. This condition causes light rays to be focused in front of the retina. Nearsightedness may be corrected by placing a concave lens in front of the eye.
c. Farsighted individuals have eyes that are too short. This results in a condition that focuses light behind the retina. Farsightedness can be corrected with a convex lens that converges the light rays, causing the focal point to fall on the retina.

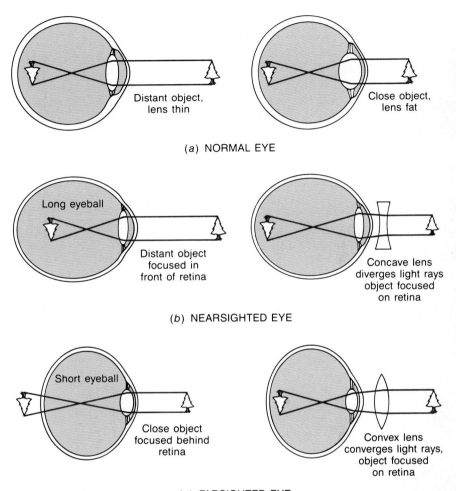

Distant object, lens thin

Close object, lens fat

(a) NORMAL EYE

Long eyeball

Distant object focused in front of retina

Concave lens diverges light rays object focused on retina

(b) NEARSIGHTED EYE

Short eyeball

Close object focused behind retina

Convex lens converges light rays, object focused on retina

(c) FARSIGHTED EYE

gamma rays at the shortest end of the spectrum to radio waves at the longest end. The visible range of the spectrum is *biologically* defined as the range from approximately 390 to 760 nm that act on the photolabile molecules in the receptor cells. See Figure 6-6, which shows the full electromagnetic spectrum.

Physicists have debated the nature of electromagnetic energy for many years. Older "wave" theories tended to treat electromagnetic energy as continuous wave motion. Some theorists suggest that electromagnetic energy is comprised of indivisible particles called **quanta** (within the range of visible light the term **photons** is often used instead of *quanta*). Each quantum, or photon, is thought to contain a precise amount of energy. A compromise between wave theory and quantum theory suggests that light is composed of particles that have wave properties.

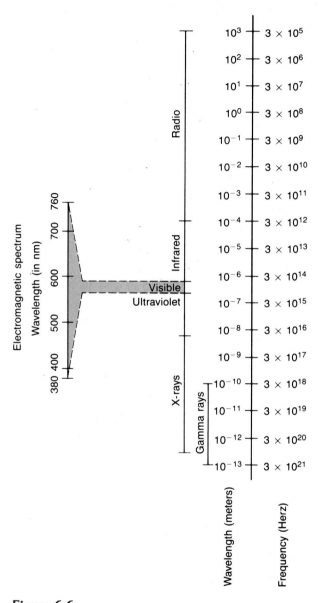

Figure 6-6
The scale represents the full electromagnetic spectrum expressed in terms of wavelength and frequency. The range of visible light has been expanded for detail. (See also Color Plate 12).

A key to understanding the optics of the eye is to know that electromagnetic energy interacts with matter in several ways. It may be transmitted through matter, reflected or refracted by it, or bent around it. Which of these events will occur is determined by the wavelength of the electromagnetic energy and the nature of the matter in question. For example, the long radio waves can bend around buildings and other terrain features. The very short gamma rays are actually reflected by molecules in the atmosphere. (This is one reason for our concern over the loss of ozone in the upper atmosphere. Ozone effectively reflects the gamma rays, which are potentially harmful to animal life.) Electromagnetic energy in the range of visible light may be reflected from some materials (e.g., metals) and transmitted through others (e.g., glass and air). Light energy is also refracted (bent) when it passes between media of different densities. For example, when light passes between a less dense medium like air into a more dense medium like water, the light is refracted by the boundary layer between the two media. You have most likely experienced this if you have ever tried to catch a fish in a pond by hand or attempted to pick up a coin at the bottom of a pool.

Now let's examine what happens to light as it interacts with the accessory structures of the eye. Light entering the eye must first pass through the cornea. For two reasons the cornea is, in fact, a very strong lens. First, the cornea is very dense relative to the air, So as light passes from the air to the cornea, it is refracted at the boundary layer. The amount of refraction produced is also determined by the shape of the boundary layer between the two media. Light that is perpendicular to the boundary is not refracted at all. The amount of refraction increases as the angle of incidence increases (see Figure 6-7).

Light then passes through the pupil and is refracted further by the lens. Contrary to what is commonly believed, the lens accounts for only a small portion of the total refractive power of the eye. When objects are viewed at a distance of 6 m or more, the cornea accounts for 70% of the eye's refractive power. There are three reasons for this. First, compared to the lens of other vertebrates such as fish, cats, and dogs, the human lens is quite flat, giving it less refractive power. Second, the lens, although made of dense material, is surrounded by fluid on both sides, and the density differential is quite small compared to the air–cornea boundary. Finally, the pupil restricts light to the central third of the lens where the angles of incidence are smallest, further limiting its refractive power. Although the lens accounts for only 30% of the refractive power of the eye, its importance is not diminished. Through the process of accommodation the lens makes fine refractory adjustments that maintain an accurately focused image on the retina.

The combined refractive power of the cornea and lens is sufficient to invert the image so that the top of the visual field is projected onto the bottom of the retina and the bottom of the visual field is projected onto

Figure 6-7
a. Light passes from a medium of one density to another without refraction when it is perpendicular to the boundary layer. *b.* When the angle of incidence is increased, the amount of refraction increases. *c.* When the rays of light contact a curved boundary, as with the cornea of the eye, the angle of incidence and the amount of refraction increase as the distance from the corneal center increases. *d.* The combined refractive power of the cornea and the lens inverts the image on the retina. Note that the top of the visual field is projected onto the bottom of the retina, and the left side of the visual field is projected onto the right side of the retina.

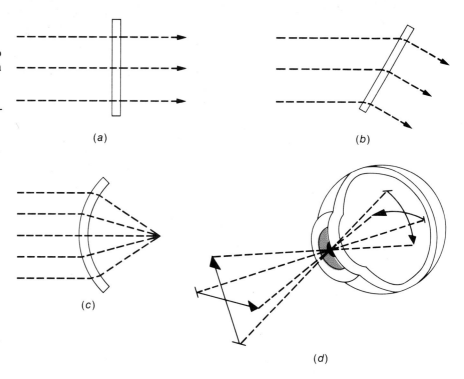

(a)

(b)

(c)

(d)

the top of the retina. The left and right portions of the visual field are, of course, also reversed. The image on the retina is upside down and backwards (see Figure 6-7d).

The cornea, lens, and pupil have provided great adaptive advantages over the simple pinhole eye that we saw in the nautilus. The cornea provides the eye with a much wider field of view than was possible with the simple pinhole. The lens permits accurate focusing of the image over a much wider range of focal distances. Finally, the pupil regulates the luminance levels that enter the eye and, in so doing, provides for normal functioning over a wide range of light intensities.

This is not to say that the optical qualities of the human eye are perfect—they are far from that. Neither the cornea nor the lens transmits light perfectly. Both have physical characteristics that produce spherical aberrations to the transmitted light. Additionally, the aqueous and vitreous humors contain tiny particles that scatter the rays of light before they reach the retina. Finally, as we discuss shortly, the retina in the vertebrate eye is "wired" backwards so that light must pass through blood vessels and several layers of neural tissue *before* it reaches the receptor cells. Fortunately, the neural tissue that lies between the receptor cells and the incoming light is very transparent.

The image that finally does reach the photoreceptors is, at best, blurry and distorted. Yet, as you are no doubt aware, our ability to see fine detail is remarkably good. Therefore, some neural-sharpening mechanism must exist. Our neural simulation of the visual world must somehow be enhanced by peripheral and/or central coding of the fuzzy image that is projected onto the retina. This mechanism is discussed in Chapter 7.

We have seen how the accessory structures of the eye have evolved to be more sophisticated and efficient processors of light. In parallel with these adaptive changes, the retinal network and the receptor cells have evolved to be more complex and sophisticated.

The Photosensitive Receptor Cells

The human retina contains approximately 130 million receptor cells. Traditionally, these photosensitive receptors have been divided into two types based on their physical appearance—**rods** and **cones**. As their names would suggest, the rods have long, rod-shaped distal segments; and the cones have shorter, cone-shaped distal segments (see Figure 6-8). This is somewhat misleading, however, because more recent evidence has shown that in some areas of the retina there are rodlike cones and conelike rods. The distal segment is connected to the inner segment by a narrow juncture that contains the connecting cilium. The inner segment contains the cell nucleus and is packed with many mitochondria. The innermost portion of the cell is a stubby unmyelinated axon that broadens into a synaptic body.

The receptor cells may be more meaningfully differentiated by their subcellular organization and by the photolabile chemicals they contain. The distal portion of the rods and cones contain hundreds of **lamellae**, thin folds of membrane. Examination with the electron microscope has shown that the lamellae are formed from invaginations of the cell membrane that begin at the narrow juncture between the inner and outer segments of the cell. In the rods the lamellae form discs that become completely separated from the outer cell membrane. Radiographic tracer techniques have shown that the discs are continuously flaking off at the most distal end and are replaced by new discs throughout the life span of the individual. The same does not appear to be true for the cones. The discs formed by the lamellae of the cones remain fused to the outer cell membrane and do not appear to be replaced. Young (1970) has suggested that the cones have their cone shape because the discs at the outer end were formed earlier in the life of the individual than the discs that are closer to the juncture.

Photosensitive Chemicals   In addition to the anatomical features that differentiate between rods and cones, these photosensitive cells differ biochemically in that each contains a different form of photolabile chemical. The rods contain **rhodopsin**, whereas the photosensitive material in cones is **iodopsin**. There are

Figure 6-8
a. Drawing of a rod and cone from the retina of the frog showing the characteristic difference in shape. The figure also shows the major intracellular structures. *b.* A greater enlargement of the outer segment of the rod (*top*) and cone (*bottom*). In the rod the discs are formed from the invagination of the cell membrane but gradually become detached. In the cone the discs remain fused to the cell membrane throughout the life of the cell.

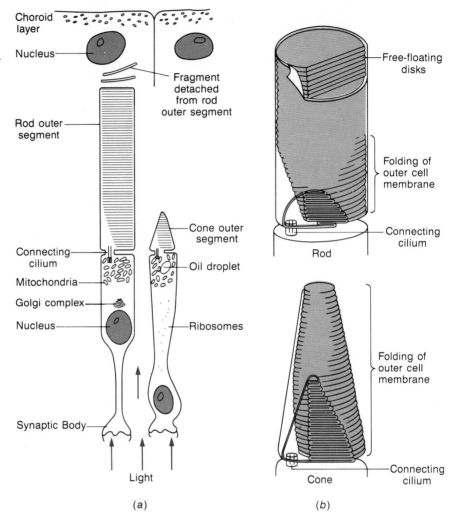

Choroid layer

Nucleus

Fragment detached from rod outer segment

Rod outer segment

Cone outer segment

Connecting cilium

Oil droplet

Mitochondria

Golgi complex

Nucleus

Ribosomes

Synaptic Body

Light

(a)

Free-floating disks

Folding of outer cell membrane

Connecting cilium

Rod

Folding of outer cell membrane

Connecting cilium

Cone

(b)

actually three different forms of iodopsin. This fact is an important consideration when color vision is discussed in Chapter 7. It is now believed that each photosensitive receptor contains only one type of photolabile molecule. This is important because the specific molecular character of each of these molecules determines the spectral sensitivity of the receptor cell. (A spectral sensitivity curve plots the varying sensitivity of the cell as a function of the wavelength of light.) This explains why some species are able to detect light in different wavelengths; they have different photosensitive chemicals in their receptor cells.

Transduction in Photoreceptors

Now let us examine how photosensitive chemicals transduce light energy into neuronal activity. In this discussion I deal only with transduction in rods because we know more about them than we do about the cones.

The Tale of Two Remarkable Pigment Molecules

Nothing is more instructive about the conservative nature of the evolutionary process than is the remarkable adaptation of organic chemicals. Some years ago I was pleasantly surprised to learn that the chlorophyll of green plants and hemoglobin in our blood are very similar chemical compounds. In fact, if you were to exchange just one atom—replace the magnesium atom in chlorophyll with an iron atom—the core of the chlorophyll molecule is identical to the porphyrin (heme) that forms the hemoglobin molecule.

At first this may not impress you. But think of this. Chlorophyll is found *only* in green plants. It is a pigment that absorbs sunlight, which is used to drive the photosynthesis process for plant growth. Hemoglobin, as you know, is found in the blood of animals, and it is essential for the oxygen exchange used in aerobic metabolism. As is so often true in evolutionary biology, something that works in one situation is simply modified and used in another way.

Another group of photopigments that are closely related to chlorophyll are the carotenoids. It is the carotenoids that give many flowers and fruits their distinctive colors, and they are responsible for the brilliant fall displays when the chlorophyll in the leaves diminishes. Chlorophyll and the carotenoids also regulate the photo-taxic behaviors of plants that cause many green plants to grow toward and orient their leaves in the direction of the source of light.

The photolabile chemicals of the human rods and cones (and indeed the photoreceptors of all animals) are based on the carotenoid compounds. Carotenoids are the building blocks for vitamin A, carotene, and the vitamin A variants that are the basic molecules of the animal photosensitive molecules. Animals, however, are unable to synthesize vitamin A and are totally dependent on plants for that purpose. (If your mother told you to eat carrots because they are "good for your eyes," she was certainly on the right track.)

It is interesting to note that the photosensitive chemicals in most green plants are found in chloroplasts, which are flattened structures filled with many lamellae. The lamellae serve the same function as the discs of rods and cones. They provide a structure that causes light to pass through many layers of photosensitive molecules, thus increasing the probability that a molecule will be struck by a photon of light. The point being made here is that nature does not "reinvent the wheel." Evolution works by building on and modifying existing mechanisms.

Rods are more numerous than cones. Of the approximately 130 million receptors in the human retina, only 6 million or so are cones. Because of this, and the fact that there are three similar forms of iodopsin, more is known about rhodopsin. There is good reason to believe, however, that the biochemical events for the transduction of light by iodopsin and rhodopsin are very similar.

Rhodopsin, like the other photosensitive chemicals, is made up of two complex molecules—**retinal** and **opsin**. In the human eye there are four forms of opsin, one for the rods and one for each of the three types of cones. Rhodopsin, then, consists of rod opsin and retinal. Retinal is synthesized from two **retinol** (vitamin A) molecules.

The retinal molecule is very long and has the ability to change shape by bending at a given place. When straight, the retinal is called **all-trans retinal**, and the bent form is called **11-cis retinal**. Only the 11-cis retinal is capable of forming a bond with rod opsin; however, the 11-cis form is very unstable and can only retain its bent form in total darkness. If struck by even one photon of light, it returns to the all-trans form and consequently breaks its bond with the rod opsin (see Figure 6-9). (Psychophysical experiments [e.g., Hallett, 1987] indicate that in the completely dark adapted human eye only 1 to 2 quanta of light are required to produce a visual sensation.)

It has been estimated that each rod cell contains upwards of 10 million molecules of rhodopsin. Yet, the action of a single photon on just one of these many rhodopsin molecules is sufficient to produce a change in the resting potential of the cell. The amount of energy produced when retinal and rod opsin separate is very small. Therefore, it is thought that the energy released when rhodopsin breaks down into rod opsin and retinal may set other chemical steps in motion that involve high-energy cyclic phosphate bonds. (See Hubbel & Bownds, 1979, and Schnapf & Baylor, 1987, for reviews.) The result of this action is to close sodium ion channels and thus restrict the flow of sodium into the cell. Limiting the flow of the positively charged sodium ions into the cell produces the hyperpolarized receptor potential.

Note that the rods and cones, unlike most of the nerve cells we have discussed so far, do not produce an action potential. The receptor poten-

Figure 6-9
The effect of light on the molecule of rhodopsin is to cause 11-cis retinal to straighten into the all-transretinal form. This causes the retinal molecule to detach from the rod opsin. The energy released by the separation of the two molecules produces a change in the permeability of the cell to sodium, resulting in the receptor potential.

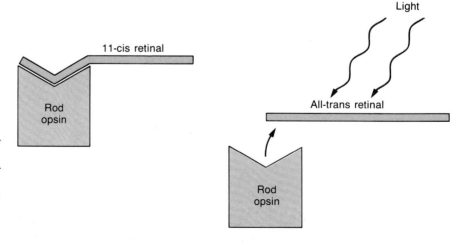

tial in the photoreceptors is *hyperpolarizing*, perhaps the opposite of what you might have anticipated it to be. How then does the receptor potential produce neuronal events that exit the eye? To deal with that question we will first need to take a closer look at the rest of the neural structure of the retina.

The Retina

When viewed through an ophthalmoscope, an instrument that provides slight magnification of the retina, it is quite apparent that the retina is not a uniform structure (see Figure 6-10). Two distinct regions can be seen on the retina, the **optic disc** (blind spot) and the **fovea centralis**.

The optic disc is located on the nasal side of each retina and is very easily distinguished by the many blood vessels that appear to converge on it. It is at this point that the veins and arteries enter and exit the eye. The optic disc is also the point on the retina where the axons carrying information from the eye exit to form the **optic nerve**. You may recall that I pointed out earlier in this chapter that the retina is "wired" backwards. The receptors face the back of the eye and must send information back toward the source of light. Then the fibers must travel to a point of exit, the optic disc. Therefore, there are no receptor cells found here, and that condition produces a small blind spot in the part of the visual field that projects onto this area.

Under normal viewing conditions you are not aware that the blind spot exists, but its presence can be demonstrated quite easily. Look at the dot on the left of Figure 6-11a with your right eye while your left eye is

Figure 6-10
The retina of the eye as seen through the ophthalmoscope. The fovea can be seen on the left, and the blind spot with its radiating blood vessels is on the right.

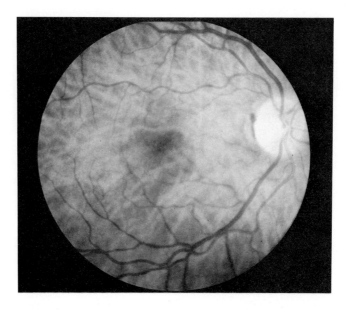

Figure 6-11

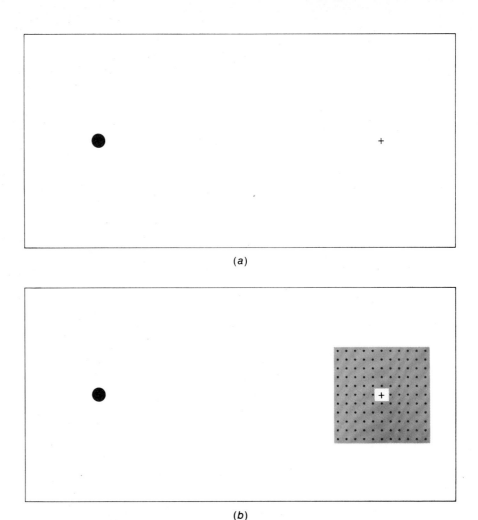

(a)

(b)

covered or closed. Then, move the text back and forth in a range of about 12 to 16 in. from your face. You will find a point where the + will disappear. At that focal distance the image of the + is being projected onto the optic disc. If you move the figure closer to you, the image of the + will move to the nasal side of the optic disc and reappear. Move the figure away and the image will pass through the blind spot, disappear, and then reappear as it is projected onto the lateral side of the optic disc.

Normally, we are not aware of the blind spot for two reasons. First, the part of the visual field that is projected onto the optic disc of one eye is also projected onto an area of the retina of the other eye that does contain receptor cells. Therefore, one eye is able to fill in what the other eye cannot see.

Now close one eye and look around. Do you detect a blind spot? No.

Figure 6-12
The visual acuity of the
eye. Note that the acuity
drops precipitously within
the first 2° of arc on either
side of the foveal center.

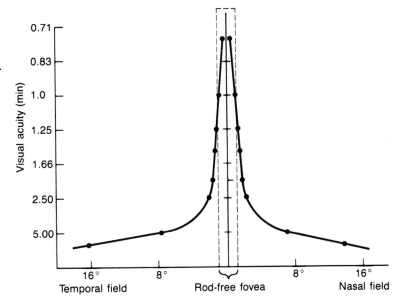

Figure 6-12
The visual acuity of the
eye. Note that the acuity
drops precipitously within
the first 2° of arc on either
side of the foveal center.

There is another mechanism at work here. Look at Figure 6-11b. As you did with the previous figure, look at the spot on the left and situate the figure so that the colored center of the matrix is projected onto the optic disc. Note that not only does the colored mark disappear, *the matrix appears to fill in!* Clearly, some central mechanism must be at work here that subjectively fills in the expected image.

The fovea centralis, as its name would suggest, is situated at the very center of the retina. When you look directly at a letter on this page, you are projecting the image of that letter onto the center of the fovea. The fovea is rich with receptor cells (primarily cones), and it is the area of the fovea that provides us with the finest levels of visual acuity. The fovea is actually formed by a pit or indentation in the retina. The pit is there because the cells that constitute the other layers of the retina have been "brushed" aside, providing direct access for light onto the receptor cells. (See the following explanation of the histological organization of the retina.) Figure 6-12 represents the level of visual acuity across the surface of the retina. Note how acuity is greatest at the point of the fovea and drops off precipitously within the first 2°of arc on either side of the foveal center. Beyond that point the decline in acuity falls off more gradually.

The most central area of the fovea is called the **macula lutea** (yellow stain or spot). When viewed with the opthalmoscope, this area has a yellow appearance, whereas the remainder of the retina is pink. The macula appears yellow because we are getting direct access to the receptor cells, and under the bright light of the opthalmoscope the iodopsin is bleached from its normal purple tint to yellow.

Note also from Figure 6-10 that the blood vessels become very delicate as they approach the fovea. Under higher levels of magnification you would see that the macular blood supply is dependent on minute capillaries—so tiny, in fact, that in some places the red blood cells must pass in single file. This too helps provide good visual acuity in this part of the retina. It is also problematical in that for many older people, particularly those who have a history of high blood pressure, the capillaries can become sclerotic (hardened) and blocked. This condition starves the receptor cells of the necessary blood supply, causing **macular degeneration**. People with macular degeneration have very limited foveal vision and, therefore, very poor acuity.

Histological Organization of the Retina

Close examination of the retina with the light microscope reveals that it is organized into several distinct layers. These layers have been identified as the receptor layer, the outer nuclear layer, the outer plexiform layer, the inner nuclear layer, the inner plexiform layer, and the ganglion cell layer (see Color Plates 7 and 8).

The outermost layer is comprised of the outer segment of the receptor cells that butt up against the choroid coat. The cell segments of the receptor cells that contain the cell bodies make up the outer nuclear layer. The receptor cells provide input to **bipolar** and **horizontal cells**. The outer plexiform (tangled) layer is made up of the processes that eminate from the bipolar and horizontal cells (see Figure 6-13). Horizontal cells receive information from many receptors and transmit information parallel to the surface of the retina. The horizontal cells appear to synapse onto adjacent bipolar cells. The bipolar cells receive information from fewer receptor cells and transmit information perpendicular to the retina. The bipolar cells synapse onto **amacrine cells** and **ganglion cells**. The cell bodies of the horizontal, amacrine, and bipolar cells make up the inner nuclear layer. Like the horizontal cells, the amacrine cells transmit information parallel to the surface of the retina, and they innervate other amacrine, bipolar, and ganglion cells. The cell processes of the bipolar, amacrine, and ganglion cells make up the inner plexiform layer. The cell bodies of the ganglion cells make up the innermost layer, the ganglion layer. The axons of the ganglion cells migrate toward and form the optic disc. They are the only fibers that transmit information from the retina to the brain.

Electrophysiological Events in the Retina

The receptor, bipolar, and horizontal cells all respond to light the same way; they produce slow, graded potentials. None of them produce the spiked action potential that we typically see in neurons. As reported earlier, the receptors invariably produce a negative-going hyperpolarizing response that reduces the release of the transmitter. The same is true for the horizontal cells. The bipolar cells, however, may produce either a hyperpolarizing or depolarizing potential in response to the onset of light.

Figure 6-13
Schematic drawing of the histological organization of the retina, not drawn to scale. See text for explanation. (Adapted from Dowling & Boycott, 1966) (See also Color Plates 7b, 8, 9, 10, and 11.)

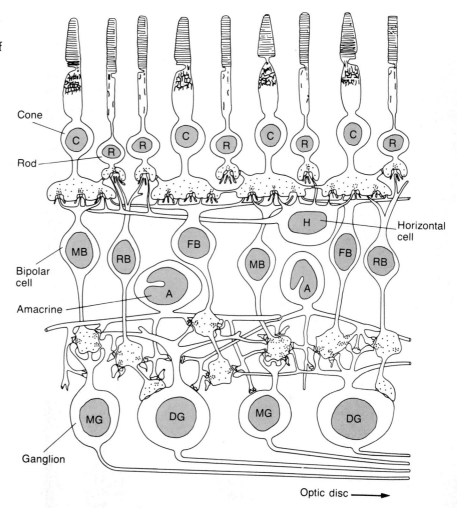

The electrical events of amacrine cells appear to be more complex. Most of them respond to both increases and decreases in light with either transient depolarizing responses, or they may produce spiked potentials. The response of ganglion cells is quite complex. Some respond with a graded depolarizing response or a spike response only to the onset of light. Others respond in a similar fashion only when light is eliminated. Still others respond to either the onset or offset of light in the same manner. Interestingly, there are some ganglion cells that are most active when the light source is moving in one direction but not the other! I have more to say about this sort of retinal coding in Chapter 7. See Figure 6-14 for a summary of the electrophysiological responses of the various retinal cells (Dowling, 1970).

Figure 6-14
See text for explanation.
(Adapted from Dowling,
1970.)

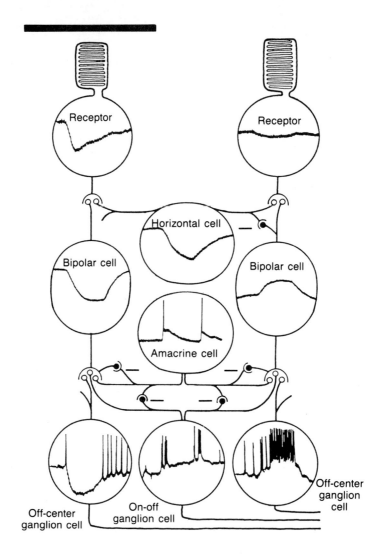

*Evolutionary Trends
in the Retina*

Much of what we know about the organization of the retina comes from the study of the primitive eye of *Necturus* (the mudpuppy), a salamander (e.g., Dowling, 1970; Dowling & Werblin, 1969). There is a great range of complexity in vertebrate retinas, and the retina of *Necturus* is among the most simple. Nevertheless, the various types of retinal cells and their interconnections seem to be relatively uniform across vertebrate species. That is, as far as we know, the bipolar, horizontal, amacrine, and ganglion cells are "wired" in similar ways in all vertebrate retinas.

A few comparisons between the retina of the mudpuppy and our own retina is instructive, because they will provide us with an insight to some evolutionary trends that have occurred in the retina. First, the mudpuppy seems to have only one type of receptor cell. It is more like our cones than our rods. The mudpuppy receptor cells are larger; and compared to the receptors in the human eye, there are far fewer receptor cells per unit/area in the mudpuppy retina. The mudpuppy has no foveal pit; rather, the organization of its retina is very uniform across all areas of the retina. Finally, the number of ganglion cells of the mudpuppy retina is very nearly equal to the number of receptor cells. This latter point is far from true in the human retina (see Color Plate 10).

Recall that there are 130 million receptor cells in the human retina—approximately 124 million rods and 6 million cones. There are, however, only about 1 million fibers in the optic nerve! This means that in humans, as compared to *Necturus*, there is much more processing and organizing of visual information taking place at the level of the retina.

The ratio of receptor cells to ganglion cells is called the **convergence ratio**. In the human eye the convergence ratio is much higher for the rods than it is for the cones. Hundreds of rods may converge through the retinal network onto a single ganglion cell. Although the rods greatly outnumber the cones, the number of ganglion cells transmitting information from the cone-rich fovea outnumber the ganglion cells that serve the remainder of the retina.

Figure 6-15
The figure on the left represents the small convergence ratio of the foveal area and its attendant narrow receptive field. The right-hand figure depicts the relatively high convergence ratio of the photoreceptors in the periphery of the retina. Note that the receptive field is determined by the convergence ratio.

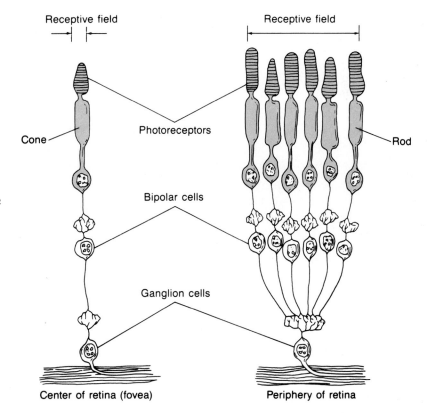

The convergence ratio reflects the size of the receptive field for the photoreceptors. What this means is that cones have a much smaller receptive field than do the rods, and therefore, the cones must be able to provide much more precise detail. See Figure 6-15 for a schematic comparison of the convergence ratio in the fovea and peripheral retina.

Judging from the differences in the organization of the retinas of the mudpuppy and the human, we begin to see that the human eye has evolved to process visual information in different and perhaps more complex ways. Examining the human retina, one gets the impression that what you really have is not one, but two eyes under one lens—a rod eye and a cone eye. Let's review the evidence that seems to support this notion.

1. There are two kinds of receptors: rods and cones.
2. Rods have rhodopsin as their photosensitive chemical. The cones have three different forms of iodopsin.
3. Rods are much more numerous and are found primarily in the periphery of the retina. The cones are concentrated primarily in the fovea. Recall that in the fovea the other retinal cells have been displaced to the side so light may impact with the cones more directly and with less distortion.
4. The rods have a very high convergence ratio and, therefore, a large receptive field. The cones have a low convergence ratio and narrow receptive field. Although the rods outnumber the cones, there are more ganglion cells for the fovea than there are for the remainder of the retina.
5. Finally, as we discuss in the next chapter, more of the visual brain is dedicated to receiving information from the small foveal area of cones than is true for the proportionately larger periphery of the retina where the rods are found

The evidence just reported has been used to describe a "duplistic" eye. The **duplicity theory**, first described by von Kris in 1896, suggests that the human eye and the eyes of all other primates have evolved to be two kinds of eye in one—a dual purpose eye. I say more about this theory in the next chapter.

CHAPTER SUMMARY   1. Many single-celled organisms are able to detect and respond to light. Unicellular receptor cells are found in a wide range of metazoans. The most simple forms of eyes with accessory structures are the *ocelli*, which are found in many species of arthropods. The *compound eye* is made of several *ommadidia* that have one or more receptor cells. The *complex eye* found in most vertebrate animals has many receptor cells under a single lens. This configuration allows for good motion detection and good pattern discrimination.

2. The eye is controlled by six *extrinsic* muscles, which direct *saccadic,* *convergent*, and *tracking* eye movements. *Intrinsic muscles* within the eye control the *accommodation* of the lens and the *pupillary reflex*.

3. The ball of the eye has three tissue layers—the sclera, choroid, and retina. The most anterior portion of the sclera is optically clear and is called the *cornea*. The interior of the eye can be divided into two chambers. The anterior chamber contains *aqueous humor* and is separated from the posterior chamber by the *iris* and *crystalline lens*.

4. The visible spectrum of light is biologically determined by the nature of the biochemical photolabile chemicals within the receptor cells, the rods and cones. The rods contain *rhodopsin*, and the photosensitive material in the cones is *iodopsin*. These photolabile chemicals are composed of *retinal* and *opsin*. There are four different forms of opsin, one for the rods and one for each type of cone.

5. The retinal molecule has the ability to change shape. When straight, it is called *all-trans retinal*; when bent, it is *11-cis retinal*. The 11-cis retinal forms bonds with opsin. If struck by one photon of light, the 11-cis retinal changes to the all-trans retinal and breaks the bond with the opsin molecule. The loss of the bond with opsin releases energy that initiates other chemical events that change the resting potential of the receptor cell.

6. The *optic disc*, or *blind spot*, is an area of the retina that has no receptor cells because it is the place where the axons exit the eye. The *fovea*, or *macula lutea*, is the place on the retina that has the greatest density of cones, and it is the place that provides the best visual acuity.

7. The receptor cells provide input to *bipolar* and *horizontal* cells. The bipolar cells synapse onto *amacrine* and *ganglion* cells. The axons of the ganglion cells migrate toward the optic disc and are the only fibers that transmit information from the retina to the brain.

8. The receptor, bipolar, and horizontal cells do not produce spiked potentials. Only the ganglion cells send coded information from the eye to the brain.

9. The primate retina is unique in that both rods and cones are present. The biochemistry, distribution, and retinal connections of the rods and cones on the retina account for the duplistic nature of the primate eye.

SUGGESTED READINGS

Brown, E. L., & Deffenbacher, K. (1979). Introduction to vision (Chapter 8). *Perception and the senses*. New York: Oxford University Press.

Schmidt, R. R. (1978). *Fundamentals of sensory physiology*. New York: Springer-Verlag.

Schnapf, J. L., & Baylor, D. A. (1987). How photoreceptor cells respond to light. *Scientific American, 256*, 40–47.

KEY TERMS

Accommodation   The reflexive adjustment of the lens by the ciliary muscle; focuses the visual image on the retina.

All-trans retinal   The light-stable form of retinal.

Amacrine cells   Neurons in the retina. They innervate with bipolar cells, ganglion cells, and other amacrine cells.

Aqueous humor   The clear, watery fluid found between the cornea and the lens of the eye.

Bipolar cells   Retinal cells that convey information from the receptor cells to the ganglion and amacrine cells.

Choroid coat   Dark layer of epithelial cells between the receptor cells and the sclerotic coat.

Ciliary muscle   Smooth muscle under the control of the autonomic nervous system. It is the intrinsic muscle that controls the accommodation of the lens.

Ciliary-type photoreceptor   One of two major types of photoreceptors—ciliary and microvillous. The ciliary type contains a cilium between the two segments of the receptor cell.

11-cis retinal   Precursor of rhodopsin; combines with rod opsin to form rhodopsin.

Cones   One of two types of photoreceptors, along with the rods, that are found in the human retina. The cones are found primarily in the central fovea.

Convergence   Crossing movement of eyes to foveate on objects that are close to the observer.

Convergence ratio   The ratio of receptor cells to ganglion cells. A high convergence ratio means that many receptor cells innervate a few ganglion cells.

Cornea   Clear anterior part of the eyeball. The cornea is responsible for the major portion of the refraction of light entering the eye.

Crystaline lens   The lens of the eye. It is controlled by the ciliary muscle and provides the fine focusing of the visual image on the retina.

Duplicity theory   Theory proposing that the primate eye (including the human eye) has evolved to be a dual purpose eye.

Extrinsic muscle   Striate muscle attached to outside of eye that moves the eye in its orbit.

Fovea centralis   Depression in the surface of the center of the retina; central point of the visual field.

Ganglion cells   Neurons found in the retina of the eye. The cell bodies of the ganglion cells form the ganglion layer. The axons of the ganglion cells migrate to the optic disc and form the optic nerve.

Glaucoma   Dangerously high pressure inside the eyeball due to poor drainage of the aqueous humor. When not treated, it can result in blindness.

Horizontal cells   Neurons in the retina that transmit information parallel with the surface of the retina.

Intrinsic muscle   One of three muscles found inside the eye. The radiating and sphincter muscles of the iris and the ciliary muscle comprise the intrinsic muscles.

Iodopsin   The photolabile pigment of the cones. There are three types of iodopsin in the human eye.

Iris   Two smooth muscles, the radius and sphincter muscles, found in front of the lens of the eye. Under control of the autonomic nervous system the iris controls the size of the pupil.

Lamellae   Subcellular folds of membrane found in the rods and cones. The photosensitive pigments are found on the surface of the lamellae.

Macular degeneration   Loss of foveal vision that results from blockage of the capillaries that serve the macula.

Macula lutea   A yellow-appearing disc in the center of the fovea. The yellow is attributable to the bleached photopigment in the cones found in this area.

Melanin   The pigment that controls the color of the skin and the color of the iris.

Microvillous-type photoreceptor   One of two major types of photoreceptors; ciliary and microvillous. The microvillous, or rhabdomeric type, usually possess a tightly packed stack of tubes or villi.

Ocelli   Simple eye having one or a few receptor cells under one lens.

Ommatidium   Single facet of a compound eye.

Opsin   Chemical precursor of visual pigments.

Rod opsin, when joined with 11-cis retinal, forms rhodopsin.

Optic disc Blind spot in eye where arteries and veins enter and exit the eye; the point on the retina where the axons of the ganglion cells converge to form the optic nerve.

Optic nerve The axons of ganglion cells that exit the eye at the point of the optic disc.

Photon A quantum of light energy in the visual spectrum of electromagnetic energy.

Primary sensory cell A receptor cell that is a true neuron.

Quantum The theoretical particle that is the smallest part of electromagnetic energy; *see also* Photon.

Retina The network of cells including the receptor cells and other supportive cells that line the back of the eye.

Retinal A chemical precursor of rhodopsin.

Retinol A chemical precursor of rhodopsin.

Rhabdomeric *See* Microvillous-type photoreceptors.

Rhodopsin The photolabile pigment found in the rods.

Rod One of two types of photoreceptors, the other being cones, found in the human eye. Rods are found primarily in the perifery of the retina and provide scotopic vision.

Saccade Rapid movement of the eye from one point of fixation to another.

Sclera (sclerotic coat) Hard, outermost layer of the eyeball.

Secondary sensory cell A highly modified receptor cell that may or may not be a true neuron, such as the hair cells for audition.

Tropism A relatively fixed form of behavior in response to a physical stimulus. For example, a positive photo tropism would be the natural tendency to move toward light.

Vitreous humor The clear viscous fluid that fills the posterior chamber of the eyeball.

Chapter 7

Seeing: Part 2
The Seeing Brain

The Visual Pathways

Anatomy of the Visual Pathways
Visual Fields

Visual Coding

Coding at the Level of the Retina
Coding at the Level of the Lateral Geniculate Nucleus
Coding in the Visual Cortex

Organization of the Visual Cortex

Ocular Dominance
Spatial Frequency Analyzers?
The Evolution of Multiple Maps on the Cortex

Seeing in Color

Photopic and Scotopic Vision
Theories of Color Vision
Coding for Color Vision

Seeing in Three Dimensions

Pictorial Depth Cues
Physiological Depth Cues

The Effects of Early Experience on the Development of the Visual System

Sensory Deprivation
Rearing in Selected Visual Environments

Chapter Learning Objectives

After reading this chapter, you should

1. Be able to trace the visual pathways from the optic nerve to the primary visual cortex.

2. Understand how the anatomy of the visual pathways determines the visual fields represented in each half of the brain.

3. Be able to discuss how the neural organization on the retina may account for lateral inhibition, receptive fields, and feature detection.

4. Be able to compare and contrast the functions of X, Y, and Z ganglion cells.

5. Know and be able to discuss how visual coding differs at the level of the retina, thalamus, and primary visual cortex.

6. Be able to compare the various levels of feature detection evidenced by the different types of sensory cells in the visual cortex.

7. Be able to discuss the evolution and the significance of multiple cortical maps of the retina on the brain.

8. Be able to compare and contrast photopic and scotopic vision.

9. Be familiar with the theories of color vision and be able to site evidence that supports or fails to support each theory.

10. Know and be able to discuss how color coding takes place at the level of the retina, thalamus, and visual cortex.

11. Be familiar with the monocular and binocular cues for three-dimensional space. Be able to describe how depth cues are coded in the visual cortex.

12. Be able to describe the various types of studies that examined the early development of the visual system and relate their results to the functional organization of the visual cortex.

In Chapter 6 we saw how the human eye has evolved from simple organelles in single-celled animals to be a complex organ comprised of several types of tissues. We examined the physical properties of light and looked at how photolabile chemicals within the photoreceptors react to light and, in so doing, produce the receptor potential. Finally, we reviewed the organization and structure of the retina, and we looked at some of the electrophysiological events that occur in the retina in response to light.

The Visual Pathways

In this chapter we outline the anatomy of the remainder of the visual system by tracing the neuronal pathways from the eye to the various cortical and subcortical structures in the brain that are associated with vision. We also examine the various types of neuronal coding that account for pattern vision, color, and the perception of depth. We begin by examining the visual pathways.

Anatomy of the Visual Pathways

You will recall that the axons of the retinal ganglion cells migrate to the optic disc and then form the optic nerve. These fibers travel toward the brain, posteriorly and medially, to meet at the **optic chiasma**. In many mammals, including humans, there is a special arrangement at the chiasma. Approximately half of the fibers from each retina cross over to the opposite side of the brain so that each side of the brain receives input from both eyes. This is a relatively new invention of evolution.

In some nonhuman vertebrates, such as amphibians and reptiles, there is complete decussation (crossing over) of the visual fibers (see Figure 7-1). That is, all of the fibers from the left eye project onto the right side of the brain, and all of the fibers from the right eye project onto the left side of the brain. This makes sense if you recall from Chapter 3 that each side of the brain controls the contralateral side of the body. The problem with this configuration, however, is that coordination of input for the two eyes is totally dependent on the commissures that connect the two halves of the brain. That is, in order for the right side of the brain to receive information from the right eye, that information must first go to the left side of the brain. Then the information must be transmitted across the commissures to the right side of the brain.

For most mammals, but especially the carnivores and primates, fibers from each eye project directly to both sides of the brain. As you will see later, this adaptation provides a particularly effective source of depth information that was well suited to the life-style of predators and the arborial primates. In humans, each retina is about evenly split so that the ganglion cell fibers originating on the nasal half of each retina cross over to the contralateral side of the brain, whereas the fibers that originate on the lateral retina remain on the ipsilateral side of the brain.

Figure 7-1
The visual system in amphibians and reptiles is organized so that all the retinal fibers from the eye cross over to the opposite side of the brain. In the frog, all the visual information from the left eye sends information to the right side of the brain. Because the right side of the brain controls the left side of the body, this arrangement makes good sense.

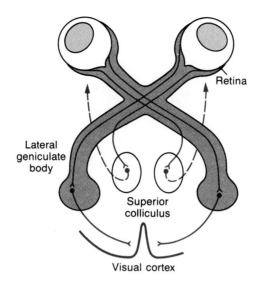

The ganglion cell axons passing out of the chiasma form the optic tract, which is the second cranial nerve. About 80% of these fibers project back to the **lateral geniculate nucleus** of the thalamus (**geniculate** means "bent," like a knee). Here the ganglion cell axons synapse onto the second sensory neurons in the visual pathway. These fibers then travel in a gentle, twisting arc, moving first in the anterior direction, then dorsally, and finally in a posterior direction to the **striate** region of the occipital cortex (see Figure 7-2). This roundabout route is due to the fact that the forebrain folds back on the midbrain during the ontological development of the brain.

The fibers in the optic nerve, the optic tract, the lateral geniculate nucleus, and the striate cortex are segregated topographically. That is, their relative position is similar to the region of the retina that they represent. Therefore, it is possible to "map" point for point a functional mosaic of the retina on the lateral geniculate nucleus and the primary visual cortex.

In addition to the fiber tracts that project to the primary visual cortex, 20% of the optic fibers terminate in a variety of subcortical structures. A large number of these fibers project to the **superior colliculi**. These nuclei are part of the corpora quadrigemina (literally, the body of four twins) which are four prominent nuclei on the posterior surface of the mesencephalon. As noted in Chapter 3, the inferior colliculi have a function in audition, and we deal with them in more detail in Chapter 8. The superior colliculi function in attention to visual stimuli and in the coordinated movement of the eyes. The superior colliculi also send and receive information from several cortical areas that function in vision.

Figure 7-2
The anatomy of the visual pathways. Visual information travels from the retina to the optic nerve. At the optic chiasma half of the fibers from each eye decussate (cross over) to the contralateral side of the brain. Most of the fibers from the left and right eye course through the optic tract to the lateral geniculate nucleus of the thalamus. Within the lateral geniculate nucleus these fibers synapse onto the next sensory neurons, which in turn project to the striate cortex of the brain. Note that the right visual field is projected onto the left half of each retina. The anatomy of the visual pathways is such that all the information from the left retina of each eye is sent to the left lateral geniculate nucleus and then on to the left hemisphere of the brain. Because the left brain controls the right side of the body, it makes good sense that the right visual field should be represented in the left brain. The opposite is true for the left visual field, which is projected onto the right side of the brain.

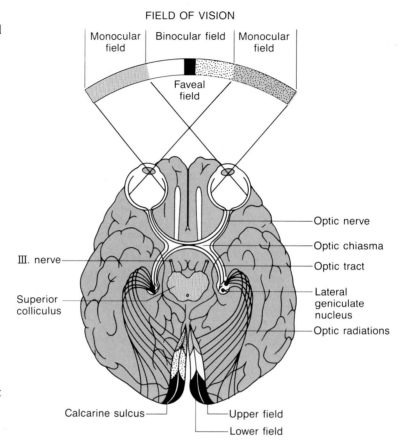

Gangion cell axons also project directly to the **ventral lateral geniculate** nucleus, which appears to be a relay station to a number of subcortical structures involved with vision. Other subcortical structures receiving direct input from the retina include the **accessory optic optic nuclei**, which play a role in the saccadic and coordinated tracking movements of the eyes; the **suprachiasmatic nucleus** of the hypothalamus, which is thought to regulate physiological processes that are under the influence of circadian (day/night) rhythms; and the **pretectum** area, which is involved in the pupillary reflex.

Visual Fields   In Figure 7-2 you will note that each eye shares a large overlapping visual field with the other eye. This is not true for all mammals. Redundant visual fields are found in those animals whose life-styles require forward-looking vision. The eyes of these animals rest in the front of the head, unlike those of most prey animals, like rabbits or deer, where the eyes are located to the side of the head. In prey animals the eyes tend to have a wider field of view, and there is very little overlap between the visual fields of each eye. The combined wide-angle fields of view can encompass a full 360°. This makes a good deal of sense for animals that must be alert for possible attack from any direction. Forward-looking eyes lose this protective capability but have other adaptive advantages, which will be discussed later in this chapter.

Tracing the path of visual information, you will note that the right visual field for each eye is projected onto the left hemiretina. This is due to the combined refractive power of the cornea and lens. This information is then projected back to the left lateral geniculate nucleus and finally to the left striate cortex. Stated more simply: All of the information from the right visual field goes to the left brain; conversely, all of the information from the left visual field goes to the right brain. Therefore, the information from the visual half field that is projected to each side of the brain is coherent with the side of the body that is controlled by that half of the brain. Visual information may also be transferred from one side of the brain to the other across the corpus callosum. In this way both sides of the brain can ultimately receive information from either side of the visual field.

Visual Coding

Now that we have a general knowledge of the anatomy of the eye and the visual pathways, we are ready to examine coding in the visual system. As you will see, the coding of visual information takes place at each level of visual processing; the retina, the lateral geniculate nucleus, and the visual cortex. We begin at the retina.

Coding at the Level of the Retina

If you place a fine black line, no wider than a human hair, on a white background and view it from a distance of 3 or 4 m, you can see the line without difficulty (assuming you have normal vision). Not only that, the line appears to be continuous, and it appears to have two clearly defined edges where the black meets the white background. How is this possible? We already know from Chapter 6 that the optical qualities of the human eye are not all that good. In fact, the image that is projected onto the receptor cells is, at best, a pretty fuzzy one.

LATERAL INHIBITION

One retinal process that appears to be at work here is **lateral inhibition**. We have known since the nineteenth century of a visual phenomenon known as **Mach bands** (named after Ernst Mach, who first described them). Mach noted that when the luminance level of light was distributed as shown in Figure 7-3, an apparent narrow band of darker or lighter luminance was perceived at the transition points. These bands are

Figure 7-3
Mach bands. The graph at the bottom of the figure plots the illumination level depicted in the top figure. Note the perceived edges of lightness and darkness at the transition points. These edges, which do not actually exist on the figure, are thought to be due to lateral inhibition at the level of the retina.

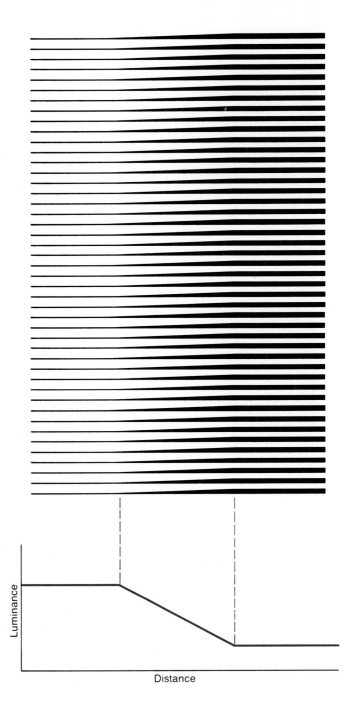

not present on the actual stimulus but are the "product" of the way our visual system processes the stimulus. With little knowledge of the biological factors involved, Mach proposed that the bands must be due to some form of lateral inhibition in the receptor cells.

The first real physical evidence for the existence of lateral inhibition came from studies of the compound eye of *Limulus*, the horseshoe crab. Hartline (1949) reported that when a very narrow beam of light is focused on a single ommatidium of the compound eye, the output of the receptor cells increases. However, if a second light is focused on a neighboring ommatidium, the activity of the first is inhibited.

In the human eye, lateral inhibition is thought to be produced by the action of the horizontal cells. When stimulated by light, the receptor cells are hyperpolarized, and this apparently reduces the release of transmitter substance from the receptor cells. This, in turn, excites the horizontal and bipolar cells that are innervated by the receptor cells. The horizontal cell then produces a graded potential that strongly inhibits large numbers of bipolar cells in its immediate area. In this manner the horizontal cells function to sharpen the boundary between the illuminated receptor and bipolar cells and the surrounding nonilluminated cells.

RECEPTIVE FIELDS

Each photoreceptor in the retina is responsive to changes in light intensity in a very small part of the total field of view of the retina. As you might expect, the particular **receptive field** for a given rod or cone is determined by its location on the retina. The other neurons in the retina—the bipolar, horizontal, amacrine, and ganglion cells—also have receptive fields. Their receptive fields, however, are determined by two factors: (1) their location on the retina and (2) the neural circuitry that innervates them. For example, ganglion cells in the periphery of the eye tend to have much larger receptive fields than do the ganglion cells that receive information from foveal receptors. This is due to the high convergence ratio of rods to ganglion cells in the periphery of the retina.

For bipolar cells the receptive field constitutes the combined receptive fields of all the photoreceptors that produce graded potentials in the bipolar cell. That is, the receptive field for any bipolar cell includes the field of any rod or cone that either inhibits or excites the bipolar cell either directly or through the action of a horizontal cell.

FEATURE DETECTORS

At the level of the ganglion cells the situation becomes somewhat more complex. Ganglion cells not only have receptive fields, as do the other retinal cells; they are also affected differently by certain features of the visual stimulus. For this reason they are called **feature detectors**.

In the early 1950s Kuffler (1952, 1953) discovered that ganglion cells had receptive fields that where roughly circular. Each field was made up of a central disc surrounded by a ring or annulus. Interestingly, Kuffler found that when a small point of light was directed at the central disc, the light produced a burst of activity. However, when the light was focused onto the surrounding annulus, the same ganglion cell was inhibited. In Kuffler's terms the cell had a "center-on, surround-off" receptive field. Other cells, however, had receptive fields that were just the opposite of this. These cells were inhibited by a spot of light focused on the central disc and excited when the spot of light was focused on any point on the annulus. These feature detectors were termed "center-off, surround-on" cells.

When exposed to diffuse light or to no light at all, these ganglion cells respond only with background levels of activity. (Keep in mind that ganglion cells, like most other neurons that produce spike potentials, have a background level of activity. They produce action potentials at a base rate, even without input from other cells. In terms of encoding information, inhibiting or slowing down the rate of the action potentials can encode meaningful information, just as does increasing the rate of activity.) The cells produce a maximal response, either excitatory or inhibitory, when the brightness level in the central disc is most different from the surround (Figure 7-4).

X, Y, AND W CELLS

Not all ganglion cells behave as just described. Those that do comprise 55% of the ganglion cells and are called **X cells**. Located primarily in the foveal area, the X cells conduct slowly, and they tend to have medium-size cell bodies and small dendritic fields. The X cells also show a sustained response to continued stimulation in their receptive fields.

A second class of ganglion cells, called **Y cells**, conduct rapidly, are large, and have large dendritic fields. The Y cells make up only 5% of the ganglion cells. They are distributed over the entire retina and respond briefly, and most strongly, to rapidly moving stimuli. A third class of ganglion cells, the **W cells**, account for about 40% of the ganglion cells and seem to respond most actively to large stimuli that are moving. The W cells have very small cell bodies, but their dentritic trees branch across very large areas of the retina. They have the slowest conduction speed of the three types of cells.

The response characteristics and the physical distribution of the X, Y, and W cells would suggest that the X cells function, primarily, to provide information about fine detail. Because the X cells are also the only ones that show different response characteristics to light of varying hues, they are also implicated in the coding of color information. (I discuss this in more depth in the section of this chapter dealing with color coding.) The Y cells seem to supply information about movement. Because both the Y and W cells send axons to the superior colliculus, they likely function in the coordination of eye movement.

Figure 7-4
Feature detectors. Some ganglion cells, on-centers (*left*), are most active in response to a spot of light surrounded by darkness. Other cells, off-centers (*right*), are most active when the ring around the center of their field is illuminated and the center is dark. Both types of cells show little response to diffuse light or darkness.

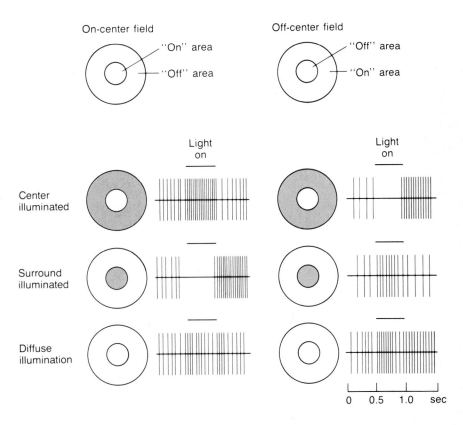

There is still considerable debate concerning the function of the three types of ganglion cells. One theory suggests that the X cells have more of a role in analyzing spatial patterns, whereas the Y cells analyze temporal patterns. Other researchers believe that the Y cells provide basic information about form and X cells fill in the fine details. One thing is clear: there is still much to be learned about the function of the different types of ganglion cells. (This brief review of X, Y, and W cells is based, mostly, on the research of Fukuda, Hsiao, and Watanabe, 1985; Rodieck, 1979; Sherman and Spear, 1982; and Stone and Fukuda, 1974.)

Coding at the Level of the Lateral Geniculate Nucleus

The next level of coding takes place in the lateral geniculate nucleus. Almost all of the X cells and many of the Y cells that originate in the retina terminate here. Single-cell recording in the lateral geniculate nucleus shows that the receptive fields are very similar to those found at the level of the ganglion cells.

Each lateral geniculate nucleus has six layers of cells. Each layer receives only information from the retina of one eye. The topographical organization of the retina is preserved in each layer. It is interesting to note that in humans the alternating layers within the lateral geniculate receive input from left and right retinas. That is, within each lateral

Figure 7-5
Section through the right-
side lateral geniculate
nucleus of the rhesus
monkey. The tissue has
been stained with cresyl
violet. From the photo
you can see how the
structure was given the
name geniculate, which
means "bent," like a
knee. Layers 1, 4, and 6
receive information from
the left (contralateral) eye.
Layers 2, 3, and 5 receive
information from the right
eye, which is on the same
side. The receptive fields
for each eye are in almost
perfect registration on
each layer. That is, the
same topographical loca-
tion would be found
along the unlabelled line.
(From Hubel, Wiesel, &
Le Vay, 1977.)

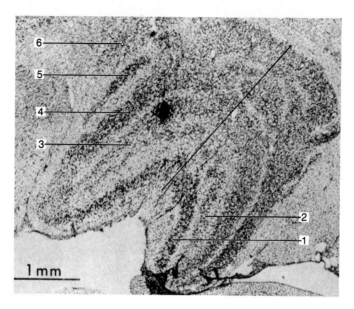

geniculate nucleus, where there is a layer receiving information from the
left eye, there is another layer receiving information from the right eye
bordering on it (see Figure 7-5).

Coding in the Visual Cortex

The coding of visual information in the cortex is more complex, by far,
than anything we have discussed. Two extraordinary researchers; David
Hubel and Torsten Wiesel, began a systematic evaluation of the visual
cortex in the late 1950s and early 1960s. Their considerable contribution
to science led to their being awarded the 1981 Nobel Prize in physiology
and medicine. (They shared the award that year with Roger Sperry,
another neuroscientist. Sperry's contributions to our understanding of
the brain are discussed at length in the final chapter of this book.) Much
of what I have to say here is based on their research, and I recommend
that those who want to know more about their work read their delightful
review article published in *Scientific American* (Hubel & Weisel, 1979).
     Early in their exploration of the visual cortex, Hubel and Weisel
discovered that, unlike the brain cells of frogs that only receive information from one eye, most of the cells in the visual cortex of cats and
primates respond to information from both eyes. Because the eyes of
these animals face forward, they have a significant portion of their visual
fields in common. The result of this is that most cells in the primary
visual cortex have binocular receptive fields. Hubel and Weisel also
found that cells in the visual cortex tended to have larger receptive fields
than did the ganglion cells or the cell of the lateral geniculate nucleus.

Most notably, they found that the cells of the primary cortex could be differentiated into three types based on the stimulus features to which they were most responsive.

SIMPLE CELLS

Many cells in the striate cortex have receptive fields similar to those shown in Figure 7-6. These **simple cells** respond with either excitation or inhibition to a spot of light in any part of their receptive field. Typically, these cells have linear fields that produce excitation or inhibition. The linear field is bordered by a field that produces the opposite effect. That is, if the cell has a linear field where a spot of light produces excitation, then it would be bordered on one or both sides by a field that produces inhibition when illuminated. The organization of the receptive field is such that several points of light forming an edge or bar of light produce the maximum effect when they are oriented in the same direction as the field.

Look at Figure 7-6a. If an edge of light is oriented so that it activates only the excitatory portion of the field, it will produce the maximum excitatory effect. Similarly, it would produce a large inhibitory effect if it were aligned with the inhibitory portion of the receptive field. Rotate the edge 90° and it passes through both excitatory and inhibitory areas of the receptive field. This produces excitatory and inhibitory effects that tend to cancel each other out. Flooding the entire field with light would also produce canceling inhibitory and excitatory effects. In effect, simple cells are "tuned" to detect edges of light with a specific orientation.

The receptive fields for simple cells are thought to be the aggregate of the receptive fields for several lateral geniculate cells. Let's see how this could be. Recall that the receptive field for each geniculate cell is an off-center/on-surround or an on-center/off-surround. Now, take several lateral geniculate fields of the same type and place them in a line, as in Figure 7-7, and you have a simple cell receptive field.

COMPLEX CELLS

Complex cells have receptive fields that are much larger than the receptive fields of simple cells. These cells are located in the striate cortex and the bordering area called the parastriate. Unlike the simple cells, complex cells do not respond to small points of light anywhere in their receptive fields. They are, however, very sensitive to stimulus patterns with a specific orientation and with a preferred direction of movement. Complex cells will respond vigorously to these stimuli if they appear anywhere within their receptive field. If, for example, a particular complex cell is sensitive to a vertical bar of light that is moving from right to left, the cell will respond to it when the bar of light appears anywhere within the cell's large receptive field.

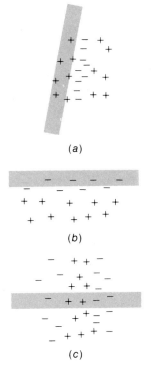

(a)

(b)

(c)

Figure 7-6
The receptive fields of the simple cells found in the striate cortex. Note that the fields have lines or edges of inhibition in response to light (indicated by minus signs) and edges of excitation (indicated by plus signs). A spot of light in an inhibitory area produces inhibition; a spot of light in the excitatory region produces excitation. The maximum effect is produced by an edge or line of light that is aligned with the inhibitory or excitatory areas as in *a* and *b*. If the edge of light is perpendicular to the receptive field, as in *c*, both inhibitory and excitatory areas are affected, and the combined effect is small.

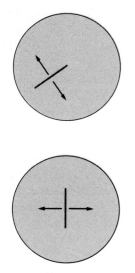

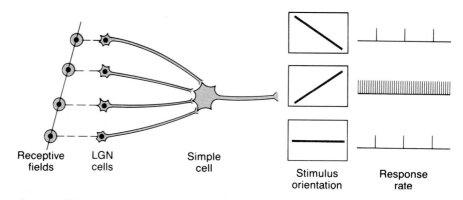

Figure 7-7
The receptive fields for simple cells are thought to be the aggregate of the receptive fields of several lateral geniculate cells.

Figure 7-8
The receptive fields for complex cells are larger than those for simple cells. Complex cells are most responsive to edges of light with a specific orientation and moving in a preferred direction.

Some complex cells will respond to movement in one direction, for example, left to right, but not to movement that is right to left. Others are not that selective and will respond to bars of light of a preferred orientation that move in either direction. Figure 7-8 illustrates receptive fields of complex cells.

HYPERCOMPLEX CELLS AND HIGHER-ORDER HYPERCOMPLEX CELLS

The **hypercomplex** and **higher-order hypercomplex cells** are very similar to the complex cells. They have an added feature in that they have a strong inhibitory response to features that extend beyond their receptive fields. These cells will stop responding to a moving bar of light if the bar extends beyond the edge of the receptive field. These cells may respond vigorously to a bar of light passing through their receptive field but suddenly "ignore" the bar if it is lengthened to extend completely through the field. Additionally, some hypercomplex cells tend to respond to stimuli of specific sizes and shapes. Some of them, for example, appear to be most responsive to two edges that meet at right angles.

Organization of the Visual Cortex

An interesting characteristic of the cortex is that it appears to have a vertical organization. When a microelectrode is moved through the cortex and visits nearby cells, the cells frequently are found to have similar characteristics. For example, several cells may all respond to stimulation from the same area of the retina, or they may all respond to bars of light having the same orientation. We note later that the columnar organization of the cortex is a common characteristic in many areas of the brain, and similar vertical patterns of organization exist for other senses as well. Actually, the vertical organization of the cortex was first reported by Mountcastle in his studies of the somatosensory (body senses) primary projection areas.

Hubel and Weisel made two important observations about the columnar organization of the primary visual cortex. First, they found that if the microelectrode was oriented perpendicular to the surface of the cortex, all of the cells in the path of the electrode had the same response characteristics. They interpreted this to mean that the electrode remained in a single column as it passed through the various layers of the cortex. If, however, the microelectrode path was at a slight tangent to the surface, they found cells that had different, but related, response characteristics. For example, the cells may all have been responsive to edges in the same part of the visual field, but each cell was most responsive to edges of a slightly different orientation. They interpreted this to mean that the electrode had passed through several columns, and the cells in bordering columns seemed to have similar response characteristics (see Figure 7-9).

Ocular Dominance

We saw earlier that animals with forward-looking eyes have visual pathways that are organized so information from both eyes is sent to the same side of the brain. The left half of each retina sends fibers to the left side of the brain, and the right half of each retina sends information to the right side of the brain. Microelectrode recordings have shown that some cells in the striate cortex respond exclusively to stimulation in the visual field of one eye. Most of the cells, however, show some responsiveness to stimuli presented in the appropriate visual field of either eye (e.g., Burkhalter & Van Essen, 1986; Poggio, 1984).

Figure 7-9
The striate cortex is organized into columns. All of the cells in a column have the same response characteristic. The response characteristics of the cells in bordering columns tend to be similar. In the figure all of the cells respond to edges of light in the same portion of the visual field. Each bordering column contains cells that respond most vigorously to edges with a slightly different orientation.

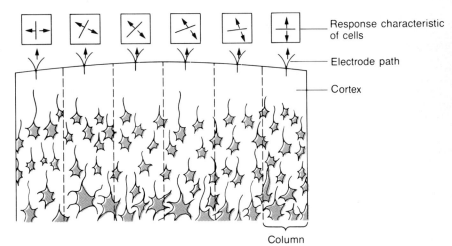

Response characteristic of cells

Electrode path

Cortex

Column

Grandmother Cells?

Cells in the primary projection area of the visual cortex have been identified that respond to a variety of stimuli, including edges of light and darkness, moving bars, and angles. But what of other parts of the brain that receive visual information from the primary projection areas? We know from clinical data that lesions to visual association areas in the occipitoparietal and occipitotemporal cortex can produce unusual visual deficits. Frequently, lesions to these areas cause difficulty with recognizing and interpreting the meaning of complex images. Are there cells in the association areas of the brain that detect more complex and cognitively meaningful stimuli like the letters on this page, a flower, or your grandmother's face?

Charles Gross and his colleagues "stumbled" on a cell in the inferior temporal gyrus of a macaque monkey that apparently would not respond to a host of simple stimuli such as bars, circles, and angles. After working with the cell for some time, one of the researchers, in frustration, stuck his hand into the cell's receptive field and waved goodbye as the research team got ready to move the recording electrode to another cell. The cell responded vigorously! The researchers quickly set about cutting complex figures out of cardboard to see what other stimuli might induce a response. They studied this same cell for 12 hours and found that it responded progressively more actively to stimuli that approximated the shape of a monkey's hand (Spotlight Figure 7-1a).

Researchers in the same laboratory have identified cells in the same general area of the cortex that act like "face de-

tectors" (Bruce, Desimone, & Gross, 1981; Desimone, Albright, Gross, & Bruce, 1984). These cells respond most vigorously to monkey and human faces. Interestingly, the cell's response rate is greatly reduced if the eyes are left off of the face. The cells completely "ignore" the stimulus when all of the component parts of the face are present but the parts are scrambled (Spotlight Figure 7-1b). Face detectors are not common. They comprise less than 10% of the neurons examined in the secondary visual projection areas of the temporal cortex. Their existence, however, has been verified by researchers in two other laboratories (Parett et al., 1985; Rolls, 1984).

Are there cells in your brain that do recognize your grandmother's face? At this time we can't say. But it seems reasonable that in highly social species like humans, quick and accurate facial recognition is an important sensory characteristic. Cells with response characteristics for detecting and analyzing facial features would be an adaptive advantage for those species that form close and durable social bonds. We know that very young human infants will attend more to facelike stimuli that any other complex visual pattern. Very recent data show that human infants have a clear preference for facial features over other stimuli of equal complexity. This preference has been shown to develop when the infants are between 6 and 12 weeks old (Dannenmiller & Stephens, 1988). Evidently, our brains are "prewired" at birth to detect and analyze facial features.

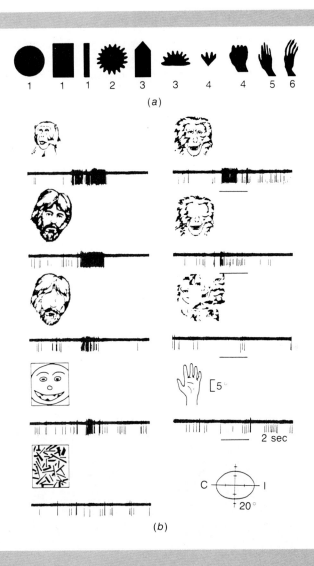

Spotlight Figure 7-1
a. Stimuli used to excite a sensory neuron in the inferior temporal cortex. The stimuli are arranged from left to right in their order of increasing effectiveness (From Gross et al., 1972) *b.* The cell response characteristics of a single cell in the temporal lobe. The cell responds most vigorously to complete faces of monkeys and humans. (From Bruce et al., 1981.)

Hubel and Weisel found that most of the cells that evidence binocular receptivity tend to respond most vigorously to input from one eye. Additionally, they noted that as the track of their recording electrode was moved parallel with the surface of the cortex, adjacent cells appeared to alternate between cells that were most responsive to stimulation in one eye to cells that were most responsive to stimulation in the other eye. They interpreted these data to mean that the striate cortex was organized into columns by **ocular dominance** as well as by stimulus orientation. Their interpretation was later confirmed by autoradiographic techniques (see Spotlight 7-2).

Spatial Frequency
Analyzers?

Recent studies have shown that sensory cells may be designed to detect sine wave gratings rather than lines, edges, and corners. Sine wave gratings are visual patterns of alternating light and dark areas that may vary along three dimensions. Sine wave patterns may vary in (1) their frequency, or the number of alternating bars in a given amount of visual field (usually expressed in terms of the visual angle—the cycles per degree of visual arc); (2) contrast, which is the difference in darkness between the light and dark areas; and (3) their orientation in the visual field (Figure 7-10).

Some investigators have shown that both simple and complex cells in the striate cortex show differing response characteristics to spatial gradings of varying frequencies (**spatial frequency**) (Campbell, Cooper, & Enroth-Cugell, 1969; DeValois, Albrecht, & Thorell, 1982; Maffei & Fiorentini, 1973). Additionally, it has been shown that X cells are more sensitive to high spatial frequency gratings, and Y cells tend to be more sensitive to low spatial frequency gratings. There is also some evidence

Figure 7-10
The sine wave pattern at the top left has a high spatial frequency compared to the pattern on the top right. The sine wave pattern on the bottom left has a high contrast level compared to the pattern on the bottom right.

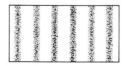

that simple and complex cells in the visual cortex encode sine wave features (Pollen, Gaska, & Jacobson, 1988). Also, the cortex may have a columnar organization based on spatial frequencies (Tootell, Silverman, & De Valois, 1981).

Finally, there is clear evidence that the spatial frequency characteristics of various stimuli govern the observation preference of very young infants (Banks & Ginsburg, 1985; Kleiner, 1987). That is, very young infants are more likely to look at stimuli with one set of spatial frequency characteristics than another. Also, the observation preferences of infants show rapid changes in the first 2 months of life, which may reflect the organizational changes of neural circuitry that underlie spatial frequency detection and processing (Stephens & Banks, 1987).

But what is the significance of this? Mathematicians tell us that through a process known as Fourier analysis any graphic pattern can be "broken down" into a combination of sine wave patterns. Thus, the combined action of several different "sine wave analysers" in the visual cortex may reconstruct more complex patterns.

Does the brain have feature detectors for edges and lines, for sine waves, or perhaps for both? If the brain has both types of feature detectors, how do they relate to each other, and how do they combine to produce cognitively meaningful images? These questions are not answerable at this time.

The Evolution of Multiple Maps on the Cortex

We have already noted that there is a topographical representation of the retina in the lateral geniculate nucleus and in the primary visual cortex. The story, however, doesn't stop here. In the hedgehog, a primitive insectavore, there is a second representation of the retina situated close to the primary projection area. In the tree shrew there are three or possibly four representations of the retina on the cortex. In the rhesus monkey one can locate eight representations of the retina in the primary receptor area and in the surrounding visual association cortex. (See Changeux 1985, pp. 115–119, for an expanded discussion of the development of multiple cortical processing levels.)

Note the progression here: more complex forms have evolved increased representations of the retina in the brain. Each additional topographical representation of the retina likely indicates a quantitative and/or qualitative increased extraction of more information. It also appears that in more complex animals the cortex has a more critical role in sensation. A decortecate rat that is deprived of its entire visual cortex can still see and learn simple discrimination tasks based on brightness cues. A cat without the visual cortex does more poorly. In humans, removal of area 17 produces a condition called **blindsight**. The person claims to be blind, however, he or she is still able to perform a number of visual tasks. Apparently the lower brain regions continue to process visual information, but the conscious awareness of sight is lost.

SPOTLIGHT 7-2

Using Radioactive Substances to Study the Organization of the Brain

A recent technological development that makes use of radioactive tracers has added much to our knowledge of the organization of the brain. This technique makes use of the fact that some substances that can be transported by the CNS can also be "tagged" with a radioactive atom that can be traced using sensitive Geiger counters or located using special films that are sensitive to the radioactive material.

In 1977, Hubel and Weisel injected a radioactive substance into the left eye of a rhesus monkey. The radioactive substance was taken up by the ganglion cells and transported via anterograde axoplasmic flow to the lateral geniculate nucleus. The radioactive material subsequently crossed the synapse in the lateral geniculate nucleus and was picked up by the second sensory neuron and finally deposited in the primary visual cortex.

Thin sections made perpendicular to the surface of the striate cortex were then placed on a special film that produces an autoradiograph, a picture that highlights those areas of the tissue containing the radioactive amino acid. The autoradiograph (Spotlight Figure 7-2) showed al-ternating light (radioactive) and dark columns, indicating that the radioactive material was concentrated in alternating vertical columns. This study confirmed the microelectrode data that found that the striate cortex was organized into columns by cells dominated by input from one eye. We would expect that if the radioactive material had been injected into the right instead of the left eye, the pattern of light and dark columns would have been reversed.

Using a similar technique, Hubel, Weisel, and Stryker (1978) injected the same radioactive substance into the eye of a rhesus monkey and then exposed the animal to a pattern of high-contrast vertical stripes. Their assumption was that exposure to vertical stripes would cause more activity in those striate cells that respond to vertically oriented features. Therefore, they predicted that the radioactive material would be concentrated in the columns of cells that had this particular orientation. The autoradiograph again showed that the radioactive material had indeed been concentrated into columns.

As we discuss in more detail later, lesions to the primary visual projection areas produce very different visual deficits than do lesions to the newer (in evolutionary terms) projection areas. For the moment I will give you just a few examples. A lesion to the primary projection area for vision (area 17) produces a **scotoma** (small blind spot in the visual field). The size and location of the scotoma is totally dependent on the size and location of the lesion in the primary cortex. Lesions to secondary projec-

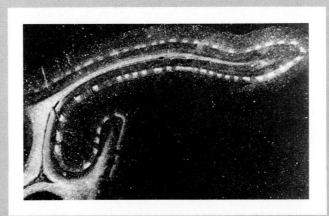

Spotlight Figure 7-2
An autoradiograph of a cross section of a rhesus monkey brain made perpendicular to the surface of the striate cortex. The animal had been injected with a radioactive substance in one eye. (From Hubel & Weisel, 1977.)

tion areas, sometimes referred to as the visual association area, impair the ability to use visual information. Reading problems, object agnosia (inability to recognize common objects), and loss of color discrimination, among other deficits, have been observed in people with lesions to the vision association areas. Again, the type and extent of the deficit are determined by the size and location of the lesion.

Seeing in Color

It was noted earlier that color vision, the ability to discriminate between various wavelenghts (hues) of light, is widely distributed in the animal kingdom. Further, we noted that color vision evolved quite early and that its presence or absence seems to be determined primarily by the need for color discrimination in the particular life-style of the organism.

Photopic and Scotopic Vision

We noted in Chapter 6 that the primate eye is quite literally two kinds of eye in one. The foveal part of the retina contains cones, and the peripheral retina is primarily rods. Cone vision is called **photopic** vision and is characterized by good acuity and chromatic (color) vision. Rod vision is called **scotopic** vision. It provides good motion detection and greater sensitivity in low levels of illumination, and it is achromatic (without color).

Does this mean that we are not able to see color in the periphery of our visual field? Yes—in the outer perimeter of the visual field we have no ability to see color. If you doubt this, you can demonstrate this with assistance from someone else. Have the person assisting you stand behind you with a colored object. It is best if you are unaware of the color. Then, while you stare at a fixed point on the wall, have the person move the object very slowly from behind you into your peripheral field of view until you are just able to detect the motion. At this point you will be unable to name the color. Then have the person continue to move the object further forward slowly until you are able to name the color. You will find that there is a wide range of the peripheral field of view where you are able to detect the motion of the object but unable to detect its color. Why, then, are we normally not aware of a transition in the visual field between the chromatic and achromatic areas? Probably for the same reason that we are not aware of the blind spot in each eye; we "fill in" the color.

Actually, you have experienced achromatic vision many times, although you may not have been aware of this. When you are out at night, in the absence of artificial light, you are unable to see color. The reason for this is that at starlight levels of illumination your foveal vision does not function and you see only with the rods. Although you know well that the grass and leaves of the trees are green, you actually see them in shades of gray.

Your photoreceptor cells adapt to the darkness. This **dark adaptation** causes the photoreceptors to be more sensitive to light. It takes some time for dark adaptation to occur. You have probably experienced this when entering a movie theater (particularly at a matinee when you go from the brightness of the street to the dimly illuminated theater). At first you may have considerable difficulty seeing as you stumble over people's feet getting to your seat. However, after 10 minutes or so your eyes adapt to the dark, and you have no difficulty seeing when you go back for the popcorn you forgot to purchase.

Figure 7-11
The dark adaptation
curve. The first part of the
curve represents the
photopic adaptation curve
of the cones. The second
segment is the scotopic
adaptation curve of the
rods.

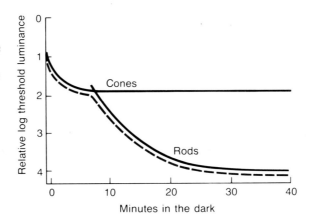

Complete dark adaptation requires between 30 and 40 minutes of exposure to darkness. Measuring the sensitivity threshold to light during the dark adaptation process produces an unusual curve having two obvious segments (Figure 7-11). The curve shows a rapid, early adaptation that levels off; this is followed by a slower, more lengthy period of adaptation. The early (photopic) part of the curve represents the adaptation of the cones. The second (scotopic) segment of the curve is the adaptation of the more sensitive rods. At the rod–cone break all sensitivity to color is lost.

Theories of Color Vision

We have known for some time that people with normal color vision are able to match any color by mixing the appropriate levels of three other colors of light. This is the principle of the color television set, which mixes blue, green, and red dots to produce the natural range of hues. In 1801, Thomas Young postulated a theory of color vision based on this phenomenon of trichromatic color mixture. Young proposed that the eye must have three, and only three, kinds of color receptors, and that each of these color receptors must have a different spectral sensitivity. In 1852, Hermann von Helmholtz, the respected physiologist, endorsed and popularized this trichromate theory. Helmholtz believed that blue-, green-, and red-sensitive photoreceptors would be found in the retina. Today, both men are recognized for their contribution, and the theory is known as the **Young–Helmholtz trichromatic theory**.

A different explanation for color vision was offered by another prominent physiologist, Ewald Hering. Hering noted that, *psychologically*, some colors appear to be **primary** in that all other colors seem to be some combination of them. He also noted that some colors seem to be perceptual opposites. For example, he pointed out that it was easy to accept the idea of colors such as reddish yellows or blueish greens, but other combinations like reddish green didn't seem possible. Therefore, Hering

Figure 7-12
a. The absorption spectra of 10 primate cones. Each curve represents the relative absorption of a single cone to various wavelengths of light. These data show that the spectral sensitivity of the cones tends to peak in three groups: the blue, yellow-green, and red portions of the spectrum. (From Marks, Dobelle, & MacNichol, 1964) *b.* The absorption spectra of the rods and the three types of cones in humans. (From Dartnall, Bowmaker, & Mollon, 1983.)

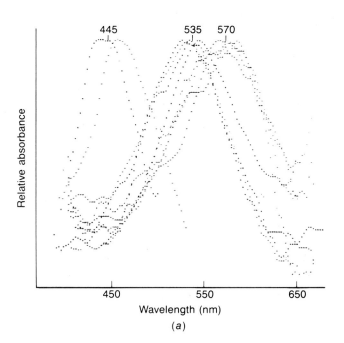

(a)

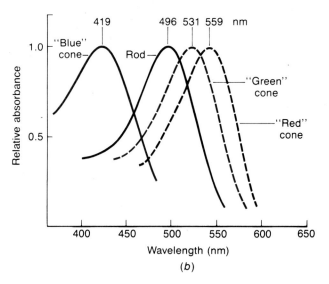

(b)

postulated that colors could be categorized into opposite pairs of primary colors. He identified the opposing pairs as red-green, blue-yellow, and white-black. (Black and white are also primary, but we typically don't think of them as colors.) He theorized further that there must be three opponent physiological processes with opposed positive and negative values, for example, positive blue–negative yellow.

Is there any physiological evidence to support either of these theories? As we discuss in the next section, there is some evidence to support both, and neither theory gives us a totally satisfactory explanation of color vision.

Coding for Color Vision We have seen how the visual system codes for various features, spatial frequencies, and movement. We now examine the physiological evidence for coding color.

COLOR CODING IN THE RETINA

You may recall from Chapter 6 that there are three types of cones but only one kind of rod in the eye. The three types of cones are differentiated by the type of cone opsin (iodopsin) they contain. The type of iodopsin determines the spectral sensitivity of the cone.

Using a technique called **microspectrophotometry**, it is possible to direct very small spots of light onto single photoreceptors. Basically, this technique uses the optical system of a microscope, but the optics are used backwards to project a very narrow beam of light through a single cone. The light passing through the cone is then analyzed with a very complex spectrometer to determine what wavelengths were absorbed by the cone. With this technique investigators (Brown & Wald, 1964; Marks, Dobelle, & MacNichol, 1964) found that the cones fell into three groups clustering in the blue, green, and red areas of the visible light spectrum. Figure 7-12a shows the absorption spectra for 10 cones in the primate eye, and Figure 7-12b shows the averaged absorption spectra for the three types of cones and the rods of the human eye.

An Observation:

Dark Adaptation in Red Light

Did you ever wonder why in the old war movies, when the pilots were getting prepared to go out on a night mission, the briefing room was illuminated in red light? The answer to that question can be found in Figure 7-12b. When the room is illuminated only with light from the red end of the spectrum, the blue and green cones and the rods, which are relatively insensitive to the red wavelength, are actually adapting as though they were in the dark. Therefore, when the pilots leave the briefing room and jump into their aircraft, they are able to see quite well with the rods and the blue and green cones that have become more sensitive to low levels of light.

This point was made very clear to me when I was in pilot training in the air force (more years ago than I really care to remember). At the beginning of a lecture on night flying, half of the class were given red goggles to wear. About a half hour into the lecture the lights were put out, and we were placed in total darkness. The lights were then turned up very slowly with a reostat. Soon, the half of the class that had been wearing the red goggles began to whistle and shout out "oohs" and "ahs," while the remainder of the class (including myself) were left wondering what was going on! When the illumination was increased sufficiently, all of us could see the life-size picture of Marilyn Monroe.

Microelectrode recordings of the receptor potential of cones in the eye of the carp produce data remarkably similar to that found using microspectrophotometric techniques. The data in Figure 7-13 show the receptor potential of three cones to light stimuli presented at 20-nm wavelength intervals (Tomita, Kaneko, Murakami & Pautler, 1967). You will note that, as was true with the microspectrometric techniques, the three cells evidence the maximum response in the blue, green, and red portions of the spectrum. Another point needs to be made here. Both sources of data show that although the three types of cones have peak responses to light of a given frequency, they are *not* narrowly tuned to that frequency. Rather, each type of cone responds to a broad range of frequencies that overlap to a large extent with the range of the other two cones.

Figure 7-13
The graded receptor potentials of three types of cones in the eye of the carp. The responses are not spike potentials; they are graded potentials to light stimuli presented at 20-nm wavelength intervals. (From Tomita, Kaneko, Murakami, & Pautler, 1967.)

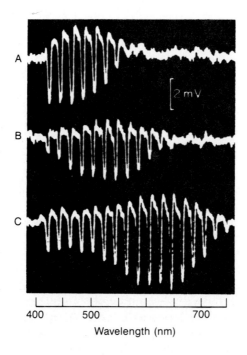

Wavelength (nm)

COLOR CODING IN THE GANGLION CELLS

The data from the cones seem to be consistent with the trichromatic theory of color vision. The ganglion cells, however, respond to specific frequencies of light quite differently than do the cones. The ganglion cells respond to the primary colors of light in an opponent manner. For example, a given cell might be excited by red and inhibited by green or excited by yellow and inhibited by blue. Additionally, some ganglion cells are not sensitive to hue and only respond to changing levels of brightness. As Hering predicted, the opposing pairs were always red-green and blue-yellow, and the brightness discriminators may be thought of as the white-black opponent cells (DeValois & DeValois, 1975).

The retinal circuitry to account for the transition from a trichromatic system to an opponent process system is not known. Figure 7-14 shows one possible way that long-, medium-, and short-wavelength cells could produce an opponent process in the bipolar and ganglion cells.

COLOR CODING IN THE LATERAL GENICULATE NUCLEUS

If there are, indeed, three opponent processes and each process has a positive and negative valence for each member of the pair, there ought to be six types or classes of cells. That is, for each opponent pair like red and green, there should be a plus red–minus green and a minus red–plus green cell. This is exactly what has been found at the level of the lateral geniculate nucleus.

Refer to Figure 7-15, which summarizes the microelectrode data from several studies completed by DeValois and his colleagues. Consider

Figure 7-14
One possible neural circuit that could produce an opponent process from long-, medium-, and short-wavelength cells.

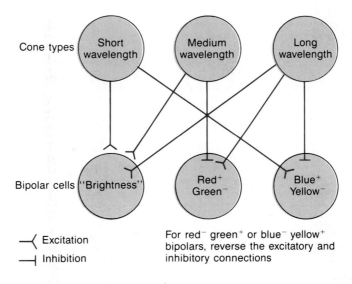

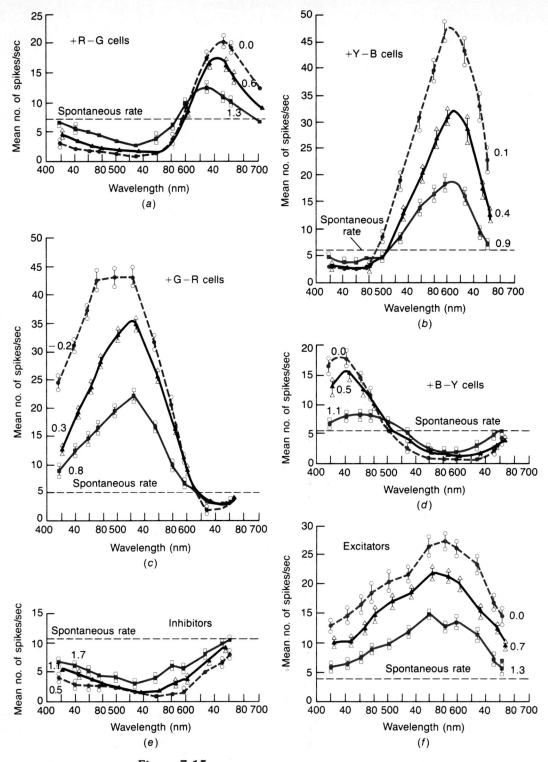

Figure 7-15
Opponent process cells in the lateral geniculate nucleus. See text for explanation. (From DeValois & DeValois, 1975.)

the data from the plus blue–minus yellow geniculate cell (Figure 7-15d). The dashed line represents the cell's background level of spontaneous activity. This cell has its highest level of excitation at approximately 420 nm (blue) and is most inhibited at approximately 600 nm (yellow). The minus blue–plus yellow cell (Figure 7-15b) shows the opposite inhibitory/excitatory pattern.

Now refer to the two bottom graphs of black-white opponent cells. Note how these cells are either excited across all frequencies of light (Figure 7-15f; plus white–minus black) or inhibited across all frequencies of light (Figure 7-15e; minus white–plus black). The plus white–minus black cells are maximally activated by a spot of light with a dark surround, whereas the opposite is true for the minus white–plus black cells.

COLOR CODING IN THE VISUAL CORTEX

Color coding in the visual cortex presents a complex and confusing picture. Most of the cells appear to operate in an opponent manner. Unlike the ganglion and lateral geniculate cells, however, the cortical cells are not necessarily "tuned" to the primary colors (Zeki, 1980). Many of the cortical cells are very selectively active to a very narrow frequency range compared to the geniculate cells. Additionally, color-sensitive cells have been located in two areas of the visual cortex identified as areas V1 and V4. The cells in area V1 act consistently with the opponent process theory. The cells in V4 do not and seem to respond only to one narrow band of light. Furthermore, the cells in V4 are affected by the contrast of hues acting on different parts of the retina (Zeki, 1983). That is, they may respond in one way to red if blue is also projected somewhere else on the retina and another way if yellow is projected elsewhere on the retina. The cell's activity apparently depends on the contrast between one area of the retina and another. The cell is not simply responding to the hue in its immediate receptive field.

How the color coding just described enables us to detect and discriminate between many subtle differences in hue is not understood. None of the color theories can account for how the visual system detects colors such as brown, metallic gold, or skin tones. Nor do we have a clear understanding of how color coding and feature detection coding are integrated into a meaningful visual perception.

Seeing in Three Dimensions

The image that is projected onto the retina of each eye is a curved two-dimensional image. Yet, we are able to make remarkably accurate depth discriminations. How is this done? There are two sources of information concerning depth: (1) pictorial depth cues, which are greatly influenced by experience and learning, and (2) the physiological depth cues, which are dependent on the organization of the visual system.

Pictorial Depth Cues   As you know from looking at photographs and paintings, the illusion of depth can be produced on a flat surface. Early in the history of human beings, artists did not understand how to use pictorial depth cues to create perspective; because of this, their paintings and drawings appear to be flat. Later, artists learned to use shading, interposition (closer objects block the view of more distant objects), relative height in the field (more distant objects appear higher in the field), relative retinal size, and other pictorial cues that produce the feeling of depth in their paintings. These pictorial depth cues are equally effective when viewed with one eye or two and because of this are sometimes referred to as monocular depth cues.

Physiological Depth   There are three sources of depth information that are based on phy-
Cues   siological mechanisms: (1) accommodation, (2) convergence, and (3) **retinal image disparity**, or **stereopsis**.

You may recall from Chapter 6 that accommodation is the change in the optical qualities of the lens produced by contraction of the ciliary muscle and mediated by the ANS. This occurs when an observer looks at objects that are about 3m or less away from him- or herself. Evidently, pressure receptors in the ligaments that connect ciliary muscle to the lens, provide feedback information concerning the state of tension on the lens. This, in turn, provides some information about depth. However, in the absence of all other depth cues, accommodation provides little usable depth information.

Convergence of the eyes to foveate on close objects is under control of the nasal and lateral rectus muscles. As in accommodation, pressure receptors in the tendons of these muscles provide feedback concerning the position of the eyes, which, in turn, provides some information concerning the distance of the object from the observer. Like accommodation, convergence provides only very rough information concerning depth.

The most accurate and most usable source of depth information comes from retinal image disparity. As noted earlier, the visual fields of the left and right eyes in forward-looking animals are very similar. That is, each eye sees much of what the other eye sees (refer to Figure 7-2). The image produced on each eye is not, however, *exactly* the same. You can demonstrate this for yourself quite easily. Just hold one finger up at arm's length and look at the background wall. Now alternately open and close first your right, then your left, eye. You will note that your finger appears to jump back and forth. The reason for this is that your finger registers in a slightly different position relative to the background in one eye than it does in the other.

Figure 7-16
The horoptor is an imaginary arc of equidistant points that passes through the point of foveation. See text for explanation.

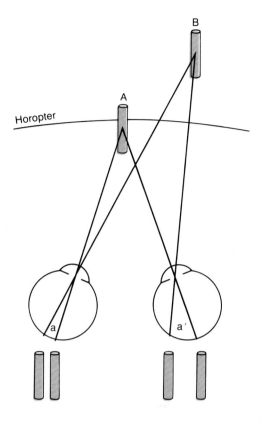

Figure 7-16
The horoptor is an imaginary arc of equidistant points that passes through the point of foveation. See text for explanation.

Look at Figure 7-16. Note that with the eyes focused on point A, the image of point A falls on identical or homologous points on each retina. If an arc were drawn through point A so that all the points on the arc were equidistant from the observer, each point on the arc would also project onto homologous points on each retina. This imaginary arc, called the **horoptor**, is formed each time the eyes foveate on some object. In the example in the previous paragraph, when you foveated on your finger at arm's length, the horoptor is an imaginary arc passing through your finger.

Now look at the retinal projection of point B in Figure 7-16. Note that the image of point B falls on slightly disparate points on each retina, represented by the difference in angles (a) and (a'). This occurs for all objects that are either closer to or farther from the observer than the objects on the horoptor. As we will see, this retinal image disparity is a powerful and accurate source of depth information.

It was noted earlier that many cortical cells respond to input from both retinas. Cells have now been identified that have response characteristics that reflect levels of retinal image disparity. These cells respond with excitation or inhibition to stimuli that project onto non-homologous retinal areas.

Refer to Figure 7-17, which is based on data from several studies reviewed by Poggio and Poggio (1984) and Poggio, Gonzalez, and Krause (1988). The top two figures (*a* & *b*) show the response characteristics of single cells to correlated (C) and uncorrelated (U) dot patterns when viewed binocularly (B) and monocularly by the left eye (L) and by the right eye (R). The correlated stimuli present identical dot matrices independently to each eye, whereas the uncorrelated condition produces retinal image disparity similar to that produced by objects that do not fall on the horoptor. (A similar technique can be used to produce the illusion of depth; see the following discussion of random dot stereograms. Figure 7-17a shows a cell that is activated when the dots do not fall on homologous retinal points (U). Figure 7-17b shows the response characteristics of a cell that is inhibited by nonhomologous retinal stimuli (U).

Figure 7-17c shows the response characteristics of six types of cells that give maximum excitation or inhibition to binocular images. The horizontal axis of each graph shows the amount of disparity expressed in degrees of visual arc. No disparity (zero degrees) occurs when the stimulus is on the horoptor. Positive numbers indicate that the stimulus is farther than the horoptor. Negative numbers indicate that the stimulus is nearer to the observer than the fixation point. The vertical axis shows the neural response rate in pulses per second.

The two graphs on the left represent cells that are excited by stimuli that are closer than the horopter. The cell represented on the top is more finely tuned. The two graphs on the right represent cells that are excited by stimuli beyond the horopter. The graphs in the center represent cells that are excited (top) and inhibited (bottom) by stimuli that fall on the horoptor. The monocular response characteristics of the various types of cells are shown by the points connected by the dotted lines.

Retinal image disparity can be used to produce the illusion of depth on a two-dimensional surface. Julesz (1964) demonstrated this with his now famous random dot stereograms (Figure 7-18). Each half field of the stereogram is made up of identical random dot matrices, with the exception that a pattern of dots in one of the matrices is shifted slightly to the right. Viewed independently, each pattern of dots presents a uniform texture. When fused with a stereoscope, the disparate dots (in this case, a square in the center) are seen "floating" above the background.

The illusory effect can be obtained without a stereoscope, but it does take a little practice. Hold the book about 18 in. to 2 ft away. Place your finger on the page and between the two dot patterns. Then move your finger closer to you and allow your eyes to cross. The two patterns will appear to divide into three. With your eyes still crossed, shift your attention from your finger to the center, fused pattern of dots and you should see the floating square. This perception of depth, in the absence of

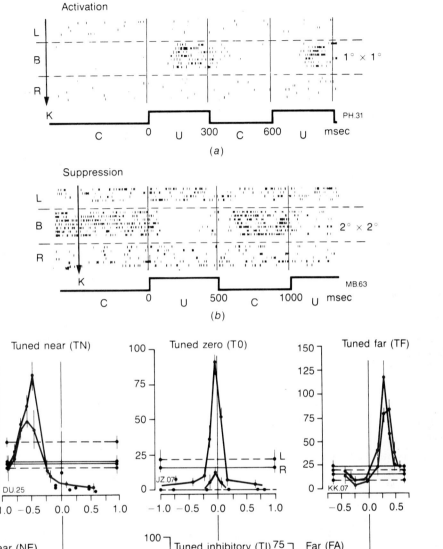

Dynamic Random-Dot Correlograms

Activation

$1° \times 1°$

PH.31

Suppression

$2° \times 2°$

MB.63

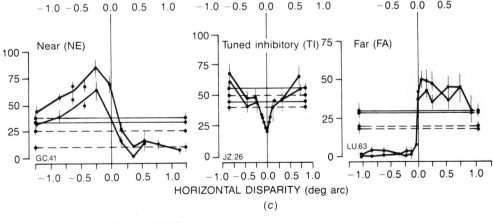

HORIZONTAL DISPARITY (deg arc)

(c)

Figure 7-17
Response characteristics of cortical cells that are responsive to retinal image
disparity. See text for explanation. (From Poggio, Gonzalez, & Krause, 1988.)

One Visual System or Two?

On occasion, people with lesions to the brain suffer some rather surprising visual losses. For example, people have lost color vision while their visual acuity, depth perception, and motion detection capabilities have remained absolutely normal. Others have lost their ability to recognize faces without loosing the ability to recognize other complex stimuli. These kinds of selective losses have caused some researchers to speculate that the visual system may be physically divided into functionally distinct subsystems.

We noted earlier that ganglion fibers from each retina project to the lateral geniculate nucleus of the thalamus, where they are organized into six rather clearly defined layers. This six-layered structure is unique to primates. The four dorsal layers (**parvocellular** layers) are very similar, if not identical, in appearance and function. However, they differ significantly from the two ventral (**magnocellular**) layers. The parvo and magno layers seem to differ in several important ways (Livingstone & Hubel, 1988).

1. Approximately 90% of the cells in the parvocellular layers are strikingly sensitive to differences in wavelength, but none of the cells in the magnocellular layers respond differently to light of varying hues.
2. The retinal fields for cells in the parvo system are consistently smaller than those found for cells in the magno system.
3. The cells in the magnocellular layers respond more rapidly and for a shorter duration than do the cells in the parvo system.
4. Finally, the cells in the magnocellular layer are more sensitive to low-contrast stimuli than are parvo cells.

The segregation of the two visual systems is continued in the cortex. (See Spotlight Figure 7-3.) The fibers of the magno and parvo systems innervate cells in different layers of the visual cortex of the primary (VI) projection area, which, in turn, project to different locations in the secondary visual projection area (V2). The cells in the V1 and V2 cortical areas behave in a manner consistent with the source of their input. Cells that receive information from the magno system have response characteristics that are most selective for stimulus orientation, movement, and retinal image disparity. The parvo system projections are selective for color, stimulus size, boundaries, and sharp changes in contrast.

These data are consistent with the notion of a two-process eye in primates, with the parvo system to provide acuity and color information and the magno system to analyze large feature elements, motion detection, and binocular depth cues. Why should there be separate visual systems?

The magno division appears to be the more primitive visual system and may be homologous to the entire visual system found in all nonprimate mammals. It provides the more basic visual information required to navigate in the environment, identify and locate prey, and avoid predators. The parvo system may be a new invention for providing additional abilities to analyze fine detail, determine borders using color information, and scrutinize the surface properties of objects.

The separation of visual functions within the CNS may help to explain why lesions to the brain may produce very specific deficits to one kind of visual processing while leaving other functions intact. Additionally, the separation of functions may help to explain visual illusions such as that shown in Figure 5-9. The parvo system many attempt to establish borders between surfaces based on color, whereas the magno system provides competing edge information. The result is the illusory "filling-in" effect in the competing areas of the figure.

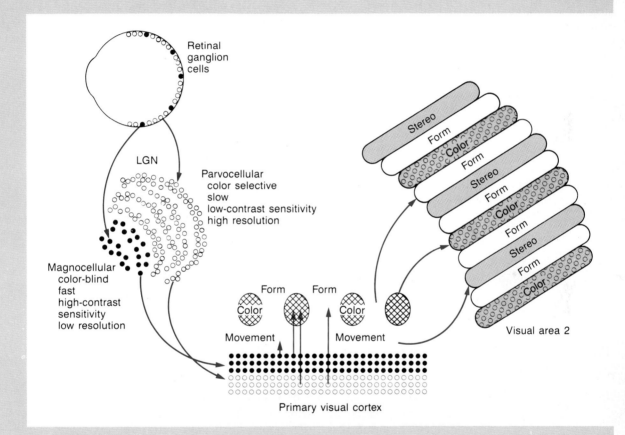

Spotlight Figure 7-3
Diagram of the functional segregation of the primate visual system. (From Livingstone & Hubel, 1988.)

Figure 7-18
A random dot stereogram developed by Bela Julesz. When the two matrices are fused, they produce the illusion of a square floating above the background. Fusing the two circular dot patterns will produce the illusion of a three-dimensional globe.

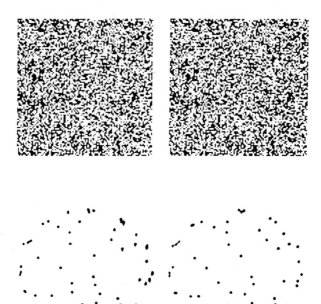

all other depth cues, is thought to be due solely to retinal image disparity. In his marvelous book, *Foundations of Cyclopean Perception* (1971), Julesz has many examples of three-dimensional stereoscopic figures, including some that appear to be solid three-dimensional objects. A few hours spent with this book would be well worth your time.

The Effects of Early Experience on the Development of the Visual System

The degree to which the brains of newborn young have developed at birth differs widely in various species. For example, in some precocial species, the brain is well developed during the gestation period and the young are ready to function independently immediately after birth. In other species such a humans, monkeys, and cats, the brain is quite immature at birth. Much of the development of the brain must take place after birth. In these more altricial species the visual experiences that occur soon after birth can greatly affect the postnatal development of the visual cortex.

Sensory Deprivation   Researchers have studied the effects of various forms of sensory deprivation on the postnatal development of the visual cortex. These studies can be divided into several kinds, depending on the type of early visual experience.

COMPLETE DEPRIVATION

The cells in the visual cortex of newborn cats are similar to the visual cells of adult cats in that they respond to input from both eyes and they show selective response characteristics for edges of specific orientations. One difference, apparently, is that fewer cells in 4- to 6-week-old kittens evidence this specificity for orientation (e.g., Bonds, 1978; Imbert, 1979).

If kittens are deprived of light by being raised in darkness or by having their eyelids sutured together, visual acuity does not develop normally, and the cortical cells either cease to respond to visual stimulation or respond abnormally. The degree of the loss is directly related to the age of the kitten at the onset of the deprivation and the duration of the deprivation. The deprivation must take place in the first 4 to 6 weeks or the effect is greatly reduced. The longer the deprivation period, the greater will be the visual decrement (e.g., Berkley, 1981; Dews & Weisel, 1970; Mitchell, 1981). Long periods of deprivation beginning at birth produce irreversible losses of visual acuity.

MONOCULAR DEPRIVATION

If kittens or monkeys are raised with just one eye occluded, vision in the unoccluded eye develops normally. The occluded eye, however, looses visual acuity; and if the deprivation is begun early enough and is maintained long enough, sight is lost in that eye.

As you might expect, monocularly reared animals have fewer cortical cells that respond to input from both eyes. Hubel and Weisel (1970) demonstrated that for kittens there is a very brief period in the maturation of the visual cortex when binocularity is established. Kittens deprived of input from one eye for only 3 days during the fourth and fifth week evidence a significant reduction in cells that respond to binocular input. Kittens that are 4 months old or older, however, can be monocularly deprived for very long periods with little or no effect on ocular dominance. Other investigators have shown that deprivation of visual input to one eye for periods of only 24 hours can significantly affect the percentage of cells responding to binocular input if the deprivation takes place during the fourth week (Olson & Freeman, 1975).

LABORATORY INDUCED STRABISMUS

Strabismus occurs naturally when the nasal and lateral rectus muscles do not function in concert so that the two eyes do not foveate on the same point. This causes the eyes to have very disparate images. The effects of strabismus can be duplicated in the laboratory either by surgically cutting one of the extrinsic muscles or by having the animal wear goggles with a prism over one eye that optically displaces the image.

When it occurs early in the development of cats and monkeys, strabismus causes a significant reduction in the number of cortical cells

Figure 7-19
a. A monkey wearing goggles that induce strabismus. *b.* The percentage of cells that respond to stimulation from both eyes after various periods of exposure to strabismus. (From Crawford & von Noorden, 1980.)

(a)

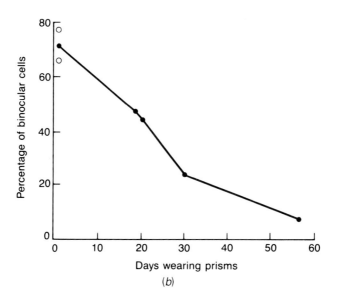

(b)

that respond to input from both eyes. Compared to the normal 80% of cells that respond to binocular input, Hubel and Weisel (1965) found only 20% in cats with surgically induced strabismus. Crawford and von Noorden (1980) found that in normal macaque monkeys 70% of the cortical cells evidenced binocularity. However, infant monkeys that wore strabismus-inducing goggles for 60 days had only 10% of their cortical cells that responded to input from both eyes (see Figure 7-19). As can be seen in Figure 7-19b, the number of cells responding to both eyes decreased as the duration of the strabismus increased.

These data may be related to naturally occurring strabismus in children. Not too infrequently, the eyes of young children are imbalanced and do not move in concert. As a result, the image in each eye is not coherent with that of the other eye. This can be repaired surgically, but not until the child is 3 to 5 years old. Typically, the child tends to favor one eye for foveating and attends less to the information from the other eye. If this goes uncorrected, the child will begin to loose acuity in the nonpreferred eye. Therefore, the prescribed treatment is to blindfold the preferred eye for some part of each day, forcing the child to use the nonpreferred eye. This procedure is continued until the situation can be dealt with surgically.

A similar problem may occur following eye surgery in young children. The patched eye may become weakened, causing **amblyopia**, or "lazy" eye. If uncorrected, children with amlyopia may have severe losses in acuity in the nonpreferred eye. Typically, this can be avoided by the use of a patch over the preferred eye for some period of time each day.

Rearing in Selected Visual Environments

The effects of the stimulus deprivation studies caused some researchers to wonder what might be the effect of exposing the developing visual system to various types of selected stimuli. In these studies, called selective rearing experiments, the animals are raised in total darkness until they are old enough to be worked with in the laboratory.

In the earliest of these studies (Blakemore & Cooper, 1970), cats wore neck ruffs so they could not turn and see their own bodies. They were placed in high-walled tubes for several hours each day. The walls of the tube were high-contrast vertical or horizontal black and white stripes. Behaviorally, the kittens were greatly affected by this treatment. Their head movements were jerky when they observed moving objects, they bumped into objects, and their depth perception seemed to be greatly diminished. Recordings from their visual cortex showed that for kittens exposed to a vertical environment, most of the cells in the primary cortex showed sensitivity to vertically, but not horizontally, oriented stimuli. The opposite was true for kittens raised with the horizontal stripes.

In a similar study kittens wore goggles instead of being placed in the tubes (Hirsch & Spinelli, 1971). The goggles had patterns of either vertical or horizontal high-contrast black and white stripes. The results of this study were even more striking in that few cells responded to stimuli that were more than 5° to 10° out of register with either the horizontal or vertical patterns in the goggles.

Taken together, the results of these deprivation and selective rearing studies tell us much about the developing brain. It is clear from these studies that the organization of the brain is not complete soon after birth and that the final organization is greatly influenced by the visual experiences of the organism. It is also clear that there are **critical periods** in the maturation of visual cortex in which certain visual experiences must occur or the brain is unalterably modified.

**CHAPTER
SUMMARY**

1. In humans, unlike many other vertebrates that have all of the visual information from each eye projected to the opposite side of the brain, half of the fibers from each eye project to the same side of the brain and half to the contralateral side. This adaptation provides a particularly effective form of depth perception.

2. Optic fibers that exit the eye form the *optic nerve*. The fibers meet at the *optic chiasm* and form the *optic tract*. Most of the fibers of the optic tract project to the *lateral geniculate nucleus* of the thalamus, where they synapse onto fibers that project to the *striate* area of the occipital lobe, which is the *primary visual cortex*.

3. Coding of visual information takes place at each level of sensory processing: the retina, the lateral geniculate nucleus, and the visual cortex. *Lateral inhibition* enhances the boundary between light and dark areas. In the human eye lateral inhibition is thought to be produced by the organization and action of the horizontal cells.

4. The receptor and sensory cells of the retina have *receptive fields* that are determined by their location on the retina and the neural circuitry that innervates them. In addition to receptive fields, ganglion cells respond to specific features of the visual stimulus. For this reason they are called *feature detectors*. Ganglion cells may be divided into at least three types: *X, Y,* and *Z cells*. Each type of ganglion cell has different response characteristics to features in the visual field.

5. Coding in the visual cortex is much more complex than coding in the retina and the lateral geniculate nucleus. Three classes of cells—*simple, complex,* and *hypercomplex*— have been identified in the visual cortex. The various types of cells encode lines, edges, and corners having various orientations in the visual field. Complex and hypercomplex cells also encode features that show movement. The visual cortex is organized into columns of cells. All of the cells in a column appear to encode the same type of visual information. Adjacent columns appear to have similar, but not identical, coding functions.

6. Most cells in the visual cortex receive information from both eyes. Many cells evidence a greater response (*ocular dominance*) for information from one eye. There is good evidence that the cortex is organized into alternating columns of cells having ocular dominance for either the left or right retina. Recent studies indicate that sensory cells may be designed to encode sine wave gratings.

7. More complex vertebrates have evolved multiple cortical representations or maps of the retina. Each additional topographical representation of the retina likely indicates a qualitative and/or quantitative increase in the processing of visual information.

8. Cone vision is called *photopic* vision, and it is characterized by good acuity and chromatic vision. Rod vision is called *scotopic* vision. It provides good motion detection and greater sensitivity in lower levels of illumination, and it is achromatic. In darkness, photoreceptors become more sensitive to light. This is called *dark adaptation*.

9. The *Young–Helmholtz trichromatic theory* proposes that there are three kinds of color receptors in the red, blue, and green spectra that encode color vision. The *opponent process theory*, proposed by Hering, attributes color vision to three opponent pairs of receptors: red-green, blue-yellow, and black-white. Psychophysical and physiological data indicate that both theories may be partially correct. Color coding at the level of the retina appears to be based on the three different types of receptor cells. Color coding at the level of the lateral geniculate nucleus and the cortex appears to support the opponent process model. Neither theory adequately explains our ability to discriminate between many subtle differences in hue.

10. Two kinds of information provide cues to depth: *pictorial depth cues* and *physiological depth cues*. *Retinal image disparity*, or *stereopsis*, provides the most accurate source of depth information.

11. Researchers have studied the effects of various environmental experiences on the postnatal development of the visual system. These studies clearly demonstrate that the maturation of the visual system is under the influence of both biological and environmental factors. Visual experience greatly influences the developing visual system. There are *critical periods* in the maturation of the visual cortex in which certain visual experiences must occur or the brain is unalterably modified.

SUGGESTED READINGS

Boynton, R. M. (1988). Color vision. *Annual Review of Psychology, 39,* 69–100.

Farah, M. J. (1988). Is visual imagery really visual? Overlooked evidence from neurology. *Psychological Review, 95,* 307–317.

Hubel, D. H., & Weisel, T. N. (1979). Brain mechanisms of vision. *Scientific American, 241,* 150–162.

Ludel, J. (1978). *Introduction to sensory processes.* San Francisco: Freeman.

Mollon, J. D. (1982). Color vision. *Annual review of Psychology, 33,* 41–46.

KEY TERMS

Accessory optic nucleus   Nucleus of cells that controls saccadic and smooth tracking movement of the eyes.

Ambliopia   Severe loss of visual acuity in one eye.

Complex cells   Cells in the visual cortex that have wider receptive fields than do simple cells and respond most vigorously to edges that move through the field.

Critical period   Period of time during the maturation of the individual when certain events must occur for normal development to take place.

Dark adaptation   The increasing sensitivity to light that occurs with exposure to darkness.

Feature detector   Afferent nuerons that respond to specific classes of stimuli; sensory cells that are most responsive to stimuli having specific characteristics.

Higher-order hypercomplex cells   Cells in the visual cortex that show strong inhibition to features that extend beyond the edge of their receptive fields.

Hypercomplex cells   Cells in the visual cortex that have response characteristics similar to those of complex cells. These cells have the added characteristic of being inhibited by stimuli that extend beyond their receptive field.

Lateral geniculate nucleus   A group of cell bodies in the thalamus. The dorsal part of the nucleus receives input from the ganglion axons forming the optic tract.

Lateral inhibition   Inhibitory effect on the surface of the retina; thought to be under the control of horizontal cells and believed to sharpen boundaries.

Mach bands   Illusion of apparent lines of brightness seen in transitional areas of homogenious bands of varying brightness.

Magnocellular visual system   Visual system that provides movement, depth, and general figure information (*see* Parvocellular visual system).

Microspectrophotometry   Technique for analyzing the spectral absorption characteristics of single receptor cells.

Ocular dominance   Visual cells in the cortex that

respond to input from one eye more than the other eye.

Optic chiasma   Juncture of the right and left optic nerves. In primates and humans, half of the fibers from each eye cross over to the contralateral side of the brain at the optic chiasma.

Parvocellular visual system   Part of the primate visual system that provides color, acuity, and detailed visual information (*see* Magnocellular visual system).

Photopic   The chromatic and detailed vision in the cone portion of the visual field.

Pretectum   Area in the midbrain that functions in the control of eye movement.

Primary color   Colors such as red, green, blue, and yellow that do not appear to be mixtures of other colors.

Receptive field   Portion of the visual field that activates a receptor cell or ganglion cell.

Retinal image disparity   Images not on the horoptor project onto nonhomologous areas of each retina; the basis for stereopsis depth information.

Scotoma   Blind spot in the visual field.

Scotopic   The monochromatic vision in the rod portion of the visual field.

Simple cells   Cells in the visual cortex that respond to edges of light of various orientations.

Spatial frequency   Gratings of alternating light and dark bars have spatial frequencies expressed in terms of the visual angle between the bars.

Stereopsis   Binocular depth cue resulting from retinal image disparity.

Strabismus   Misalignment of the eyes causing each eye to have largely disparate images.

Striate cortex   The primary visual cortex; receives input from the lateral geniculate nucleus and has a topographical representation of the retina.

Superior colliculus   Prominent nucleus on the posterior surface of the mesencephalon. The superior colliculi function in the coordinated movement of the eyes. Together with the inferior colliculi they comprise the corpora quadrigemina.

Suprachiasmic nucleus Group of cells that receive information from the retina; thought to function in physiological mechanisms that are regulated by circadian rhythms.

Ventral lateral geniculate nucleus Group of cell bodies in the lateral geniculate nucleus of the thalamus; a relay point between the ganglion cell axons and subcortical structures associated with vision.

W cells Type of ganglion cell with a very large receptive field; responds to large moving stimuli.

X cells The most prevalent type of ganglion cell; found primarily around the fovea; have narrow fields that are organized in an opponent/surround fashion.

Y cells Type of ganglion cell; respond briefly to moving stimuli; have a smaller receptive field than W cells but a larger one than X cells.

Young–Helmholtz trichromatic theory Theory proposing that color coding is based on the combination of three colors.

Chapter 8

Hearing, Balancing, and the Chemical Senses

PART I   HEARING

Sound and the Auditory Mechanism

Physical Properties of Sound
Anatomy of the Ear
Mechanics of the Inner Ear
Auditory Pathways

Auditory Coding

Coding for Pitch
Coding for Loudness
Coding for Timbre
Localization of Sound

PART II   BALANCING AND THE CHEMICAL SENSES

Balancing

Anatomy of the Vestibular Organ
The Vestibular Pathways
Neural Coding in the Vestibular Mechanism

The Chemical Senses

Olfaction
Adequate Stimulus for Olfaction
Stereochemical Theory of Odor
Gustation
Receptors for Taste
Adequate Stimulus for Gustation
Neural Coding for Taste

Chapter Learning Objectives

After reading this chapter, you should

1. Be familiar with the physical properties of sound that account for frequency, loudness, and timbre.

2. Know the structures that make up the outer, middle, and inner ear and be able to describe their function.

3. Understand the mechanics of the accessory structures of the ear.

4. Be familiar with the auditory pathways beginning from the eighth cranial nerve to the primary auditory cortex.

5. Understand auditory coding for pitch and loudness and be familiar with species differences in audition.

6. Know how timing and loudness cues may be used to localize the source of sound.

7. Know the structures of the labyrinth organ and be able to describe their function.

8. Understand how the ear and the labyrinth sense evolved from the lateral line organ in fishes.

9. Understand how rotational and gravitational cues are encoded by the vestibular mechanism.

10. Be familiar with the anatomy and neural pathways for olfaction.

11. Be familiar with the stereochemical theory of coding for odor.

12. Be able to compare and contrast the taste receptors on the tongue.

13. Know the primary qualities of taste and be able to discuss how each quality of taste is coded.

In Chapter 5 we discussed the different classes of receptors. This classification scheme was based on the type of physical energy that the receptor cells were "designed" to transduce into neuronal activity. Specifically, it was noted that receptor cells could be divided into those receptors that are responsive to specific chemicals in solution, radiant energy, thermal energy, electric charges, and mechanical stimulation. Audition, and the closely related labyrinth sense (the vestibular system), have both evolved from the lateral line organ in fishes. The lateral line organ is a mechanoreceptor organ that detects vibration in water, and in some of the more complex aquatic vertebrates it also functions as an organ of balance.

PART I   HEARING

Sound and the Auditory Mechanism

How did the auditory system evolve from an organ that senses vibrations in water into an organ that interprets vibrations in air as sound? To understand how this transition occurred, we must first look at the physical properties of sound.

Physical Properties of Sound

The speakers on your stereo system produce sound by creating systematic variations in the density of air. Inside each speaker there is a flexible diaphragm that is pushed back and forth electrically. Because the molecules in air are not densely packed together, the outward motion of the diaphragm causes the molecules to become more closely packed together, whereas the inward motion of the diaphragm has the opposite effect (see Figure 8-1).

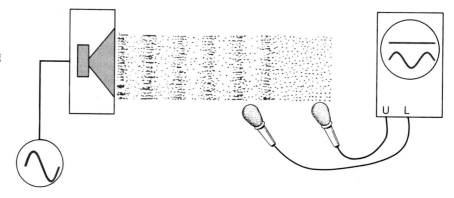

Figure 8-1
The speaker creates sound by mechanically compressing and rarefying molecules of air by pushing a diaphragm out and in. The microphone picks up these variations in air pressure and converts them through the electrical circuitry of the oscilloscope into a sine wave pattern.

Table 8-1. The Sound Pressure Levels (dB) of Several Representative Sounds

Sound Level, dB SPL	Typical Example
180	*Saturn* rocket from 150-ft distance
140	Loud rock concert at stage
110	Jet engine on the tarmack
100	Shouting at close range
80	Busy truck traffic at street level
70	Human voice at conversation level
50	Quiet conversation
30	Softest whispered voice
20	Soft breeze in wooded area
6.5	Pin striking hard floor

The alternating compression and expansion of the molecules of air cause variations in the pressure they may exert. This variation in pressure is referred to as the **sound pressure level (SPL)** of the waves of sound. SPL is a measure of force expressed in dynes per square centimeter of surface area. When your stereo is turned up high, you can actually feel this vibrating force on your body. This is particularly true for deep sounds like those produced by a kettle drum or a tuba.

Sound waves can vary along three dimensions: (1) frequency, (2) amplitude, and (3) complexity. The **frequency** of sound waves is expressed in cycles per second or **hertz (Hz)**. In your stereo, high- and low-frequency sounds are produced by vibrating the diaphragm rapidly or slowly. Perceptually, we refer to the varying frequency of sound as **pitch**. The amplitude of sound is expressed in **decibels (dB)**, which is just another way of expressing sound pressure level. The speaker in your stereo produces high- and low-amplitude sounds by moving the diaphragm greater and lesser distances. The perceptual experience of amplitude is called **loudness**. Table 8-1 shows the decibel levels for a variety of commonly experienced sounds. Complexity of sound waves accounts for their unique signature. It is complexity that produces the "brassy" sound of a trumpet as compared to the "shrill" sound of a whistle or the "warm" sound of a bassoon. The speaker in your stereo produces complexity by superimposing (mixing) several frequencies. The term **timbre** is used to describe complex sounds (see Figure 8-2).

Anatomy of the Ear The ear is divided into three main regions: the outer, the middle, and the inner ear (see Figure 8-3).

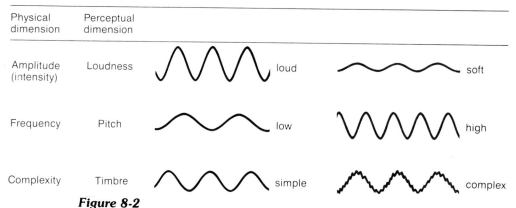

Physical dimension	Perceptual dimension		
Amplitude (intensity)	Loudness	loud	soft
Frequency	Pitch	low	high
Complexity	Timbre	simple	complex

Figure 8-2
The physical dimensions of sound waves and their psychological equivalents.

Figure 8-3
The anatomy of the ear.

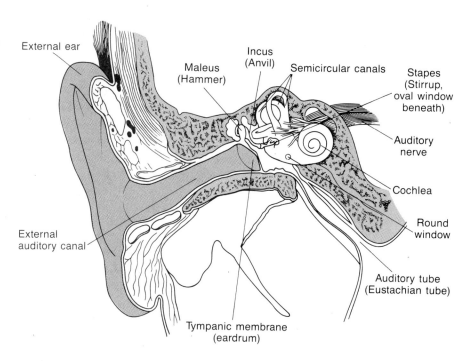

THE OUTER EAR

The most noticeable part of the outer ear is the **pinna** (feather), which is the visible flap of skin and cartilage. In some animals, like dogs and horses, the pinnae are movable and thus aid in locating the source of sound. Some humans exhibit a vestige of this capability, and they can "wiggle" their ears. This movement is very limited, however, and no longer serves a useful purpose. In humans the pinna functions to collect and direct high-frequency sound into the **external auditory meatus**. The external auditory meatus, or auditory canal, is approximately 2.7 cm long. The canal's length and shape cause it to resonate in response to frequencies in the range of 2000 to 4000 Hz (von Békésy, 1960). These frequencies are very important to us because much of the human voice falls within this range.

THE MIDDLE EAR

The **eardrum**, or **tympanic membrane**, is located at the medial terminus of the auditory canal. The eardrum is a cone-shaped membrane. It is the transition point between the outer and middle ears. The evolution of the eardrum and the middle ear was a necessary adaptation for terrestrial vertebrates. This makes good sense if you keep in mind that the lateral line organ of fishes and the inner ear of mammals are filled with fluid.

It is relatively easy to translate the vibrations in the water surrounding a fish to the fluid inside the fish's lateral line organ. Transmitting vibrations from air to a dense medium like fluid is much more difficult and results in a significant (30 dB) loss in energy. Therefore, the middle ear evolved as a mechanism to provide a mechanical advantage at the transition point between the air and the fluid-filled inner ear (see Spotlight 8-1).

The eardrum is very thin, and it moves freely in response to sound waves. It moves inward when the air pressure in the outer ear is greater than that in the middle ear, and the eardrum moves outward when the opposite pressure conditions exist. This motion of the eardrum is transmitted to three small bones in the middle ear, the **ossicles**. In the following order, the **malleus** (hammer), **incus** (anvil), and **stapes** (stirrup) communicate movement of the eardrum to a small oval-shaped membrane on the cochlea. A small muscle, the tensor tympani, is attached to the malleus. This muscle acts reflexively to very high intensity sounds and restricts the movement of the maleus. In this manner prolonged overstimulation of the inner ear is prevented.

The mechanical advantage of this system is derived in two ways. First, relatively large movements of the eardrum result in much smaller movements of the oval window. This provides a mechanical advantage just like placing the fulcrum on a lever closer to the object that is to be lifted. Large movements on the long side of the lever produce smaller, but more forceful, movements on the short side of the lever. Second, the surface area of the tympanic membrane is 14 times greater than the surface of the oval window. Therefore, pressures that are distributed over the larger surface area are concentrated (focused) onto the smaller surface.

The middle ear opens into the oral cavity through the **eustachian tube**. This is necessary to allow the air pressure in the middle ear chamber to equalize with the pressure outside of the body. If the pressure

SPOTLIGHT 8-1

From Jaw bone to Ear

a. The early vertebrate ear served both to detect vibrations in water and to govern balance. Vibrations were transmitted from the surrounding water to the inner ear through the hyomandibular bone.

b. In the terrestrial reptiles the hearing mechanism becomes more intricate. A membrane (the eardrum) transmits variations in air pressure to the air-filled middle ear, which, in turn, communicates with the fluid-filled inner ear. Also, a portion of the fluid-filled inner structure becomes specialized for detecting vibrations while another portion continues to serve as an organ of balance.

c. In the early mammal two bones that once served as the joint of the jaw migrate to join the modified hyomandibular bone (now the stapes). The three ossicles provide the mechanical advantage required to compensate for the energy that is lost in the transition from air to water. Note that the inner ear now has evolved into a spiral structure, whereas the balance organ has developed into three circular canals.

d. The human ear is simply a well-developed mammalian ear (see Spotlight Figure 8-1).

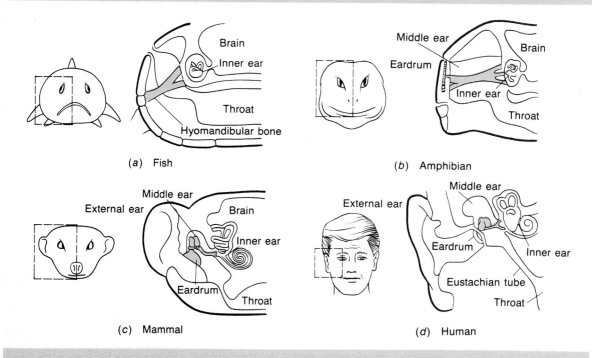

(a) Fish

(b) Amphibian

(c) Mammal

(d) Human

Spotlight Figure 8-1
The evolution of the ear from the lateral line organ of fishes. See text for explanation.

on the sides of the tympanic membrane is not equal, it restricts the free movement of the membrane and appear to be muted. You have likely experienced this when flying in an airplane or in a rapidly moving elevator. Usually the imbalance in pressure is cleared with the characteristic "squeaking" or "popping" sound as air rushes into or out of the middle ear.

An Observation:
A Very Delicate
Balance

An imbalance of air pressure on the eardrum can be a potentially dangerous and painful experience for aviators and skydivers, who can experience very rapid and very large changes in air pressure. If the eustachian tube is blocked, due to swelling of its mucous membrane lining or to fluid buildup, as is common with head colds, then the pressure differential can cause the eardrum to rupture.

Part of the required training for pilots is to "fly" in an altitude chamber. Evacuating the air from the chamber produces conditions similar to flying at various altitudes. In this way the trainees can experience conditions such as anoxia (lack of oxygen) and rapid decompression in the relative safety of the chamber. On my very first "flight" in the chamber, I experienced a blockage in my left ear. As we passed through the equivalent of 10,000 ft above sea level, the pain I experienced in that ear defies description! No other source of pain will grab your attention more quickly or more completely than that.

THE INNER EAR

The inner ear is comprised of the **cochlea** and the balance organs—the utricle, saccule, and semicircular canals, which we discuss later. The cochlea (the term comes from the Greek word for "snail") is a spiral-shaped structure embedded in the bony mass of the skull. The cochlea is about the size of the last segment of your small finger. If the cochlea could be uncoiled, as in Figure 8-4, its total length would be just over an inch (3.38 cm).

Viewed in cross section, the cochlea can be seen to have three fluid-filled chambers. The upper and lower chambers, the **vestibular canal (scala vestibuli)** and the **tympanic canal (scala tympani)**, are connected by a hole (the **helocotrema**) at the apex of the spiral. These two chambers share a common fluid, the **perilymph**. The middle chamber, called the **cochlear canal**, is separated from the lower and upper chambers by the **basilar membrane** and **Reisner's membrane** (Figure 8-5). Reisner's membrane is only one cell layer thick, and its only function is to keep the two types of fluid found in the cochlea separated.

A complex structure, the **organ of Corti**, rests on the basilar (base) membrane, and the structure is partially covered by the **tectorial** (roof)

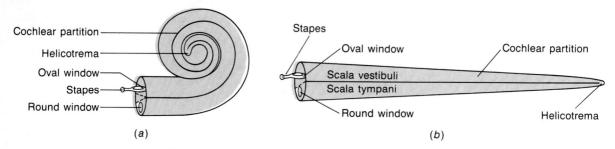

Figure 8-4
The cochlea in the normal spiral condition (*a*) and uncoiled (*b*).

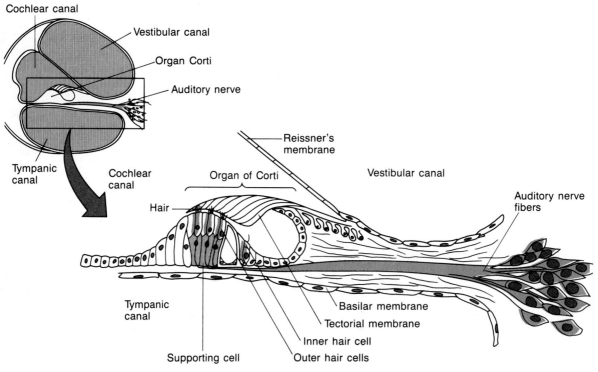

Figure 8-5
Cross section through the cochlea. (See also Color Plate 14.)

membrane. The organ of Corti contains the hair cells that are the receptor cells for audition (see Figure 8-6a). The human cochlea has approximately 12,000 outer and 3,400 inner hair cells. The stereocilia, or hairs of the outer receptor cells, are in physical contact with the tectorial membrane. The hairs of the inner receptor cells come close to the tectorial membrane but do not actually make contact with it. Each hair cell is embedded in a supporting cell (Deitier's cell). The hair cells form synapses with the dendrites of sensory neurons that form the auditory nerve (Figure 8-6a). Figures 8-6b and 8-6c show the damaging effects of

Figure 8-6
a. The organ of Corti.
b. Scanning electron micrograph of the upper surface of the cochlea after the tectorial membrane has been removed. The inner hair cells can be seen above arranged in three curved rows. The outer hair cells are the V-shaped structures at the bottom of the micrograph.
c. Scanning electron micrograph showing damage to the hair cells resulting from exposure to high-intensity sound.

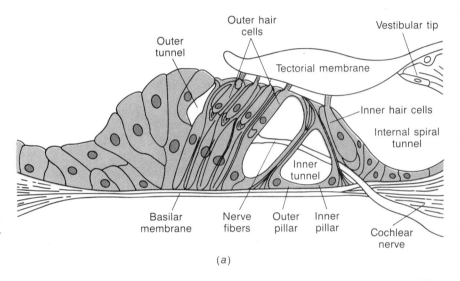

(a)

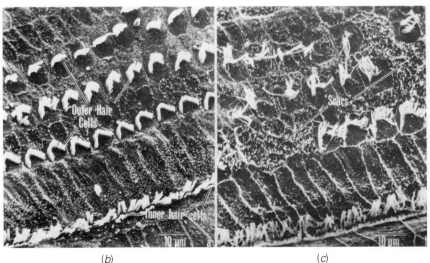

(b)   (c)

long-term exposure to high intensity sound to the hair cells of the organ of Corti. (See Anniko, Thornell, & Wróblewski [1988] for a review of the anatomy of the inner ear.)

Mechanics of the Inner Ear

We noted earlier that vibration of the tympanic membrane was translated by the ossicles to produce smaller, but more forceful, movements of the oval window. We also noted that the cochlea is filled with fluid and that it is encased in bone. The fluid inside the cochlea cannot be compressed; therefore, any movement of the oval window must produce an opposite movement at the point of the **round window** (refer to Figure 8-4). As the oval window is pushed in by the stapes, the pressure generated by that movement causes the round window to be pushed outward.

It might be helpful here to think of a short segment of pipe filled with water and having a flexible membrane covering each end. If you push in on the membrane at one end of the pipe, the membrane at the other end will bulge outward. Release the pressure, and both membranes will return to their original position. Therefore, if a 2000-Hz sine wave pattern enters the ear, the oval and round windows would oscillate back and forth, in opposite directions, at a frequency of 2000 Hz.

The alternating movements of the oval and round windows cause movement of the fluid inside the cochlea. This, in turn, produces movement of the basilar and tectorial membranes. Here is the key to how the adequate stimulus for audition is produced. Try this. Place your hands together so that the tips of the fingers of each hand are aligned. Now push back the tips of the fingers of your left hand with the fingertips of your right hand. Reverse this process several times and note the shearing action that is taking place at the palms of your hands.

Now visualize movement of the basilar and tectorial membranes. Deflection of the basilar membrane produces a shearing effect between the basilar and tectorial membranes. This sets into motion a series of complex actions. Because the body of the outer hair cells is embedded in the basilar membrane and the hairs of the cells are in contact with the tectorial membrane, the shearing motion produces a deflection of the hairs. Adjacent hairs are attached to each other at the tips. Therefore, movement of the longest stereocilia produces shearing forces on the adjacent hairs. These forces are translated to the **cuticular plate**, the point where the stereocilia are attached to the soma of the receptor cell. The result of all of this touching and shearing is the production of a receptor potential in the hair cell.

The inner hair cells appear to be activated in a slightly different manner. The inner hair cells have one third fewer cilia than do the outer hair cells, and their cilia do not come into direct contact with the tectorial membrane. It is thought that the cilia of the inner hair cells are stimulated by movement of the fluid that fills the space between the two membranes. Apparently, this is a less efficient mechanism; consequently, the inner hair cells are only stimulated by the larger movements of the basilar membrane. This notion is supported by the fact that the inner hair cells only respond to SPLs of 50 to 60 dB or higher (Scharf, 1975).

The subcellular events that produce the receptor potential are not well understood (Hudspeth, 1983). It is known that the endolymph surrounding the hair cells is rich in K^+ but low in Na^+. Also, there is a "plus" 80 mV differential between the ion concentrations in endolymph relative to that in the perilymph. This charge, in addition to the charge produced by the resting potential of the hair cells, provides a combined potential of "minus" 150 mV between the cilia and the endolymph.

The mechanical stimulation of the cilia appears to open channels that are specific for K^+. This is supported by the fact that removing K^+ from the endolymph effectively eliminates the receptor potential (Valli, Zucca, & Casella, 1979). The flow of K^+ ions into the hair cells is the apparent source of the depolarizing receptor potential. Depolarizing the receptor cells causes the release of transmitter substances across the synapse to sensory cells that form the auditory nerve. Interestingly, both the inner and outer hair cells also receive efferents from neurons in the medulla. These efferents (see Figure 8-7) secrete acetylcholine and appear to have an inhibitory effect on the hair cells. The function of these efferent fibers in auditory processing remains a mystery.

Figure 8-7
The synaptic connections of (*a*) the inner hair cells and (*b*) outer hair cells. Note that both types of auditory receptor cells have afferent and efferent connections. The efferent connections originate in the medulla and are thought to be inhibitory. (Adapted from Spoendlin, 1973.)

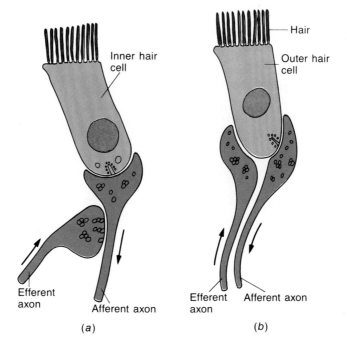

Inner hair cell

Hair

Outer hair cell

Efferent axon

Afferent axon

Efferent axon

Afferent axon

(*a*)

(*b*)

Auditory Pathways   The auditory pathways from the ear to the brain are very complex, and frankly, a bit confusing. Recall that as the brain evolved over time, newer processing centers have been added to existing brain structures. In the less complex vertebrates, audition is a hindbrain function. Therefore, the addition of midbrain and forebrain auditory processing centers has greatly complicated the anatomy of the auditory system. You will find it helpful to refer to Figure 8-8 as we trace the various fiber tracts and nuclei that are associated with audition.

The receptor cells in the organ of Corti innervate with the dendrites of sensory neurons, which in turn form the cochlear nerve. These fibers are joined by axons originating in the balance organ. They form the **statoacoustic**, or **eighth cranial, nerve**, which attaches at the level of the medulla. The fibers of the statoacoustic nerve synapse within the medulla in the **ventral cochlear** and **dorsal cochlear nuclei**. The majority of the fibers exiting these nuclei cross over (decussate) to the **superior olivary nucleus** on the contralateral side of the medulla. The remainder of the axons terminate in the ipsilateral olivary nucleus.

From the superior olives on each side of the medulla, the fibers project dorsally toward the midbrain and join other axons that form the **lateral lemniscal track**. Most of these axons terminate at the midbrain level in the **inferior colliculi**. You may recall that the superior colliculi rest adjacent to the inferior colliculi and that they function in vision. (Together the superior and inferior colliculi form the corpora quadrigemina.) It is thought that coordination between the two senses occurs at this level of the midbrain.

Figure 8-8
Schematic representation of the anatomy of the auditory pathways. (Adapted from Norman & Lindsay 1977.)

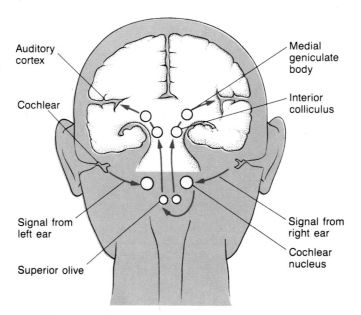

Auditory fibers exiting the inferior colliculi project to the medial geniculate nucleus of the thalamus, where they synapse with the next level of sensory neurons. From the medial geniculate nucleus the auditory fibers project to the primary auditory cortex, which forms the ventral portion of the Sylvian fissure.

Not shown in Figure 8-8 are the efferent fibers that project from the auditory cortex through several synaptic levels all the way back to the hair cells in the cochlea. As noted earlier, these centrifugal fibers have an inhibitory effect on the hair cells (Desmedt, 1962).

Auditory Coding

Unlike the visual system, which acts like a *synthesizing* organ, the auditory system appears to behave more like an *analytical* organ. In order to encode for color, the eye "mixes" two or three wavelengths of light, and we perceive a color that is different from the original hues. The auditory system does not work the same way. If two pure tones are presented to the ear, we do not detect the sum of the tones or some intermediate tone. Rather, both tones are detected and may be analyzed individually. It is this characteristic of the auditory system that provides the capacity to interpret complex sounds.

Coding for Pitch   The human ear is sensitive to sound in a range of frequencies from approximately 20 to 20000 Hz. The sensitivity to different frequencies varies considerably across this range, with the greatest levels of sensitivity being in the range between 1000 and 8000 Hz. This makes sense for humans, because the most critical frequencies for the human voice are found in this range. The specific range of frequencies that are audible to a given species is determined primarily by the acoustical and mechanical characteristics of the auditory accessory structures (pinna, external auditory meatus, eardrum, ossicles, and cochlea).

It is commonly held that other species—dogs and cats, for example—have more sensitive hearing than do humans. As was noted in Chapter 5, this is not necessarily true. Psychophysical studies have shown that for those frequencies of sound to which humans are most sensitive, the sensitivity of the human ear is quite remarkable. What is true concerning species-specific sensitivity to sound is that various species evidence remarkable differences concerning what frequencies they are most able to detect (see Spotlight 8-2).

Theories concerning the coding for pitch may be divided into two types: timing and place theories. Timing theories propose that pitch is encoded by the rate or pattern of neuronal activity. Place theories suggest that pitch is determined not by the frequency of neuronal response but by which neurons are responding. We will see that, as was true for the two

Auditory Offense of the Bat and the Countermeasures of the Moth

Insectivorous bats have the remarkable ability to fly through complex terrain, and to detect and capture insects in flight while in total darkness. The bats accomplish this remarkable feat by emitting high-frequency sounds. The sounds are emitted in pulses, which are reflected off objects in the environment. The reflected sound is detected by the bat much like a submarine emits and detects reflected sonar signals for underwater navigation. Actually, bats emit two kinds of auditory signals: (1) a lower frequency, longer duration signal that helps them detect and avoid larger solid objects and (2) a very high frequency, very short duration signal that they use to capture insects in flight (Novick, 1963).

Spotlight Figure 8-2a shows the intricate maneuver of a bat as it catches a moth in midair. The drawing was made from multiple-exposure, strobe-lighted photographs. The numbers in the drawing indicate the simultaneous positions of the moth and bat. Point 6 represents the position the moth would have been in if it had not been captured by the bat.

It is interesting to note that some species of moth have evolved a passive bat detection system as a countermeasure to escape hunting bats. A tympanum has evolved on the thorax of these moths which is "tuned" to the 70000- to 100000-Hz sound emitted by the bat just prior to the terminal phase of its attack. When the distinctive frequency and pulse pattern of the terminal phase is detected, the moth takes an evasive dive (see Spotlight Figure 8-2b), causing the bat to miss (Roeder & Treat, 1962).

Spotlight Figure 8-2
a. The insectivorous bat is able to detect and capture insects in flight using an active sonar system. (Adapted from Webster, 1963.) b. The evasive maneuver of a moth that has a tympanum tuned to the frequency emitted by the bat. (Adapted from Roeder & Treat, 1962.)

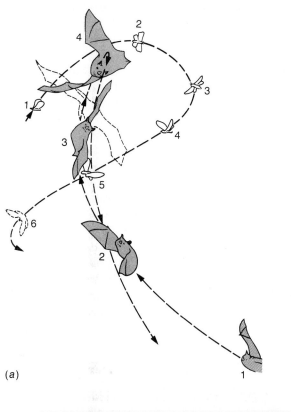

(a)

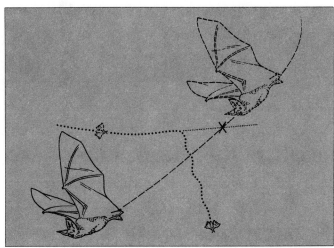

(b)

theories proposed for the encoding of color, neither the place nor the timing theories can adequately explain the encoding for pitch. Rather, some combination of the two theories appears to be necessary to explain the data.

CODING FOR PITCH AT THE LEVEL OF THE COCHLEA

There is a tonotopic distribution along the basilar membrane. The highest frequencies are located at the base of the cochlea, and the lowest frequencies are found at the apex. If an animal is exposed to high-intensity sound for a long time, measureable damage occurs on the organ of Corti. Figure 8-9 shows the results of such an experiment done on pigs (Smith, 1947). These data show that as the frequency of sound increases, the area of the ensuing lesion occurs closer to the base of the cochlea.

This finding is consistent with Békésy's model of the cochlea, which predicts that sounds of different frequencies cause wave patterns to form at different locations along the basilar membrane (Békésy, 1960). Békésy's **place theory** of frequency coding is based on the physical characteristics of the cochlea. The theory predicts that high frequencies will produce the maximum deflection of the basilar membrane at the base of the cochlea, where the membrane is most narrow. Low-frequency sounds produce the maximum deflection at the apex of the cochlea, where the basilar membrane is widest. (This may seem backwards to

Figure 8-9
Lesions to the organ of Corti in the pig produced by high-intensity sounds of different frequencies. The horizontal axis shows the distance from the base of the cochlea. The whitened area indicates the location of the lesion. (From Smith, 1947.)

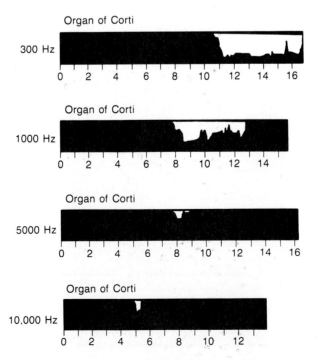

Figure 8-10
The basilar membrane is widest at the apex of the cochlea and becomes progressively more narrow as it approaches the base of the cochlea.

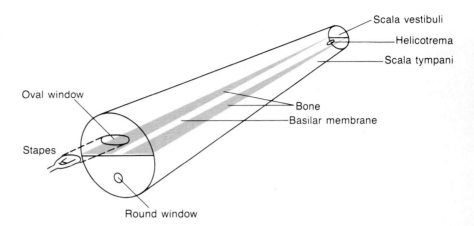

you, but a close examination of the organ of Corti shows that the basilar membrane is widest at the apex and narrowest at the oval window; see Figure 8-10.)

The displacement of the basilar membrane that is produced by any given frequency is quite large. Nevertheless, people are able to make very fine frequency discriminations, in the range of just 2 or 3 Hz. This presents some serious problems for the place theory, which cannot account for such fine frequency discriminations based on very broad wave forms on the basilar membrane. Also, although the place theory seems to hold fairly well for frequencies above 5000 Hz, it does not account very well for lower frequencies. At lower frequencies encoding of pitch may be accomplished by another strategy. The **volley theory** argues that pitch is related to the sequence and rate of receptor activity, and it suggests that the rate and the order of receptor activity encode frequency. The theory proposes that a single neuron can represent a range of frequencies by changing its rate of activity. That is, the cell may respond 20 times per second to a 20-Hz sound and 200 times per second to a 200-Hz sound. Further, several cells responding in volleys may be responsible for coding a given frequency. The volley and place theories are not necessarily mutually exclusive. There is some evidence that below 1000 Hz, pitch may be encoded by the timing or rate at which cells respond and that some combination of timing and place may account for the coding of frequencies between 1000 and 5000 Hz (Attneave & Olson, 1971; Rose et al., 1967).

CODING FOR PITCH BEYOND THE COCHLEA

Single-cell recordings made in the cochlear nerve and at higher levels in the auditory system show that auditory cells have rather precise frequency tuning. Figure 8-11 shows the typical V-shaped frequency response characteristics of cells in several structures in the auditory

298

Figure 8-11
Frequency sensitivity of
auditory cells from several
structures in the auditory
system. (Adapted from
Katsuki, 1961.)

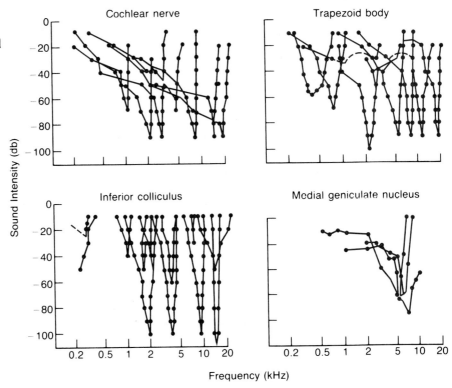

pathways. These data show rather clearly that although these cells tend
to respond to a wider range of frequencies at high intensity levels, their
selectivity becomes increasingly narrow as the decibel level decreases
(Katsuki, 1961).

Recordings made from the various nuclei along the auditory pathway and at the level of the auditory cortex all show a tonotopic distribution similar to that found at the level of the basilar membrane. That is, a
tonotopic map spanning the full range of audible frequencies can be
identified at the level of each auditory nucleus and at the level of the
primary auditory cortex as well.

Coding for Loudness   The human ear possesses an enormous range of sensitivity for the amplitude of sound. It has been estimated that the human ear can detect sound
at levels that are only 100 trillionth of the intensity needed for sound to
be harmful to the cochlea (Uttal, 1973)! If you are like me, numbers like
100 trillion are more than a little mind boggling. To get a "feel" for the
sensitivity of the ear, think of this: If you were to be placed in an anechoic
chamber (a sound isolation chamber that has sound-absorbing materials
on the walls, ceiling, and floor) and you were totally isolated from
external sound, you would still detect sounds. What sounds? The sounds

of your own bodily processes—your respiration, the blood coursing through the arteries and veins in your head, and perhaps the churning of food in your stomach and intestines.

It has been estimated that detectable sounds would be produced by vibrating the tympanic membrane a distance less than the diameter of a hydrogen atom or by moving the tip of the hair cells less than 100 picometers (trillionths of a meter)! (See Hudspeth, 1983, for a review.) This sounds like the kind of stuff that belongs in Ripley's Believe It or Not.

At the base of the cochlea, where pitch is encoded by which hair cells are activated, intensity appears to be encoded by the frequency or rate of cell activity. Higher-intensity sounds produce a more rapid rate of response in the cochlear nerve than do lower-intensity sounds. At the apex of the cochlea, where pitch is determined by the timing of cell activity, a different coding strategy is needed for loudness. Most researchers believe that in the apex loudness is encoded by the number of hair cells that are activated at any given point in time.

At the level of the cortex loudness appears to be spatially coded in a fashion similar to the tonotopic distribution for pitch. Recording of evoked potentials on the surface of the cortex produces a pitch-by-amplitude matrix (Figure 8-12). The matrix has the frequency characteristic distributed in one direction and increasing and decreasing loudness mapped in the other dimension.

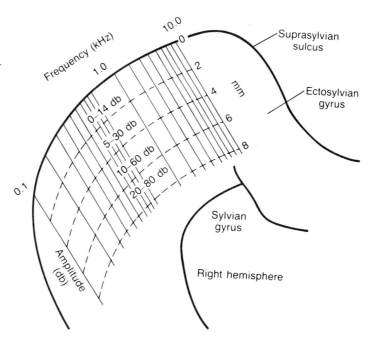

Figure 8-12
Coding of intensity and frequency of auditory stimuli on the auditory cortex of the dog. Increasing frequency, expressed in kHz, is distributed in an arc from left to right. Increasing intensity, expressed in dB, is plotted from top to bottom. (Adapted from Tunturi, 1952.)

Coding for Timbre   Most of the sounds that we encounter in the natural environment are not pure tones of only one frequency. The human voice, the bark of a dog, and an orchestra are all complex sounds that may be broken down into many component frequencies. When a great tenor like Luciano Pavarotti or Placido Domingo hits a C note, it is not the same as a pure 262-Hz C tone produced by a frequency generator. Nor do the two C notes produced by Pavarotti and Domingo sound exactly the same. Rather, each of their voices has a unique timbre that is easily distinguished by opera lovers like myself.

Complex tones have a **fundamental**, or **carrier**, **frequency** and many **overtones**. The overtones produce the distinctive timbre of the complex sounds. The basilar membrane responds to a complex sound wave by producing a complex and dynamic wave form along the basilar membrane. The pattern of the wave form produces the complex activity of the cochlear nerve. Unfortunately, little is known about the specifics of this process.

Localization of Sound   The source of sound may be determined with one or two ears. Monaurally, we are able to detect the source of a sound with surprising accuracy by moving our head and using the ear like a rotating antenna. Some species, as I mentioned earlier in this chapter, are able to move the pinna of the ear and in so doing facilitate sound localization.

We are able to detect the source of sound binaurally using two types of cues: (1) timing cues and (2) intensity cues. Look at Figure 8-13a. Note that a sound coming from one side of the head will first reach the ear that is closest to the origin of the sound. This timing cue is an effective mechanism for the localization of sound, particularly for high-frequency sounds of short duration. If the sound is of a lower frequency, different parts of the wave form may enter the two ears at any point in time. This phase difference may also serve as a cue to localize the source of the sound (see Figure 8-13b). Finally, the head will effectively block higher-frequency sounds from the distant ear. This produces a binaural intensity differential that aids in determining the source of the sound.

There are several places along the auditory pathways leading to the brain where comparisons may be made between the information coming from each ear. Thus, single cells in various auditory nuclei can receive information from both ears. Using single-cell recording techniques, several investigators have shown that many auditory cells are sensitive to binaural intensity differences (e.g., Ivarson, de Ribauprene, & de Ribauprene, 1988). Figure 8-14 shows the response characteristics of cells in the right inferior colliculi to sounds originating from different axes. These data show two types of cells. The cell in the left graph is most responsive when input from both ears is balanced. The cells in the middle and right graphs respond maximally to input from the contralateral ear (Leiman & Hafter, 1972).

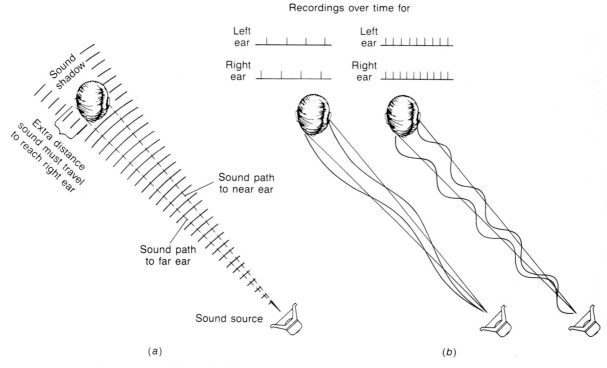

Figure 8-13
Timing and intensity cues for the binaural localization of sound. *a.* The head casts a "shadow," which decreases the intensity of the sound on the far side. *b.* A different part of the wave form enters each ear at any point in time. This phase difference is most noticeable with low-frequency tones.

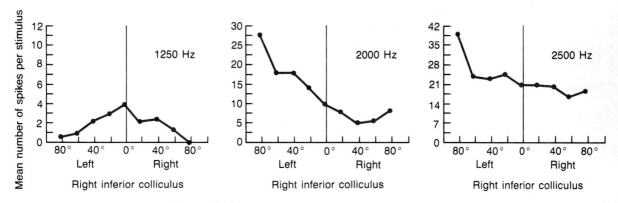

Figure 8-14
The mean number of neural impulses from cells in response to sound originating from various axes. The speakers were positioned at angles ranging from 80° left and right of center at 20° intervals. The frequency of the sound is shown within each graph. (From Leiman & Hafter, 1972.)

PART II BALANCING AND THE CHEMICAL SENSES

Balancing

I noted earlier that the organ of balance and the cochlea both evolved from the lateral line organ in fishes. Physically, they are both embedded in the same bony labyrinth within the skull. For this reason, they are often referred to as the labyrinth sense. The balance organ shares the same endolymph and perilymph fluids that are found within the cochlea. Additionally, as is true in the cochlea, the balance organ depends on the mechanical displacement of hair cells as its adequate stimulus.

Anatomy of the Vestibular Organ

The part of the labyrinth sense concerned with balance is called the **vestibular system**. The vestibular system is composed of two component parts: (1) the **vestibular sacs**, which are two ball-shaped structures called the **utricle** and **saccule**, and (2) the **semicircular canals**.

SEMICIRCULAR CANALS

There are three semicircular canals in each labyrinth organ. Each of the canals is oriented along one of the three cardinal planes of the head— sagittal, coronal, and horizontal. This is an important feature, as it allows each canal to be particularly sensitive to movement in only one of the cardinal planes of the head. Each canal has an enlarged area called the **ampulla**. The ampulla contains a complex structure called the **crista**, which is the part of the semicircular canal that contains the receptor cells. The receptor cells are very similar in appearance to the hair cells found in the cochlea. The hairs of the receptor cells on the crista, however, are embedded in a gelatinous mass called the **cupula** (see Figure 8-15).

Figure 8-15
Two views showing that the three semicircular canals are oriented approximately 90° apart.

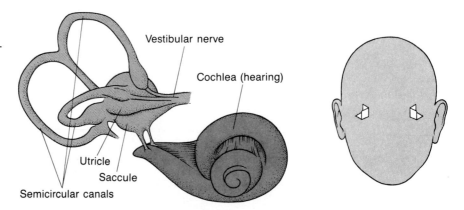

Vestibular nerve

Cochlea (hearing)

Utricle

Saccule

Semicircular canals

To understand how the semicircular canals operate, it might be helpful to think of a bicycle tube filled with water. If you turn the tube around its axle, there is a tendency for the water to resist the movement. Momentarily, the tube will tend to move around the water. If the movement is sustained, the water in the tube will eventually catch up and move at the same rate as the tube. Now imagine the water-filled tube suspended by a cord that has been tied to the rim. If the tube is spun from the cord like a top, the tube and the water will both move at the same rate.

The semicircular canals operate on this very same principle. When the head is turned along one of the cardinal axes, the fluid in the semicircular canal that is aligned with that axis will tend to resist the movement, and the canal will, quite literally, move around the fluid. The fluid in the other two canals, however, is unable to resist the motion.

Now let's take this one step further. Movement of the endolymph within the semicircular canal bends the cupula in the direction opposite to that of the rotation of the head. (Actually, the cupula, which is attached to the crista and therefore to the wall of the canal, is pushed through the endolymph.) Because the cupula is gelatinous, the flow of the endolymph causes it to bend. When the endolymph catches up with the movement of the canal, the cupula returns to its original upright position. Bending the cupula in either direction causes the hairs of the receptor cells to be bent, and this is the adequate stimulus for the receptor cells (Figure 8-16).

THE VESTIBULAR SACS

The utricle and saccule have a very different mechanism. Both sacs are ball-shaped, and they have a flat internal structure that holds the

Figure 8-16
Movement of the semi-circular canal in one direction causes the cupula to be bent in the opposite direction.

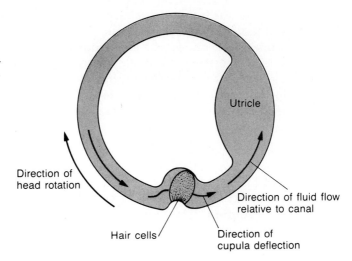

Figure 8-17
The organization of the receptive tissue in the utricle and saccule.

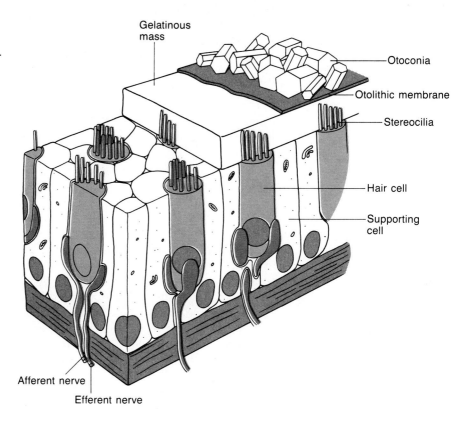

Figure 8-17
The organization of the receptive tissue in the utricle and saccule.

receptor cells in place. The hairs of the receptor cells in the utricle point toward the top of the head. The hairs within the saccule point laterally toward the side of the head.

As was true in the semicircular canals, the hairs of the receptor cells in the vestibular sacs are embedded in a gelatinous mass. Unlike the semicircular canals, the gelatinous mass is flat, and there is a layer of calcium carbonate crystals (otoconia) embedded in its surface (see Figure 8-17). The otoconia are very dense relative to the other structures in the vestibular sacs, and movement of the head causes them to shift their position. This, in turn, produces a shearing action in the gelatinous mass that causes the hair cells to be deflected.

The Vestibular Pathways

Fibers that exit the vestibular mechanism join fibers from the cochlea and form the eighth cranial nerve. The afferent neurons that exit the vestibular mechanism are bipolar, and their cell bodies form the **vestibular ganglion**. The vestibular fibers enter the CNS at the level of the medulla, where most of the afferents synapse in the vestibular nuclei. The remainder of the vestibular fibers project directly to the cerebellum.

The pathways within the CNS are somewhat confusing. Fibers

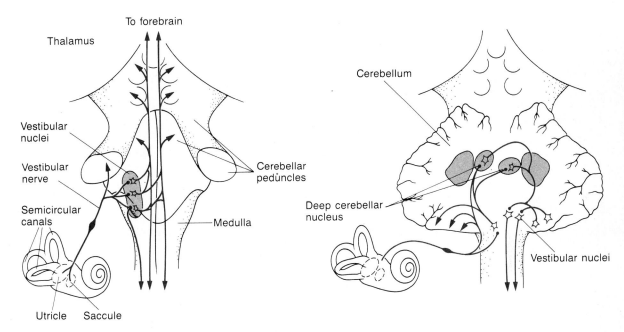

Figure 8-18
The neural pathways of the vestibular mechanism.

originating in the vestibular nuclei project to the cerebellum, the spinal cord, nuclei in the medulla and the pons, and the temporal cortex (see Figure 8-18). The projection to the cerebellum and the spinal cord functions in the coordination of balance, shifts in body position, and body movement. (I say more about this in Chapter 9.) The projections to the medulla- and pontine-level nuclei are particularly important in that they integrate head movement with eye movement. The vestibular mechanism has direct influence over the extrinsic muscles of the eye. In this manner, the vestibular mechanism feeds information to the eyes to compensate for the movement of the head. The projections to the temporal cortex are not well understood. It is thought that they function to provide conscious awareness of dizziness and imbalance.

As was true for the cochlea, there are efferent fibers that project from the CNS to the receptor cells of the vestibular mechanism. These fibers originate in the cerebellum and in the medulla and have an inhibitory effect on the receptor cells.

Neural Coding in the Vestibular Mechanism

Recall that the adequate stimulus for the receptor cells in the vestibular mechanism is the deflection of the hairs. In the semicircular canals this was accomplished by the deflection of the cupula. In the saccule and utricle the hair cells are deflected by the shearing actions produced by the weight of the otoconia.

Motion Sickness

Most of us have experienced the very uncomfortable feeling associated with motion sickness—dizziness, sweating, and queasiness. In severe cases, motion sickness can be very disabling. Motion sickness most often occurs under two conditions. The first condition is when there is inconsistent information between motor action and vestibular stimulation. This occurs when your body is passively moved without motor input, as happens when you ride in a car or airplane. Under these conditions your vestibular mechanism reports that you are moving, but there is no motor action to correlate with the motion. The second and most powerful source of motion sickness is when the information concerning movement from the vestibular system is inconsistent with the movement information coming from the eyes.

Consider the following experiment. You are placed in a barber chair and blindfolded. The chair is rotated clockwise until you are turning at a steady rate, several revolutions per minute. At first the semicircular canal that is oriented in the horizontal plane will report that movement. As the endolymph inside that canal

"catches up," the hairs of the receptor cells will return to their upright position, and the vestibular nerve fibers will return to their base rate of activity. Now, you are still rotating at a steady rate; however, the vestibular mechanism reports that you are not moving.

Let's take this one step further. Now the rotation of the barber chair is slowed and stopped. As the chair slows, the fluid inside the horizontal canal will tend to stay in motion. This will deflect the cupula, causing the vestibular mechanism to report rotation in the counterclockwise direction! If the blindfold is removed at this point, your eyes will accuarately report no motion while your vestibular mechanism is erroneously reporting motion in the counterclockwise direction. This causes rapid nystagmoid (side-to-side) movements of the eyes as the visual system attempts to compensate for the motion cues coming from the vestibular mechanism. Additionally, the inconsistent motion cues can produce severe symptoms of motion sickness (Spotlight Figure 8-3).

To understand neural coding in the vestibular system, it will be helpful to remember that most sensory cells have a normal background level of spike activity. Slowing the rate of the background spike activity encodes information, just as does increasing the frequency of activity. The hairs of the receptor cells are aligned in order of increasing length in one direction. Movement of the hairs from the short to the long side of the cell produces excitation. This causes the spike output of the fibers in the vestibular nerve to increase over their background level. Movement in the opposite direction produces inhibition, decreasing the frequency of spikes below the background rate (Figure 8-19).

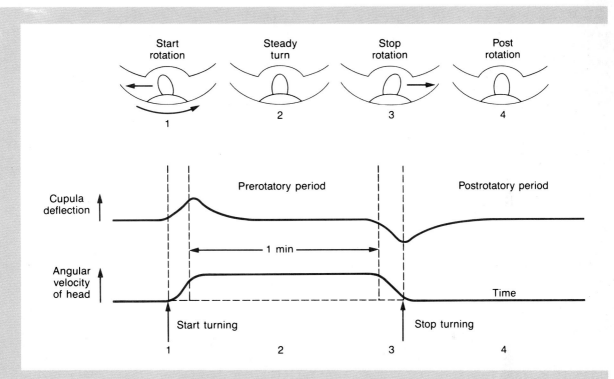

Spotlight Figure 8-3
Clockwise movement is reported at first. After several revolutions at a constant rate, the vestibular mechanism stops reporting the rotation. When the chair is slowed to a stop, the vestibular mechanism reports motion in the counterclockwise direction. Opening the eyes causes nystagmoid movement of the eyes and the symptoms of motion sickness.

The Chemical Senses

Sensitivity to chemicals, particularly the organic chemicals, is an essential characteristic for all animals. All animals must be able to detect plant and/or animal compounds if they are to survive. As pointed out in Chapter 5, even single-celled organisms are able to detect and react to specific chemicals that are in solution. The amoeba, for example, is able to locate a distant food source by detecting just a few molecules from the food source that have entered into solution. Most free-swimming protozoans also can detect toxic substances, in their environment, and they can take action to avoid them.

Figure 8-19
The background rate of spike activity in the vestibular nerve is increased or decreased by deflection of the hairs in the receptor cells. Given a base rate (*a*), moving the hairs in one direction (*b*) produces excitation; movement in the opposite direction (*c*) produces inhibition.

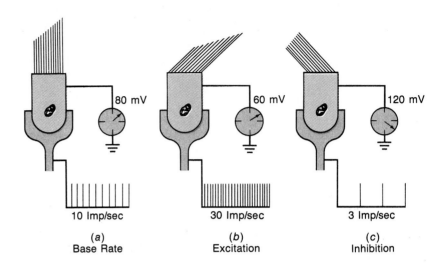

Typically, when we refer to the chemical senses in vertebrates, we tend to think of taste (gustation) and smell (olfaction). These are, most certainly, chemical senses. However, they are not the only chemically sensitive processes that we possess. There are many receptors inside of our bodies that gather information from the digestive system, the blood, the lymphatic fluids, and other aspects of the internal environment. It is our olfactory and gustatory senses, however, that provide us with chemical knowledge concerning our environment. I will concentrate on these two chemical senses in the remainder of this chapter.

An Observation:

Tasting with Your Feet?

For many species of invertebrates we may have some difficulty defining the nature of their chemical senses. Think of the following examples for a moment. Many insects, like the blowfly, have chemical receptors on the tongue. We would have little difficulty accepting these sensory cells as "taste" receptors. The blowfly also has chemical receptors in the last segment of their front limbs (their feet?) that are sensitive to the same chemical substances. The blowfly uses these receptors to locate food sources. Are these "taste" receptors as well? Does the blowfly "taste" with its "feet"?

You doubtlessly know that many insects "feel" with the antennae on their heads. Just think of how ants or bees use their antennae to investigate their environment. Other insects, like the saturniid moths, use their antennae for a very different purpose. The males of this species use their antennae to detect a specific chemical substance that is emitted by the female. Using this mechanism, the male is able, under ideal conditions, to locate a receptive female at distances of a mile or more (Schneider, 1969)! Is this an example of taste or smell or something else altogether?

It is interesting to note that the saturniids are found in the adult form for only a very brief period of time. They spend most of their life cycle in the immature form. As caterpillars, they feed on the leaves of trees. As adults, their mouth parts are incompletely formed, and they are unable to feed. Their sole purpose in the few days of their life as adults is to find a mate and reproduce. In the Northeast, where the saturiids are pests on fruit trees, the males are lured by the thousands into traps that have been baited with the substance emitted by the female.

Olfaction   The olfactory receptor cells are located in a small patch of skin, the **olfactory epithelium**, which is located at the top of the nasal cavity (see Figure 8-20). Turbinate bones inside the nasal cavity act to direct and mix air that is drawn through the nose and into the lungs. Only a small portion of the airborne molecules come into contact with the receptor cells in the olfactory epithelium.

The receptor cells have a long narrow process that terminates in several cilia. The cilia are completely surrounded by a mucus layer, and presumably, molecules must penetrate the mucus layer before coming into contact with the cilia. Axons from the receptor cells pass through a perforated bony structure, the **cribriform plate**, and terminate in the **olfactory bulb**. Within the olfactory bulb the receptor cells synapse onto the dendrites of **mitral cells**. The axons of the mitral cells form the first cranial nerve and project to the **uncus** (primary olfactory cortex), the

Figure 8-20
Two views of the olfactory apparatus. The receptor cells have hairlike cilia that project into the olfactory mucosa. Odor molecules dissolve in the mucus before coming into contact with the receptor cells.

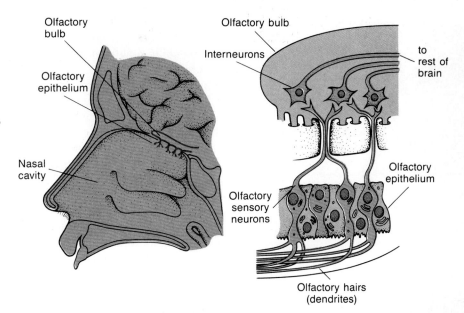

anterior olfactory nucleus, the **olfactory tubercle**, and various parts of the limbic system including the amygdala, and the septal area.

Unlike the cortical projections of vision and audition, the olfactory pathways do not have clearly defined projection areas in the neocortex. The primary olfactory projection area of the cortex is in the uncus, which is comprised of older paleocortex. There is evidence that some olfactory fibers do project to the pyriform cortex located below the occipital cortex and to the frontal lobe, but the function of these projection areas is not understood (Tanabe et al., 1974; Tanabe et al., 1975).

The limbic areas that receive olfactory input are known to control behaviors related to sexual activity, territoriality, and aggressiveness. This should not be surprising to you. Most mammals use pheromones (chemical signals) to mark territorial boundaries, establish social hierarchies, and identify females in estrus. Anyone who has owned a male dog is very familiar with that species's manner of marking territorial boundaries with urine. Olfaction clearly has a very important role in emotional behaviors.

Adequate Stimulus for Olfaction

Not all substances have a detectable odor. We are unable to smell gold, salt, quartz, and many other substances. To be "available" for olfaction, chemicals must be volatile. Individual molecules must escape into the air so that they may enter the nasal cavity and come in contact with the receptor cells located in the olfactory epithelium. It is also true that not all volatile substances have a detectable odor. Many of the most volatile gases—hydrogen, oxygen, nitrogen, and so on—have no odor at all. Evidently, chemicals that have an odor must possess some additional quality that causes them to interact with the lipid and/or protein elements of the receptor cell membrane. Although there are some exceptions, most of the substances that we are able to smell are small organic compounds (molecular weight in the range of 15 to 300) that are soluble in lipids or proteins.

We know very little about the process of transduction in the olfactory system. It is thought that odor-inducing molecules come into contact with "receptor molecules" that are present on the membranes of the receptor cell ciliary processes (see Figure 8-21). This, in turn, causes unspecified ion channels to open and depolarize the cell. Depolarizing the olfactory receptors increases their firing rate (Lancet, 1984).

One of the reasons why we know so little about olfaction is that we have not as yet been able to identify any physical property about olfactory stimuli that would allow us to predict something about how they produce different sensory experiences. With vision and audition it was possible to make some intelligent predictions about what sensory experiences would occur as frequency or wavelength changed. No analogous properties have been identified for olfactory stimuli.

Figure 8-21
The olfactory receptors and mucosa. Cilia of the olfactory receptor cells are surrounded by a thin mucous layer. Each receptor cell is isolated from its neighbors by support cells. The odor-producing chemicals must dissolve in the mucous layer before they come into contact with the cilia of the receptor cells.

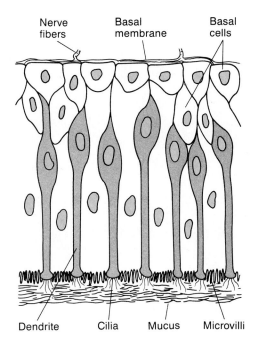

Stereochemical Theory of Odor

We are able to discriminate between many different odors, yet our vocabulary for these many olfactory experiences lacks precision. Terms like *pungent, ethereal, camphoraceous,* and *musky* seem to be "fuzzy" compared to *red, blue, orange,* and *purple.* Several theories have been advanced that attempt to classify odors; none have been very satisfactory.

One of the more widely accepted theories of olfaction is Amoore's **stereochemical theory** (Amoore, 1970; Amoore, Johnston, & Rubin, 1964) proposing that there are seven primary odors. These primary odors and substances that are representative of them are shown in Table 8-2.

Table 8-2. Amoore's Classification of Odors and Representative Substances

Primary Odor	Substance
Ethereal	Dry-cleaning fluid
Camphoraceous	Mothballs
Musky	Angelina root oil
Floral	Roses
Minty	Peppermint candy
Pungent	Vinegar
Putrid	Rotten eggs

Figure 8-22
Amoore's stereochemical theory of odor. Molecular models and the proposed receptor sites into which the molecules fit. (From Amoore, 1970.)

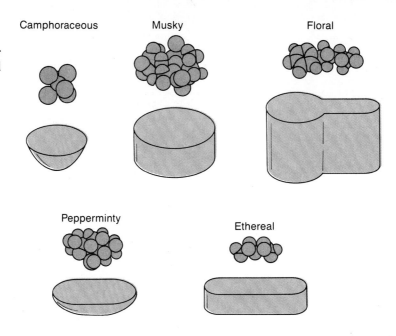

An intriguing feature of Amoore's theory is his proposal that the odor of a given chemical is determined by its shape. Amoore built many models of chemicals, and he noted that many substances that looked alike, smelled alike. His theory suggests that there are receptor sites of various shapes into which odor-producing molecules fit—like a key in a lock (Figure 8-22). Transduction is then induced somehow when a molecule of the correct shape comes into contact with the receptor site.

There are two serious limitations to the stereochemical theory. First, no shape-specific receptor sites have ever been identified on the membrane of the olfactory receptor cells. This does not mean that they do not exist, only that they have not as yet been identified. Second, there are too many exceptions to the shape–odor relationship proposed by the stereochemical theory. Many molecules with similar shapes have been shown not to have similar odors, and there are many examples of molecules having very different shapes and similar odors.

Gustation   Much of what we call "flavor" is in reality a combination of gustatory and olfactory cues. People who are **anosmic** (lack the sense of smell) do not experience the enormous variety and complexity of flavors that others can experience. You can test this for yourself by pinching your nostrils closed and sampling a variety of foods. Without prior knowledge of what you were tasting, you would have difficulty distinguishing between different flavors such as chocolate, banana, and vanilla pudding or between pineapple and potatoes.

Figure 8-23
The distribution of the papillae on the surface of the tongue.

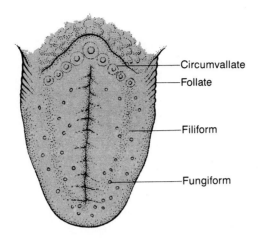

Circumvallate

Follate

Filiform

Fungiform

Receptors for Taste

The taste receptors are distributed on the tongue surface in clusters of 20 to 30 cells called taste buds. The taste buds are found in groups located within complex structures called **papillae** which is derived from the Latin word for "pimple." The papillae are what give the tongue its coarsely textured surface.

There are four types of papillae, which can be distinguished by their characteristic shape (see Figure 8-23). **Fungiform papillae** are shaped like mushrooms and are located on the sides and the tip of the tongue. **Circumvallate papillae** are the largest of the four types of papillae. They resemble low mounds that are surrounded by a deep trench. The circumvallate papillae form a V-shaped pattern on the back portion of the tongue. **Foliate papillae** are located on the sides and toward the back of the tongue. As their name would suggest, these papillae are located in a series of folds on the surface of the tongue. The **filiform papillae** are the most numerous, and they are distributed over most of the tongue's surface. Of the four types of papillae, they are the only ones that do not have taste buds (Moncrieff, 1967).

The receptor cells for taste are unique in that they are the only type of receptors that have a very short life span. The taste receptors are in a continuous process of maturing and dying. The cells are viable for approximately 10 days. Old cells atrophy, and they are replaced by new cells that develop from surrounding epithelial tissue (Graziadei, 1977).

The neural pathways for gustation are complex. Taste fibers from the tongue are carried by the seventh, ninth, and tenth cranial nerves. A given taste bud may innervate more than one nerve (Keverne, 1982). These fibers synapse in the **solitary nucleus**, which is located within the medulla. From the medulla taste fibers project to the **parabrachial nucleus** in the pons. From the pons, fibers project to the ventral posterior portion of the thalamus, the lateral hypothalamus, and various parts of the limbic system. Two cortical projection areas for taste have been identified: (1) the postcentral gyrus and (2) the anterior part of the insula.

Adequate Stimulus for Gustation

It is generally accepted that there are just four "primary" qualities of taste—sweet, salty, sour, and bitter. Unfortunately, the specific chemicals that account for these tastes are not easily grouped into four categories. Hydrogen ions appear to be essential for the experience of sour. This accounts for the sour taste of acids like citric acid and vinegar. Chloride ions are associated with salty taste. Chemicals that facilitate the passage of Cl⁻ across the cell membrane enhance the sensation of salty (Schiffman, Simon, Gill, & Beeker, 1986). However, Cl⁻ alone cannot account for the intensity of the salty taste, and there are some substances that do not contain chlorine yet also produce a salty taste. Most sweet-tasting substances are complex carbon molecules such as sucrose and fructose, but there are many exceptions to this. Artificial nonnutritive sweeteners such as sodium saccharine and aspartame attest to this fact. Bitter-tasting substances are quite varied. Many poisonous substances are bitter; however, there is no common chemical characteristic about poisonous substances that causes their bitter taste.

Not all parts of the tongue are equally sensitive to the four primary tastes. As shown in Figure 8-24a, the sides of the tongue are more sensitive to sour. The back of the tongue is most sensitive to bitter substances. Sweet and salty sensations are produced at the tip of the tongue.

Neural Coding for Taste

Is taste encoded by the pattern of activity produced by many fibers (across-fiber coding), or are there specific fibers for each of the primary tastes (labeled line coding)? As is typical with these either–or questions, the answer seems to be a little bit of both. The response pattern of most

Figure 8-24
a. The distribution of sensitivity to the four primary tastes on the surface of the tongue. *b.* The structure of the taste bud. Each taste bud contains supporting cells and a number of taste receptor cells. Receptor sites on the membrane of the receptor cell bind with taste-producing molecules.

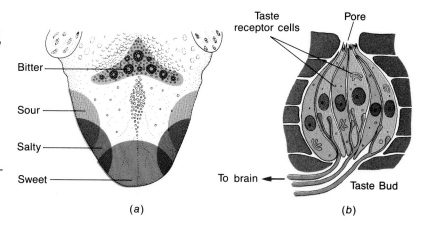

(a)   (b)

Figure 8-25
The response characteristics of a single cell in the chorda tympani of the monkey. See text for explanation. (From Sato et al., 1975.)

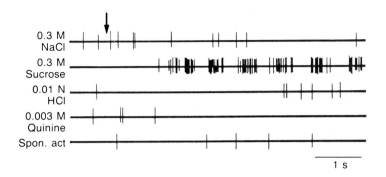

taste fibers indicates that few cells are highly specific to a specific taste. Rather, the majority of the taste fibers respond to a variety of substances. There are taste fibers that show a preference for substances that produce similar taste experiences. As you might have predicted, these fibers are most specific for the primary taste qualities—sour, salty, sweet and bitter.

Figure 8-25 shows the response characteristics of a single cell in the chorda tympani of a monkey. The bottom trace represents the background level of activity for the cell. The four other traces show the response rate of the cell when the receptor was exposed to NaCl (salty), sucrose (sweet), HCl (sour), and quinine (bitter). Clearly, this cell is most responsive to sweet. Other cells have been identified that respond most vigorously to salty, sour, and bitter (Sato, Ogawa, & Yamashita, 1975).

Currently it would be premature to attribute gustatory coding to across-fiber or labeled line neural activity. As seemed to be true for the coding of color and pitch, no single theory can account for all of the data.

CHAPTER SUMMARY

1. Sound waves vary along three dimensions: frequency, amplitude, and complexity. The frequency characteristic of sound (*hertz*) is experienced as *pitch*. The amplitude (expressed in *decibels*) is experienced as *loudness*. The complexity of sound waves is experienced as *timbre*. The ear evolved from the lateral line organ in fishes, which detects vibration in water. Complex accessory structures were needed for this vibration system to be sensitive to the weaker sound waves in the air.

2. The ear can be divided into three main regions: the outer, middle, and inner ear. The *outer ear* is comprised of the *pinna* and *auditory meatus*. The *middle ear* includes the *tympanic membrane*, the *ossicles*, and the *eustachian tube*. The *cochlea* is the *inner ear*. The cochlea has two chambers: the *scala vestibuli* and the *scala tympani*, which are separated by the *basilar membrane*. The *organ of Corti* contains the receptor cells for audition and rests on the basilar membrane. The adequate stimulus for audition is the movement of the hairlike processes on the receptor cells, which results from a shearing action between the basilar membrane and the *tectorial membrane.*

3. The human ear is sensitive to sound in the range of 20 to 20000 Hz. Theories concerning the coding for pitch may be divided into two types: timing and place theories. However, neither the place nor the timing theories can adequately explain the encoding of pitch. Single-cell recordings show that sensory cells in the cochlear nerve and several nuclei along the auditory pathways are tuned to specific frequencies. There is a *tonotopic* distribution on the auditory cortex similar to that observed on the organ of Corti.

4. The coding for loudness appears to differ at the basal and apical ends of the cochlea. At the base of the cochlea loudness appears to be encoded by the rate of cell activity. Loudness appears to be encoded near the apex by the number of cells that are activated.

5. Sound is localized using timing and loudness cues. Timing cues are more effective for localizing high-frequency sounds of short duration. Phase differences of sounds entering each ear are useful for the localization of low-frequency sounds.

6. The *vestibular mechanism* is composed of two component parts: the *vestibular sacs* (the *utricle* and *saccule*) and the *semicircular canals.* Movement of the hair cells within the *cupula* of each semicircular canal encodes rotation of the head in a given plane. The force of gravity on the *calcium carbonate otoliths* within the saccule and utricle triggers hair cells, which provide information about the position of the head in relation to the ground.

7. The sense of smell is poorly understood. The olfactory receptor cells are located in the olfactory epithelium. The receptor cells have ciliary processes that are surrounded by a layer of mucus. Unlike the cortical projections of vision and audition, the olfactory pathways do not have clearly defined projection areas in the cortex. Most olfactory fibers project to paleocortex and to structures in the limbic system.

8. Olfaction is important in sexual behavior, territoriality, and agressiveness. Many terrestrial animals use *pheromones* (chemical signals) to mark territorial boundaries, establish social hierarchies, and identify females in estrus.

9. Little is known about transduction in the olfactory system. It is thought that odor-inducing molecules come into contact with "receptor molecules" on the membrane of the receptor cells. One of the more widely accepted theories of olfaction is the *stereochemical theory*, which proposes that odor-producing molecules fit into receptor sites like a key in a lock. However, no receptor sites have, as yet, been identified.

10. *Taste buds* are found in complex structures called *papillae*. There are four types of papillae identified by their shape: *fungiform, circumvallate, foliate,* and *filiform.* The filiform, which are the most numerous, do not contain taste buds. The receptor cells for taste are unique in that they have a short life span and must be replaced continuously.

11. Much of what we call "flavor" is really a combination of taste and olfaction. There are four primary qualities of taste: salt, sweet, sour, and bitter. The specific chemicals that account for these tastes are not easily grouped into four categories. Hydrogen ions appear to be essential for sour, and chloride ions are important for salty. A wide variety of chemicals can produce sweet and bitter.

12. Neural coding for taste is complex and poorly understood. A majority of taste fibers respond to a variety of substances. A few fibers seem to be specific for substances that produce a similar taste. Generally, these fibers are most specific for one of the primary taste qualities.

SUGGESTED READINGS

Békésy, G. von. (1972). The ear. In *Perception: Mechanisms and models* (a *Scientific American* publication). San Francisco: Freeman.

Green, D., M. (1976). *An introduction to hearing.* Hillsdale, NJ: Erlbaum.

KEY TERMS

Ampulla Enlarged area of the semicircular canals.

Anosmic Without the sense of smell.

Circumvallate papillae Mound-shaped structures on the tongue that are surrounded by a deep trench.

Basilar membrane Membrane separating the upper and lower chambers of the cochlea.

Cochlea Spiral-shaped structure of the inner ear.

Cochlear canal Small chamber located between the vestibular and tympanic chambers. The organ of Corti is located in the cochlear canal.

Cribiform plate Perforated bony structure at the top of the nasal cavity. Axons of the olfactory receptor cells pass through this structure.

Crista Structure within the ampula of the semicircular canals that contains the receptor cells.

Cupula Gelatinous structure within the ampula of the semicircular canals. The hairs of the receptor cells are embedded in the cupula.

Cuticular plate Point of attachment for the cilia of the hair cells.

Decibel (dB) A measure of the amplitude of sound expressed in dynes per unit area of surface.

Dorsal cochlear nucleus Projection area of the cochlear nerve at the level of the medulla.

Eardrum The cone-shaped membrane that is the transition area between the outer ear and middle ear.

Endolymph Fluid found in the cochlear canal.

Eustachian tube Tubular structure connecting the middle ear and the oral cavity.

External auditory meatus Tube-shaped structure between the pinna and the tympanic membrane.

Filiform papillae   The most numerous form of coarse structures found on the surface of the tongue. Of the four types of papillae the filiform are the only ones that do not have taste buds.

Foliate papillae   Folds in the tissue of the tongue that contain taste buds.

Fundamental frequency   The carrier frequency of a sound.

Fungiform papillae   Mushroom-shaped structures found on the surface of the tongue.

Helocotrema   A small opening between the vestibular and tympanic canals of the cochlea.

Hertz (Hz)   The frequency characteristic of sound expressed in cycles per second.

Incus   *See* Ossicles.

Inferior colliculi   Pontine-level nuclei that function in audition.

Lateral lemniscal track   A spinothalamic track. Fibers from the auditory pathway join the lateral lemniscal track at the level of the *medula*.

Malleus   *See* Ossicles.

Mitral cells   Located in the olfactory bulb; receive input from the olfactory receptor cells.

Olfactory bulb   Situated above the cribriform plate; contains sensory cells for olfaction.

Olfactory epithelium   Tissue at the top of the nasal cavity that contains the receptor cells for olfaction.

Organ of Corti   Complex structure on the basilar membrane; contains the receptor cells for audition.

Ossicles   Three small bones—the malleus, incus, and stapes—that transmit vibration between the eardrum and the oval window of the cochlea.

Oval window   Thin membrane at the entrance to the vestibular chamber of the cochlea.

Overtones   Characteristic of complex sounds that produce distinctive tonal qualities.

Papillae   Coarse structures on the surface of the tongue. The taste buds are located in the papillae.

Perilymph   Fluid found in the vestibular and tympanic chambers of the cochlea.

Pinna   The fleshy outer portion of the ear.

Pitch   The psychological experience of the frequency of sound.

Place theory   Theory of frequency coding in the cochlea proposed by Békésy.

Reisner's membrane   Thin, one-cell, layered membrane separating the vestibular chamber and the cochlear canal.

Round window   Thin membrane at the end of the tympanic chamber of the cochlea.

Saccule   *See* Vestibular sacs.

Semicircular canals   Three tubular structures in the vestibular mechanism. Each of the tubes is oriented in one cardinal plane of the head and reports head movement in that plane.

Stapes   *See* Ossicles.

Statoacoustic nerve   The eighth cranial nerve comprised of fibers from the cochlea and the vestibular mechanism.

Stereochemical theory of olfaction   Theory that relates the quality of olfactory experience to the shape of the odor-inducing chemical.

Stereocilia   The cilia or hairs of the auditory receptor cells.

Superior olivary nucleus   Nucleus in the auditory pathway; receives fibers from the ventral and dorsal cochlear nuclei.

Taste buds   Clusters of receptor cells for gustation.

Tectorial membrane   Thin membrane that covers the top of the organ of Corti.

Tensor tympani   A small muscle attached to the malleus; reacts reflexively to high-intensity sound by limiting the movement of the ossicles.

Timbre   The psychological experience of complex sound waves that provide the unique signature of the sound; for example, the brassy sound of a trumpet is due to its unique complexity, or timbre.

Tympanic canal   Lower canal of the cochlea.

Tympanic membrane   *See* Eardrum.

Uncus   The parahippocampal gyrus; the primary olfactory projection area.

Utricle   *See* Vestibular sacs.

Ventral cochlear nucleus   Projection area for the cochlear nerve located at the level of the medula.

Vestibular canal   Upper canal of the cochlea.

Vestibular ganglion Bulbous ganglion on the vestibular nerve. The cell bodies of the bipolar vestibular cells are located in the vestibular ganglion.

Vestibular sacs Two rounded structures in the labyrinth—the utricle and saccule.

Vestibular system Part of the labyrinth organ that is concerned with balance.

Volley theory Theory of coding for sound. The volley theory proposes that frequency is coded by the timing and sequence of neuronal activity.

Chapter 9

Sensing and Moving the Body

PART 1 SENSING

The Somatosensory System

The Anatomy of the Skin
Receptors in the Skin

Transduction and Encoding of Sensory Information

Temperature
Touch
Active versus Passive Touch
Pain

Anatomy of the Somatosensory System

The Lemniscal Pathways
The Spinothalamic Pathways
Organization of the Somatosensory Cortex

PART 2 MOTOR CONTROL

The Muscles

How Skeletal Muscles Work
The Reflex Arc Revisited

Brain Structures in the Control of Movement

The Pyramidal System
The Extrapyramidal System
The Cerebellum

Chapter Learning Objectives

After reading this chapter, you should

1. Be familiar with the anatomy of the skin.

2. Be able to identify the various receptors in the skin and know the adequate stimulus for each.

3. Understand how transduction occurs in the different types of somatosensory receptor cells.

4. Be able to discuss touch mechanisms for localization, discrimination, and feature detection.

5. Be able to compare and contrast active and passive touch.

6. Be familiar with bright and dull pain and be able to give evidence that they are based on different neural mechanisms.

7. Understand the relationship between endogenous opiates and the perception of pain.

8. Be able to compare the lemniscal and spinothalamic somatosensory pathways from the receptor cells to the somatosensory cortex

9. Know the evidence regarding the lemniscal system as a newer evolutionary development.

10. Be able to discuss the organization of the somatosensory cortex.

11. Be familiar with the anatomy and neuronal control of smooth, striate, and cardiac muscle.

12. Be able to describe events at the neuromuscular junction that initiate muscle contraction and understand the physical events within the muscles that cause them to shorten.

13. Be familiar with monosynaptic and polysynaptic reflexes and understand the feedback mechanisms that control muscle action.

14. Know how the pyramidal and extrapyramidal motor systems differ in anatomy and function.

15. Be familiar with the evolution of the three divisions of the cerebellum and be able to discuss the role of the cerebellum in motor control.

PART 1   SENSING

In Chapter 5 we noted that multicellular animals have evolved specialized receptor cells. Each type of receptor cell appears to have evolved in a
way that makes it particularly effective at detecting and transducing one
kind of physical energy. Multicellular organisms developed receptors
that could detect, differentiate, and integrate information from both the
external and internal environments of the organism. This specialization
has provided a very significant adaptive advantage over single-celled
organisms.

The Somatosensory System

Now we turn to the body senses. The **cutaneous** (skin) sense provides
information about environmental influences on the surface of our body.
Various forms of touch, temperature, and the report of painful stimulation originate from receptors found in the skin. Similar sensations can
also arise from receptors found around internal organs. Also, there are
kinesthetic sensors in our joints and muscles that provide us with
information about the position and movement of parts of our bodies.
Together these body senses are called the **somatosensory** system.

You should recall from the previous chapters on vision and the
labyrinth sense that there are two major theoretical views concerning
how sensory information is coded. Specificity theory proposes that coding
is attributable to the specific kinds of receptor cells. Simply put, the
specificity theory would point out that cones in the retina report information about vision, and hair cells in the cochlea report information about
sound. Conversely, pattern theory proposes that sensory coding is the
result of the pattern of neural activity from many nerve fibers. Pattern
theorists would point out that it is the combined report of several cones
that encodes light of a specific hue. We know from our discussion of
vision and audition that neither theory can adequately account for all of
the data. There is, in fact, considerable evidence to support both theories.

The study of the body senses has done little to simplify this issue.
As was true with vision and audition, the evidence suggests that the physical nature of the receptor cell and the pattern of activity produced in
many receptor cells are both important factors in sensory coding of body
information. Additionally, in some cases such as the Pacinian corpuscle,
specific types of receptors seem to respond to a very narrow range of
physical stimuli. Other receptors, such as the free nerve endings, appear
to respond to many different forms of environmental stimulation and
may report very different sensations, depending on the type of physical
energy they transduce.

Let us begin by looking at the cutaneous senses—touch, temperature, and pain.

The Anatomy of the Skin

The skin is a vital organ, although we don't tend to think of it in this way. With the exception of the outermost layer, the **epidermis**, the skin is a living and complex organ that, among other things, helps to regulate body temperature, filters sunlight, maintains the body fluids, and protects us from a host of noxious chemicals in air and water.

The **dermis** is the living part of the skin. It is located beneath several layers of dead epidermal tissue. The dermal layer is composed of a complex matrix of glands, blood vessels, muscle, connective tissue, fat, and hair. There are also a variety of receptors and nerves in the dermal layer. The kind and number of receptor cells found in the skin vary greatly in different parts of the body. Hairy skin, like the skin that covers most of your body, tends to have fewer receptors than hairless (**glabrous**) skin. Glabrous skin, like the skin on your fingers, the palms of your hands, and your lips, is thinner than hairy skin; and it contains higher concentrations and a greater diversity of receptor cells. Figure 9-1 shows representative sections through hairy and glabrous skin.

Receptors in the Skin

There is still considerable debate concerning the number of different types of skin receptors and their proposed functions. Actually, the reported number of receptor types has decreased in recent years. As histological techniques have improved, some receptors previously thought to be unique have been grouped together and others have been shown to be nothing more than artifacts of staining techniques (Iggo and Andres, 1982). The types of receptor cells listed below and summarized in Table 9-1 represent the major classes of cutaneous receptors.

1. *Pacinian corpuscle.* The Pacinian corpuscle was already discussed at length in Chapter 5 where it was used as a model to explain transduction in receptor cells. The Pacinian corpuscle has the largest encapsulated end organ of any receptor cell. It is large enough to be seen without the aid of magnification. These receptors are found at relatively deep layers of both hairy and glabrous skin. They are also located in the connective tissues of skeletal joints. The Pacinian corpuscles report pressure and they are particularly sensitive to vibrations in the 150- to 300-Hz range. These receptors have large, highly myelinated axons, and they therefore have a very rapid conduction rate.

2. *Merkel's disks.* Merkel's disks are found just below the epidermis in both hairy and glabrous skin. Typically, these receptors are found in association with specialized epitheleal cells called Merkel's cells. Little is known about transduction in Merkel's disks. They respond to mechanical stimulation and probably are involved in reporting light touch.

3. *Ruffini endings.* Ruffini endings are found primarily in hairy skin. They are also found in fewer numbers in glabrous skin and skeletal joints.

Figure 9-1
a. The anatomy of gla-
brous (hairless) skin.
b. The anatomy of hairy
skin (see also Color
Plate 15).

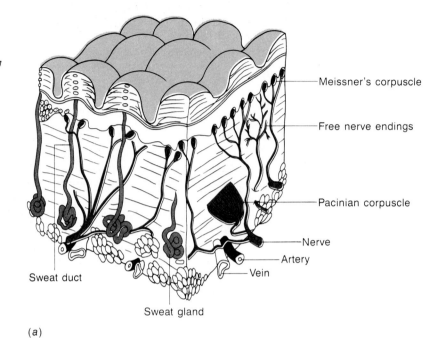

Meissner's corpuscle

Free nerve endings

Pacinian corpuscle

Nerve

Artery

Vein

Sweat duct

Sweat gland

(a)

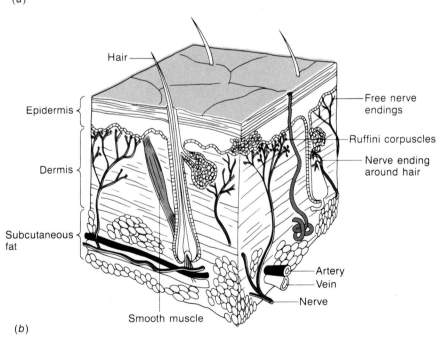

Hair

Epidermis

Dermis

Subcutaneous
fat

Smooth muscle

Free nerve
endings

Ruffini corpuscles

Nerve ending
around hair

Artery

Vein

Nerve

(b)

Table 9-1 Characteristics of Primate Receptors

Ending Type	Fiber Size	Function
Pacinian corpuscles	Large	Most sensitive to deep touch and vibrations
Merkel's disks	Large	Pressure receptors in both hairy and glabrous skin
Ruffini endings	Large	Pressure receptors in both hairy and glabrous skin
Krause end bulbs	Large	Pressure receptors in the lips, tongue, and external genitalia
Meissner corpuscles	Large	Most sensitive to light touch and vibrations
Hair follicle spirals	Large	Most sensitive to displacement of hair—report light touch
Free nerve endings	Medium	Some respond to temperature; others report pain with strong mechanical stimulation
Free nerve endings	Small	Some respond to temperature; others report pain with noxious heat, cold, or mechanical stimulation

They were once thought to be associated with temperature; however, more recent evidence has shown that they respond to very low frequency vibration. Mechanical stimulation that produces a distortion of the encapsulated ending of the Ruffini cells is thought to be the adequate stimulus.

4. *Meissner corpuscles.* These vibration-sensitive cells are located exclusively at the upper levels of the dermis in the papillae of glabrous skin. The papillae are the folds that produce the characteristic prints of the fingers and palmar skin. The Meissner corpuscles have a coiled nerve ending, and there are stretchable fibers that penetrate and surround the coils in the corpuscle. It is thought that deformations of the skin that stretch these fibers activate the nerve ending.

5. *Krause end bulbs.* These receptors are unique in that they are only found in the **macocutaneous** zones where mucous membrane and dry skin meet, such as the lips, the eyelid, and the glans of the penis and clitoris. Typically, the Krause end bulbs have neural endings that tangle into ball-shaped structures. Several of these balls send fibers to a common axon. It is thought that these receptors respond to the mechanical distortion of the ball-shaped structures.

6. *Hair follicle spirals.* As is obvious from the name, these receptors are located only in hairy skin. A network of fine filaments surround the base of each hair follicle. These receptor cells are sensitive to any movement of the follicle. You can demonstrate this for yourself by displacing a

single hair on the back of your hand or your forearm with the tip of your pen or pencil. These receptors report the sensation of light touch.

7. *Free nerve endings.* Each of the receptor cells mentioned thus far can be distinguished by some unique feature of the neural ending. The free nerve endings are just that—free. The receptor cells terminate in a series of branches that are not encapsulated and that have no special structural features. As noted in Table 9-1, free nerve endings are associated with a variety of skin senses, including temperature, mechanical stimulation, and pain. The cornea of the eye, which is sensitive to touch, warm, cold, and pain, contains only receptor cells with free nerve endings.

It has been suggested by some investigators that all receptors having free nerve endings are capable of reporting pain when they are intensely stimulated (e.g., Lindahl, 1974; Weddell & Verrillo, 1972). That is, thermal and mechanical receptors may also report pain when the level of stimulation is high enough to cause tissue damage. Some free nerve endings, however, may be specialized **nociceptors** (pain receptors). For example, free nerve endings found in the walls of blood vessels in the head are the likely source of headache pain, and free nerve endings in the lining of the intestines are the source of abdominal pain that results from trapped gases.

Transduction and Encoding of Sensory Information

As we have noted already, the somatosensory system is diverse encompassing the sensory qualities of touch, temperature, kinesthesis, and pain. We now examine transduction and coding of each of these sensory qualities individually although kinesthesis is discussed later in the part of this chapter dealing with the integration of sensory information and motor control.

Temperature   The sensation of warmth or coolness is somewhat unique in that the reference point is not fixed. What you experience as warm or cool is dependent to some degree on what you have experienced recently. I can make this point most clearly with an example.

Look at Figure 9-2 and follow the sequence of events. First, the left and right hands are placed in a water bath that contains water that is the same temperature as the skin surface. Because the water is neither warmer nor cooler than the skin, the experience is "neither warm nor cool." Now the left hand is placed in a bath that is 2° cooler and the right hand is placed in a bath that is 2° warmer than the first bath. The experience now is that the left hand feels coolness and the right hand feels warmth. After a few minutes, adaptation will take place and both hands will experience neither warm nor cool. (If the temperature of the bath is

Figure 9-2
See text for explanation.

Bath temperature
the same as
skin temperature

After adaptation

very different from the temperature of the skin, 20° for example, the adaptation would not be as complete and the coolness or warmness would still be experienced, but at a lesser level than when the hands were first placed in the bath.) Now for the final step. Both hands are now placed in the original bath that was previously neutral. The left hand will now experience this as warm; whereas the right hand has the experience of cool.

Within a finite range of skin temperatures, the temperature of the stimulus is experienced as either warm or cool relative to the temperature of the skin. The reference temperature of the skin is sometimes referred to as physiological zero.

An Observation:

Psychological Heat—Warm + Cool = Hot?

When I was an undergraduate student and taking the introductory psychology course, my instructor demonstrated the perceptual phenomenon of **psychological heat**. The apparatus he used to demonstrate this "psychological" phenomenon was quite simple. Two lengths of copper tubing were bent into 180° curves to form a repeated pattern of "S" shapes. The two "S" patterns were then positioned so that they formed alternating cross-members. Cool water (30°C) was run through one copper tube and warm water (44°C) was run through the other. This produced on alternating pattern of warm and cool tubes. (It has been demonstrated that cool fibers are most active to 30°C and warm fibers are most active to 44°C.)

As student "volunteers," we were asked to come forward and test the temperature of the water coming out of each tube to "prove" to ourselves that the water was truly warm and cool. Then we were asked to place our forearm on the alternating pattern of warm and cool stimuli and report our perception. You might think that the perception would be that of alternating warm and cool, or that the two stimuli would cancel each other out and produce a neutral experience. The subjective experience, to the enormous amusement of my somewhat sadistic instructor, was that of very uncomfortable heat!

Observation Figure 9-1
a. The apparatus used to demonstrate the phenomenon of psychological heat.
b. The response characteristics of warm and cool fibers. Note that there is considerable overlap between the two curves. The cool fibers are most active at 30° C and the warm fibers are most active at 44° C. (From Kenshalo, 1976.)

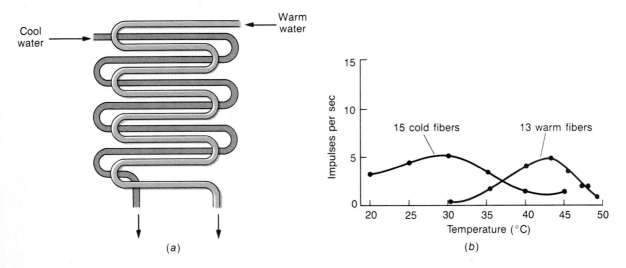

Apparently, simultaneous stimulation of adjacent warm and cool receptors, which is an unlikely condition under normal environmental conditions, produces the subjective experience of heat. Here we can see that the subjective perception (the internal simulation) is not necessarily consistent with the real world.

The weight of evidence now supports the notion that warmth and coolness are detected by different populations of receptors having free nerve endings. That is, there are cool receptors and warm receptors (Sinclair, 1981). Warm fibers respond most vigorously to increases in temperature and continue to respond at an elevated rate if the warm temperature is maintained. Additionally, warm fibers are inhibited by decreasing temperatures (Duclaux & Kenshalo, 1980). The response characteristics of cool fibers are, as you might predict, just the opposite. Figure 9-3 shows the response characteristics of warm and cool fibers.

Figure 9-3
a. The response rate of a cool and warm fiber expressed in impulses per second for a range of steady skin temperatures. Note that the cool fiber is most responsive to a skin temperature of approximately 26° C. The warm fiber is most responsive at skin temperatures around 47° C. Both fibers show some response to temperatures between 30° and 43°. (Adapted from Hensel & Kenshalo, 1969). *b.* Note that the cool fiber shows a momentary increase in response rate when the temperature is decreased from 20.5° to 15.2°. A similar momentary increase in activity occurs when the temperature is decreased from 35° to 31.5°. *c.* The response of a warm and cool receptor to increases and decreases in temperature. Note that the cool receptor is excited by a decrease in temperature, whereas the warm fiber is inhibited by the same change. The opposite response characteristics occur when the temperature is increased.

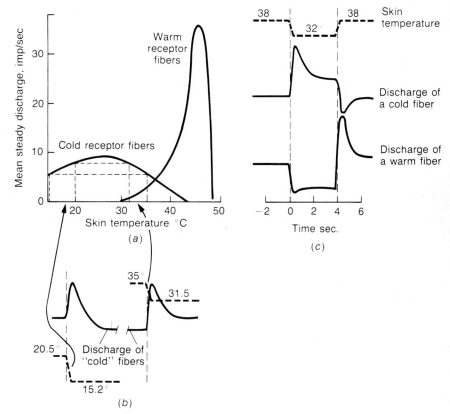

Touch   Touch is a very complex sense that includes the experience of light touch, pressure, deep pressure, and vibration. As you might expect, because touch encompasses such a diverse range of experiences, there are several kinds of receptor cells associated with it. If you refer again to Table 9-1, you will see that all the various types of encapsulated receptor cells are associated with some aspect of touch, and many, but not all, receptors having free nerve endings report touch as well.

RECEPTIVE FIELDS

The sensation of touch varies widely from one part of the skin to another. Variations in two characteristics of touch, **localization** and **discrimination**, are particularly informative about the distribution and the response characteristics of receptors cells.

Localization is the ability to accurately report where the skin has been stimulated without the benefit of seeing the point being touched. Discrimination refers to the ability to differentiate between two points of stimulation that are in close proximity. Discrimination is usually correlated with the **two-point limen**, which is the smallest distance between two points of stimulation that are perceived as two points. As it turns out, localization and discrimination are related in that they are both regulated by the size of the touch receptor's receptive fields.

Figure 9-4 shows the two-point limen, expressed in millimeters of separation between the two points, for various parts of the female body. (The pattern for males is essentially the same.) The figure should confirm what you might have guessed from your personal experience. Discrimination ability is far superior for locations such as the fingers and the lips than it is for the back, the thigh, or the calf. The two-point limen is almost 10 times larger for the calf than it is for the thumb or first finger. This makes good sense. Tactile exploration is done with our hands and not with our backs or calves (see Spotlight 9-1).

Recordings from single neurons have shown that the receptive fields for touch cells vary widely (Vallbo & Johansson, 1976). Some neurons respond only to stimulation applied to small spots, whereas others respond to stimulation over large areas of skin (see Figure 9-5). Interestingly, those areas of skin that have very small receptive fields also have very accurate localization and a small two-point limen. Also, as you might predict, the density of receptors is greatest in those areas having the smallest receptive fields.

FEATURE DETECTORS

You may have noticed a parallel between the description of receptor field size in touch and what was noted concerning receptive fields for ganglion cells in the visual system. The similarities between touch and

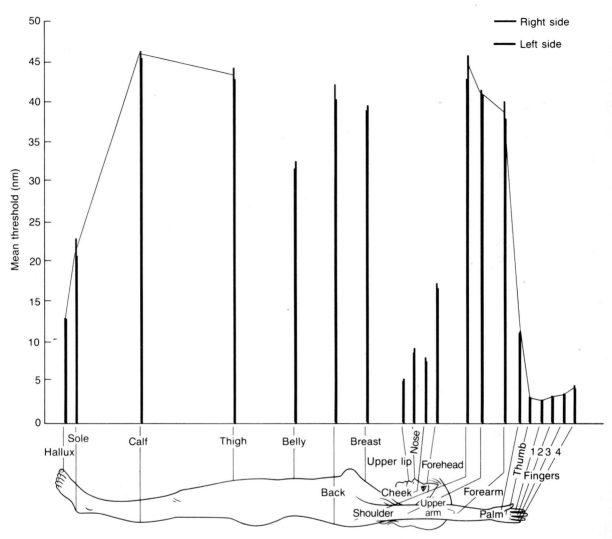

Figure 9-4
The two-point limen expressed in millimeters for various parts of the female body. The color lines are for the right side of the body, and the black lines represent the data from the left side of the body. (From Weinstein, 1968.)

vision do not end here. Recordings of the response characteristics of sensory cells in the thalamus has provided evidence for the encoding of specific features for touch.

Mountcastle and his colleagues were among the first researchers to report the existence of touch cells that respond to special sensory features. They found these cells in the somatosensory projection areas in the

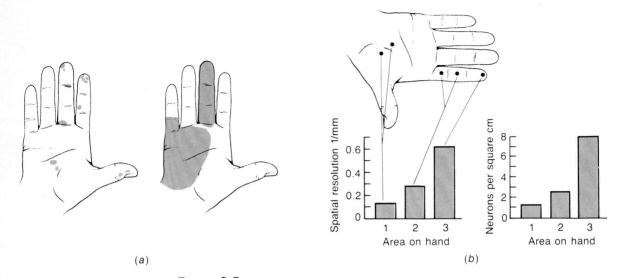

(a)   (b)

Figure 9-5
a. The receptive fields of single neurons in the human hand. At left the hand
shows a number of small receptive fields. Two larger receptive fields are
plotted on the right figure. b. The bar graph on the left shows the spatial
resolution at three locations on the hand and fingers. (Taller bars indicate finer
resolution.) The density of receptor neurons is plotted on the right for the
same three locations. The data show that areas with high spatial resolution
have high densities of neurons with small receptive fields. (Both figures from
Vallbo & Johansson, 1978.)

thalamus. Figure 9-6 illustrates the receptive field for a single touch
neuron in the thalamus of a rhesus monkey. This particular cell is excited
by mechanical stimulation in the center of the field and inhibited by
mechanical stimulation in the surrounding area. This on-center/off-
surround cell is remarkably similar to the on-center fields that were identified in the visual system (Mountcastle & Powell, 1959).

Other cells have been identified in the primary somatosensory
projection areas of the cortex (the postcentral gyrus) that have response
characteristics very similar to those observed in simple and complex cells
found in the visual cortex. These cells are most active when mechanical
stimulation of the skin is of a specific orientation or when the pattern of
stimulation moves across the surface of the skin in a given direction
(Hyvärinin & Poranen, 1978). Look at Figure 9-7. Part a illustrates the
response characteristics of a neuron in the parietal cortex of the monkey
brain. This particular cell responds most actively to a metal bar when it
is pressed against the skin in the horizontal position. The cell responds
progressively less vigorously as the bar is rotated toward the vertical
orientation.

Figure 9-6
Receptive field for a touch cell found in the thalamus. The cell is excited by mechanical stimulation in the center of the field but inhibited by mechanical stimulation in the surround. (From Mountcastle & Powell, 1959.)

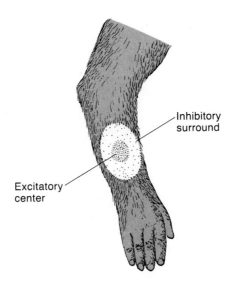

Inhibitory surround

Excitatory center

Figure 9-7
The receptive fields of cells in the parietal cortex of monkeys. *a.* This cell responds most actively when a metal edge is placed on the skin in the horizontal position. The response rate drops off as the edge is rotated to the vertical orientation. *b.* This cell responds most actively to movement across the skin in one direction but does not respond when the movement is in the opposite direction. (From Hyvärinen & Poranen, 1978.)

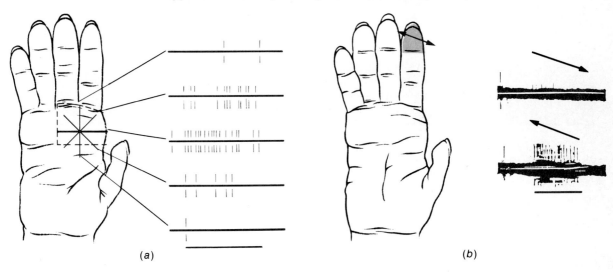

(*a*) (*b*)

Sensory Substitution—Seeing with Touch?

You no doubt are aware that blind people can be taught to read using the braille system. Braille was invented by a blind Frenchman, Louis Braille, in 1824. Braille substituted patterns of raised dots for each letter of the alphabet. Proficient braille readers can process these tactile cues very accurately, and some expert users of braille can read up to 125 words per minute.

More recently, using more sophisticated technology, researchers have attempted to substitute tactile stimulation in a more complex way, hoping that blind people could learn to "see with their skin." A small television camera is attached to the subject's head. The image from the camera is processed through a small computer, which, in turn, controls a matrix of stimulating probes that can be placed against the skin. Each probe in the matrix can stimulate the skin either by vibration or with a small electric charge. The pattern of stimulation produced by the computer roughly approximates the shape of objects in the visual environment. (Bach-y-Rita, 1972; Bach-y-Rita and Hughes, 1985; Bach-y-Rita, 1988) See Spotlight Figure 9-1.

After training, subjects have been able to identify ("see") a variety of geometric figures as well as common objects, such as telephones, toy cars, and dinnerware. Additionally, the portable device allows the subject to detect when he or she is getting closer to objects, and to detect when one object obscures the "view" of other objects in the environment.

Clearly there are limitations to this type of sensory substitution device. Detail is severely limited by the poor localization and discrimination of tactile receptors on the torso. Because of this, only very crude images can be presented onto the skin. Nonetheless, research of this type may someday produce a workable prosthesis that substitutes tactile stimulation for vision. The hope is that someday the blind will be able to use this device to move about freely in the environment.

Figure 9-7b illustrates the response characteristics of a cortical cell that responds vigorously to movement in one direction. The same cell shows no response to movement over the same area but in the opposite direction. The similarities between these neurons and neurons in the visual cortex are inescapable. In both sense modalities the more peripheral cells respond to a wide variety of stimuli. Cells at the thalamic and cortical levels appear to have increasingly more selective response characteristics. Similar coding strategies seem to operate in both systems (Constanzo & Gardner, 1980; Goldstein, 1984).

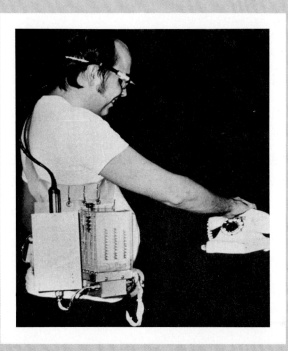

Spotlight Figure 9-1
A blind subject with a portable sensory substitution system. The camera
attached to the eyeglass frame sends the image to the small computer
(attached to the harness), which in turn controls the stimulating matrix, in this
case, comprised of 256 electrodes. The electrodes stimulate the skin in a
pattern that approximates the shape of a telephone. (From Bach-y-Rita, 1972.)

Active versus
Passive Touch

If someone placed common objects such as a door key, a bottle cap, or a
quarter in your hand and then asked you to identify the objects just by
"feeling" them, you could do this with little difficulty. Given the same
task but denied the opportunity to manipulate the objects in your hand,
you would then find the task close to impossible to do. What is the
difference?

Clearly, in the first condition you are more active. The movements
of your hand and fingers over the object are purposive. You are able to
correlate changes in the position of your hand and fingers with the
pattern of mechanical stimulation those changes produce. Also, as you

palpate the unknown objects, you can obtain other cues about the objects concerning their hardness, smoothness, and texture.

What we have here is the difference between touching and being touched. It might be helpful to think of three levels of information processing. When objects are placed onto the skin passively, we have the experience of being touched, but little more. If the objects are then moved over our passive hand and fingers, we have more information concerning shape, hardness, and texture (Schwartz, Perez, & Azulaz, 1975). The highest level of information becomes available when we actively explore the objects. This final level adds kinesthetic feedback and the additional information that purposeful and planned movements provide (Gibson, 1962).

A relatively new technology permits recording the activity of single cells in the brains of awake and active animals. Figure 9-8 shows the response of neurons in the postcentral gyrus of a monkey's brain while the animal is actively manipulating objects of various shapes and sizes. It is important to note that these cells do not respond to passive mechanical stimulation of the skin. They do, however, become active when the monkey grasps certain objects. The cell on the left responds when the monkey grasps a ruler or a block, objects that have edges, but it does not respond when the monkey grasps a cylinder. The cell on the right responds when the monkey grasps round objects like a cylinder or a ball, but it does not respond to the block. Neurons like these may play a role in the process of active touch.

Pain   Unlike temperature and touch, the sensation of pain can be induced by a variety of physical stimuli. It appears that almost any type of physical energy that is capable of causing tissue damage will also produce the sensation of pain. Certain forms of radiation that can cause tissue damage, like X-rays and gamma rays seem to be the exception to the rule. Irritating chemicals, intense heat or cold, excessive pressure or stretching, and cutting or piercing objects can all cause pain.

The fact that stimuli capable of causing tissue damage also produce the experience of pain seems to make good evolutionary sense. Pain and the natural tendency of animals to avoid painful stimuli have obvious adaptive advantages for the survival of species. The importance of pain for survival is evident in those few people who have congenital insensitivity to pain. These people, especially when they are children, are in constant danger of serious and potentially fatal injury because they fail to feel pain. Leaning on a hot stove or stepping on a piece of glass does not produce the sensation of pain or the appropriate reflexive avoidance response.

Because of its importance as a danger signal concerning injury and potential life-threatening events, pain also has an emotional component (Melzack, 1980; Sternbach, 1968). There is some evidence that the

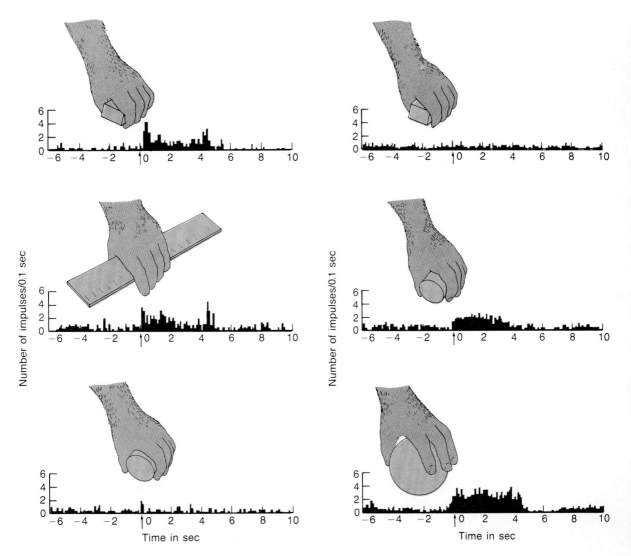

Figure 9-8
The response characteristics of neurons in the postcentral gyrus of monkeys during active touch. The arrow on each graph indicates the time that the monkey grasps the object, and the firing rate of the neuron is indicated by the height of the bars. The cell on the left responds most actively to objects with edges. The cell on the right responds most actively to round objects. (From Sakata & Iwamura, 1978.)

emotional experience of pain is somewhat independent of pain itself. That is, the sensation of pain and the unpleasant feelings that pain produces may well depend on different brain circuits. We have known for some time that **prefontal lobotomies** (lesions that isolate the most anterior pole of the cortex from the remainder of the brain) have little effect on the sensation of pain but greatly diminish the emotional qualities of experiencing pain. Lesions made to specific thalamic nuclei, notably those nuclei that are intimately associated with the limbic system, can have the same emotional blunting of pain. The basal ganglia, through connections with the prefrontal lobes and the thalamus, also appear to be implicated with the perception of pain (Barker, 1988).

Most investigators associate networks of free nerve endings with pain. There is, however, considerable controversy over the nature of the adequate stimulus for pain. The problem, quite obviously, is that so many different stimuli can result in the perception of pain. It has been proposed that pain is a special form of chemical sense. When cells are broken open by a cut, a burn, or another strong physical force, the contents of the cell empty into the extracellular space. Several "candidate" substances have been suggested, including K^+, histamine, acetylcholine, and serotonin (Sinclair, 1967). Recent investigations have shown that body cells contain an enzyme that converts certain blood proteins into a chemical called **bradykinin**. The membranes of free nerve endings are thought to contain specific receptor sites for bradykinin. When bradykinin binds to the cell membrane, it causes a change in the resting potential of the receptor cell (Fields, H. L., & Besson, J. -M., 1988; Besson, Guilbaud, Abdelmoumene, & Chaouch, 1982). This mechanism would not, however, explain some forms of pain that are not associated with tissue damage, for example, the intense pain from touching the sclera of the eye or the tympanic membrane in the ear. This suggests that there may be more than one mechanism for the sensation of pain.

ONE OR TWO TYPES OF PAIN

The picture concerning pain is made all the more confusing by the possibility that there may be more than one kind of pain. There is good reason to believe that "dull" pain, the kind of pain you experience with a stomach ache, and "bright" pain, the pain you experience when you prick your finger with a pin, are mediated by two separate sensory systems.

Dull pain appears to be mediated by more lightly myelinated and unmyelinated fibers. The axons carrying bright pain tend to have a larger diameter, and they are more highly myelinated. Therefore, bright pain is conducted more rapidly. Dull pain tends to adapt more slowly. (If you have ever suffered from gastritis or if you have ever had a hangover from heavy drinking, you can attest to that fact.) Dull pain tends to be sensed more generally and is difficult to localize accurately. Generally, bright pain can be localized more precisely than dull pain. However, precise localization, even of bright pain, can be problematical. It is often difficult to identify which tooth is the source of a toothache. Physicians know that sharp pain from internal organs, such as the gall bladder and appendix, is frequently referred to parts of the body that are quite distant from the actual source of the problem.

Finally, as you will see later in this chapter, dull and bright pain fibers do not share the same pathways to the brain. Lesions made to specific thalamic nuclei can abolish the sensation of bright pain but leave dull pain unaffected—a clear indication that the two types of pain are mediated by separate neural networks.

THE BIOCHEMISTRY OF PAIN

We have known for many years that a variety of environmental factors seem to moderate the perception of pain. For example, there are many documented cases of individuals who fail to experience pain during the heat of battle or in other emotionally charged situations. Using self-hypnosis, people are able to undergo dental surgery without the benefit of anesthesia. Similarly, acupuncture has been used in China for centuries as a substitute for chemically induced anesthesia. People have undergone major surgery with acupuncture as the only source of pain control.

These events have caused speculation in the scientific community concerning the existence of some naturally occurring process or processes within the brain that have the ability to blunt or completely eliminate the experience of pain. One other source of data has caused neuroscientists to wonder about the existence of naturally occurring substances that moderate pain. Simply put, brain scientists have wondered why receptor sites exist in the brain for powerful analgesic substances such as morphine and other derivatives of the opiates. Could these receptor sites be there to accommodate naturally produced analgesic opiatelike substances?

Recently, investigators have discovered analgesia-inducing neural circuits within the brain (Herz et al., 1970). Among other pain-regulating loci, the periaqueductal gray matter and rostroventral area of the medulla appear to be important centers that inhibit pain (Basbaum & Fields, 1978; Mayer & Liebeskind, 1974). Morphinelike neuromodulators called **endogenous opiates** (**endogenous** means "to be produced from within") appear to be associated with these neural circuits, which block the experience of pain (Hughes et al., 1975). To date, a number of endogenous substances with opiate qualities have been identified. These substances—which have been termed **enkephalins, endorphins**, and

dynorphins—are all derived from much larger peptides that are their precursor molecules (Akil et al., 1984).

The regulation of pain experience by acupuncture appears to be related to the action of endogenous opiates. The analgesic characteristics of acupuncture are eliminated if subjects are first given naloxone, a chemical that blocks the effect of opioids. It is interesting to note that the **placebo effect** may also be due to endogenous opiates. (A placebo is an inert or nonmedicinal substance that is "prescribed" by a physician. Evidently, placebos produce the desired relief of symptoms because the patient *believes* that they will.) The ability of a placebo to affect the experience of pain is blocked by naloxone (Levine, Gordon, & Fields, 1979). This would indicate that the placebo actually does produce a pharmacological effect through endogenous opioides. How this is accomplished is not understood.

Anatomy of the Somatosensory System

Somatosensory information from the body enters the central nervous system via the dorsal root of the spinal nerves. Information from the face and head enters through the cranial nerves, primarily the trigeminal nerve. The cell bodies of the primary sensory cells are located in the dorsal root or cranial ganglia. Typically, the somatosensory pathway is divided into two distinct anatomical systems: the **lemniscal** and the **spinothalamic pathways**.

For the reasons that follow, the lemniscal system is thought to be a newer evolutionary development.

1. The lemniscal fibers tend to be more heavily myelinated and, therefore, conduct information more rapidly.

2. The lemniscal system provides precisely localized information about touch and pressure. The spinothalamic pathways provide less precise information concerning temperature and pain.

3. The first-order sensory cells of the lemniscal system project to nuclei in the medulla before they synapse onto second-order sensory neurons. The first-order sensory cells of the spinothalamic system synapse in the dorsal horn at the entry level of the spinal cord.

4. Decussation (crossing over of information to the contralateral side) occurs at the level of the medulla in the lemniscal system. Spinothalamic fibers decussate at the point of entry as would be true in segmented invertebrate animals.

5. The spinothalamic system sends many fibers into the reticular formation, a structure that has an important sensory-motor function in primitive vertebrates. Neocortical projections from the spinothalamic system tend to be less precise. This is particularly true for pain fibers.

Figure 9-9
a. The lemniscal somato-sensory pathways.
b. The spinothalamic somatosensory pathways.

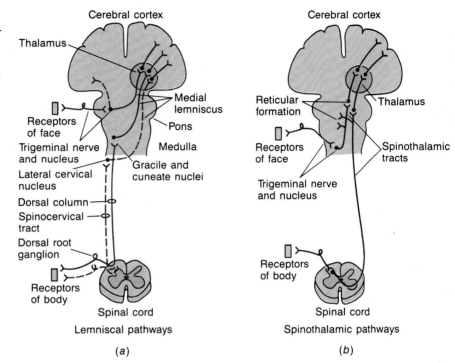

Lemniscal pathways

(a)

Spinothalamic pathways

(b)

Now let us examine the lemniscal and spinothalamic pathways in some detail (Figure 9-9).

The Lemniscal Pathways

The lemniscal pathways are shown in Figure 9-9a. The first-order unipolar sensory neuron has an exceptionally long axon. For example, a touch fiber from the tip of your toe travels all the way up the leg and across the body to enter into the dorsal root at the lumbar level of the spine. The soma for this cell is located in the doorsal root ganglion. A fiber from the same cell enters the spinal cord and immediately courses in the rostral direction through the dorsal column to nuclei located in the medulla (the **nucleus gracilus** and the **nucleus cuneatus**). The cell that started in the toe ends up in the medulla.

At the level of the medulla the first-order cells make a synapse onto the second-order neurons. These cells decussate immediately and enter the **medial lemniscal** pathway, which projects to the ventral posterior nucleus of the thalamus. The neurons synapse in the thalamus and the third-order neurons project to the somatosensory cortex. Muscle, tendon, and joint receptors follow a similar pathway to the somatosensory cortex. Because these neurons are so closely related to muscle control, they are discussed in more detail later in this chapter.

Somatosensory information from the head is carried by the trigeminal, facial, and vagus nerves. Most of this information is carried by the trigeminal nerve through the trigeminal ganglion to the trigeminal nucleus, where the first synapse occurs. The second-order fibers decussate immediately and form the trigeminal lemniscus, which courses toward the ventral posterior nucleus of the thalamus. As was true with the other lemniscal fibers, these neurons synapse in the thalamus with third-order neurons that, in turn, project to the somatosensory cortex.

The Spinothalamic Pathways

The spinothalamic pathways are depicted in Figure 9-9b. Note that unlike the lemniscal system, the first-order neurons synapse immediately in the dorsal horn on the ipsilateral side of the spinal cord. Second-order neurons decussate at the same vertebral level and then course upward, forming the spinothalamic tract. Many of these neurons send branches to the reticular formation. Some of the second-order fibers follow a polysynaptic pathway through the reticular formation (the **reticulothalamic tract**). All of the second-order neurons, however, terminate in either the ventral posterior nucleus (temperature) or the **parafascicular nucleus** (pain) of the thalamus.

Sensory information from the head enters the CNS through the trigeminal nerve. The fibers synapse in the trigeminal nucleus and decussate immediately, forming the **trigeminothalamic tract**, which terminates in the ventral posterior and parafascicular nuclei of the thalamus. As was true for the lemniscal pathways, the temperature fibers then project to the primary receptor area of the neocortex. The third-order pain fibers appear to project to many higher cortical structures.

Organization of the Somatosensory Cortex

It was noted earlier that Mountcastle (1957) was among the first to report that the somatosensory cortex is organized into columns of cells. Each column is composed of cells that have a similar function. Additionally, the somatosensory cortex appears to be organized in a manner that reflects a topographical representation of the body. That is, a map of the body (called a **homunculus**) is represented across the surface of the cortex. Interestingly, the homunculus is quite distorted. Not all areas of the body have equal representation. Rather, those areas that have greater sensory fidelity and are more "important" in our behavior have a disproportionate amount of cortical representation. Figure 9-10 is the somatosensory homunculus that was produced by Penfield and Rasmussen (1950) by direct stimulation of the postcentral gyrus.

It was originally thought that there was only one primary somatosenory projection area on the surface of the cortex and that this area sent out information to surrounding "association" areas. More recent studies have shown that there are many cortical representations for the body senses. As was true with vision, the number of cortical representations seems to increase in the more complex vertebrates. For example, Merzenich and Kaas (1980) have mapped at least seven somatosensory

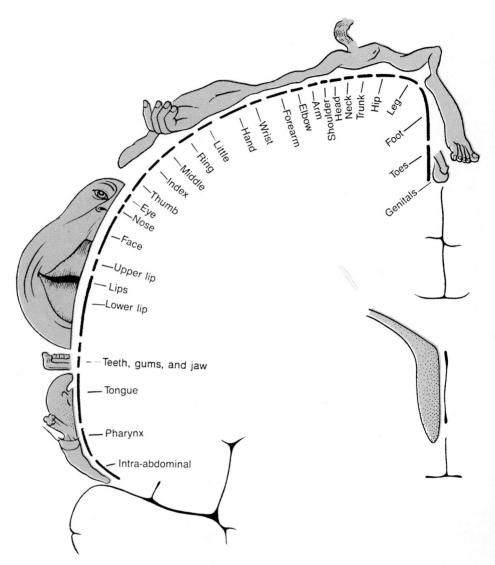

Figure 9-10
The somatosensory homunculus mapped across the postcentral gyrus.
(Adapted from Penfield & Rasmussen, 1950.)

representations (**animunculi**) on the surface of the owl monkey brain. Each animunculus appears to be a complete and orderly representation of the surface of the body or of deep body tissues. It now appears that each cortical map responds to a specific submodality (e.g., receptors that detect muscle length, receptors for vibration) of the somatosensory system (Dykes, 1983). There is still much to be learned about the function of the many cortical somatosensory maps in primate brains. Further research will undoubtedly provide important new insights.

PART 2 MOTOR CONTROL

Clearly, information about changes in our environment, as well as changes in the internal state of our bodies, is of limited use unless we are able to do something about that information. The ability to act on sensory input is the domain of the efferent portion of the CNS. The efferent neuronal system acts on sensory information by modulating the activity of glands and muscles. In the remainder of this chapter we examine the muscles and motor control by the CNS.

The Muscles

There are three distinct kinds of muscle tissues: striate, smooth, and cardiac muscle (Figure 9-11). **Striate muscles** account for most of the muscle mass in the body. The striate muscles, which get their name from the distinctive stripes that run perpendicular to the length of the muscle fibers, are sometimes referred to as skeletal muscles because most of them are attached to bones and control skeletal movement. (The extrinsic muscles of the eye, which move the eye in its orbit, and some stomach muscles are exceptions to this general rule.) The striate muscles are under the direct conscious control of the CNS.

Smooth muscle, unlike the striate muscles, is controlled by the autonomic nervous system. Because of this we have little conscious control over the action of the smooth muscles. Smooth muscles are found, primarily, in and around internal organs such as the bladder and the uterus, and in the walls of blood vessels. In the digestive system, smooth muscle is found in the walls of the stomach and the small and large intestines. The smooth muscles produce the rhythmic peristaltic move-

Figure 9-11
The three types of muscle: (a) smooth, (b) striate, and (c) cardiac.

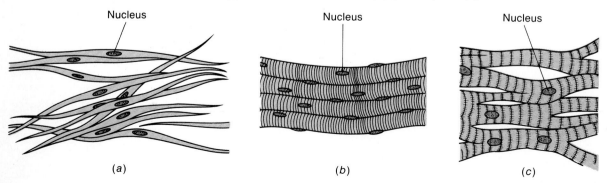

Nucleus	Nucleus	Nucleus
(a)	(b)	(c)

ments that churn the food in the stomach and move the solid matter through the gut.

Smooth muscle also constitutes the intrinsic muscles of the eye—the ciliary muscle that controls the shape of the lens and the radiating and sphincter muscles of the iris, which control the size of the pupil. Finally, smooth muscles are found at the base of some body hairs, where they control **piloerections** (elevating the hair). The "chicken skin" or "goose bump" effect that results from sympathetic nervous system activation is due to the constriction of smooth muscle in hairy skin.

An Observation: From Threat Display to "Chicken Skin"

Did you ever wonder why people get "goose bumps" or "chicken skin" when they are frightened or angered? Many vertebrate animals have developed characteristic visual displays that communicate their level of agitation to other animals. Most birds, for example, have characteristic postures, with the head elevated, when they threaten each other. Many reptiles and amphibians have evolved specialized patches of skin on the head and/or back that can be elevated or inflated to make threatening displays.

In many mammals body hair, which is controlled by smooth muscles, is used to signal agitation. You have no doubt observed that cats elevate the hair on their necks and backs when they are threatened. The piloerection is produced by sympathetic activation of the smooth muscles at the base of the hair follicle. This is just a part of the cat's threat display, which is clearly understood as a threat by members of the same species. The complete threat display in domestic cats includes arching the back, pulling back the ears, baring the teeth, and producing the characteristic hissing sound.

Among the primates, the baboon is without doubt the champion at producing impressive threat displays. The male baboon has very long, stiff hairs on the neck, back, and shoulders that, when elevated, cause him to appear much larger. This piloerection, along with an impressive set of canine teeth, makes a most effective threatening display toward other males and for potential predators as well.

Humans have lost much of their body hair. With the exception of the head and face, the body hair that remains is sparce and quite short compared to that of other primates. Nevertheless, when frightened or angry we too experience a piloerection in the form of "goose bumps." This vestigial form of behavior is likely the remnant of a more effective threat display of our more hairy ancestors. The ineffective "chicken skin" effect makes more sense if we view it in an evolutionary perspective. I say more about threatening displays when we discuss emotional behavior.

As its name suggests, **cardiac muscle** is only found in the heart. This type of muscle looks very similar to striate muscle. Cardiac muscle is unique in that it continues to function rhythmically in the abscence of all neuronal input. This fortunate characteristic of cardiac muscle is what permits successful surgical heart transplants. The characteristic pattern and rate of cardiac constrictions are controlled by a small group of "pacemaker" cells. The pacemaker is modulated by hormones, particularly the catecholamines, that are in the blood.

For the remainder of this chapter I concentrate on skeletal muscle and the integration of sensory information and motor control.

How Skeletal Muscles Work

Striate muscle is made up of two very different kinds of muscle fibers, extrafusal and intrafusal muscle fibers. The **extrafusal fibers** are thicker, and they are controlled by **alpha motor neurons**. The extrafusal fibers provide almost all of the motor force produced by striate muscles. Each alpha motor neuron innervates a number of extrafusal fibers. The number of muscle fibers controlled by an efferent neuron varies widely. In those muscles that have greater precision, like the muscles in the fingers of the hand, the number of muscle fibers controlled by a single neuron is small. In other muscles having less precision, like the diaphragm or the muscles in the buttocks, a single motor neuron may innervate hundreds of muscle fibers.

The **intrafusal fibers** are thin, and they contract when activated by **gamma motor neurons**; however, the contraction of these fibers has very little motor force. The intrafusal fibers contain specialized structures called **muscle spindle organs**, which contain afferent neurons. The spindle receptor cells are stretch receptors that provide information about the length of the muscle.

HOW MUSCLES CONTRACT

Efferent neurons terminate at the **neuromuscular junction**, where the motor neurons synapse on the **motor end plate**. When the propagated action potential reaches the motor axon, terminal calcium channels are opened, allowing Ca^+ to enter releasing the neuromuscular transmitter. The transmitter substance, acetylcholine, causes a depolarization of the postsynaptic membrane that is propagated down the length of the muscle fiber. The acetylcholine is then broken down by its enzyme, acetylcholine esterase.

Each muscle fiber contains a bundle of myofibrils that consists of overlapping strands of protein, **actin** and **myosin**. The myosin component is studded with motile, paddlelike structures that insert into the adjacent actin molecule. Depolarization of the muscle membrane causes the paddles on the myosin molecules to bind to the actin strands and bend in one direction, release from the actin molecule, bend back, attach

Figure 9-12
The anatomy of the skeletal muscles shown in increasing levels of magnification. *a.* The muscle is made of (*b*) individual muscle fibers. *c.* The muscle fiber is divided into smaller divisions called myofibrils by a reticulated membrane called the sarcoplasmic reticulum. *d.* The myofibrils are composed of sarcomeres, which are attached end to end. *e.* Within each sarcomere alternating fibers of actin and myosin are connected by cross bridges from the myosin molecules. *f.* In vertebrate skeletal muscle the actin and myosin filaments are in register, giving the muscle a striped appearance.

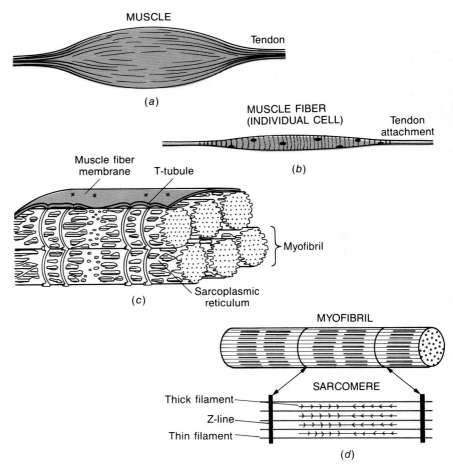

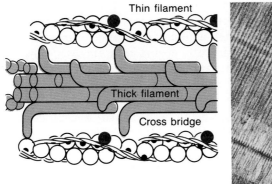

to the actin and bend again. This ratchetlike action causes the myosin and actin strands to slide across each other in small steps, shortening the overall length of the muscle. The amount and the force of the contraction are, as you might expect, modulated by the number of alpha neurons involved and their firing rate.

As you know, the contraction of muscles takes energy. The energy comes from adenosine triphosphate (ATP), which has high-energy phosphate bonds (Figure 9-13). When the ATP attaches to the myosin paddles, it breaks down to adenosine disphosphate, releasing the energy from one of its phosphate bonds.

FEEDBACK FROM THE MUSCLES

The muscle spindle organs are designed to provide information concerning the length of the muscle. They are not, however, the only afferent neurons to be found in the muscles. Stretch receptors, **Golgi tendon organs**, are located in the tendons where the muscles attach to the bone. Unlike the spindles, these stretch receptors detect the force exerted by the muscle through the tendons by increasing their firing rate as force increases. Therefore, while the spindles of the intrafusal muscles encode the length of the muscle, the Golgi receptors report how hard the muscle is pulling.

The Reflex Arc Revisited   In Chapter 3 we examined the anatomy of the spinal cord. You probably recall that the afferent neurons enter the spinal cord through the dorsal root and that efferent fibers exit through the ventral root. This configuration is the basis of the sensory-motor reflex arc.

MONOSYNAPTIC REFLEX

The muscle reflex is dependent on both sensory and motor fibers. Let us first examine the simplist form of spinal reflex, the **monosynaptic** (meaning "only one synapse") **reflex** arc. I don't mean to imply here that there are only two neurons involved. In fact, most reflexive circuits require the combined action of thousands of sensory and motor neurons. *Monosynaptic* in this case means that there is only one synaptic *level* between the afferent and efferent neurons.

The **patellar reflex** (knee jerk) is an example of a monosynaptic reflex. Striking the ligament that is attached to the patella with a soft mallet causes the muscle to be stretched. Receptors in the tendons of the quadracept muscle send this information back to the spine, where they synapse onto efferent neurons at the same spinal level. The efferent fibers, in turn, cause the muscle to shorten, resulting in the knee jerk response. Figure 9-14 shows the monosynaptic reflex.

Monosynaptic reflexes take place very rapidly. The time delay between the activation of the tendon receptor and the muscle response is approximately 50 msec. Making the same motor action voluntarily

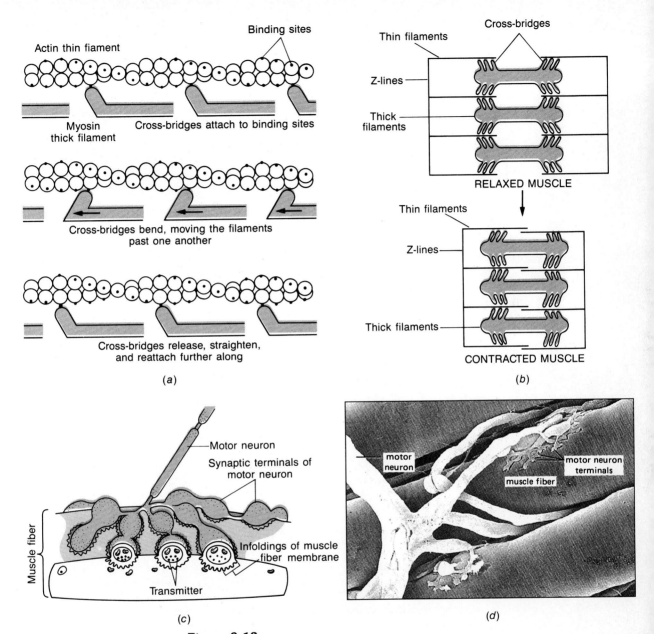

Actin thin fiament

Binding sites

Myosin thick filament

Cross-bridges attach to binding sites

Cross-bridges bend, moving the filaments past one another

Cross-bridges release, straighten, and reattach further along

(a)

Cross-bridges

Thin filaments

Z-lines

Thick filaments

RELAXED MUSCLE

Thin filaments

Z-lines

Thick filaments

CONTRACTED MUSCLE

(b)

Motor neuron

Synaptic terminals of motor neuron

Muscle fiber

Infoldings of muscle fiber membrane

Transmitter

(c)

motor neuron

muscle fiber

motor neuron terminals

(d)

Figure 9-13

a. Muscle contraction. In response to the depolarization of the muscle membrane, the paddlelike structures of the myosin bend in one direction, release from the actin, bend back, attach to the actin, and bend again. *b.* The resulting ratchetlike action causes the actin and myosin filaments to move relative to each other, shortening the muscle fiber. *c.* The neuromuscular junction. Action potentials reaching the terminus of the motor neuron cause the release of the transmitter, which binds to receptor sites on the membrane of the muscle fiber. *d.* Scanning electron micrograph showing the neuromuscular junction. (See also Color Plate 16.)

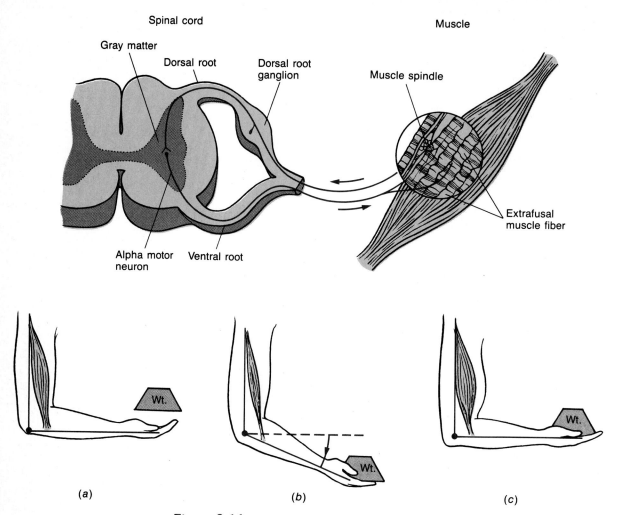

Figure 9-14
The monosynaptic reflex. Dropping the weight onto the hand causes the bicep to lengthen (*a & b*). The spindle fibers in the bicep activate the alpha motor neuron in the ventral horn, causing the reflexive shortening of the bicep (*c*).

would take 200 msec or more. This large difference can be attributed to the fact that monosynaptic spinal reflexes have only one synapse and do not require the multisynaptic participation of neural centers in the brain.

You can demonstrate this to yourself quite easily. Have someone hold an ordinary playing card between your thumb and first finger. Then, without your accomplice giving you prior warning, try to catch the card between your fingers when the card is released. It can't be done.

Too much time is required to detect the motion of the card with the visual system, decide to close your grip, and finally send this information to the muscles in the hand.

POLYSYNAPTIC REFLEX

Most synaptic reflexes require more than one synapse. These **polysynaptic** reflex circuits vary widely in complexity. Some are relatively simple and involve afferent and efferent neurons and interneurons at just one level of the spinal column. Others include neurons at two or more levels of the spinal cord, and neural centers in the brain may be included as well.

Think of what would happen if you were to pick up a very hot cup. In addition to the reflexive action to let the cup go, there would also be associated postural changes to withdraw the whole body and control balance. These other reflexive motor reactions are mediated by other levels of the spinal cord. The conscious experience of the event does not take place at the spinal level at all. Rather, this requires participation of higher neural centers in the brain. Let's take this example one step further. Suppose that the cup is a rare and expensive piece of china. Central inhibition may come into play here, blocking the reflexive tendency to drop the cup!

COORDINATION OF OPPONENT MUSCLES

Muscles cannot push; they can only pull. Because of this obvious fact, muscles must be organized into opponent pairs sometimes referred to as **flexors** and **extensors**. (It should be noted that not all striate muscles move limbs. Some, like the muscles that raise and lower the eyelids or the muscles in the lips, serve a very different function.) Each muscle of the opponent pair serves as the antagonist to the other, moving the limb in the opposite direction. The two muscles work in concert so that when one is contracting, the antagonist is relaxing and lengthening.

The reciprocal action of the opponent muscles is controlled by the stretch receptors in the intrafusal muscle fibers. These afferents send axons to inhibitory interneurons, which synapse on the alpha motor neurons of the antagonist muscle. Therefore, contraction of one muscle of an opponent pair produces inhibition of the antagonist muscle, thus permitting smooth movement of the limb.

Brain Structures in the Control of Movement

Complex motor action is under the control of a variety of structures in the brain, including the cerebellum, the basal ganglia, the thalamus, motor areas of the cerebral hemispheres, and a number of brain stem nuclei. Traditionally, the motor areas of the brain have been divided into two

The Evolution of Muscle Control—Variations on a Common Theme

The movement of the body, or parts of the body, is dependent on a support system and muscles that work in opposite directions. This basic theme can be seen throughout much of the animal kingdom. (Refer to Spotlight Figure 9-2.)

Hydrostatic Skeletons: Many marine animals are basically hollow, fluid-filled tubes with soft walls. The fluid pressure inside and outside of the animal is essentially the same, therefore, the soft walls need little structural firmness. These animals, such as the sea anemone, have two layers of muscles that are arranged perpendicular to each other. A circular layer of muscles forms a band around the circumference of the tube, and a layer of longitudinal muscles runs the length of the body.

The two bands of muscles work in concert so that when one constricts the other relaxes. When the longitudinal band constricts, the circular band relaxes. This causes the animal to constrict, forcing fluid out of the apical opening of the body. The opposite muscle action leng-thens the animal and consequently draws fluid into the hollow center of the body.

Exoskeletons: Arthropods, such as crabs and insects, have evolved a rigid, protective outer skeleton. Flexible joints, or hinges, permit movement between segments of the exoskeleton. Each joint has two muscles spanning the flexible hinge, a flexor and an extensor. As was true with the anemone, the two muscles work in a cooperative fashion so that when one constricts the other relaxes. Constricting the extensor while relaxing the flexor causes the joint to straighten. The opposite muscle action causes the joint to bend.

Endoskeletons: Humans and other vertebrates possess a rigid internal skeleton. Generally, the bones of the skeleton meet at one of two types of joints: (1) hinged joints, such as the elbow, and (2) ball-and-socket joints, such as the hip. Pairs of antagonistic muscles are attached on either side of the joints. When extensors contract and flexors relax, the joint straightens.

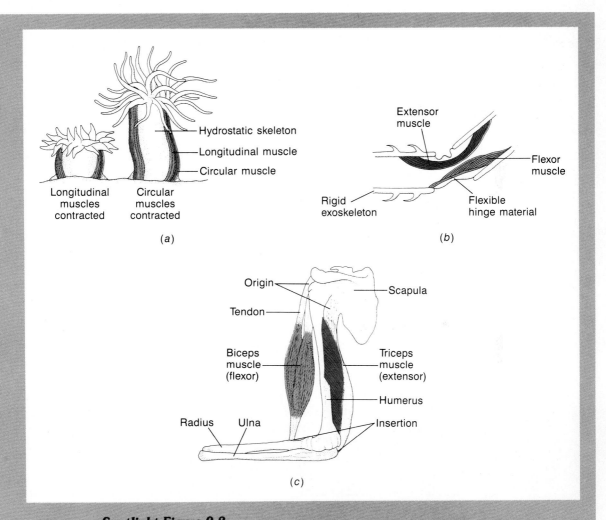

Spotlight Figure 9-2
a. The hydrostatic skeleton as seen in the anemone. *b*. The exoskeleton of arthropods. *c*. The endoskeleton of the vertebrates.

separate, yet interrelated, systems: (1) the pyramidal system and (2) the extrapyramidal motor system. This division is based on anatomical differences between the two systems. Also, clinical data derived from individuals who have experienced brain damage show that the two motor systems control different aspects of motor behavior.

The Pyramidal System

The **pyramidal system** includes neurons that have their cell bodies in the motor cortex. The axons of the pyramidal system are heavily myelinated and pass through the brain stem to form the **pyramidal tract**. Most of the axons (85–90% of the pyramidal tract decussate in the medulla and form the lateral cerebrospinal tract. The remainder stay on the ipsilateral side, forming the ventral cerebrospinal tract. Information from these fibers decussates at lower levels of the spinal cord where the fibers synapse onto other efferent neurons in the ventral horn (see Figure 9-15).

As noted earlier, the pyramidal system is a relatively new evolutionary invention. Among all of the contemporary vertebrates it is found only in the mammals. It has been estimated that in humans the pyramidal tract has approximately one million fibers. This figure is about double that found in the cow and horse, animals that are considerably larger than humans (Towe, 1973). Lesions to the pyramidal system produce profound motor dysfunctions in humans. Similar, but less severe, motor losses have been noted in other primates. In mammals other than primates the impairments resulting from lesions to the motor cortex are much less debilitating. From these data it would seem reasonable to think that the pyramidal system has evolved to serve increasingly important executive functions controlling precise, voluntary motor actions.

By far, the largest number of pyramidal cells originate in a narrow strip of motor cortex, the **precentral gyrus**. Clinical data have shown that lesions to this area of the brain result in partial flacid paralysis of striate muscle on the contralateral side of the body. Typically there is some recovery of function following lesions to the precentral gyrus. Reflexive movements tend to return first, followed by a partial recovery of voluntary movements. It is not clear whether the recovery is attributable to yet undamaged portions of the pyramidal system or to other motor centers (Wiesendanger, 1984). As you might predict, stimulation to the motor cortex produces movement of muscles on the contralateral side of the body.

Wilder Penfield and his colleagues (1975) found that direct stimulation of the precentral gyrus reveals a topographical representation of the body. As was true for the sensory homunculus, the motor homunculus is a distorted representation of the body. Muscle groups having greater precision, like the muscles in the fingers, have cortical representations that are very large, whereas muscle groups in the torso, legs, buttocks, and so on are underrepresented. This makes sense if you recall that for

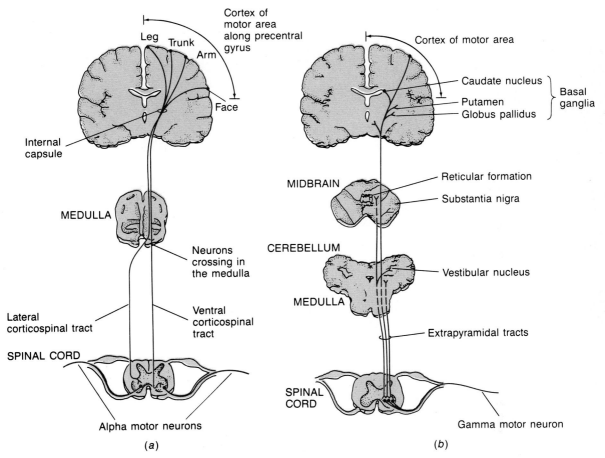

Figure 9-15

a. The anatomy of the pyramidal motor system. *b.* The anatomy of the extrapyramidal motor system.

muscles having greater precision, a single motor neuron innervates a few muscle fibers, whereas for less precise muscles many hundreds of muscle fibers are activated by one efferent axon.

You have probably noted the remarkable similarity between the motor homunculus found on the precentral gyrus (Figure 9-16) and the sensory homunculus located on the postcentral gyrus (Figure 9-10). The fact that the two homunculi are situated like mirror images of the body is instructive. It shows the intimate and rapid communication that exists between the homologous points of the sensory and motor portions of the cortex.

In a particularly instructive series of studies Evarts (1968, 1972, 1974) demonstrated that pyramidal neurons in the precentral gyrus are

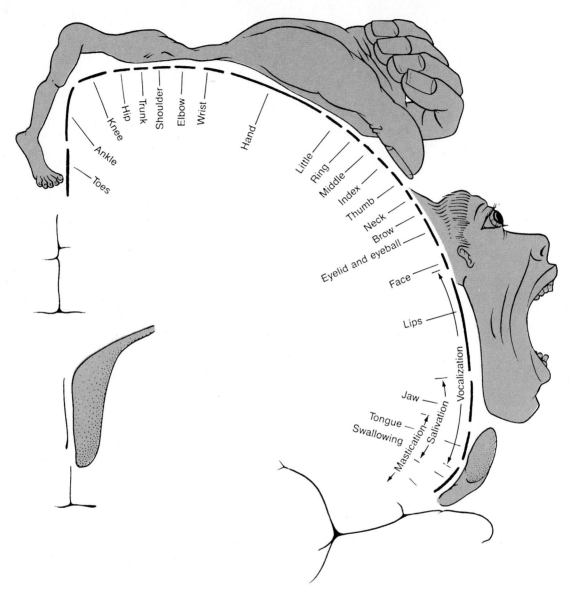

Figure 9-16
The motor homunculus mapped on the precentral gyrus. Note that those muscle groups having greater precision are exaggerated in size. (Adapted from Penfield & Rasmussen, 1950.)

Figure 9-17
The experimental paradigm used by Evarts (*a* & *b*) *c*. Activity of the precentral neurons (*top*) is greatest prior to the motor response indicated by the R arrow. The cells in the postcentral gyrus are most active following the onset of the motor response. (Adapted from Evarts, Shinoda, & Wise, 1984.)

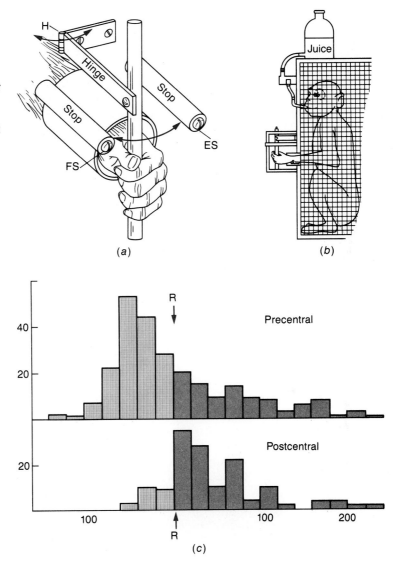

important in planning and executing fine motor behaviors. Evarts recorded single-cell activity in rhesus monkeys that had been trained to make very specific, fine, voluntary motor actions (see Figure 9-17). The monkeys were required to flex or extend the wrist to move a lever in response to various stimuli. If the monkey moved the lever correctly within a given amount of time, it was rewarded with a squirt of fruit juice.

The graph in Figure 9-17 shows clearly that the cells in the precentral gyrus are most active just *prior* to initiating the movement, whereas cells in the postcentral gyrus fire most rapidly after the movement starts. Evarts also demonstrated that the firing rate of some precentral gyrus cells was directly related to the force that would be required to make the motor response.

Finally, Evarts was able to demonstrate that the reaction time required to elicit the motor response was more rapid when the monkey was cued by cutaneous stimulation than when a visual cue was used. This was interpreted as behavioral confirmation that the motor cells forming the motor homunculus along the precentral gyrus receive rapid feedback from the sensory cells that form the homologous points along the somatosensory homunculus on the postcentral gyrus.

An Observation: "I Didn't Move My Finger—You Did!"

Typically, when planned surgery on the brain is done, the patient is given a local, rather than a general, anesthetic. This can be done because there are no pain receptors in the brain. Beyond that, there is a very good reason for doing the surgery with a local anesthetic. It is important for the neurosurgeon to remain in communication with the patient during the surgery. As the operation proceeds, the surgeon stimulates the surface of the cortex with a small electric probe. This is done to establish the function of each area of cortex *before* the scalpel is put to work.

Because the patient is awake, he or she is able to report to the surgeon what experiences occur as a result of the stimulation. As you might expect, what the patient experiences is determined by the part of the cortex receiving the stimulation. Stimulation of the sensory cortex produces sensory experiences. Placing the probe on primary visual or auditory cortex produces visual and auditory experiences.

Stimulation of the motor cortex along the precentral gyrus produces movement on the contralateral side of the body. It is interesting to note that when a motor area is stimulated, for example, the cortical area that controls the hand, the patient is likely to report, "My hand moved" or "You moved my hand," not, "I moved my hand." Thus, direct stimulation to the motor cortex produces movement without volition (Penfield, 1975). The patient is very much aware that he or she did not initiate the movement and further that the movement was beyond his or her control.

The Extrapyramidal System

The **extrapyramidal system** has been loosely defined as all of the cerebral motor structures that do not follow the pyramidal neural pathways. Neuroanatomists disagree concerning what structures should or should not be included in the extrapyramidal system. For our purposes we will include those cortical motor neurons that do not follow the

Figure 9-18
Shadow drawing of the brain showing the anatomy of the basal ganglia.

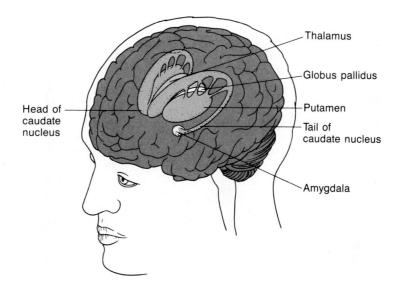

Thalamus

Globus pallidus

Head of caudate nucleus

Putamen

Tail of caudate nucleus

Amygdala

pyramidal tract, the forebrain nuclei (also known as the **basal ganglia**), and some brain stem nuclei, most notably, the substantia nigra and the red nucleus (see Figure 9-18).

The extrapyramidal system differs from the pyramidal motor system in several important ways.

1. Unlike the pyramidal system, which has neurons that originate primarily from the precentral gyrus, the extrapyramidal neurons originate from many cortical areas plus the basal ganglia.

2. The extrapyramidal pathways follow a more complicated, multisynaptic pathway and interact with brainstem nuclei before entering the spinal cord.

3. Whereas the pyramidal system controls fine motor action, particularly on the more peripheral muscles, the extrapyramidal system controls posture and general body movements like walking and bending, and it is more involved with muscles closer to the center of the body.

4. Finally, as I indicated earlier, the pyramidal system is a more recent evolutionary development found only in mammals.

THE ROLE OF THE BASAL GANGLIA

The basal ganglia are a group of forebrain nuclei including the putamen, the globus pallidus, and the caudate nucleus. Some anatomists include the substantia nigra and the subthalamic nuclei in this grouping. The basal ganglia receive input from many areas of the cortex, the thalamus and the cerebellum. Lesions to the basal ganglia result in slow, weak, and poorly coordinated movements (Delong et al., 1984). Generally, large movements of the limbs and torso are most affected.

Disorders of the Basal Ganglia

Two relatively common medical disorders are associated with dysfunction of the basal ganglia. **Parkinson's disease** results from the degeneration of the dopaminergic pathways projecting from the substantia nigra to the caudate nucleus and the putamen. Among others, the symptoms of Parkinson's disease include slow and halting movements, rigidity, resting motor tremors, and difficulty in initiating purposive movements. Although the cause of Parkinson's disease is still not known, it is thought to be due to toxins in the environment rather than to hereditary factors.

Huntington's disease, or **Huntington's chorea** (the word *chorea* means "dance") is caused by degeneration of the caudate nucleus and the putamen. The symptoms of the disease start with facial tremors, which eventually spread to all muscle groups. In the later stages walking, standing, and even sitting unsupported become impossible. Psychological symptoms include difficulty with memory, impaired judgment, delusional thought patterns, emotional lability, and socially inappropriate behaviors. Unlike Parkinson's disease, Huntington's chorea appears to be genetically determined. The disease is controlled by an autosomal dominant gene, and the offspring of individuals who carry the gene have a 50% chance of inheriting the disease (Sanberg & Coyle, 1984).

Interestingly, the symptoms of Huntington's chorea do not appear until later in life. The most common time of onset is between 30 and 50 years of age. Therefore, individuals who are the offspring of someone who has the disease will not know their own fate until much later in life. As you can imagine, this can be quite stressful. Therefore, a search for a presymptomatic test of the disease is under way. Small doses of L-dopa (a chemical precurser of dopamine) trigger Huntington's symptoms in individuals who carry the gene, but it has no effect on normal people. Although this test appears to be reliable, there is some risk that the L-dopa may accelerate the onset of the disease (Klawans, Goetz, Paulson, & Barbeau, 1980).

The Cerebellum   In Chapter 3, I noted that the cerebellum (literally, "little brain") is an extremely complex structure that is associated with motor function. Comparing the cerebellum in various species shows that there is a clear relationship between the size and complexity of this structure and the complexity of the motor behaviors evidenced by the species. For example, flying animals such as birds and bats tend to have a more complex cerebellum than the more sedentary species like the sloth or the turtle.

The cerebellum is connected to the hindbrain and brainstem by three stalks: the superior, middle, and inferior peduncles. Like the two cerebral hemispheres, the cerebellum has several internal nuclei and an outer cortex that is highly convoluted. Much of the cortex is hidden in deep fissures. In humans, only one sixth of the total surface can be seen from the outside.

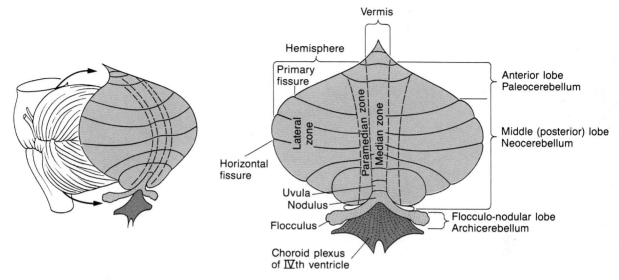

Figure 9-19
The lobes of the cerebellum.

Traditionally, the cerebellum has been divided into three parts based on the timing of their evolutionary development: the archicerebellum, the paleocerebellum and the neocerebellum (see Figure 9-19). As its name suggests the archicerebellum is the oldest part of the cerebellum. It is comprised of the **flocculonodular lobe** (the **flocculus**), and it is functionally associated with the vestibular mechanism. The paleocerebellum is roughly comprised of the **vermis** (the worm). It too is old and is associated primarily with fibers from the spinal cord and the lower brain stem. The remainder of the cerebellum is the neocerebellum. It is the newest part, and it is associated with the motor centers in the cerebral cortex, the thalamus, the upper levels of the brain stem, and the basal ganglia (Noback, 1967).

The cerebellum receives input from the spindle organs of the skeletal muscles. Additionally, somatosensory information from all parts of the body is projected to the cerebellum. Similar to the cerebral cortex, the cerebellum has somatotropic representation (a homunculus) on the cortical surface.

The cortex of the cerebellum has three distinct cellular layers. There is a uniform appearance across most of the surface of the cortex. Efferent fibers from the cerebellum originate in the **Purkinje cells**. These cells synapse onto other efferent neurons in the deep cerebellar nuclei, which, in turn, send axons via multisynaptic pathways through the cerebral peduncles to other brain centers. Recent studies have shown that all of the Purkinje cells produce postsynaptic inhibition on all of their target cells via the inhibitory transmitter substance, gamma-aminobutyric acid (GABA). This does not mean that the cerebellum serves only to inhibit motor activity. Many of the Purkinje cells innervate other efferents in the deep cerebellar nuclei, which normally show a high level of activity. Evidently, the Purkinje cells modulate and tune the activity of these cells, which have both excititory and inhibitory functions (see Color Plate 6).

Due to the inhibitory nature of the Purkinje cells it was originally thought that the cerebellum only functioned to produce the unconscious control of muscle tone and balance. It is now known that the cerebellum does this and more. Single-cell recordings similar to that used by Evarts (as just described) have shown that, like motor cells in the cerebral cortex, cells in the cerebellum become very active prior to motor action. This suggests that the cerebellum may have a function in planning and initiating conscious motor activity.

Lesions to the cerebellum invariably cause characteristic motor symptoms. The specific symptoms are determined by the size and location of the lesion. Additionally, the symptoms can be attributed to the other motor centers in the brain that depend on the cerebellar input. For example, the flocculus is so intimately involved with the vestibular mechanism, problems with posture and balance occur when this structure is damaged.

Damage to the area bordering the vermis causes motor weakness and discontinuity of motor action. As an example, following a lesion to this area, the coordinated shoulder, arm, wrist, and hand movements required to toss a Frisbee would be accomplished serially rather than simultaneously. That is, the individual may first move the shoulder, followed by the arm, the wrist, and then the hand movement rather than making one coordinated and simultaneous movement of all the associated muscles.

Lesions to the lateral areas of the neocerebellum impair the timing and force of ballistic movements. Following these lesions, people tend to make errors in the direction, intensity, and timing of many movements like typing, clapping hands, and hitting or kicking a ball (Brooks, 1984). Some people evidence **hyperkineticdystonia**, which is characterized by exaggerated, ballistic movements. For example, when reaching for a cup, the person is unable to stop the movement in time and literally reaches through the cup, knocking it over. Evidently, we cannot rely on visual feedback to control the duration and force of ballistic movements. By the time we perceive that the movement is sufficient, it is too late to stop it in a timely manner. The cerebellum does this for us by timing the contraction of the agonist muscles needed to counter the movement.

CHAPTER SUMMARY

1. The *cutaneous* sense, which provides information about the surface of the body, and the *kinesthetic* sense, which provides information concerning our joints and muscles, make up the *somatosensory system*. The skin is

composed of the *epidermis*, which is several layers of dead tissue, and the *dermis*, which contains the receptor cells for cutaneous sensation.

2. Some receptor cells such as the *Pacinian corpuscle* appear to be specific for one or a few qualities of sensation, whereas others such as the *free nerve endings* appear to be much less specific. All cutaneous receptors respond to changes in the level of the adequate stimulus and show adaptation to steady states.

3. Touch is the most complex cutaneous sense and includes the experience of light touch, pressure, deep pressure, and vibration. The distribution and variety of touch receptors vary widely in different parts of the body. The density of touch receptors is greatest in those areas of the skin where localization, discrimination, and feature detection are most clearly developed.

4. The sense of pain is important for the survival of the species. A wide range of stimuli, all of which could produce tissue damage, are associated with pain. Unlike with other senses, the projection of pain fibers in the brain is not localized. Some researchers believe that there are two types of pain—*dull pain* and *bright pain*. Dull pain is carried by thin, slow, unmyelinated fibers, whereas bright pain is carried by fat, rapid, highly myelinated fibers.

5. Morphinelike neuromodulators called *endogenous opiates* are present in the brain. These substances—called *enkephalins, endorphins,* and *dynorphins*—appear to moderate the sensation of pain.

6. The two major somatosensory pathways are the *lemniscal* and the *spinothalamic* pathways. The lemniscal system is thought to be a newer evolutionary development. With the possible exception of pain fibers, both somatosensory pathways project to the somatosensory cortex of the brain, where they form a topographical representation of the body called an *animunculus* or *humunculus*. As was true with vision, the number of cortical representations seems to increase in the more complex vertebrates.

7. There are three kinds of muscles: *smooth, cardiac,* and *striate*. Smooth muscle is controlled by the ANS. Cardiac muscle is only found in the heart and continues to function in the absence of all neuronal input. Striate, or skeletal, muscle is made up of *extrafusal* fibers, which cause the muscle to shorten, and *intrafusal* fibers, which provide feedback concerning the length of the muscle. Both types of fibers are innervated by efferent fibers at the *neuromuscular junction*. The neuromuscular transmitter is acetylcholine.

8. Each striate muscle fiber contains bundles of *myofibrils* that consist of overlapping strands of *actin* and *myosin*. When excited by depolarization of the muscle fiber, the two molecules move across each other in ratchetlike action. This causes the muscle to become shorter. The amount of contraction is determined by the number of alpha neurons involved and their firing rate.

9. Skeletal muscles are organized into opposing pairs—*flexors* and *extensors*. The reciprocal action of the opponent muscles is controlled by the stretch receptors in the intrafusal muscle fibers.

10. The motor areas of the brain have been divided into two separate but interrelated systems—the pyramidal and the extrapyramidal motor systems. This division is based on anatomical and functional differences. The pyramidal system is a relatively new evolutionary development and functions in voluntary, precise motor action. The extrapyramidal system is quite diverse and includes those cortical motor fibers that do not follow the pyramidal pathways, the *basal ganglia*, and motor areas in the brain stem. The extrapyramidal system controls posture and general body movements like walking and bending.

11. The cerebellum has been divided into three parts based on the timing of their evolutionary development. The *archicerebellum* is the oldest part and innervates the vestibular mechanism. The *paleocerebellum* is associated with structures in the spinal cord and the hindbrain. The *neocerebellum* is the newest structure and is associated with motor areas in the cerebral cortex. Efferent fibers from the cerebellum originate in the *Purkinje cells*, which produce postsynaptic inhibition via the inhibitory neurotransmitter *GABA*. Lesions to various areas of the cerebellum produce motor deficits. The specific motor loss varies with the location of the cerebellar lesion.

SUGGESTED READINGS

Davis J. (1984). *Endorphins: New waves in brain chemistry*. New York: Doubleday.

Evarts, E. V. (1979). Brain mechanisms of movement. In *The brain* (a *Scientific American* book). San Francisco: Freeman.

Iggo, A., & Andres, K. (1982). Morphology of cutaneous receptors. *Annual Review of Neuroscience, 5*, 1–32.

Miles, F. A., & Evarts, E. V. (1979). Concepts of motor organization. *Annual Review of Psychology, 30*, 327–362.

KEY TERMS

Actin   Together with myosin, one of the two protein molecules that mediate the contraction of muscle fibers.

Alpha motor neuron   Efferent neuron that originates in the ventral horn and causes the contraction of extrafusal muscle fibers.

Animunculus   Schematic topographical representation of the surface of the animal body on the cortex of the brain; *see also* Homunculus.

Bradykinin   Substance produced by the action of cell enzymes on certain blood proteins.

Thought to be the adequate stimulus for some forms of pain.

Cardiac muscle   The type of muscle found in the heart.

Cutaneous   Pertaining to the skin.

Dermis   Living skin found beneath the epidermis.

Dynorphins   *See* Endogenous opiates.

Endogenous opiates   Neuromodulator substances, including enkephalins, endorphins, and dynorphins, that are associated with pain-blocking circuits in the brain.

Endorphins   *See* Endogenous opiates.

Endoskeleton   The rigid internal skeleton of vertebrates.

Enkephalins   *See* Endogenous opiates.

Epidermis   Nonliving outermost layer of the skin.

Exoskeleton   The rigid outside skeleton that is characteristic of the arthropods.

Extensor (muscle)   Muscle of opponent pair of muscles; extensors tend to extend joints; *see also* flexors.

Extrafusal muscle   Large striate muscle fibers that are responsible for the motor force of the skeletal muscles.

Extrapyramidal system   Diverse motor system comprised of structures not included in the pyramidal motor system.

Flexor (muscle)   Muscle of opponent pair of muscles; flexors tend to bend joints; *see also* extensor.

Gamma motor neuron   Efferent neuron that causes the contraction of intrafusal motor fibers.

Glabous skin   Hairless skin such as the skin found on the fingertips and the palms of the hand.

Golgi tendon organ   Stretch receptor in the tendons of striate muscle; encodes the force applied by the muscle through the tendon.

Homunculus   Schematic topographical representation of the surface of the human body on the cortex of the brain; *see also* Animunculus.

Huntington's disease   Muscle disorder related to degeneration of the caudate nucleus; also known as Huntington's chorea.

Hydroskeleton   The fluid-supported, soft-walled skeleton characteristic of many marine animals.

Hyperkineticdystonia   Exaggerated movements resulting from lesions to the cerebellum.

Intrafusal muscle   Muscle fiber that functions primarily as a stretch receptor that reports the length of the muscle.

Kinesthesis   Part of the body senses that reports body position and movement.

Lemniscal pathway   Somatosensory pathway for touch and pressure.

Monosynaptic reflex   The most simple form of reflex; has one synapse between sensory and motor fibers.

Motor end plate   The postsynaptic region of the neuromuscular junction.

Muscle spindle organ   Sensory structures of intrafusal muscle fibers; provide feedback about the length of the muscle.

Myosin   *See* Actin.

Neuromuscular junction   The synapse between the motor neuron and the muscle fiber.

Nociceptor   Receptor cells having free nerve endings; may be specialized for reporting pain.

Nucleus cuneatus   Relay nucleus of the lemniscal pathway located in the medulla.

Nucleus gracilus   Relay nucleus of the lemniscal pathway located in the medulla.

Patellar reflex   The knee jerk reflex; based on a monosynaptic reflex arc.

Piloerection   Elevation of the hair by smooth muscles at the base of the hair follicle.

Placebo effect   The response to an inert or nonmedicinal substance sometimes given by a physician to please the patient.

Precentral gyrus   Motor cortex located anterior to the central sulcus.

Prefrontal lobotomy   The surgical isolation of the most anterior pole of the cortex from the remainder of the brain.

Psychological heat   The subjective experience of heat produced by stimulating the skin with an alternating pattern of warm and cool.

Purkinje cells   Output cells located in the cortex of the cerebellum.

Somatosensory   The body senses.

Smooth muscle   Muscle found in internal organs; controlled by the ANS.

Spinothalamic pathway   Somatosensory pathway for temperature and pain.

Spindal organ   Stretch receptor organ associated with the intrafusal muscles.

Striate muscle   Skeletal muscles that control body movement.

Chapter 10

Consuming: Eating and Drinking

PART 1   CONSUMMATORY BEHAVIOR AND THIRST

Consummatory Behavior

Homeostasis
Drives versus Mechanisms

Thirst

Drinking Strategies
The Partitioning of Fluid in the Body

Mechanisms for the Control of Water Balance

Kidney Function
Drinking Initiators and Inhibitors
Volumetric Thirst
Osmometric Thirst
The Role of the Lateral Hypothalamus
Terminating Drinking Behavior

PART 2   EATING BEHAVIOR

Hunger

Feeding Strategies
Eating Mechanisms in the Blowfly

Neural Centers for Eating

Problems with the Dual Center Model
Centers or tracts?

Hunger and Satiety

The Stomach
Sham Feeding
Glucose and Hunger
Cholecystokinin and Hunger

Learning and Experience Effects on Eating

Set Points?
Eating Disorders

Chapter Learning Objectives

After reading this chapter, you should

1. Be able to define and give examples of homeostatic mechanisms.

2. Be able to compare and contrast drive theories and mechanism models of consummatory behaviors.

3. Be able to discuss the drinking strategies of various species and relate them to their biological niche.

4. Understand how fluid is partitioned in intracellular and extracellular partitions of the body.

5. Be able to discuss how the kidney controls fluid and salt balance.

6. Know the difference between volumetric thirst and osmometric thirst and be able to describe how these two sources of thirst are related.

7. Be familiar with the role of the hypothalamus in the control of drinking behavior.

8. Be able to explain how peripheral and central mechanisms influence the termination of drinking.

9. Understand how ecological factors affect the eating strategies of various species.

10. Be familiar with the strengths and weaknesses of the dual center model of eating behavior.

11. Be able to describe how peripheral and central mechanisms influence the onset and termination of eating.

12. Know how learning and experience can influence eating behaviors. Specifically, be able to explain how experience may influence eating disorders.

PART 1   CONSUMMATORY BEHAVIOR AND THIRST

Consummatory Behavior

To sustain the basic processes of life, all living things must consume matter from the environment. Plants consume water, minerals, and other essential elements from the soil and the air. They thereby create the essential organic materials that sustain, either directly or indirectly, all animal life. All animals, ranging from the simplest to the most complex species, must consume organic material in the form of plants or other animals (or both), which, in turn, they use as the source of biological energy. Additionally, animals must maintain an adequate level of intracellular and extracellular fluids if they are to function normally.

The issues that concerns us in this chapter deal with consummatory behaviors. Specifically, we attempt to identify the physiological and neural mechanisms that initiate, modulate, and terminate eating and drinking behaviors. We begin with a look at homeostatic mechanisms.

Homeostasis   In the early 1920s Walter Cannon introduced the term *homeostasis* to describe a variety of regulatory biological processes. These homeostatic processes govern a host of physiological activities, which include the control of body temperature, the regulation of heart rate and blood pressure, the maintenance of the desired concentrations of various ions in the body fluids, and the regulation of appropriate fluid levels inside and outside the cells.

Homeostatic mechanisms are **negative-feedback systems** in that they actively return the process under control back toward some desired level called the **set point**. An analogy of a thermostat may be helpful at this point. As you know, a room thermostat is set at some desired temperature. If the temperature in the room should rise above the desired level, the thermostat detects this variation and causes cooler air to enter the room. The temperature is returned to the desired level. Should the temperature drop below the set point, the thermostat causes warmer air to enter the room, again bringing the temperature back to the desired level.

Most thermostats are purposely designed to be a little "sloppy." That is, they allow the room temperature to deviate a few degrees before they go into corrective action. If this were not so, the heating and cooling system would be constantly switching on and off. Instead of a set point there is actually a set *range*. (The thermostat in my university office is particularly sloppy. It has a very large range so the temperature of the room is, more often than not, too warm or too cool, and it seems to pass only very briefly through the comfort zone!) Most biological homeostatic

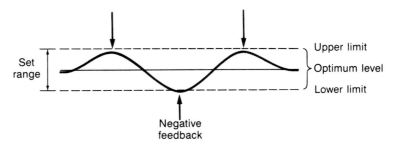

Figure 10-1
A homeostatic mechanism. Variations in either direction from the desired level, indicated by the colored line, result in corrective action back to the set point. The figure shows a homeostatic mechanism as it would work in a system where there is a range of acceptable variance, a set range.

mechanisms evidence similar characteristics. They actively correct deviations from the desired set point, and they have a range of "acceptable" deviations from the set point before corrective action is initiated (see Figure 10-1).

Drives versus Mechanisms

There are at least two commonly accepted ways of explaining consummatory behavior. We can be very **reductionistic** and attempt to define consummatory behaviors at the cellular and even subcellular level. That is, we can explain goal-directed behaviors such as eating and drinking in terms of physical events taking place between the within cells. This approach is sometimes referred to as a **mechanistic model** of explanation because the emphasis is placed on the role of smaller parts of the overall system. It is similar to explaining the operation of a machine in terms of how the component parts function.

From a "scientific" point of view reductionistic models of behavior are appealing. With this approach explanations are founded in physical, and therefore, measurable events. As noted later in this chapter, investigators have been quite successful in explaining consummatory behaviors in relatively simple organisms that possess correspondingly simple nervous systems. As you might expect, this becomes a much more formidable task when we attempt to apply this level of explanation to human behavior.

The second way to describe consummatory behavior is based on the **drive reduction model**. Unlike the mechanistic model, the drive reduction model attempts to explain consummatory behavior in more global terms. With this approach behavior is generally viewed as being under the control of internally experienced urges or drives. The outward expression of these drives is evident in the strength or frequency of certain overt behaviors that they induce (Geen, Beatty, & Arkin, 1984). Terms such as *hunger drive, thirst drive*, or *sex drive* are commonly used in our society, and they are doubtlessly familiar to you.

The model proposes that the intensity of drives is variable; that is, they may increase or decrease as a function of the time of deprivation. The longer you have been denied the appropriate goal object (food, water, sex), the stronger the drive will become. If, however, you have just eaten a filling meal, for example, the hunger drive would be quite low.

The model does not deny the existence of underlying physiological mechanisms for the drives, it simply places emphasis at a different level of explanation.

If you were to ask a group of people to describe what they feel or experience when they are "hungry," you might be surprised by the diversity and the imprecision of the responses. Adjectives such as *empty, nervous, headachy, fidgety, bitchy, impatient, agitated, uneasy*, and so on tend to be the best that we can come up with. The problem associated with drives is that they are difficult (if not impossible) to measure directly.

In a sense, drives are like *hypothetical constructs*, concepts concerning things that we believe exist but that we can only assess indirectly. Common sense tells us that the hunger drive exists because we see the resulting behavior—we eat. However, defining the hunger drive with any degree of precision or trying to measure it in meaningful terms is quite another matter.

As is so often true in science, both models have something useful to offer, and they both can help us understand goal-directed behaviors better. Both models, however, have their limitations.

I noted earlier that we have difficulty explaining the complex consummatory behavior of humans using very reductionistic models. Similarly, you may have some difficulty applying the drive reduction model to very simple animals. The thought of a hungry amoeba, a thirsty planaria, or a sexually aroused earthworm may be a little difficult for you to deal with intellectually.

The problem that we have here is that it is difficult to talk about "drives" or complex "motivated" behaviors without also thinking in human terms. Clearly, all animals eat; however, do all animals feel hungry in the same sense that you feel hungry? Are simple animals such as insects, fishes, birds, horses, or dogs capable of feeling or consciously experiencing anything? What do words like *feel* and *experience* mean when they are applied to animals other than humans? We come to grips with these difficult questions in the last chapter of this book. Here we deal with eating and drinking behaviors in animals and humans at a biological level.

Thirst

Humans are approximately 70% water. Water is the main constituent of all of the tissues of our body. This makes sense if you consider that animals evolved in a fluid environment—the sea. All of our critical life-supporting activities—the transport of nutrients, minerals, and oxygen to the cells; the elimination of waste; indeed, all biological activity—takes place in an aqueous environment. Each day the average person consumes approximately 2,500 ml of water. An equal amount of water is lost, primarily through the elimination of waste (urine and fecal matter), evaporation from the lungs and skin, and active perspiration to control body temperature.

Maintaining the correct balance of bodily fluids and ions in solution is essential for sustaining life. The most primitive single-celled organisms evolved in the sea, where the composition of the water in their environment was very similar to their internal fluids. As marine animals invaded fresh-water environments, more complex systems evolved to deal with the lower osmotic pressures (lower concentrations of ions in solution) found in these waters. Special mechanisms developed to allow these animals to hold higher ionic concentrations in the internal fluids relative to the surrounding water. The fluid balance problem became even more complex as animals moved from a marine to a terrestrial environment. The sealike aqueous internal environment needed to be maintained in a nonfluid external environment. Therefore, in terrestrial animals both water and minerals must be consumed, and their elimination must be accurately regulated to maintain the essential balance.

Drinking Strategies

Different animals evidence drinking strategies that fit their particular ecological niche. For obvious reasons, marine animals and animals that live near aquatic environments do not need to search for water, nor do they need complex mechanisms for retaining the water that they consume. Animals that live in the sea, even mammals such as seals and birds like the penguin, never drink. They obtain almost all of the fresh water they need from the organic matter (plants and animals) that they eat. There is a good reason for this. The dissolved salts in seawater are too highly concentrated for most animals; therefore, they are totally dependent on the consumption of other organisms for their source of fresh water. Many animals that live in the sea have evolved special organs that concentrate the salts in solution and excrete them as waste. This is also true for some seabirds that necessarily consume some seawater when they eat.

Ironically, many desert-dwelling animals—including many insects, reptiles, and even some mammals—do not drink at all. As is true with the marine animals, they obtain the fluids they require from the food they eat. Of necessity, these animals have evolved special behavior patterns and physiological mechanisms for conserving water and maintaining the proper balance of ions in solution. Most desert mammals are nocturnal and avoid the strongly evaporating rays of the sun. Additionally, these animals excrete very little urine. Their urine, however, is very highly concentrated.

The drinking strategy (or total lack of drinking) evidenced by a given species serves one purpose: to maintain the vital balance of intracellular and extracellular fluids necessary to support life. In the next section we look at the various organs that are involved in regulating drinking. We examine those structures that monitor fluid supplies in the body, and we examine the physiological mechanisms that initiate, modulate, and terminate drinking behaviors.

The Partitioning of Fluid in the Body

Although fluids can move from one part of the body to another, it is helpful to think of the body fluids as being partitioned into four different compartments. By far, the greatest amount of fluid, approximately 67%, is located within the cells. Fluid within the cells is called **intracellular fluid**. The fluid that is outside of the cells, **extracellular fluid**, can be divided into three divisions. **Interstitial fluid** is the fluid that surrounds the outside of the cells, and it accounts for approximately 26% of the body fluids. In a sense, interstitial fluid *is* the seawater environment that we now carry internally. The remaining extracellular fluid is found in the blood plasma and the cerebrospinal fluid, which together account for approximately 7% of the total body fluids.

As stated earlier, the fluids of the body can move from one compartment to another. One factor that influences this movement is the relative concentration of solutes in the fluid compartments. Active homeostatic processes attempt to maintain **isotonic** conditions in the intracellular and extracellular fluids. That is, there is a natural mechanism to balance the concentration of ions on either side of the cell membrane. If the amount of interstitial fluid is increased without a concurrent increase in solute, the fluid outside of the cells would become **hypotonic** relative to the intracellular fluid. Under these conditions osmotic pressure would cause fluid to cross the cell membrane and enter the cell. Conversely, if interstitial fluid was decreased, an extracellular **hypertonic** condition would exist, and osmotic pressure would move fluid out of the cells (Figure 10-2).

In a similar fashion, the fluid levels of the blood plasma and cerebrospinal fluid are maintained within narrow limits. For example, the amount of blood plasma must be relatively constant to avoid dangerous increases or decreases in blood pressure and to ensure the normal

Figure 10-2
a. Osmotic pressure causes fluids to move across a semipermeable membrane from the hypotonic to the hypertonic side. *b*. Under nearly isotonic conditions, where the concentration of solute is almost identical on either side of the membrane, small amounts of water move in both directions, maintaining the homeostatic balance.

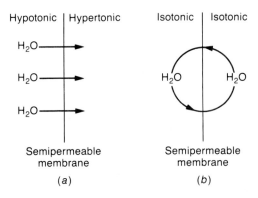

pumping efficiency of the heart. If blood is lost, through an accident for example, osmotic pressure will pass water through the capillary walls into the blood vessels from the surrounding interstitial fluid.

Mechanisms for the Control of Water Balance

The fluid balance is maintained by periodic ingestion and excretion of water. You cannot discuss water balance without simultaneously considering the concentration of solutes, primarily sodium, in the body fluids. Both water and sodium levels are controlled primarily by the excretion of urine by the kidneys.

Kidney Function

The kidneys extract fluid, water, and a variety of waste substances from the blood. Most of the water is returned to the body by the kidneys. The fluid that is retained by the kidneys is then stored in the bladder as urine. When sufficient levels of urine accumulate, it is excreted through the urethra. The concentration of sodium in the urine can vary widely. If the organism has consumed large quantities of water, the amount of urine produced will increase and the sodium level of the urine will be low. Conversely, if the organism is dehydrated, little urine will be produced and the urine will be highly concentrated.

An Observation:
"Urine" My
Territory Now

You may recall from earlier chapters that many terrestrial animals scent mark the boundaries of their territories with urine. Male dogs are well known for this sometimes annoying practice. Some years ago I was active in an obedience training club for dogs. Before a regional match the club had a photo session for about 50 dogs in my backyard. The male dogs took that opportunity to cover all of the carefully placed urine deposits made by my male Pekingese, making the boundaries of his territory tenuous at best.

His behavior for the next two days was quite remarkable. His water intake increased by two or three times his normal consumption level. Additionally, his pattern of urination changed markedly. Every time he was let out into the backyard, he deposited small amounts of urine in many locations as he frantically attempted to reestablish his territory.

The amount of water and sodium excreted by the kidneys is under the control of two hormones: **aldosterone** and **antidiuretic hormone (ADH)**. Aldosterone is a steroid hormone that is produced by the cortex of the adrenal gland. The hormone modulates the activity of sodium ion pumps in the kidneys that control the reabsorption of sodium into the body. Low levels of aldosterone cause higher concentrations of salt in the urine. High levels of aldosterone cause salt to be conserved in the body fluids.

Aldosterone levels in the blood are elevated by two factors: (1) increased sympathetic activity to the kidneys and (2) a decrease in blood flow through the kidneys. When either of these conditions exists, the kidneys secrete renin. Once absorbed into the blood, renin goes through several transformations which terminate in the formation of **angiotensin II** (see Figure 10-3). Angiotensin II, in addition to several other effects, stimulates the adrenal cortex to produce aldosterone.

Antidiuretic hormone is released into the bloodstream by the posterior portion of the pituitary gland. ADH controls the reabsorption of water in the kidneys. Higher levels of ADH increase the reabsorption rate. Therefore, ADH is released by the pituitary when the body becomes dehydrated.

Figure 10-3
The transformation of renin to angiotensin II. In response to sympathetic activation or low blood flow, the kidneys produce renin. In the blood the renin changes to angiotensin, which converts to angiotensin I and in turn to angiotensin II. Angiotensin II stimulates the adrenal cortex to produce aldosterone.

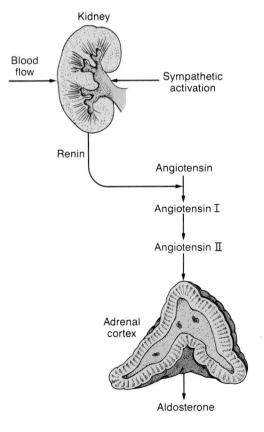

Addison's Disease

In 1855, Thomas Addison, an English physician, provided the first detailed clinical description of primary adrenal insufficiency. This is an extremely rare disorder in which there is progressive atrophy of the adrenal cortex. (Secondary adrenal insufficiency, which may produce very similar symptoms, is due to a disorder of the hypothalamic-pituitary-adrenal hormone system.) Addison's disease can be treated successfully with hormone replacement therapy. Because the disorder is so rare and because there are usually abnormal behaviors associated with the loss of minerals in the body fluids, Addison's disease can be misdiagnosed as a behavioral, rather than a physiological, problem (Porth, 1982).

As the disorder progresses, aldosterone levels decrease, causing the excessive loss of both sodium and potassium salts through the urine. Additionally, there is a loss of extracellular fluids. Behavioral correlates of the disorder include fatigue, irritability, and depression; and in some cases, more severe mental disturbances may appear. Interestingly, some individuals show a markedly increased appetite for salt. They may add salt liberally to their food or even consume it in large quantities directly from the shaker. In at least one such case, a young boy was misdiagnosed, and his mother was instructed to limit his salt intake carefully. Shortly thereafter the boy experienced a cardiovascular collapse and died.

This is an unfortunate example of a **specific hunger**, the natural tendency of the body to detect deficiencies of essential substances. The specific hunger for salt has been demonstrated in laboratory rats that have been deprived of salt in their diets. These animals show a clear preference for food containing high concentrations of salt. They will even drink salty water, which most animals naturally avoid.

Antidiuretic hormone is actually produced by the **supraoptic nucleus** and the **paraventricular nucleus** of the hypothalamus. The selective inhibition of either of these nuclei has been shown to decrease water consumption in water-deprived animals (Ukai & Holtzman, 1987). The antidiuretic hormone is transported in vesicles down hypothalamic axons to the posterior portion of the pituitary, where it is released when the hypothalamic neurons are activated. The production and release of ADH from within the supraoptic and paraventricular nuclei may be influenced by yet another hypothalamic center, the **nucleus circularis** (Hatton, 1976). Cells within this nucleus seem to function as **osmoreceptors** that respond to the loss of intracellular fluid (see Figure 10-4). Hatton reported that electrical stimulation to the nucleus circularis caused water

Figure 10-4
Two photomicrographs in
cross section through the
hypothalamus of the rat.
The *top* figure shows the
relative position of the
hypotholamic nuclei
associated with drinking;
PVN = paraventricular
nucleus, SON = supraop-
tic nucleus, n circ = nucleus circularis, OC = optic
chiasm. The *bottom* figure
is the nucleus circularis
under higher magnifica-
tion. Note that the cells of
the nucleus form a tight
ring around a capillary
(cap). Both figures from
Hatton, 1976.)

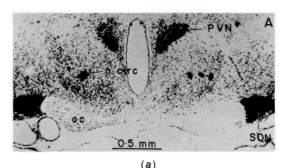

(a)

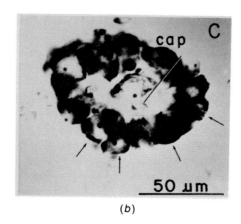

(b)

to be retained, presumably from the release of ADH. This finding,
however, has not been verified by other investigators and must be viewed
tentatively.

Drinking Initiators   We have seen that the kidneys play a central role controlling water and
and Inhibitors   salt in the body. We reviewed the feedback mechanism between the
kidneys and the adrenal cortex that regulates the release of aldosterone,
which in turn controls the reabsorption of sodium in the kidneys. Finally,
we outlined the role of hypothalamic and pituitary mechanisms that
control ADH levels in the blood. Antidiuretic hormone controls the
reabsorption of water by the kidneys.

    Several important questions concerning water consumption remain.
Specifically, we need to examine how the body monitors fluid levels and
the concentration of salts. That is, we need to know how we detect the
fact that fluid levels in the body are low, high, or about right. How do
we monitor the concentration of salts in intracellular and extracellular

fluids? Additionally, we need to examine those peripheral and central nervous system structures that are involved in initiating and terminating drinking behaviors.

To understand the physiological mechanisms that modulate, initiate, and terminate water consumption, it is important to remember that there are two factors that regulate water intake: (1) the volume of fluid in the body and (2) the concentration of solute in the body fluids. When an animal drinks because the level of fluid in the body is lower than desired, it is known as **volumetric** (to meter volume) **drinking** or **volumetric thrist**. When an animal consumes water in order to decrease the concentration of solute in the body fluids, it is called **osmometric** (to meter osmotic pressure) **drinking** or **osmometric thirst**.

Obviously, volumetric and osmometric thirst are not totally independent from each other. For example, the normal loss of water through the lungs and skin decreases the volume of fluids in the body, increasing volumetric thirst. However, the amount of solute in the body is not changed by this water loss. The evaporated water loss causes the concentration of solute in the remaining water to increase, thereby increasing osmometric thirst. But now consider what would happen if you were to donate blood. The blood that is lost is isotonic with the remaining body fluids. Therefore, volume is decreased without a concomitant increase in solute concentration. In this example volumetric thirst would be increased, but osmometric thirst would be unaffected.

Research has shown that different mechanisms seem to be at work to control volumetric and osmometric thirst. This is sometimes referred to as the "double depletion theory" of thirst. We will deal with them separately.

Volumetric Thirst   The loss of extracellular fluid produces a condition called **hypovolemia** (lower than normal volume), which increases drinking (see Spotlight 10-2). When the hypovolemic condition affects the blood serum levels, it can be quite dangerous because it causes the output of the heart to drop. To deal with this situation, the walls of the right atrium of the heart contain pressure-sensitive receptors that detect venous blood pressure. Decreased activity from these cells produces two effects: (1) messages are sent to the brain, causing ADH to be released by the pituitary, and (2) the kidneys secrete more renin. The combined effect is to increase the readsorption of water and conserve sodium.

This response to the hypovolemic condition prevents further loss of extracellular fluid but does nothing to replace the fluid that has been lost. Replacement of the lost fluid requires the animal to consume water. What then initiates drinking?

There is good evidence to show that reduced blood flow in the kidneys alone initiates drinking behavior. Fitzsimons (1972) demon-

How to Get Water from a Rat

One way to reduce fluid volume in a laboratory animal would be to draw off some blood. The obvious disadvantage to this method is that you get not only the fluid but also the blood cells making the animal anemic. A better solution would be to extract only the extracellular fluid. But how can this be done?

In 1961, Fitzsimons introduced a clever technique to draw extracellular fluid. The procedure begins by injecting polyethylene glycol that is suspended in a liquid into the peritoneal cavity of rats. The substance has very large molecules that cannot pass through cell membranes; therefore, it stays in the peritoneal cavity. The presence of the polyethylene glycol does increase the osmotic pressure and in so doing causes extracellular fluid to move into the peritoneum. Next, the polyethylene glycol is extracted from the peritoneum along with the extracellular fluid, making the animal hypovolemic (Spotlight Figure 10-2, steps 1 to 3). (If

polyethylene glycol sounds to you like something you would put into your car radiator, you are not on the wrong track. Ethylene glycol *is* used as antifreeze. *Poly*ethylene glycol is simply a large number of these molecules in a chain.)

The loss of fluid causes considerable thirst, and the rats consume a great deal of water over the next few days. Note, however, that the fluid removed from the rats was isotonic; therefore, solute was lost as well as solvent. If the rats are given a choice between water and a hypertonic saline solution (which they normally refuse to drink), they chose the saline solution to replace the salt that was lost.

Stricker (1973) used the same procedure with rats that had their kidneys removed. Again the induced hypovolemia caused the rats to drink. This study demonstrates that even without the renin produced by the kidneys, the pressure sensors in the heart were sufficient to stimulate volumetric thirst.

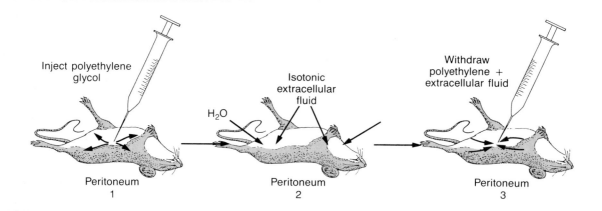

Spotlight Figure 10-2
Step 1: Inject polyethylene glycol into peritoneum. Step 2: Increased osmotic pressure draws extracellular water into the peritoneum. Step 3: Water and polyethylene glycol are withdrawn from the peritoneum.

strated that partially constricting the flow of blood to the renal artery, which does not affect venous pressure, increased drinking. It can be assumed that this procedure increased renin output from the kidneys. It is tempting to suggest that the renin, actually angiotensin II, triggers drinking by activating some center or centers in the brain.

Angiotensin is a peptide, and we know that neurons have receptor sites on their membranes for peptide transmitters. Are there angiotensin-sensitive neurons in the brain? And if so, where are they located?

Two brain centers have been associated with angiotensin-induced drinking: (1) the **subfornical organ (SFO)** and (2) the **median preoptic nucleus**. Injections of small amounts of angiotensin in the SFO increase neural activity and induce drinking (Epstein, Fitzsimons, & Rolls, 1970; Phillips & Felix, 1976; Simpson, Epstein, & Camardo, 1978). Drinking behavior is also induced by injections of angiotensin into the median preoptic nucleus (Shrager & Johnson, 1980). There is some evidence that the SFO innervates the median preoptic nucleus via angiotensin-secreting terminals (Lind & Johnson, 1982). (See Figure 10-5.)

Osmometric Thirst

I am sure that you have experienced thirst after eating a particularly salty meal. Personally, I am addicted to salty foods like potato chips, pretzels, nuts, and pizza with anchovies. However, I can't eat these salty foods without also consuming a beverage.

There is a good reason why sodium chloride so effectively induces thirst. You may recall from our discussion of the neuron in Chapter 3 that some ions such as potassium (K^+) pass rather freely through the cell membrane. The cell membrane is much less permeable to other ions, and sodium (Na^+) is in that category. The extracellular fluids—interstitial fluid, blood plasma, and cerebrospinal fluid—contain about 0.9% salt (NaCl). If you consume a large amount of salty food, the concentration of salt in the extracellular fluid rises above this level, producing a hypertonic condition. Because the Na^+ cannot enter the cells, an unequal concentration of solute will exist on either side of the cell membrane. The resulting osmotic pressure (osmosis) causes water to move from the area of low concentration inside the cell across the membrane to the interstitial fluid. As the cells dehydrate, they become smaller.

One of the most generally accepted hypotheses concerning osmotic thirst is that the dehydration of special **osmoreceptor cells** initiates drinking (Gilman, 1937). It is important to note that the dehydration may be due to water loss or due to any solvent (not just salt) that increases the concentration of extracellular fluid relative to intracellular fluid (Fitzsimons, 1972). But where are the osmoreceptors to be found?

The search for the osmoreceptors that induce drinking, as you might have predicted, begins in the hypothalamic nuclei of the brain. In the early 1950s researchers demonstrated that small injections of

Figure 10-5
Schematic representation of the kidney and neural mechanisms that control the onset of volumetric drinking. Low blood volume causes the kidney to release renin, which is transformed to angiotensin II in the blood plasma. Agiotensin II activates the subfornical organ, which in turn activates the median preoptic nucleus, leading to drinking behavior.

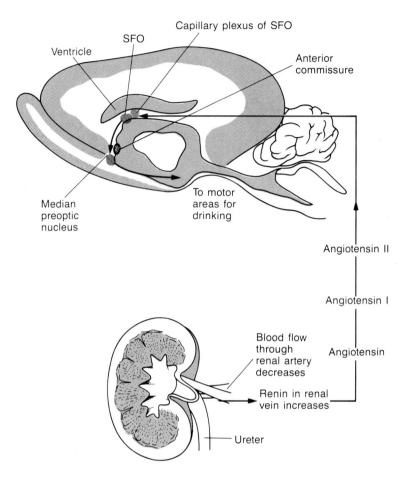

hypertonic NaCl into regions of the hypothalamus caused animals to drink. These studies suggest that osmoreceptors are located in the brain, but they do not eliminate the possibility that pressure-sensitive cells could be located in other body structures.

In a very clever study, Ramsay, Rolls, and Wood (1977) demonstrated that varying the concentration of salt in the cerebral circulatory system modulates drinking but that changing salt concentrations in other parts of the body did not have a similar effect. Using dogs as subjects, they first exposed the carotid artery on either side of the neck. The carotid artery is the primary source of blood to the brain. (See Figure 10-6.) Injections into these arteries can alter the concentration of solute in the blood that reaches the brain without significantly altering the blood concentration in other parts of the body. The dogs were deprived of

Figure 10-6
Experimental paradigm used to modify the concentration of cerebral blood flow without significantly changing the concentration of blood in the periphery of the body.

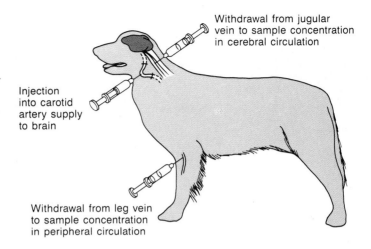

Withdrawal from jugular vein to sample concentration in cerebral circulation

Injection into carotid artery supply to brain

Withdrawal from leg vein to sample concentration in peripheral circulation

water, and the concentration of cerebral blood was monitored by sampling venous blood exiting the cerebrum through the jugular vein. Then water was injected into the carotid artery at a rate that dropped the jugular venous blood concentration to predeprivation levels. This treatment reduced water intake by 75% compared to dogs that received carotid injections of isotonic saline solution. (The concentration in the blood sampled from the leg did not vary noticeably.) These results show that cellular hydration in the brain, but not in the periphery of the body, influences drinking.

In 1971, Blass and Epstein showed that injections of water directly into the **lateral preoptic area** of the hypothalamus reduced drinking in rats that had received subcutaneous injections of hypertonic saline solution. However, the same treatment had no effect on rats that had been stimulated to drink by injections of angiotensin. Their data suggest that the preoptic area is specific for osmometric thirst.

Introducing hypertonic sucrose into the extracellular fluid has the same effect as hypertonic solutions of NaCl. Using this technique, Peck and Blass (1975) located a small region between the lateral preoptic area and the lateral hypothalamus that appears to be most active in controlling osmometric thirst (see Figure 10-7).

The Role of the Lateral Hypothalamus

One other structure, the *lateral hypothalamus*, appears to play a central role in drinking. Lesions to this structure produce a temporary loss of both eating and drinking behaviors. Recovery of eating and drinking following lateral hypothalamic lesions is not complete. The animals will drink only when eating (perhaps to lubricate food), and they never respond normally to osmotic and volemic thirst cues. Injecting hypertonic saline

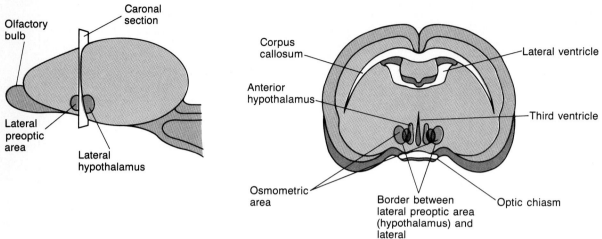

Figure 10-7
Hypothalamic area at the junction of the lateral preoptic area and the lateral hypothalamus found to induce osmometric drinking in rats. (Adapted from Peck & Blass, 1975.)

solution or causing hypovolemia with polyethylene glycol no longer stimulates drinking. Apparently, the lateral hypothalamic region, or neural pathways that pass through this region, modulate the motor mechanisms that control drinking.

Terminating Drinking Behavior

Consider the following: (1) If you drink to correct hypovolemic or hypertonic conditions in the body, and (2) you continued to drink until one or both of these thirst-inducing conditions is corrected, (3) you would always consume much more water than is actually needed. If a dog is deprived of water and then given free access of water, it will drink for a few minutes until it consumes the water it needs. However, it takes 10 to 12 minutes for the water to get through the digestive system and start entering blood. It will take three fourths of an hour before all the water consumed is distributed in the body. Clearly, there must be some peripheral mechanism that meters water consumption.

Receptors in the mouth, throat, stomach, and intestines could influence water consumption. One laboratory technique that has helped to identify the role that these peripheral structures have in metering water intake is the esophageal bypass (see Figure 10-8). Using this surgical preparation, it is possible for animals to **sham drink** or the stomach can be loaded with water directly, bypassing the mouth. Sham drinking allows the animal to consume water by the mouth; however, the ingested water flows into a pan on the floor and not into the stomach.

Although the mouth, tongue, and throat seem to have a secondary role in the metering of water intake (Miller, Sampliner, & Woodrow,

Figure 10-8
Surgical preparation that permits sham drinking or direct loading of water into the stomach.

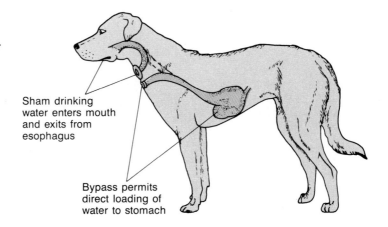

Sham drinking water enters mouth and exits from esophagus

Bypass permits direct loading of water to stomach

1957), sham drinking by itself is not satiating. Animals that have been deprived of water will sham drink for long periods of time, not stopping until they are physically exhausted (we note later that sham eating has a somewhat different effect). Apparently, receptors in the stomach (Maddison, Rolls, Rolls, & Wood, 1980) and small intestines (Hall & Blass, 1977) have a more critical role in the peripheral regulation of water intake.

We have seen that both cellular dehydration and reduced fluid volume influence thirst. Figure 10-9 summarizes, in graphic form, the homeostatic mechanisms involved in the double depletion of causal factors of thirst.

Figure 10-9
Summary diagram of the double depletion theory of thirst.

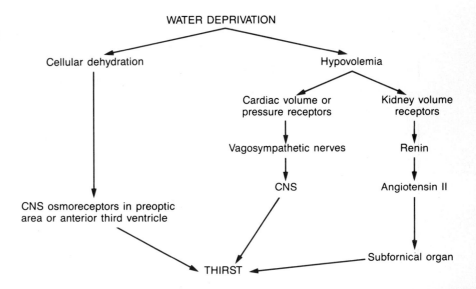

WATER DEPRIVATION

Cellular dehydration

Hypovolemia

Cardiac volume or pressure receptors

Kidney volume receptors

Vagosympathetic nerves

Renin

CNS

Angiotensin II

CNS osmoreceptors in preoptic area or anterior third ventricle

Subfornical organ

THIRST

PART 2   EATING BEHAVIOR

Hunger

As I noted earlier, consummatory behaviors are phylogentically ancient. All of our ancestors had to eat to live. It should not be surprising, then, that eating behaviors in mammals are controlled by older subcortical structures. Norgren and Grill (1982) have shown that decerebrate rats (the brain was transected between the diencephalon and the midbrain) are still able to feed. Indeed, these animals were able to distinguish between various foods by their taste.

Feeding Strategies   Not all animals have the same food requirements and eating strategies. Some marine forms are completely sedentary and feed on food particles that are carried to them on ocean currents. Some browsing species live entirely on plants that are available to them year-round, whereas others must migrate to follow the available plants as seasons change. Predators and scavengers that live exclusively on other animals must follow the prey animals that live on the lower part of the food chain.

Typically, zoologists classify animals into five main groups based on their primary source of food (see Table 10-1). The anatomy of the animal, its primary food source, and its eating strategy are closely linked. As an example, nectivorous animals like the butterfly and the humming-bird have evolved long styluslike mouthparts that enable them to gain access to fluid meals that are likely to be deep within the flowering parts of plants. Herbivorous animals, sheep, and wildebeasts, for example, have evolved heavy, crushing and grinding molars, flexible lips and tongue, and multilevel stomachs that enable them to eat and digest coarse, poor-quality, grasses and seeds that have relatively little caloric

Table 10-1   **Categories of Animals Based on Their Primary Food Source**

Class	Diet	Examples
Herbivorous	Only plant matter	Deer, hippopotamuses, elephants, many birds
Insectivorous	Only insects	Many birds, some bats, some frogs, anteaters
Carnivorous	Only meat	Dogs, cats, some reptiles, many fishes
Nectivorous	Only plant nectar	Bees, butterflies, hummingbirds
Omnivorous	Mixed diet of meat, plants, and/or insects	Raccoons, some birds, chimpanzees, and humans

energy. The carnivorous animals like the big cats and the wolf have evolved large canine teeth and sharp, cutting molars for piercing, tearing, and cutting flesh. Omnivorous animals like humans have evolved teeth that appear to be a compromise between the crushing teeth of the herbivore and the cutting teeth of the carnivore.

The frequency and duration of meals are determined by the caloric quality of the food and the metabolic level of the animal. Some species eat continuosly over much of the day. Zebras, rhinoceroses, and elephants, for example, must consume enormous quantities of food each day. The high bulk and low caloric value of the plant material that makes up their diets require that they spend most of their waking hours eating. The nutritive characteristics of the nectar eaten by hummingbirds are quite good. However, the metabolic activity of these lightweight dynamos is so high that they too must consume large quantities relative to their diminutive size. A python, due to its low metabolic rate and high-energy (meat) diet, may only feed on one large meal every other month.

The temporal pattern of eating may also be determined by other factors that are important to the life -style of the species. Migratory birds may eat heavily in preparation for long periods of fasting during migration. Similarly, bears "overeat" and build up large reservoirs of adipose tissue in preparation for the winter hibernation. Polar bears may lose as much as one third of their body weight during the long winter fast. Finally, as we discuss later in this chapter, learning and, for humans, custom may also influence the pattern of eating behaviors.

Eating Mechanisms in the Blowfly

We begin our discussion of the physiological mechanisms of eating by examining the eating behavior of the blowfly. This may seem a bit unusual to you, but consider that the evolution process tends to build on successful adaptations and that the common blowfly is, in a real sense, a "living fossil." They have survived and successfully competed for food in essentially the same way for millions of years. The term *blowfly* is actually given to several species of flies in the family Caliphoridae. They range in size from that of the common housefly to that of large horseflies. Many of these flies have bodies that are metallic blue or green. They can be found on all of the major land masses of the world.

Vincent Dethier, a behavioral biologist, has studied the eating behavior of the blowfly in great detail. The blowfly appears to fly randomly until it senses a source of food upwind. After landing in the vicinity of the odor-producing substance, the fly walks about until it senses ("tastes") food with sensory hairs in its feet (tarsi). Dethier (1967a, 1967b) inserted a recording electrode through a hole drilled in a single taste hair (a technical tour de force). Recordings from the taste hairs demonstrated the existence of two types of sensory neurons. One of these neurons is most sensitive to sugar, and the other is most sensitive to salt. The rate of activity of these two cells is directly correlated to the concentration of its specific stimulus.

The Teeth Tell the Tale

The shape and pattern of an animal's teeth can tell us much about the eating habits of their owner. Look at the skull and teeth of the three animals shown in Spotlight Figure 10-3a. The skull on the left is that of an ungulate and herbivore, the black rhinocerous. The skull in the middle is that of the omnivorous black bear. The skull on the right is a carnivore, the coyote. Look carefully at the canine teeth and molars of the coyote. Clearly, these teeth have evolved for piercing, cutting, and tearing flesh. The bear also has piercing canine teeth, but note how the molars are better shaped for crushing and grinding. Now look at the teeth of the rhinocerous. There are only remnants of canine teeth, and the molars are massive, designed to crush and grind coarse plant foods.

You may recall from Chapter 1 that paleontologists and anthropologists have reconstructed the evolution of humans based mainly on a fossil record comprised mostly of teeth, skull bones, and a few other skeletal fragments. Teeth, because of their density, fossilize particularly well. Just as we are able to make some conclusions about the eating behaviors of contemporary animals from their teeth and skull, it is possible to make some assumptions about the eating behaviors of extinct species from the fossil record.

Compare the skull, jawbone, and teeth of the gorilla (*Gorilla gorilla, Pongidae*) and humans (Spotlight Figure 10-3b). Several obvious differences are evident. The jaw of the gorilla is much more massive, and there is a large sagittal crest along the length of the skull for attaching the equally large mandibular muscle that moves the jaw. The gorilla has retained prominent canine teeth (primarily for threat displays). The gorilla is a herbivore and is capable of crushing 4-in. diameter bamboo with his teeth. Humans, as you know, are omnivorous animals.

The evolutionary trend in dentation (and presumably, diet) in the hominid lineage is quite clear. Canine teeth decrease in size and prominence, the molars become less massive, and the jaw becomes lighter, with the teeth forming a more circular arch. This trend is quite obvious in the comparisons of the arch and palate of a contemporary great ape, *Ramapithicus*, and humans seen in Spotlight Figure 10-3c. Based on this type of data, anthropologists have suggested that the hominids developed an omnivorous diet that likely consisted of seeds, grains, fruit, roots, tubers, insects, and meat (probably in the form of carrion).

Spotlight Figure 10-3
a. From left to right, the skull and teeth of a herbivore (black rhinoceros), omnivore (black bear), and carnivore (coyote). (Adapted from Vaughan, 1978.) b. The skull of a gorilla and a human. (Adapted from Poirier, 1977.) c. From left to right, the teeth and palate of the great ape, the fossil *Ramapithecus* (from two fossil fragments), and a human. (Adapted from Poirier, 1977.)

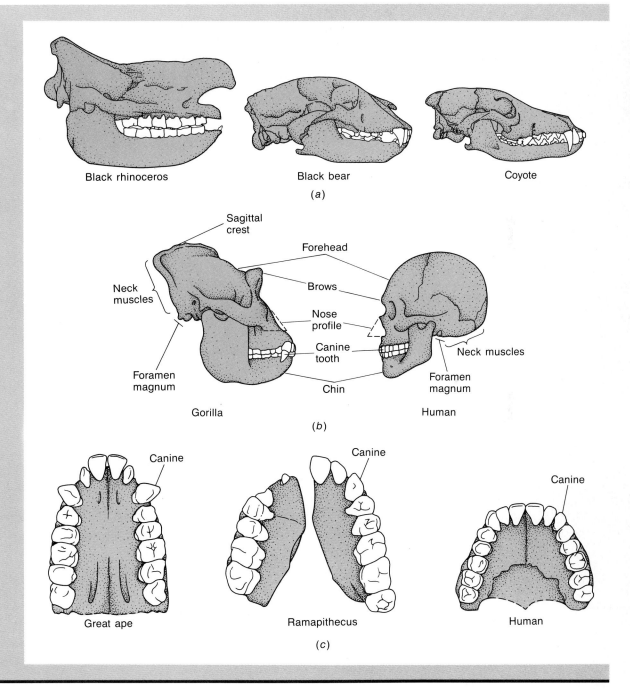

Black rhinoceros   Black bear   Coyote

(a)

Sagittal crest

Forehead

Neck muscles

Brows

Nose profile

Canine tooth

Foramen magnum

Chin

Neck muscles

Foramen magnum

Gorilla   Human

(b)

Canine

Canine

Canine

Great ape   Ramapithecus   Human

(c)

Increased activity in the tarsal sensory hairs triggers extension of the proboscis. Sensory hairs on the labellum (lip) of the proboscis contain receptor cells for salt and sugar, as well as a third receptor cell that is sensitive to water. Activation of one or more of these receptors causes the food to be sucked up by the fly until the receptors adapt to the stimulus and cease firing. This defines one eating episode, or one meal. The sequence begins again when a new source of food is encountered (Figure 10-10).

So far, we have an effective system for detecting and ingesting food. An additional mechanism is needed to inhibit eating when the animal has consumed enough food even when a new source of food is present. The signal to inhibit eating comes from the crop (the fly's equivalent to the stomach). Stretch receptors in the wall of the crop send inhibitory signals that prevent extension of the proboscis. Dethier demonstrated that cutting the fibers from the crop to the brain resulted in **hyperphagic** (overeating) behavior. In some instances the flies would repeat the episodic feeding cycles until they literally burst. Hyperphagia may also

Figure 10-10
The anatomy of the blowfly. *a.* The external anatomy. *b.* Enlarged detail of the proboscis and labellum.

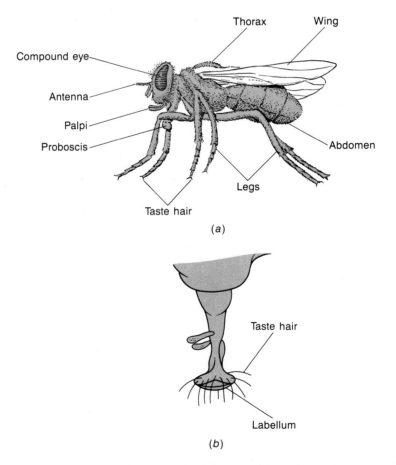

(a)

(b)

occur by cutting the nerve bundle that runs along the ventral side of the body. In this case the fly does not respond to adaptation of the sensory hairs and eats one long continuous meal. These findings demonstrate that both internal (crop) and external (sensory hairs) cues control feeding.

Are there similar neural mechanisms that mediate eating behaviors in more complex animals? We turn now to an examination of brain mechanisms in mammals and humans.

Neural Centers for Eating

In the early to mid-1950s a "dual center theory" for the control of eating developed. The theory proposed that a "hunger" center was located in the **lateral hypothalamus (LH)**, and a "satiety" center was found in the **ventromedial hypothalamus (VMH)**. Although support for this hypothesis persists, more recent data have shown that the dual center theory may have some weaknesses and does not adequately explain eating behavior. (See Grossman, 1984, Keesey & Powley, 1986, and Stricker & Verbalis, 1987, for reviews). In retrospect, however, it is easy to see how the theory developed and received an early acceptance. The issue is by no means settled.

In 1940, Hetherington and Ranson reported that bilateral lesions to the ventromedial hypothalamus of rats caused the animals to become very obese. Normal adult albino rats weigh between 450 and 550 g. Some of the hyperphagic rats have weighed in at over 1,000 g! (See Figure 10-11.) Other researchers replicated this effect in monkeys, dogs, cats, and even some species of birds. Additionally, electrical stimulation to the VMH terminated eating in animals that had been deprived of food. With these data the VMH was quickly accepted as the "satiety center" of the brain because lesions to it seemed to prevent animals from becoming satiated, whereas stimulation seemed to satiate hungry animals.

Eleven years after Hetherington and Ranson demonstrated that lesions to the VMH produced obesity, Anand and Brobeck (1951) reported that bilateral lesions to the nearby lateral hypothalamus (LH) caused rats to refuse to eat. Although some recovery was noted, the **aphagia** was in many cases so severe that the animals died of starvation even when their usual food was available to them ad libitum (by free access). These findings were replicated elsewhere, and it was not long before the LH was labelled the "feeding center."

Electrical stimulation of the LH was found to induce eating even in animals that had been recently satiated with food. This finding brings up an important theoretical question. Does electrically induced behavior like that resulting from stimulation of the LH represent automatic stereotypic behaviors, or is the animal responding to an electrically induced drive? That is, does the electrical stimulation produce automatic

Figure 10-11
Hypophagia in the rat.
The animal on the left
has received a lesion to
the ventromedial
hypothalamus that causes
overeating. (From Hether-
ington & Ranson, 1940.)

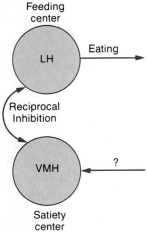

Figure 10-12
Model of the dual center
theory of eating behavior.
The lateral hypothalamus
(LH) is the "feeding" or
"on" center for eating,
and the ventromedial
hypothalamus (VMH) is
the "satiety" or "off"
center. Activation of the
VMH in response to feed-
back from substances in
the blood inhibits the LH.

preprogrammed motor behaviors like a robot or automaton, or does the
animal eat because it "feels" hungry?

First, it should be noted that electrically induced eating is stimulus
specific. That is, the animal will consume appropriate substances (food)
but will not indiscriminately consume anything in the cage. The locomotor response to direct stimulation of the brain is dependent on where the
food is located when the stimulation is begun. The animal does not move
randomly until food is encountered; rather, it moves purposively toward
the food. The induced motor responses for consuming the food are
appropriate for the kind of food that is present—liquid, mash, or hard
pellets. Finally, and perhaps most telling, if the animal has been trained
to press a lever for a food reward, it will press the lever when the LH is
stimulated. These data suggest that stimulation of the LH induces sensations not unlike those experienced through food deprivation. The animal
appears to be responding to a hunger drive. (See Valenstein et al., 1970,
and Wise, 1974, for reviews.)

The dual center model for eating behavior is depicted in Figure
10-12. The model proposes that the LH initiates eating and the VMH
terminates eating via inhibitory control of the LH. Several sources of
information suggest that the LH and the VMH actually have reciprocal
inhibitory connections (Hernandez & Hoebel, 1980). The VMH is
thought to be under the control of some feedback factor in the blood
serum. (Suggested by the question mark in Fig. 10-12.)

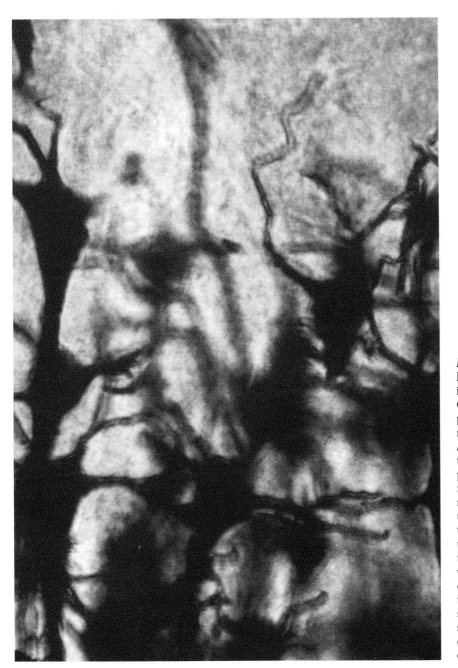

Plate 1.
Fox Golgi stain of neurons in the human cortex. The Golgi stain technique completely coats the outer membrane of the cell. Additionally, this staining technique has the unusual property of staining just a few cells in the tissue (the mechanism for this is not understood). This staining technique provides an unusually clear picture of the shape of each cell. At very high levels of magnification, the focal depth of the microscope is very shallow. For this reason some of the cells at varying depths in the tissue appear out of focus.

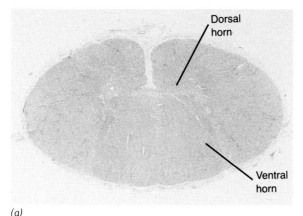

Dorsal horn

Ventral horn

(a)

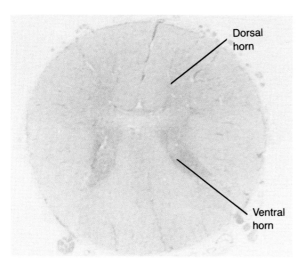

Dorsal horn

Ventral horn

(b)

Plate 2.

Cross section through four levels of the spinal cord. The staining technique used causes the lipoproteins in myelin to be stained light blue and the nucleoproteins in the cell bodies to be stained light red. The dorsal and ventral horns (the unstained grey matter) contain many cell bodies and, therefore, appear red in this preparation. The heavily myelinated tracts (the unstained white matter), which are rich in lipoproteins, surround the central area and are stained blue. The cervical section (a) is closest to the brain, followed in order by the thoracic (b) lumbar (c), and sacral (d) regions. Note that the dorsal and ventral horns, relative to the heavily myelinated area, appear to increase in size as the sections get more distant from the brain. This is because the number of fibers in the spinal nerve tracts decrease as information exits and enters the spinal cord at each vertebral level. Therefore, fewer fiber tracts are found in the spinal segments that are furthest from the brain.

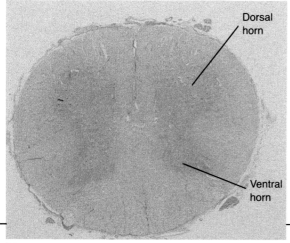

Dorsal horn

Ventral horn

(c)

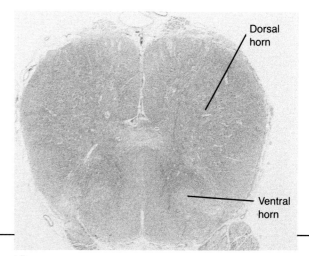

Dorsal horn

Ventral horn

(d)

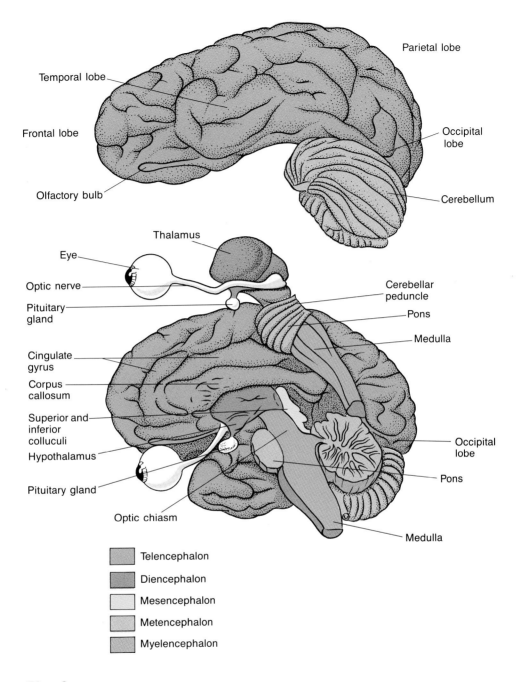

Plate 3.
The major structures of the human brain (the major subdivisions of the brain are color-coded, based on the key at the top of the figure). The left cerebral hemisphere and cerebellum have been cut away to expose the structures that are normally hidden from view. Additionally, the brain has been cut in the mid-sagittal plane to provide access to midline structures.

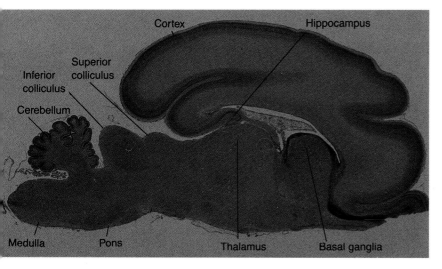

Plate 4.
Sagittal section of the human fetal brain. Between 100 and 150 days gestation, the developing human brain exhibits physical characteristics that are very similar to the structure of other vertebrate central nervous systems. As the brain develops, the cerebral hemispheres fold back and cover the remainder of the brain structures (see Fig. 3-8a). Note that even at this early stage of development almost all of the major brain structures are already in place. Continued development results in the elaboration of the existing structures.

Plate 5.
Coronal section of the rat brain. In this tissue preparation, myelinated fiber tracts are stained blue and cell bodies are stained light pink. Some of the major fiber tracts have been identified. The appearance of the myelinated fibers is determined by the direction in which the microtome blade has passed through the tissue. Fibers that are oriented parallel to the knife cut appear as lines. Fibers that are perpendicular to the knife cut appear as dots, like a bundle of cut wires viewed from the end. The enlarged area shows some fiber tracts at a much higher level of magnification. The thin blue lines on the top are myelinated fibers within the cortex that are coursing to and from the corpus callosum. The dotted pattern in the middle is caused by fibers that are oriented perpendicular to the knife cut. The matrix of horizontal tracts immediately below are fibers within the corpus callosum that course laterally and medially. The cell bodies of neurons and glial cells appear as small pink dots.

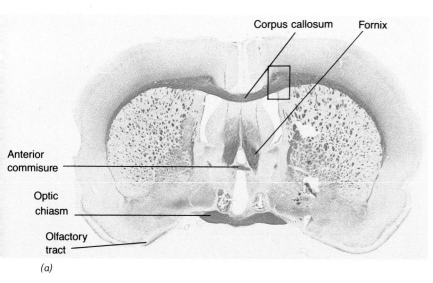

(a)

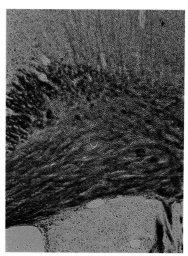

(b)

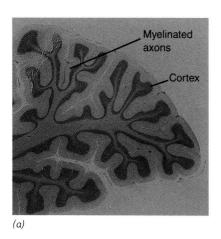

(a)

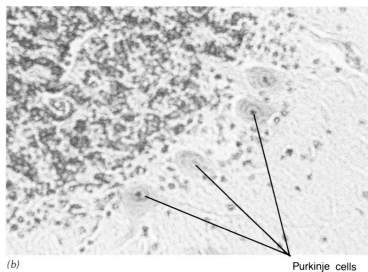

(b)

Purkinje cells

Plate 6.
Human cerebellum. Different staining techniques may provide complementary information.
a. & b. The section of the cerebellum on top has been treated with a crystal violet stain that
is selective for proteins found within the cell body and the cell membrane. The large purkinje
cells of the cerebellum can be seen on the border of the cortex. Note that the nucleus of
each cell, which is composed of highly concentrated nucleoproteins, is stained more darkly
than the other structures. c. & d. The tissue section on the bottom shows the same tissue
stained with a much more complex stain. This staining technique tends to coat the membrane of some fibers. This preparation shows the fine (black) hairlike fibers that innervate the
dendrites of the purkinje cells that could not be seen in the crystal violet preparation.

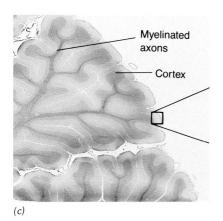

(c)

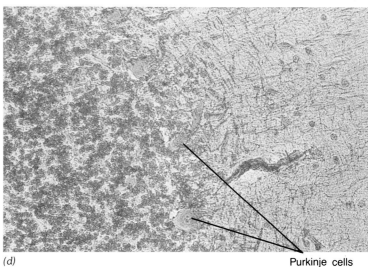

(d)

Purkinje cells

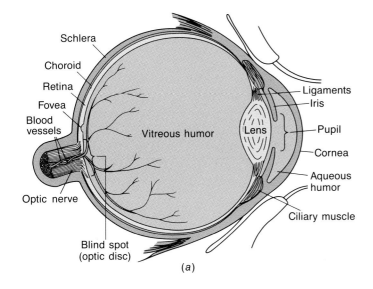

Schlera
Choroid
Retina
Fovea
Blood vessels
Vitreous humor
Lens
Optic nerve
Blind spot (optic disc)
Ligaments
Iris
Pupil
Cornea
Aqueous humor
Ciliary muscle

(a)

Plate 7.

a. The anatomy of the human eye. b. The retina of the eye has several distinct layers (see also Plates 8, 9, and 10). Light must pass through a number of these layers before reaching the photolabile molecules in the receptor cells. Therefore, the tissue of the retina is optically clear. The rods and cones have long extensions that are packed with a highly convoluted membrane that provides a large surface area to hold the photolabile molecules (rhodopsin in the rods; iodopsin in the cones).

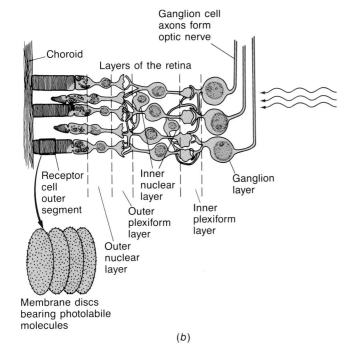

Choroid
Layers of the retina
Ganglion cell axons form optic nerve
Receptor cell outer segment
Outer nuclear layer
Outer plexiform layer
Inner nuclear layer
Inner plexiform layer
Ganglion layer
Membrane discs bearing photolabile molecules

(b)

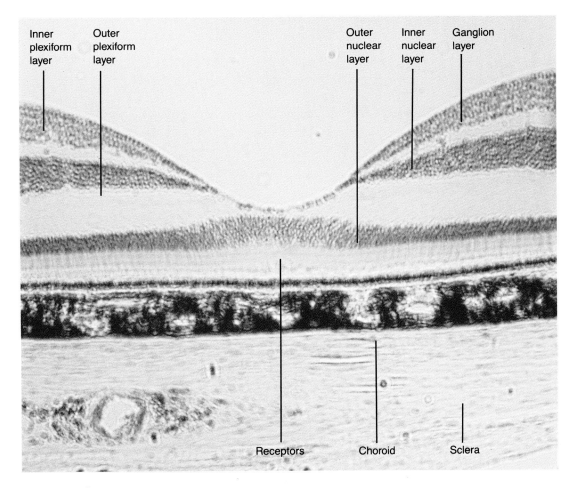

Inner plexiform layer   Outer plexiform layer   Outer nuclear layer   Inner nuclear layer   Ganglion layer

Receptors   Choroid   Sclera

Plate 8.

Fovea of the eye of a rhesus monkey. Light passes through the retina from the top. The retina, which is optically clear, must be stained to expose its cellular structure. This staining technique shows that the retina is composed of several distinct layers. The ganglion layer contains the cell bodies of the ganglion cells, which are the only cells that send information from the eye to the brain. The inner plexiform layer is comprised of lightly stained cell processes (dendrites and axons). The inner nuclear layer contains the cell bodies of amacrine, bipolar, and horizontal cells. The outer plexiform layer contains the cell processes that communicate between the receptor cells and the cells in the inner nuclear layer. The outer nuclear layer is comprised of the cell bodies of the receptor cells (rods and cones). In the fovea, the cell bodies of the ganglion and inner nuclear layers are "brushed aside" to provide light with more direct access to the receptor cells. Note that the cones that make up the receptor layer in the fovea are very densely packed causing the outer segments of the cells to appear as fine lines. Also note the high concentration of ganglion cells on either side of the foveal pit. The low convergence ratio between the cones and the ganglion cells, the high concentration of cones, and the direct access of light to the receptor layer all contribute to the extraordinary visual acuity in the fovea. The choroid layer is a dense black color even without staining. It serves to absorb light rays after they pass through the receptor cells.

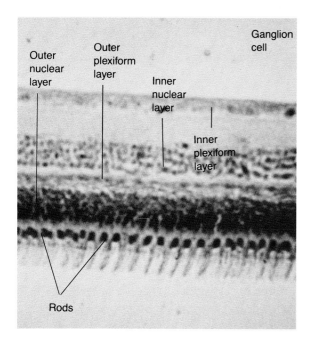

Outer nuclear layer

Outer plexiform layer

Inner nuclear layer

Inner plexiform layer

Ganglion cell

Rods

Plate 9.

Segment of the peripheral retina of the rhesus monkey. The peripheral retina contains the same cellular layers that are found in the fovea. However, the rods that make up the receptor layer are less densely packed together. Additionally, the ratio of rods to ganglion cells is quite high. That is, the receptor cells greatly outnumber the ganglion cells. The result is poorer visual acuity, a wider visual field for each ganglion cell, and better motion detection.

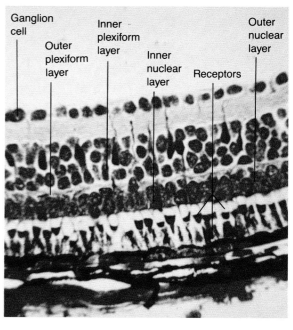

Ganglion cell

Outer plexiform layer

Inner plexiform layer

Inner nuclear layer

Receptors

Outer nuclear layer

Plate 10.

Segment of the retina of the Necturus. The Necturus, or mudpuppy, is related to the salamander and the newt. These animals have very simple retinas compared to those of mammals. The mudpuppy retina is organized into layers similar to those found in more complex retinas, however, it has fewer receptor cells that are quite large.

Plate 11

Eye of a human fetus. The major structures of the fetal eye are identified (the shape of the cornea and the retina have been distorted in the tissue processing). The cell structure at this stage of development is relatively homogeneous across the retina. The cells of the retina continue to differentiate and migrate during the gestation period. The process of cell differentiation and migration in the retina is not complete even at birth. The incomplete development of the retina and visual centers in the brain account for the limited visual capabilities of newborn infants.

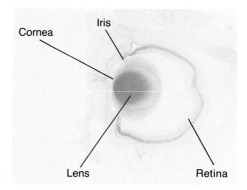

Cornea

Iris

Lens

Retina

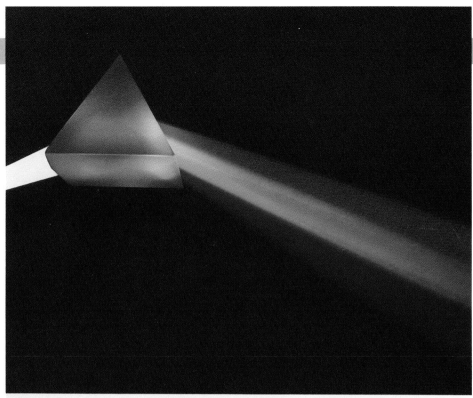

Plate 12.
The electromagnetic spectrum. The band of visible light has been expanded for detail.

SPECTRUM ANALYSIS

| COSMIC RAYS — GAMMA RAYS — X-RAYS — ULTRA VIOLET | INFRA RED — SHORT WAVE RADIO — LONG WAVE RADIO |

VISIBLE SPECTRUM
3900 TO 7600 ANGSTROM UNITS (1X10⁻⁸ CM.)

CONTINUOUS SPECTRUM

4000   4500   5000   5500   6000   6500   7000   7500

Continuous Spectra are produced by incandescent solids, liquids and gases under high pressure.

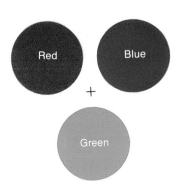

Red   Blue
+
Green

Plate 13.
The primary colors. Stare at the figure for at least one minute without moving your eyes. Then stare at a white surface or simply close your eyes. Note that the color of the after-image is the complimentary color of that on the figure.

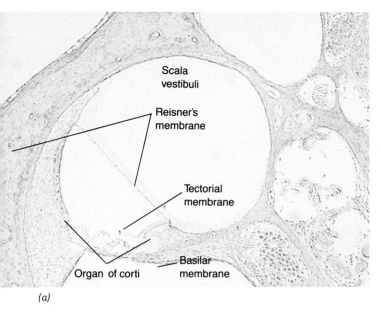

Scala vestibuli

Reisner's membrane

Tectorial membrane

Organ of corti

Basilar membrane

(a)

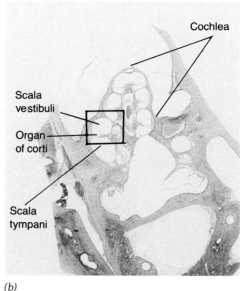

Cochlea

Scala vestibuli

Organ of corti

Scala tympani

(b)

Plate 14.
The cochlea. The cochlea is comprised of a fluid-filled, spiral tube. The tube is divided into two chambers, the scala vestibuli and the scala tympani, by the basilar membrane. The complex organ of Corti rests on the basilar membrane. Movement of fluid within the cochlea causes deflection of the basilar membrane that, in turn, produced a shearing action by the tectorial membrane. The relative movement of the two membranes causes the deflection of hair processes on the receptor cells located within the organ of Corti.

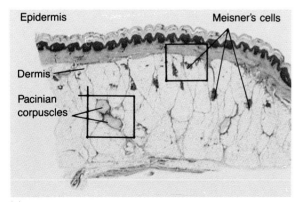

Epidermis

Meisner's cells

Dermis

Pacinian corpuscles

(a)

Plate 15.
Thin section of the finger tip. *a.* Meisner's cells and Pacinian corpuscles are two types of touch receptors found in the dermis layer of the skin. *b.* Meisner's cells, which are like a tube that is folded upon itself, are located closer to the surface and detect light touch and vibration. The Pacinian corpuscle has a rod-like receptor cell that is enclosed in an onion shaped encapsulating end organ. *c.* & *d.* Pacinian corpuscles report deep touch and pressure. Note that the appearance of the Pacinian corpuscle varies depending on how the microtome knife passed through the tissue. *c.* When cut in cross section, the rod appears as a small dot surrounded by the concentric rings of the end organ. *d.* When cut longitudinally, the receptor ending appears as a rod surrounded by oval layers of the end organ.

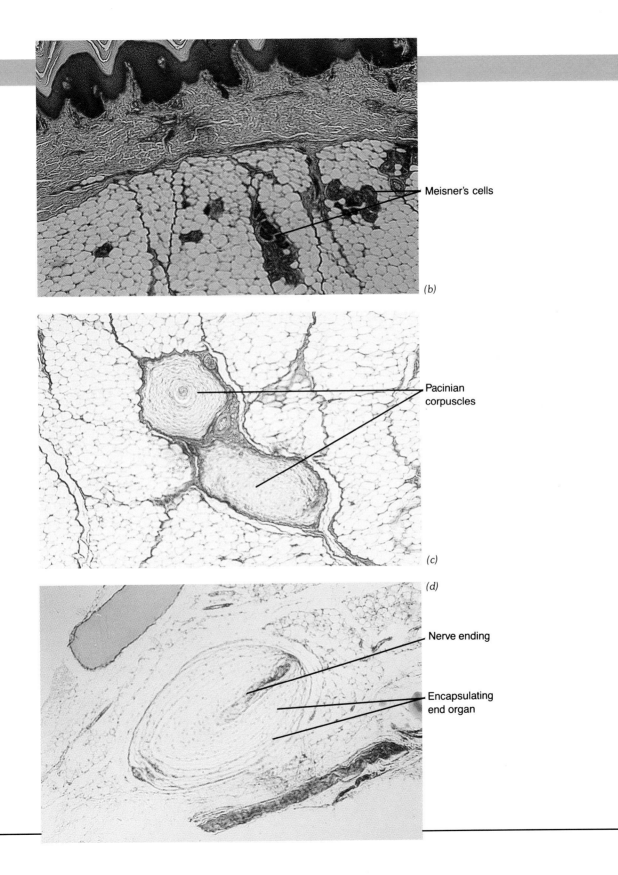

Meisner's cells

(b)

Pacinian
corpuscles

(c)

(d)

Nerve ending

Encapsulating
end organ

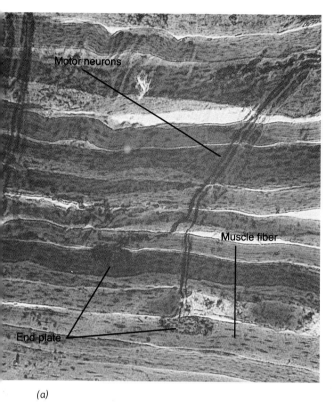

(a)

Plate 16.
The neuromuscular junction. *a.* Motor neurons terminate on muscle fibers. *b.* The enlarged micrograph
shows the neuromuscular junction on striate (skeletal)
muscle. Neural signals arriving at the neuromuscular
junction cause the release of acetylcholine, which
causes the muscle fibers to shorten.

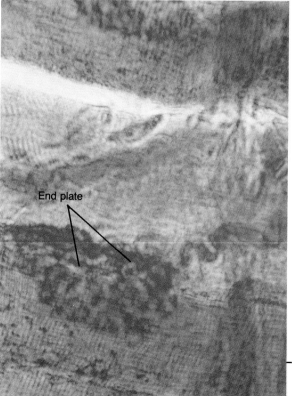

(b)

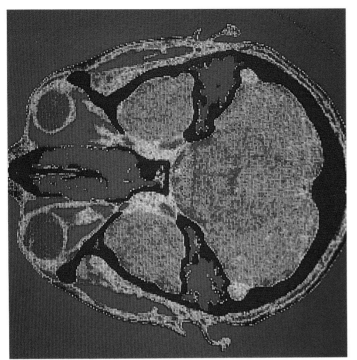

Plate 17.
Horizontal image of the head generated by computerized axial tomography (CAT scan). A dye is injected into the blood. X rays are passed through the head from many different directions, recorded, and processed through a very sophisticated computer program. The computer reconstructs the image, which represents a thin slice through the tissue.

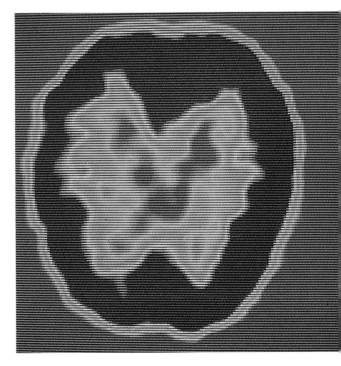

Plate 18.
A horizontal image of the normal human brain generated by positron emission tomography (PET). The person is injected with radioactive 2-deoxy-glucose, which enters the brain and is subsequently metabolized like glucose. Sensors around the head detect the levels of radio emissions at any given point in time and provide a measure of activity in different areas of the brain. The image produced is color-coded and represents the level of activity in the various structures in a thin slice of tissue.

Plate 19.

a. A saggital view of the living brain generated by nuclear magnetic resonance (NMR) also known as magnetic resonance imaging (MRI). The head is placed in a powerful magnetic field. Then a burst of radio-frequency energy is passed through the tissue at right angles to the magnetic field causing the molecules in the tissue to align along the axis of the electromagnetic pulse. When the pulse ends, the molecules realign their axis of spin; each molecule wobbles back to its original orientation, producing a characteristic "resonant" frequency. The characteristic resonant energy emitted by various molecules can be detected, analyzed by a computer, and converted into an image. In this way very detailed images of the living brain are possible without causing discomfort (courtesy of Dan McCoy/Rainbow).

(a)

b. New developments in mathematics and computer science now permit the construction of 3-dimensional images from many MRI "slices" through the brain. The operator is able to select which parts of the tissue mass will be shown. The surface of the skin, the skull, and the cortex are shown in the upper left figure. The upper right provides a horizontal section at the level of the eyes while retaining the 3-dimensional view of the ventricles. The bottom figures provide the frontal and lateral aspects of the brain and spinal cord; the lower right figure retains the major arteries that serve the brain. The color was added by the computer program (courtesy of Professor K. H. Höne, Institute of Mathematics and Computer Science in Medicine, University of Hamburg).

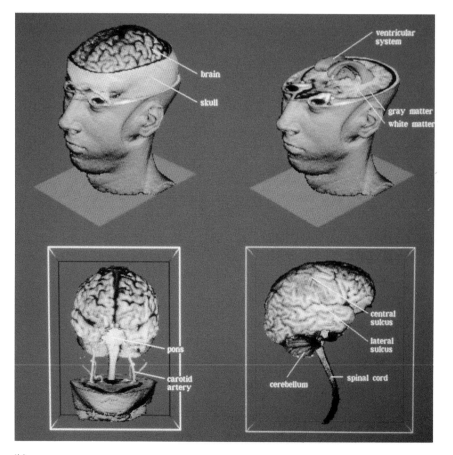

(b)

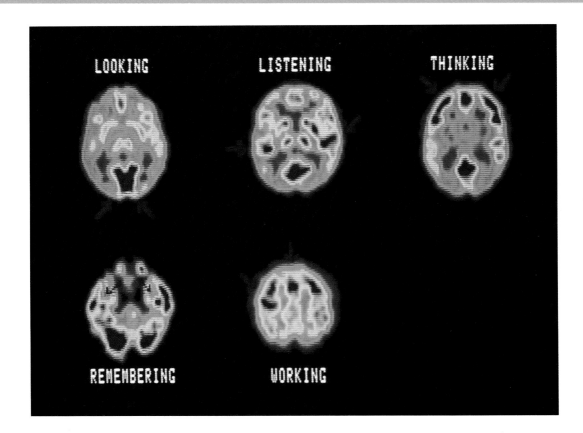

Plate 20.
Positron emission tomography of normal people showing varying metabolic patterns of activity related to different mental tasks. The scans are color-coded, with red indicating the highest levels of metabolic activity and blue the lowest. The images across the top row show the brain activity levels for passive exposure to visual stimuli (*left*) and auditory stimuli (*center*), and while working on a cognitive task (*right*). The two bottom figures show the brain activity during an auditory memory task (*left*) and a task requiring the person to move the fingers of the right hand (*right*).

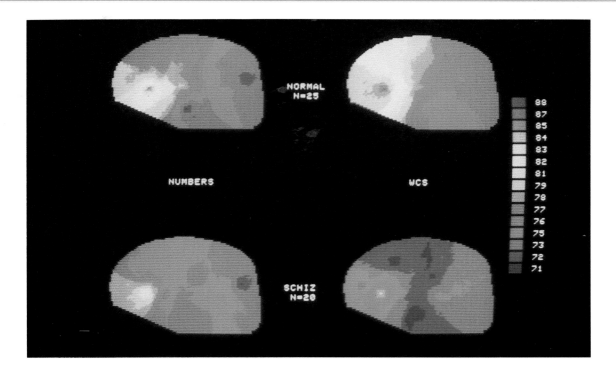

Plate 21.

Images of the regional blood flow in normal people and schizophrenic patients. The subjects are administered a radioactive tracer substance that enters the brain through the vascular system. Sensitive geiger counters monitor the level of radioactivity in various areas of the brain, which provides an indirect measure of the level of activity in various brain regions. The images on the top represent the average data for normal subjects performing a simple numbers matching task (left) and a task that activates the prefrontal cortex (right). The bottom two images represent similar data for a group of schizophrenic patients. Note that the schizophrenic patients do not show the normal activation expected in the prefrontal region of the brain.

*Problems with the
Dual Center Model*

As researchers examined the role of the lateral hypothalamus and the ventromedial hypothalamus more closely, it became apparent that the dual center model for eating behavior had some serious problems. First, lesions to the LH seemed to have an effect on both eating and drinking; the animals had adipsia (refusal to drink) as well as aphagia. Second, and perhaps more important, the adipsia and the aphagia were not permanent (Teitlebaum & Stellar, 1954). Animals that were kept alive by force feeding eventually began to feed spontaneously. The "recovery" is never complete, and the animals never regain the ability to regulate their water intake, nor do they regain normal responses to certain characteristics of food.

Alan Epstein (1971) has noted four progressive stages in the recovery from lateral hypothalamic lesions (Figure 10-13). The animals never drink spontaneously. In the final stage the animal survives on dry food, drinking only to lubricate the food. This type of drinking is called **prandial drinking**. Evidently, LH-lesioned rats do not produce sufficient levels of saliva and must consume water with virtually every bite of food. The animals never recover their normal, presurgery weight. If nursed until they eventually feed spontaneously on dry food and water, they maintain reduced body weight. These data indicate that other brain structures must be involved with feeding in addition to the LH.

Lesions to the VMH, the satiety center, do not result in unbridled eating. The animals do consume larger and higher-caloric meals. However, after a rapid increase in weight (called the dynamic phase), they reach a plateau and maintain their body weight at the higher level (static phase). Animals with lesions to the VMH show a variety of unusual eating characteristics. Together they are referred to as the VMH syndrome. The list of eating abnormalities includes the following:

1. When compared to normal animals, if food is available ad libitum, VMH animals have fewer eating periods in a day, but they consume much larger meals at each feeding.

2. VMH animals are very reactive to the quality of food. If the food is very palatable, they will increase their daily intake; however, if the food is adulterated with quinine to make it taste bitter, they will lower their consumption to levels even below that of normal animals. If powdered food is offered (a texture rats do not prefer), VMH rats will eat much less than normal animals.

3. VMH animals will not work hard for food. If the animal must press a lever to receive small pellets of food, it will decrease its caloric intake; under these conditions normal animals will not change their caloric intake significantly.

4. Finally, VMH animals seem to be easily distracted from eating, and once distracted, they do not return to complete the meal.

Hyperphagia in Humans

Many people have problems controlling their weight. Obesity, however, may be caused by a variety of physiological and psychological factors. Most overweight people, like myself, have a developmental history of weight problems. They are likely to have been heavy as infants and throughout most of their adolescent and adult years. These people also tend to have a history of poor dietary practices. They tend to eat less often or irregularly, and as you might expect, they tend to consume many more calories in a given meal than normal-weight people do.

There have been several cases reported of individuals who have experienced sudden pathological changes in eating behaviors resulting from lesions to the brain (Beal et al., 1981). Reeves and Plum (1969) documented a particularly interesting case of a 20-year-old woman who was first brought to their attention one year after she had developed an abnormal appetite that caused her to gain weight at an alarming rate. In addition to the eating behavior problems, she complained of frequent headaches and the termination of menstruation. In all other regards she appeared to be mentally alert and intelligent, and she showed no emotional disturbance.

A year later she returned to the clinic. The eating behavior had not improved, and now she evidenced other behavior disturbances, including mental confusion, memory loss, uncooperativeness, and unprovoked aggressiveness. Physical tests revealed reduced endocrine function in both the thyroid and the adrenal cortex. Exploratory surgery revealed a neoplasm (tumor) at the base of the brain, but its location made it inoperable.

The patient died 3 years after the onset of the illness. In the months just before her death, she had to be fed almost continuously to avoid violent outbursts. Even with the moderate control exerted on her by the hospital staff, she was eating almost 10,000 calories per day! A postmortem examination determined that the tumor had destroyed the ventromedial nucleus of the hypothalamus (Spotlight Figure 10-4). Additionally, the tumor had invaded the connecting pathways between the hypothalamus and the pituitary gland. This latter condition was the likely cause of the reduced endocrine function.

Humans may also become anorexic as a result of bilateral lesions to the lateral hypothalamus. As was true with hyperphagia resulting from brain damage, anorexia resulting from damage to the hypothalamus is very rare.

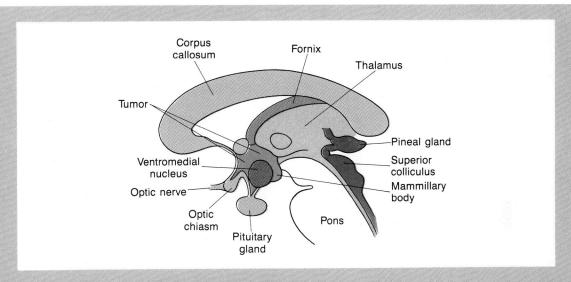

Spotlight Figure 10-4
The location of the neoplasm that caused obesity.

SPOTLIGHT 10-5

VMH Syndrome in Humans?

Stanley Schachter and his colleagues completed a series of studies on the eating behaviors of obese humans, with some interesting results (Schachter, 1971). Being a social psychologist, Schachter was the first to admit that he was not intimately familiar with the anatomy and physiology of the hypothalamus. He confessed that he may have eaten one once in a French restaurant, but beyond that he was unwilling to commit himself.

Schachter was interested in the unusual eating characteristics of VMH-syndrome animals. He wondered if there was a parallel between what was being reported in the laboratory concerning brain-lesioned hyperphagic rats and the eating characteristics of obese people. Schachter used as his subjects people who were, according to insurance company standards, mildly to moderately obese (15–25% overweight).

Survey data showed that, like the VMH rats, the obese people ate less regularly and ate fewer meals a day than did the normal-weight controls. The data also showed that obese humans tended to consume much larger meals and, therefore, more calories each day than did the control subjects. Schachter was interested in knowing whether obese humans were particularly sensitive to the quality of food. Were obese humans overly sensitive to external food cues such as taste and texture? To get at this question, he set up a clandestine situation where subjects were given free access to milkshakes ostensibly as a reward for waiting to participate in a study dealing with a totally different matter. Obese subjects consumed more milkshakes than did normal-weight controls. However, when the milkshake was adulterated with quinine, the obese subjects consumed about half as much as that drunk by the normal-weight people.

In another study Schachter looked at the willingness of obese people to work for food. In a research paradigm similar to the one in the study just described, the subjects were offered free access to almonds while waiting to participate in the fictitious experiment. When the almonds had already been shelled, the obese subjects ate more than did the controls. When the almonds were still in the shell and needed to be cracked open, the obese people ate less than the normal-weight controls.

Schachter interpreted these data as support for the notion that obese humans evidence similar eating irregularities as do VMH rats. Schachter would not go so far as to suggest that obese humans have malfunctions in their ventromedial hypothalmus (and neither would this author). His research does tentatively suggest the possibility that physiological, as well as psychological, factors may be correlated with human obesity.

More recent studies question the interpretation of some of Schachter's research. Some studies suggest that some people in all weight categories are highly responsive to external food cues (Novin, 1979; Rodin, 1976, 1978). Furthermore, there is some evidence that very obese people are *less* responsive to external food cues than are moderately obese and normal-weight people.

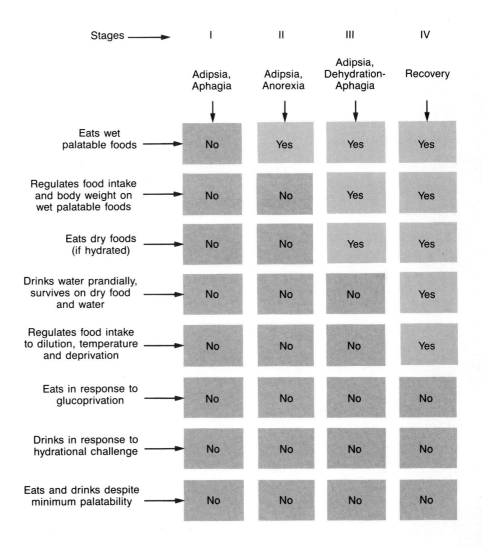

Stages ⟶	I	II	III	IV
	Adipsia, Aphagia	Adipsia, Anorexia	Adipsia, Dehydration-Aphagia	Recovery
Eats wet palatable foods ⟶	No	Yes	Yes	Yes
Regulates food intake and body weight on wet palatable foods ⟶	No	No	Yes	Yes
Eats dry foods (if hydrated) ⟶	No	No	Yes	Yes
Drinks water prandially, survives on dry food and water ⟶	No	No	No	Yes
Regulates food intake to dilution, temperature and deprivation ⟶	No	No	No	Yes
Eats in response to glucoprivation ⟶	No	No	No	No
Drinks in response to hydrational challenge ⟶	No	No	No	No
Eats and drinks despite minimum palatability ⟶	No	No	No	No

Figure 10-13
The stages of recovery from lesions to the lateral hypothalamus. (Adapted from Teitelbaum & Epstein, 1962.)

Clearly, the hyperphagia is not related simply to the VMH animals being hungry or being unable to experience satiation.

Centers or Tracts?   The early studies of the behavioral correlates of lesions to the LH focused on eating and drinking anomalies. However, lesions to the LH produce a variety of other behavioral deficits. The animals show a loss of motor abilities; they stop grooming, fail to right themselves when placed on their back, and lose the ability to cling to an inclined floor onto which normal rats cling quite easily. This has led some investigators to propose that the abnormal eating and drinking behaviors simply represent an overall loss of behavioral functioning.

It now appears that the eating and drinking deficits attributed to the LH may be due to the destruction of the **nigrostriatal bundle**, a group of fibers that pass through the lateral hypothalamic area. This fiber tract runs from the substantia nigra to the caudate nucleus. You will recall that degeneration of this dopaminergic circuit was the causal factor for Parkinson's disease.

Electrolitic or chemical lesions to the nigrostriatal bundle cause aphagia and adipsia as well as motor deficits (Ungerstedt, 1971). Other research implicates dopaminergic pathways with eating and drinking behavior. (See Stricker, 1982, for a review.) LH-lesioned animals that have recovered to stage 4 eating and prandial drinking become aphagic and adipsic if given dopamine antagonists (drugs that block the effect of dopamine). Conversely, dopamine agonists facilitate recovery from LH lesions (Ljungberg & Ungerstedt, 1976). These studies provide strong evidence for the importance of dopaminergic fiber tracts in eating, drinking, and motor behaviors. These data also would suggest that the concept of an LH "feeding center" is too simplistic.

Obesity resulting from lesions to the VMH may also be the result of damage to fiber tracts (Gold et al., 1977; Swanson & Sawchenko, 1983). Recent evidence suggests that damage to fibers connecting cells of the paraventricular nucleus with brain stem regions is likely to be one cause of hyperphagia in VMH-lesioned animals. These fibers innervate nuclei in the brain stem that modulate the parasympathetic control of the vagus nerve. The loss of input to these brain stem nuclei causes increased insulin output from the pancreas. Additionally, the paraventricular nucleus modulates the pituitary gland, which in turn controls the output of a variety of hormones that indirectly control the release of **glucagon** from the pancreas. Glucagon promotes the production of glucose. The combined effect of disrupting the fibers that pass through the VMH is that insulin output is increased and glucagon output is decreased. This condition causes glucose and amino acids to be stored and prevents their use as metabolic fuel. Therefore, the animal must overeat because it cannot get access to its stored nutrients. See Figure 10-14 for a summary of effects resulting from interruption of efferent fibers from the paraventricular nucleus.

Figure 10-14
Summary of effects resulting from interruption of the efferent fibers from the paraventricular nucleus.
1.   Lesion to the VMH destroys efferent fibers from the paraventricular nucleus.
2.   Loss of paraventricular output to sympathetic nervous system increases the output of epinephrine from the medulla of the adrenal gland.
3.   Loss of paraventricular output to the pituitary increases the output of adrenocorticotropic hormone (ACTH), which in turn increases the output of corticosteroids from the adrenal cortex, thus increasing the release of epinephrine from the adrenal medulla.
4.   Elevated levels of epinephrine in the blood decrease the output of glucogon from the pancreas.
5.   Loss of paraventricular output to the dorsal

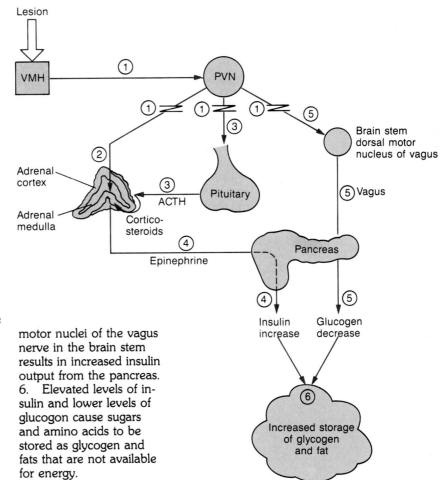

motor nuclei of the vagus nerve in the brain stem results in increased insulin output from the pancreas.
6.   Elevated levels of insulin and lower levels of glucogon cause sugars and amino acids to be stored as glycogen and fats that are not available for energy.

Hunger and Satiety

As was true with thirst, some internal homeostatic mechanism(s) must exist that initiate and terminate eating behaviors. Some of the earliest research on the signals that control eating behaviors, predictably, centered around peripheral mechanisms for metering food intake such as the mouth and the stomach.

The Stomach   In 1912, Cannon and Washburn completed an experiment that recorded the activity of the muscles in the wall of the stomach. The human subjects first had their stomachs emptied. Next, the subjects swallowed a rubber, inflatable bladder that was connected to a pen recorder by a pneumatic tube. Contractions of the stomach muscles caused movement of the pen. They found a consistent correlation between constrictions of the stomach and the subject's subjective report of "hunger pangs." Subsequent research, however, has shown that the link between stomach cues and the sensations of hunger is a weak one at best. Cutting the vagus nerve, the only neural connection between the stomach and the brain, does not eliminate the sensation of hunger nor the regulation of food intake. Also, cancer patients that have had their stomachs removed still report feeling hungry. They also have no difficulty regulating their caloric intake even though they must eat smaller, more frequent meals.

Sham Feeding   Sham-feeding studies have shown that consummatory cues from the mouth have a greater influence on eating than they do on drinking behavior. Recall that esophagotomized animals that have been deprived of water drink until they are exhausted. Drinking cues from the mouth, tongue, and throat appear to have little or no effect on satiety for water. Unlike drinking, cues from the head seem to influence eating behavior even when the food does not enter the stomach. When sham feeding, animals consume approximately the same quantity of food as do normal animals. As you might predict, the animal that sham feeds returns shortly to eat again. The satiety produced by the previous feeding is very short-lived.

As was true with drinking, peripheral metering of intake makes sense. The time delay between the consummatory behavior and the actual nutritive outcome of that behavior can be measured not in minutes but in hours. Metering of food intake by the mouth (and stomach) is necessary quite simply to avoid overeating. Clearly, other more central mechanisms must control hunger and satiety.

Glucose and Hunger   Glucose has long been thought to have a central role in eating behavior (Mayer, 1955). There are several very good reasons for this. Carbohydrates and proteins that are consumed as food are eventually broken down into glucose and amino acids, which can be "burned" as energy. Because amino acids normally are prevented from entering the CNS, only glucose is available as fuel in the brain. Therefore, glucose has garnered a good deal of attention in theories of eating. (Under conditions of prolonged food deprivation the brain can use ketones as fuel. This is one way that the brain is protected from starvation even at the expense of other body tissues.)

Excess glucose and amino acids are stored in the body for future use as glycogen. When food intake greatly exceeds the body requirements, the glycogen can be converted into fat and stored as adipose tissue. When food is not available in the intestines, the stored fat can be converted to free fatty acids and glucose and used as food.

Glucostatic theories of eating maintain that it is the level of *available* glucose in the blood that determines hunger and satiety. When glucose is available and being metabolized rapidly, as should be the case immediately following a meal, then the organism is satiated. When blood sugar levels are low, the organism should be hungry. (Paradoxically, diabetics tend to be hungry even though they have high levels of glucose in their blood. Apparently, this is due to the fact that they also have low insulin levels, and insulin is necessary for the effective utilization of glucose in body tissues. In their case the glucose is present, but it is not readily *available*.)

There is good evidence that glucose levels influence eating behavior. Injections of insulin into the peritoneal cavity of laboratory animals produce the rapid onset of eating. The insulin causes the rapid uptake of glucose into the cells, resulting in a hypoglycemic condition. Theoretically, there are receptors in the body that are sensitive to glucose levels—but where are they to be found?

Glucose receptors have been identified in the lateral hypothalamus. Lesions to this part of the brain eliminate hypoglycemia-induced eating resulting from injections of insulin. However, the animals continue to modulate their eating behavior appropriately in response to other cues. For example, they will correctly increase or decrease their intake when given a diluted or concentrated liquid food (Blass & Kraly, 1974). Apparently, the glucose receptors in the brain do not play a critical role in the regulation of food intake.

The liver has also been found to have glucose-sensitive cells. The injection of glucose into the haptic portal vein, which feeds blood directly to the liver, produces rapid and long-lasting satiety (Novin et al., 1983; Russek, 1971). These cells have been shown to send information to the brain via the vagus nerve (Niijima, 1969, 1982). However, denervation of the liver does not significantly modify eating behavior. Clearly, the liver does have a role in eating, but it is not the only source of hunger signals.

The role of glucose in hunger and satiety is certainly complex and confusing, and the picture is far from complete. More research is needed to better define the effects of sugar on eating behavior. At this time, the glucostatic theory alone cannot adequately explain the behavior.

Cholecystokinin and Hunger

Recently, the hormone **cholecystokinin (CCK)** has been reported to have hunger-reducing properties. CCK is secreted from the duodenum of the small intestine, and the hormone has been found in a number of species, including humans. Actually, the term *cholecystokinin* is used to refer to a large group of heterogeneous hormones. The original CCK hormone identified was composed of a string of 33 amino acids and is therefore called CCK-33. Shorter strings of CCK have been identified and two of these, CCK-8 and CCK-4, have also been implicated in hunger.

CCK is known to be released by the duodenum when food is passed from the stomach. The presence of the hormone in the blood causes the gallbladder to constrict, which aids the digestive process. Because the blood levels of CCK are related to the amount of nutrients passing through the duodenum, researchers proposed that the level of CCK could possibly be monitored as a satiety signal. More recent evidence suggests that CCK produces its effect in a circuitous fashion by first activating cells in the small intestine. These cells then communicate with the brain through the vegas nerve. This notion is supported by the fact that cutting the vegas nerve eliminates the hunger-reducing effect of CCK.

Several studies have shown that injections of CCK suppress eating in a variety of species (e.g., Smith, Gibbs, & Kulkosky, 1982; Strohmayer & Smith, 1986). These data are somewhat difficult to interpret because the CCK may also induce nausea and pain, and it inhibits motor activity—factors unrelated to hunger that could also influence the amount of food consumed. For example, when injections of CCK are associated with a specific food, the animals show a subsequent learned aversion for that food (Deutsch & Hardy, 1977). This phenomenon is sometimes referred to as **bait shyness**. Data on human subjects are too limited and the results too variable to permit a clear analysis. Intravenous injections of CCK have been shown to decrease eating in normal weight (Kisseleff et al., 1981) and in obese men (Pi-Sunyer et al., 1982). If these results can be replicated consistently; and if no unwanted side effects are found, CCK may be a valuable treatment for obesity.

Learning and Experience Effects on Eating

When we eat, what we eat, and how often we eat are influenced greatly by learning and experience. For humans, culture and tradition play an important role in eating habits. In Western cultures, having three main meals each day is the norm. Many Asian and African peoples traditionally have one, two, or four main meals a day. In some primitive cultures the number and timing of meals are far less predictable, and eating seems to be regulated more by the availability of food than by "scheduled" mealtimes.

An Observation:

Changing Your Dog's Eating Habits

Genie, my West Highland terrier, like all dogs, is a carnivore. Her natural tendency is to consume enormous meals when food is available, as it would be following a kill. The remainder of the time she would tend to be inactive, as would be true between times for hunting. (I must admit it is sometimes difficult to think of Genie as a hunter/killer/carnivore, especially when she is lying on her back, all four legs in the air, and sound asleep!) Genie, however, has been fed ad libitum (free access to food) ever since she was weaned from her mother's milk. Because of this, her eating behavior is not at all like that of her cousins, the wild dogs of Africa or the dingo from Australia. Genie eats 8 to 10 small meals dispersed throughout the day, and she regulates her caloric intake with remarkable precision. If her food is changed from one brand having 21% protein to another having 15% protein, she adjusts her intake accordingly.

Many domestic dogs are fed just once each day. If placed on an ad libitum schedule, they will overeat at first. However, they too "learn" to distribute their feeding and to regulate their intake appropriately once they adjust to the continuous presence of food. Clearly, experience can modify their eating pattern.

Set Points?   Humans and animals are able to regulate their caloric intake with surprising accuracy. Studies have shown that even under conditions where the food is pumped directly into the stomach using a **nasopharyngeal gastric tube** (see Figure 10-15), animals can still adjust their intake based on the caloric value of the food. In this laboratory situation the animals have fixed amounts of liquid food pumped directly into the stomach by performing some operant (e.g., press a lever). The animals are able to control the volume of food ingested based on the caloric value of the food. With enough experience, the animals will ingest less of a high-concentration food and more of food that has low caloric value.

Figure 10-15
a. The apparatus for intra-gastric self-injection. When an animal presses the lever, liquid food is pumped directly into the stomach, bypassing all oral and olfactory cues.
b. The surgically implanted nasopharyngeal gastric tube. (Adapted from Epstein & Teitelbaum, 1962.)

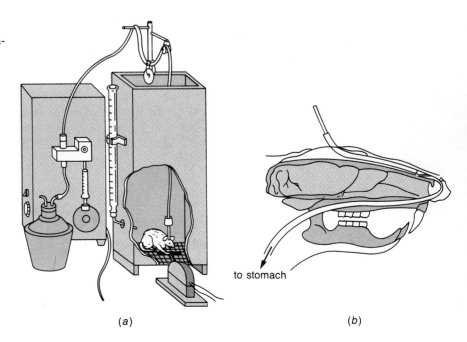

to stomach

(a)   (b)

Humans may also be able to regulate food intake based on the caloric richness of the food. For example, Foltin et al. (1988) have shown that people can accurately regulate food intake based on the caloric content of the food. In their study the subjects lived in a "residential laboratory" so that the researchers could accurately monitor food intake. The subjects, who had unrestricted access to food, accurately changed food consumption to compensate for dilution of the food's caloric content.

The fact that humans and animals are able to regulate their caloric intake and maintain their body weight within rather narrow limits has led some researchers to hypothesize the existence of long-term weight-regulatory mechanisms. Because fluctuations in weight are attributable primarily to gains and losses of stored fats, some theorists have focused on the state of adipose tissue deposits as the long-term signal for weight control. In one of the better known of these theories, the **set point theory**, Kennedy (1966) proposed that body weight fluctuates around a certain **set point**. The set point is thought to be determined by the amount of stored fat. Large deviations from the set point cause the animal to increase or decrease consumption in the appropriate direction. According to the theory, the set point can vary with experience. Overweight or underweight people establish new set points around which they regulate their food intake(Keesey & Powley, 1986).

Set point theory is not without its detractors. One difficulty with the theory is that fat does not circulate in the blood. How then does the brain monitor the amount of fat stored in the body? Are there fat detectors, and if so, where are they to be found?

I noted earlier that fat is used as a source of energy when glucose resources are not available. Stored fat is broken down and released into the blood as free fatty acids and glycerol. Thre is clear evidence that the level of free fatty acids in the blood does fluctuate and that the free fatty acids cross the blood–brain barrier. Cells have been identified in the medial and lateral hypothalamus that respond to changing levels of fatty acids in blood (Oomura et al., 1979). These data do provide support for the notion that lipostatic detectors may exist in the brain; however, much more research is needed before set point theory can be accepted or rejected.

Eating Disorders

Earlier in this chapter we noted that eating disorders may result from brain lesions. Abnormal weight and eating are also associated with hormone imbalance. For example, people with higher than normal levels of insulin tend to overeat because insulin enhances the entry of glucose into the cells, leaving the blood with lower than normal glucose levels. The insulin also increases the conversion of glucose into fats; therefore, these people tend to be obese.

Some eating abnormalities are not easily correlated with any physiological problems. One of the most notable of these is **anorexia ner-**

vosa. Not all physicians agree on the diagnostic criteria for anorexia. The condition is generally defined by an unreasonable fear of gaining weight, an unrealistic body image (anorexics perceive themselves to be bigger and heavier than they actually are), and refusal to eat enough to maintain normal body weight. It is commonly thought that anorexia nervosa is a relatively new phenomenon. It is not. The report of symp-similar to anorexia nervosa date back to the late 1600s. The term itself, which means "the nervous loss of appetite," was coined by William Gull in the 1870s. The occurrence of anorexia has had a sudden and rapid increase in our society, and this accounts for the widely held misconception that it is a new syndrome (Garfield, 1984).

Anorexia nervosa occurs most commonly in white, middle- and upper-class young women. This has caused speculation that there may be biological as well as psychological explanations for the eating disorder. There is some evidence to suggest that women may have a physiological predisposition for anorexia that is related to lower concentrations of reproductive hormones (Brauman & Gregoire, 1979; Gold et al., 1986; Schwabe, 1981). It has also been proposed that anorexia may result from problems associated with the neural control of eating by the paraventricular nucleus (Leibowitz, 1983). To date, however, the evidence for a physiological causal factor in anorexia remains weak.

Independent of the etiology of anorexia, it remains a very serious condition. Many of those who suffer from excessive weight loss associated with this eating abnormality greatly decrease their resistance to disease. In addition, menstruation may become irregular or even stop, and organ failure may prove to be life-threatening. Severe anorexics may even evidence deterioration of brain mass, as seen in increased ventricle size and enlarged space between the convolutions of the brain surface (Dolan, Mitchell, & Wakeling, 1988). The seriousness of this finding is heightened by the fact that these brain changes are not reversed by weight gain that may follow successful treatment of anorexia.

Most available evidence indicates that psychological and sociological factors are the more likely determinants of the eating disorder. Some theorists see anorexia as a form of depression (e.g., Bemporad et al., 1988; Logue, Crowe, & Bean, 1989). Others view it as a maladaptive response to perceived ineffectiveness—a way of demonstrating control over oneself, and perhaps a way of manipulating others. The most prevalent theory is that both anorexia and the related eating disorder **bulimia** are inappropriate reactions to the contemporary emphasis on thinness and its importance to physical attractiveness. (Bulimia is characterized by alternating dieting, binge eating, and self-induced vomiting.) Irrespective of the causal factors, anorexia and bulimia are serious conditions that result in significant, life-threatening biological stresses. Death-rate estimates range from 5 to 10%, often from heart failure or complications from infectious disease. As you may know, Karen Carpenter, the popular singer, suffered from anorexia and eventually died from

SPOTLIGHT 10-6

Beauty—In the Eye of the Beholder, but a Moving Target

Women tend to store fat somewhat differently than do men. The distribution pattern of stored fat can vary even between various groups of women. Hottentot women, for example, tend to store fat in the buttocks and thighs (see Spotlight Figure 10-6a). This condition, known as *steatopygia*, is most pronounced in older women, and Hottentot men consider it very desirable and attractive. The Masai judge taller and thinner women as beautiful, whereas the Yoruba find shorter, full-bodied women more attractive (Ford & Beach, 1951).

The concept of beauty also changes over time (see Spotlight Figure 10-6b-c). The nudes painted by the famous Dutch artist Rubens represent the epitomy of beauty and sensuality of his culture during his lifetime. By contemporary standards, these women are clearly overweight, if not obese. In an interesting study (Garner et al., 1980), researchers compared the "vital statistics" of the *Playboy* magazine centerfold models from 1960 to 1980. They found a clear trend toward thinner, more "tubular" bodies among the models from more recent years. This likely represents one example of the emphasis on thinness in our society.

Paleontologists have been fascinated by small female figurines found in the artifacts of early human beings. Some researchers have speculated that the figures resent fertility images because of the "exaggeration" of the female proportions—the breasts, thighs, and buttocks being quite large. The figurines may not be exaggerations at all. They may, in fact, be accurate representations of what was perceived by early men and women as beautiful. We will never know for sure.

physical complications induced by self-starvation. (See Levy, Dixon, & Stern, 1989, for a review.)

Standards of feminine beauty vary among and within different cultures, and they change over time. The ideal of feminine attractiveness in the Soviet Union is considerably different from that in the United States. Russian women (and men) prefer a more full figure. There are also very clear differences between technologically advanced and third world countries. In technologically advanced countries, there is a reverse correlation between affluence and obesity. That is, there is a tendency for people who are lower on the socioeconomic scale to be more obese. The trend is just the opposite in third world countries, where there

(a) (b) (c) (d)

Spotlight Figure 10-6
The image of beauty changes over time. *a.* Steatopygia in a 16-year-old Hottentot woman. *b.* This figurine of a woman is the Venus of Willendorf from the artifacts of early *Homo sapiens. c.* A Rubens painting. *d.* The contemporary concept of beauty in our society.

is a positive relationship between affluence and obesity (Sobal & Stunkard, 1989).

Within our own culture blacks and people of Hispanic origin do not place as great an emphasis on thinness as do white people from the middle- and upper-socioeconomic classes. It is interesting to note that anorexia is quite rare in men. Men account for less than 10% of the reported cases (some estimates are less than 5%). However, among men the incidence of anorexia in homosexuals appears to be much higher, perhaps reflecting the heightened concern for physical attractiveness in this group (Herzog, Norman, Gorden, & Pepose, 1984; Mishkind et al., 1986).

CHAPTER   **1.** Eating and drinking behaviors are regulated by *homeostatic mechanisms*.
SUMMARY   Homeostatic mechanisms operate on a negative-feedback principle that
maintains various physiological processes at desired levels called *set
points*.

2. Two commonly accepted ways of explaining consummatory behavior
are the drive reduction model and the mechanism model. Typically, the
more reductionistic mechanism model works more effectively with simple
organisms.

3. Animal life began in the sea, where the balance of intracellular and
extracellular fluids is relatively simple. Terrestrial animals have evolved
complex mechanisms to maintain a sealike environment within their
bodies. Animals evidence different drinking strategies that fit their particular ecological niche.

4. Humans, like most mammals, are approximately 70% water, which is
partitioned in the intracellular and extracellular parts of the body.

5. The kidneys play a central role in maintaining the water balance as
well as regulating the concentration of ions in the body fluids. The
amount of water excreted by the kidneys is under the control of two
hormones: *aldosterone* and *antidiuretic hormone*.

6. Drinking is initiated by at least one of two factors: (1) decreased levels
of bodily fluids (*volumetric thirst*) or (2) increased concentrations of solutes
in the bodily fluids (*osmometric thirst*). Volumetric thirst is controlled by
pressure-sensitive cells in the right atrium of the heart, which, in turn,
influence the levels of antidiuretic hormone. Osmoreceptors in the
hypothalamus control osmometric thirst. The lateral hypothalamus and
the lateral preoptic area of the hypothalamus have been identified as
important brain structures in drinking behavior.

7. The mouth, throat, stomach, and small intestines all seem to have a
role in the peripheral control of water consumption.

8. Animals can be classified into five main groups based on their primary food source: carnivorous, herbivorous, insectivorous, nectivorous,
and omnivorous. The feeding strategies of most animals are determined
by such factors as the caloric value of their food, the availability of food,
and seasonal influences on food.

9. Among mammals, the shape of the teeth and jaw reflect the eating
strategy. Paleontologists use the fossil record of the teeth and jaw to make
hypotheses about the feeding habits of extinct animals including the
hominids.

10. Early theories proposed that eating was controlled by neural centers
in the brain. Specifically, the *lateral hypothalamus (LH)* and the *ventromedial*

hypothalamus (VMH) were identified, respectively, as the "hunger" and "satiety" centers. Later evidence proved that this simple model was flawed.

11. Dopaminergic fiber tracts including the nigrostriatal bundle appear to be involved in eating, drinking, and general motor activity.

12. Sham feeding studies have shown that the mouth and stomach have a peripheral role in metering food intake. However, central brain mechanisms appear to control caloric intake. Glucose-sensitive cells in the hypothalamus and the liver appear to be involved in satiety; however, they alone cannot account for the termination of eating.

13. Cholecystokinin (CCK), a hormone released by the duodenum, reduces hunger. This substance may have some use as a diet aid for overweight people.

14. For humans, learning, culture, and tradition have an important influence on eating behavior.

15. Some weight problems in humans can be attributed to biological factors such as hormone imbalance. Most severe eating disorders such as *anorexia nervosa* and *bulimia* appear to be maladaptive reactions to social values placed on thinness.

SUGGESTED READINGS

Pirke, K. M., & Ploog, D. (1986). Psychobiology of anorexia nervosa. In R. J. Wurtman and J. J. Wurtman (Eds.), *Nutrition and the brain* (Vol 7). New York: Raven Press.

Rolls, B. J., Wood, R. J., & Rolls, E. T. (1980). Thirst: The initiation, maintenance, and termination of drinking. In J. M. Sprague and A. N. Epstein (Eds.), *Progress in psychobiology and physiological psychology (Vol. 9)*. New York: Academic Press.

Schachter, S. (1971). Some extraordinary facts about obese humans and rats. *American Psychologist, 26,* 129–144.

Thompson, C. I. (1980). *Controls of eating*. New York: SP Medical & Scientific Books.

KEY TERMS

Aldosterone A steroid hormone produced in the cortex of the adrenal glands that modulates the level of salt in the body.

Aphagia Loss of eating behavior.

Angiotensin II Metabolized from renin; stimulates the release of aliosterone from the adrenal cortex.

Antidiuretic hormone (ADH) Hormone produced by the posterior portion of the pituitary gland. ADH controls the reabsorption of water in the kidneys.

Bait shyness The tendency to avoid specific foods that have caused illness or discomfort.

Cholecystokinin Hormone produced in the small intestine reported to reduce eating behavior.

Extracellular fluid All of the body fluids located outside the cells, including the interstitial fluid, blood plasma, and cerebrospinal fluid.

Glucagon   Pancreatic hormone that promotes the conversion of glycogen into glucose.

Homeostasis   An active, negative-feedback mechanism that maintains some process at a desired level.

Hyperphagia   Overeating.

Hypertonic   Having a higher concentration of solute.

Hypotonic   Having a lower concentration of solute.

Hypovolemia   Lowered extracellular fluid condition that increases drinking.

Interstitial fluid   That portion of the body fluid that surrounds the cells.

Intracellular fluid   That portion of the body fluid that is located inside the cells.

Isotonic   A condition where two areas of fluid have the same level of solute concentration.

Lateral hypothalamus   Cluster of cell bodies in the hypothalamus associated with the initiation of eating behavior.

Median preoptic nucleus   Hypothalamic structure associated with volumetric drinking.

Nasopharyngeal gastric tube   A surgically implanted device that permits food to be pumped directly into the stomach, bypassing the mouth.

Negative-feedback system   An active process that detects deviations from a given level; *see* Homeostasis.

Nucleus circularis   A center within the hypothalamus that is responsive to intracellular water loss.

Osmoreceptor cell   Cell in the body that is sensitive to dehydration.

Osmoreceptors   Cells that respond to the loss of intracellular water.

Osmometric thirst   Drinking that is initiated by the increased concentration of solute in the body fluids.

Prandial drinking   Drinking associated with the consumption of food.

Set point   The desired level for a given homeostatic process.

Set point theory   Weight-regulation theory based on the condition of stored fats in the body.

Specific hunger   An innate preference for specific substances needed in the diet.

Subfornical organ   Structure in the hypothalamus associated with volumetric thirst.

Ventromedial hypothalamus   Group of cell bodies in the hypothalamus associated with satiety.

Volumetric thirst   Drinking that is initiated by the decrease in body fluid volume.

Chapter 11

Sleeping and Waking

Biological Rhythms
Biological Clocks
Pacemaker Neurons?
Annual Clocks?
Environmental Influences on Biological Clocks

Theories of Why We Sleep
Sleep as an Adaptive Mechanism
Sleep as a Restorative Process

Characteristics of Human Sleep
Stages of Sleep
REM Sleep
Changes in Sleep over the Lifetime
Dreaming and REM Sleep
The Importance of REM Sleep

Neural Mechanisms in Waking and Sleep Cycles
The Brain's Biological Clock
The Role of the Brain Stem

The Biochemistry of Sleep
Hypnogenic Substances?
The Role of Neurotransmitters

Sleep Abnormalities
Insomnia
Narcolepsy

Chapter Learning Objectives

After reading this chapter, you should

1. Be familiar with the various types of biological rhythms—circadian, ultradian, and infradian.

2. Be able to discuss the reasons why some biological rhythms need to be resistant to environmental influences.

3. Understand how some biological rhythms can be influenced by environmental stimuli such as the intensity and duration of light.

4. Be able to compare and contrast adaptation and restorative theories of the need to sleep.

5. Know how the electrical activity of the brain may be used to characterize the stages of sleep.

6. Be able to describe and compare slow-wave sleep and REM sleep.

7. Be able to identify the various brain structures that are known to be active in sleep and waking behavior.

8. Be able to discuss the transmitter substances that are associated with the neural circuits related to sleep and wakefulness.

9. Be familiar with the various types of sleep abnormalities.

To the best of my knowledge, all vertebrate animals spend at least some part of each day in a resting state that is similar to what we call sleep. There may be some exceptions to this generalization that have not as yet been documented. For example, very little is known about the sleeping behavior of fish. This is particularly true for those fish that live at great ocean depths where light is absent. Similarly, little is known about the sleeping behavior of cave-dwelling fish and reptiles that live in total darkness. Of those animals that have been studied extensively, researchers report finding alternating patterns of arousal—sleep and waking—that are pervasive and very predictable.

In this chapter we examine sleep in some detail, and we grapple with some rather difficult questions concerning altered states of consciousness. We want to know, Why is sleep such a common phenomenon in such a wide variety of animals? Is sleep, like food and water, necessary for survival? If so, how much sleep do we need? Why are periods of sleep and waking cyclical, and what factors regulate the cyclical pattern of sleep? Are there inter- and intraspecies differences in sleep patterns; and if there are, what is the significance of these differences? What happens during the period of time when we sleep? Is sleep nothing more than a period of quiescence, or is it a period of active repair and restoration? What physiological mechanisms influence waking and sleeping cycles? We begin by examining biological rhythms.

Biological Rhythms

Our planet is in constant motion. It revolves around the sun and rotates on its north-to-south axis. The earth's annual movement around the sun (365.25 days), combined with the tilt of the earth's axis, causes the yearly cycle through the four seasons—spring, summer, fall, and winter. The rotation of the earth on its axis produces the daily, 24-hour (actually, 23-hour and 56-minute) cycle of light and darkness. These two kinds of planetary motion are the bases of many cyclical biological rhythms.

Daily rhythms are called **circadian** (literally, "about a day"). We noted in Chapter 4 that some biological rhythms, like the human menstrual cycle, occur over periods that are longer than a day. These rhythms are called **infradian** because their frequency is lower than once a day. Some infradian rhythms can be quite long indeed. The life-cycle of the 7-year cicada is a good example of a very long infradian rhythm. These insects spend very long periods in their larval form as subterranean grubs. As grubs, however, they are sexually immature and unable to mate. They go through adult metamorphosis once every 7 years, mate, and start the infradian cycle again. Biological rhythms that occur more than once a day are called **ultradian** rhythms. Fluctuations in the patterns of brain wave activity evidence ultradian rhythmic patterns. I say more about the pattern of brain wave activity in the section of this chapter dealing with stages of sleep.

Some biological rhythms such as the annual migration of birds and the daily cycle of waking and sleeping in humans is quite obvious and easily observed. Most biological rhythms, however, go on without our awareness. These rhythms include, fluctuations in body temperature, cycles of fast and slow brain wave activity, and periodic variations of hormone levels in blood serum. See Figure 11-1 for some examples of circadian rhythms.

Although many biological rhythms are overtly subtle, they are nonetheless important. For example, Halberg et al. (1960) demonstrated very clearly that resistance to toxic agents varies dramatically with the time of day. Their research showed that mice, which are nocturnal animals, are four times more resistant to toxic substances at night when they are active than in the daytime when they are normally asleep. In a similar way, certain medications are more or less effective at a given time of the day, depending on fluctuations in our body chemistry. Our resistance to physical stressors like major surgery is lowest when our core body temperature is lowest, as it is at the end of our nocturnal period of sleep.

Biological Clocks

More than 250 years ago, the French astronomer d'Ortous de Mairan proved that flowering plants that apparently open and close their petals in response to light and darkness continue to do so even when they are placed in continuous darkness. He made this observation by simply placing one plant in a dark closet and comparing its behavior to that of a second plant that was exposed to the normal pattern of light and darkness. The petals of both plants opened and closed in perfect synchrony. This simple experiment demonstrated, without doubt, that the plant's rhythmic activity was under the control of an internal clock. The questions remain: What makes the clock tick? What underlying physiological mechanism(s) regulates the biological clock?

We noted earlier that a complex CNS is not necessarily required to regulate rhythmic patterns of behavior. Apparently, even simple single-celled plants and animals possess some form of timing mechanism. What is most interesting is that these biological clocks are very resistant to change. Researchers have exposed single-celled organisms to heat, cold, and a host of potentially disruptive chemicals with no effect. Even removal of the cell nucleus by microsurgery, which eventually causes the organism to die, does not disrupt the timing of cyclical behaviors for the period of time that the organism survives the surgery.

Pacemaker Neurons?

More complex organisms seem to have evolved special cells that play a central role in regulating rhythmic patterns of behavior. In 1972, Strumwasser, Schlechte, and Bower noted that neurons around the eye of

Figure 11-1
Many aspects of human physiology and behavior show circadian rhythms. The shaded area represents sleep. The figures for the three hormones and for grip strength are expressed as deviations from the 24-hour mean. (Modified from Krieger & Hughes, 1980.)

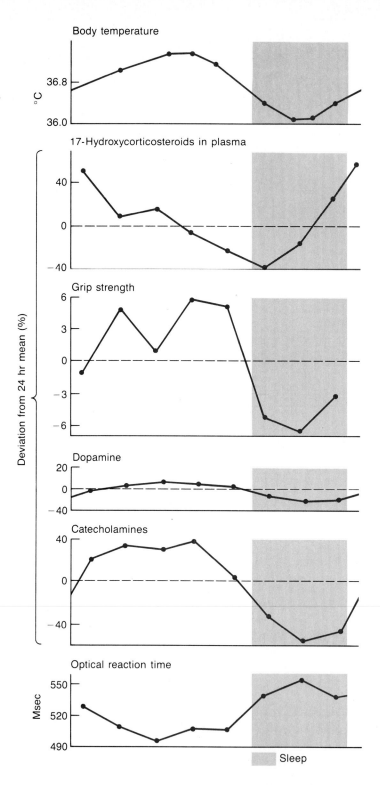

Aplysia californica seem to serve as pacemakers that regulate feeding and resting cycles.

You may recall that the sea slug *Aplysia* is a favorite subject of many biologists because it has very large neurons and a very simple nervous system. The neurons located in the outer rim of the eye fire more rapidly when exposed to light and more slowly in darkness. These neurons have been surgically removed from the animal and nurtured in a special bath in the laboratory. When the isolated cells are maintained in complete darkness, they fire in the same pattern as the cells of the living animal. Evidently, the timing mechanism is genetically coded within these neurons, and it operates somewhat independently of environmental stimuli. The process that regulates the pacemaker neurons in *Aplysia* is not well understood.

Annual Clocks?

Some animals, like the golden-mantled squirrel of the Rocky Mountains, inhabit environs that can only support them for a part of the year. Unable to migrate to more supportive terrain, as their neighbors the Rocky Mountain sheep do, these animals are forced to hibernate over the winter months if they are to survive. Unlike bears that sleep for long periods during the winter, true hibernators go into a deep comalike condition where their metabolic activity is greatly reduced. During the hibernation period heart rate, blood pressure, respiration rate, and body temperature all decrease to levels that could not support any overt activity (see Figure 11-2).

Animals that hibernate must have an ultradian cycle (in the case of the golden-mantled ground squirrel, an annual biological clock) that is very *resistant* to vagaries in the weather. These animals must increase their food consumption and gain weight in September and October, before they hibernate in late November, independent of the specific weather conditions that year. If the fall months were unseasonably warm in a given year and this were to cause the squirrels to delay their weight gain, they could be caught by a sudden onset of winter unprepared for the long period of hibernation. How then do hibernating animals time their annual cycle?

Pengelley and Admunson (1971) kept populations of golden-mantled ground squirrels in the laboratory. Some were kept at a constant 32° F; others were housed at normal room temperature. The lighting for both groups alternated in 12-hour cycles of light and dark. Both groups of animals increased their food intake in September and October, gaining the expected amount of weight, and then went into hibernation. They awakened in the spring right on schedule with the animals in the field. In another study, animals that where raised in the laboratory under constant light and temperature conditions from birth still evidenced the same rhythmic pattern of behavior after 3 years. The ultradian cycle is, necessarily, quite independent of environmental cues. Rather, this

SPOTLIGHT 11-1

Cellular Clocks?

Biological rhythms are not new inventions of evolution. Clearly, there must have been selective pressures for organisms to develop adaptive mechanisms that were linked to planetary movement. Evidence of the early evolution of biological rhythms can be found in very simple plant and animal life forms.

There is a species of golden-brown algae that inhabits the coastal sands of the northeastern part of the United States. This algal form is quite interesting in that it migrates to various levels of the sand in synchrony with the ocean tides. When the tide is high, this single-celled organism migrates to lower levels of the sand. However, when the tide recedes during daylight hours, the algae move up to the surface to take advantage of the sunlight, which is necessary to drive photosynthesis. When the tide rises again, the algae migrate back to the relative safety of the lower levels of sand (see Spotlight Figure 11-1).

As you know, the ocean tides are controlled by the moon and cycle in time to the lunar day, which is 24.8 hours. This means that each day the algae must migrate upward (or downward) 56 minutes later than they did the previous day. How do these little plants regulate this intricate schedule? Are they perhaps responding to some relatively straightforward environmental cue such as moisture, temperature, light, or pressure?

Palmer (1975) took populations of the golden-brown algae into the laboratory, where they were maintained in continuous light. All other physical cues were held constant. The algae continued to migrate through the sand in perfect synchrony with the tides on the beaches that were 27 mi away! Clearly, the algae respond to some internal biological clock that is set to lunar time.

---

annual cycle seems to be the genetic heritage of these animals. It is clearly the evolutionary end product of genetically programmed instructions that have adapted them to survive in their unique niche. How the genetic program keeps the clock on schedule is not known at this time, nor do we understand the specific physiological mechanisms and neural centers involved in running the clock.

Environmental Influences on Biological Clocks

Not all biological clocks are as inflexible as the lunar clock of the algae and the annual clock of the golden-mantled squirrel. Some biological clocks appear to be influenced by environmental cues. (See Spotlight 11-3 for an example of how the human circadian rhythm is altered when environmental cues are absent.) Stimuli in the environment that influence cyclical behaviors are called **zeitgebers**, a German word that

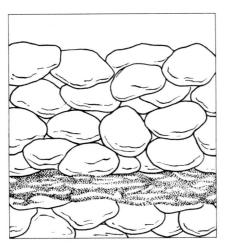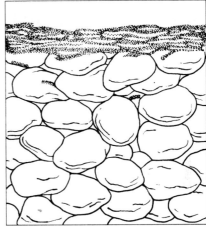

Spotlight Figure 11-1
Two views of golden-brown algae migrating through coastal sand in synchrony with the tides.

means "time giver." Zeitgebers appear either to initiate or regulate biorhythms. One environmental stimulus that appears to serve as a zeitgeber is light. This is particularly true for plants and some nonhuman species of animals. For example, some seedlings show no rhythmic pattern at all if they are made to germinate in constant darkness. However, a single exposure to light is enough to trigger the genetically programmed response to light and dark (Bünning, 1973).

The activity of the **pineal gland** seems to be directly influenced by the intensity and pattern of environmental light conditions. In birds the pineal gland is able to sense light directly through the skull as well as indirectly via signals from the optic nerve. In some mammals, like the rat and the bat, there is a branch of fibers projecting from the optic tract to the pineal gland. Cutting this fiber tract eliminates the influence of light on circadian rhythms (Menaker, 1974).

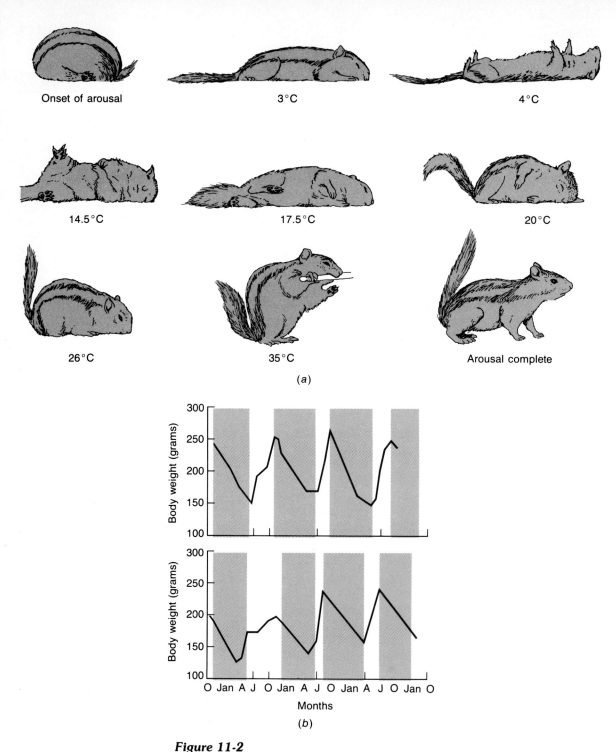

Figure 11-2
a. As the golden-mantled squirrel revives from hibernation during a 2-hour period, its body temperature rises from just above freezing to normal. *b.* The graph represents a typical 4-year record of hibernation cycles and the colored line shows the animal's fluctuations in body weight. (From Pengelley & Admundson, 1971.)

The pineal gland controls the amount of **melatonin** in the blood. Melatonin is a hormone that regulates physiological cycles such as body temperature and behavioral cycles such as wake and sleep in a variety of animals (Wurtman & Lieberman, 1987). Melatonin itself is synthesized from another hormone, serotonin. Two enzymes in the pineal gland accomplish this transformation. One of these enzymes, N-acetyltransferase, seems to be most closely related to the release of melatonin into the blood. N-acetyltransferase and melatonin are always at the highest levels during periods of darkness. In chickens N-acetyltransferase and melatonin are, respectively, 27 times and 10 times higher at night than during the day.

The sensitivity of the pineal gland to light was shown quite graphically by Binkley (1979). When light was introduced during the normal dark phase of the day/night cycle, the level of N-acetyltransferase in the blood dropped precipitously. The resulting drop in melatonin caused the temperature of the birds to rise, and they initiated eating and scratching behaviors. Returning the birds to darkness reversed this effect. Because the onset of dawn and sunset varies over the course of the year, the pineal gland must somehow reset the biological clock with the changing seasons. The pattern of light and dark appears to be the zeitgeber on which the pineal gland depends for this adjustment.

Theories of Why We Sleep

Humans spend almost a third of their lives asleep. Why should this be so? Isn't this a terrible waste of valuable time. Would it not be better if we could be active and productive 24 hours a day? Just think about how much more time you could spend studying for this course! Perhaps you don't find that a particularly attractive way to spend those additional waking hours. Then imagine spending those hours doing whatever pleases you the most. I once posed this to a class, and one student shouted out, "Sleeping pleases me the most!"

Sleep researchers and theorists have grappled with this question for many years. Generally, theories concerning the need for sleep fall into three categories; (1) theories that view sleep as an *adaptive mechanism* that contributes to the survival strategy of the species, (2) theories that see sleep as an essential period of *construction* or *repair*, and (3) theories that attribute a *psychological need* for sleep, and particularly for the dream experiences that occur during sleep. The emphasis of this book is biological; therefore, I concentrate on the first two theoretical positions.

Sleep as an Adaptive Mechanism

I have heard one sleep researcher say that the purpose of sleep is "to prevent us from wandering around in the dark and bumping into things." This may sound like a flippant remark, but if you think about it

When a Day Isn't 24 Hours

We are constantly surrounded by environmental cues that inform us about when we should be awake and when we should be asleep. There are clocks, radio, television, and the behaviors of other people to signal us. Perhaps the most salient cue is the alternating periods of light and darkness. What do you suppose would happen if these natural and manmade cues were absent? What sort of waking and sleeping cycle would you keep in the absence of any external cues to tell you that it is time to go to sleep or that it is time to get up from sleep?

Many studies have addressed this issue (e.g., Aschoff, 1979; Aschoff, von Goetz, Wildgruber, & Wever, 1986; Weitzman, 1981). Typically, the subjects are placed in deep caves where the temperature is constant and there are no cues about natural light. The subjects are provided with a communication link to the outside (for safety and data collection purposes) but they are denied all information about time. Each of the subjects has control of the artificial light and goes to sleep and awakens according to his or her own schedule.

Under these conditions the human biological clock continues to function. Interestingly, the clock invariably slows and drifts away from the "normal" 24-hour day/night cycle. Some individuals adopt very long days, lasting up to 35 to 37 hours. Most of the subjects settle into a wake/sleep cycle that approximates the length of the lunar day, 25 hours. Once a new day is established, the subjects establish a very regular wake/sleep cycle. See Spotlight Figure 11-2.

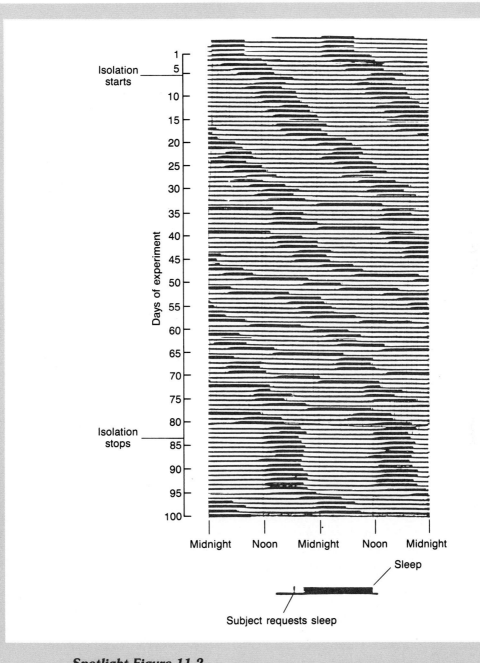

Spotlight Figure 11-2
The sleep and waking pattern of a subject isolated from all external cues concerning night and day. The shaded area indicates the period of time in isolation. Sleep periods are indicated by solid black lines. (From Weitzman, 1981.)

for a moment, I believe you will see the wisdom behind his comment. If you have ever camped out in the wilderness, away from all sources of human-produced light, in much the same manner as our primitive ancestors lived, you have experienced just how inadequately prepared we are to cope with the night environment.

An Observation:

Do Not Venture Into the Dark

Some years ago I spent 2 weeks in the triple canopy rain forest on the island of Luzon in the Philippines. The various species of trees in the rain forest branch out at three different levels. The shorter species are just 20 to 30 ft high, whereas the tallest of the trees are over 150 ft above the ground. The foliage produced by the three canopies of leaves is so dense that the sunlight never penetrates to the jungle floor.

At night you are plunged into absolute darkness without even the benefit of reflected moonlight or starlight. Quite literally, you cannot see your hand in front of your face. The Negritos, a primitive people who live in the area, keep camp fires burning all through the night. They never venture from their campsites after sunset. As experienced as they are with this environment, it is simply too dangerous for them to move about at night.

The primary premise of adaptive theories of sleep is that various species have evolved to be *most* effective during some part of the day/night cycle. Nocturnal animals, like most rodents, bats, owls, and so on, are simply more efficient at night. Therefore, they are more likely to survive if they are restive in the daylight hours. Conversely, diurnal animals, like most monkeys, hooved animals, humans, and so on, are most effective in daylight and are more likely to survive if they are quiescent at night (Webb, 1982).

The duration and pattern of sleep observed in various species lend support to the notion that animals have evolved sleep characteristics that "fit" their ecological niche. (See Table 11-1 for a comparison of sleep states for some representative species.) Herbivores such as cattle and deer tend to have much less sleep than do the carnivores. This is apparently an adaptation that helps to protect prey animals from predators. Some species, by necessity, have frequent, but very short, sleep cycles. This is true for dolphins, who must frequently rise to the surface to breathe. Some sea birds like the terns spend months gliding over open water. These birds have very brief sleep cycles while gliding.

It has been suggested that the adaptive usefulness of sleep is no longer relevant for humans. The use of artificial light and the elimination of human predators make sleep obsolete. This has caused at least one researcher to hypothesize that as a species we can dispense with sleep altogether (Meddis, 1979; 1975). This, of course, is not very likely—at

Table 11-1 **Comparison of Waking and Sleep States in Various Mammals**

Animal	% of Time per 24-hr Period, by State			
	Waking	Slow-Wave Sleep*	REM Sleep	Total Sleep
Cow	82.6	15.8	1.6	17.4
Dog (pointer)	66.2	30.0	3.0	33.0
Echidna	64.2	35.8	0.0	35.8
Human	60.6	32.8	6.6	39.4
Fox	59.2	30.8	10.0	40.8
Kangaroo rat	55.7	38.5	5.8	44.3
Seal	55.7	33.5	10.7	44.3
Rabbit	50.0	48.0	2.0	50.0
Rat	42.9	48.2	8.6	57.1
Cat	42.3	42.2	15.5	57.7
Armadillo	28.0	59.0	13.0	72.0
Opossum	19.2	76.7	4.1	80.8
Baboon	18.0	71.3	10.5	82.0
Squirrel monkey	17.0	59.3	22.9	83.0

* See section on stages of sleep for definitions of slow-wave and REM sleep.
Note: Modified from Rojas-Ramirez and Drucker-Colìn, 1977.

least not in the near future. The mechanisms that control sleep are programmed into our genes, and they are physiologically based. To live without sleep, we must change our genetics, our anatomy, and our biochemistry. Furthermore, sleeplessness would need to have a significant adaptive advantage for survival! After all, that is the basis of the evolutionary process.

Sleep as a Restorative Process

We have all felt the compelling nature of sleep. If you have ever "pulled an all-nighter" preparing for an examination, you know how difficult it is to "fight off" the need to sleep. Is sleep, like food or water, a basic, life-supporting physiological requirement? Some sleep researchers believe that sleep is essential because it is a period of time when the body repairs itself. The basic premise of this view of sleep is that the body must go into a period of quiescence to catch up or restore itself in ways that it cannot during the active waking period.

One way to address this issue is to observe the effects of sleep deprivation. If sleep is required for the organism to restore itself, then the prolonged absence of sleep should cause the machinery of the body to break down. Anecdotal evidence suggests that sleep deprivation causes serious physical and psychological harm to humans. Reports from American prisoners of war during the Korean conflict suggest that sleep deprivation was one of the most potent factors in the brainwashing techniques employed by their North Korean captors. The evidence from more carefully studied instances of prolonged sleep deprivation provide mixed results.

In 1959, as a publicity stunt, a New York disc jockey stayed awake for 200 hours. Toward the end of his vigil, he experienced hallucinations and delusions that he was being poisoned, symptoms similar to a paranoid psychosis (Dement, 1974). More recently, a 17-year-old boy remained awake for 264 hours. (He did so to be listed in the *Guinness Book of World Records*.) Although he experienced difficulty staying awake and had to engage in frequent physical activity to fight off sleep, the young man evidenced no significant mental or physical problems. Following his prolonged abstinence from sleep, he slept for less than 15 hours and awoke feeling fine. The next night he slept his normal 8-hour sleep period (Gulevich, Dement, & Johnson, 1966). The great difference in the response to sleep deprivation experienced by these two people suggests that the effect of prolonged sleep deprivation may be related to the mental and physical state of the individual.

Laboratory studies of sleep deprivation in animals are difficult to interpret. In the typical laboratory study the animals must be forcefully exercised or prodded with noxious stimuli to keep them awake. You can't simply ask the animal to avoid falling asleep, as you can with human subjects. Therefore, no research paradigm has, as yet, been found that can deprive animals of sleep without also producing other forms of physical stress. Laboratory studies do indicate that the combined effect of sleep loss and physical stress is much more devastating than physical stress alone (Rechtschaffen, Gilliland, Bergmann, & Winter, 1983). These data indicate that the loss of sleep produces an additional physiological stress on the animals. This may help to explain why the loss of sleep had such a profound effect on prisoners of war. As you can imagine, prisoners of war are under much physical and psychological stress. The effect of sleep deprivation could have been compounded by their already stressed condition.

Oswald (1980) has noted that sleep time is a period of increased anabolic activity. Cell division, protein synthesis, and long-bone growth in children occur at higher levels during sleep. This effect is likely due to fluctuations in the secretion of growth hormone (GH). Takahashi (1979) showed that GH levels in blood serum evidence a marked increase during the early part of the sleep cycle (Figure 11-3). Additionally, Drucker-Colín and Spanis (1976) showed that the amount of protein found in the interstitial fluid of the brain increased significantly during sleep. They interpreted their findings to mean that protein synthesis was at its highest level during sleep. Furthermore, the plasma levels of steroid hormones, which are important for a wide variety of bodily defenses, increase during sleep (Born, Kern, Bieber, & Fehrn-Wolfsdorf, 1986). These data lend strong support to the notion that the sleep period serves a restorative function.

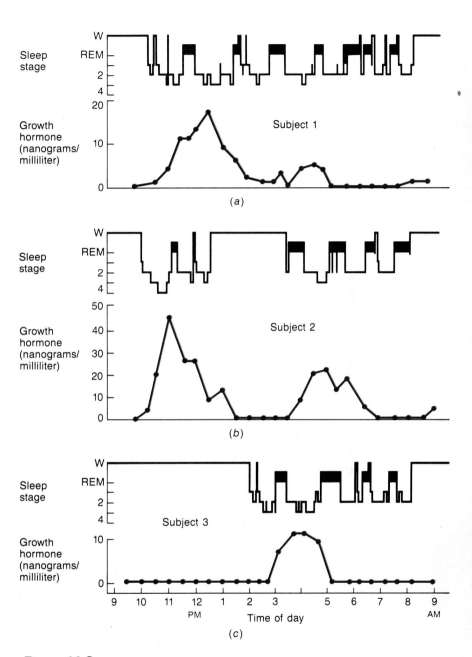

Figure 11-3
Graphs of blood plasma levels of growth hormone during the sleep cycle for three subjects. In the *a* and *c* graphs the subjects experienced a sudden rise in GH shortly after entering the sleep cycle. In the middle graph (*b*) the subject's sleep is interrupted, causing a biphasic rise in GH after the onset of each sleep cycle. (From Takahashi, 1979.)

Clearly, the two theories concerning the need for sleep are not mutually exclusive. It is not difficult to imagine that sleep, which may have evolved as an adaptive behavior, has also come to serve other functions after its biological mechanism was established. As is so often the case with theoretical issues like this one, there is evidence to support both positions.

Characteristics of Human Sleep

Up to this point I have been discussing sleep as though it were a simple homogeneous state. Based on the patterns of electrical activity in the brain, sleep researchers have shown that sleep can be divided into several distinct stages or periods. (See Spotlight 11-3). Each stage of sleep appears to have its unique characteristics and functions.

Stages of Sleep   During periods of wakefulness the EEG pattern shows two basic types of activity. **Alpha activity** occurs when the individual is resting quietly and is particularly evident when the eyes are closed. **Beta activity** occurs when the individual is mentally alert and active. When you are actively solving word problems or trying to remember a mathematical formula, your brain wave activity is dominated by beta waves. The pen movement generated by the two forms of activity appear to be quite different. Beta activity is characterized on the EEG by low-amplitude, irregular, high-frequency waves. By contrast, the alpha activity is high amplitude, more regular, and lower frequency.

The more regular activity seen in alpha waves is the result of the synchronized firing of large populations of neurons, probably in the cortex. This synchrony is thought to reflect a resting or depressed state. (People who use meditation techniques to relax are generating alpha activity. In fact, there are commercially available alpha biofeedback devices that can be used to facilitate the meditation process.) The desynchronized pattern of beta activity is thought to reflect the active processing of many smaller populations of neurons.

When you go from a waking to a sleeping state, the pattern of brain wave activity passes through a predictable sequence of changes. In the transition period between waking and sleeping the brain wave activity is dominated by irregular, low-amplitude activity interspersed with short periods of alpha activity. In the first stage of sleep the amount of alpha activity increases; however, the record still shows short periods of desynchronous, low-amplitude activity. About 10 minutes after the onset of stage 1 sleep the amount of alpha decreases, and the record shows short bursts of very high amplitude activity called the **K complex**. This signals the onset of stage 2. Fifteen minutes or so into stage 2 **delta waves**

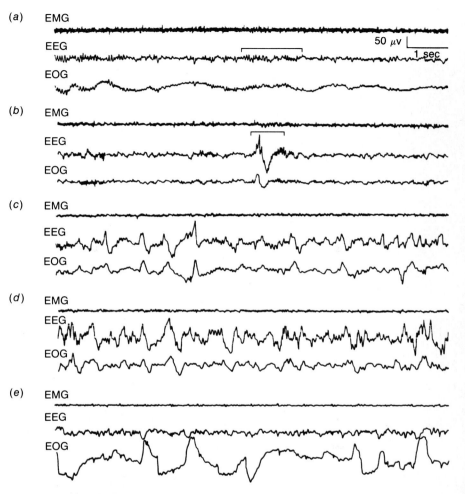

Figure 11-4
An EEG recording showing the various stages of sleep. The three traces are, from top to bottom, the EMG, EEG, and EOG. *a.* Stage 1 sleep. The bracket indicates a period of alpha activity. *b.* Stage 2 sleep. The bracket marks a K complex. *c.* Stage 3 sleep with periods of delta activity. *d.* Stage 4 sleep. The record is dominated by delta activity. *e.* REM sleep. The EEG pattern has become desynchronous. The EMG activity is greatly reduced. Note the prominent eye movements as indicated by the EOG. (From Cohen, 1979.)

appear, signaling the beginning of stage 3. Delta activity is characterized by very slow (1–4Hz) high-amplitude waves. Throughout the third stage of sleep the delta activity increases. When the EEG pattern of activity becomes dominated by delta activity, the individual is in stage 4 (see Figure 11-4).

EEGs, EOGs, and EMGs

As you know from our earlier discussions, neurons and muscle cells function via electrochemical actions. The electrical activity of each cell is measurable, and as we noted in previous chapters, recording the activity of single cells is a very useful research tool. Before microelectrode techniques were developed, researchers were able to record the activity of "populations" of cells by using comparatively large electrodes fixed to the surface of the skin. Each electrode is coated with a special conducting cream or gel that helps the electrode make good contact with the skin. Additionally, an abrasive cleanser may be used to remove excess layers of dead cells from the epidermis. See Spotlight Figure 11-3.

Electrodes placed at carefully mapped locations on the scalp record the activity of large populations of brain cells. This procedure, called an **electroencephalogram** (**EEG**) has been used by sleep researchers to monitor the activity of the brain during periods of waking and sleeping. In a similar fashion, electrodes

(a)

Spotlight Figure 11-3
a. The typical surface electrode used to record brain wave and muscle activity. b. The typical placement of surface electrodes to record brain wave and muscle activity during sleep. c. A commercially available multiple-pen recorder used to make simultaneous EEG, EOG, and EMG recordings.

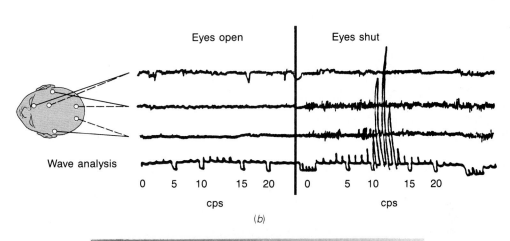

Eyes open | Eyes shut

Wave analysis

0 5 10 15 20 | 0 5 10 15 20

cps | cps

(b)

(c)

Spotlight Figure 11-3 (Continued)

SPOTLIGHT 11-3

can be placed over large numbers of muscle fibers like the frontalis muscle group on the forehead. The electrical activity produced by the constriction of the muscle fibers is recorded in the form of an **electromyogram** (**EMG**). One special form of EMG records the activity of the rectus muscles that move the eyes in their orbit. This type of recorded activity, called an **electro-oculogram** (**EOG**), provides an indication of eye movement.

Sleep researchers use all three forms of macroelectrode recordings to help them define the various stages of sleep. The output of the electrodes is processed through special electrical filters that help to detect activity within certain frequency ranges and eliminate unwanted noise. The filtered signals are then amplified and recorded by multiple-pen recorders that provide a permanent record. A single night of sleep will produce hundreds of recorded pages of EEG, EOG, and EMG data. In the past these records had to be scored visually, page by page and line by line, by human observers. New computer-scoring techniques hold promise for a less labor-intensive method of data analysis (Haustein, Pilcher, Klink, & Schulz, 1986; Stanus, Lacroix, Kerkhofs, & Mendlewitz, 1987).

REM Sleep Approximately 90 minutes after sleep begins there is a sudden change in the EEG record. The pattern of EEG activity becomes desynchronized, and the waveform looks remarkably like that of an awake and alert brain. The EMG activity of the skeletal muscles is now greatly diminished. Muscle tonus is lost, and the major skeletal muscles have become very flaccid. With the exception of the muscles of the diaphragm, which are essential for breathing, and the small muscles at the extremities of the body—fingers, toes, mouth, and so on—the individual is motionless. If at this point you were to attempt to elicit a spinal stretch reflex by tapping on a tendon, the response would be negligible. Although the brain wave activity looks similar to an awake brain, the individual is clearly very much asleep. For this reason, this unusual sleep period has been called **paradoxical sleep** (Aserinsky & Kleitman, 1955).

The EOG record during this period of sleep reflects rapid and large movements of the eyes (refer to Figure 11-4). For this reason, this period of the sleep cycle is also known as **rapid eye movement (REM) sleep**. During REM sleep the individual is likely to evidence signs of sexual arousal. In males, the penis becomes erect, and in some cases semen may be ejaculated. (This is what has been referred to as "nocturnal emissions," "wet dreams," or "sex dreams.") However, the changes observed in the genitals are not necessarily associated with dreams having sexual content (Fisher, Gross, & Zuch, 1965). Women, too, evidence genital

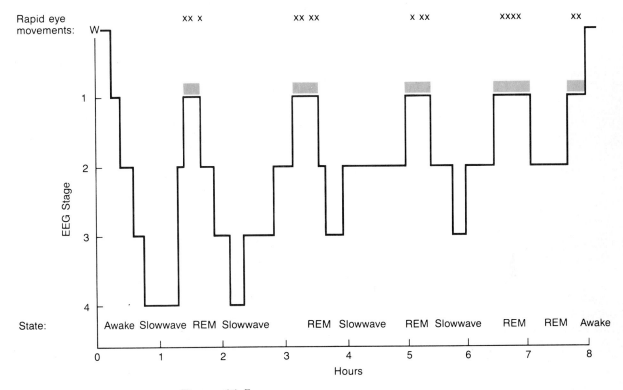

Figure 11-5
Graphic representation of a typical pattern of sleep during a single night.
(From Hartmann, 1967.)

activation during REM sleep and have increased secretions of vaginal lubricant. Women may also experience orgasm during REM sleep.

During the remainder of the sleep cycle the person will alternate between REM and slow-wave sleep about every 90 minutes. Each 90-minute infradian rhythm contains between 20 and 30 minutes of REM. Therefore, an 8-hour sleep period will usually have four or five periods of REM sleep. See Figure 11-5 for a typical pattern of sleep stages in a sleep cycle.

The 90-minute infradian rhythm is not unique to the pattern of REM and slow-wave sleep. Ninety-minute cycles of rest and activity have been noted in a variety of behavioral and physiological activities, including eating, drinking, heart rate, oxygen consumption, peristaltic action of the digestive tract, and the production of urine. Additionally, performance on a variety of tasks that have high attentional demands seems to fluctuate on a 90-minute cycle. Kleitman (1982) called this phenomenon the **basic rest–activity cycle (BRAC)**. We note later in this chapter that the BRAC is likely the effect of an internal clock located in the medulla.

Changes in Sleep over the Lifetime

Newborn infants spend much of their day asleep. As most parents know from their own loss of sleep, the pattern of an infant's sleep is quite unpredictable. It takes several weeks before some evidence of a 24-hour pattern of waking and sleeping emerges (see Figure 11-6). A clear circadian pattern does not develop until the infant is 16 weeks old.

Ontological studies of sleep have shown some interesting relationships between age and sleep behavior. One obvious relationship between age and sleep is that the amount of daily sleep decreases steadily with age. Each day newborn infants sleep close to 16 hours; 2- to 3-year-olds sleep about 12 hours; 5- 9-year-olds, 10 hours; 18-year-olds, 8 hours; 50-year-olds, about 6 hours. The progression is quite clear. Apparently, our need for sleep decreases as we get older.

Figure 11-6
Development of the circadian rhythm of waking and sleeping in the infant. The solid lines represent periods of sleeping, and the clear areas are periods when the infant is awake. The weeks following birth are shown on the left. The right side of the graphic shows the percentage of time spent in sleep. The 24-hour clock is presented at the bottom of the figure. (From Kleitman & Engelman, 1953.)

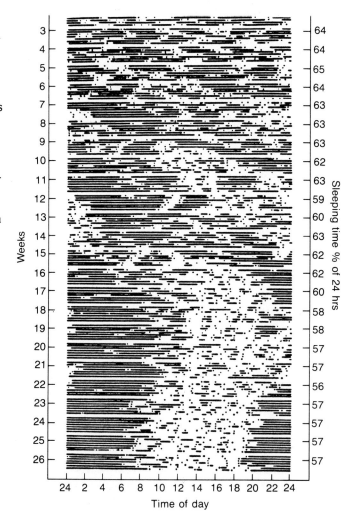

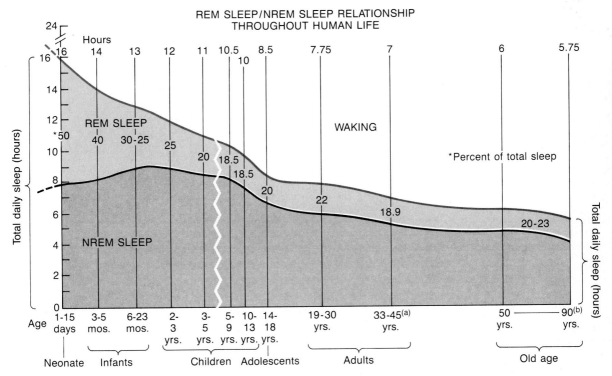

Figure 11-7

Changes in sleep over the life span. (From Roffwarg, Muzio, & Dement, 1966.)

A close examination of the stages of sleep shows that the proportion of the sleep cycle spent in REM also decreases with age. Newborn infants spend fully half of their sleep time in REM. (There is still some doubt concerning this figure, because the EEG pattern of very young children does not show the adult pattern for the various stages of sleep. The adult pattern of EEG activity does not begin until age 5 or 6.) The percentage of REM sleep drops to approximately 20% during adolescence and to less than 15% in old age. (See Figure 11-7.)

The greater percentage of REM sleep seen in infants and children has caused some theorists to propose that REM is an important time period for brain development. This hypothesis is supported by at least two other pieces of data. First, infants born prematurely, when the brain is in its fastest period of growth, evidence an even greater amount of REM sleep than do other newborns. Second, precocial animals (e.g., guinea pigs, horses) that have well-developed brains at birth evidence much less REM than do altricial animals (e.g., dogs and cats) that have poorly developed brains at birth.

***Table 11-2* Differentiating Characteristics of REM and Slow-wave Sleep**

REM Sleep	*Slow-wave Sleep*
EEG pattern desynchronized	EEG pattern synchronized
Rapid eye movements	Eye movement slow or absent
Flaccid muscle tone	Normal muscle tone
Sexual activation (penile erection, vaginal secretion)	Sexual activation absent
PGO waves present*	PGO waves absent
Vivid action-oriented dreams	Passive, less detailed dreams

* PGO waves are bursts of activity starting in the pons followed by activity in the lateral geniculate area of the thalamus.

Dreaming and REM Sleep

Many sleep laboratory studies have shown that REM sleep is associated with periods of vivid storylike dreaming. (See Dement, 1974, for a review.) Subjects aroused during REM are four times more likely to report experiencing a dream than subjects aroused during slow-wave sleep. The content of dreams appears to take place in real time. The length of dreams is closely related to the duration of the REM period. This is contrary to the once popular belief that dreams last only a few seconds. Dreaming also appears to take place during other stages of sleep; however, these dreams are more like thoughts or static images rather than the action dreams elicited during REM. We noted earlier that muscle tone for the large skeletal muscles is all but absent during REM sleep. This paralysis may have evolved as a mechanism to protect the dreaming organism by preventing motor responses to the content of the dream. You can readily imagine that many motor responses to the content of dreams could be dangerous for a sleeping organism. Table 11-2 summarizes the major differences between REM and slow-wave sleep.

In the early years of psychology many psychologists and psychiatrists placed much significance on the content of dreams. Followers of the Freudian and Jungian models of personality theory thought that the content of dreams could be useful for interpreting the "hidden" and underlying motives of overt behaviors. Some contemporary psychologists still believe that the interpretation of dream content is a useful method of gaining insight to the dynamics of behaviors, both normal and maladjusted. They are, however, an ever-decreasing minority. Most psychologists now feel that the interpretation of dreams cannot be tested in any meaningful way. (See Pivicki, 1988, for a review.)

An Observation:

Does Genie Dream?

Some questions that seem on the surface to be relatively simple to answer can be devilishly difficult to prove. For example, do dogs dream? If you have ever had a dog as a pet, I am relatively sure that you *think* they do. When I observe my West Highland terrier, who like most carnivores sleeps a good part of the day, it isn't difficult for me to imagine that Genie dreams. Frequently, her feet and tail will twitch, and she will emit soft, muffled growls and yelps. At these times I can also see her eyes moving rapidly from side to side under her closed lids—REM. Is she dreaming about chasing squirrels or driving off the pesky tabby cat that has the unmitigated gall to sleep on the hood of our car? (Cats have a lot of unmitigated gall.)

If I suggested to you that apes dream, you might, without any real data, find that idea easy to accept. But what about horses, cows, giraffes, wildebeests, and musk-oxen; or what of monkeys, deer, rats, hedgehogs, platypuses, and snakes? As we move from the familiar to the unfamiliar or from the humanlike to the less humanlike, it becomes less and less probable to us that these animals dream.

Many mammals show EEG patterns that are similar to human REM sleep. The amount of REM observed in different species seems to be closely correlated with the total amount of sleep. For example, cats sleep about 16 hours a day and experience nearly double the amount of REM sleep as do humans. Fish, birds, reptiles, and many other vertebrates do not have a cerebral cortex. Comparisons between the EEGs of these animals and our own are not really possible. These animals seem to have just one kind of sleep, but it is not possible to determine if it is REM or non-REM. Clearly definable REM and non-REM patterns of sleep seem to be limited to the mammals. The alternating pattern between slow-wave and REM sleep is a relatively new evolutionary development.

It is risky to generalize from the human experience to animals. The sleep of premature infants is predominantly REM. Do these infants dream—and if they do, of what do they dream? What experiences can they draw on to experience dreams as we know them?

You could no more *prove* that Genie dreams than you could prove that premature infants dream. Neither dogs nor the infants can tell us about their sleep experiences. It is altogether possible that REM may serve a very different purpose for premature infants and infrahuman organisms than it does for you or me. It is also possible that REM sleep provides the same yet-unknown function for both. The dreams we experience during sleep may be nothing more than the by-product of that yet poorly understood process.

The Importance of REM Sleep

Research has shown that REM is an important part of the sleep cycle. It is possible to deprive subjects of REM sleep without greatly affecting other stages of sleep. This is done by monitoring the EEG of sleeping subjects and arousing them when the EEG pattern shows that they are about to enter the REM stage.

The need for REM sleep may be separate and independent from the need for sleep in general. Dement (1960) found that humans who were selectively deprived of REM tended to enter REM more frequently. That is, the time between episodes of REM became shorter. Dement also noted that after several days of REM deprivation the subjects had a marked increase of REM during the next night of uninterrupted sleep. The amount of REM was still greater during the second night of postdeprivation sleep. The total REM sleep evident for the two nights of uninterrupted sleep almost equaled the amount lost from the selected deprivation. This **rebound effect** caused Dement to conclude that a certain amount of REM sleep was needed. The rebound effect would also indicate that there is some regulatory mechanism for this particular stage of sleep.

Early studies of REM deprivation suggested that the selective loss of REM in humans produced emotional changes including anxiety, irritability, and impaired concentration and judgment. More recent studies have failed to provide consistent support of the earlier findings. For example, there is at least one individual case study that would suggest that the complete loss of REM resulting from a pontine lesion caused no observable negative behavioral effects (Lavie, Pratt, Scharf, Peled, & Brown, 1984).

Research with laboratory animals (cats) suggests that protein synthesis, which normally increases during sleep, reaches its highest levels during periods of REM sleep (Drucker-Colìn & Spanis, 1976). This finding has suggested to some theorists that REM may be relatively more important for the restorative function of sleep than are other phases of the sleep cycle, as noted earlier. Additionally, some researchers propose that REM sleep may have important functions in learning and the incorporation of new memory (Bloch, Hennevin, & Leconte, 1977). As we discuss in Chapter 12 dealing with that subject, there is much evidence that protein synthesis is intimately associated with the learning process.

Generally speaking, there is not enough solid evidence to support any theory concerning the importance of REM. The function of REM remains unclear, and it is likely to be the subject of much research in the near future.

Neural Mechanisms in Waking and Sleep Cycles

In single-celled organisms the mechanism for the regulation of rhythmic behavior is, necessarily, within the cell. As the CNS evolved, specialized groups of cells developed that assumed these functions. We turn now to examine the neural centers that control waking and sleeping cycles.

The Brain's Biological Clock

We have already noted that the 24-hour pattern of light and darkness is an important environmental cue that influences circadian rhythms. Rats that have been blinded or kept in total darkness develop free-running biological clocks. These animals sleep approximately the same amount of time as intact animals. Their sleep pattern, however, is irregular and independent of the influence of light.

Information about light is passed through nonvisual neural tracts from the optic nerve to the hypothalamus. Lesions to the medial hypothalamus interrupt the normal circadian activity of rats (Richter, 1967), suggesting that the biological clock may be located here. More specifically, the **suprachiasmatic nucleus (SCN)** of the hypothalamus appears to be the primary locus of the circadian clock. Autoradiographic techniques have shown the existence of direct projections of ganglion fibers from the retina to the SCN. Bilateral lesions of the SCN produce disruptions of the sleep and waking cycle that are very similar to that of blinded animals (Stephan & Nuñez, 1977). The lesions affect the pattern, but not the amount of sleep, suggesting that other mechanisms may serve to regulate the total sleep need.

In an elegant study, Schwartz and Gainer (1977) demonstrated circadian fluctuations in the activity of the cells in the SCN. Rats were injected with radioactive 2-deoxyglucose, which is taken up like ordinary glucose by cells that are metabolically active. The radioactive material enters the active cells freely; however, it cannot be metabolized. Therefore, the relative activity of cells can be determined by measuring the radioactivity buildup within the cells. The amount of radioactivity found in the cells of the SCN was closely related to the time of day when the substance was injected into the rats. Rats receiving daylight injections (when rats normally sleep) had high concentrations of radioactivity in the SCN. Nighttime injections resulted in little radiocative accumulations in the SCN (see Figure 11-8). These data show quite clearly that the SCN is most active when the organism is in the quiescent phase of the day/night cycle.

As we have seen, two bits of data implicate the SCN as the brain center that serves as the light-driven biological clock. First, islolating the SCN from retinal input disrupts the clock. Second, the neural activity of the SCN is entrained to the day/night cycle. Is it possible that the SCN is influenced indirectly by other brain centers that receive visual information from the retina? A study by Inouye and Kawamura (1979) would

Figure 11-8
Autoradiographs of the brains of rats injected with carbon-14-labelled 2-deoxyglucose during daylight (*left*) and at night (*right*). The darkened regions in the hypothalamus at the left (arrows) indicate increased metabolic activity. (From Schwartz & Gainer, 1977.)

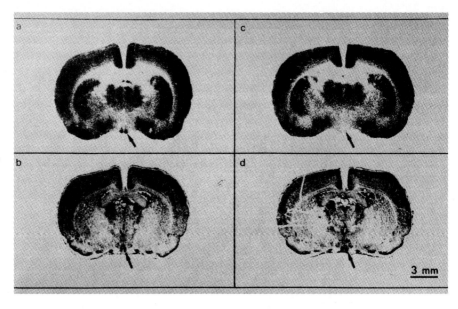

argue against that possibility. They lesioned the optic fibers caudal to the optic chiasm. This surgical procedure blinds the animal by cutting all of the fibers that project to the lateral geniculate nucleus, but it does not interrupt the retinal fibers that course directly to the PCN. These animals retain rhythmic activity that is synchronized with the light/dark cycle.

The Role of the Brain Stem

In the late 1930s the Belgian neurophysiologist Frédérick Bremer completed some experiments that focused attention on the importance of the brain stem in waking and sleeping behavior. Bremer made knife cuts at various levels of the brain stem and then recorded the electrical activity of the brain. He noted that the placement of the lesion made a very significant difference in both the overt behavior and the EEG activity of his animal subjects. When the brain stem was lesioned at a point below the medulla, the animal showed the normal EEG activity associated with waking and sleeping states. This surgical preparation, which Bremer called the **encéphale isolé** (isolated brain) caused paralysis because the motor fibers in the spine were cut. However, the encéphale isolé preparation did not disrupt the normal rhythmicity of the wake and sleep cycle. When the animal was awake, as indicated by the EEG pattern, the pupils were dialated and the eyes followed moving objects. When the EEG pattern indicated that the animal was asleep, the pupils constricted and the eyelids closed (Bremer, 1937).

When the cut was made at the upper level of the midbrain, between the superior and inferior colliculi, the result was quite different. This

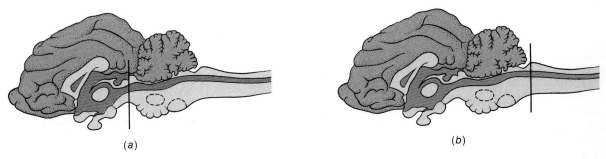

Figure 11-9
Schematic representation comparing (*a*) the cerveau isolé and (*b*) the encéphale isolé.

preparation, termed the **cerveau isolé** (isolated forebrain), caused persistent EEG sleep patterns with no periods of wakefulness. See Figure 11-9 for a comparison between the two lesions. At the time it was thought that the constant sleep induced by the cerveau isolé was due to the loss of sensory input. The knife cut at this level eliminates all somatosensory input from the body and the head (only the olfactory and optic cranial nerves are spared). With the encéphale isolé, however, all of the cranial nerves are spared.

This interpretation was consistent with the **passive sleep theory** that was commonly accepted at that time. The passive theory of sleep assumed that sleep starts because the mechanisms that support the waking state simply run down. In this case somatosensory input was considered to be the necessary source of wakefulness.

In the late 1940s and early 1950s new data caused sleep researchers to question the earlier interpretation of Bremer's research. Giuseppe Moruzzi and Horace Magoun (1949) found that direct electrical stimulation to specific nuclei within the **brain stem reticular formation (BSRF)** could induce arousal. The reticular formation consists of diffuse groups of cells whose axons and dendrites project in many directions throughout the medulla and the thalamus, and through the thalamus to a number of cortical areas. The BSRF receives collateral fibers from ascending sensory tracts, which presumably provide information about sensory events.

Lindsley, Schriener, Knowles, and Magoun (1950) found that lesions to the reticular formation could produce results similar to those seen with the cerveau isolé. Lesions made to the somatosensory pathways that spared the collateral sensory projections to the reticular formation failed to affect the wake/sleep cycle. Further, these animals could be aroused by sensory stimulation even though the direct sensory pathways to the thalamus were lesioned. See Figure 11-10 for a model of the activating role of the BSRF resulting from the work of Lindsley and his

Figure 11-10
The Lindsley et al. model
of the activating role of
the BSRF. Note that the
somatosensory fibers that
project to the thalamus
are lesioned. Sensory stimulation continues to
produce arousal through
collateral fibers to the
BSRF, which activates the
cortex directly and in-
directly through synapses
in the thalamus. (Modified
from Lindsley et al.,
1950.)

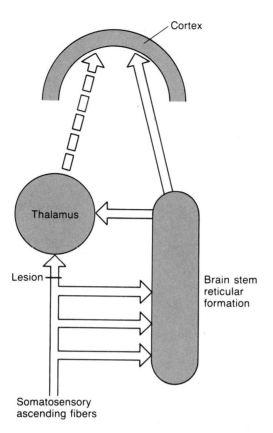

colleagues. These data called for a new interpretation of Bremer's research. Evidently, the persistent sleep that results from the cerveau isolé
can be attributed to the disruption of projections from the reticular
formation and not to the loss of somatosensory input. (See Gottsmann,
1988, for an updated review of the cerveau isolé preparation.)

The work of Moruzzi, Magoun, Lindsley, and others focused attention on active neural centers in the brain stem that could control waking
and sleeping behaviors. From this new perspective the onset of sleep can
be attributed to the action of excitatory and inhibitory centers that act on
the mechanism(s) that promote the waking state. This is an **active sleep
theory**. From this perspective, sleep is viewed not as the absence of
behavior but as simply another form of behavior. Thus, sleep is an active
process that is evident in different (not less) brain activity than that seen
in the waking state.

Just as direct electrical stimulation in the BSRF can produce
arousal, researchers discovered that electrical stimulation in other brain
stem regions of the cat can induce sleep in waking animals (Batini et al.,
1959). These findings supported the notion that active neural centers
controlled the onset of sleep.

In the 1960s and 1970s the renowned French sleep researcher Michel Jouvet developed a comprehensive theory concerning the neural control of sleep. This theory centered on two interrelated systems in the brain stem, the **raphe nuclei**, or the **raphe system** (*raphe* means "crease" or "seam"), and the **locus coeruleus** (from the Latin for "blue place") (Jouvet, 1967, 1974). The raphe system is actually a series of nuclei that cluster along the midline of the brain stem (see Figure 11-11). Lesions that are confined to the raphe system can produce total insomnia lasting for several days. This is followed by a period of recovery; however, the animals never return to their normal amount of sleep.

Jouvet found that cats given injections of **parachlorophenylalanine (PCPA)** could not sleep for over 40 hours. Additionally, these animals did not return to their normal sleep cycle for almost 10 days (Jouvet, 1974). This finding has important implications for several reasons:

1. PCPA is known to block the synthesis of the neurotransmitter serotonin.
2. The cells in the raphe system are rich with serotonin. In fact, the raphe system is thought to be one of the primary sources of serotonin in the CNS.
3. Small lesions to the raphe system reduce the overall level of serotonin in the brain.
4. The amount of serotonin loss due to lesions of the raphe system is closely correlated with the amount of sleep. The less serotonin available, the greater the insomnia.

These facts lead Jouvet to propose that serotoninergic circuits originating in the raphe system are responsible for the induction of sleep. He proposed that the serotoninergic fibers produce their effect by inhibiting the action of nearby arousal neurons in the reticular formation.

The second neural center prominent in Jouvet's sleep model, the locus coeruleus, is located in the dorsal pons. Its noradrenergic neurons send axons and dentrites to a wide variety of brain centers including the cortex, the hippocampus, the thalamus, the cerebellum, and the medulla (see Figure 11-12). Jouvet and his colleagues found that lesions to the ascending fibers of the locus coeruleus greatly increased both slow-wave and REM sleep (Jones, Bobillier, & Jouvet, 1969). More recently it has been shown that lesions to the locus coeruleus can increase the amount of REM sleep without affecting other stages of sleep (Caballero & de Andrés, 1986). A similar effect is seen with the chemical suppression of the neurotransmitter noradrenalin. These findings led Jouvet and others to propose that the locus coeruleus produces its effect by suppressing the activity of the raphe system.

Specifically, Jouvet hypothesized that the raphe system initiated slow-wave sleep, and the locus coeruleus, by its suppression of the raphe

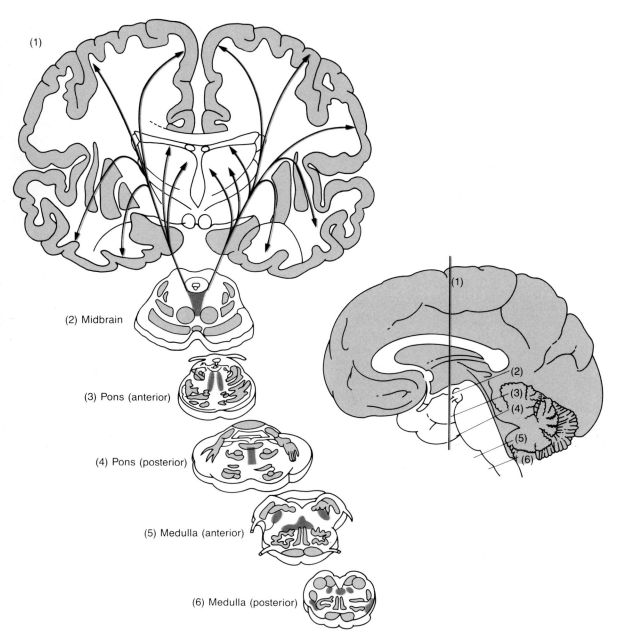

(1)

(2) Midbrain

(3) Pons (anterior)

(4) Pons (posterior)

(5) Medulla (anterior)

(6) Medulla (posterior)

(1)

(2)
(3)
(4)
(5)
(6)

Figure 11-11
The location of the raphe system and the locus coeruleus, including their
cortical and subcortical projections.

Figure 11-12
The location of the reticular formation, the raphe system, and the locus coeruleus in the cat. The dashed lines show the location of the (*a*) cerveau isolé and (*b*) encéphale isolé.

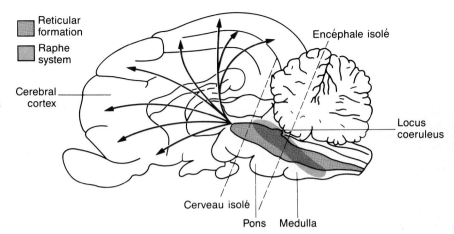

system, initiated the REM stage of sleep. The onset of REM is signaled by very high amplitude **PGO waves** (pons-geniculate-occipital). The PGO waves begin just as REM sleep begins and continue throughout the REM period. Each PGO wave is synchronized with the eye movements noted during REM. There is some evidence that the PGO activity is modulated by the amygdala, although the role of the amygdala in sleep is not clear (Calvo et al., 1987). Jouvet believed that the PGO waves originate in the locus coeruleus; however, attempts to verify the source of PGO waves have not met with success.

More recent studies have shown that Jouvet's model is not without its limitations (e.g., Hobson & McCarley, 1977; Kelly, 1981; Ramm, 1979). Nevertheless, his pioneering research firmly entrenched the active neural center theory of sleep. Most contemporary sleep researchers agree that sleep is the result of active processes induced by neural centers probably located in the brain stem and the nearby hypothalamus.

The Biochemistry of Sleep

The notion that some chemical or set of chemicals can induce sleep is not new. In fact, some of the earliest theories of sleep attributed the need for sleep to "toxins" that accumulated in the body during the active period of the day. We now examine the evidence for the existence of biochemical regulators of sleep and arousal.

Hypnogenic Substances?   In 1913, Legrende and Piéron kept dogs awake for long periods of time. Their intent was to allow the toxin, or "hypnogenic substance," in the animals to rise to abnormally high levels. They then extracted cerebrospinal fluid from the sleep-deprived animals and injected it into the

Passing on Sleep

If sleep and wakefulness were controlled by substances in the blood, you would expect that two individuals who share the same blood would have synchronized sleeping cycles. The evidence, however, does not meet with this expectation. Human Siamese twins who share a common cerebral blood supply have independent sleep cycles. *Parabiotic twins* (animals that are joined surgically and share the same blood supply) do not evidence synchrony in their waking and sleeping cycle.

There may be substances that control sleep, but cannot cross the blood–brain barrier. In that situation levels of the substance found in the brain and in the blood could be quite independent. An interesting study by Drucker-Colín and Spanis (1976) tested this hypothesis. Their research adopted a technique developed by Myers in 1970 that permits the extraction of cerebrospinal fluid from freely moving animals.

The device called a **push–pull cannula** is chronically implanted through the skull and projects into the brain. The cannula is actually a narrow-diameter tube within a larger tube (see Spotlight Figure 11-4a). The device permits the experimenter to pump **Ringer's solution** (a solution that approximates the salts found in the interstitial tissue) slowly through the narrow tube and extract the fluid and other substances found in the extracellular fluid of the brain through the larger tube. With this technique the intracranial pressure is not significantly altered.

Druker-Colin and Spanis implanted push–pull cannulas in the brains of cats. Ringer's solution was then perfused into the brain of a donor cat, and the extracted fluid was perfused into the brain of the recipient cat. They found that Ringer's solution perfused through the brain of a sleeping cat induced the recipient to go to sleep more rapidly than control animals that received injections of plain Ringer's solution (see Spotlight Figure 11-4b). They also found that solution passed through the brain of an alert donor cat caused a sleeping recipient to wake up. These data support the hypothesis that the brain chemistry of sleeping and waking animals differs.

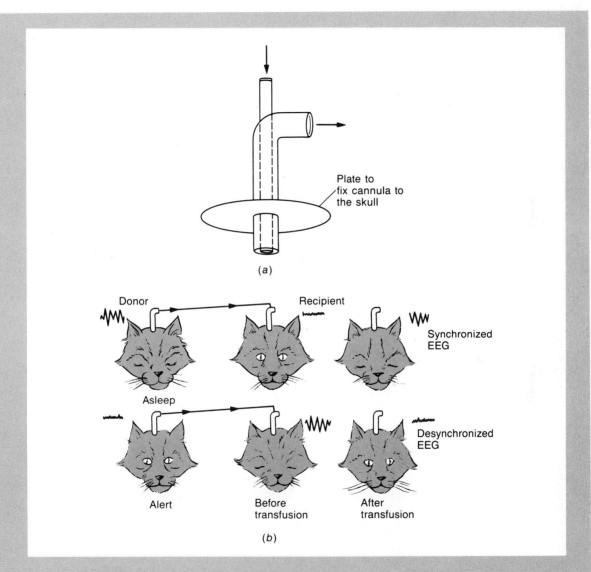

Spotlight Figure 11-4
a. The push–pull cannula. *b.* The research setup used by Drucker-Colin and Spanis. Perfusate obtained from the donor animals on the left is perfused into the recipient animals on the right. (Adapted from Drucker-Colin & Spanis, 1976.)

ventricular cavity of animals that had not been deprived of sleep. The nondeprived dogs immediately went to sleep and slept for 2 to 6 hours. Legrende and Piéron concluded that the sleep was induced by some yet unidentified hypnogenic substance. Subsequently, researchers who replicated this study noted that the data could not be interpreted quite so cleanly. They noted that the injections of cerebrospinal fluid increased intracranial pressure and caused hyperthermia. The sleep could have been the result of these unwanted side effects of the injections.

More recent studies have identified a small glucopeptide, called **factor S**, which appears to induce sleep (Fencl, Koski, & Pappenheimer, 1971; Inoué, Uchizono, & Nagasaki, 1982; Krueger, Pappenheimer, & Karnovsky, 1982). Factor S, which has two amino acids, has been found in very small quantities in the nervous system, blood, and urine of animals and humans. When injected into laboratory animals, factor S hastens the onset and increases the duration of sleep. A second substance, produced in the thalamus, has been implicated with slow-wave EEG activity. The substance called **delta sleep-inducing peptide**, is thought to initiate synchronized brain wave activity.

The evidence to support specific chemicals as candidate sleep-inducing substances is still quite limited and should be dealt with cautiously. However, it is evident that some yet unidentified substance(s) does induce sleep and wakefulness. See Spotlight 11-4 for data that support this notion.

The Role of Neurotransmitters

We have already seen that serotoninergic and adrenergic circuits are very much involved in sleep. Logically, sleep researchers were interested in what possible role these neurotransmitters have in the regulation of sleep and waking cycles. Unfortunately, the data are inconsistent and confusing, and they do little to advance our understanding of sleep.

It was noted earlier that PCPA blocks the synthesis of serotonin. The lower levels of serotonin, in turn, decrease the amount of sleep. However, if PCPA treatments are maintained over a longer period of time, the long-term depletion of serotonin loses its effect. The amount of sleep approaches pretreatment levels (Morgane, 1981). It is not at all clear how short-term reductions in the level of serotonin produce an effect on sleep when long-term reductions of the same neurotransmitter do not.

One way to increase the availability of serotonin in the CNS is to introduce its chemical precursor. The amino acid *L-tryptophan* is converted into serotonin after it enters the brain. Some researchers have found that relatively large doses of L-tryptophan taken before retiring help some people with sleeping problems to sleep (e.g., Schneider-Helmert & Spinweber, 1986). The treatment of sleeping problems with L-tryptophan appears to be most effective with younger people. Why this should be is unclear.

The role of noradrenalin in sleep is just as tenuous and unclear as serotonin. It was noted earlier that the adrenergic circuits of the locus coeruleus appear to stimulate REM by suppressing the slow-wave sleep under control of the raphe system. The data, however, show that lesioning the locus coeruleus or depleting the amount of noradrenalin may increase, decrease, or have no effect on REM (Jones, Harper, & Halaris, 1977). What is most clear about the data concerning the role of neurotransmitters in sleep is that more study is needed before any sort of a coherent picture can be painted.

Sleep Abnormalities

It has been estimated that 8 to 15% of U.S. adults have chronic complaints concerning sleep (Weitzman, 1981). In many instances sleep disturbances are just one symptom of a psychological or neurological problem. Most often abnormal sleep is associated with psychological depression or substance abuse.

Insomnia   How much sleep is enough? Some people sleep 4 or 5 hours each night and feel perfectly satisfied. Others feel that they must have at least 8 or 10 hours each night before they have had a "full" night's sleep. There have been several well-documented cases of individuals who for most of their adult life sleep just 1 hour a night (without unreported naps). So, how much sleep is enough? It seems to depend, at least to some degree, on the individual.

We have two problems in dealing with sleep disturbances. One is a problem of definition. As I just noted, the amount of sleep that is "normal" for one person is not necessarily normal for others. Second, there is a problem of perceptions. If I sleep 5 hours a night (as I do) and I am satisfied with that amount of sleep (as I am), then I perceive that I don't have a sleep disorder. On the other hand, if I sleep 5 hours a night and feel that I need more sleep, then the perception of a problem exists.

Insomnia, or sleeplessness, is the most common form of sleep abnormality. Insomnia has been associated with a variety of psychological and neurological factors. Typically, sleeplessness is categorized into three types: (1) onset insomnia refers to difficulties falling asleep, (2) maintenance insomnia occurs in individuals who awaken frequently during the night, and (3) termination insomnia applies to people whose sleep period ends too soon. The three types of insomnia are not mutually exlusive, and it is possible to suffer from more than one kind of insomnia. It should be noted that some people report sleeping much less than they actually do. Often the actual amount of sleep people have, as measured by natural observation or EEG, is considerably more than they report.

Paradoxically, one of the most common causes of insomnia is sleeping pills. Insomnia is *not*, at this time, a disease that can be cured by medication. Sleep medications are usually prescribed to deal with sleep loss that is a secondary symptom of physical or psychological problems. Of particular concern is that people develop a tolerance to most drugs that are prescribed for sleeplessness (Weitzman, 1981). The drugs loose their effectiveness, which, in turn, requires higher dosages to accomplish the same effect. The result is termed *drug-dependency insomnia*, a condition in which the individual experiences insomnia from the withdrawal from sleep medication.

One source of insomnia is associated with breathing problems during sleep. The condition known as **sleep apnea** is not uncommon, and most people experience relatively brief (10-sec) periods when breathing stops during sleep. These lapses in breathing are not problematical and do not interfere with sleep. This less severe form of sleep-related breathing problem is particularly common among people who snore. However, the condition can be quite severe. Breathing stops long enough for carbon dioxide to accumulate in the blood. This triggers CO_2 chemoreceptors, and the person awakens, gasping for air.

Sleep apnea has been linked to *sudden infant death syndrome (SIDS)*. This refers to otherwise normal children who die suddenly in their sleep. It is thought that for some unexplained reason these children fail to react to the CO_2 buildup in their blood. There is some evidence that the potential for a SIDS death is inherited. The parents and siblings of some SIDS children do not react normally to heightened levels of CO_2.

Narcolepsy The term *narcolepsy* refers to a cluster of sleep disorders characterized by the onset of sleep at inappropriate times. Narcoleptic people (and animals) do not necessarily have more sleep than normal individuals. The primary symptom of narcolepsy is the **sleep attack**, which is the uncontrollable urge to sleep. Typically, the narcoleptic sleep attack lasts for a very short period of time (usually 2 to 5 minutes).

I am sure that you can imagine how disruptive sleep attack can be to normal life. One form of narcolepsy, **cataplexy**, is more than disruptive—it is extremely dangerous. The cataplectic attack causes the skeletal muscles to go limp, causing the person to collapse. The person does not loose consciousness but is completely paralyzed. It is thought that the cataplectic attack is attributable to the sudden onset of REM or at least that part of the REM sleep phase that causes the paralysis of skeletal muscle. Unlike other forms of narcolepsy, cataplexy usually occurs when the person is emotionally aroused. Any emotion—laughter, anger, or shock—can trigger a cataplectic attack.

There is good reason to believe that narcolepsy is a heritable condition. The relatives of narcoleptic people are 60 times more likely to have the disorder than the percentage found in the normal population

(Kessler, Guilleminault, & Dement, 1974). Additionally, through selective breeding, Dement and his colleagues have successfully bred dogs that are very susceptible to cataplectic attack (Kartin, Kilchiff, & Dement, 1986).

Unlike insomnia, which cannot be treated effectively with medication, narcolepsy can be successfully treated with drugs. Specifically, imipramine, which facilitates the activity of the neurotransmitters serotonin and catecholamine, is an effective treatment for cataplexy. Sleep attack can be controlled to some degree by stimulants such as amphetamines.

CHAPTER SUMMARY

1. Rhythmic activity appears to be pervasive in all species of animals as well as many species of plants. Even some single-celled organisms possess predictable, time-linked forms of behavior. These biological rhythms are classified into *circadian rhythms*, which are tied to the 24-hour cycle of the day; *ultradian rhythms*, which occur more than once a day; and *infradian rhythms*, which are cyclical behaviors that are longer than a day.

2. Many biological rhythms are very resistant to changes in environmental conditions. Some rhythms, however, are dependent to some degree on environmental stimuli. The research evidence would suggest that most forms of rhythmic behaviors are under the control of *biological clocks*. The way in which these biological clocks control behavior is often poorly understood.

3. When deprived of all cues concerning time, the human biological clock tends to drift away from the 24-hour day/night cycle. Under these conditions some people adopt very long days, lasting up to 35 to 37 hours. Most people settle in on a 25-hour day, which is close to the lunar day.

4. There are two theories concerning the origin of sleep. The *adaptive theory* of sleep maintains that circadian rhythms, like sleep, have evolved as adaptive mechanisms that help to ensure the survival of the species. Restorative theories view sleep as a necessary period of quiescence when the body repairs itself. There is considerable evidence to support both theories.

5. Human sleep is characterized by several distinct stages. These stages of sleep can be readily identified by measuring brain wave activity on an *electroencephalogram*. One stage of sleep, *rapid eye movement sleep (REM)*, is paradoxical in that the brain wave activity is very similar to that of an alert brain. There is considerable evidence to suggest that detailed, storylike dreams occur during REM sleep.

6. The pattern of sleep activity changes greatly over the life span of the individual. Two general trends concerning sleep have been noted: (1) the total amount of sleep decreases with age and (2) the percentage of total sleep spent in REM decreases with age.

7. The hypothalamus appears to be central to the control of the brain's biological clock. Specifically, the *suprachiasmatic nucleus (SCN)* appears to be the primary locus of circadian rhythms.

8. Knife cuts made to the medulla and the midbrain (*encéphale isolé* and *cerveau isolé*) helped to focus attention on the role of the brain stem in arousal and sleep. More precise lesion studies identified the *brain stem reticular formation (BSRF)* as an arousal center. The BSRF receives information from the various sensory systems and projects fibers diffusely through much of the forebrain.

9. One theory of sleep proposed by Jouvet has focused on two brainstem centers: the *raphe system* and the *locus coeruleus*. Although this theory has received much support, recent data have shown that the model cannot account for all of the data on sleep.

10. The biochemistry of sleep and arousal is still poorly understood. Several chemicals including *serotonin, norepinephrine, acetylcholine,* and *factor S* have been implicated in sleep and wakefulness.

11. The most common sleep abnormalities are generally divided into two types. *Insomnia*, or sleeplessness, is the most common form of sleep abnormality. Paradoxically, one of the most common causes of insomnia is the misuse of sleep-inducing drugs. *Narcolepsy* refers to sleep disorders characterized by the inappropriate onset of sleep.

SUGGESTED READINGS

Dement, W. C. (1974). *Some must watch while some must sleep*. San Francisco: Freeman.

Moore-Ede, M. C., Sulzman, F. M., & Fuller, C. A. (1982). *The clocks that time us*. Cambridge, MA: Harvard University Press.

Pengelley, E. T., & Admundson, S. J. (1971). Annual biological clocks. *Scientific American, 224,* 72–79.

Pivik, R. T. (1986). Sleep: Physiology and psychophysiology. In, M. G. H. Coles, E. Donchin, & S. W. Porges, (Eds.). *Psychophysiology: Systems, processes, and applications.* New York: Guilford.

Turek, F. W. (1985). Circadian rhythms in mammals. *Annual Review of Psychology, 47,* 49–64.

KEY TERMS

Active sleep theory Theory that the onset of sleep is controlled by the action of an active neural center.

Alpha brain wave activity Slow-wave, high-amplitude, synchronous brain wave activity that occurs when the individual is quiet and resting.

Beta brain wave activity High-frequency, low-amplitude, dysynchronous brain wave activity that is associated with an active, alert brain.

Brain stem reticular formation (BSRF) Hind brain structure associated with CNS arousal.

Cataplexy A type of narcoleptic attack that causes the person to collapse due to the loss of muscle tonus in the skeletal muscles.

Cerveau isolé Sectioning the midbrain at the

level between the superior and inferior colliculi. This surgical preparation results in constant sleep; *see* Encéphale isolé.

Circadian rhythm A biological rhythm that is synchronized to approximately 24 hours.

Delta waves Synchronous, high-amplitude brain wave activity that is seen in stages 3 and 4 of the sleep cycle.

Drug-dependency insomnia The loss of sleep that is the direct result of withdrawal from sleep medication.

Electroencephalogram (EEG) Electrical recording of large populations of neurons in the brain.

Electromyogram (EMG) Surface recording of the activity of large populations of muscle fibers.

Electro-oculogram (EOG) Surface recording of the rectus muscles around the eye that provides an indication of eye movement.

Encéphale isolé Sectioning the spinal column below the medulla. This surgical preparation does not interrupt rhythmic wake and sleep cycles. *See* Cerveau isolé.

Factor S A small glucopeptide thought to induce sleep.

Infradian rhythm A biological rhythm that occurs less often than once each day.

Insomia Sleep disorder characterized by less than normal amounts of sleep.

K complex Very high amplitude spiking EEG patterns seen in stage 2 of the sleep cycle.

Locus coeruleus Dark colored pontine level group of cell bodies associated with sleep and arousal.

Narcolepsy The sudden and inappropriate onset of sleep.

Nucleus coeruleus A brain stem structure associated with REM sleep.

Paradoxical sleep Period in the sleep cycle during which the EEG pattern is desynchronized and appears similar to that of an alert brain; *see also* REM sleep.

Passive sleep theory Theory that the onset of sleep occurs when the mechanism for arousal runs down.

PGO waves Distinctive high-amplitude waves that precede the onset of REM sleep.

Push–pull cannula A device that permits the extraction of cerebrospinal fluid from freely moving animals.

Raphe system A cluster of brain stem nuclei thought to control slow-wave sleep.

Rapid eye movement (REM) sleep Period of sleep that is characterized by rapid movement of the eyes and desynchronous brain wave activity; *see also* Paradoxical sleep.

Rebound effect The increased percentage of REM sleep resulting from the earlier deprivation of that stage of sleep.

Sleep apnea When breathing stops during sleep, causing the person to awaken, gasping for air.

Suprachiasmatic nucleus (SCN) Hypothalamic nucleus that serves as the light-driven biological clock.

Ultradian rhythm A biological rhythm that occurs more often than once each day.

Zeitgeber Environmental stimulus that influences biological rhythms.

Chapter 12

Learning and Remembering

PART 1   BASIC CONCEPTS AND SIMPLE SYSTEMS

Plasticity of Behavior

What Are Learning and Memory?
Forms of Learning
Forms of Memory

Learning in Simple Systems

Habituation
Sensitization
Classical Conditioning

Intra- and Intercellular Mechanisms in Learning

Proteins, RNA, and Learning
The Synapse and Memory

PART 2   STRUCTURE OF LEARNING AND MEMORY

Brain Mechanisms Involved in Learning

In Search of the Engram
The Hippocampus, the Temporal Lobe, and Long-term Memory
Other Brain Structures Associated with Learning

The Evolution of Brain Complexity and Learning

Brain Size and Intelligence
The Role of the Cortex
Cell Complexity and Learning

Labile and Stable Memories

Consolidation Theory
ECS and Consolidation

Chapter Learning Objectives

After reading this chapter, you should

1. Understand the adaptive advantage of learning and memory for all species, including humans.

2. Be able to define and give examples of the following terms: *habituation, sensitization, classical conditioning,* and *instrumental learning.*

3. Be able to compare and contrast associative and nonassociative forms of learning.

4. Understand how learning psychologists differentiate memory in terms of the duration of the memory trace.

5. Know the intracellular and intercellular events that account for habituation, sensitization, and classical conditioning in simple invertebrate nervous systems.

6. Be able to review the evidence that implicates RNA and protein synthesis in learning and memory.

7. Know and be able to discuss the ways the synaptic organization of the brain may be changed by environmental experience.

8. Be familiar with the attempts to isolate the engram and be able to discuss why these efforts failed.

9. Be able to discuss the clinical and laboratory evidence that implicates the hippocampus and other temporal lobe structures in learning and memory.

10. Understand how evolutionary changes in the CNS relate to increased behavioral flexibility and intelligence.

11. Be able to discuss retroactive inhibition and retrograde amnesia as they relate to the consolidation theory of memory.

12. Know and be able to discuss how studies of memory that use electroconvulsive shock (ECS) support and fail to support the consolidation theory of memory.

PART 1   BASIC CONCEPTS AND SIMPLE SYSTEMS

Plasticity of Behavior

Behavior changes over time. As you will see later in this chapter, this rather straightforward statement is a central component of any satisfactory definition of learning. Typically, learning is thought of as some relatively long term *change* in the behavior of an organism resulting from *past experience.* I would like for you to think of behavioral change in another way. Think of behavioral change in a broader sense. Think of the changes that occur in behavior as species evolve.

The evolutionary pressures that drive changes in the morphology of species simultaneously induce changes in species behavior. That is, behavior and morphology evolve in parallel. In Chapter 1 we saw some examples of how selective breeding (e.g., the Tryon maze dull and maze bright rats) can produce dramatic changes in behavior over just a few generations. This too is an example of behavioral change, not within an individual organism but across generations of organisms.

The point here is that there are two related forms of behavioral plasticity: (1) behavioral changes resulting from the lifetime experiences of individual organisms and (2) behavioral changes that occur as the result of environmental pressures across generations of organisms. These two forms of behavioral plasticity are not totally independent of each other. As discussed in the following sections, both of these forms of behavioral change reflect environmental influences on the biology and chemistry of the organisms.

This raises an important question: If natural selection produces animals whose *physical* and *behavioral* characteristics are specifically adapted to their environments, what additional adaptive advantages do learning and memory provide? Natural selection occurs slowly and determines inherited potentials for behavior that are specific for the species. Learning allows individuals within the species to alter their behaviors (within limits) more rapidly in response to specific events in the environment. Think of the following example.

Many wasps make nests from mud that they collect at the edge of ponds or streams and fashion into larval chambers. Other wasps build nests comprised of hexagon-shaped chambers made from a paperlike material. These wasps make their paper nests by masticating wood fibers and mixing them with an oral secretion that makes the fibers pliable. Some species of wasps build very large nests that have many dozens of larval cells. Others, like *Polistes*, fashion a single-layered nest that usually has less than 15 larval cells (see Figure 12-1).

Figure 12-1
An adult queen and the nest of the wasp *Polistes.* (From Ross, 1965.)

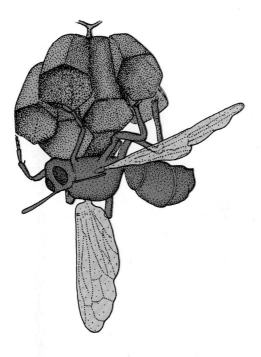

The nest size and the material used to make the nest are innately determined. Every individual of a given species builds essentially the same nest. However, each wasp must select a building site that is both protected and within a reasonable distance of the raw materials used for the nest construction. Each time the wasp leaves the nest site, she "remembers" and returns to the same source of building materials. Each time a wasp returns to the nest site after foraging for construction materials, she must "assess" the progress of the project in order to continue. If you were to intervene by blocking her route to the raw materials or by "undoing" some of the completed nest, she would adjust to these new conditions and modify her behavior appropriately.

Learning and memory provide the flexibility to adjust rapidly to the existing environmental conditions. This is a profound adaptive advantage, and it is evident even in some of the simplest organisms. However, the ability to learn, to remember, and to behave in nonstereotypic ways does vary widely from one species to another. Generally speaking, the organisms with larger and more complex CNSs evidence more learning ability. Before we can examine the biological and biochemical factors concerned with learning in humans and other species, we first need to come to grips with a working definition of learning and memory.

What Are Learning and Memory? The concept of learning is extremely complex. Depending on how one defines the term, *learning* may encompass biochemical events that occur at the subcellular level of organization as well as complex changes in the observable behavior of the entire organism. Because learning is such a complex concept, it is tempting to begin by identifying behaviors that are *not* considered to be learned.

Fundamental to any definition of learning is the presence of behavioral change or plasticity resulting from experience. There are, however, many examples of behaviors, some of which are very complex, that do not satisfy this condition. Consider the following examples. A moth that has just emerged from its cocoon is drawn to light. A newborn rat reflexively rights itself if placed on its back. A human infant, just minutes old, responds to touch on its cheek by turning its head in the direction of the stimulation and opening its mouth (the rooting reflex). The kangaroo, which is born naked, blind, and just a few inches long, makes its way from the vaginal opening across the mother's abdomen and into the marsupial pouch where it seeks out and attaches itself to one of the nipples.

All of these complex behaviors have something in common. They occur without the benefit of previous experience. They are stereotypic for the species, genetically programmed, and innately determined. These behaviors are the end product of millions of years of adaptive changes to environmental pressures. Although these are "intelligent" behaviors, in the sense that they serve a useful purpose for the organism, they are not learned.

If learning is a change in behavior that results from previous experience, what is memory? It is tempting to simply say memory is what has been learned. However, is memory the newly changed behavior itself, or is it something physical that "causes" the newly changed behavior? This is not a benign question.

Let us suppose for a moment that memory is in fact the newly changed behavior. If this is true, we can measure memory directly by measuring the behavior. Now suppose that I teach a hungry rat a complex new task—negotiating a multiple corridor maze for a food reinforcement. After many practice trials the rat eventually reaches the point where it can negotiate the maze from the start box to the goal box without error. This change in behavior certainly meets our definition of *learning* and the rat's ability to negotiate the maze, by definition, is a measure of its memory for the learned behavior.

Now let's follow this line of thought to its logical (or illogical) conclusion. Suppose that we feed the rat ad libitum until it is satiated and place it in the start box. You may not be surprised to find that the rat now makes many "mistakes" and enters blind alleys the way it did in its early training trials. Has it forgotten? Is the memory lost? No. The animal is simply not motivated to reach the goal box. At that moment its natural tendency to explore is having a greater influence on its behavior than is its need for food. The problem is quite clear. Measuring the behavior is a direct measure of *performance*, but it is an indirect measure of memory.

What, then, is *memory*? Memory is the aggregate biochemical and neural changes that result from experience. Memory is the subcellular, cellular, and intercellular reorganization that underlies the new behavior. It is our task in the remainder of this chapter to identify the physical changes that account for learning and memory. First, we need to examine the various categories of learning and memory that have been identified.

Forms of Learning   Psychologists have divided learned behavior into several categories. Not all forms of learned behavior are evident in all species. In fact, the various types of learned behaviors can be placed on a continuum ranging from the most basic to the most complex. Generally speaking, as you go from lesser to more complex organisms, the number of learning categories in the behavioral repertoire increases.

HABITUATION AND SENSITIZATION

The most basic forms of learned behaviors are **habituation** and **sensitization**. Actually, these very simple forms of learning are nothing more than changes in the strength of preexisting responses to a given stimulus. Habituation takes place when an organism stops responding or reduces the strength of its response to a stimulus that is experienced frequently. Sensitization is the opposite of habituation and occurs when the organism increases the strength of response to a relatively neutral stimulus. Both habituation and sensitization are important for survival and can be seen in a wide spectrum of organisms including those having the most primitive nervous systems.

It is difficult to demonstrate learning in very simple organisms because their range of behaviors is so limited. There is some data showing that even single-celled organisms evidence sensitization. For example, the amoeba moves by extending pseudopods. This movement can be inhibited by strong light. Lights occurring late in a series produce greater inhibition than lights of the same intensity that preceded them (Mast & Pusch, 1924). The changes in the protoplasm that account for this sensitization are not known.

The sea anemone belongs to the first phylum of animals to have an identifiable nervous system, a nerve net. Anemones have a limited behavioral repertoire; however, they do have a characteristic response to touch. If the anemone is poked, it contracts its body wall. If touched again, the strength of the contraction lessens. Habituation then, is evident even in a nerve net, the simplest form of nervous system.

The value of these behaviors is quite clear. Habituation conserves energy by eliminating unnecessarily strong responses to repeated

Figure 12-2
a. The research laboratory as used by Pavlov to study classical conditioning of salivation in the dog. *b.* The process of classical conditioning.

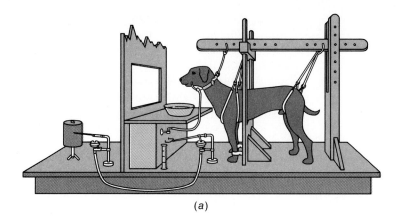

(a)

Before conditioning

 Neutral stimulus (bell)　No salivation

 Unconditioned stimulus (food)　Unconditioned response (salivation)

An unconditioned stimulus produces an unconditioned response

During conditioning

 Neutral stimulus (bell) Unconditioned stimulus (food)　Unconditioned response (salivation)

The unconditioned stimulus is presented along with a neutral stimulus.
The unconditioned stimulus continues to produce an unconditioned response.

After conditioning

 Conditioned stimulus (bell)　Conditioned response (salivation)

The neutral stimulus has become a conditioned stimulus.
It is now capable of producing a conditioned response–the same response
which was previously produced by the unconditioned stimulus.

(b)

stimulation by a neutral stimulus. In more complex animals the attenuation of response to familiar, nonthreatening stimuli permits more effective responses to novel stimuli. Sensitization may serve a useful purpose for avoidance of noxious and potentially harmful stimuli.

ASSOCIATIVE LEARNING

Habituation and sensitization are often referred to as **nonassociative learning** because the likelihood of occurrence and the magnitude of the behavior are determined solely by the strength and temporal characteristics of the stimulus. The anemone does not associate touch with any possible consequences, nor does the anemone recognize any conditions that lead to the stimulation. **Associative learning**, which is considerably more complex, requires a more complex nervous system. This type of learning occurs when a connection or association is made between two stimuli or between a particular stimulus and a response. Two types of associative learning have been studied extensively in the laboratory: **classical conditioning** and **instrumental learning**.

1. *Classical conditioning*. The famous Russian physiologist Ivan P. Pavlov studied classical conditioning in great detail. For this reason classical conditioning is often referred to as **Pavlovian conditioning**. As is often the case in science, Pavlov uncovered classical conditioning accidentally. While studying how various characteristics of food determined the output of the salivary gland in dogs, Pavlov noted that his subjects would increase the output of saliva *before* the experiment began (Figure 12-2a). Pavlov correctly hypothesized that the dogs had become familiar with the laboratory routine, and they salivated because they associated food with being in the laboratory environment.

Pavlov confirmed his hypothesis by demonstrating that dogs could be made to salivate to a neutral stimulus (i.e., a stimulus that does not normally cause salivation in dogs) when it was repeatedly paired with the presentation of food. Over several trials a bell (**conditioned stimulus [CS]**) was sounded just prior to the presentation of the food (**unconditioned stimulus, [US]**). Salivation, which is an **unconditioned response (UR)** to food, occurred after each pairing of the two stimuli. After many trials the dogs salivated (**conditioned response [CR]**) to the sound of the bell even in the absence of the food (Figure 12-2b).

An Observation: Classical Conditioning of a Single Cell?

Recently, E. N. Sokolov and his colleagues at the University of Moscow have completed some studies indicating that classical conditioning can be accomplished within a single neuron that has been isolated from the remainder of the CNS. The researchers isolated neurons from the CNS of the snail and maintained them in a solution that kept the cells viable for some period of time.

The isolated cells can be activated one of two ways: chemically with the neurotransmitter acetylcholine (ACh) or by electric pulses. The researchers paired subthreshold levels of the ACh with suprathreshold electric shocks. After several such trials the original subthreshold level of ACh (CS) was found to produce the action potential in the absence of the electric shock (US). The researchers maintain that the cell's response is learned because the response only occurs when the ACh precedes the shock within 120 msec. The response does not occur if the stimuli are presented in reverse order, noncontiguously, or separately. Therefore, habituation or sensitization cannot account for the results.

The researchers proposed that the CR of the cell results from an increase in the number of active ion channels on the cell membrane. The research raises questions concerning the nature of the memory trace. Is learning dependent on the interaction between neurons, as most theories maintain, or can learning occur at the level of a single cell (Sinz, Grenchenko, & Sokolov, 1982)?

---

2. *Instrumental learning*: If you think about it, you will note that the learner in the classical conditioning paradigm is not very active in the learning process. Bells go off, food is placed in the dog's mouth, and salivation occurs. Instrumental learning is a bit more complex in that the learner must participate in the process for learning to occur. In this type of associative learning a stimulus is matched to a response. The learner must *do something*—push a lever, press a button, go to a designated place, and so forth—in order to receive a reinforcement or to avoid a punishment. The stimulus/reward is contingent on the learner's action or manipulation of some object. For this reason this type of learning is sometimes referred to as *operant conditioning* (Figure 12-3).

3. *Discrimination learning*: A more complex form of associative learning requires the learner to choose or discriminate between the outcomes of a response to two or more stimuli—ergo, the name **discriminant learning**. The learner is rewarded for choosing one stimulus but is not rewarded for choosing another. Said another way, the animal must learn to select one stimulus but *inhibit* selecting the other. Figure 12-4 shows devices used to study discriminant learning in three laboratory species.

There are several variations of discriminant learning, including *reversal learning* and *delayed response learning*, which are more complex and demanding learning tasks. Reversal learning requires the subject to stop responding to a stimulus that was previously rewarded and start responding to a stimulus that was not rewarded previously. In delayed response learning the subject is shown which stimulus will be rewarded but is prevented from responding for some period of time. Reversal learning and delayed response learning require a complex CNS. When

Figure 12-3
A typical operant cham-
ber used to study in-
strumental learning.

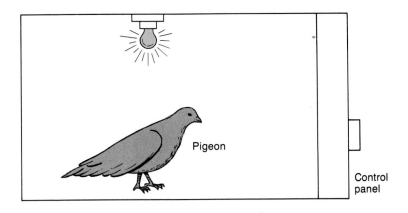

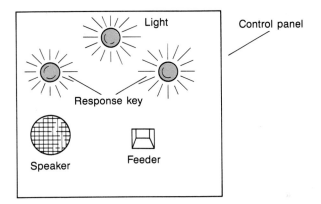

exposed to a series of problems of the same type, such as a reversal learning task, most animals evidence an improvement of performance with each new problem. This is referred to as *learning set* or "learning to learn." As we see later in this chapter, there is a wide variance in learning set ability across species. Generally, animals with larger and more complex brains develop learning sets more rapidly.

Forms of Memory   The terms *learning* and *memory* are so frequently paired that we tend to think of them as being synonymous. Indeed, it is difficult to think of learning without memory. Based primarily on what we know from the study of human learning, psychologists have identified three types of memory. This division is based on the duration of the memory trace, which is the physical representation of memory in the brain (McGaugh, 1968).

1. *Sensory memory*: The briefest memories are **sensory memories**. Suppose you were to look at a complex scene projected tachistoscopically (very briefly) onto a screen. For a second or two you would perceive

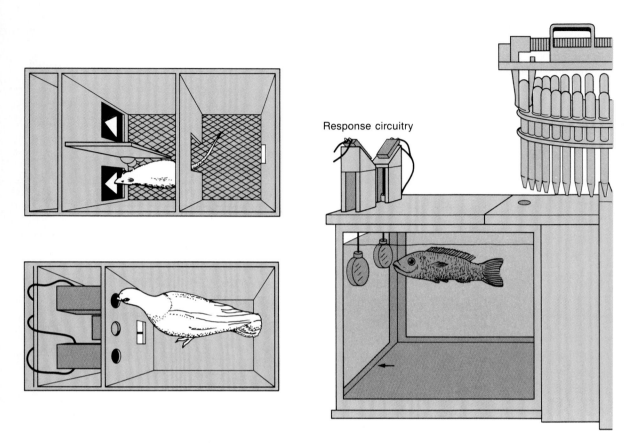

Response circuitry

Figure 12-4
Examples of discriminant learning in the rat, pigeon, and fish.

many elements of the image. However, after a few seconds, much of the picture would fade from memory and you would only be able to recall one or two details. The brief, but large, storage capacity of sensory memory is attributed to the **sensory buffer**. This sensory buffer can be thought of as the active neural processing taking place in the sensory circuitry of the brain.

Sensory memory can be divided further based on the specific sense modality involved. **Iconic** (Greek for "image") **memory** is sensory memory in the visual system. **Echoic** and **haptic memories** are, respectively, very brief auditory and tactile memories. Because vision and audition are very important senses in humans, iconic, and echoic memory have been studied extensively. Consequently, we know more about these two forms of sensory memory.

2. *Short-term memory*: Somewhat longer memories are referred to as **short-term memory**. Suppose that you need to find the telephone num-

ber of a restaurant. You find the number, close the directory, dial the number, and get a busy signal. It is likely that you will need to look up the number again. Note that you held onto the memory of the number long enough to complete the task at hand, but then lost it. For this reason, this type of memory is sometimes called **working memory**.

The duration of working memory can vary significantly. For example, you probably can remember where you sat in the library to study yesterday or this morning. However, it is not likely that you would remember where you sat 4 or 5 days ago. This is an example of what is sometimes called intermediate-term memory.

3. *Long-term memory*: Memories that last for weeks, months, and years are called **long-term memories**. Your memory of your own telephone number, the name of your psychology professor, or the name of the last president of the United States fall into this category. Many long-term memories fade with time; others seem to last for a lifetime. The term **permanent memory** is used for memories such as the memory of your mother's face, the names of family members, and other memories that appear to endure without fading.

Some learning psychologists believe that there may be a different neural mechanism involved for each type of memory. The multiple-trace hypothesis, for example, suggests that at least some of the neural circuits responsible for the short-term memory trace differ from the brain circuits necessary for establishing long-term memory. Figure 12-5 depicts a model of the multiple-trace hypothesis of memory storage. Indeed, there is a large body of clinical and experimental data suggesting that different brain structures underlie long- and short-term memory. Before we can examine this issue further, we need to review learning in simple neural systems.

Figure 12-5
Diagram of the multiple-trace hypothesis of memory storage. (Based on model described by McGaugh, 1968.)

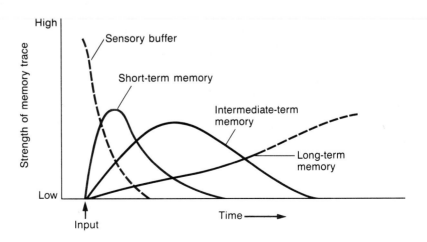

Learning in Simple Systems

The trend in evolution is to be conservative—to build on mechanisms and systems that have been proven to be successful adaptations. For this reason, it is instructive to study learning and memory in very simple organisms. We can assume that the subcellular, cellular, and intercellular mechanisms that underlie learning in the most simple nervous systems have been retained and that they serve as models for more complex learning in the most advanced nervous systems, including our own.

There are other reasons for studying simple organisms. The most obvious is that their simplicity makes them easier to understand. For this reason researchers have turned to invertebrates for the study of the more basic forms of learning. One invertebrate, the sea hare, *Aplysia californica*, has received a good deal of attention for several important reasons.

1. The number of nerve cells in the ganglia that make up its nervous system are few compared to vertebrate brains. The entire nervous system of *Aplysia* has upwards 18,000 neurons located in several ganglia. The abdominal ganglia, which has been the object of much attention, has approximately 1,000 neurons (see Figure 12-6).

2. The invertebrate ganglion is organized with the cell bodies of the neurons on the outside and the dendrites in the core. (The ganglia of vertebrates have the cell bodies in the core.) This configuration of the neurons in the invertebrate ganglion makes it easier to identify and easier to record from individual cells.

3. The individual cells in the invertebrate ganglion are very large. Some have distinctive shapes and can be seen without the aid of a microscope.

4. The cellular organization within the ganglion is consistent from individual to individual. Because of this, it is possible to generalize the function of a given cell between individuals. That is, once you have identified what a specific cell does in one individual, you know what the same cell does in all individuals.

Eric Kandel and his colleagues have made an extensive study of the neural mechanisms that control the gill-withdrawal reflex in *Aplysia* (Kandel, 1976, 1979). The gill-withdrawal reflex is controlled by neurons located in the abdominal ganglion. The delicate gill is usually extended on the animal's dorsal surface. A mantle provides some protection to the gill, and there is a siphon on the posterior end of the mantle that draws water across the gill. In rough water, or if the mantle or siphon is touched by a piece of debris, the gill is reflexively withdrawn. In the laboratory this reflexive response is induced by a carefully controlled jet of water.

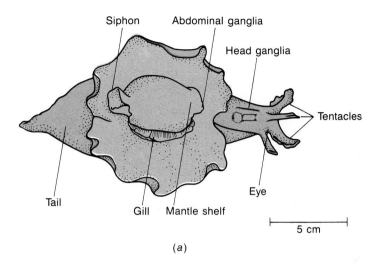

Siphon · Abdominal ganglia · Head ganglia · Tentacles · Eye · Mantle shelf · Gill · Tail

5 cm

(*a*)

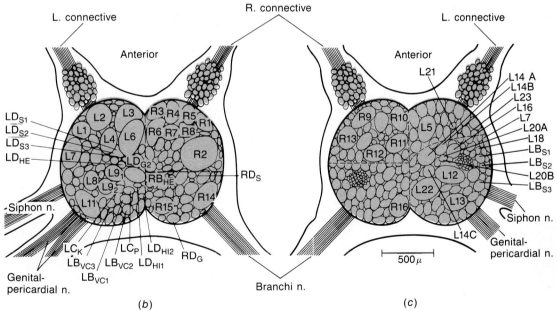

L. connective · R. connective · Anterior · L. connective

(*b*)

LD_{S1} · LD_{S2} · LD_{S3} · LD_{HE}

L2 · L3 · R3 · R4 · R5 · R1 · L1 · L4 · L6 · R6 · R7 · R8 · L7 · R2 · LD_{G2} · LD_{HE} · L9_1 · RB_{HE} · RD_S · L8 · L9_2 · L11 · R15 · R14

Siphon n.

LC_K · LB_{VC3} · LB_{VC2} · LC_P · LD_{HI2} · LD_{HI1} · RD_G · LB_{VC1}

Genital-pericardial n.

Branchi n.

(*c*)

Anterior · L21 · L14 A · L14B · L23 · L16 · L7 · L20A · L18 · LB_{S1} · LB_{S2} · L20B · LB_{S3}

R9 · R10 · L5 · R13 · R11 · R12 · L12 · L22 · L13 · R16 · L14C

Siphon n. · Genital-pericardial n.

500 μ

Figure 12-6
a. The dorsal view of *Aplysia*. *b*. and *c*. The abdominal ganglion from the dorsal and ventral perspectives. (Modified from Frazier et al., 1967.)

Learning Without a Brain

You may find it a bit hard to believe that many insects can live for a period of time after the head has been removed. In fact, the males of some species of mantids are able to mate after the female has eaten their head as part of their mating behavior. The complex copulatory movements of the male appear to be completely under the control of ganglia in the body and function quite independently of input from the head ganglia.

Learning researchers frequently attempt to study the neural basis of learning in very simple nervous systems. In the early 1960s Horridge demonstrated learning in the body ganglia of insects. Using the cockroach as his subject, Horridge cut the connections between the head of the insect and the rest of the body. The roach was suspended above a water bath with one wire from an electric stimulator connected to one of its legs. A second wire was placed in the water bath so that the insect's leg would complete the circuit when it touched the water. (See Spotlight Figure 12-1.)

Each experimental insect was yoked to a control insect, which received shocks of the same intensity each time the experimental animal received a shock. In a few minutes the experimental animals learned to fold their legs under the body to avoid the shock. The control animals that received shocks that were not correlated with the leg position showed no evidence of learning. Some years later researchers demonstrated that learning could take place even when the ganglion that innervates the leg is totally isolated from the rest of the roach's nervous system.

In a similar fashion, learning at the spinal level has been demonstrated in a variety of vertebrate species that have had the spinal cord severed from the brain. Together these studies demonstrate that simple forms of learning can occur in isolated neural circuits. It is likely that the physical mechanisms at the subcellular, cellular, and intercellular levels that account for learning in small groups of cells outside the brain are the framework upon which more complex types of learning are built.

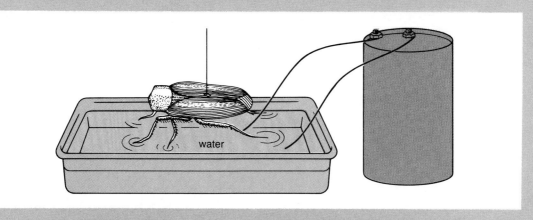

Spotlight Figure 12-1
The apparatus used by Horridge to demonstrate learning in decapitated insects. (Redrawn from Horridge, 1962.)

Habituation   The gill-withdrawal response habituates readily. After repeated stimulation the strength of the response lessens and may stop completely. The
gill withdrawal is controlled by 6 motor neurons and 24 sensory neurons.
A simplified diagram of the circuitry is shown in Figure 12-7. Sensory
cells in the siphon and mantle send excitatory signals to motor neurons in
the abdominal ganglion. This occurs either directly through a monosynaptic circuit or indirectly through interneurons. The motor neurons then
send excitatory signals to the muscles that retract the gill.

As you might predict, single-cell recordings show that the firing rate
of the motor neurons decreases during habituation. The reduced activity
of the motor neurons was found to be related to a change at the synapse
between the sensory and motor neurons. Specifically, the researchers
found that as stimulation continued, the size of the excitatory postsynaptic potentials (EPSPs) decreased. Further study showed that the depression of the EPSPs was due to a decrease in the amount of neurotransmitter released into the synapse.

There are two possible mechanisms that could account for the
decrease in neurotransmitter release. Repeated activation could close
Ca^{2+} channels, which would limit the flow of Ca^{2+} into the presynaptic

Figure 12-7
Diagram of the basic neu-
ral circuits involved with
the gill-withdrawal reflex
in *Aplysia*. A monosynaptic circuit from the mantle
or siphon excites motor
neurons L7, LDG1, *etc*.
Other excitatory signals
project to interneurons,
which in turn send excit-
atory signals to the motor
neuron. (Adapted from
Kupferman, Carew, &
Kandel, 1974.)

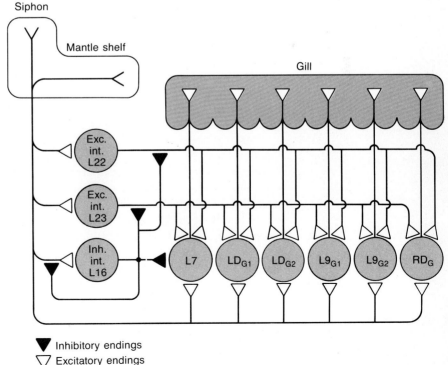

terminal (Klein & Kandel, 1980). Remember that the Ca^{2+} concentration in the axon terminal controls the release of neurotransmitter at the presynaptic membrane. It is also possible that repeated activation of the sensory neuron causes a depletion of the amount of neurotransmitter available in the presynaptic cell (Bailey & Chen, 1983). If stimulation is halted for a period of time, the EPSPs return to their original amplitude. These findings show that short-term habituation in *Aplysia* results when the level of excitation in an existing neural circuit is decreased.

It is interesting to note that habituation of the gill-withdrawal reflex is specific for the locus of stimulation. Habituation to repeated stimulation of the mantle has no effect on stimulation to the siphon. That is, the habituation was specific for those circuits between the sensory cells in the mantle and the motor cells in the abdominal ganglion. An animal that shows complete habituation due to repeated stimulation of the mantle shows a normal reflexive withdrawal when the siphon is stimulated, and vice versa. This finding lends further support to the idea that habituation is due to decreased excitation in specific, preexisting circuits.

Studies of several other species of invertebrates have shown similar results. There is also reason to believe that habituation of spinal reflexes in vertebrates operates on a similar principle. Therefore, across a wide spectrum of species where habituation has been studied, the underlying mechanism appears to be synaptic depression.

Sensitization   Very strong stimulation can produce sensitization of the gill-withdrawal response in *Aplysia*. If the animal is given a strong electric shock to just about any part of the body, it will subsequently show an increased response to touch of the mantle or siphon. The sensitized response may last just a few seconds or as long as a day, depending on the intensity and the number of repetitions of the noxious stimulus. Thus, the same response that can be habituated can also be sensitized.

As was true for habituation, the mechanism underlying sensitization is related to a change in the amount of neurotransmitter released by the sensory (presynaptic) neuron. The mechanism, which has been well documented, is a bit complicated. You need to read the following carefully.

The sensitization process begins by activating a "facilitating" interneuron (Kandel & Schwartz, 1982). This neuron has been clearly identified and can be located in each organism. The facilitating interneuron has presynaptic connections with the sensory neurons at their juncture with the excitatory interneurons and with the motor neurons (refer to Figure 12-8). The neurotransmitter released by the facilitating interneuron has been identified as seratonin (5HT). The release of seratonin onto the membrane of the sensory neuron induces the production of cyclic AMP within the sensory cell. This, in turn, causes an increase in the levels of a cyclic AMP-dependent enzyme. The enzyme blocks the potassium-specific channel in the membrane.

Figure 12-8
Diagram of the neural circuit involved in the sensitization of the gill-withdrawal reflex. Presynaptic serotoninergic connections on the sensory neuron cause an increase in the amount of excitatory neurotransmitter released at the connections between the sensory neuron and the excitatory interneuron and the motor neuron. (Redrawn from Kandel & Schwartz, 1982.)

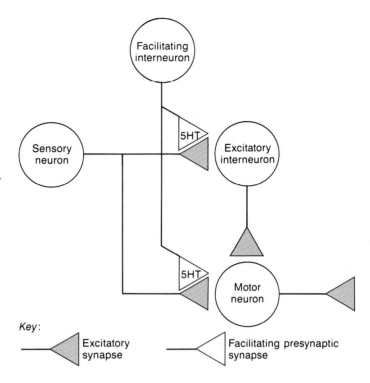

We are now at the point where activating the facilitating neuron closes potassium channels in the sensory neuron. You recall from Chapter 2 that following an action potential, it is the flow of potassium ion out of the cell that returns the cell to the resting potential. The result of closing some of the potassium channels is to retard the restoration of the resting potential and *prolong* the effect of the action potential. This has the effect of prolonging the release of neurotransmitter from the sensory cell, resulting in an increase of the gill-withdrawal reflex. Figure 12-9 depicts the presynaptic events that account for sensitization and habituation.

Long-term sensitization appears to be determined by the production of a yet unidentified protein in the sensory cell. Support for this hypothesis comes from the fact that chemicals that block or retard protein synthesis prevent long-term sensitization but have no effect on brief sensitization. As you will see later in this chapter, protein synthesis is an important factor in more complex learning as well.

As was true for habituation, sensitization results from changes in the strength of preexisting neural circuits. There is some evidence that classical conditioning may also work on the same principle.

Classical Conditioning

We noted earlier that simple organisms such as *Aplysia* have a limited repertoire of behaviors. For this reason researchers were hard pressed to find a way to demonstrate classical conditioning in this organism. After

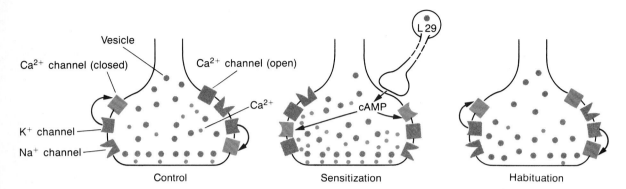

Figure 12-9
Hypothesized presynaptic events that account for habituation and sensitization of the gill-withdrawal reflex in *Aplysia*. The membrane of the axon terminal is covered with ion channels that are specific for K^+, Ca^{2+}, and Na^+. Dark symbols represent channels that are closed. In the sensitized condition the facilitating neuron causes an increase in cyclic AMP, which in turn closes K^+ channels and allows Ca^{2+} channels to remain open; this causes an increase in the release of excitatory neurotransmitter. In the habituation condition repeated stimulation causes Ca^{2+} to close, resulting in fewer vesicles binding to the presynaptic membrane. (Redrawn from Klein & Kandel, 1980.)

many years and many failed attempts, a classically conditioned response in *Aplysia* was successfully demonstrated by Kandel and his colleagues (Carew, Walters, & Kandel, 1981).

The gill-withdrawal reflex habituates to repeated light touch to the siphon. However, strong electric shock to the tail produces a vigorous gill-withdrawal reflex that does not habituate. Light touch was followed rapidly by shock to the tail. After several pairings of the shock (US) and the touch (CS), a vigorous reflex occurs to light touch in the absence of the shock.

Although the exact circuitry is not known, it is thought that the electric shock activates neurons, which facilitate the release of neurotransmitter by the sensory cell that responds to touch on the siphon. Touch to the mantle or other parts of the organism does not produce the classically conditioned response. The mechanism resembles sensitization, but it is more specific (Kandel & Schwartz, 1982).

A more complex conditioned response has been studied in a related organism, the nudebranch mollusk *Hermissenda crassicornis*. This colorful marine snail feeds on small organisms that gather in well-lighted water near the surface. Therefore, the snail naturally moves toward light. Because the animal's soft body is vulnerable, the snail also has a natural tendency to move away from light into deeper and more calm waters when the sea is rough.

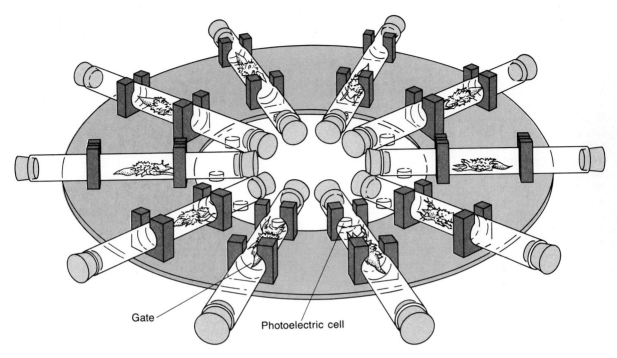

Gate

Photoelectric cell

Figure 12-10
Apparatus used to condition *Hermissenda*.

The animal's rate of movement toward light was timed in a laboratory apparatus (see Figure 12-10). Some of the animals were then submitted to turbulence (US) in the presence of light (CS). The pairing of the turbulence with the light caused the snails to approach light much more slowly (CR) than control animals that also experienced turbulence but not in the presence of light. The CR was noted to last for days and weeks (Alkon, 1984; Lederhendler, Gart, & Alkon, 1986).

The neural circuitry involved in this learned response is now well understood. *Hermissenda* has two kinds of photoreceptor cells in its eye. They have been named the "A" and "B" receptors. The two light-sensitive receptors have the opposite effect in response to light. The type B cell inhibits, and the type A cell promotes movement toward the source of light. The conditioned decrease in the approach to light is attributable to changes in the activity of the type B cells. During conditioning the concentration of Ca^{2+} in the B cell increases, and the outflow of K^+ from the cell is decreased. The net result is to increase the release of neurotransmitter from the B cell. As you can see in Figure 12-11, increasing the activity of the B cell inhibits the A cell, which decreases the motion toward the light.

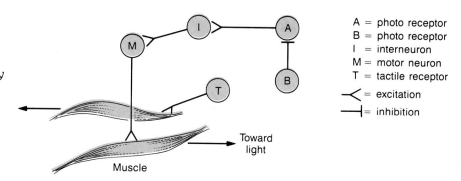

Figure 12-11

Neural connections in *Hermissenda* that control the response to light and turbulence. The A sensory cell promotes movement of a group of muscles, which moves the organism towards light. The B cell inhibits the A cell. Tactile information from sensory hairs detects turbulence and excites a second group of muscles that move the organism away from light. (Figure based on Alkon, 1984.)

Although the level of calcium within the B cells increases during training, it returns to pretraining levels rather rapidly. Nonetheless, the CR persists for days and weeks after the calcium concentrations have returned to their pretraining levels. How does this happen? The high levels of calcium during training activates enzymes, which attach phosphate molecules to molecules of protein. This process, known as **phosphorylation**, changes the character of the proteins in the cell membrane that act as ion channels (Goh, Lederhendler, & Alkon, 1985). The result of the phosphorylation is to close some of the potassium-specific channels in the cell membrane for long periods. The decreased flow of potassium out of the cell prolongs the effect of the B cell. In this manner the classically conditioned response persists over long periods of time.

We have seen that learning in very simple organisms depends on biochemical events within the cells and on the cell membranes that produce changes in the strength and duration of synaptic activity between cells. In *Aplysia*, habituation and sensitization are determined by events that either increase or decrease the release of neurotransmitter by the presynaptic cell. In *Hermissenda*, the learned decrease in speed to approach light is determined by changes in the physical properties of proteins in the cell membrane. The modification of the proteins produces long-term changes in the activity between the neurons in the light-sensitive circuits.

The completeness of our knowledge concerning the mechanisms that underlie learning in simple nervous systems such as the invertebrates far exceeds what we know about learning in our own brains. We know, however, that the process of evolution is conservative and tends to build on existing mechanisms that have stood the test of time. It is likely, therefore, that the biochemical and cellular mechanisms of learning and memory used by invertebrates have been preserved. It is also likely that they serve as the building blocks for additional brain mechanisms and systems for memory storage yet to be found in the mammalian brain.

Intra- and Intercellular Mechanisms in Learning

In this section we deal with those events within the cell that may influence the process of learning. Additionally, we examine the cellular mechanisms for the storage and recall of memory. Before we do this, however, it must be noted that complex learning and memory in humans are likely to involve the intracellular and intercellular activity of many thousands of cells in diverse areas of the brain. Trying to understand these enormously complex systems is an awesome task. We are just beginning to put the pieces of the puzzle together.

Understanding basic intracellular events is an important first step to the understanding of more complex mechanisms of learning and memory. It is important to understand, however, that the neural mechanisms underlying learning and memory that result in observable and measurable behaviors are dependent on large ensembles of interacting neurons. Trying to understand learning and memory on this large scale in terms of events that occur in one or a few neurons is a little like trying to make sense out of the image on a television screen by looking at one or two pixels. Clearly, the action of large cell assemblies is determined by the action of the individual cells that make up the assembly, but it is *not* reducible to the activity of units (John & Schwartz, 1978).

Proteins, RNA, and Learning Soon after the molecular structures of DNA and RNA were discovered, scientists began to speculate that these complex molecules could be the molecular foundation of memory. After all, if DNA could carry the "genetic memory" for such complex physical structures as the eye, the ear, and indeed the brain itself, it could also encode complex memories. Unfortunately, the DNA molecule is very stable and resistant to change. RNA, however, is continually being synthesized in the cell, and it acts as the template for the manufacture of proteins. Could learning and memory be attributable to changes in these complex molecules?

Research on the role of RNA and protein in learning and memory falls into three general areas. One group of studies has examined how radioactive precursors for the synthesis of RNA and proteins, such as radioactive amines, are incorporated into the brain during learning. Second, the influence of drugs that either facilitate or retard the synthesis of proteins has been studied. Finally, there are those studies that attempted to transfer training chemically from one organism to another (see Spotlight 12-2).

RNA AND PROTEIN SYNTHESIS DURING LEARNING

Protein is a major component of every part of the cell, including the cell membrane that forms the synapse between neurons. Many of the

Passing Memory from One Organism to Another?

In the mid-1950s James McConnell and Robert Thomspon started a series of studies that were to shake the conventional thinking of that time concerning the biological bases of learning and memory. As doctoral students at the University of Texas, they began to study learning and memory in planaria (flatworms). In their earliest research they successfully trained planaria to "wriggle" to the onset of a light by pairing the light (CS) with a mild electric current (US) using classical conditioning techniques (Thompson & McConnell, 1955).

The conventional wisdom of the time supported a model of learning which maintained that new behaviors were due to new connections in the brain (refer to the accompanying section on consolidation theory). Following this model, McConnell set out to demonstrate that the learned response in the planaria was due to the formation of new connections between the neurons in the cerebral ganglia (the worm's equivalent to the brain). Taking advantage of the remarkable regenerative powers of the flatworms, McConnel trained two groups of worms and then cut the worms in one group in half. Each half of the worm regenerates the missing half to form a whole worm.

McConnell logically hypothesized that worms which regenerated from the head end would retain the training in subsequent testing. Worms that regenerated from the tails would, of necessity, need to regenerate a new brain and therefore should not retain the new circuitry formed during the training. When tested for retention of the original training, all three groups—the intact worms, the worms that regenerated from the head end, and the worms that regenerated from the tail end—had equal retention of the original learning (McConnell, Jacobson, & Kimble,

1959)! See Spotlight Figure 12-2. This finding led to speculation that the physical substrate of the memory could be represented by something inside the cell as much as by the connections between cells.

To test this hypothesis McConnell came upon an unusual idea. He knew from his study of planaria that under certain conditions they are cannibalistic—they would eat other planaria. He trained a group of worms and ground them into a paste—"smart paste." A second group of control worms that were not trained were also ground into a paste—"dumb paste." Worms were then fed either smart paste or dumb paste and tested for the acquisition of the conditioned response. The worms fed on smart paste apparently "remembered" the training. At least they learned the conditioned response more rapidly than did the planaria that fed on untrained paste (McConnell, 1962).

Subsequently, researchers in other laboratories began to report similar findings in other species, including mammals. As an example, Babich, Jacobson, Bubash, and Jacobson (1965) trained rats to approach a clicking sound for food. The animals were killed, their brains were removed and crushed, and the RNA was extracted. The RNA was injected into the peritoneum of untrained rats. The recipient rats learned to approach the clicking sound more rapidly. Research findings such as these sparked a great deal of interest and controversy. Unfortunately, the results tended to be plagued with inconsistencies (Smith, 1975), and alternative explanations of the data were proposed (Hartry, Keith-Lee, & Morton, 1964; Jensen 1965). Because of these concerns, research funds for this area of research quickly dried up, and the whole research area has slipped into obscurity.

DRUGS, PROTEIN SYNTHESIS, AND LEARNING

If the synthesis of protein is a central factor in learning and memory, it follows that drugs which modulate protein synthesis should produce an effect on learning. Pursuing this line of thinking, it follows that drugs which inhibit protein synthesis should also inhibit learning. Generally, this seems to be borne out by the research data.

Early research in this area used the protein synthesis inhibitors puromycin, cycloheximide, and acetoxycycloheximide to study learning and memory. These antibiotic drugs were typically administered prior to training in dosage levels that inhibit protein synthesis by as much as 90%. All of the research using these drugs suffered from three problems that could influence the interpretation of the results. First, the dosage levels required to produce an observable effect where also toxic levels and therefore had an effect on most aspects of the animal's behavior. Second, in many studies the drugs were administered directly into the brain, producing a traumatizing effect from the drug administration. Finally, the results, although generally supportive of the protein synthesis hypothesis, tended to be small and inconsistent.

Many of the problems associated with the earlier inhibitors were overcome by another antibiotic, **anisomycin**. This drug is much safer and can be given subcutaneously; and because of its low toxicity, it can be administered repeatedly without danger to the subject (Flood, Bennett, Rosenzweig, & Orme, 1973). This last feature permits researchers to study how the inhibitor affects learning over longer periods. Figure 12-12 shows the results of a study in which mice were given one, two, or

Figure 12-12
Interaction of dose and strength of training in anisomycin-induced amnesia for a passive avoidance task. Injections were administered 2 hours apart. Inhibition of learning was greater when training was weaker and when protein synthesis was inhibited for a longer time. (Redrawn from Flood et al., 1973.)

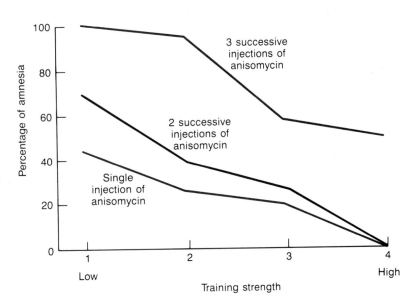

three injections of anisomycin. The first injection was administered 15 minutes prior to training. The second and third injections were given at 2-hour intervals following the first injection The data clearly demonstrate that both the duration of protein synthesis inhibition and the strength of training are important factors. All three levels of inhibition had some effect on animals that were weakly trained. However, it took three successive injections to affect animals that received stronger training. That is, the stronger the training, the longer the inhibition had to be maintained to cause the desired effect.

The Synapse and Memory Most learning theorists believe that the changes in the cell that influence learning and memory must ultimately effect changes in interneuronal communication. That is, the changes must ultimately affect communication across the synapse.

NEUROTRANSMITTERS ASSOCIATED WITH LEARNING

In 1973, Deutsch hypothesized that learning depends on an increase in the activity of cholinergic circuits in the brain. Deutsch predicted that cholinergic antagonists (blockers) should impair memory, whereas cholinergic agonists (facilitators) should enhance memory. The data appear to bear out his hypothisis. For example, scopolomine, a drug that blocks the acetylcholine synapse, weakens memory; and physostigmine, a cholinergic agonist, enhances memory on a variety of tasks in laboratory animals (Aigner & Mishkin, 1986; Deutsch, 1973; Murray & Fibiger, 1986). Additionally, drugs that damage acetylcholine neural circuits significantly impair learning and memory (Sandberg et al., 1984). (See Levin, 1988, for a review of ACh involvement in spatial learning tasks.)

There is evidence that acetylcholine circuits are important in learning in both humans and laboratory animals. Memory impairment that normally occurs with human aging has been correlated with a decrease in brain levels of acetylcholine (Davies, 1985). Scopolomine, which we noted earlier blocks cholinergic synapses, causes young adults to show marked deficiencies on a variety of learned tasks. In many ways their performance is similar to that of senile older persons (Beatty, Butters, & Janowsky, 1986).

You might predict that a cholinergic facilitator, such as physostigmine, would enhance learning and memory; and indeed it does. Physostigmine appears to be particularly effective with older individuals and others who have poor memories (Davis et al., 1978; Sitaram, Weingartner, & Gillin, 1978). Early hope that this drug could serve as a therapeutic intervention for poor learning was not borne out, because it produces severe, unwanted side effects.

Similar to acetylcholine, levels of norepinephrine and serotonin decrease in old age. Damage to adrenergic and serotoninergic circuits have been shown to produce learning deficits in monkeys that are similar to the learning deficits observed in older monkeys (Arnsten & Goldman-Rakic, 1985). Drugs that increase the activity of adrenergic circuits appear to improve learning in older mice (Zornetzer, 1985); however, this effect may be attributable in part to a general increase in metabolic activity.

Glutamic acid (glutamate) appears to be the primary excitatory transmitter substance in the hippocampus. (We will see later in this chapter that the hippocampus is an important structure in learning and memory.) Changes in the sensitivity of postsynaptic glutamate receptors have been associated with the phenomonon known as **long-term potentiation**, which appears to be associated with some forms of learning (Lynch & Baudry, 1984).

The term "long-term potentiation" refers to an increase in the activity of cells in the hippocampus following brief periods of electrical stimulation. The increased activity of the hippocampal cells may last for a few hours or, in some instances, as long as a month or more. Researchers now believe that the underlying mechanism that results in long-term potentiation is directly associated with the number of active glutamate receptors found on the postsynaptic membrane of hippocampal neurons (Thompson, Mamounas, Lynch, & Baudry, 1983).

Apparently, the stimulation of the neurons within the hippocampus opens calcium-specific ion channels that, in turn, causes the production of a specific protein enzyme that acts to expose additional glutamate receptors on the surface of the post-synaptic membrane. The effect of the additional receptors is to make the neurons more sensitive to the glutamate transmitter. Because normal hippocampal activity is thought to be associated with certain kinds of learning (e.g., spatial learning tasks), the potentiation resulting from the increased number of glutamate receptors is believed to be associated with these types of learning. Support for this notion comes from studies that show that lesions to the hippocampus and conditions that inhibit the formation of glutamate receptors in the hippocampus have similar negative effects on the acquisition of spatial learning tasks (Lynch & Brady, 1984).

MORPHOLOGICAL CHANGES OF THE SYNAPSES

The connections between neurons in the brain appear to be in a constant state of flux. The number and size of the synaptic connections on a given neuron change continuously (Cotman & Nieto-Sampedro, 1982). There is now very good evidence to support the notion that these synaptic changes can be influenced by the environment.

In the early 1960s, Rosenzweig, Krech, and Bennett (1961) demonstrated that simply manipulating the complexity of the environment could produce a number of changes in the brains of rats. They raised rats under three conditions: (1) alone, (2) in groups of three, and (3) in groups of 10 to 12. In the latter condition they provided the animals with a variety of stimulus objects that were exchanged daily. This last

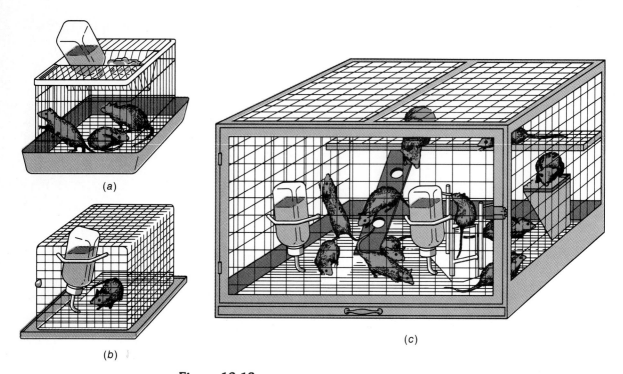

(a)

(b)

(c)

Figure 12-13
Laboratory environments that provide differential opportunities for learning.
a. The standard colony environment with 3 animals per cage. *b.* Impoverished
environment with the rat housed alone. *c.* The enriched environment with 10
to 12 rats per cage and a variety of stimulus objects. (Rosenzweig, Bennett, &
Diamond, 1972.)

condition they referred to as the enriched condition, because it provided
opportunities for informal learning that the other conditions did not.
Litter mates were assigned to one of the three conditions immediately
after weaning, and they were kept in their assigned condition for 80 days
(see Figure 12-13).

In the earliest of a long series of studies the researchers found that the
animals which were raised in the enriched condition (EC) developed a
greater amount of acetylcholine esterase (AChE) than did the animals
raised in the isolated condition (IC). Because AChE is the enzyme that
breaks down the neurotransmitter acetylcholine, this finding was interpreted to mean that the enriched environment increased the levels of the
neurotransmitter (Rosenzweig, Krech, & Bennett, 1961). Further study
also showed that the animals raised in the enriched environment developed
cerebral cortices that were thicker and heavier than those of the rats raised in
isolation (Diamond, Krech, & Rozensweig, 1964; Rozensweig et al., 1962).
These findings supported the notion that the morphology of the brain was
indeed being influenced by the complexity of environmental experience.

Figure 12-14
The technique used to quantify dendritic branching. Using an enlargement of a microphotograph of the neuron, branching is determined by counting the number of branches of different orders, as shown on the left, or by counting the number of branches within concentric rings, as shown on the right. (From Greenough, 1976.)

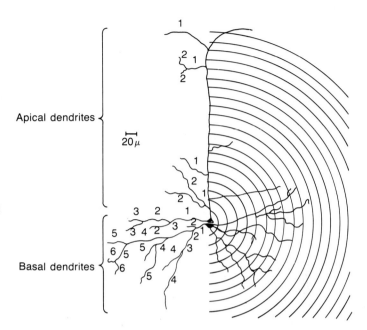

Apical dendrites

20 μ

Basal dendrites

Further research in this vein provided evidence that the number of spines per unit of length of the dentrite was significantly higher for the EC animals compared to the IC group (Globus, Rosenzweig, Bennett, & Diamond 1973). Additionally, the amount of dentritic branching was greater for the EC animals compared to that seen in the two other conditions (Greenough & Volkmar, 1973). (See Figure 12-14 for the method used to quantify the amount of dentritic branching.) Finally, the length of the thickened portion of the postsynaptic membrane was found to be greatest for animals raised in the enriched environment (Diamond et al., 1975; West & Greenough, 1972). Together these data show that an enriched environment (1) leads to development of an increased number of synaptic connections and (2) produces greater dentritic branching required to support additional synaptic connections; furthermore, (3) the size (and perhaps the strength) of synaptic connections can be modified by the complexity of life experiences.

Is it possible that the neuroanatomical changes in the brain found in these studies could be attributable simply to higher levels of activity? The additional social stimulation found in the EC groups could account for the changes in the brain. More recent studies (Bennett et al., 1979; Chang & Greenough, 1984) have dealt with this issue. These studies provide strong evidence that it is learning and not just increased activity that produces the brain changes reported in the earlier studies. The weight of the evidence supports the conclusion that learning can bring about identifiable and measurable changes in the organization of the brain.

PART 2   STRUCTURE OF LEARNING AND MEMORY

Brain Mechanisms Involved in Learning

As we have seen, there is good evidence that learning involves both inter- and intracellular changes in the brain. Several important questions remain. Where in the brain do these changes take place? Do all structures of the brain serve some function in learning and memory, or are some brain structures more important for this function than are others? Are specific brain structures involved with one kind of learning, but not another? Are there separate neural circuits for encoding memory and others for the retrieval of memory?

In Search of the Engram   If you had to look for the location within the brain where memory is stored, where would you look, and how would you know you had found it? This is the exact problem that faced Karl Lashley, who embarked on a long series of studies to find the **engram**, the physical substrate of memory (Lashley, 1929, 1950).

The research paradigm Lashley employed was straightforward enough. He trained animals on various tasks, selectively lesioned parts of their brains, allowed them to recover from the surgery, and then tested them for recall of the task. That is, he tested the animals for the amount of memory for the task that was saved. (For this reason the test performance is called a **savings score**.) Lashley compared the postlesion performance of the test animals to the performance of other animals that received sham surgery. These control animals underwent the same surgical procedure as the test animals, except that their brains were not lesioned. Thus, Lashley could control for the effect of the surgical experience.

Consistent with the thinking of his time, Lashley made the lesions to the cortex of the rat's brain. The prevailing theory in the 1920s held that memory was the result of new connections between cortical areas of the brain. Lashley reasoned that by removing areas of the cortex or making knife cuts through the cortex (see Figure 12-15), he would disrupt these connections and in so doing eliminate memory. The results of his carefully conducted research where far from what was predicted.

Lashley found that large lesions to the cortex could indeed produce a profound loss of performance on the previously learned tasks. Smaller lesions, as you might predict, caused smaller losses. However, the locus of the small lesions seemed to have no effect. A small lesion to one part of the cortex produced essentially the same decrement in performance as a similar sized lesion in any other part of the cortex (see Figure 12-16)! Further, Lashley found that none of the knife cuts, or any combination of knife cuts, made to the cortex produced any effect at all. These findings

Figure 12-15
Incisions in the rat brain that have no effect on the recall of a maze task. (Redrawn from Lashley, 1950.)

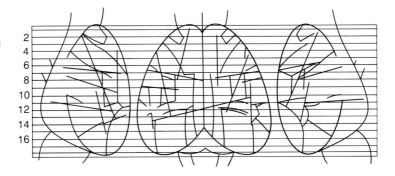

Figure 12-16
The relationship between maze difficulty and the percentage of brain cortex lesioned. Mazes 1, 2, and 3 are in increasing order of difficulty. The first two mazes show a "floor effect"; the tasks are so easy that even large lesions to the brain fail to produce a significant effect. The third maze shows a clear relationship between the size of the brain lesion and the number of errors. (Redrawn from Lashley, 1929.)

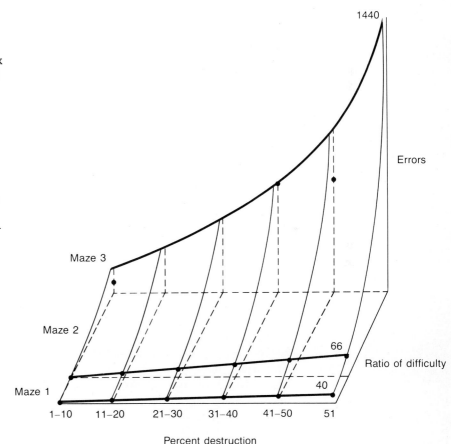

definitely challenged the prevailing *connectionist* view of the organization of the brain, which maintained that new behaviors were due to new connections between neurons, similar to the way a telephone switchboard connects telephones.

Based on this research Lashley proposed two basic principles of brain organization:

1. **Mass action**. The cortex functions as a unit. The more cortex available, the better the brain functions. Memory following lesions to the cortex is affected more by the size of the lesion than it is by the location of the damage.
2. **Equipotentiality**. Within the cortex one area is as good as another for storing memory. No part of the cortex is more specialized for learning and memory than any other part.

Subsequent research has failed to provide much support for Lashley's ideas of mass action and equipotentiality. Lashley himself realized that his research did not shed much information about the true nature of the engram. In 1950 he wrote:

> This series of experiments . . . has discovered nothing directly of the real nature of the engram. I sometimes feel, in reviewing the evidence on the localization of the memory trace, that the necessary conclusion is that *learning just is not possible*. [Emphasis mine.]

The cause of Lashley's frustration lies in some central, but erroneous, assumptions in his research. As "Monday morning quarterbacks," it is easy for us to look back and point out the errors in these assumptions; however, I suspect that at the time we could have done no better.

1. Lashley assumed that memory was restricted to the cortex. As we note later in this chapter, many subcortical structures are important and even critical for learning and memory to take place.
2. Lashley assumed that one kind of learning was pretty much the same as any other kind of learning. He thought that the data he collected on maze learning would generalize to other learning tasks. Maze learning is a very complex task that could include sensory processing from the visual, olfactory, and proprioceptive senses. As such it must involve many more areas of the brain than tasks that require just one sense. It does not seem reasonable that all parts of the brain would have equal input on very different tasks. For example, you would expect that a visual pattern recognition task is not likely to involve the same brain structures as those required to learn and recall the name of the thirtieth president of the United States. (Calvin Coolidge—just in case you did not recall.)
3. All of Lashley's work was done with the rodent brain, which, compared to the human brain, has a cortex that is relatively primitive and poorly differentiated. You recall from Chapters 1 and 3 that in the

evolution of the verebrate brain the cerebral hemispheres became increasingly more complex and more important in the control of overt behavior. If you were to replicate Lashley's research using humans (this is, of course, a very unethical suggestion), the results would probably be quite different.

4. Lashley assumed that a specific memory is localized in a place, like filing data in a single partition of computer disc. The component parts and the various characteristics of a given memory may be encoded in many different ways and distributed in many parts of the brain. Hundreds and thousands of neurons distributed in widely dispersed areas of the brain may be active to some degree for various aspects of a certain memory or task. A lesion that damages a small subset of those neurons may not, necessarily, erase the memory. Rather, it may only weaken some aspects of the memory that only partially affect performance.

5. Finally, there is the problem of *diaschesis*. A lesion made to one part of the brain is likely to cause functional disturbances in other brain areas that receive and/or send information to the lesioned structures. Because of this, it is not possible to state unequivocally that the effects observed from a given lesion are due soley to the part of the brain that was lesioned.

The Hippocampus, the Temporal Lobe, and Long-term Memory

We have noted that there is good reason to think that memory is dispersed in many areas of the brain. One brain structure, the hippocampus, seems to play a particularly central role in the active process that leads to the long-term storage of information. Some of the more persuasive evidence to support the importance of the hippocampus in memory comes from human clinical data (see Spotlight 12-3).

CLINICAL EVIDENCE

Lesions to the hippocampus resulting from infection (Starr & Phillips, 1970), alcohol-related vitamin B_1 deficiency (Rozin, 1976), and surgical intervention (Scoville & Milner, 1957) may produce profound impairments in long-term memory. Independent of the source of the trauma, the symptoms associated with hippocampal lesions are consistent. Memory for events that occurred prior to the lesion remain essentially normal. However, the person has difficulty putting new experiences into long-term memory.

Lesions to the hippocampus, which have a profound effect on the ability to store information such as names, dates, and events into long-term memory, do not eliminate some other forms of long-term memory. H. M., the patient described in Spotlight 12-3, and other patients who have had extensive damage to the hippocampus can learn finger mazes, their performance on mirror-reading tasks shows improvement with experience, and they can learn to solve complex problems such as the

SPOTLIGHT 12-3

The Case of H. M.

In the mid-1950s Brenda Milner and her colleagues reported the amazing case of a young man who, as a result of damage to his hippocampus, lost the ability to transfer short-term memory into long-term memory. The man, known in the literature by his initials H. M., had suffered for some years with grand mal epilepsy. Surgical intervention was attempted to remove the brain tissue in the medial basal regions of the temporal lobes that were the focal points initiating the epileptic seizures. This surgical procedure had been proven effective in the past. Unfortunately for H. M., a significant portion of the hippocampus was removed from each temporal lobe of the brain (see Spotlight Figure 12-3a). As a result of this surgery, H. M. lives entirely in the present.

H. M. can remember events only for the time they remain in short-term memory. If you were to introduce yourself to him, chat with him for a few minutes, leave the room, and return five minutes later, he would not recall your name, nor would he have any recall of ever having met you. H. M. would read the newspaper or magazines over and over again with the same interest level because he had no recall whatsoever for the previous reading. For many years after the surgery he continued to report his age and the date as being 27 and 1953, which was correct at the time of the surgical lesion to his brain.

The following excerpt comes from Dr. Milner's observations:

On one occasion, he was asked to remember the number 584 and was then allowed to sit quietly with no interruption for 15 minutes, at which point he was able to recall the number correctly without hesitation. When asked how he had been able to do this, he replied,
"It's easy. You just remember 8. You see 5, 8, and 4 add to 17. You remember 8, subtract it from 17 and it leaves 9. Divide 9 in half and you get 5 and 4, and there you are: 584. Easy."
In spite of H. M.'s elaborate mnemonic scheme, he was unable, a minute or so later, to remember either the number 584 or any of the associated complex train of thought; in fact, he did not know that he had been given a number to remember. (Milner, 1972)

It is important to note that although H. M. has some loss of memory for events that preceded the surgery, his very long term memory is, for the most part, quite normal. His recall of dates, names, and events that occurred in his youth is similar to your own. His IQ, as measured by standardized tests, is also normal. The damage to the hippocampus appears to have impaired his ability to place new information into storage. It is also important to note that although H. M. is unable to put certain kinds of information into long-term memory, like names, dates, and specific events, he is able to profit from

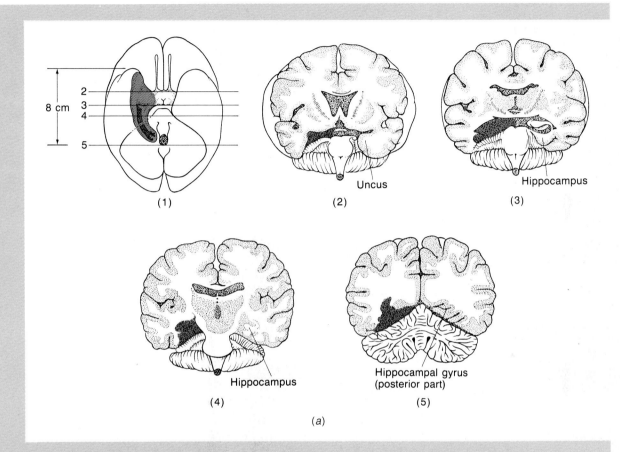

(a)

Spotlight Figure 12-3
a. Brain tissue removed in the operation on the patient H. M. The operation
was performed bilaterally, but the diagram shows only unilateral removal so
that the form of the lesioned structures can be seen. (1) The base of the brain,
showing the extent of the operation, and the levels of the sections shown in
2–5. (From Scoville & Milner, 1957) *b.* (2) Performance of H. M. over three
consecutive days on a mirror tracing task. The data clearly show learning from
trial 1 to trial 10 within each daily session (short-term memory) and retention
from day to day (long-term memory). (Data redrawn from Milner, 1965.)

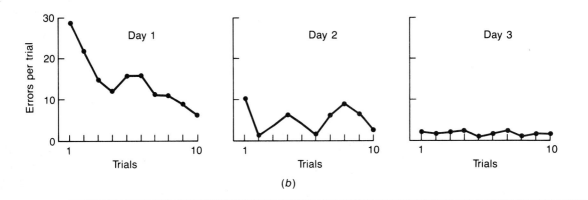

(b)

Spotlight Figure 12-3 (*Continued*)

some experiences. For example, when tested over 3 days on a mirror-tracing task (see Spotlight Figure 12-3b) his performance showed considerable improvement. Yet each day he denied having ever seen the apparatus before, nor did he remember the nature of the task (Milner, 1965).

H. M. is quite aware of his condition. As you can imagine, this causes him considerable concern. He lives in a constant state of "now" with no recall of what he has experienced just a few minutes earlier.

He described this strange state as follows (Milner, 1970, p. 37):

Every day is alone in itself, whatever enjoyment I've had, and whatever sorrow I've had.... Right now, I'm wondering, have I done or said anything amiss? You see, at this moment everything looks clear to me, but what happened just before? That's what worries me. It's like waking from a dream. I just don't remember.

Tower of Hanoi puzzle (see Figure 12-17). (Mirror reading requires the subject to read words printed backwards like this: *enalpria, euqitsym, lufreehc.*)

The fact that lesions to the hippocampus in humans produce an effect on some kinds of long-term memories, but not others, has caused some researchers to speculate that there may be separate processess that underlie each kind of memory. That is, the storage and retrieval of the different types of information could depend on independent structures and processes. Cohen and Squire (1981) believe that **procedural knowledge**, or how to do something, is quite different from **declarative knowledge**, which can be thought of as an accessible record of previous

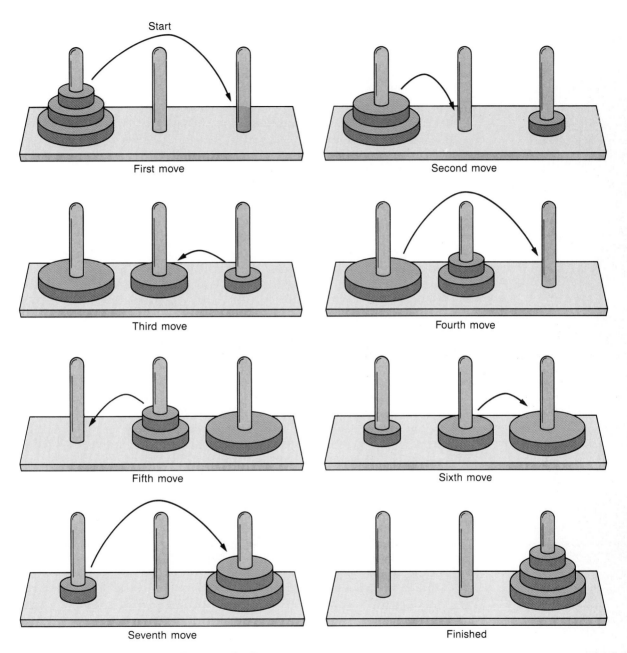

Figure 12-17
The Tower of Hanoi puzzle. The task is to move all of the discs, one at a time, to another peg without ever placing a larger disc over a smaller one. The figure shows the optimal solution to the puzzle. Hippocampal lesioned individuals like H. M. can learn to solve this puzzle and improve with each trial. In H. M.'s case, he denies having seen the puzzle or knowing the nature of the task, even though his performance shows memory of the solution.

experiences. It is the difference between knowing *how* to do something and knowing *that* something has happened. It is thought that procedural knowledge evolved before declarative knowledge. This view is based on the belief that declarative knowledge is dependent on higher brain structures in the temporal lobe. Procedural knowledge, which includes more simple forms of learning such as habituation, sensitization, psychomotor learning, and classical conditioning, is, at least in part, dependent on lower brain centers.

LABORATORY EVIDENCE

The clinical reports implicating the hippocampus in long-term memory spurred a flurry of laboratory investigations using a variety of nonhuman species. Generally, the laboratory data show that complete bilateral lesions to the hippocampus do produce some deficits in a variety of learning tasks. The severity of the deficit varies widely, depending on the nature of the learning task and the species under study (e.g., Bingman et al., 1987; Chrobak, Aanin, & Walsh, 1987; Jarrard et al., 1984; Kimble, 1968; Olton & Papas, 1979; Staubli, Fraser, Kessler, & Lynch, 1986; Whishaw, 1987). However, the laboratory data obtained from several species using a variety of learning tasks suggest that even total lesions to the hippocampus and to other temporal lobe structures do not produce the profound loss of memory seen in human clinical cases. In one extensive series of studies of learning in primates (Mishkin, 1978; Salmon, Zola-Morgan, Squire, 1987; Zola-Morgan, Squire, & Mishkin, 1981) showed rather clearly that neither the hippocampus nor other temporal lobe structures such as the amygdala are essential for the formation of memory for a complex visual and recognition task. However, bilateral lesions to both the amygdala and the hippocampus produce severe deficits in learning.

There is considerable data suggesting that lesions to the hippocampus produce deficits which are most sensitive to tasks in which information must be held for a short period of time, that is, working-memory tasks (Baddeley, 1986, 1988; Barnes, 1988; Olton, 1983; & Kesner, 1985). Patricia Goldman-Rakic and Harriet Friedman (1988) have recently shown that selected hippocampal structures are quite active in working-memory tasks but not in other forms of learning. In their research rhesus monkeys were injected with 2-deoxyglucose before receiving training on a variety of learning tasks. (The 2-deoxyglucose is taken up by the brain and may be traced.) In this way it is possible to get a rough measure of local brain metabolism rates during a given task. Their results show that the hippocampus is most active in delayed response tasks which require the monkeys to hold information in working memory.

Why should there be such enormous differences between the role of the hippocampus in human memory compared to that in other species? Is this due to some artifact in the few clinical cases on record? I think not.

You must keep in mind that it is not possible to generalize results between species without some risk. There are species-specific aspects to learning, just as there are species-specific differences in sensory systems (D'Amato, 1974).

It should not be surprising that the function of the hippocampus and other temporal lobe structures differ across species. Recall from Chapters 1 and 3 that as the brain evolved, new structures developed and the function of older structures changed. The function of a given brain structure in one species is not necessarily equivalent to the function of the same structure in other species. This is a particularly reasonable idea when we are dealing with forebrain structures and complex behaviors.

CLASSICAL CONDITIONING IN THE HIPPOCAMPUS

Several recent studies have shown that the activity of single cells in the hippocampus reflect learning. In one study the researchers used classical conditioning techniques to cause reflexive movement of the nictitating membrane in rabbits to an auditory signal. (The nictitating membrane covers the eye briefly to clean and protect the eye from foreign particles). A tone (CS) preceded a puff of air (US) directed at the rabbit's eye. After several pairings of the tone with the puff, the nictitating membrane responded to the tone alone (CR).

The researchers recorded the activity of the nictitating membrane and firing rate of single cells in the hippocampus during the classical conditioning trials. Single-unit recordings from within the hippocampus showed that cells become conditioned to the tone (Berger & Thompson, 1978). Before the conditioning, the hippocampal neurons were unresponsive to the CS. After a few trials they began to fire before the response (see Figure 12-18).

To verify the relationship between the hippocampal activity and the CR of the nictitating membrane, the researchers lesioned the hippocampus bilaterally. With the hippocampus lesioned, conditioning the nictitating response was not possible (Weisz, Solomin, & Thompson, 1980). Also, as shown in Figure 12-19, the researchers found that pseudoconditioning controls (where the tone and puff are presented at the same frequency but not correlated with each other) evidence no change in hippocampal activity.

The exact mechanism that underlies the conditioning of cells in the hippocampus is not known. Recent research has shown that the conditioned eyeblink remains after acute decerebration (Mauk & Thompson, 1987). It appears that although the hippocampus is necessary for establishing the CR, the learned response is maintained by centers in the brain stem and cerebellum (McCormick & Thompson, 1984). However, the plasticity of cells in the hippocampus provides clear evidence for a physiological basis of conditioning.

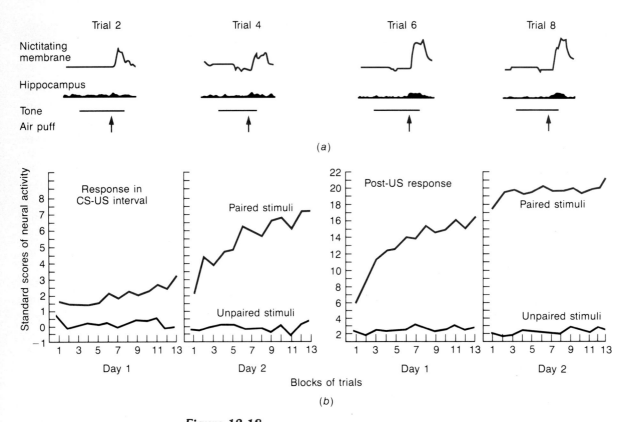

Figure 12-18
Conditioning in the hippocampus. a. Responses in the hippocampus and the nictitating membrane during early conditioning trials. The nictitating membrane response comes after the air puff, and the hippocampal single-unit response gradually increases. b. Further enhancement of the hippocampal response during 2 days of training. The lower curve, labelled "unpaired stimuli," is a pseudoconditioning control. (Redrawn from Berger & Thompson, 1978.)

Other Brain Structures Associated with Learning

A number of brain centers in addition to the hippocampus and temporal lobe structures appear to function in learning and memory. Each of these brain structures appears to have somewhat unique characteristics that vary with the nature of the learning task and the species under consideration.

MIDBRAIN STRUCTURES

Midbrain structures, including the thalamus and the mammalary bodies, have been associated with learning and memory. Long-term alcoholics suffering from **Korsakoff's syndrome** experience memory problems that are less severe, but similar to, those found in hippocampal patients. Prolonged alcoholism affects many areas of the brain; however,

Figure 12-19
The activity of the nictitating membrane and hippocampal firing rates before and after conditioning. The width of each bar in the histograms is 15 msec. The tone (CS) duration is 350 msec. The vertical arrows indicate the time of the air puff. *a.* The nictitating membrane and hippocampal responses begin after the air puff in the early conditioning trials. *b.* Nictitating and hippocampal responses begin prior to the air puff after conditioning. *c–f.* Pseudoconditioning controls show no evidence of hippocampal activity, although there is a vigorous response of the nictitating membrane to the air puff. (Redrawn from Berger & Thompson, 1978.)

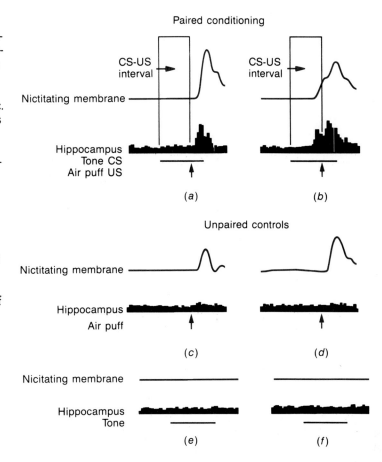

the mammalary bodies and the medial dorsal nucleus of the thalamus appear to be the structures that are most affected (Mair, Warrington, & Weiskrantz, 1979; Victor, Adams, & Collins, 1971). Unlike people with hippocampal amnesia, Korsakoff patients frequently deny their memory problems and confabulate (make up) memories to cover for their deficiency.

An independent source of evidence from the well-documented case of the patient N. A. provides further confirmation that a focal lesion to the medial dorsal nucleus of the thalamus can impair memory formation. N. A. received a focal lesion to the medial dorsal nucleus from a fencing accident. The fencing foil entered his nostril and penetrated the brain, producing the lesion shown in Figure 12-20. N. A. has normal memory for events that preceded the accident, but he is markedly amnesic for events that followed the brain damage. His amnesia is particularly noticeable for verbal material (Squire & Moore, 1979; Teuber, Milner, & Vaughan, 1968). Although the lesion to N. A.'s brain was thought to be

Figure 12-20
Magnetic resonance imaging showing the lesion in the patient N. A. The images are consecutive 3 mm thick coronal slices through the diencephalic region of the brain. The open arrows (A., B., and C.) show an opening at the floor of the third ventrical. The solid white arrow (A through F) shows a large lesion that extends from the third ventricle into the thalamus. An enlargement of the lateral ventrical (V) may also be seen on the right side (A). (From Squire, Amaral, Zola-Morgan, Kritchevsky, & Press, 1989.)

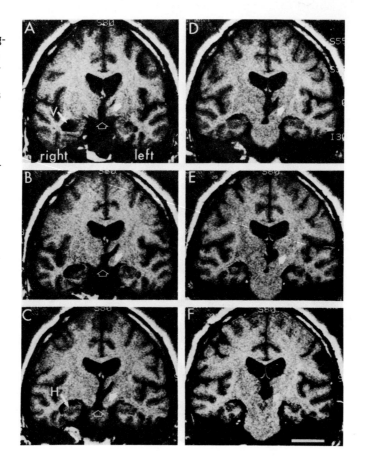

focused in the medial dorsal thalamus, based on CAT scan data, recent examination of the lesion using newer and more accurate magnetic resonance imaging techniques indicates that the affected area is somewhat larger and includes the regions shown in Figure 12-20.

PREFRONTAL CORTEX

The extreme anterior tips of the frontal lobes are referred to as the prefrontal cortex. When the prefrontal cortex is lesioned in primates, predictable deficits in learning occur. Most affected are tasks that require a delayed response (e.g., Bachevalier & Mishkin, 1986; Brush, Mishkin, & Rosvold, 1961). Typically, in delayed response tasks the animal sees the cue to an appropriate response but must delay responding for some period of time. The fact that prefrontal lesions disrupt this type of learning suggests that this region of the brain may be important for short-term, or working, memory. The data may also be explained in terms of a disruption of attentional processes.

Primates with prefrontal lesions also show a tendency to perseverate with responses that had been previously rewarded. For this reason they tend not to perform well on tasks such as reversal learning tasks that alternate the rewarded stimulus (Mishkin, 1964). This could be due to a disruption of inhibitory connections that are necessary to allow the animal to stop responding to stimuli that were previously rewarded.

Prefrontal lesions in humans produce less specific deficits than those observed in other primates. Generally, performance decrements are small, and these individuals do not score differently from normal subjects on standardized intelligence tests. Patients who have had prefrontal lobectomies do tend to evidence perseveration on some tasks (Milner, 1965; Shallice, 1982), and they do evidence difficulties with forgetting intentions (Hécaen & Albert, 1978). Deficits have been reported for a variety of visuospatial tasks, but they may be attributable to occulomotor abnormalities rather than problems with learning and memory (Luria, Karpov, & Yarbuss, 1966; Stuss & Benson, 1984).

The Evolution of Brain Complexity and Learning

The powerful and flexible brain mechanisms for learning found in humans and other complex organisms have been built on simple and specific adaptations in preceding species. Over the course of time very specific circuits in the more simple animals came to be used in more general and more plastic ways in larger and more complex brains.

We noted in Chapters 1 and 3 that there are several consistent patterns of change in the evolution of the brain. Generally, the brain increases in size relative to the weight of the body; this is called the brain–body ratio. There is a tendency for the newer forebrain structures to increase in size relative to older hindbrain structures; this is termed the encephalization process. Finally, the complexity of the circuitry associated with a given cell increases, further increasing the possible number of interactions between neurons. Each of these evolutionary changes has the potential to affect learning and memory.

Brain Size and Intelligence

We noted earlier that there is a clear relationship between the size and complexity of the CNS and the range and flexibility of potential behaviors of specific species. Simple nervous systems are only capable of supporting very few, rigid, stereotypic behaviors; therefore, they are less plastic in response to environmental influences. The progression in the complexity of the behavioral repertoire between the paramecium, planarian, fish, canine, primate, and humans is patently clear.

Riddel and Corl (1977) developed a brain index called **Nc** that is based on the ratio of brain to body weight. When this index is applied to the ability of various species to form learning sets, there is a rather clear

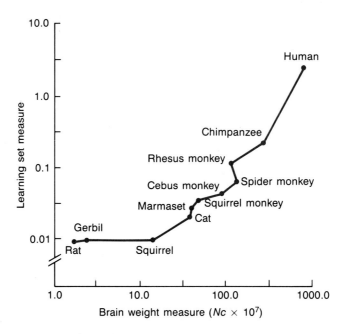

Figure 12-21
Correlation between the rate of acquisition of learning sets and brain size for 11 mammalian species. The brain measure is Nc, which is related to the encephalization index. (From Riddell & Corl, 1977.)

positive relationship between Nc and the rate of acquisition of learning sets. Figure 12-21 shows this data. The rank-order correlation between the behavioral measure and the brain index was 0.98, which is an extremely high value. They interpreted these data to mean that the rate of formation of learning sets is closely related to the relative brain size of the species tested.

In a similar study Riddell (1979) tested five species of mammals on a task that required the subjects to inhibit responding to a recently rewarded stimulus and to return to a previously rewarded stimulus (reversal learning). The scores were quantified using an index K, which is the Nc index multiplied by a constant. The rank-order correlation was 0.94. These data supported the conclusion of the earlier study that related brain size to intelligence (see Figure 12-22).

Additional support for the correlation between brain size and intelligence comes from studies that have compared the behavior of animals of the same species but having various brain sizes. Large- and small-brained animals from heterogeneous strains of mice were tested on four learning tasks. The results indicate that large-brained animals of the same species do perform better on some tasks (Jensen, 1979). Additionally, animals born from small litters have larger brains and perform better on a variety of tasks than animals born in normal-sized litters of six or more pups (Marthens et al., 1974).

The Role of the Cortex

Clearly, the neocortex is not essential for learning and memory in all species. We noted earlier that species without a brain structure that is the equivalent to the cortex are capable of learning. Additionally, some forms

Figure 12-22
Plot of performance of five species on a reversal task using Riddell's index K, which is a measure of the flexibility of behavior. The lower the K index, the greater the behavioral flexibility. (From Riddell, 1979.)

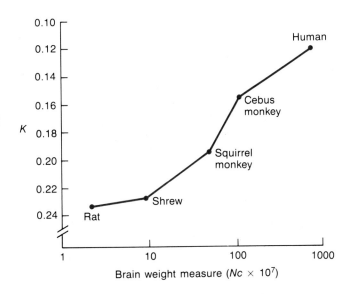

of learning such as habituation and sensitization can occur in subcortical structures. However, in the more complex vertebrate brains the cerebral cortex appears to account for an increasing amount of observable behavior including those behaviors that depend on learning and memory. This is, of course, one of the major points of the encephalization theory concerning the evolution of the CNS.

The problem-solving ability of several strains of rats has been shown to be positively correlated with the weight of the cerebral cortex (Rosenzweig, Bennet, & Diamond, 1967). Research that has examined the effects of environmental complexity on the development of the brain has demonstrated convincingly that:

1. Enriched environments increase the weight of the cerebral cortices but does not influence the weight of subcortical structures (Rozenzweig et al., 1962).
2. Enriched environments increase the thickness of the cortex (Diamond, 1976).
3. Enriched environments increase the size of neuron cell bodies in the cortex, but not in other brain regions (Diamond et al., 1975).

Clearly, the cerebral cortex is plastic and does reflect environmental experience. The more complex cortices of some species provides the necessary brain circuitry for more complex learning.

Cell Complexity and Learning   We have already noted that complex learning requires changes in synaptic transmission between neurons. There is excellent evidence that complex learning increases the number and complexity of the interactions between neurons. In a recent study, Spinelli, Jensen, and DiPrisco (1980)

Figure 12-23
Dendrites of neurons from trained somatosensory cortex (*a*) and untrained somatosensory cortex (*b*) using reduced silver Golgi stain. (From Spinelli, Jensen, & DiPrisco, 1980.)

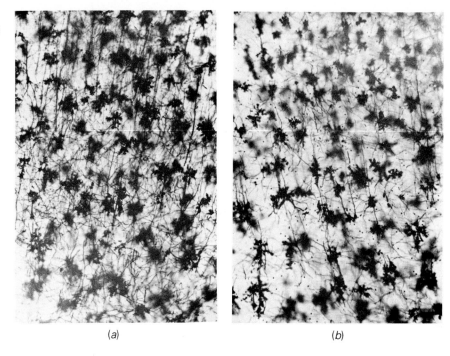

(a)   (b)

trained young kittens to avoid mild shock by flexing a leg. Following the training, the somatosensory cortex was stained with the Golgi technique. You will recall that this stain makes the entire membrane of the cell visible. The neurons of the trained animals evidenced a significant increase in the number and complexity of dendritic branching. The effect was truly remarkable, as you can see in Figure 12-23.

The complexity of the neuron has increased over evolutionary time. It follows that the more complex neurons have greater opportunities for synaptic interaction with other neurons. Thus, the power of the brain is determined by both the number and the complexity neurons.

An example may be helpful at this point. The Purkinje cells in the cortex of the cerebellum are the output cells that transmit information from the cerebellar cortex to deep nuclei in the cerebellum. From there the information is transmitted to other centers in the brain. You will recall from Chapters 3 and 9 that the cerebellum is responsible for much of the unconscious motor coordination associated with precise muscle action. In the process of learning a new motor skill, such as swinging a golf club or balancing a dowel on the tip of your finger, arrays of new neural circuits in the cerebellum are formed that coordinate, at the unconscious level, the action of the different motor groups involved in the task.

The size of the cerebellum, the surface area of the cerebellar cortex,

Figure 12-24
Purkinje cells in several representative species. They are ordered, left to right and top to bottom, in terms of the complexity of the motor behavior of the species. (Adapted from Nieuwenhuys, 1969.)

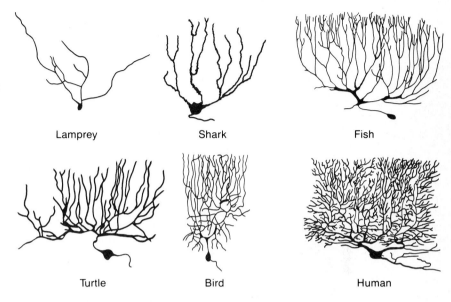

Lamprey   Shark   Fish

Turtle   Bird   Human

and the complexity of the neurons within the cerebellum correlate closely with the flexibility and complexity of the motor repertoire of the species. Figure 12-24 depicts the Purkinje cells of several representative species. They are arranged, left to right and top to bottom, in order of increasing complexity of the motor behavior of the species. The elaboration of dentritic processes in the more complex vertebrate brains reflects the increased processing capability of the cells.

Labile and Stable Memories

We have now established that memory for complex tasks is dependent on intra- and intercellular changes that affect the activity of large groups of cells. We have also seen that memories can be classified in terms of their duration, with some memories lasting fractions of a second and others appearing to be permanent.

Learning theorists have wondered about the process that turns short-term memories into those that can last a lifetime. The fact that only some memories become long-term or permanent ones was interpreted to mean that for some period of time all memories are in a labile state. Only some memories, for whatever reason or method, become permanent. Many learning theorists assumed that during the time period when memories are labile, they are sustained by a transient neuronal process or activity. Long-term memories, however, were thought to be the result of some structural change in the neurons that required a long period of time to complete.

Consolidation Theory   The ancient Greeks knew that head injury caused the loss of memory for events that preceded the trauma. With head injury, not all memory is lost—rather, just memories for some period of hours, days, weeks, or even years prior to the incident. Typically, trauma-induced amnesia lessens with time, and recall of some events does return. However, events that immediately precede the trauma may be totally lost. It appears that older memories are more resistant to the trauma than newer memories. Because the trauma has greater effects on memories that precede it, this type of memory loss is called **retrograde amnesia**.

The labile nature of memory was also observed in studies of verbal learning conducted in Germany at the end of the nineteenth century. Researchers noted that learning new material, like nonsense syllables, interfered with the recall of previously learned material. That is, if subjects memorize a list of words and then study a second list, their recall for the first list is adversely affected compared to subjects that were not required to study the new material. This effect is known as **retroactive inhibition** because the newly learned material inhibited recall of the previously learned material. In 1900, Müller and Pilzecker proposed the **perseveration–consolidation** hypothesis to account for this well-documented phenomenon. Their hypothesis suggested that memories first enter a labile state where they perseverate (continue to be actively processed) but where they are subject to disruption. Over time these perseverating memories consolidate (become fixed) into a more permanent form that is resistant to disruption. This notion was consistent with the clinical data concerning retrograde amnesia and was widely accepted.

In 1949, Hebb proposed that the perseveration–consolidation hypothesis could be explained in terms of the development of neural circuits. Hebb suggested that temporary memories, such as working memory, could be the result of reverberating activity between groups of neurons. The reverberating process was thought to continue while the memory was still accessible. Memories were thought to become stronger as the reverberating process continues. If the reverberating process continued uninterrupted for some period of time, then structural changes would take place that would fix the memories and make them permanent. If the consolidation theory is correct, then anything that interferes with or interrupts the reverberating circuit would weaken or eliminate the memory trace.

ECS and Consolidation   Laboratory studies to test the hypothesis subjected animals to a variety of treatments that could potentially interrupt neuronal activity. One such treatment passed an electric current through the animal's brain that induced unbridled neuronal activity resulting in seizures. The general research paradigm for these studies was to teach the animals a specific task and then apply **electroconvulsive shock (ECS)** at various times after the learning had taken place. It was reasoned that the longer the ECS was delayed the more resistent the memory would be to disruption. If successful, the studies would support the consolidation theory and tell us something about the temporal factors governing the fixation of the permanent memory trace.

An Observation: From Slaughterhouse to Psychiatric Ward?

In the late 1930s, an Italian psychiatrist named Cerletti noted that pigs in the local slaughterhouse were made much more manageable by an electric shock administered across the temples. He decided to try this treatment on a schizophrenic patient who had not spoken coherently in many years. (Evidently, malpractice suits were not much of a consideration in Italian medicine at that time.) The first shock he applied to the patient was not strong enough to produce the desired effect. Cerletti then announced to the others in the room who were observing the treatment that he would try again with a stronger shock. The patient cried out, "Not another one—it's deadly!" Encouraged by this lucid (and totally reasonable) response, Cerletti gave the patient a second, and stronger, shock. The shock produced a seizure, and the patient lost consciousness. Later, when asked what had happened to him, the patient replied, "I don't know. Maybe I was asleep."

Exaggerated reports of the success of the treatment ensued, and ECS became an enormously popular therapeutic treatment, which is now referred to as electroconvulsive therapy (ECT). ECT is still used clinically, primarily to treat certain forms of depression. Exactly how ECT works to reduce the symptoms of depression is not well understood. The amnesic effect of ECT, however, is well documented.

I once interviewed a 26-year-old man who had received more than a dozen ECT treatments over the period of a year for the treatment of very severe depression. At one point when I asked him if he intended to pursue the career he had begun, he replied; "You know, I've been to four different colleges, and I have a bachelor's and a master's degree. I have trouble remembering the names of the courses I've taken—much less remember what I studied in those courses."

The earliest studies that used ECS to study memory consolidation were encouraging. Chorover and Schiller's work (1965) showed that ECS indeed seemed to interfere with the consolidation of the memory trace. The ECS produced amnesia when applied immediately following learning, and the amnesic effect diminished as the time between learning and the ECS increased (Figure 12-25). These data were interpreted to mean

Figure 12-25
Consolidation curve for a passive avoidance task. The verticle axis indicates the percentage of animals that avoided stepping down on a floor that had given them a foot shock. The horizontal axis shows the time delay between the foot shock and the ECS. (Redrawn from Chorover & Schiller, 1965.)

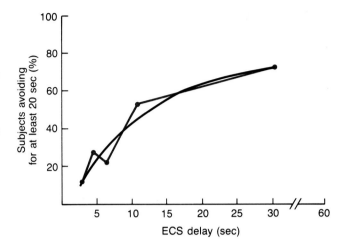

(1) that the ECS treatment interrupted the perseverative process, and (2) that the longer the perseverative process was allowed to persist, the stronger the memory became fixed or consolidated. (See Figure 12-25.)

Subsequent studies began to cast doubt on this interpretation. First, researchers began to question why the time course for the ECS studies was so brief. Retrograde amnesia in humans can reach back days, weeks, and even years. The ECS treatment in the laboratory only seemed to be effective for a few seconds or minutes. Further, it appeared that the amnesia was not permanent. If the animals were tested a few days or weeks after the treatment, the memory seemed to strengthen. Additionally, it was shown that memories which had considerable time to consolidate could be disrupted if the ECS was applied when the memory was active (see Maki, 1986, for a review). For example, if rats were trained on a task and then several hours later retrained and given the shock, the ECS caused amnesia for the original learning (Lewis, Misanin, & Miller, 1968). It seems that ECS could affect well-consolidated memories if they were active at the time of the treatment. Finally, it was shown that ECS-induced amnesia could be eliminated by giving the animals a "reminder" stimulus. For example, if rats had been made amnesic for a strong foot shock, the amnesia could be eliminated by a mild shock given to the tail 24 hours later (Galluscio, 1971; Miller & Springer, 1972).

What can be concluded from these studies? Clearly, ECS does impair memory. However, the effect seems to be on active memories independent of consolidation time. Furthermore, the ECS does not eliminate all traces of memories, because they return in time. Perhaps the treatment does not effect the encoding of memory at all. The ECS may temporarily disrupt the retrieval mechanism that is necessary to bring the memory out of storage.

CHAPTER SUMMARY

1. Behavioral plasticity takes two forms. First, behavior changes through natural selection in the evolution of species-specific behaviors. Behavioral change also occurs within individuals, in the form of learning, as organisms adjust to current environmental conditions.

2. Learning is a change in behavior resulting from previous experience. Memory is the aggregate of the subcellular, cellular, and intercellular changes that result from experience. When we test for learning by observing behavior, we are actually measuring *performance*. It is not possible to measure learning directly by observing overt behavior.

3. The most simple forms of learning such as *habituation* and *sensitization* are changes in the strength of preexisting responses to a stimulus. These *nonassociative* forms of learning can be found in the most simple organisms. Associative forms of learning, such as *classical conditioning* and *instrumental learning*, are more complex and require a more complex nervous system. More complex forms of associative learning require the organism to discriminate between the outcomes of a response to two or more stimuli. Several forms of discriminant learning have shown wide variance in learning ability across species.

4. Learning psychologists have classified memory into several types based on the duration of the memory trace. The briefest memories are *sensory memories*. *Short-term*, or *working*, memories are just long enough to complete the task at hand. *Long-term* and *permanent memories*, such as the name of your mother, may last a lifetime, as long as the brain remains healthy. Some learning theorists believe that different brain structures underlie each type of memory.

5. Habituation, sensitization and classical conditioning have been studied in simple, invertebrate nervous systems. Using invertebrate models, researchers have shown that habituation, sensitization, and classical conditioning result from changes in the strength of preexisting neural circuits. We know much more about the neural events that underlie learning in simple organisms than we do about learning in our own brains.

6. A variety of research studies have implicated changes in RNA and protein synthesis during learning. Drugs that inhibit protein synthesis also inhibit learning. By tracing how radioactive amines are incorporated into the brain, researchers have been able to identify specific changes in RNA and proteins following learning. Some researchers believe that long-term memory requires the synthesis of proteins.

7. Acetylcholine circuits are important in learning and memory. Drugs that block cholinergic circuits weaken learning and memory. Conversely, drugs that enhance or mimic cholinergic synapses enhance memory.

8. Learning can bring about identifiable and measurable changes in the organization and biochemistry of the brain. Animals raised in an enriched environment evidence consistent changes in their brains, including increased levels of acetylcholine esterase, thicker and heavier cortices, increased number of dendritic spines, and larger pre- and postsynaptic membranes.

9. Learning psychologists have attempted to find the locus of memory, called the *engram*. Based on the results of a long series of studies that systematically lesioned areas of the cortex in rats, Lashley proposed that it is the amount of brain tissue lesioned—and not the location of the lesion—that is important in learning. This position is stated in his two basic principles of brain organization called *mass action* and *equipotentiality*. Lashley's theory did not hold up with the evidence of further study.

10. The data from clinical studies of brain lesions in humans and from animal studies in the laboratory have shown that the hippocampus is an important brain structure for the formation of long-term memories. In laboratory animals the learning deficit resulting from lesions to the hippocampus varies widely depending on the nature of the learning task and the species under study.

11. The study of the activity of single cells in the hippocampus has demonstrated learning (classical conditioning) at the cellular level.

12. Many brain structures, in addition to the hippocampus, may be involved in learning and memory. Some of the more notable structures associated with learned behavior are the amygdala, the cerebellum, the thalamus, and various areas of the cerebral cortex.

13. The size of the brain has been correlated with behavioral flexibility and intelligence. In more complex vertebrates the cortex appears to account for an increasing amount of the observable behaviors, including those behaviors that depend on learning and memory.

14. The transfer of short-term memory into long-term memory is not well understood. Donald Hebb proposed that long-term memories require time to be *consolidated* or *fixed*. He hypothesized that this consolidation was attributable to a *perseveration* of neuronal activity that resulted in a physical change at the synapse.

15. Clinical data on *retrograde amnesia* and laboratory studies of *retroactive inhibition* support a *perseveration–consolidation* hypothesis of the transfer of short-term memory to long-term memory.

16. Attempts to interfere with memory consolidation indicate that memory can be disrupted. However, the data do not support the notion that memory consolidates over long periods of time. Head trauma appears to affect active memories independent of consolidation time. The effect of head trauma on memory may be due to the disruption of retrieval mechanisms rather than storage processes.

SUGGESTED READINGS

Alkon, D. L. (1983). Learning in a marine snail. *Scientific American, 249,* 70–84.

Baddeley, A. (1988). Cognitive psychology and human memory. *Trends in Neurosciences, 11,* 176–181.

Changeux, J. P., & Konishi, M. (Eds.). (1987). *The neural and molecular basis of learning.* New York: Wiley.

Domjan, M. P., & Burkhard, B. (1985). *The principles of learning and behavior* (2nd ed.). Monterey, CA: Brooks/Cole.

Dunn, A. J. (1980). Neurochemistry of learning and memory: An evaluation of recent data. *Annual Review of Psychology, 31,* 343–390.

Greenough, W. T., & Bailey, C. H. (1988). The anatomy of a memory: Convergence of results across a diversity of tests. *Trends in Neuroscience, 11,* 142–147.

Maki, W. S. (1986). Distinction between new and used traces: Different effects of electroconvulsive shock on memories for places presented and places past. *Quarterly Journal of Experimental Psychology: Comparative and Physiological Psychology, 38,* 397–423.

McConnel, P. S., Boer, G. J., Romijn, H. J., van de Poll, N. E., & Corner, M. A. (1980). *Adaptive capabilities of the nervous system.* Amsterdam: Elsevier.

Rosenzweig, M. R. (1984). Experience, memory, and the brain. *American Psychologist, 39,* 356–376.

Zechmeister, E. B., & Nyberg, S. E. (1981). *Human memory: An introduction to research and theory.* Monterey, CA: Brooks/Cole.

KEY TERMS

Anisomycin An antibiotic that inhibits the synthesis of protein within the cell.

Associative learning Learning characterized by the connection or association between two stimuli or a stimulus and a response.

Classical conditioning Associative learning between the occurrence of two stimuli.

Conditioned response (CR) In classical conditioning, the learned response to the previously neutral conditioned stimulus.

Conditioned stimulus (CS) In classical conditioning, the previously neutral stimulus that elicits the conditioned response.

Declarative memory Accessible record or memory for past events; The type of memories that can be put into words; *see* Procedural memory.

Discriminant learning Associative learning that requires the learner to respond to one stimulus, but not others.

Echoic memory Sensory memory associated with audition.

Electroconvulsive shock (ECS) Electric shock passed across the temples and through the brain that causes convulsions.

Engram The physical substrate of memory.

Equipotentiality Lashley concept concerning the organization of the brain; states that one part of the brain has the equal potential to store memory as any other part of the brain; *see* Mass action.

Habituation The elimination or reduction of the strength of a preexisting response to a stimulus.

Haptic memory Sensory memory associated with the skin senses.

Iconic memory Sensory memory associated with the sense of vision.

Instrumental learning Also known as Pavlovian conditioning; requires the learner to manipulate something in order to receive a reinforcement.

Korsakoff's syndrome Pattern of behavioral deficits, including memory loss, resulting from chronic alcohol abuse.

Long-term memory Memories that are stored for periods lasting weeks, months, and years.

Long-term potentiation Prolonged activation of neurons in the hippocampus resulting from brief electrical stimulation.

Mass action Lashley theory of brain organization that hypothesises that the size of a brain lesion is more important than the location of the lesion in determining the performance deficit; *see* Equipotentiality.

Nonassociative learning Learning that is solely dependent on the strength and temporal qualities of the stimulus.

Perseveration–consolidation hypothesis Theory proposing that memories are labile for some period of time before they become permanent.

Procedural memory Memory for the rules or procedures of how to do tasks; *see* Declarative memory.

Retroactive inhibition Learning new material interferes with recall of previously learned material.

Retrograde amnesia Memory loss following head trauma.

Savings score Test score that is a measure of the amount of memory retained for a given task.

Sensitization An increase in the strength of a preexisting response to a stimulus.

Sensory buffer The action of the sensory circuitary that is thought to provide the large storage capacity of sensory memory.

Sensory memory The most brief form of memory attributed to the sensory buffer.

Short-term memory Sometimes referred to as working memory; the active memory store used to accomplish a given task.

Unconditioned response (UR) In classical conditioning, the response to a stimulus that is independent of learning.

Unconditioned stimulus (US) In classical conditioning, the stimulus that produces the unconditioned response independent of learning. Working memory; *see* Short-term memory.

Feeling: The Emotional Mind

Chapter Learning Objectives

After reading this chapter, you should

1. Be able to discuss the relationship between the increasing complexity of emotional behavior and the evolution of forebrain structures.

2. Be able to cite evidence that some forms of emotional behavior are innate in human infants.

3. Understand and be able to describe the physiological concommitants of strong emotional arousal in animals and humans.

4. Be able to compare and contrast the James–Lange and Cannon–Bard theories of emotion.

5. Understand the role of the Papez circuit in emotional behavior.

6. Be able to explain the function of the sympathetic and parasympathetic divisions of the autonomic nervous system in emotion and stress reactions.

7. Be able to describe the three stages of the general adaptation syndrome.

8. Know which brain structures are associated with affective and predatory attack.

9. Understand the relationship between testosterone levels and overt aggressive behavior in animals and humans.

10. Be able to review the evidence for reward-inducing structures in the brain.

11. Be familiar with the role of serotonin and endogenous opiates in reward systems.

The Evolution of Emotions

Think of an angry spider, a frightened worm, or a frustrated fish. Clearly, emotionally charged words like *angry, frightened,* and *frustrated* seem inappropriate when they are associated with very simple animals. With a dog or a cat we have something that is much more complex, and words with emotional qualities no longer seem quite so incongruent. Nevertheless, you may still have some difficulty with the notion of a frustrated dog or a happy cat. On the other hand, we have no difficulty at all applying these emotionally laden terms to ourselves or to the people around us. Donald Hebb suggests that humans are the most emotional of all the animals; both in the diversity of emotional expression and in the pervasiveness of the expression of emotions in our daily lives (Hebb & Thompson, 1968). Let's examine this point a bit more closely.

When two males of a specific species of lizards confront each other to gain access to a female, food, or a sheltered place, they turn their side to their rival, stand motionless, and expose a large flap of skin called the **dewlap** (see Figure 13-1). This threat display may be sufficient to avoid more direct conflict. Failing to avoid conflict, the animals may begin to fight—pushing, biting, and clawing at each other until one retreats in defeat. During the conflict, did they feel angry? Does the winner feel the "thrill of victory"? Does the defeated male lizard stop and retreat because he is frightened? When beaten by his adversary, does he feel "the agony of defeat"? Hardly.

The behavior I have just described is very rigid and stereotypic and does not require learning. It is controlled by structures in the brain stem and other centers in the hindbrain. This form of behavior is "hard wired" into the lizard's central nervous system because it is critical for the survival of the species. Are similar behaviors "hard wired" in our own brains? The evidence appears to suggest that they are.

Figure 13-1
Aggressive display of the South American *Anolis* lizard.

Expression of Emotion in Infants

We are all familiar with the fact that human infants are able to cry immediately following birth. This genetically determined distress call produces strong emotional responses in adults; however, it may or may not reflect emotion in the infant. Within a few weeks the crying behavior of the infant develops some complexity, and you may be able to distinguish between a "distress/frightened" cry and an "angry/frustrated" cry.

A second emotional expression is also evident in very young infants: the smile. Almost immediately after birth the first signs of smiling appear. Within a few weeks the infant produces a well-defined smile to a variety of visual, auditory, and tactile stimuli. (Some anthropologists and developmental psychologists equate the smile in infants with the "fear grin" seen in infant monkeys and apes. The fear grin is a protective gesture that appears to communicate submissiveness to adults and juveniles.) By the time the infant is $2\frac{1}{2}$ months old, it produces a "social smile"—a smile directed at another human face that invites a social response.

It is important to note that this pattern of smiling behaviors is very consistent in all infants across all cultures. Additionally, the same maturational pattern of smiling behaviors can be seen in many brain injured infants. Many elements of this behavior pattern are even present in children who are born blind (Fraiberg, 1971). These facts support the notion that smiling behavior is innately determined in humans.

The adaptive value of crying and smiling behaviors seems quite clear. Crying communicates to the caregiver that a biological need has not been met. Smiling elicits the caretaker's attachment to the infant and promotes social interaction.

Overt Expression of Emotion

Can you tell, just by looking at the expression on someone's face, what emotion he or she is experiencing? Let's put this idea to the test. Look at the faces in Figure 13-2. Can you accurately apply the following emotional terms to each face? anger sadness surprise fear happiness disgust

Figure 13-2
What emotions are being expressed?

 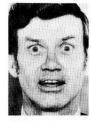   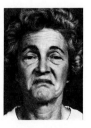 

Figure 13-3
Agreement on judgments
of emotion in five literate
cultures. (From Ekman,
1973.)

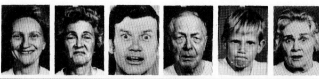

	Happiness	Disgust	Surprise	Sadness	Anger	Fear
United States	97%	92%	95%	84%	67%	85%
Brazil	95%	97%	87%	59%	90%	67%
Chile	95%	92%	93%	88%	94%	68%
Argentina	98%	92%	95%	78%	90%	54%
Japan	100%	90%	100%	62%	90%	66%

The faces in Figure 13-2 come from a cross-cultural study that examined how people from different countries judge the expression of emotion in faces (Ekman, 1973). The data showed that there was a remarkable degree of agreement across the various cultures tested. Ekman interpreted these findings to mean that facial expressions of emotions have a strong genetic component.

Now look at Figure 13-3, which matches the emotions with the faces and shows the percentage of agreement on judgment of emotions from five cultures. How did you do? The students in my classes consistently match five or six accurately.

The muscles of the human face permit a greater range of expression than is true with any other organism. These muscles are present and functioning at birth (Ekman & Oster, 1979). We have already noted that newborns can smile and cry. They are also able to knit their brow, squint their eyes, and purse their lips. When given a wedge of lemon to suck on, an infant only a few days old can produce a remarkable range of facial movements.

There is a clear evolutionary trend for increasing muscular control of facial features. With the exception of the muscles that open the mouth, the face of fishes is without expression. Some lizards, as we have noted, have evolved movable flaps of skin that provide two facial expressions—normal and aggressive. Muscles have migrated forward to move the ears, lips, and snout in the primitive mammals. However, in the primates, facial muscles have become increasingly specialized, and a variety of facial expressions are available that communicate emotional states. Humans possess specialized muscles for controlling the movement of the brows and nostrils, (see Figure 13-4) and there is more precise control over the lips and tongue (which is also a necessary component for the production of complex sounds in human language). It seems sensible that the variety of potential facial expressions parallels the evolving complexity of emotions across species.

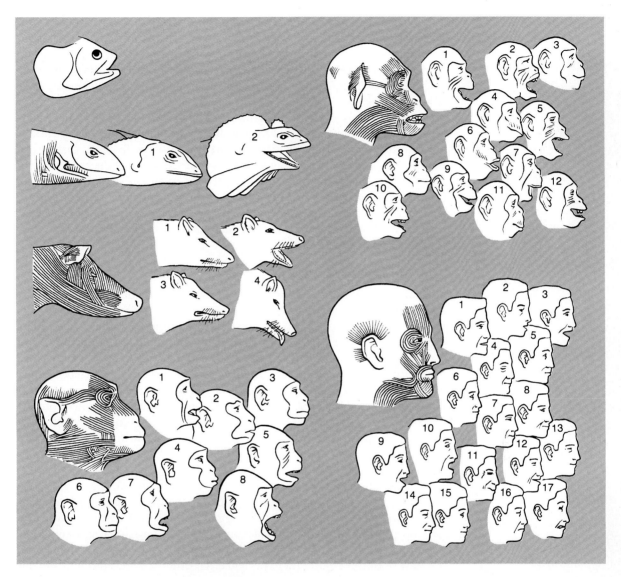

Figure 13-4
The evolution of the expression of emotion in the face. The numbers refer to
specific emotional states. (Redrawn from Gregory, 1929.)

Emotions Defined

You may be somewhat surprised to learn that scientists who study the
biological mechanisms of emotion have been unable to agree on a satisfactory working definition of the term *emotion*. In fact there is significant
disagreement on the number of different emotions. We have been

singularly unsuccessful in arriving at a definition that does not rely on subjective terms. Words like *fear, sorrow, anger, remorse*, and *jealousy* transmit a good deal of information about our emotional states. However, if asked to define what you feel when you experience fear, you are likely to resort to other terms that are equally subjective—*scared, jumpy, nervous, edgy, terrified*, and so on. Scientists do no better.

One thing we can all recognize are the visceral changes that accompany emotional arousal—changes in heart rate, breathing, perspiration, and intestinal and stomach contractions (that queasy feeling). One problem facing those who study emotions is that the same general physiological changes seem to take place almost independently of the nature of the emotional experience. It is difficult, if not impossible, to differentiate accurately and consistently between the physiological responses that result from intense sexual arousal, fear, anger, depression, or joy (Ekman, Levenson, & Friesen, 1983).

THE JAMES—LANGE THEORY

In the late 1800s William James proposed a theory of emotions that was based on the ideas of the Danish psychologist Carl Lange. For this reason it is known as the **James–Lange theory**. James noted that sometimes there are clear reasons for our emotional experiences. If you are swimming at the beach and see the dorsal fin of a shark in close proximity, it is totally understandable that you would experience physiological changes such as an increase in heart rate, respiration, and blood pressure. However, have you ever felt suddenly afraid without an obvious cause? Sitting alone in a darkened room, you feel your face flushing, beads of perspiration forming on your forehead, and your heart beginning to race. You notice these changes and think, Gosh, I'm frightened!

The James–Lange theory proposes that we consciously experience emotions *after* we react to our own physiological changes. James proposed that environmental events trigger physiological changes, and the specific physiological changes account for the conscious experience of emotion. The specific pattern of physiological response would determine the nature of the emotional experience. In other words, emotions *are* the physical sensations we experience from our body. As James put it, "We feel sorry because we cry, angry because we strike, afraid because we tremble" (James, 1884).

THE CANNON—BARD THEORY

As I noted earlier, we are not able to differentiate accurately between emotions based on different patterns of physiological change. Walter Cannon suggested that James's theory was flawed. The various forms of emotional experience could not be attributed to unique patterns of physiological response. Cannon (1927, 1929) pointed out that the very same physical reaction—for example, goose bumps could be elicited by hearing a beautiful piece of music or the screech of chalk on the chalkboard, or by watching an autopsy for the first time.

Cannon proposed a theory of motivation, later modified by Phillip Bard (thus the name **Cannon—Bard theory**), which stated that emotion-inducing events send signals to various locations in our brains. Some of those signals go to the hypothalamus, which, in turn, produces physiological responses through the autonomic nervous system. Other signals go to the cerebral cortex, where they produce the subjective experience of fear, anger, or happiness. The nature of the emotion is determined by the subjective interpretation of the environmental situation. Although the theory was not totally correct in some particulars, it was correct in placing the source of emotions in the brain and not in the peripheral organs.

The Limbic System and Emotions In 1937, James W. Papez proposed that emotions could not be isolated in a specific brain "center." Rather, Papez proposed that emotions are governed by a complex, interacting network of brain circuits. Papez based his theory in part on the fact that the senses of smell, taste, and pain appear to be closely associated with an interconnected group of structures and neural pathways now called the **Papez circuit**. Papez reasoned that these three sense modalities are central to most emotional behaviors. Taste and smell are important in a variety of behaviors, including those in establishing territories, hunting, eating, having sex, and maintaining social dominance. Pain, of course, is important in fear and aggression.

Paul MacLean expanded on Papez's theory and redefined the Papez circuit into what is now known as the limbic system (MacLean, 1949, 1970). Some of the structures within the *limbic system* are either poorly developed or not present in the brains of premammalian vertebrates. The presence of a well-developed limbic system in mammals permits more varied and complex emotional behaviors. The limbic structures (see Figure 13-5) are quite prominent in all mammals. However, the limbic system has remained relatively unchanged in the evolution of the mammalian brain. As you can see from Figure 13-6, the size of the limbic structures has remained relatively stable, whereas that of other, newer brain structures (especially the neocortex) has increased markedly (Russell, 1961).

The structures of the limbic system tend to border the midline of the brain (*limbic* comes from the Latin *limbus*, which means "border"). The most prominent structures of the limbic system include some nuclei within the anterior portion of the thalamus, the hypothalamus, the olfactory bulbs and the olfactory cortex, the hippocampus, the amygdala, the septum, the cingulate and dentate gyri, and the fornix. MacLean has proposed that there are three circuits within the limbic system (1970).

Figure 13-5
The major structures and pathways of the limbic system.

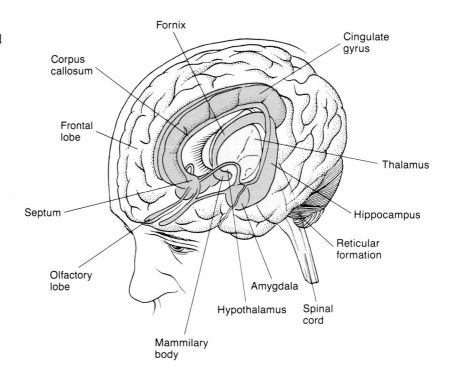

Fornix

Cingulate gyrus

Corpus callosum

Frontal lobe

Thalamus

Septum

Hippocampus

Reticular formation

Olfactory lobe

Amygdala

Hypothalamus

Spinal cord

Mammilary body

Figure 13-6
The brains of a rabbit, a cat, and a monkey, showing the relative size of the limbic structures (shaded area) compared to the remainder of the brain. Note that the forebrain structures increase greatly, whereas the limbic system remains relatively stable.

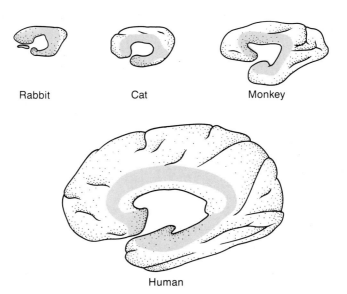

Rabbit   Cat   Monkey

Human

(1) One circuit includes the amygdala and hippocampus and functions in behaviors essential for self-preservation. As we discuss later in this chapter, lesions in this part of the limbic system can eliminate aggressive behaviors. (2) The second circuit includes the cingulate gyrus, the septum, and some areas in the hypothalamus. This circuit appears to be related to pleasurable emotions including sexual excitement. (3) The third system is comprised of the anterior portion of the thalamus and some nuclei within the hypothalamus. According to MacLean, this system is important for socially relevant behaviors. This last circuit is found to be largest in the primates, including humans.

The Role of the Autonomic Nervous System

You will recall from Chapter 3 that the ANS has two anatomically distinct divisions. The sympathetic division mobilizes the body's resources and produces the flight-or-fight response. The parasympathetic division functions in concert with the sympathetic division and generally works to conserve energy and resources. The effects of sympathethic and parasympathetic activation are summarized in Figure 13-7.

Pick (1970) has proposed that, in evolutionary terms, the sympathetic portion of the ANS is the newer of the two divisions. In ectothermic animals such as the reptiles the ANS functions primarily to conserve energy during periods when the environment is warm. The sympathetic system evolved slowly in early mammals probably as a mechanism to eliminate excessive heat generated during periods of high metabolic activity. Pick proposed that the sympathetic division evolved slowly into a mechanism for expending energy rapidly during conflict and stress.

Fear, anger, sexual arousal, and other strong emotional experiences activate the sympathetic division of the ANS. This, is turn increases heart rate and blood pressure; causes bronchia in the lungs to open in order to facilitate the uptake of oxygen and the elimination of carbon dioxide; increases perspiration to provide cooling for the body; causes blood vessels to the muscles and the brain to dilate, thus increasing blood flow; decreases the activity of smooth muscle in the stomach and intestines, allowing energy normally used for digestion to be diverted to other muscles and organs; and finally, causes smooth muscles attached to hair follicles to constrict, producing a piloerection. (The piloerection serves as part of the threat display in many mammals. In humans it produces the familiar goose bumps that are a vestige of that behavior.) All of these responses to sympathetic activation prepare the organism to expend a great deal of energy in a short period of time.

Recall from Chapter 3 that the endocrine system is also affected by emotional arousal. The hypothalamus induces the release of ACTH from the pituitary, which, in turn, stimulates the secretion of a number of adrenal glucocorticoids from the cortex of the adrenal gland. These steroid hormones serve a variety of functions designed to protect the

Figure 13-7
The sympathetic and pa-rasympathetic divisions of the autonomic nervous system, the organs they innervate, and the effects each produces.

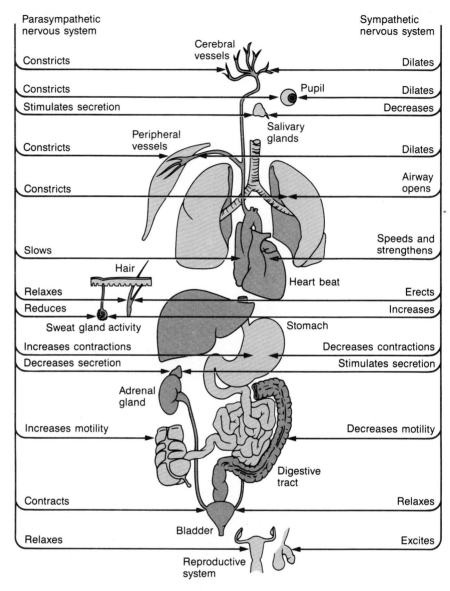

stressed organism (e.g., see Delahunt & Mellsop, 1987). The glucocorti-coids also stimulate the conversion of fats and proteins to sugars, provid-ing energy to deal with the presenting situation. The medulla of the adrenal gland is activated directly by the hypothalamus and secretes epinephrine and norepinephrine, which have a general activating effect on the organism. Additionally, hormones from the pituitary that activate the thymus gland are released into the bloodstream. It is thought that the thymus gland influences the production of *leukocytes*, which help the body

Figure 13-8
The actions of the hypothalamus, the autonomic nervous system, and the endocrine glands in reaction to emotional arousal.

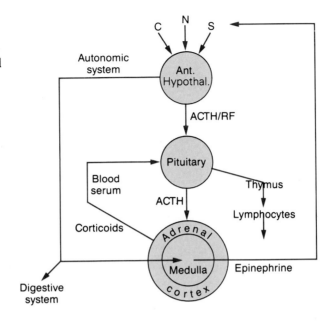

to fight infections of bacteria and other foreign matter. The actions of the hypothalamus, the ANS, and the endocrine system are summarized in Figure 13-8.

Stress and Reactions to Stress

In 1935, Hans Selye was studying the effects of injecting various hormones into rats. The treatment apparently caused considerable physical stress to the animals, and some of them died. Selye noted that many of the deceased animals had developed gastric ulcers. He also noted that the adrenal glands were enlarged, and the thymus gland and the lymph nodes had deteriorated. Because a variety of hormone treatments produced the same effect, Selye hypothesized that the symptoms he observed might be a general reaction to any kind of stressor. He tested this hypothesis by subjecting animals to a variety of other stressors such as exposure to severe cold or prolonged sleep deprivation. The effect was always the same: gastric ulcers, enlarged adrenals, and deterioration of the *thymicolymphatic system*. Selye termed this triad of symptoms the "general stress syndrome."

Selye noted that all the organisms he studied reacted to stress in three stages. Together, the stages are called the **general adaptation syndrome (GAS)**, which is depicted in Figure 13-9. As the figure suggests, each individual has a normal or desired level of resources that are available to resist life stressors. In the first stage of the GAS, the *alarm stage*, there is an alarm reaction that is characterized by sympathetic activation that results in a rapid depletion of stress-related resources (e.g., epinephrine, norepinephrine, glucocorticoids).

Figure 13-9
The three stages of the
general adaptation syn-
drome: alarm, resistance,
and exhaustion. (From
MacLean, 1954.)

In the second stage, the *resistance stage*, the animals appear to adapt to the presence of the stressor. However, stored fats and proteins continue to be depleted by the higher levels of glucocorticoids in the blood. Also, these hormones inhibit the formation of antibodies by the thymus gland, and they decrease the number of white blood cells in the blood. Because of this, the animal becomes more susceptible to other stressors. Selye (1974) noticed that many stress-related diseases develop during the resistance stage. Another part of the resistance stage is the suppression of many of the bodily functions related to sexual behavior and reproduction. In males, sperm production drops, as does the secretion of male sex hormones. In females, the menstrual cycle is disrupted or suppressed. Sexual interest decreases, and sexual behavior may terminate.

If stress is maintained at a high enough level for a long enough period of time, the animal enters the *exhaustion stage*. In this the last stage, the resources for dealing with stress fall well below normal, and the animal dies. Death may result from a variety of stress-related organ failures. In some cases death is due to peritonitis (inflammation and infection of the peritoneal cavity) resulting from a perforation of the stomach or intestinal wall.

An Observation:

**Voodoo Curse—
Is There Anything
to It?**

Do you ever wonder if there is any truth in the stories of voodoo curses. Can anyone really die because some voodoo doctor has stuck a pin in an effigy doll or splattered chicken blood on a doorway? Although it does not seem plausible to well-educated and sophisticated people, there just may be something to it.

Most people in the scientific community viewed voodoo magic as illogical nonsense until a very respected researcher, Walter Cannon, published a series of well-documented cases of *voodoo death* (1942). The scenario for each case had a common thread. First, the person who died strongly believed in the power of voodoo, magic spells, and supernatural phenomena. Second, the person believed that he or she was going to die because of a specific incident, a transgression of voodoo rules, some taboo behavior, a curse placed by someone with voodoo power, and so on. Finally, the people around the victim also believed in the voodoo magic and acted as though they too expected the person to die. Somehow, the terror and hopelessness associated with the belief in certain death actually caused the victim to succumb. But how?

The answer may lie in the results of some interesting studies completed by Curt Richter (1957). Richter was interested in the swimming behavior of rats. He found that ordinarily rats could swim for very long periods without rest. Most of his subjects could swim nonstop for as long as 2 days even when the bath was made very turbulent by a high-velocity jet of water. (It would be similar to you trying to swim in a whirlpool.)

Richter found that clipping the rat's whiskers just prior to placing them in the bath made an enormous difference in their ability to survive the stress of the turbulent water. In fact, many of these shaved rats could only swim for a few minutes. Then, they would sink to the bottom of the tank—dead. It didn't seem logical that rats without whiskers could not swim. In fact, Richter found that if the whiskers were removed several days prior to placing the rat in the bath, the effect was greatly reduced, and the animals could swim almost as long as rats whose whiskers were intact.

What was going on here? Postmortem examination of those animals that succumed quickly showed that indeed they did not drown at all. They died of cardiac arrest! A rat's whiskers are critical for orientation. Evidently the combination of the turbulent water and the inability of the rat to use tactile information obtained from the whiskers was doubly stressful. This caused a very large sympathetic response. However, after a few minutes in a bath from which the rat could find no escape, the parasympathetic system became highly activated. Apparently, the parasympathetic response, both to the hopelessness of the situation and as a homeostatic rebound to the sympathetic response, was enough to stop the rat's heart.

The results from Richter's work suggest a possible explanation for voodoo deaths and for other unexplained deaths associated with terrifying events leading to a sense of hopelessness. People in the medical profession have often noted that patients who become convinced of imminent death give up and, in turn, may hasten their own death.

CONTROL AND STRESS

One important factor concerning stress seems to be the "psychological" impact of the stressful situation. It appears that physical stressors also induce emotional stress—fear, anxiety, depression. The emotional stress adds to, and in fact, may be more stressful than, the physical stressor.

Figure 13-10
The experimental conditions used in the "executive" monkey study. When the executive monkey (*left*) depresses the lever, both monkeys avoid the shock. (From Brady et al., 1958.)

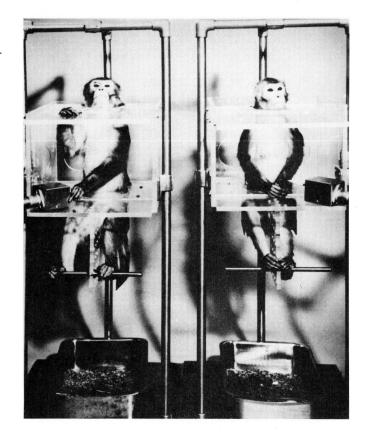

The first formal study to address this issue (Brady, Porter, Conrad, & Mason, 1958) examined the combined effect of physical stress and each individual's state of control over the physical stressor. Two rhesus monkeys were placed in restraining chairs, as shown in Figure 13-10. There was an electrode attached to the foot of each monkey that would provide an electric shock to both of the monkeys every 20 seconds. The shock could be avoided if a control lever was pressed within the 20-second period. Although each monkey had access to a control lever, only one lever could actually control the onset of the shock.

The animals were tested in 6-hour sessions twice each day. That is, they were placed in the experimental situation for 6 hours, followed by 6 hours of rest. That sequence was followed for 24 hours a day. After a number of days the monkey that had access to the lever controlling the shock, the so-called *executive monkey*, developed gastric ulcers. The monkey in the yoked condition showed no evidence of ulcers. Because both animals received the same level and number of shocks, these data were interpreted to mean that the ulcers resulted from the additional "emotional stress" experienced by the decision-making executive monkey.

In the study completed by Brady and his colleagues, the executive monkey learned the task rather quickly, and neither monkey received many shocks. Further study showed that control over the shocks (decision making) was not the key factor for developing ulcers (Foltz & Millett, 1964). Rather, the ulcers could be attributed to higher states of arousal. In fact, when similar studies were done with rats (Weiss, 1968, 1971, 1972), the yoked animals evidenced more gastric ulcerations than did the executive rats. This finding was likely due to the fact that the yoked animals could neither control the shocks nor predict their onset. Therefore, the yoked animals were in a higher state of emotional arousal. The ulcers are not due directly to the high level of emotional arousal. Rather, they appear to be due to the high level of parasympathetic activation that follows the periods of excitation.

Activation of the parasympathetic system causes the secretion of the stomach acids that are essential for digestion of food. In these studies, the excessively high levels of parasympathetic activation cause the release of large amounts of stomach acid, which damages the lining of the stomach, duodenum, and small intestine, resulting in ulcers.

As was true for the physically stessed animals studied by Selye, animals subjected to long periods of emotional arousal also evidence enlarged adrenal glands and deterioration of the thymolymphatic system. Additionally, studies with rats have shown that the anterior nuclei of the hypothalamus (the area of the hypothalamus that controls the pituitary gland) enlarges following prolonged emotional arousal. This is likely due to enlargement of the neurosecretory cells located in these brain structures (Galluscio et al., 1974).

Aggression and Dominance

In complex societies such as our own, the word *aggression* has a negative connotation. We tend to think of aggressive behavior as being self-serving, antisocial, and generally unwanted. I would have you think of aggressiveness in another way—as assertive behavior that is absolutely essential for the survival of the species.

Think of the least aggressive species of animals. Perhaps rabbits, canaries, sheep, and similar "docile" animals come to mind. Although the animals in these species do not typically show much aggressive behavior toward animals of other species, they do evidence intraspecies aggression. Two male rabbits or sheep will put on quite an aggressive display if placed in the same pen with a female that is sexually receptive. Both the male and female canary will drive other canaries away from their nest, particularly if the nest contains eggs or newly hatched young. Animals that are unable or unwilling to fight for territory, to protect their young, to possess a mate, or to gain access to the resources that sustain life (food, water, shelter, and so on) simply do not survive.

TYPES OF AGGRESSIVE BEHAVIORS

The adaptive advantage for most forms of aggressiveness is quite clear. Ultimately, the aggressive behavior increases the probability that the animal will mate or compete more effectively for the resources required for survival. Wilson (1975) has classified aggressive behaviors into several types based on function.

1. *Territorial aggression.* This form of aggression is usually directed at members of the same species. Aggressive displays and overt attack are used to drive intruders from the defender's territory. Territorial aggression may be directed at animals of other species that compete for the same food and shelter resources.

2. *Dominance aggression.* This form of aggression is seen primarily in social animals. The behavior is directed at members of the social group. Its purpose is to establish a social dominance hierarchy. In some species dominance aggression is enhanced by characteristic features and postures that designate those possessing higher social rank. The silver hair on the back of older and more dominant gorillas, the characteristic high position of the tail in some canines and primates, and the facial color patches and large canine teeth of the mandril baboon are examples of features and behaviors that enhance dominance.

3. *Sexual aggression.* We have already noted that males of many species compete for access to females. Additionally, the males of some species threaten or attack females solely to mate or to force them into a prolonged sexual alliance. The females of some species can evidence aggressive behaviors toward sexually aroused males when the female is not ready for mating.

4. *Parental aggression.* Parents of many animals show mild forms of disciplinary aggression toward their own young. In mammals, the female often must attack her own young at weaning to force them to be self-sufficient feeders.

5. *Predatory aggression.* Some researchers do not consider predation for food to be aggressive behavior (e.g., Davis, 1964). However, many elements of predatory behavior are seen in intraspecies fighting, and the young of most carnivores "practice" predatory behaviors as part of their play activity. It is difficult to think of predatory aggression as an entirely different process.

6. *Antipredatory aggression.* Purely defensive behaviors can, at times, develop into focused attack. For example, when cornered, the deer or elk can very effectively fend off a pack of wolves, in some cases seriously wounding or killing the predator.

AGGRESSIVE BEHAVIOR IN HUMANS

Human's long history is replete with examples of intra- and inter-species aggressiveness. Our willingness to kill other animals for our own purposes has completely eliminated some species and placed numerous others on the endangered list. Our history of intraspecies brutality in territorial and ideological wars is well documented. Is aggression in humans innate? Is aggression in humans adaptive? Certainly, from an evolutionary and biological perspective aggression is both adaptive and innate. It is unlikely that any characteristic that is as pervasive and apparently easily elicited could have evolved without some adaptive purpose.

Please do not misunderstand. I am not suggesting that war, criminal violence, and wanton killing of other species can be justified or explained away because of our evolutionary history. Nor do I think it wise to ignore the existence of our aggressive nature or to attribute human aggression to the "abnormal circumstances" associated with our complex society (e.g., Montague, 1968). It is important to understand that aggressiveness is a natural form of behavior in every species, including humans. It is also important to understand that, in a very real way, human technology has outgrown human biology. Clubs, spears, handguns, bombs in airplanes, and now the nuclear-tipped ICBMs have provided us with the ability to extend the potential destructiveness of our innate aggressiveness at an exponential rate. With that reality to deal with, it is far better to recognize and accept our biological tendency for aggressive behavior, to modify our social structures in ways that minimize the occurence of antisocial aggression, and to find positive ways of expressing our aggressive tendencies.

Brain Structures Associated with Aggressive Behavior

Behaviors of various kinds can be either modified, strengthened, or diminished by lesioning various structures in the brain. Additionally, behaviors such as aggression can be elicited in the laboratory by stimulating specific brain structures. Much of the study of the brain mechanisms associated with aggression has made use of this type of methodology.

THE HYPOTHALAMUS

In 1928, Hess reported that he could elicit a full-blown rage response in intact cats by stimulating the hypothalamus. (Hess pioneered many of the techniques used for long-term implants of stimulating electrodes. He received the Nobel Prize in 1949 for his work. See Hess, 1957, for a review of his careful study of the hypothalamus and midbrain.) That same year, Bard (1928) had shown that lesions to the hypothalamus eliminated integrated aggressive behaviors. The animals in Bard's studies only evidenced fragments of the normal attack behaviors seen in intact cats. Bard also demonstrated that he could elicit a complete rage response in cats with all brain tissue above the level of the hypothalamus removed. Bard described the rage response in these animals as **sham rage** because all of the typical attack behaviors were evident (spitting,

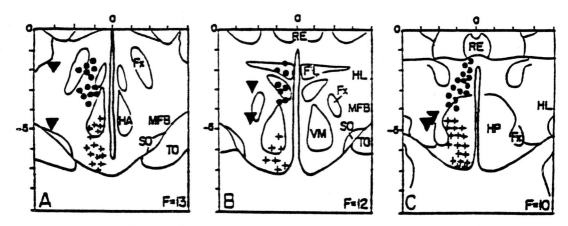

Figure 13-11
The distribution of sites in the hypothalamus of cats from which electrical stimulation elicits flight, attack, and killing of prey. (+, defense; ●, flight; ▼, prey killing). Three different cross sections of the hypothalamus are shown. A is the most anterior cross section. (FIL, nucleus filigormis; Fx, fornix; HA, anterior hypothalamus; MFB, median forebrain bundle; SO, supraoptic nucleus; TO, optic tract; VM, ventromedial nucleus) (Adapted from Kaada, 1967.)

snarling, biting, clawing, piloerection, etc.); however, the rage was not associated with a directed attack. This is understandable because the animals are made blind by the surgery.

The pioneering work of Hess and Bard directed much attention on the hypothalamus. Subsequent research has shown that not all parts of the hypothalamus are associated with aggression (Masserman, 1941). Stimulation to the anterior regions of the hypothalamus, most notably the portion surrounding the fornix (Akert, 1961) and the medial hypothalamus (Delgado, 1969; Flynn, Vanegas, Foote, & Edwards, 1970), produce the strongest and most consistent ragelike responses. Stimulation to the lateral hypothalamus produces behaviors normally seen in predation—stalking and capturing prey. These data have been interpreted to mean that there are at least two types of aggressive behaviors under the influence of the hypothalamic nuclei: (1) **affective attack**, which is controlled by the more anteromedial nuclei, and (2) **predatory attack**, which is controlled by the lateral nuclei. Affective attack includes those aggressive behaviors commonly seen in inter- and intraspecies fighting. Predatory attack is more closely related to the stalking and capture behaviors that lead to killing for food (Glickman, 1977). (See Figure 13-11.)

THE AMYGDALA

The amygdala is known to be important for feeding, drinking, and sexual behavior. It is also important for aggressiveness. The amygdala

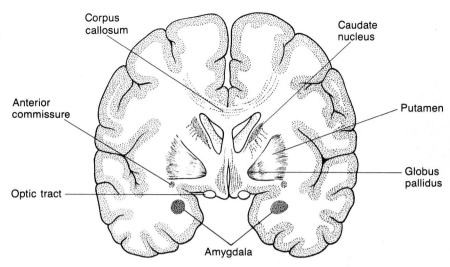

Figure 13-12
Coronal section of the human brain showing the location of the amygdala.

contains several nuclei, which can be divided into two groups: (1) the **corticomedial nuclei** are older and have been shown to be involved in predatory attack (Vergnes, 1975); (2) the **basolateral nuclei** evolved more recently and appears to be associated with affective attack (Vergnes, 1976). (See Figure 13-12).

Bilateral lesions to the amygdala can produce either remarkable tameness or heightened aggressiveness, depending on the size and location of the lesion. Amygdalectomized animals (complete bilateral removal of the amygdala) do not appear to recognize social aggression, and they fail to respond appropriately when threatened. When placed in colonies, most social animals will naturally establish a "pecking order" of social dominance. (The term *pecking order* comes from the social hierarchies found in barnyard chickens.) The number one rooster in the pecking order or in the colony, the **alpha animal**, is dominant over all others. The second animal is subordinate to the alpha animal, but dominant over the remainder, and so on.

Pribram and his colleagues (Pribram, 1962; Rosvold, Mirsky, & Pribram, 1954) found that rhesus monkeys do not respond appropriately to the aggressive behaviors that monkeys use to establish social hierarchies. In rhesus monkeys, dominance is established and maintained primarily using facial displays that emphasize the canine teeth. The researchers performed an amygdalectomy on the most dominant animal in the colony. After the animal recovered from the surgery, he was returned to the colony, and he promptly dropped to the bottom of the social hierarchy. Surgery to the new alpha animal produced the same effect. However, when the third alpha animal received the surgery, he did not loose dominance. Rather, he became even more dominant, vicious, and aggressive. This was apparently due to the fact that the new number

Psychosurgery for the Control of Aggressive Behavior

Psychosurgery, or surgery performed for the sole purpose of modifying behavior, is not a new idea. Ancient civilizations used **trephinations** (holes chipped or bored in the skull) in an apparent attempt to let evil spirits escape. It is interesting to note that some of these people actually survived this primitive surgery! We know this because healing is evident around the edges of the holes in the skull. However, we do not know whether the treatment had any effect (positive or otherwise) on the behavior, because there is no written record to tell us.

In more modern times psychosurgery had a resurgence in the mid-1930s. Egas Moniz, a Brazilian neuropsychiatrist had attended a research meeting in which Jacobsen (1936) reported that lesions to the prefrontal lobe of chimpanzees made the animals tame and easier to handle. Moniz wondered if a similar effect could be obtained in anxious human patients. He performed several *prefrontal lobectomies* (removal of the frontal lobes) and reported glowing results (1936).

That was the beginning. More effecient procedures were developed, the latest being the *leucotomy*. In this procedure the surgeon forces a curved blade through the upper orbit of the eye (between the upper eyelid and the ball of the eye). The blade is then swung back and forth to sever the fiber tracts that project to and from the prefrontal cortex. This procedure became a very popular treatment for many patients who did not respond to other forms of treatment. In fact, it was considered to be safe enough to be done in the surgeon's office. By the end of the 1950s more than 40,000 patients in the United States alone had received one of the various forms of prefrontal psychosurgery.

Psychosurgery is still used to treat aggressive behavior. For example, people with focal epileptic seizures in the temporal lobe often have a history of unprovoked violence toward others or themselves. Most often these people are treated successfully with antiepileptic drugs such as Dilantin. However, in some cases the drug therapy is ineffective, and the episodes of violence continue unabated. To deal with cases that are resistant to treatment with drugs, some neurosurgeons have turned to the selective destruction of specific structures in the brain, including the amygdala, cingulate gyrus, hypothalamus, and other limbic structures (e.g., Balasubramaniam & Kanaka, 1976; Kelly, Richardson, & Mitchell-Heggs, 1973).

Because the amygdala and other brain centers associated with violent behavior are located deep within the brain, the surgeon must use stereotaxic surgical techniques to gain access to the tissues that are to be lesioned. Spotlight Figure 13-1 has two X-ray photographs (*a* and *b*) showing the head placement in a stereotaxic device and the placement of tandem electrodes, one in each amygdala; *c* shows a pair of lesioning electrodes placed over the coronal section of the brain.

The following case history is typical of the type of patient considered to be a reasonable candidate for this type of surgical intervention.

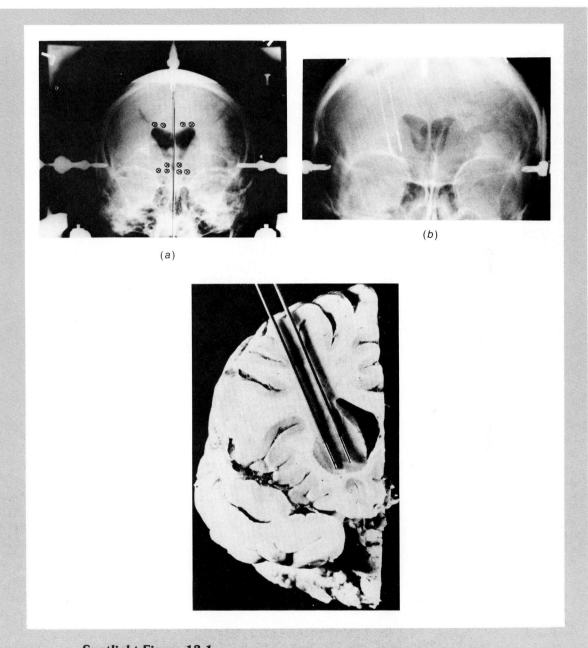

Spotlight Figure 13-1
a. X-ray photograph of the head placed in the stereotaxic instrument. (From Kelly et al., 1973.) *b.* X-ray showing simultaneous bilateral localization for amygdala lesions. (From Brown, 1973.) *c.* A pair of lesioning electrodes shown in place on a dissected brain. (From Bingley et al., 1973.)

SPOTLIGHT 13-1

A 24-year-old white female with a 9-year history of intermittent depression coupled with self-mutilation, three suicidal episodes including wrist-slashing, and explosive physical violence against others without external provocation. Additionally, there were lapses into alcoholic excess and sexual promiscuity. Several years of psychotherapy with concurrent chemotherapy and two courses of ECT were not fruitful. Patient was observed in our secured unit because of her marked hostility towards nurses and attendants.

    Following bilateral amygdalotomy ... the patient remained moderately depressed and anxious but her hostility and antisocial behavior were controlled. Subsequent cingulotomy produced good emotional balance ... In January ... she returned to work in San Francisco and has been gainfully employed without

difficulty since that time. (Brown, 1973, pp. 191–192.)

    There are many people who question whether or not psychosurgery can be justified. Opponents point out that the surgical procedures are not reversible, as are most chemotherapy techniques. Further, they suggest that the procedures are done primarily to protect society and not to help the patient. Defenders of psychosurgery point out that the surgery does indeed help the patient, and that the surgery is usually a last resort attempted only after other, less invasive, forms of intervention have been tried and have failed. The debate is likely to continue for some time. We hope that the occurrence of psychosurgery will decrease as our knowledge of brain chemistry becomes more precise.

two animal was quite passive and made no real challenge to unseat the alpha monkey. (Refer to Figure 13-13.)

OTHER BRAIN CENTERS ASSOCIATED WITH AGGRESSION

The **septum** lies between the walls of the anterior portion of the lateral ventricles. In some animals aggressive behaviors are inhibited by electrical stimulation to the septum. Lesions to the septum appear to lower the threshold for rage responses (Brady & Nauta, 1953). Rats with bilateral lesions to the septum can be extremely emotional and evidence ragelike attack with little provocation. This behavior is short-lived, and the animal's aggressiveness appears to return to normal. In some species such as mice, lesions to the septum increase flight behavior rather than aggressiveness.

The **periaqueductal grey matter** is the region in the midbrain that surrounds the cerebral aqueduct. Electrical stimulation in this area of the brain elicits affective attack that is very similar to that seen with stimulation to the anteromedial portions of the hypothalamus (Edwards & Flynn, 1972). Lesions to the **ventromedial tegmentum**, an area below the tectum, eliminates affective attack but appears to leave predadory

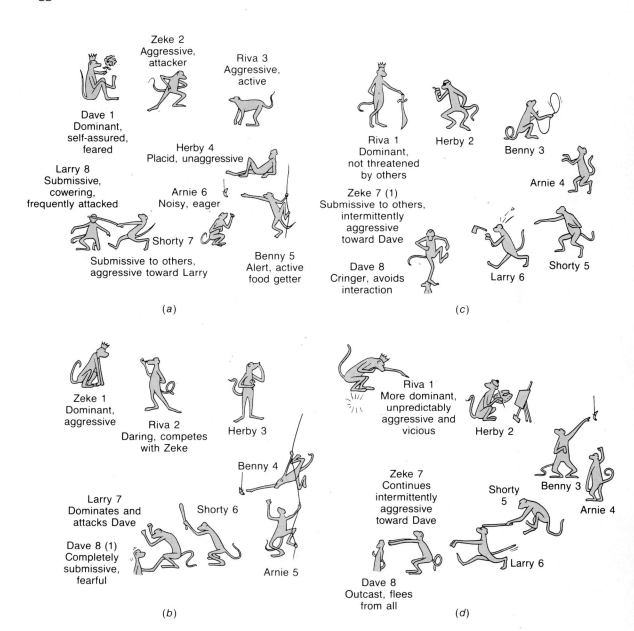

Figure 13-13

Social dominance hierarchies in a group of male rhesus monkeys following repeated amygdalectomy of the dominant monkey. *a.* Before surgery was begun. *b.* Dave, the alpha monkey prior to surgery falls to the bottom of the hierarchy. *c.* After Zeke, the new alpha monkey, was amygdalectomized. *d.* After Riva received surgery he did not loose his dominance status. This was attributed to the passiveness of Herby, the new number two monkey. (Redrawn from Pribram, 1962.)

attack unaffected (Adams, 1986). For an extensive and systematic review of the neural systems associated with aggressive behavior in animals and humans, see Weigner and Bear (1988).

Hormones and   You may have noted in the amygdalectomy study discussed earlier that
Aggression   all of the monkeys were males. There is a good reason for this. Male animals of many species tend to evidence more aggressive behaviors than do the females. One reason for this is the male steroid hormone testosterone. It has been known for a very long time that the castration of male animals reduces their tendency to be aggressive. However, the aggressive behavior of castrated animals can be restored by injections of the male sex hormone.

Figure 13-14 shows the results of castration and hormone replacement treatment on the aggressive behavior of mice. In this particular study aggressiveness was determined by the number of biting attacks directed at an inanimate object placed in the animal's cage. The data clearly show that castration reduced aggressive behaviors and that injection of testosterone restored the behavior. Additionally, the level of aggressive behavior was directly correlated with the dosage of the hormone. The female data are also informative. Note that removing the ovaries had essentially no effect on the aggressive behavior of the females. Also note that, compared to males, the aggressive behavior of the females is quite limited (Wagner, Beauving, & Hutchinson, 1980). Similar results have been reported by Barr, Gibbons, and Moyer (1976); DeBold and Miczek, (1981); and Albert, Walsh, Gorzalka, Siemens, and Louie (1986).

Attempts to correlate testosterone levels with overt aggressive behavior in humans have been less dramatic. It has been noted that male aggressiveness and intermale fighting show a marked increase during pubescence in the early teens years when testosterone levels increase (Mazure, 1983). However, the studies of normal male adult populations have found either no significant correlations, or low but positive correlations between aggressiveness and blood serum testosterone levels (e.g., Rose, 1978; Rubin, 1982). There is some evidence from prison populations that inmates convicted of violent crimes tend to have higher testosterone levels than do other prisoners (Rada, Laws, & Kellner, 1976).

Other hormones such as the glucocorticoids and ACTH also influence aggressive behavior in males. These hormones, however, do not appear to influence the overt behavior directly. They produce their effect by modulating the amount of testosterone in the blood, which, in turn, influences the aggressiveness (Leshner et al., 1973).

There is good evidence that the serotoninergic neural circuits may influence aggressive behavior in both animals and humans. (See Pank-

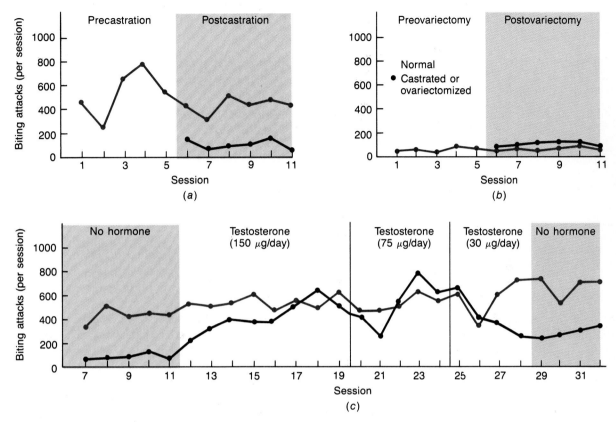

Figure 13-14
Behavioral effects of castration and testosterone replacement therapy in mice. *a.* Male behavior before and after castration. *b.* Female behavior before and after removal of the ovaries. *c.* Effects of hormone replacement on attack behavior of castrated males. (Adapted from Wagner et al., 1980.)

sepp, 1986, for a review.) Serotonin appears to inhibit many forms of aggressive behavior, including predation and offensive and defensive attack (Sheard, 1983). Decreased serotonin turnover (the term *turnover* relates to the rate of release and syntheses of serotonin) has been associated with aggressive behavior in rats (Valzelli & Garattini, 1972). Additionally, drugs that inhibit the release of serotonin, such as PCPA (para-chloro-phenylalanine), tend to increase aggressive behavior. People with a history of violent behavior and people who have attempted suicide by violent means have lower than normal serotonin turnover (Edman, Åsberg, Levander, & Schalling, 1986; Yaryura-Tobias & Neziroglu, 1981).

Pleasure and Reward Systems

We have seen that there are specific brain mechanisms that control rage and aggression. Are there similar mechanisms that make us "feel good" and provide a sense of reward? The answer appears to be yes. However, as was true for other forms of emotion, we have some difficulty in defining our terms. Just what do we mean when we say that an experience was pleasurable or rewarding? One problem we have defining positive emotions is that in some instances the very same stimulus that produces a pleasurable effect may at other times and under different conditions accomplish just the opposite effect.

Think of the following example. You are very hungry, and someone offers you one of your favorite desserts. (In my case there is no contest here—it's chocolate cheesecake with a large topping of freshly whipped sweet cream.) Eating your favorite dessert while you are hungry can be pleasurable. However, how would you respond to a large serving of your favorite dessert if you had just completed an enormously heavy meal, or if you had a severe case of stomach flu? What was pleasurable under one set of circumstances can be quite aversive in another.

For our purposes it is better to deal with the term *reinforcing* rather than *pleasurable*. We can consider some event to be reinforcing if it is likely to elicit some form of behavior. From this point of view *eating* food is reinforcing, not the presence of food. That is, we focus on the occurrence of observable behaviors rather than the stimuli that may, or may not, elicit the behaviors. This approach avoids some of the pitfalls of stimuli that appear to be motivating in one set of conditions but not another.

Brain Structures Associated with Reward

Direct stimulation to the brain can be used as reinforcement. (See the observation on "Serendipity and Discovery.") In fact, animals will work harder and longer for direct stimulation to some reward-inducing structures in the brain than they will for more natural forms of reinforcement such as food or sex. The apparent strength of the various reward-evoking structures varies widely; some are only mildly reinforcing, whereas others are potently reinforcing. Figure 13-15 shows some of the laboratory techniques that have been used to study the effects of direct stimulation to reinforcement-inducing areas of the brain.

Unlike natural reinforcers, the reinforcement derived from brain stimulation does not seem to produce normal satiety. Rats and monkeys have been known to press a lever thousands of times an hour for direct stimulation to the brain. Apparently, they stop only when fatigue prevents them from continuing. (This may be attributable to the fact that no consummatory response is made.) Animals will choose direct stimulation to the brain over other forms of reinforcement. For example, rats that were kept on a near starvation diet or deprived of water chose direct stimulation to the brain more often than they chose access to food or

Figure 13-15
Several laboratory techniques used to study the reinforcing properties of direct stimulation to the brain. *a.* The self-stimulation technique. The animal receives a short train of electric pulses to the brain after pressing the lever. *b.* Maze-running technique. The rat receives a limited number of electrical stimulations at one end of the maze and then must go to the other end of the maze for additional stimulation. *c.* Runway. The rat must cross a grid floor that shocks the feet to receive brain stimulation. *d.* T maze. The animal chooses between a natural reinforcement (food) and direct brain stimulation.

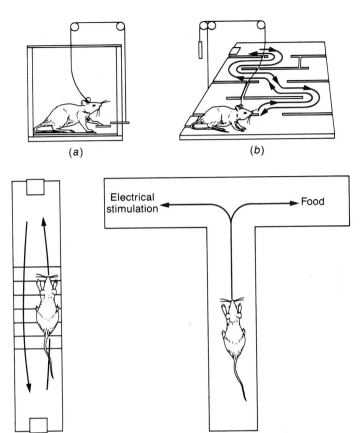

water. Additionally, animals have endured considerable punishment in the form of shock to the feet to gain access to brain stimulation (e.g., Spies, 1965; Valenstein & Beer, 1962).

An Observation:

Serendipity and Discovery

I am often amazed at how frequently important scientific discoveries occur in seridipitous ways. In 1954, James Olds and Peter Milner were investigating the aversive effects of electrical stimulation on parts of the reticular formation in rats. Unfortunately—or fortunately—there was an error made in the placement of one of the electrodes, and the tip missed its target by several millimeters. (The electrode was most likely placed somewhere in the hypothalamus. The exact location of the electrode placement is not known, because the brain was lost, and no histological confirmation of its placement could be made.)

In their research, Olds and Milner had been testing their animals in an open field. The animals were connected to the stimulator by a flexible wire and were free to move about in the enclosure. Typically, the animals avoided locations in the open field where they had been given stimulation that produced an aversive effect. Below is Olds's description of the response of the animal that had received the errant electrode.

> I applied a brief train of 60-cycle sine-wave electrical current whenever the animal entered one corner of the enclosure. The animal did not stay away from the corner, but rather came back quickly after a brief sortie which followed the first stimulation and came back even more quickly after a briefer sortie which followed the second stimulation. By the time the third electrical stimulus had been applied the animal seemed indubitably to be "coming back for more." (Olds, 1973, p. 81)

Olds and Milner were quick to recognize that they had stumbled onto something important. They later implanted electrodes into the brains of rats and placed the animals into an operant chamber that would allow the rats to press a lever in order to administer their own stimulation. The researchers found that some rats would press the lever hundreds of times an hour just to receive a brief train of electric pulses after each response. Later Olds carefully mapped what he termed the "pleasure centers" of the brain.

The list of structures known to reinforce behavior is quite large, including many areas of the limbic system, as well as some midbrain and cortical structures (Olds & Fobes, 1981). However, most of the brain structures known to be reinforcing are part of the evolutionarily older forebrain and midbrain structures (see Figure 13-16). The strongest and most reliable effects of electrical stimulation are found within targets in the **medial forebrain bundle (MFB)**. This group of fibers runs along the sagittal axis of the brain. The MFB contains long ascending and descending axons that interconnect forebrain and midbrain structures. There are also many shorter axons that connect areas adjacent to the sagittal pathway of the fiber tract. Additionally, serotoninergic and catecholaminergic fibers that course from the brain stem to forebrain and mid-brain regions pass along the tract of the MFB. The large number, complexity, and diversity of fibers coursing along the MFB make inter-pretation of the stimulation data quite difficult. However, two general conclusions do seem possible. First, the portion of the MFB that courses through the lateral hypothalamic area produces the most consistently reinforcing effects. Second, as you will see shortly, the catecholaminergic fibers within the MFB appear to be those most central to emotional behavior.

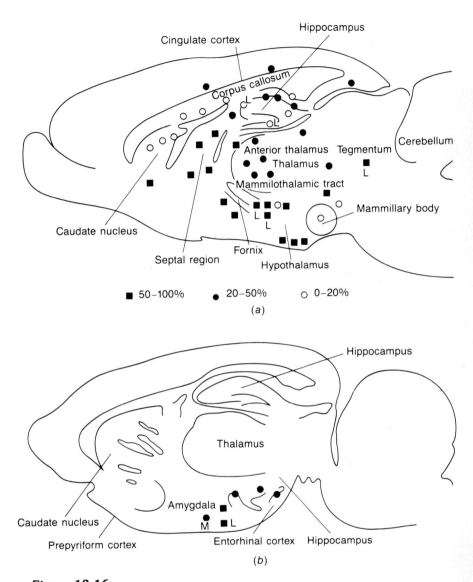

Figure 13-16
Reinforcing centers in the rat brain. *a.* Sagittal section near the midline of the brain showing loci that support self-stimulation. *b.* Sagittal section 2 to 3 mm lateral from figure *a.* (Redrawn from Olds, 1956.)

Humans have had the opportunity to self-stimulate various areas of the brain. As you might imagine, the number of cases is quite limited. In the 1960s, Heath implanted stimulating electrodes in the brains of several patients who had a variety of behavior problems, including narcolepsy, epilepsy, and uncontrollable aggressiveness. The patients were provided with a portable stimulator that allowed them to self-stimulate at will. The stimulators were also configured so that they would record the number of stimulations (Heath, 1963).

Unlike laboratory animals, humans can tell us what they experience when their brains are stimulated. The subjective experiences of one patient who had several electrodes implanted in a number of target sites is particularly instructive. Electrodes placed in the septal area were reported to be most rewarding and produced a "good" feeling that was similar to building up to sexual orgasm. Other sites produced feelings of euphoria, a dizziness akin to drunkenness, anger, and frustration. It is interesting that humans do not become slaves to the stimulation, as is seen in laboratory animals. They are able to control the stimulation quite well, and the frequency of stimulation decreases as the "novelty" decreases. In fact, the site in one patient that was stimulated most was actually mildly aversive. However, stimulation there (the electrode was in the centromedial thalamus) produced a feeling similar to having a memory on the "tip of your tongue" but being unable to bring it out. Apparently, the patient's frequent stimulation of this area was his attempt to bring out the elusive memory.

Neurochemistry of Reinforcement

We have seen that direct stimulation to a number of locations in the brain will reinforce specific behaviors. A careful examination of the location of these reinforcement-generating sites shows that they tend to cluster along a few neural pathways. This fact has caused some researchers to believe that reinforcement may be limited to just one or a few neurotransmitters (Gallistel et al., 1985).

CATECHOLAMINES

The first of the neurotransmitters to receive attention as the possible candidate for reinforcing circuits was the catecholamine norepinephrine (Stein & Ray, 1960). Animals will self-stimulate with electrodes placed in the locus coeruleus, a noradrenergic nucleus in the pons. Additionally, amphetamines, which are agonists for norepinephrine, facilitate self-stimulation. However, later research (e.g., Cooper, Konkol, & Breese, 1978; Phillips, Van der Kooy, & Fibiger, 1977) showed that the norepinephrine hypothesis was a false direction.

Attention then shifted to dopamine, the other catecholamine neurotransmitter. Dopaminergic fibers pass along the MFB near the lateral hypothalamus. Electrodes placed in this location produce particularly strong episodes of self-stimulation. However, when given *sprioperidol*, a dopamine antagonist, these animals stop self-stimulation. Similar effects also occur with a number of other dopamine blockers including pimozide and haloperidol. (See Fibiger, 1978, for a review.) Because dopaminergic circuits are also involved with motor activity, the dopamine antagonist data could be attributed to the influence of the catecholamine blockers on motor behavior and not the reinforcement resulting from the electrical stimulation to the brain. Research by Fouriezos and Wise (1976) show rather clearly that the suppression of self-stimulation is due to the inhibition of reward mechanisms rather than suppression of motor activity.

OPIATES

Although there is general agreement that dopamine circuits are important in reinforcement, most researchers believe that other neurotransmitters must be involved as well. Specifically, endogenous opiates are known to play some role in reinforcement.

You will recall from our discussion of pain perception in Chapter 9 that endogenous opiates—the enkephalins and endorphins—moderate the sensation of pain. You are also doubtlessly aware that opiate substances like heroin, morphine, and methadone are psychoactive drugs capable of causing strong psychological dependency. These facts have caused some researchers to hypothesize that opiate circuits in the brain function in the reinforcement of behavior.

Neurons that contain opiate receptors are known to be in several areas of the brain that have reinforcing effects when stimulated electrically. These include the hypothalamus, the periaqueductal grey matter, the locus coeruleus, and the nucleus accumbens. Research has shown that rats will press a lever to have minute quantities of opiates injected directly into these structures. (The needle of the microsyringe is chronically implanted, with the tip in the target site. The syringe is controlled automatically and injects a fixed amount of the drug when the lever is pressed by the animal.) Additionally, the injection of opiates increases the rate of responding for electrical stimulation. Naloxone, an opiate antagonist, decreases the response rate for electrical stimulation. Together these data provide excellent evidence for an opiate-mediated reinforcement mechanism. (See Olds and Fobes, 1981, and Schaefer, 1988 for a review.)

In this chapter we have reviewed the evolution, anatomy, and biochemistry of emotional behavior. In Chapter 14 we direct our attention to maladaptive behavior—the malfunctioning mind.

CHAPTER SUMMARY

1. Primitive vertebrates have a limited repertoire of emotional behaviors. Both the complexity and the pervasiveness of emotional behavior increase with the complexity of the CNS. More complex emotions are controlled by forebrain structures that are poorly developed or absent in the primitive vertebrates such as the fishes, reptiles, and amphibians.

2. The consistent pattern of emotional development in human infants and the similarity of emotions across various cultures support the notion that emotions are "hard wired" in the human nervous system.

3. There is significant disagreement concerning the definition of emotions. There is even disagreement concerning the number of basic emotions in humans. The *James–Lange theory* proposes that the pattern of physiological response determines the nature of emotional experience. The *Cannon–Bard theory* of emotions stresses the sameness of physiological response to emotional arousal and states that the nature of a given emotional experience is due to the subjective interpretation of the environmental situation.

4. Papez suggested that emotions could not be localized in "centers" in the brain. Papez proposed that emotions were governed by a complex, interacting network of brain circuits. The *Papez circuit* is comprised of many structures that are included in the limbic system.

5. The *autonomic nervous system* can be divided into the *sympathetic* and *parasympathetic* divisions. The parasympathetic division is phylogenetically older and evolved to conserve energy in cold-blooded vertebrates. The sympathetic system evolved slowly in mammals and is used to expend energy in the *flight-or-fight reaction*. The ANS operates in concert with the hypothalamus and endocrine system to control many homeostatic processes such as heart rate, blood pressure, and respiration.

6. The *general adaptation syndrome* proposed by Hans Selye is a three-stage reaction to prolonged physical and psychological stress. The three stages are the *alarm stage*, the *resistance stage*, and the *exhaustion stage*. The symptoms associated with the GAS are gastrointestinal ulcers, thymolymphatic deterioration, and enlargement of the adrenal gland. Early studies that examined the role of control on stress reactions (the *executive monkey studies*) stressed control as an important contributor to the formation of gastric ulcers. Later studies showed that ulcers are due primarily to the parasympathetic rebound following intense emotional arousal.

7. The hypothalamus is a key structure in the control of aggressive behavior. *Affective attack* is controlled by the *anteromedial nuclei* of the hypothalamus. *Predatory attack* is controlled by the *lateral nuclei* of the hypothalamus. The *amygdala* is an important structure in aggressive behavior. In monkeys, bilateral lesions to the amygdala influence the reaction to aggressive social cues that establish and maintain social dominance hierarchies. Other brain centers associated with aggressive behavior include the *septum* and the *periaqueductal grey matter*.

8. Aggressiveness in males is related to levels of *testosterone*. Castration reduces aggressiveness in a variety of mammals, including mice, rats, monkeys, and humans. The therapeutic injection of male sex hormone increases aggressiveness. The level of aggressive behavior is positively correlated with the level of blood serum testosterone. Serotoninergic neural circuits have an influence on aggressive behavior. People with a history of unprovoked violence have lower than normal serotonin turnover.

9. Electrical stimulation to various locations in the brain can be rewarding. Animals will work harder and longer for direct stimulation to the brain than they will for normal reinforcers. Although many structures in the brain have been found to be reward inducing, the most consistent and strongest reward is found with stimulation to the *medial forebain bundle*.

10. Some researchers believe that reinforcement may be limited to brain circuits containing just one or a few neurotransmitters. *Dopaminergic* circuits appear to be central to reward mechanisms in the brain. The fact that *endogenous opiates* are known to moderate the sensation of pain and that opiates like heroin and morphine produce strong psychological dependence has led some researchers to propose an opiate mechanism for reinforcement.

SUGGESTED READINGS

Blanchard, D. C., & Blanchard, R. J. (1988). Ethoexperimental approaches to the biology of emotion. *Annual Review of Psychology, 39,* 43–68.

Lorenz, C. (1966). *On aggression.* New York: Harcourt, Brace.

Levine, P. (1986). Stress. In Coles, M. G. H., Donchin, E., & Porges, S. W., *Psychophysiology: Systems, processes, and applications.* New York: Guilford.

Pribram, K. H. (1981). Emotions. In S. Filskov and T. Boll (Eds.), *Handbook of clinical neuropsychology.* New York: Wiley.

Svare, B. B. (Ed.). (1983). *Hormones and aggressive behavior.* New York: Plenum Press.

Stellar, J. R., & Stellar, E. (1985). *The neurobiology of motivation and reward.* New York: Springer-Verlag.

Valenstein, E. S. (1980). *The psychosurgery debate: Scientific, legal and ethical perspectives.* San Franciso: Freeman.

Weigner, W. A., & Bear, D. M. (1988). An approach to the neurology of aggression. *Journal of Psychiatric Research, 22,* 85–98.

Wilson, E. O. (1975). *Sociobiology: The new synthesis.* (Chap. 11 & 13). Cambridge, MA: Harvard University Press.

KEY TERMS

Affective attack Ragelike behaviors similar to those seen in inter- and intraspecies fighting; *see* Predatory attack.

Basolateral nuclei (amygdala) Part of amygdala that has evolved most recently and is associated with affective attack.

Cannon–Bard theory Theory of emotions which proposes that emotions are centered in higher brain centers rather than in the response of peripheral organs.

Corticomedial nuclei (amygdala) Phylogenetically older part of the amygdala that is associated with predatory attack.

General adaptation syndrome (GAS)   A generalized pattern of stress reactions identified by Hans Selye.

James–Lange theory   Theory of emotions that stresses the physiological response to environmental events as the source of emotions.

Medial forebrain bundle   Tract of fibers that run sagittally along the midline of the brain.

Papez circuit   A complex neural circuit associated with emotions and comprising much of what is now called the limbic system.

Periaqueductal grey matter   Midbrain structure that surrounds the cerebral aqueduct and is associated with aggressive behavior.

Predatory attack   Aggressive behaviors associated with stalking and capturing prey; *see* Affective attack.

Psychosurgery   Neurosurgery that is performed solely to modify behavior.

Septum   Forebrain structure located between the walls of the lateral ventricles; is included in the limbic system and is associated with aggressive behavior.

Sham rage   Aggressive attack behavior that is not directed at a specific object.

Ventromedial tegmentum   Midbrain area below the tectum associated with aggressive behavior.

Malfunctioning: The Abnormal Mind

Chapter Learning Objectives

After reading this chapter, you should

1. Be familiar with the various criteria by which abnormal behavior may be defined.

2. Be able to compare and contrast the organic and functional forms of abnormality.

3. Know how neuropsychological test batteries may be used to diagnose and differentiate between organic and functional abnormal behavior.

4. Be able to describe the new technologies for imaging the living brain, including the CAT scan, the PETT scan, and the MRI.

5. Be able to differentiate between the acute and chronic forms of schizophrenia and be able to cite evidence that they may represent different disease processes.

6. Understand and be able to discuss the evidence for a genetic component in schizophrenia.

7. Be able to review the evidence implicating various brain mechanisms in schizophrenia.

8. Know what evidence supports or fails to support the dopamine hypothesis of schizophrenia.

9. Be able to compare and contrast the unipolar and bipolar forms of affective disorders.

10. Be able to review the biochemical factors associated with affective disorders.

11. Understand how antidepressant drugs moderated the symptoms of depression.

12. Be familiar with the use of electroconvulsive shock therapy to treat depression.

A large and complex brain is in some ways a "two-edged sword." Our large brain provides us with a complexity and diversity of mental abilities unrivaled by any other animal on the face of the planet. However, like any complex system, our large brain is subject to various forms of malfunction. Bigger and more complex machines have a greater number of ways in which to break down. Similarly, the downside of a large brain appears to be an increased risk of malfunctioning.

Abnormal behavior in one form or another has likely been a part of our evolutionary history since before the dawn of human beings. Some of the earliest surviving records indicate that abnormal behavior has always been with us. As early as 3500 B.C. humans had written about the relationship between brain function and abnormal behavior. We noted in the previous chapter that primitive people made holes in the skulls of those whose behavior was viewed as abnormal. We have no way of knowing why these crude attempts at "psychosurgery" were made or if they produced positive or negative effects. Nor do we have any accurate way of determining when "abnormal" behavior evolved.

As noted later in this chapter, abnormal behavior may be due to specific physical abnormalities within the CNS, or it may result from social-psychological factors. It is not unreasonable to assume that many, if not all, of the physical causes of abnormal behavior that are known today predate humankind. Clearly, some forms of physically induced abnormal behaviors (e.g., caused by tumors, epilepsy, infectious disease) have been observed in other species. It is likely that early humans and those who preceded them suffered from similar afflictions.

Some of the nonorganic forms of abnormal behavior (e.g., character and personality disorders, neuroses, substance abuse) may or may not be the modern inventions of a complex society. Maladaptive behaviors are not unknown in primitive cultures. Psychoactive drugs have been used and misused by many primitive peoples. Additionally, behavioral patterns that are very similar to those recognized as abnormal or maladaptive in our own society are seen in almost all of the primitive cultures that have been studied (Murphy, 1976).

What Is Abnormal?

How would you define "abnormal" behavior. For that matter, how would you define "normal" behavior? You may be surprised to discover that the distinction between what is normal and what is abnormal is rarely clear.

The word *abnormal* implies *deviating* from what is commonly observed. However, it means much more than that. For example, very few people have scaled Mt. Everest. Does this fact make that form of behavior "abnormal"? In a statistical sense it does, but it falls short of what we really mean by the term *abnormal*. The word *abnormal* connotes the idea that the behavior is not only uncommon but also in some way *maladaptive* or *self-defeating*. There is also a problem defining abnormal behavior using these criteria. Specifically, whose standards of maladaptive behavior do we use?

Hunting for human heads and eating the brains of your dead relatives is not particularly abnormal if you belong to certain tribes in Borneo. What about the behavior of the terrorist who, in the name of country or religion, plants a bomb in a crowded restaurant, killing dozens of innocent bystanders? Is this abnormal? Consider the behavior of Jean Rath, the self-styled "purple lady." Jean believes that the color purple has "chosen" her. Her home, her car, every piece of clothing she owns is some shade of purple. In all other regards she appears to be no different from most people. Is this benign eccentricity more or less abnormal than that of the headhunter or the terrorist?

Clearly, behavior that is abnormal in one setting may be quite normal in another. If I entered the Metropolitan Opera House during a performance of Verdi's *Aida*, wearing a ball cap, tie-dyed sweatshirt, and jeans and started to jump around and shout out loud, you might consider my behavior quite abnormal. However, the very same behavior at a football game would seem quite appropriate, perhaps even a little subdued.

The definition of *abnormal* also assumes that the behavior has some persistence. Everyone experiences fluctuations in mood. Most people have periods of depression on the anniversary of the death of a loved one. If I am suffering from a high fever, I may become delirious and perhaps experience hallucinations for a few minutes or hours. Immediately after witnessing a horrible automobile accident, a person may become incoherent and highly agitated, and may walk about "wild eyed," yet you are not likely to consider that behavior in that context to be abnormal. These transient deviations from "normal" clearly do not qualify as truly abnormal behavior. (See Gorenstein, 1984, for a review of these issues.)

Finally, the term *abnormal* typically communicates that the individual could benefit from some form of professional intervention—physical or psychological therapy, or some combination of the two.

In summary, abnormal behavior appears to have at least some combination of the following characteristics.

1. The behavior is *statistically* different from that which is seen in the majority of people.
2. The behavior is *maladaptive* or *self-defeating* for the person.
3. The behavior is *inappropriate in a given social context*.
4. The behavior is *relatively long lasting*.
5. Perhaps what is most important, the behavior is perceived to be abnormal by society.
6. Finally, physical or psychological *therapeutic intervention* is often appropriate.

Table 14-1 **Summary of the official diagnostic categories of the major psychiatric disorders.**

1. **Disorders Usually First Evident in Infancy, Childhood, or Adolescence.** Includes mental retardation, hyperactivity, childhood anxieties, eating disorders (for example, anorexia and bulimia), speech disorders, and other deviations from normal development.

2. **Organic Mental Disorders.** Disorders in which the functioning of the brain is known to be impaired, either permanently or transiently; may be the result of aging, degenerative diseases of the nervous system (for example, syphilis or Alzheimer's disease), or the ingestion of toxic substances (for example, lead poisoning or drugs).

3. **Psychoactive Substance Use Disorders.** Includes excessive use of alcohol, barbiturates, amphetamines, cocaine, and other drugs that alter behavior. Marijuana and tobacco are also included in this category, which is controversial.

4. **Schizophrenia.** A group of disorders characterized by loss of contact with reality, marked disturbances of thought and perception, and bizarre behavior. At some phase of the illness, delusions or hallucinations almost always occur.

5. **Delusional (Paranoid) Disorders.** Disorders characterized by excessive suspicions and hostility, accompanied by feelings of being persecuted; reality contact in other areas is satisfactory.

6. **Mood Disorders.** Disturbances of normal mood; the person may be extremely depressed, abnormally elated, or may alternate between periods of elation and depression.

7. **Anxiety Disorders.** Includes disorders in which anxiety is the main symptom (generalized anxiety or panic disorders) or anxiety is experienced unless the individual avoids certain feared situations (phobic disorders) or tries to resist performing certain rituals or thinking persistent thoughts (obsessive-compulsive disorders). Also includes post-traumatic stress disorder.

8. **Somatoform Disorders.** The symptoms are physical, but no organic basis can be found and psychological factors appear to play the major role. Included are conversion disorders (for example, a woman who resents having to care for her invalid mother suddenly develops a paralyzed arm) and hypochondriasis (excessive preoccupation with health and fear of disease when there is no basis for concern).

9. **Dissociative Disorders.** Temporary alterations in the functions of consciousness, memory, or identity due to emotional problems. Included are amnesia (the individual cannot recall anything about his or her history following a traumatic experience) and multiple personality (two or more independent personality systems existing within the same individual).

10. **Sexual Disorders.** Includes problems of sexual identity (for example, transsexualism), sexual performance (for example, impotence, premature ejaculation, and frigidity), and sexual aim (for example, sexual interest in children). Homosexuality is considered a disorder only when the individual is unhappy with his or her sexual orientation and wishes to change it.

Table 14-1 (Continued)

11. **Sleep Disorders.** Includes chronic insomnia, excessive sleepiness, sleep apnea, sleepwalking, and narcolepsy.

12. **Factitious Disorders.** Physical or psychological symptoms that are intentionally produced or feigned. Differs from malingering in that there is no obvious goal, such as disability payments or the avoidance of military service. The best-studied form of this disorder is called Münchausen syndrome: the individual's plausible presentation of factitious physical symptoms results in frequent hospitalizations.

13. **Impulse Control Disorders.** Includes kleptomania (compulsive stealing of objects not needed for personal use or their monetary value), pathological gambling, and pyromania (setting fires for the pleasure or relief of tension derived thereby).

14. **Personality Disorders.** Long-standing patterns of maladaptive behavior that constitute immature and inappropriate ways of coping with stress or solving problems. Antisocial personality disorder and narcissistic personality disorder are two examples.

15. **Conditions not attributable to a Mental Disorder.** This category includes many of the problems for which people seek help, such as marital problems, parent-child difficulties, and academic or occupational problems.

Source: Based on the *Diagnostic and Statistical Manual* (3rd ed.), by the American Psychiatric Association, 1987, Washington, DC.)

Table 14-1 summarizes the categories of abnormal behaviors that are currently recognized by American psychiatrists and clinical psychologists. The table is extracted from the *DSM III-R.*

Functional versus Organic Abnormality

Abnormal behaviors may be classified in terms of their **etiology**, that is, in terms of the causal factors in the pathology. Generally, two broad classes of abnormal behavior have been identified. First, those due to poor adjustment to social or interpersonal factors are called **functional** disorders. The term *functional* is intended to communicate that the behavior, although maladaptive, can be viewed as serving some function from the perspective of the affected individual. Functional maladaptive behaviors are also frequently referred to as "adjustment to life" problems.

The second type of abnormal behaviors are related to physical factors. These are called **organic** disorders. Organic disorders may be caused by a wide variety of factors, including head trauma, genetic defects, reactions to toxic substances, abnormal brain biochemistry, infectious diseases of the central nervous system, chronic abuse of some drugs, vascular disorders (hemorrhage; disruption of arterial or venous flow; and **aneurysms**, or bulges and thinning of the blood vessel walls), tumors, multiple sclerosis, and atrophy related to the aging process (Golden, 1978).

It is often difficult to distinguish between abnormal behaviors that are functional and those having and organic origin (see "Organic or Functional?" observation). There are several reasons for this: (1) The presenting behavior that results from organic problems often appears to be very similar to that seen with functional problems; (2) some organic problems (e.g., tumors, aneurysms, atrophy) may be difficult to diagnose, particularly in their early stages; and (3) organic and functional problems are not mutually exclusive, because patients who have organic problems also have life histories that may be conducive to functional abnormalities.

An Observation:

Organic or Functional?

When I was a graduate student and taking the first of a series of courses in psychopathology, the professor took our class to a state mental hospital some miles from the university. He had prearranged to have several of the patients available and waiting in a small auditorium. The class assignment was for each of the students to, individually, spend 15 to 20 minutes with each patient. We were to conduct a brief diagnostic interview and then meet as a group and diagnose each of the patients in accordance with the mental disorder classification system in use at the time.

There were five patients in all. The first, an elderly woman, laughed continuously and inappropriately to all questions. She was not aware of the correct day or time and instructed us that it was springtime, even though it was really winter. She seemed to be incredibly silly—laughing at every comment or gesture the students made. She reported that she frequently heard voices when there was no one in the room. She believed that the voices were her dead ancestors trying to tell her what she should do. (We diagnosed her as schizophrenia, hebephrenic type.)

The second patient was a very elderly man whose speech was slurred. He gave only one- or two-word responses to our questions. It was very difficult to get him to speak much above a whisper. He knew his first name but wasn't sure about his surname. There was no clear pattern of hallucinations or delusional thought. (We weren't as sure about this one. He was probably an involutional psychotic—psychosis associated with old age.)

The third patient was a young man, perhaps in his late twenties. Speaking to him was like turning on a switch: out came a rush of words—a complex story of mystery and intrigue. According to his story, he was a very powerful person in the CIA who was being held against his will. Radio signals were being transmitted by communists—his eyeglasses were receiving the signals, the signals were controling his mind, the hospital staff were all communists, our conversation was being tapped by a "hard wire triangulating pickup device," the pickup was in the light bulbs so you had to turn off the lights if you didn't want the communists to hear, and on and on. (There was no doubt about this one. He was clearly a paranoid schizophrenic.)

The fourth patient was totally unresponsive. She held her body in an awkward, leaning position. If you moved her arms, she would keep them wherever you put them for a long time, no matter how awkward the position. No effort on our part could get her to respond to any of our questions. (We were confident that this person was a catatonic.)

The last patient was a woman in her late forties or early fifties. She appeared to bear the weight of the world on her shoulders. She told us that God was punishing the world because of her sins. Her insides were rotting away with the "pestilence of the Four Horsemen of the Apocalypse." No one in the hospital could possibly help her. It was God's just will that she suffer this way. What had she done to be in this state? "It's too terrible to say out loud—only God and me know for sure." She thought that she had been in the hospital for 12 to 15 years. In fact, it had been less than 3 months. (We settled on schizophrenia—affective type.)

When we were through, the patients were returned to their rooms, and we reviewed our diagnoses. At that point our instructor notified us that each of the patients was in fact suffering from an organic disorder. Each had been clinically diagnosed as suffering from the advanced stages of a syphilitic infection of the brain. The point he was making is that it is not patently obvious when the etiology of maladaptive behavior is functional, organic, or a combination of the two.

Look at the Venn diagrams in Figure 14-1. Venn diagrams are useful tools for depicting classification schemes. Figure 14-1a is a simple example of how the Venn diagram can be used to provide a pictorial representation of classes of objects. The circle on the right represents all things that are furry, such as fake fur or powder puffs. The circle on the left represents all living animals. Where the two circles overlap, we have

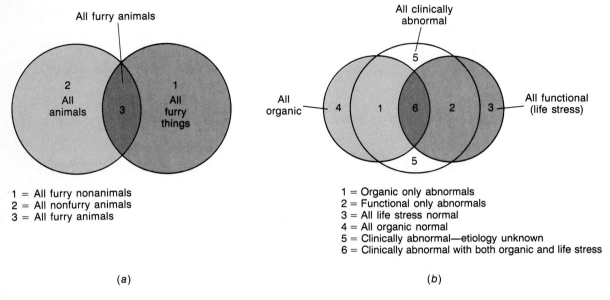

1 = All furry nonanimals
2 = All nonfurry animals
3 = All furry animals

1 = Organic only abnormals
2 = Functional only abnormals
3 = All life stress normal
4 = All organic normal
5 = Clinically abnormal—etiology unknown
6 = Clinically abnormal with both organic and life stress

(a)   (b)

Figure 14-1
a. Venn diagram used to depict classes of objects. *b.* Venn diagram showing the possible groups of individuals who have abnormal behavior. See text for explanation.

all furry animals such as bears, dogs, and giraffes. By elimination, the remainder of that circle includes all nonfurry animals, such as snakes, frogs, and birds. The remainder of the circle on the right contains all nonliving furry things.

Now look at Figure 14-1b. The large oval represents all people who, by whatever criteria we may wish to use, are perceived to be abnormal. The smaller circle on the right represents those individuals who have life histories that are likely to produce functional disorders, whereas the circle on the left represents all people who clearly have organic problems. The areas marked by the numbers 3 and 4 show that some people with organic problems and some people with stress-filled life histories do not have abnormal behavior. The area marked by 5 shows that there will be some people whose behavior is abnormal although they show neither organicity nor a clear pattern of life experiences that could produce a functional reaction. Area 6, in the middle of the figure, represents those people whose behavior is abnormal who have some evidence to support both organic and functional causality. This latter group can be the most difficult to diagnose accurately.

I hope the point is clear that both organic and psychological factors may work either independently or in concert to produce abnormal behavior. The emphasis of this book is on physiological psychology. Therefore, the remainder of this chapter concentrates on the organic causal factors of abnormal behavior. Because of this bias, a large part of the body of literature that deals with personality development, abnormal psychology, and psychiatry cannot be dealt with here.

Neuropsychology   The systematic study of the behavioral effects of brain dysfunction is a relatively new phenomenon. Following World War II, a large number of brain-injured patients were available for study by neurologists, psychiatrists, and psychologists. Research teams like those guided by Alexandre Luria, Hans-Lucas Teuber, Wilder Penfield, Arther Benton, Donald Hebb, Ward Halstead, and others began large-scale projects that attempted to correlate specific behavioral deficits that followed lesions to the brain. The modern discipline of **clinical neuropsychology** developed out of this enormous data base.

Over the years neuropsychologists have developed a wide variety of standardized tests that are used to assess the behavioral losses that occur with organic brain dysfunction. Many of these assessment tools have developed into large standardized test batteries such as the Luria Nebraska and the Halstead—Reitan Battery, which attempt to assess a wide variety of human behaviors.

The test batteries contain many subtests designed to assess one or more forms of behavior. There are subtests for evaluating motor function, sensory processing, receptive and expressive language skills, verbal and quantitative information processing, memory, and abstract thinking. The test batteries contain only those tests that are particularly sensitive to brain injured performance deficits, and therefore they are able to distinguish between functional and organic behavioral problems. No single score on any of the subtests is sufficient for making a diagnosis; rather, the pattern of subtest scores determines the diagnosis.

The processes used for standardizing a neuropsychological test battery are quite complex and beyond the scope of this book. Generally speaking, many subtests that may be included in the test battery are administered to known populations of organic and nonorganic subjects. The scores of the two groups are compared using sophisticated statistical techniques such as factor analysis, and only those tests that can reliably differentiate between the two groups are retained in the final form of the test battery (Costa, 1988; Golden, 1978; Swiercinsky, 1978).

The purpose of the neuropsychological test battery is to do more than differentiate between functional and organic patients. The test battery also attempts to differentiate between focal lesions and more general organic problems such as infectious disorders. When focal lesions exist, the tests are able to quantify the approximate size and location of the lesion.

*Imaging the
Living Brain*

The neuropsychological assessment is an indirect measure of organic dysfunction that relies on the analysis of performance decrements. The specific lesions to the brain may only be inferred from these performance decrements. In recent years there have been enormous technical advances that permit direct examination of the living brain. It is now possible to make images of the brain that provide us with much greater detail than could even be imagined in the 1940s and 1950s. These developments in imaging the brain have also provided us with many new insights concerning the relationships between organic dysfunction and abnormal behavior.

The first effective imaging technique, the X-ray, was of limited value in examining the CNS. The problem with X-rays is that they are so powerful and are not impeded by soft tissues. As you know, X-rays are effective in providing images of dense tissues such as bone and teeth; however, they do little more than provide shadowy images of the other organs in the body.

ANGIOGRAMS

One way to deal with the limitations of the X-ray is to inject radio-opaque substances into the body tissues. This is exactly what is done with the **angiogram**. The opaque dye is injected into the carotid artery while several X-ray exposures are taken. In this manner the flow of the dye through the vascular system can be tracked. This technique is particularly useful for identifying aneurysms and **strokes** (blockages in the blood flow). However, the angiogram does little to enhance the image of structures within the brain (see Figure 14-2).

COMPUTER AXIAL TOMOGRAPHY

In the 1970s computer technology and the X-ray were joined into a new and powerful imaging technique called **computer axial tomography (CAT scans)**. Unlike the conventional X-ray, which is processed on a surface like a photographic plate, the CAT scanner fires pulses of pencil-thin X-ray beams at sensitive detectors. The detectors, which completely encircle the head, measure the amount of X-ray energy that reaches them. Because more dense tissues absorb greater amounts of the X-ray energy, this provides a measure of the density of the tissue in the path of each beam. By making many scans along the same plane, the CAT scanner can provide information about the various densities in a "slice" through the head (see Figure 14-3).

The information from the CAT scanner is processed by a computer that analyzes the differences in the total radiation emitted and the amount that reaches each of the detectors. This requires very sophisticated and powerful computing capabilities, as many thousands of simultaneous equations must be solved. It is interesting that the physical technology required for producing CAT scans existed for several years

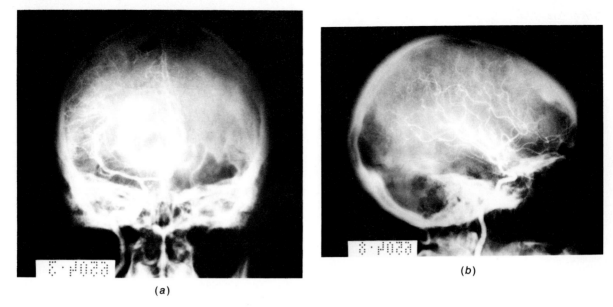

(a)

(b)

Figure 14-2
Two X-ray images of the head following injection of a radio-opaque dye into the carotid artery. The figure on the right shows the right lateral aspect. The left figure is the posterior view following injection of the opaque material into the left carotid artery. (From The American College of Radiology Institute.)

Figure 14-3
The CAT scanner circles the head, directing pinpoint pulses of X-ray energy at the ring of sensitive detectors. By combining many of these tracts, the scanner is able to produce a two-dimensional image of a slice through the brain. Color can be added to enhance the image. (See also Color Plate 17.)

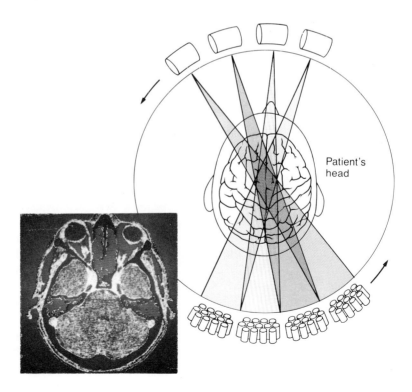

Patient's head

before the technique became practical. The actual production of usable images was dependent on the development of advanced mathematical algorithms and computer programs for processing the digitized data from the detectors.

A new development in CAT scan technology is the dynamic spatial reconstructor (DSR). This highly sophisticated device constructs three-dimensional video images from as many as 75,000 cross sections that are each similar to one CAT scan image. The computer technology then permits the three-dimensional image to be viewed from various angles, or it can be electronically "dissected" so the interior of the tissue can be examined. DSR holds much promise for the future; however, its 3 to 5 million dollar cost is a significant drawback.

NUCLEAR MAGNETIC RESONANCE

The detailed imaging of soft tissues that is possible with the CAT scan is far superior to that which can be obtained with conventional X-rays; however, it pales when compared to the images that are possible with a new technique called **nuclear magnetic resonance (NMR)**. The first time I saw a photograph of the brain using this technique, I literally came out of my seat with excitement. The image looked like a photograph of a real midsagittal slice of a dissected brain.

NMR, which is also called *magnetic resonance imaging (MRI)*, takes advantage of the fact that the nuclei of all atoms have a characteristic spin. By placing the tissue (in this case, the entire head) in a strong magnetic field, it is possible to align the spinning nuclei along the axis of the magnetic field. Then a strong burst of radio-frequency electromagnetic energy is passed through the tissue perpendicular to the magnetic field. This causes the nuclei of each kind of atom in the tissue to resonate momentarily at a characteristic frequency. The resonating nuclei generate a very small current, which can be detected and measured. The detectors can be "tuned" to pick up the energy emitted by the specific resonant frequency of only one kind of atom. In a process not unlike the CAT scan, the NMR takes measurements from several directions. A sophisticated computer analysis combines the information from each measurement and creates a two-dimensional image (Fullerton & Cameron, 1985). (See Figure 14-4.)

An added attraction of the NMR technique is that it does not subject the patient to the potentially harmful effects of X-rays. NMR technology is quite expensive, and for this reason it is still in very limited use.

POSITRON EMISSION TRANSAXIAL TOMOGRAPHY

The imaging techniques we have discussed so far provide information concerning the anatomy of the brain. Other ways of imaging the brain can provide information about the ongoing processes within the

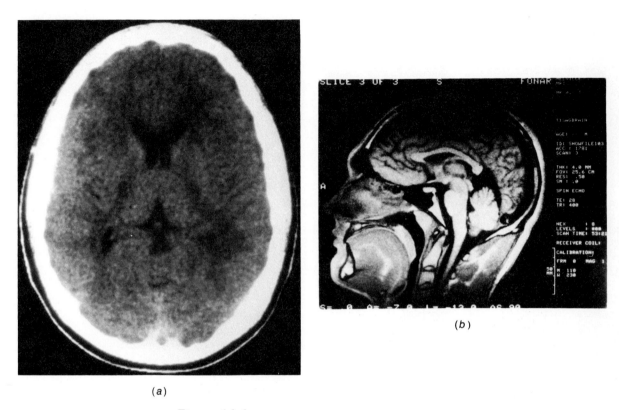

(a)

(b)

Figure 14-4
Nuclear magnetic resonance images. (a) Horizontal section, and (b) the midsagittal section of the brain. (See also Color Plate 19.)

brain. These imaging techniques, such as **positron emission transaxial tomography (PETT scan)**, utilize unstable radioactive isotopes that are injected into the patient. The isotopes are tracked as they are carried through the brain in the bloodstream.

The isotope used in the PETT scan emits positrons (positive electrons). The positrons collide with electrons. The collision causes the two particles literally to annihilate each other. This very small, but spectacular, explosion releases energy in the form of gamma rays. A circular array of detectors records the emission of the gamma activity. A computer interprets these data and produces an image of a slice through the brain. The specific slice that is imaged is determined by the position of the detector array (see Figure 14-5).

In some PETT scans a radioactive form of glucose is injected into the blood. Glucose is the primary source of energy for metabolism in the CNS. The radioactive isotope of glucose is carried by the blood to all parts of the brain. Greater levels of radioactivity are correlated with the

Figure 14-5
Positron emission trans-
axial tomography (PETT
scan) of the brain. (See
also Color Plate 18.)

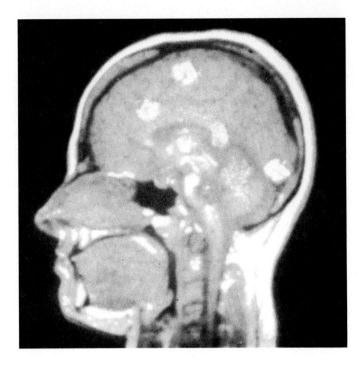

rate of blood flow, which is, in turn, interpreted as indicating those areas of the brain that have higher levels of metabolic activity. Thus, we have a noninvasive technique for measuring the activity of various structures in the brain. For example, an area of very low or no activity could indicate necrotic (dead) tissue. An area of very high intensity may indicate the location of a particularly active tumor.

PETT scanning is still somewhat experimental, but it has already provided information about the brain that was never before available. As discussed later in this chapter, PETT scans have been particularly useful for examining variations in the patterns of brain activity of mental patients.

Schizophrenia

Schizophrenia is a serious form of **psychosis** that affects as many as 2 million people in the United States (Holden, 1987), or between 1 and 2% of the entire population. The term *schizophrenia*, however, is one of the most misunderstood and misused words in the psychological vocabulary. There are at least two reasons for this. The diagnostic criteria used by psychiatrists and clinical psychologists to define schizophrenia are vexingly broad and in some cases inconsistent. Second, the term *schizophrenia* comes from the Greek and literally means "split mind." Because of this, many nonprofessional people think that the term is synonymous with "split (multiple) personality" or that it refers to people who have had the corpus callosum severed. The *schizo* part of the term actually refers to splitting off from or loss of contact with reality.

Classification of Schizophrenic Disorders

There are a number of kinds of schizophrenia. Each subtype is determined by a somewhat different pattern of symptoms. A common theme in all forms of schizophrenia is that the person, at times, experiences delusions (strong beliefs that are not based on fact), hallucinations (sensory experiences in the absence of sensory input), and bizarre ideation. These are the so-called **positive symptoms** of schizophrenia. Additionally, schizophrenics show a lack of emotional expression, and they fail to interact socially with other people; these are the **negative symptoms**. They are given this name because they represent behaviors that are present in normal individuals but absent in schizophrenics. Also, the abnormal behavior is severely incapacitating and often chronic, and it always warrants professional intervention. The following interview with a chronic paranoid schizophrenic illustrates the delusions and bizarre thinking associated with this particular form of schizophrenia.

THERAPIST: What are you doing here?

PATIENT: Well, I've been sent here to thwart the Russians. I'm the only one in the world who knows how to deal with them. They got their spies all around here though to get me, but I'm, smarter than any of them.

TH: What are you doing to thwart the Russians?

PT: I'm organizing.

TH: Whom are you going to organize?

PT: Everybody. I'm the only man in the world who can do that, but they're trying to get me. But I'm going to use my atomic bomb media to blow them up.

TH: You must be a terribly important person then.

PT: Well, of course.

TH: What do you call yourself?

PT: You used to know me as Franklin D. Roosevelt.

TH: Isn't he dead?

PT: Sure he's dead, but I'm alive.

TH: But you're Franklin D. Roosevelt?

PT: His spirit. He, God, and I figured this out. And now I'm going to make a race of healthy people. My agents are lining them up. Say, who are you?

TH: I'm a doctor here.

PT: You don't look like a doctor. You look like a Russian to me.

Imaging the Brain at Work

Is it possible to take a picture of mental activity? Not in the same sense as taking a photograph of a solid object. However, it is possible to make images that show the dynamic pattern of brain activity as the brain goes about sensing, thinking, directing actions, and solving problems.

The technique used to accomplish this is similar to that used in making PETT scans (see the discussion of positron emission transaxial tomography in this section). Subjects inhale a radioactive isotope of xenon gas (xenon-133). The xenon is taken into the blood from the lungs in the same way that oxygen is transported from the lungs to the blood. The radioactive substance moves through the brain, and as was true with the PETT scan, higher concentrations of radioactivity are correlated with increased metabolic activity. Unlike the PETT scan, which makes images of a slice of the brain using a ring of detectors, this technique surrounds the head with many individual detectors. Each detector measures the radioactivity in just the one small area of brain at which it is focused. These data are converted by the computer into a measure of blood flow for the specific location (Ingvar & Lassen, 1974).

Spotlight Figure 14-1 shows data taken from a number of subjects under a variety of mental conditions. Each drawing in the figure is of the left side of the brain, with the anterior part of the brain facing to the left. The dark circles represent those parts of the brain that have blood flow rates that are 20% or higher than the average for the entire surface of the brain. The open circles represent places where the blood flow is 20% or lower than average. The number in the small boxes represents the mean blood flow rate for the entire hemisphere of the brain. (Note that in the resting condition [upper left figure] the blood flow tends to be higher in the anterior part of the brain.)

The figures marked Sens 1 and Sens 2 represent the pattern of blood flow for low-intensity and high-intensity tactile stimulation on the contralateral side of the body. The figure labelled *hand* represents the pattern of blood flow when the subject voluntarily moves the right hand. Note the patterns of brain activity for the four kinds of verbal tasks; talking, reading, reasoning (verbal problem-solving task), and a digit span recall task. Clearly, different kinds of mental activity depend on different patterns of brain activity.

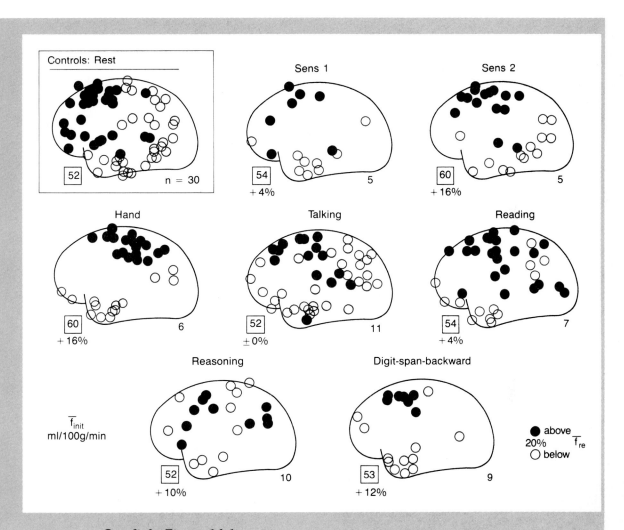

Spotlight Figure 14-1
The pattern of blood flow during various forms of mental activity. See text for
explanation. (From Ingvar, 1979.)

TH: How can you tell a Russian from one of your agents?

PT: I read eyes. I get all my signs from eyes. I look into your eyes and get all my signs from them.

TH: Do you sometimes hear voices telling you someone is a Russian?

PT: No, I just look into eyes. I got a mirror here to look into my own eyes. I know everything that's going on. I can tell by the color, by the way it's shaped. (Coleman, Butcher, & Carson, 1980, p. 407)

The progress of schizophrenia appears to take one of two courses. **Acute schizophrenia** (sometimes called *reactive* schizophrenia) has a rapid onset that may be followed by several periods of remission of the symptoms. In many cases the onset of acute schizophrenia can be related to a recent and particularly traumatic experience or set of experiences. **Chronic schizophrenia** (sometimes referred to as *process* schizophrenia) develops much more slowly, with few if any periods of normalcy following the onset of the disease. Of the two, the prognosis for chronic schizophrenia is much worse. There is considerable debate among psychiatrists concerning the nature and etiology of these two forms of schizophrenia. Central to this debate is the basic question over whether or not the acute and chronic forms of schizophrenia represent two variations of what is essentially the same disease or two totally different disorders of the brain. I discuss this issue later in this chapter.

Genetics and Schizophrenia

Schizophrenia tends to run in families. This fact could be attributed to genetic causal factors, or it is quite possible that environmental/experiential factors are at work. It is also possible that both genetic and environmental factors may play some role. That is, there may be some people who have a genetic "predisposition" for schizophrenia that is triggered by certain environmental events.

TWIN STUDIES

If it could be demonstrated that schizophrenia is truly inherited like diabetes or hemophilia, this would be a powerful statement in support of the notion that schizophrenia has an organic, rather than environmental, origin. The incidence of schizophrenia in the population is just about 1 to 2%. That is, 1 to 2 people in 100 are likely to be diagnosed as being schizophrenic at some point in their lifetime.

If you have a brother or sister who is schizophrenic, the chances that you too will have the disease are 10 times greater than that observed in the general population. The risk factor jumps to 50 times greater than

Figure 14-6
Lifetime risk of developing schizophrenia for individuals with different levels of genetic relatedness. (The genetic relatedness of individuals having two schizophrenic parents cannot be expressed as a percentage; however, it approximates the relatedness for identical twins.) (From Nicol & Gottesman, 1983.)

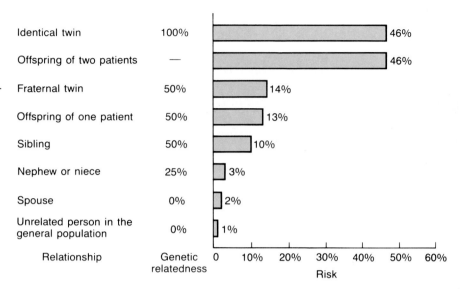

Relationship	Genetic relatedness	Risk
Identical twin	100%	46%
Offspring of two patients	—	46%
Fraternal twin	50%	14%
Offspring of one patient	50%	13%
Sibling	50%	10%
Nephew or niece	25%	3%
Spouse	0%	2%
Unrelated person in the general population	0%	1%

the population incidence rate if you have an identical twin that is diagnosed with schizophrenia (Gottesman & Shields, 1976; Nicol & Gottesman, 1983). Figure 14-6 shows the risks (**concordance**) of developing schizophrenia for individuals with different levels of genetic relatedness.

Fraternal (dizygotic) twins have one half of their genetic inheritance in common and have a concordance for schizophrenia of 15%. Identical (monozygotic) twins share the same genotype. However, the concordance for schizophrenia in monozygotic twins is about 50%. This is quite high, but it is not a perfect concordance rate. (Often the nonschizophrenic twin of a schizophrenic person evidences other, but less severe, abnormal forms of behavior.) Clearly, schizophrenia is a heritable trait, but its development is not controlled in a simple way. This point is highlighted by the fact that schizophrenia and handedness appear to be related in some as yet unknown way. The concordance for schizophrenia in monozygotic twins who have the same preferred hand (both right-handed) is about 92%. However, the concordance drops to only 25% for monozygotic twins that differ in handedness (Boklage, 1977).

The phenotypic expression of schizophrenia is not free from environmental influences. The famous Genain sisters are a case in point. The Genains are identical quadruplets, all four of whom have been diagnosed as being schizophrenic. (The probability of this occurring purely by chance is about one in one billion!) The age of onset of the schizophrenic symptoms and the severity of the disease both vary widely between the sisters. Researchers believe that these differences reflect subtle differences in the individual experiences of the four women.

PEDIGREE STUDIES

A landmark study of the heritability of schizophrenia was done in Denmark by Kety, Rosenthal, Wender, and Schulsinger (1968). The Danish government maintains exceptionally complete family records, which allowed the researchers to identify both the biological and adopted families of schizophrenic patients. The researchers found that the incidence of schizophrenia in the adopting families of the patients was no different from that normally expected in the general population. This could be interpreted to mean that environmental factors had little or no effect on the occurrence of the disease. The researchers did find an unusually high incidence of schizophrenia in the patients' biological parents. These data provide strong support for a genetic causal factor in schizophrenia. An additional finding is particularly instructive. The researchers found that the genetic factor only held for patients who had the chronic form of schizophrenia and not for those diagnosed as acute schizophrenics. They interpreted this result to mean that chronic and acute schizophrenia may have different causal factors.

Other studies have provided evidence for a genetic causal factor for schizophrenia (e.g., Gottesman & Shields, 1976; Heston, 1966). One recent study of a small group of individuals in a remote area of Sweden is particularly enlightening (Wetterberg, 1982). Apparently, a small number of families settled this remote area of Sweden about 350 years ago. The remoteness of the village resulted in the frequent intermarriage of relatives. The population, which now numbers about 6,000 has, by chance, a large incidence of schizophrenia. The risk for children in this group of people is 10 times that of other populations. Fortunately, much is known about the history of these people, and very complete pedigrees have been developed. The people in the last three generations have all been observed by professionals; therefore, the incidence of schizophrenia is well documented. Figure 14-7 is the pedigree for one such family.

Brain Mechanisms in Schizophrenia

Most people who have suffered from chronic schizophrenia evidence neurological symptoms that suggest a neurological disorder. There is now considerable evidence that brain deterioration in some form is associated with chronic schizophrenia.

Postmortem studies of the brains of mental patients who had been hospitalized for some time have shown that the brains of chronic schizophrenic patients have more signs of damage than do the brains of other mental patients, including those who suffered from the acute form of schizophrenia (e.g., Benes, Davidson, & Bird, 1986; Bogerts, Meertz, & Schönfeldt-Bausch, 1985; Stevens, 1982). Specifically, there are signs of decreased numbers of neurons. As you might predict, the loss of neurons tends to be most noticeable in limbic system structures including the hippocampus, amygdala, and the hypothalamus—structures associated with emotional behavior. Additionally, postmortem examination shows

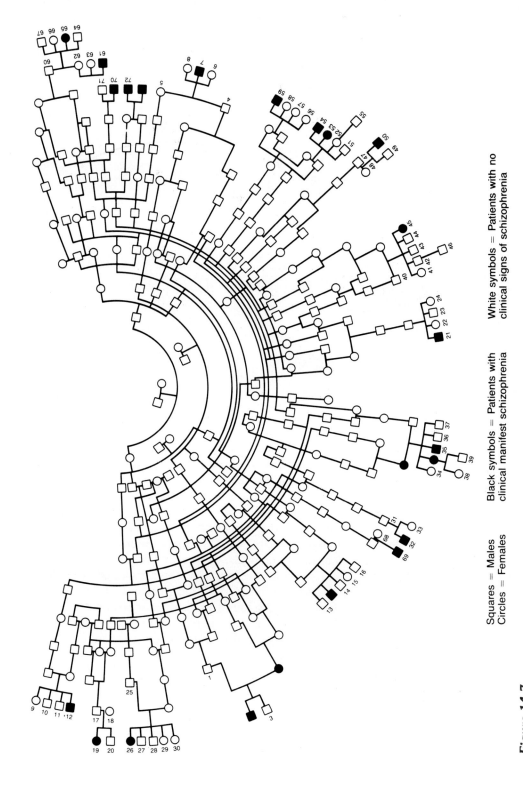

Figure 14-7

The pedigree for one family showing the genetic relationship among schizophrenic patients. Only those individuals in the last three generations (the outer three semicircles) were examined for schizophrenia. (From Wetterberg, 1982.)

Squares = Males
Circles = Females

Black symbols = Patients with clinical manifest schizophrenia

White symbols = Patients with no clinical signs of schizophrenia

Figure 14-8
Cross section of the hippocampus of (a) two normal people and (b) two people diagnosed with chronic schizophrenia. (From Bogerts, Meertz, & Schönfeldt-Bausch, 1985.)

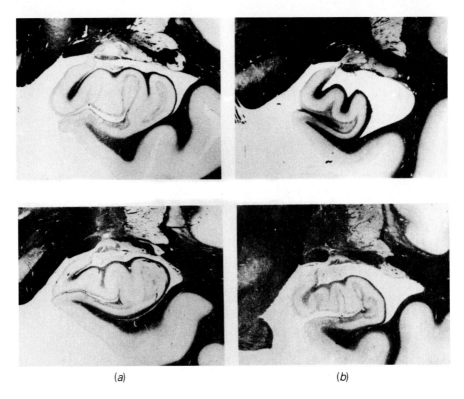

(a)   (b)

that the brains of schizophrenic patients weigh about 6% less than those of other mental patients (Brown et al., 1986). (See Figure 14-8.)

Several studies have found evidence for brain damage in living schizophrenic patients. CAT scans have shown rather clearly that ventricle size tends to be larger in schizophrenics than in other mental patients or normal controls (e.g., Stratta et al., 1989; Weinberger & Wyatt, 1982). The **ventricular brain ratio (VBR)**, that is the size of the ventricular space relative to brain tissue mass, is greatest for chronic schizophrenics (Rossi et al., 1988). Because the increase in ventricular size could not be attributed to increased cerebrospinal fluid pressure, it can be assumed that the increase in the VBR found in chronic schizophrenics is due to atrophy of the brain tissues. Researchers have also demonstrated pathological development of the **limbic allocortex** (Jakob & Beckmann, 1986) and of the **entorhinal cortex** (Falkai, Bogerts, & Rozumek, 1988) and the corpus callosum (Stratta et al., 1989) of chronic schizophrenic patients with the use of CAT scan and NMR techniques (see Figure 14-9).

Studies of blood flow in the brains of chronic schizophrenic patients suggest the presence of problems with brain metabolism. For example, Ariel et al. (1983) found reduced blood flow in all brain regions of schizophrenics. Gur et al. (1985) found a consistent imbalance in blood flow between the right and left hemispheres in chronic schizophrenic

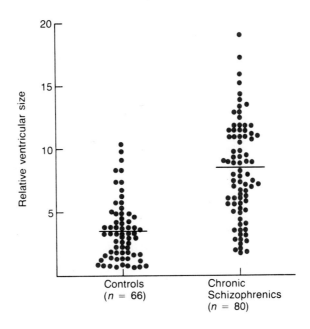

Figure 14-9
The relative ventricular size in chronic schizophrenics and controls. (From Weinberger & Wyatt, 1982.)

patients. Others have found that schizophrenics evidence unusual patterns of blood flow during a variety of tasks. (See Mirsky and Duncan, 1986, for a review.) Although there is no general concensus regarding the interpretation of these disturbances of blood flow, there seems to be agreement that blood flow abnormalities are one indication of the pathophysiology of schizophrenia.

Biochemistry of Schizophrenia

We have seen that schizophrenia is most likely an inherited disease, that its expression may be influenced to some degree by environmental factors, and that there are clear organic concommitants in the brains of people who suffer from the disease. In the 1950s it was found that the symptoms of schizophrenic patients could be moderated with antipsychotic drugs. These drugs produce their effects by changing the biochemistry of the brain. We now examine the biochemical factors that influence schizophrenia.

THE DOPAMINE HYPOTHESIS

In 1950, Henri Laborit, a French surgeon, was testing antihistamine drugs that would control dangerously low blood pressure during surgery. One such drug, promethazine, had the unusual effect of reducing presurgical anxiety without producing mental confusion. Encouraged by this finding, Laborit collaborated with Paul Charpentier, a chemist with a French pharmaceutical company. It was Charpentier who later developed **chlorpromazine**, which would later prove to be particularly effective for treating the symptoms of schizophrenia (Snyder, 1974). (Drugs have a chemical name, a family name, and a trade name under which they are marketed. Chlorpromazine is one drug in a family of drugs called **phenothiazines**. The trade name for chlorpromazine is Thorazine.)

After encouraging laboratory tests on animals, chlorpromazine was tried on a variety of mental patients. The drug had little effect on neurotic patients or those with affective (mood) disorders, but it was remarkably effective for reducing hallucinations and thought disorders in schizophrenics (Delay & Deniker, 1952a, 1952b). The use of chlorpromazine and other antipsychotic drugs spread widely in the mid-1950s. Perhaps the best metric of their usefulness is the fact that the number of hospitalized schizophrenics in this country had steadily increased since the turn of the century; however, with the widespread adoption of antischizophrenic drugs, that trend was stopped and actually reversed.

A large number of drugs are now in use for treating the symptoms of schizophrenia. Most of these drugs belong to three families of drugs; (1) the **phenothiazines**, (2) the **butyrophenones**, and the (3) **thioxanthenes**. Figure 14-10 shows most of the commonly used antischizo-

Figure 14-10
Antischizophrenic drugs. The drugs are arranged along the horizontal axis in terms of the average daily dose prescribed to elevate the symptoms of schizophrenia. (The horizontal lines indicate the dosage range.) The vertical axis indicates the amount of drug required, in moles per liter, to achieve a given degree of postsynaptic blocking of dopamine receptors. (Redrawn from Seeman, Lee, Chau-Wong, & Wong, 1976.)

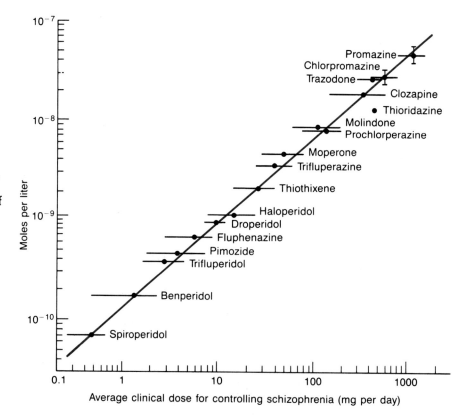

phrenic drugs. They are listed from lower left to upper right in order of their average daily prescribed dose. What do these drugs have in common? They all block postsynaptic dopamine receptors, and they block the release of dopamine from the presynaptic membrane. They are, therefore, dopamine antagonists (Pickar et al., 1986; Sahebarao et al., 1988).

It is interesting to note that antipsychotic drugs appear to be much more effective in eliminating the positive symptoms of schizophrenia than they are the negative symptoms (Angrist, Rotrosen, & Gershon, 1980). Additionally, it has been observed that schizophrenic patients having brain deterioration, as indicated by enlarged ventricles, are less responsive to antishizophrenic drug therapy than patients who do not evidence brain damage (Weinberger et al., 1980). It would appear that the negative schizophrenic symptoms (lowered affect and social withdrawal) are related to brain deterioration and that these two factors, negative symptoms and brain deterioration, are associated with a poor response to chemotherapy and a poor prognosis for eventual recovery.

The data shown in Figure 14-10 show that there is a clear correlation between a given drug's ability to block dopamine and its effectiveness in alleviating the symptoms of schizophrenia. This is a powerful argument to support the **dopamine hypothesis** of schizophrenia. The hypothesis states that schizophrenia is due to excessive activity of dopaminergic neural pathways in the mesolimbic system, a tract of fibers that project from the midbrain tegmentum to the limbic system. Therefore, drugs that retard the activity in these neural pathways relieve schizophrenic symptoms (e.g., White & Wang, 1983). (Refer to Figure 14-11.)

Figure 14-11
Dopamine pathways in the brain. (Redrawn from Iverson, 1979.)

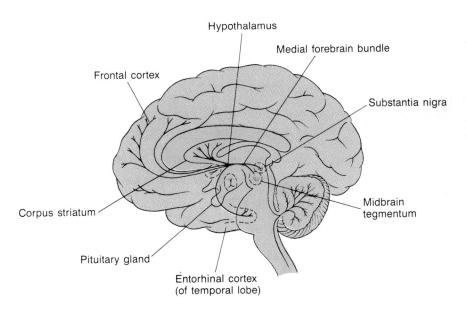

SPOTLIGHT 14-2

Tardive Dyskinesia—A Vicious Cycle

Antischizophrenic drugs reduce the symptoms of schizophrenia; they do not "cure" the disease. For this reason the patient usually must continue the chemotherapy for many years, if not the remainder of their life. Unfortunately, many drugs that have therapeutic value also produce unwanted side effects. **Tardive dyskinesia** (literally, late-appearing movement disorder) is a particularly serious side effect that occurs with the prolonged use of some antischizophrenia drugs.

Tardive dyskinesia occurs because the drug therapy retards the levels of dopamine in the brain. The target neurons for dopamine "compensate" for this lowered level of dopamine by increasing the number of dopamine receptors on the membrane. After prolonged use of the antischizophrenia drugs, the number of receptors becomes so great that the postsynaptic cells become extremely sensitive to even the smallest levels of dopamine. Because dopamine receptors in the basal ganglia produce movement, the increased sensitivity to dopamine in this part of the brain causes abnormal motor behavior in the form of bursts of involuntary movement. The motor dysfunction usually begins with jerky, ticlike movement of the tongue and face. However, as the condition worsens, the whole body may be affected.

Once the symptoms of tardive dyskinesia become apparent, the motor dysfunction is permanent. Withdrawal from the drug therapy does nothing to eliminate the motor abnormality. In fact, discontinuing the use of the antischizophrenic drug causes the symptoms of tardive dyskinesia to *worsen*! Why should this be so? Discontinuing the dopamine blocker allows the dopamine levels to increase but does nothing to reduce the abnormally high number of dopamine receptors. The only way to treat tardive dyskinesia is to *increase* the dosage levels of the dopamine antagonist, the same drug that caused the motor dysfunction in the first place! This will, in turn, increase the sensitivity to dopamine by increasing the receptor sites, and the viscious cycle continues.

Fortunately, new drugs have been developed that seem to reduce the potential danger of tardive dyskinesis. These drugs, including clozapine and thioridazine, appear to be more focused in the location of their site of action. They effectively block the dopaminergic circuits in the mesolimbic system but have little effect on the dopamine circuits that innervate targets in the basal ganglia. For this reason they effectively reduce the symptoms of schizophrenia but are less likely to produce tardive dyskinesia.

Is there any other evidence that would support the dopamine hypothesis? Consider the following:

1. Amphetamines, L-DOPA, and methylphenidate—drugs that produce the opposite effect of chlorpromazine—can induce schizophrenic symptoms if administered in high dosage levels (Lickey & Gor-

don, 1983). You may recall that L-DOPA, which is a precursor for dopamine, is used to treat Parkinson's disease. One of the negative side effects of this treatment is the production of schizophrenia-like symptoms.

2. Dopamine levels in the cerebrospinal fluid are higher in schizophrenics; however, the elevations are not very impressive.

3. The number of dopamine receptors, particularly the D_2 autoreceptors, tend to be higher in schizophrenics (e.g., Cross, Crow, & Owen, 1981; Williams et al., 1986; Wong et al., 1986). (Autoreceptors are neurotransmitter receptors located on the same neuron that secretes the neurotransmitter. Although the possible function of the additional D_2 receptors in schizophrenics is not well understood, these data do implicate dopamine in the disease process.)

4. Drugs that block the synthesis of dopamine facilitate the effect of antischizophrenic drugs.

It must be noted that not all patients diagnosed as being schizophrenic respond to antischizophrenic drugs. In fact, about 20% of the schizophrenic patients do not respond to dopamine-blocking agents. This fact does not negate the dopamine hypothesis. Rather, it suggests that there may be more than one form of schizophrenia—a dopaminergic form and one or more others that are less well understood (Herbert, 1982; Holden, 1987). It is also important to recall that there is still some confusion concerning the relationship between the chronic and acute forms of schizophrenia. It is not at all clear whether these disorders represent two forms of the same disease or two totally different diseases having independent origins and outcomes. Psychiatrists have struggled with this problem for some time. Some acute or reactive forms of schizophrenia may reflect functional reactions to life stressors and problems in social development. These "learned" maladaptive behaviors are less likely to be responsive to chemotherapy and may represent a significant portion of those patients that are insensitive to dopamine antagonists. (See Mirsky and Duncan, 1986, for an extensive review of the etiology of schizophrenia.)

Affective Disorders

In clinical terms, the word *affective* relates to mood or feelings. The major affective disorders are characterized by abnormal deviations in mood. We have all at times been depressed or greatly agitated. It is not abnormal to be depressed for some time following the loss of a loved one. Nor is it abnormal to feel euphoric in anticipation of a particularly pleasing experience. What differentiates affective disorders from normal variations in mood is that the mood state is often not related to events in the environment. The person's intense mood state may come to dominate the total of his or her conscious life, and it may result in loss of contact with reality. It has been estimated that approximately 5% of all people will suffer from a major affective disorder at some time in their lives.

Classification of Affective Disorders

Generally, affective disorders are differentiated in terms of the type and pattern of the abnormal mood state. At one end of the spectrum there are people who have inappropriate feelings of extreme elation (**mania**). They tend to be excessively active and talkative, and are generally a blur of activity. The level of euphoria does not seem to be justified by the circumstances. Frequently, these people will maintain high levels of activity for long periods, sometimes working feverishly on projects that are impossible to complete. They may go without sleep for days. The following excerpt from an interview with a 60-year-old manic woman should give you a feel for the mental state of an individual experiencing intense mania.

> (Singing) By yon bonny briefs—my briefs are entirely outrageous but God take me you'd best like it—(in normal voice) the world is round the world is crown'd—illusions of Georgie, once a porgie— can't you see?—I am worth more than all the cherries in the universe—red is beautiful, red is ripe—bow ye before me and receive my blessing—thank God I'm not the devil—the freshest thing on this earth is a newborn clod—to work is to win—twin is as twin does—I sing a song of sexpot—hand me your head on a platter and I will forgive all your sins—my plan will earn you a hundred-thousand-fold—mishmoshmoneymash—slippery-dicherypop—damn it all full speed abreast—my head is gold, my hands are silver, my tail is platinum—Where am I? What time is it? Who goes there? Gee, but it's marvelous to be alive ... (Suinn, 1970, p. 367)

The other end of the mood spectrum is depression. Again, what differentiates abnormal depression from normal event-related depression is that the mood does not fit the circumstances. Pathologically depressed individuals may become very lethargic, complain of nonexisting physical problems, lose their appetite, evidence abnormal sleep patterns, and have uncontrollable fits of crying. Additionally, they may withdraw from social contact, lose sexual interest, and communicate only when questioned. Frequently, they are riddled with guilt and feel great personal responsibility for the ills that face them and the people around them. The following excerpt from an interview between a therapist and a 47-year-old institutionalized male is indicative of the mental processes of a deeply depressed patient.

> (After several attempts to greet the patient without a response.)
> THERAPIST: What seems to be your trouble?
> PATIENT: ... There is just no way out of it ... nothing but blind

alleys ... I have no appetite ... nothing matters anymore ... it's hopeless ... everything is hopeless.

TH: Can you tell me how your trouble started?

PT: I don't know ... it seems like I have a lead weight in my stomach ... I feel different ... I am not like other people ... my health is ruined ... I wish I were dead.

TH: Your health is ruined?

PT: ... Yes, my brain is being eaten away. I shouldn't have done it ... If I had my willpower I would kill myself ... I don't deserve to live ... I have ruined everything ... and it's all my fault.

TH: It's all your fault?

PT: Yes ... I have been unfaithful to my wife and now I am being punished ... my health is ruined ... there is no use going on ... (sigh) ... I have ruined everything ... my family ... and now myself ... I bring misfortune to everyone ... I am a moral leper ... a serpent in the Garden of Eden ... why don't I die ... why don't you give me a pill and end it all before I bring catastrophe on everyone ... No one can help me ... It's hopeless ... I know that ... it's hopeless. (Coleman, Butcher, & Carson, 1980, p. 374)

Generally, severe affective disorders are divided into two types: (1) **bipolar affective disorders** and (2) **unipolar affective disorders**. The **bipolar disorder** is characterized by alternating periods of mania and depression. The episodes of mania may last a few days or may extend to a month or more before they run their course. The alternating periods of depression usually are longer lasting. **Unipolar depression** is, as its name suggests, depression without the periods of mania. The depression may be continuous, or more commonly, it is characterized by long periods of depression with periods of apparent remission. For reasons that are not well understood, unipolar depression is more common in women. Mania in the absence of depression is quite rare (Coleman, Butcher, & Carson, 1980).

Genetic Factors in Depression

As was true for schizophrenia, there is good evidence that affective disorders may be inherited. That is, affective disorders tend to run in families. Close relatives of people who suffer from affective disorders are 10 times more likely to develop these disorders than are people who do not have relatives with affective disorders (e.g., Rosenthal, 1971; Smeraldi et al., 1979; Weissman et al., 1984). The concordance rate for bipolar depression in monozygotic twins is 67%. The concordance rate for fraternal twins drops to 16%—much less than that for monozygotic twins, yet far greater than what would be expected by chance (Slater & Cowie, 1971).

These data make a strong case for the genetic predisposition to acquire affective disorders. However, they do not eliminate the contribution of environmental factors. A more compelling case for a genetic causal factor for affective disorders comes from the study of adopted children. Children who were adopted at an early age into families without a history of affective disorders but whose biological parents were afflicted with the disease are much more likely to develop affective disorders than what would be expected in the normal population (Wender et al., 1986).

The case for the role of genetics in affective disorders is quite clear. However, the disease does not appear to be inherited in a simple way. For example, it is not uncommon for an individual with no familial history of affective disorder to develop the disease, nor is it uncommon for people with a clear family history of affective disorders to be normal. As we noted with schizophrenia, it is likely that both organic and environmental factors, jointly or independently, have some role in the etiology of affective disorders. (See Loehlin, Willerman, and Horn, 1988, for a review of genetic factors associated with psychopathology.)

Brain Mechanisms in Depression

Unlike schizophrenia, there is little direct morphological evidence that can shed much light on the brain mechanisms that account for affective disorders. There are, however, several sources of data that suggest major depression may be associated more with left brain, rather than right brain, dysfunction.

People with lesions to the left brain are more likely to develop symptoms of depression and pessimism. Conversely, right brain damage is more likely to produce emotional blunting or euphoria (Davidson, 1984). EEG recordings typically show more right brain activation when normal people deal with cognitive problems. Depressed patients show exactly the opposite pattern of hemisphere activation. PETT scans made of patients during episodes of mania show clearly that the overall metabolic activity of the brain is elevated. During periods of depression the metabolic activity falls below normal. This is particularly true for the metabolic activity in the left frontal lobe (Baxter et al., 1985) and the left dorsal prefrontal cortex (Baxter et al., 1989).

Although these data are difficult to interpret, they do provide some evidence that the patterns of activity in the working brains of depressed and manic patients are not the same as those observed in the normal population. The primary problem for interpreting these data is not unlike the "chicken and egg" problem. That is, we can ask what came first—the abnormal behavior or the abnormal pattern of brain activity? Does the abnormal behavior produce the unusual pattern of brain activity, or does the abnormal pattern of brain activity produce the unusual behavior?

Biochemistry of Depression

In the late 1950s and early 1960s it became apparent that affective disorders could be treated effectively with chemotherapy. The activity of two classes of neurotransmitters, the catecholamines (norepinephrine, epinephrine, and dopamine) and serotonin, seemed to be most central to the process of affective disorders. Drugs that decreased the biological activity of catecholamines reduced the symptoms of mania. Drugs that increased the activity of the catecholamines and/or serotonin moderated the symptoms of depression. (See Schildkraut and Kety, 1967, for a review.) This led to a rather simplistic view of affective disorders which basically maintained that mania and depression were, respectively, the result of an excess or deficiency of catecholamines and serotonin. Unfortunately, the story is a bit more complex than that.

THE MONOAMINE HYPOTHESIS OF DEPRESSION

The catecholamines and serotonin are grouped together chemically with all other **monoamine** molecules (molecules that have a single amine group NH_2). The idea that the monoamine neurotransmitters could be related to emotional behavior was actually stumbled on in a somewhat serendipitous way. It was noted that *reserpine*, which was originally prescribed to treat high blood pressure, had an unwanted side effect: it caused severe depression in 10 to 15% of the patients to whom it was administered. (Why reserpine does not cause depression in all patients is not known.)

At about the same time it was noted that *iproniazid*, a drug used to treat tuberculosis, caused many patients to feel euphoric. It wasn't long before researchers put these two facts together to form a **monoamine hypothesis of depression**. Reserpine lowered the amount of catecholamines at the synapse, and iproniazid produced the opposite effect (see to Figure 14-12).

The monoamine hypothesis at first received widespread acceptance; however, more recent data have cast some doubt on the role of

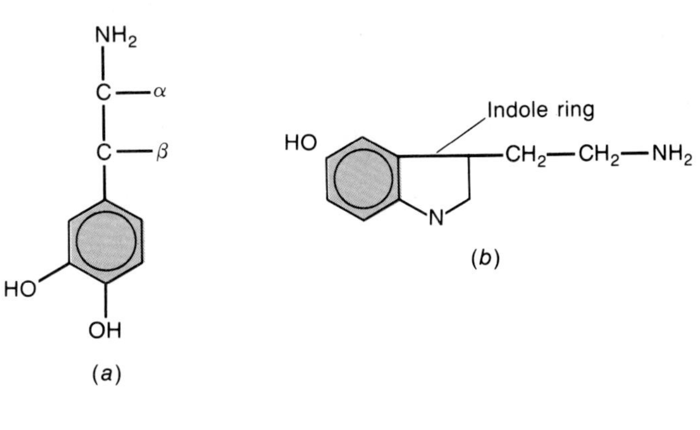

Figure 14-12
The catecholamine molecule (*a*) and the serotonin molecule (*b*) have the single amine group, which makes them both monoamines.

(a)

(b)

monoamines in depression. Two families of drugs have been shown to be particularly effective in treating unipolar depression: the **tricyclics** and the **monoamine oxidase inhibitors (MOAIs)**. Both families of drugs, it was thought, produce their antidepressant effect by increasing the amount of monoamines available at critical synapses in the brain. As you will see, this is not necessarily the case.

MOAIs slow the breakdown of monoamine transmitters and thus increase their concentrations at the synapse. The picture for the effect of MOAIs became somewhat clouded, however, when it was found that some depressed patients responded better to drugs that primarily affect the catecholamines, whereas others were more responsive to drugs that had a greater effect on serotonin (Gastpar, 1979). Could it be that some forms of depression are due to reduced levels of serotonin, whereas others due to depleted levels of catecholamines? Is depression perhaps attributable to an imbalance in the proportion of both transmitter substances.

Some of the tricyclics block the reuptake of catecholamines and in this way prolong the effect of the transmitter. However, some tricyclics have no known effect on catecholamine levels. It turns out that all of the tricyclic drugs that are effective antidepressants do have one common attribute—they block **histamine** receptors (Kanof & Greengard, 1978). Histamine is known to be a neurotransmitter in the medial forebrain bundle. You will recall that stimulation in this part of the brain is reinforcing. The MOAIs *do not* affect histamine. To complicate the picture a bit more, some drugs known to block histamine receptors apparently have no effect on the symptoms of depression (Maayani, Hough, Weinstein, & Green, 1982).

What are we to make of these inconsistent and apparently contradictory findings? Apparently, monoamines (catecholamines and serotonin) and/or histamine are important in unipolar depression. Whether or not this means that there are two or more separate biological causal factors of unipolar depressed states cannot be determined at this time; the answer awaits further research.

MOAIs and tricyclic drugs are not effective for the treatment of bipolar affective disorders. The preferred treatment for these disorders are light metallic ions. The most effective and most commonly used treatment is **lithium** in the form of lithium carbonate (Li_2CO_3). Lithium ions are known to affect catecholaminergic and cholinergic neurons as well as amino acid transmitters (Fieve, 1979). However, there is no satisfactory explanation for why lithium is clinically effective. The fact that lithium is an effective treatment for bipolar depression but not unipolar depression, whereas the tricyclics and monoamine oxidase inhibitors are effective for treating unipolar but not bipolar depression, is a good indication that these two forms of affective disorder have different biological bases (see Table 14-2).

Table 14-2 Suspected Biochemical Factors of Abnormal Behavior

Abnormality	Suspected Neurotransmitter	Most Effective Drug
Schizophrenia	Dopamine	Dopamine antagonists phenothiazines, butyrophenones, and thioxanthenes
Unipolar depression	Norepinephrine Serotonin Histamine (?)	Tricyclics, MOAIs
Bipolar depression	Norepinephrine	Lithium

ECT and Depression

We discussed the effect of ECT on memory in Chapter 10. You may recall from that discussion that ECT was first used in clinical settings to treat a variety of psychotic behaviors. Over a period of years the effectiveness of ECT for treating most forms of abnormal behavior came into question. This form of treatment did prove to be particularly effective for reducing the symptoms of depression. The use of ECT remains relatively common. However, with the advent of effective forms of chemotherapy, the frequency with which ECT is used has dropped markedly.

Because ECT is known to produce memory loss, you may wonder why it is still in use when depression can be treated with chemotherapy. There seem to be two principal reasons for the continued use of ECT. First, there is a significant delay between the onset of chemotherapy and the reduction of the symptoms of depression. The delay may be as much as 2 to 3 weeks. Depressed patients present a significant risk of suicide. For these reasons ECT is often prescribed to obtain more immediate results that will protect the patient. Second, for reasons that are not known, some patients do not respond well to chemotherapy. ECT is seen as the only viable form of treatment for these patients (Paul et al., 1981).

After more that 50 years of continuous use there is still no satisfactory explanation for how ECT reduces the symptoms of depression. An electric shock that is strong enough to produce seizures probably affects the biochemistry of the brain in more ways than we know. The use of ECT is likely to continue until more rapid acting forms of chemotherapy are discovered.

CHAPTER SUMMARY

1. Defining what is abnormal behavior is a complex task. Typically, the term suggests that the behavior is statistically different, maladaptive, self-defeating, inappropriate in the given setting, or relatively long lasting, and that it requires professional intervention.

2. Abnormal behaviors can be classified in terms of the *etiology* of the disease. *Organic* abnormality is due to dysfunction of the brain. *Functional* abnormality is thought to be due to problems associated with adjustment to life. It is difficult to distinguish between functional and organic forms of abnormality simply by observing the overt behavior.

3. *Neuropsychology* is a relatively new area of study that is concerned with the relationships between brain dysfunction and abnormal behavior. *Neuropsychologists* typically use standardized test batteries to distinguish between abnormal behaviors that have an organic, versus a functional, etiology. Neurological test batteries are able to detect the existence, extent, and location of brain dysfunctions.

4. Emerging technology has resulted in the development of many new ways to make images of the brain. Some of these imaging techniques, such as the *angiogram, CAT scans,* and *MRI,* provide detailed pictures of the brain's anatomy. Other imaging techniques, such as the *PETT scan,* are able to provide images of the ongoing activity of the brain. These new imaging techniques hold great promise for the better understanding of brain function and behavior.

5. Psychoses are serious forms of mental disease. Schizophrenia is a relatively common form of psychosis that affects between 1 to 2% of the population. There are several variants of schizophrenia; however, the disease is usually characterized by *delusions, hallucinations,* and *bizarre ideation* (the *positive symptoms*). Additionally, schizophrenics usually evidence a *lack of emotional expression* and *social withdrawal* (the *negative symptoms*).

6. *Acute schizophrenia* has a rapid onset and may be followed by periods of remission. *Chronic schizophrenia* develops more slowly and is much more resistant to treatment. There is some evidence that these two forms of schizophrenia have different causes and outcomes and in fact represent two distinct forms of mental illness.

7. There is strong evidence from *pedigree studies* and the study of *monozygotic* and *dizygotic* twins that some forms of schizophrenia are genetically determined. There is a clear relationship (*concordance*) between the degree of genetic relatedness of relatives and the probabilty of developing the disease. Exactly how genetic factors cause schizophrenia is poorly understood. It is likely that the phenotypic expression of the genetic "predisposition" for the disease is under the influence of environmental factors.

8. Postmortem examinations and measurements of the brains of living schizophrenics both show morphological evidence of the disease. The loss of neurons and an increase in the ventricular *brain ratio* (*VBR*) indicate atrophy of the brain in chronic schizophrenics.

9. The discovery of effective antischizophrenic drugs such as the *phe-*

nothiazines, the *butyrophenones*, and the *thioxanthenes* provides good evidence for a biochemical factor in some forms of schizophrenia. All of these drugs act as antagonists for dopamine. The *dopamine hypothesis* states that schizophrenia is due to excessive activity of dopaminergic neural pathways in the mesolimbic system. Not all schizophrenic patients respond well to dopamine blockers, suggesting that there is more than one form of biochemical factor associated with schizophrenia.

10. *Affective disorders* are characterized by abnormal mood or feelings, with *mania* at one end of the spectrum and *depression* at the other. Affective disorders are divided into two types: *bipolar affective disorders* and *unipolar affective disorders*. Affective disorders tend to run in families; however, it is likely that both genetic and environmental factors have some role in the etiology of the disease.

11. EEG and PETT scan data indicate that the left brain is involved in depression and the right brain is associated with mania. However, it is not possible to determine whether the abnormal behavior produces the differences in hemispheric activity or vice versa.

12. Drugs that mimic the monoamine transmitters appear to reduce the symptoms of depression. This fact has lead to the *monoamine hypothesis of depression*. In addition to the *catecholamines* and *serotonin*, there is also some evidence that *histamine* levels may affect depression. Drugs such as the *tricyclics* and the *monamine oxidase inhibitors*, which effectively reduce the symptoms of unipolar depression, are not effective for the treatment of bipolar depression. Bipolar affective disorders respond best to light metals such as *lithium*. This finding suggests that the two forms of affective disorder have different biological bases.

13. *ECT* effectively and rapidly reduces depression. There are considerable delays following the onset of chemotherapy for depression and symptom relief. For this reason ECT continues to be used to treat depression, although its mode of action is still unknown.

SUGGESTED READINGS

Beatty, J., Barth, D. S., Richer, F., & Johnson, R. A. (1986). Neuromagnetometry. In M. G. H. Coles, E. Donchin, & S. W. Porges (Eds.), *Psychophysiology: Systems, processes, and applications*. New York: Guilford.

Buchsbaum, M. W. (1983). Psychopathology: Biological approaches. *Annual Review of Psychology, 34*, 401–430.

Dimond, S. J. (1978). *Introducing neuropsychology*. Springfield, IL: Thomas.

Jernigan, T. L., & Hesselink, J. (1985). Human brain-imaging: Basic principles and applications. In R. M. Michels & J. O. Cavenar (Eds.), *Psychiatry*, Philadelphia: Lippincott.

McNeal, E. T., & Gordon, B. (1986). Antidepressants and biochemical theories of depression. *Psychological Bulletin, 99*, 361–376.

Nicol, S. E., & Gottsman, I. I. (1983). Clues to the genetics and neurobiology of schizophrenia. *American Scientist, 71*, 398–404.

KEY TERMS

Acute schizophrenia A form of schizophrenia characterized by rapid onset followed by periods of remission; *see also* Chronic schizophrenia.

Allocortex A term used to refer to primitive cortex such as the limbic cortex and the olfactory cortex.

Angiogram X-ray image of blood vessels that have been injected with radio-opaque dye.

Aneurysm Ballooning and thinning of the walls of blood vessels.

Bipolar affective disorders Maladaptive behaviors characterized by alternating shifts in mood.

Bipolar depression A form of affective psychosis in which the individual has alternating periods of depression and mania; *see also* Unipolar depression.

Butyrophenones Family of dopamine antagonists used to treat schizophrenia.

Chlorpromozine One of several phenothiozine dopamine antagonists used to treat schizophrenia; *see* Thorazine.

Chronic schizophrenia Schizophrenia characterized by slow but steady increase in symptoms. This form of schizophrenia is more resistant to treatment; *see also* Acute schizophrenia.

Clinical neuropsychology The study and treatment of abnormal behavior resulting from organic dysfunction.

Computer axial tomography (CAT scan) X-ray imaging made from thin scanning images that produce a two-dimensional "slice" through the tissue.

Delusions Strong beliefs that are not founded in reality; *see* Positive symptoms of schizophrenia.

Dopamine hypothesis Theory that attributes the symptoms of schizophrenia to excessive activity in dopaminergic neural pathways.

Entorhinal cortex The part of the limbic cortex that communicates with the hippocampus.

Etiology The causes of disease.

Functional (maladaptive behavior) Abnormal behavior that results from psychological, rather than biological, factors.

Hallucinations Sensory experiences in the absence of sensory stimulation; *see* Positive symptoms (schizophrenia).

Histamine A neurotransmitter substance found in the medial forebrain bundle.

Limbic allocortex Simple, four-layered cortex; part of the limbic system.

Lithium An element whose salts are used to treat bipolar affective disorders.

Mania Affective disorder characterized by a euphoric state and high levels of activity.

Monoamine Any complex molecule having a single NH_2 amine group.

Monoamine hypothesis (of depression) Theory that correlates affective disorders with transmitter substances having a single amine group.

Monoamine oxidase inhibitors (MOAIs) A group of compounds that effectively reduce the symptoms of unipolar depression in some patients.

Negative symptoms (schizophrenia) Forms of normal behavior that are absent in schizophrenics, such as normal affect and social interaction.

Neuropsychological test battery Any combination of specific performance tests designed to identify organic dysfunction in the central nervous system.

Nuclear magnetic resonance (NMR) Technique to make images of the brain by detecting the nuclear resonant spin frequency of atoms; also known as magnetic resonance imaging.

Organic (abnormal behavior) Behavior that may be attributed to head trauma, genetics, biochemistry of the brain, or other physical causes.

Phenothiozines Family of dopamine antagonists that are used to treat schizophrenia.

Positron emission transaxial tomography (PETT scan) Imaging technique that detects and measures the concentration of radioactive isotopes in body tissues.

Positive symptoms (schizophrenia) Forms of abnormal behavior observed in schizophrenics, including delusions, hallucination, and bizarre ideation.

Psychoses A generic term usually applied to severe, long-term mental disorders.

Schizophrenia A mental illness characterized by irrational thought, hallucinations, and/or delusions.

Tardive dyskinesia Abnormal involuntary motor activity following prolonged use of certain antischizophrenic drugs.

Thioxanthenes Family of dopamine antagonists that are used to treat schizophrenia.

Thorazine Trade name for chlorpromazine.

Tricyclics A group of compounds that are effective in the treatment of unipolar depression.

Unipolar affective disorders Maladaptive behaviors of mood that do not show alternating patterns of agitation and depression.

Unipolar depression Affective disorder characterized by unwarranted guilt, feelings of poor well-being, disturbances of sleep, and social isolation; *see also* bipolar depression.

Ventricular brain ratio (VBR) The size of the ventricles relative to the remainder of the brain mass.

Chapter 15

Communicating

Evolution of Communication
The Characteristics of Biological Communication
Communication in Primates
The Evolution of Language in Humans

Neural Mechanisms in Language and Speech
Lateralization of Language in the Brain
Brain Mechanisms in Speech
Brain Mechanisms in Language

Chapter Learning Objectives

After reading this chapter, you should

1. Be able to discuss the importance of intraspecies communication as an adaptive form of behavior.

2. Be able to define and give examples of discrete and graded signals in animal communication.

3. Understand how genetic and environmental factors may influence the expression of some forms of human and animal communication.

4. Know what is meant by the term *signal economy* and be able to give specific examples of this concept in animal and human communication.

5. Be able to describe the attempts to teach language to nonhuman primates and be able to provide evidence that supports and evidence that fails to support true language ability in these studies.

6. Be able to discuss the difficulties associated with tracing the evolution of language in humans.

7. Be able to discuss the biological and behavioral evidence for lateralization of language function in the human brain.

8. Understand the difference in language ability evident in people with expressive, receptive, and conduction aphasia.

9. Know the role of Broca's area, Wernicke's area, and the primary motor cortex in speech and language.

10. Know and be able to discuss the evidence that supports the disconnection theory of aphasia.

Evolution of Communication

I want to propose that we do an interesting but absolutely horrible experiment: interesting, because it would tell us something of great importance about the nature and origin of language; horrible, because it would be totally unethical. Suppose that you could take two human infants, immediately after birth, separate them from their parents, and raise them together in total isolation from all other humans by using mechanical robots. Their environment would be a veritable Garden of Eden having all of the resources to sustain the children. The robots would protect the infants and assure that all of their physical needs were cared for. The infants would be fed, cleaned, held, and rocked by the robots. Additionally, all of their medical needs would be attended to so that they could develop and mature into healthy adults.

With the exception of the slight whirring sound of the servo motors within the robots and the natural sounds of their garden environment (animal sounds such as birds singing and insects chirping, wind and rain noise, and so on) each of the developing infants would only experience the sounds produced by him- or herself and the other infant. They would never hear the sound of any other human voice. Twenty-one years after the experiment began, we return to observe the adult pair to determine the outcome of the sole purpose of this admittedly bizarre experiment. Are the two humans communicating with each other? If so, how are they communicating? Let's make a field observation check list. (You may want to make some personal predictions to these questions as you read them.)

1. Yes _____ No _____ Do they make different facial expressions to communicate various forms of emotion such as fear, anger, and affection?
2. Yes _____ No _____ Do they use hand and/or body gestures to signal information?
3. Yes _____ No _____ Do they appear to have specific hand and/or body signals that represent different objects in the environment?
4. Yes _____ No _____ Do they make vocal emissions to communicate emotions?
5. Yes _____ No _____ Do they make different vocal emissions to communicate various forms of emotion such as fear, anger, and affection?
6. Yes _____ No _____ Do they make vocal emissions to communicate to each other when they are not in direct visual contact?
7. Yes _____ No _____ Do they appear to have different vocal emissions for specific objects in the environment?
8. Yes _____ No _____ Do they appear to use vocal emissions and hand gestures in combination?

9. Yes _____ No _____ Do they, at times, use chains or combinations of vocal emissions rather that single emissions?
10. Yes _____ No _____ Does the order of the emissions change under different environmental situations? That is, is the order of the emissions situation specific?
11. Yes _____ No _____ Is the meaning of a given emission dependent on the specific emission that immediately precedes or follows it?
12. Yes _____ No _____ Are the humans using some form of language?

If you are like the students in my classes, you had little or no difficulty indicating yes to the first few questions on this proposed field observation form. These are the forms of communicative behavior that most of us are able to recognize in other, less advanced, animals. However, you may have found it difficult to accept the idea that two humans could develop the more sophisticated forms of oral communication without the benefit of instruction.

The point I am trying to get at here is directly related to the nature–nurture controversy. In this case the question is as follows: Is language in humans innately determined, or is it primarily a learned form of behavior that is passed on via cultural mechanisms? You know from our discussion of the nature–nurture controversy in Chapter 1 that this question, as I have just phrased it, is incorrect. This is not an either/or situation. Rather, language, like most other forms of human behavior, is the result of the dynamic interaction of our genetic potential and our life experiences.

Clearly, no one could deny the fact that the specific language we speak—and to a certain degree, how well we are able to speak it—is determined by environmental factors. That I speak English, German, or Chinese is determined greatly by such factors as where I was born, what language my parents spoke, and the language taught in the school system. How well I am able to use the language is influenced by my socioeconomic level, how well my parents speak, and the quality of my education. The question we are really concerned with here is whether or not there is a genetic predisposition for language.

We will never know whether the two humans in this experiment would develop language. The experiment simply cannot (and should not) be done. We can, however, make some intelligent predictions about the outcome of this experiment based on what we know about communication in other animals and the development of language in children. My own belief (based on the data we will discuss in the remainder of this chapter) is that our isolated humans would indeed be communicating with a complex mixture of facial expressions, gestures, and oral signals. Their expressions of emotion would be similar to our own, and it would not be difficult for us to interpret them. They are likely to have specific visual signals and oral emissions for different events and objects in their environment. Their system of communication may even have some elementary rules concerning the order of symbols; however, I feel somewhat less confident of this prediction.

Would the humans in our experiment be using "language"? I suppose the answer to that question is dependent to some degree on how we define our terms. One of the definitions of language in my desk dictionary is "any set or system of symbols used in a more or less uniform fashion by a number of people, who are thus enabled to communicate intelligibly with one another." If that is what we mean by the term *language*, then I would venture to say that our two humans will have it or at least something that comes very close to that definition. Surely, their communication system (language) would lack the depth and complexity of our own. Don't forget that our dictionaries are filled with words that were passed on to us by many people who are long gone. We have not been required to reinvent the wheel, so to speak. The humans in our experiment would not have the benefit of this long and rich cultural history. Their language would be rudimentary at best, but it would, I believe, be language.

If my prediction is correct, language in humans is truly determined by our genetic composition. Let us see on what data I base this somewhat bold prediction.

The Characteristics of Biological Communication

Biological communication is the action of one organism that alters the pattern of behavior in another organism in a way that is beneficial to the sender or the receiver of the signal. Starting with this very general definition of communication, it is clear that some form of biological communication can be identified even in the most simple organisms. The adaptive advantage of intraspecies communication is so profound that this form of behavior is ubiquitous throughout the animal kingdom. Even single-celled animals that practice sexual reproduction are able to detect and advance toward others of the same species by sensing chemical substances called *pheromones*. This basic form of signal detection is quite clearly adaptive for the survival of these species.

As was true with all the other forms of behavior that we have discussed in this book, intraspecies communication is present in a wide variety of forms and in a wide range of complexity across the various species. Generally, the communication signals produced by different organisms may be shown to have several basic structural characteristics.

DISCRETE SIGNALS

Discrete signals are those that can be given in a simple "on" or "off" fashion. For example, the patterns of bioluminescent flashing produced by different species of fireflies are discrete signals. The males of each species use this visual signal to attract females. The females are only

Figure 15-1
Discrete signals and the sexual communication of fireflies. The flashing and flight paths of the males belonging to nine species of fireflies are shown here as they would appear in a time-lapse photograph. Each species has a distinct, and relatively invariable, flashing pattern. (From Loyd, 1966.)

attracted to the appropriate pattern of flashes. For this reason, the pattern and intensity of flashing for each species are very constant (see Figure 15-1). (It is interesting to note that some fireflies prey on other species of fireflies. The predators evolved to have the ability to mimic the pattern of flashing of the species on which they prey. The females that are attracted to false sexual displays come to an unexpected end.)

Discrete signals have evolved to be progressively less variable (more discrete) because they represent a unique signal for a specific purpose within the species (Morris, 1957). Discrete signals remain constant irrespective of the strength of the stimulus that serves as their trigger. For example, the territorial threat songs of most species of birds do not change in pattern or intensity in order to indicate the level of threat. Rather, the songs are produced in identical ways independent of the strength of the stimulus that elicits them.

GRADED SIGNALS

Graded signals have evolved in a way that increases variability. Variations in intensity and/or duration of the signal may communicate different levels of motivation or intended action. The well-known waggle dance of the honeybee which was first decoded by the German biologist Karl Von Frisch, is an excellent example. When a foraging bee returns to the hive after locating a food source, she communicates this information to the other bees by performing a complex waggle dance. The pattern of her dance is a figure 8 repeated over and over again in the midst of many of her sister workers (see Figure 15-2).

The most cogent part of the dance is the straight run (the middle of the figure 8) where the bee vibrates her body from side to side. The orientation of the straight run communicates the direction to fly relative to the position of the sun. If the bee performs the dance on a horizontal surface, the orientation of the straight run is consistent with the actual position of the sun (Figure 15-2a). However, if the dance is performed on the vertical comb of the dark interior of the hive, gravity is used as the referent (Figure 15-2b). The intensity and duration of the dance communicate the distance to the food source. These distance data are actually encoded in time-to-fly, rather than actual, distance. In this way the information compensates for the effect of the wind. It takes longer to fly the same distance into a head wind than in calm conditions (Frisch,

Figure 15-2
The waggle dance of the honeybee is used to communicate the direction and time to fly to a source of food. See text for an explanation. (Redrawn from Curtis, 1968.)

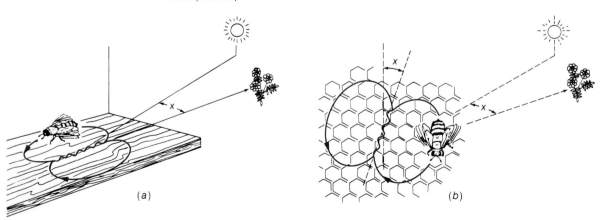

(a)   (b)

1965). (It is interesting to note that if the bee is captured and her return to the hive is delayed, she is unable to compensate for the delay time and will communicate the direction to fly at the time of her capture. The direction of flight taken by her co-workers will be incorrect by the number of degrees the sun moved during the period of her capture.)

An Observation: How to Communicate with an Ant

Many species of ants use chemical trails to guide others of their colony to sources of food. Ants returning to the nest with food attract the attention of other ants and communicate the richness of the food source by tapping the other ants with their antennae. The number of ants activated to follow the trail is determined by the intensity and duration of tactile stimulation. The strength of the chemical trail is also related to the size of the food source, and when the food source is depleted, the returning ants no longer leave a trail (see Figure 15-3).

You can do a little experiment to verify the use of chemical signals in ants. The next time you see ants on the ground, look for individuals that are stepping in the same tacks of those that preceded them. Sometimes you will actually see outbound ants meet returning foragers on the trail. Rub your fingers vigorously across the invisible

Figure 15-3
The active space of the trail of a fire ant at various times after the forager reaches the nest. (Redrawn from Wilson & Bossert, 1963.)

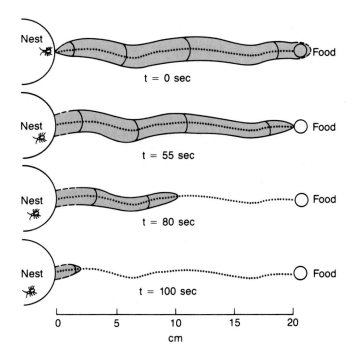

trail and wait for the next outbound ant. The ant will stop abruptly at the break in the chemical trail, backtrack, pick up the trail again, stop at the break again, and so on. When a returning forager lays down a new trail, the interrupted journey of your experimental ant will resume.

Graded communication can be strikingly complex in the aggressive displays of many animals. In the rhesus monkey, for example, the lowest level of aggressive display is the hard stare. (This may explain why staring is considered to be impolite in many cultures.) The level of the aggressive display can be increased by the addition of other components singly or in combination. Standing, opening the mouth, exposing the canine teeth, bobbing the head up and down, and making vocal emissions incrementally increase the strength of the aggressive display (see Figure 15-4). The probability of actual attack increases as the intensity of the display increases. Usually, all levels of the aggressive display come into play before an actual physical attack occurs (Altmann, 1962). Graded communication through facial expression in the African elephant is shown in Figure 15-5.

SIGNAL SPECIFICITY

The communication systems of most animals are characterized by very stereotypical signals. That is, for each signal there is only one or a very limited number of appropriate responses (**signal specificity**). The signals are also stereotypical in the sense that identical signals are used by all individuals of the species.

In Chapter 8 we discussed the remarkable ability of the male silkworm moth to detect the presence of females of that species at considerable distances. The female emits the pheromone *bombykol*, which is a

Figure 15-4
Graded signals in the aggressive display of the rhesus monkey. (Based on description in Altmann, 1962.)

Figure 15-5
African elephants use their trunk, head, and ears expressively to produce graded signals relating to their emotional state. A neutral, resting elephant is shown above for comparison. With the ears forward, as in *a*, the elephant is slightly aroused. In *b*, with the head raised, the animal is more aroused. In *c* the combined elevation of the head and forward position of the ears indicate a third level of arousal. The levels of aggressive mood are shown in *f*, *d*, and *e*. The sequence *f–j* indicates increasing levels of aggressiveness leading to attack. The levels of defensive display are shown in the two sequences below *k*. (From Brown, 1975, redrawn from Kühme, 1963.)

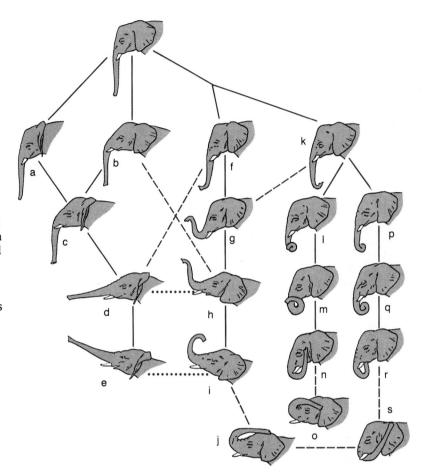

biological agent. The male moth has 10,000 sensory hairs on each of its feathery antennae. Each hair has one or two receptor cells that are receptive to bombykol and *no other substance*. In the adult form, the male silkworm has but one function in life: find a female and mate. The specificity of this chemical signal insures the survival of the species (Schnieder, 1969).

THE INFLUENCE OF ENVIRONMENT ON COMMUNICATION SIGNALS

I noted earlier that environmental factors greatly influence human communication. Learning and experience appear to affect the development of communication in other species as well. Bird song of some species appears to have different "dialects" for groups of individuals found in separated locals (e.g., Marler & Tamura, 1964). (See Figure 15-6.) Additionally, there is good evidence that normal bird song will not

Figure 15-6
Dialects in the white-crowned sparrow populations inhabiting the San Franciso Bay area. The time marker in the bottom left of each figure represents .5 sec. (From Marler & Tamura, 1964.)

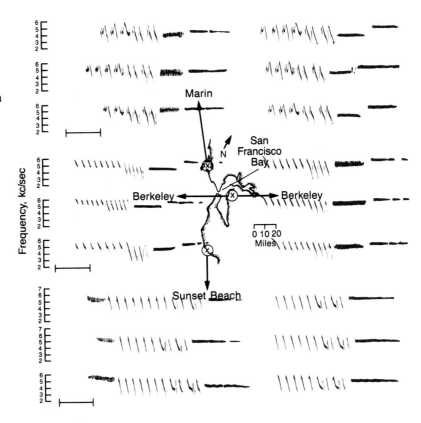

develop in some species unless they experience normal bird song. It has been shown that early deafening or raising of birds with other species changes the vocalizations of ring doves (Nottebohm, 1980). The songs produced by some species of sparrows that are raised in isolation are more simple than the normal adult songs. When deafened as infants, these birds produce even less complex songs than animals raised in isolation (Marler & Peters, 1981). (See Figure 15-7.) Apparently, similar to the development of human speech, the potential for complete communication in birds is built into the brains of these species; however, experience is required for them to reach this potential.

Birds such as parrots, mynah birds, and parakeets are able to mimic many of the sounds that they experience. What adaptive function this special ability has is not clear. It is possible that mimicking the territorial threat songs of other birds may function to drive off the birds of those species that compete for the same resources (Welty, 1975). This phenomenon has not been carefully studied. Nevertheless, mimicry in birds does represent a rather clear example that acoustic experience can have a strong role in the development of bird song. (When I was a boy we had a parakeet that could mimic human voice with remarkable fidelity.

Figure 15-7
The effects of early sound isolation and deafening on the characteristics of the typical song of two species of sparrow. The top row shows the adult pattern, the middle row shows songs produced by males reared in isolation from other birds, and the bottom row shows the song of birds deafened in infancy. (From Marler & Peters, 1981.)

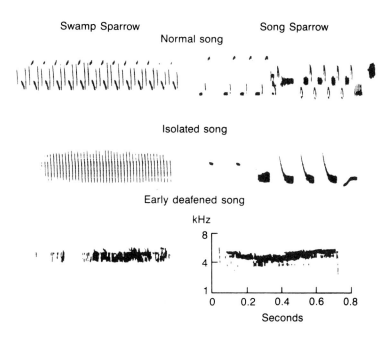

As I recall, his most frequently produced vocalization was, "Eugene, get out of bed!" Why he should have learned that particular utterance is a mystery to me.)

SIGNAL ECONOMY

When evaluated against human standards, the number of signals utilized by any given species seems to be quite limited. Field studies would suggest that even the most social animals have no more than 30 or 40 identifiable displays or signals in their entire repertoire (Moynihan, 1970). Smith (1969) has categorized the various displays and vocalizations of a number of social animals into just 12 "clusters" of messages, as follows:

1. *Identification*: distinguishes individual or species.
2. *Probability*: likelihood that the signaler will follow through with an act.
3. *General set*: components or separate messages that have no independent meaning but indicate that the signaler is very likely to take some unspecified action.
4. *Locomotion*: messages associated with the onset or termination of movement.
5. *Attack*: any hostile act or display.
6. *Escape*: messages emitted when the animal is retreating from an aggressive interaction or aversive stimulus.

7. *Nonagonistic subset*: any signal that communicates that the animal will not attack.
8. *Association*: special messages that are given when an animal is trying to approach another without attempting hostile or sexual behavior.
9. *Bond-limited subset*: messages connected with the formation and maintenance of social bonds, as between a mated pair or infants and parents.
10. *Social play*: used to initiate play.
11. *Copulation*: messages used just before or during copulation.
12. *Frustration*: signals that occur only when the animal is thwarted from the execution of other acts such as aggression and copulation.

The number of signals in human communication seems to be almost limitless. The complexity of human language, however, is not due simply to the number of signals per se. The number of **phonemes**, or smallest units of sound, that make up human language varies from as few as 20 to approximately 60, depending on the specific language and culture. This limited number of phonemes can be ordered in a much larger number of combinations that make up individual words. With the advent of cultural history the number of words has grown at a fantastic rate. The rate of growth has increased even more rapidly with the invention of written symbols to represent the words. (Just 100 years ago words such as *radar, transistor, television, polymer, supermarket, microwave, software, six-pack, rock star, yuppie, acid rain, urban blight*, and thousands more did not exist.)

The complexity of human language is increased further because the order of the words determines their meaning (**syntax**). The sentences "John eats the fish" and "The fish eats John" have totally different meanings. Additionally, the meaning of a given word may change depending on the word that immediately precedes or follows it. For example, the word *rock* has a totally different meaning if it is preceded by *the* versus *to*. The complexity of human language is more attributable to the many ways signals can be ordered and to linguistic rules than it is to the number of signals. Furthermore, true language has **grammar**, a set of rules by which words may be combined. The grammatical rules for various languages vary, but all have some basic rules in common. For example, all grammars distinguish between subject, verb, and object, and they all have ways of distinguishing between present, past, and future. As you will see, true syntax and grammar have not been demonstrated unequivocally in the communication of any other species.

Communication in Primates

Psychologists have a strong interest in primate communication because primates are so closely related to humans. Monkeys and apes communicate using a variety of sensory mechanisms. Olfactory signals are impor-

Figure 15-8
Distinctive facial displays in rhesus monkeys. Different facial patterns are achieved by combinations of graded visual and vocal components. (Redrawn from Hooff, 1962.)

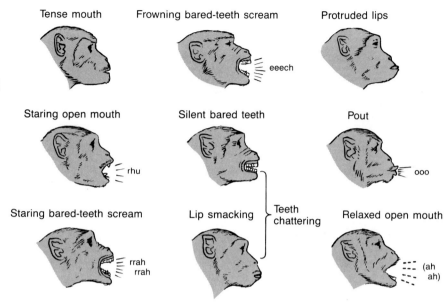

tant in sexual and social behavior. The tactile senses, particularly touch in the form of grooming behavior, play a key function in establishing social bonds. As is the case with most other arborial animals, primates rely most heavily on audition and vision for communication. Most intraspecies communication in primates is determined by graded visual and auditory signals used individually or in combination. Van Hooff (1962; 1967) has identified several "typical" facial expressions that appear to be consistent across a number of monkey species. Graded components of these facial expression include the muscles around the lips, ears, eyes, and nostrils. When combined with vocal emissions, these typical expressions allow for a variety of basic displays and the expression of a large range of emotional intensity (refer to Figure 15-8).

TEACHING CHIMPS TO TALK?

In the early 1950s researchers began to examine the language capabilities of primates in rather unique ways. Researchers began to question whether it is possible that other primates may have linguistic potential approximating that observed in humans. An underlying premise of this research suggests that the natural habitat of other primates does not stretch the limits of their language capablities. Furthermore, if given the same sort of cultural advantages and technical training experienced by humans, other primates could learn to communicate in ways similar to our own language.

The first researchers to address this issue where Hayes and Hayes, a husband and wife team who raised a female chimpanzee as you would raise a human child (Hayes, 1951). The chimp, named Viki, was raised in the home and treated in every way possible like a human infant, which included wearing diapers and eating at the table. Most important, the Hayeses talked to Viki as you would talk to a human child.

The Hayeses found that Viki's motor and cognitive development was more rapid than that of a human infant for the first year. Thereafter, Viki's intellectual development fell well behind. Adult chimpanzees are quite powerful and difficult to handle in a humanlike environment. The Hayeses were forced to stop the project while Viki was still, by human standards, a young adolescent. At that time Viki was able to say (providing the listener had a good imagination) "cup" and a few other words.

The somewhat less than exciting language ability developed by Viki can be attributed to at least three factors. First, chimpanzees do not vocalize spontaneously unless they are very emotionally aroused. Second, the chimpanzee anatomy does not permit them to produce the motor movements necessary to form human speech. The fine neuromotor control of the lips, tongue, and larynx necessary to produce words is simply not available to them. Finally, the position of the larynx in humans is much further back in the throat, allowing for a greater flexibility in the shape of the pharyngeal space. This latter factor is important, because flexibility in the shape of the phyryngeal space is required for producing the many phonemes in human language (see Figure 15-9).

A second husband and wife research team, the Gardners, had seen film of Vicki's vocalizations. They noted that while attempting to communicate vocally, the chimp was also gesturing vigorously. Recognizing the physical limitations of the chimpanzee vocal mechanism, and knowing that chimps use many gestures in the natural setting to communicate, the Gardners determined to try and teach a nonvocal language to a chimpanzee. The language they selected was American Sign Language (Ameslan), the most commonly used language for the deaf in North America.

Washoe, the young chimp selected by the Gardners, learned to model the Ameslan signs with relative ease. She eventually developed a vocabulary of several hundred signs. It is interesting to note that in the beginning Washoe learned signs at about the same rate as do human children (Gardner & Gardner, 1969). However, this may be due, at least in part, to the more rapid motor development of the chimpanzee. Later, she fell well behind. At the age of 4 Washoe had learned 132 signs, compared to the more than 3,000 words a 4-year-old human child might know.

Washoe learned signs for objects (e.g., banana, drink, door), actions (open, give, tickle), and modifiers (more, enough). The Gardners believe there are the beginnings of primitive grammar in the signing observed in Washoe (Gardner & Gardner, 1975). They point to the fact that Washoe produces novel combinations of signs. For example, after learning to combine the signs for "more" and "tickle" (she greatly

Figure 15-9
The human vocal apparatus has been modified in a way that increases the variety of sound that can be produced. The vocal apparatus of the chimpanzee, shown in the upper right, lacks the motor control and the flexibility of the pharyngeal space to produce the phonemes that compose human speech. (Redrawn from Denes & Pinson, 1973; Howells, 1973.)

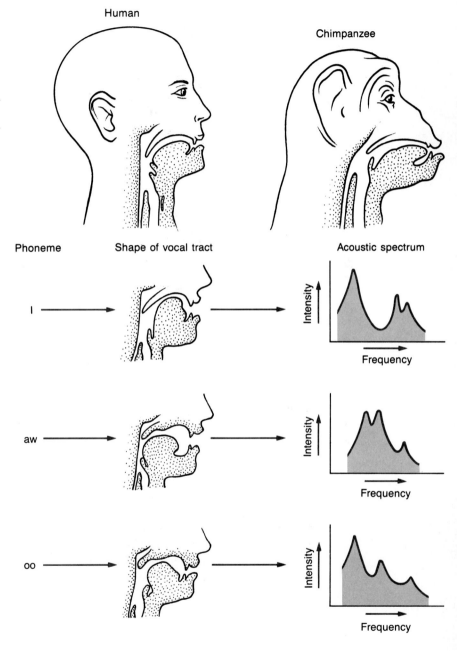

enjoyed being tickled), she later made the combined sign for "more" and "sweet," indicating that she wanted more candy to eat. On the very first occasion that Washoe experienced watermelon, she signed "water—fruit" a combination that had never been linked together previously.

Washoe shows clear signs of generalization. Once having learned "open" for the house door, she later applied the term to other doors such as the refrigerator and automobile doors. It is also interesting that Washoe used signing in the absence of her trainers. Video of Washoe alone in her room shows that she signed to herself (sort of like talking to yourself), and she signed to her toys.

Similar signing abilities have been demonstrated in the gorilla. Penny Patterson has taught a young gorilla, Koko, to use Ameslan. As was true with Washoe, Koko evidences signs of primitive grammar in her use of sign language.

Using another approach, David and Ann Premack have taught several chimpanzees to communicate using plastic symbols placed on a magnetic board (Premack & Premack, 1972). The first of their subjects, a young chimp named Sarah, was trained to associate variously shaped symbols with words and relationships. Once this was accomplished, Sarah was rewarded for constructing sentences that combined several of the plastic tokens. A key element in Sarah's training was the importance of word order. That is, she would be rewarded for constructing the word set "Sarah-insert-apple-dish" but would not be reinforced for inappropriate orders such as "dish-apple-insert-Sarah." Sarah was able to act appropriately 70 to 80% of the time to commands made of such compound sentences. The Premacks were able to demonstrate that with this "language" tool their chimpanzees were able to communicate their understanding of logical relationships such as "larger," "smaller," and "brighter."

Recently, researchers at the Yerkes Regional Primate Center near Atlanta, Georgia, have taken a different approach to teaching language to chimpanzees. The researchers constructed a huge wall-mounted computer keyboard. (Yes—even chimpanzees have entered the age of the computer.) Each key on the keyboard has a symbol that stands for a word or relationship. The computer is programmed in a very simple language, which the researchers call "Yerkish," that has simple grammatical rules. The chimp was required first to press the "please" key, which activated the computer; then she had to identify an agent (machine, attendant), followed by a verb (give, make, bring, etc.), followed by an object (fruit, music, bread, etc.) (Rumbaugh, 1977; Savage-Rumbaugh et al., 1986).

BUT IS IT REALLY LANGUAGE?

Some researchers seriously doubt that the communication skills taught to chimpanzees and gorillas really constitute language (e.g., Chomsky, 1980). Herbert Terrace and his colleagues at Columbia University taught Ameslan to a chimp they named Nim Chimpsky (an obvious play on the name of the famous linguist Noam Chomsky). At first the researchers were excited by Nim's rapid acquisition of a large vocabulary (Terrace, 1979; Terrace et al., 1979). However, close examination of Nim's use of language and observations of his interactions with his trainers led the research team to a different set of conclusions than that reached by other language researchers (Sanders, 1985).

Terrace makes the following points:

1. Almost all signs produced by chimps mimic signs recently produced by the trainer; therefore, the chimps are probably imitating their handlers' actions.
2. Grammatical strings produced by the chimps are almost invariably imitations of other grammatical strings, with an occasional substitution.
3. Chimps seldom make spontaneous statements without some prompting or questioning by humans.
4. Chimps do not systematically rely on symbol or word order. This is particularly true when three or more symbols are required.

Other researchers question whether there is any evidence of syntax in chimp language. Brown (1986) noted that the mean length of utterances in children grows rapidly as they develop. Nim's utterances held very steady between 1.1 and 1.6 signs, and the longer strings appear to be profoundly redundant (e.g., "Give orange me give eat orange me eat orange give me eat orange give me you").

The case for or against chimpanzee language is not yet closed. The research has shown rather clearly that chimps can learn to associate symbols with objects. The evidence for syntax and grammar is somewhat less convincing. Some of the differences found in chimpanzee language acquisition may be attributable to variances in training techniques and the overall environment provided for the animals. For example, the Gardners provided Washoe with much more human interaction than did Nim's trainers.

It is not realistic to think that apes who have brains that are one third the size of our own can ever acquire language similar to our own. In some respects, the whole question of ape language is ill-conceived. For the ultimate understanding of the evolution of human language it may be more instructive to understand how ape communication evolved than it is to determine whether apes can learn human language.

The Evolution of Language in Humans

When did language evolve in humans? This is a difficult question to answer because there is little in the fossil record to help us. The only really direct evidence we have of language is writing. The earliest signs of true writing known to date are the 5,000-year-old clay imprints of

Sumerian farmers. The Sumerian symbols were made in wet clay and allowed to dry as permanent records. It is thought that the clay tablets represent records of stock holdings.

It is safe to assume that our ancestors had developed a sophisticated language long before this. Just how long ago, it is impossible to know. However, there are some clues in the fossil record and enough evidence concerning the life-style of our early ancestors that we can at least make some educated guesses.

SOCIAL STRUCTURE

Throughout the animal kingdom there is a general positive correlation between the level of social complexity and the sophistication of intraspecies communication. This relationship appears to hold rather well for primates. Relatively solitary primates such as the orangutan lack social complexity; therefore, their repertoire of vocal and visual signs is less complex than that of their close cousins the gorillas and the chimpanzees.

Forms of social behavior that require particularly effective communication are cooperative defense and cooperative hunting. We see cooperative defense in the gorilla and chimpanzee, but it is most clearly evident in some species of baboons (*Papio*) that move about in the open savanna (DeVore, 1965; Washburn & Devore, 1961). (See the observation "When to Fight and When to Run.") For these animals cooperative defense is essential for survival, and they have developed elaborate vocal and visual displays to effect this form of behavior.

Some researchers suggest that the early hominids that ventured onto the savanna were faced with similar environmental pressures to become more social and, therefore, to develop more elaborate forms of communication. This process could have begun as early as 10 to 14 million years ago when *Ramapithecus* moved from the tropical forest into the woodlands that border the savanna. It is likely that *Homo habilis* enjoyed a more complex social structure than did *Ramapithecus*. There is no direct evidence to show that *Homo habilis* hunted in groups or made use of cooperative defense; however, there is evidence that these hominids did occupy the open savanna. It is difficult to imagine how such a small and fragile primate without stabbing teeth or tearing claws could survive in the open grasslands without cooperative hunting and gathering, foodsharing, and a complex social organization. It would seem reasonable that some 2 to 5 million years ago there was significant environmental pressure on this small primate to work cooperatively to survive in the open grasslands.

TOOLS, HUNTING, AND LANGUAGE?

There is very tenuous evidence that *Ramapithecus* was a tool maker. However, the evidence that *Homo habilis* developed a tool technology is

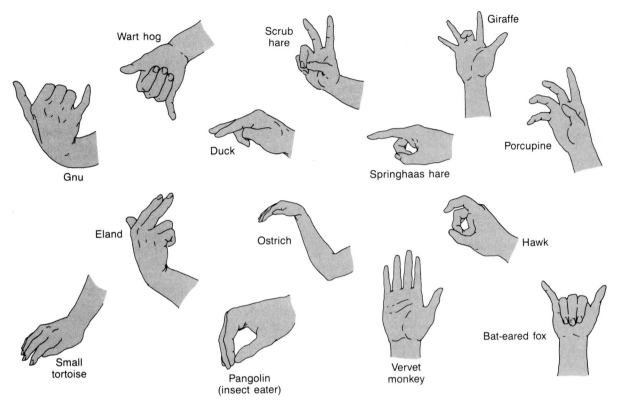

Figure 15-10
The Bushmen of South Africa rely on hand signs to communicate the various forms of animals in the wild. They use their hands and fingers to mimic the most cogent feature of the animal.

quite substantial (Leakey & Lewin, 1977). To make a tool from an amorphous bit of rock, you must first have an internal image of what the finished object should look like. The stone is modified, chip by chip, to match that internal image and the *intended* use of the tool.

Unlike the chimpanzee that modifies a twig to probe for termites *after* the termite mound is located, the stone tool maker crafts the tool *before* the hunt begins. Each tool-making hominid did not need to "reinvent the wheel"; tool making was learned from other tool makers. To communicate this form of information, the hominid must have been able to evoke cognitive images in others (Jerison, 1973). This is a much more sophisticated form of communication than a distress call or an aggressive display.

Cooperative hunting and gathering require a division of responsibility and ways of coordinating the actions of the various individuals involved in the activity. Perhaps some individuals would scout ahead while others remained concealed in relative safety. Returning scouts would need to communicate cogent information from their foraging, signs that would evoke images of objects and events in the environment such as the kind and number of animals encountered and their relative direction. This could very well have been accomplished with a combination of vocal emissions and visual signs not unlike those used by the contemporary Bushmen (see Figure 15-10). Each sign represents a different object in the environment. The externalization of names and concepts—either in vocal emissions, specific gestures, or some combination of the two—is what turns thoughts into language.

An Observation:

When to Fight and When to Run

The hamadryas baboons (*Papio hamadryas*) travel in the open savanna in troops of about 20 or more. Specific vocal calls emitted by dominant members control the activity of the troop. For example, there are specific calls that cause the troop to group together, to move, to stop and forage, and to head to the trees where they bed down for the night.

   The primary predators of this species of baboon are the cheetah and the lion. The baboons have evolved different distress calls, depending on which predator confronts them at the moment. When confronted by a cheetah, which hunts alone, the dominant males of the troop emit distress calls, which cause the largest and most dominant males to form a defense line between the cat and the remainder of the troop (see Observation Figure 15-1). A line of six or eight large males with their 4-in. canine teeth is often enough to discourage the cheetah.

Observation Figure 15-1
The threat display of the male baboon.

However, when confronted by a pride of lions, a force they are unable to handle, a different distress call is given, and the troop disperses for the safety of nearby trees.

The specificity of these distress calls can be empirically demonstrated in the field. First, the calls are recorded so that they can be played back later over loudspeakers. The audio playback of the "cheetah" or "lion" distress call produces the appropriate effect (Washburn & DeVore, 1961).

THE HUMANLIKE BRAIN

We have noted in several places in this book that one trend in the evolution of the brain is a steady increase in brain size relative to the size of the body. Recall that the human brain is almost three times the size of that of the gorilla, who outweighs us by a considerable amount. A second factor in the evolution of the brain that is central to the issue of communication is related not to the size but to the organization of the brain.

You will see later in this chapter that the temporal and parietal lobes of the brain have central roles in speech and language behaviors. The expansion of the parietal and temporal lobes in humans has forced much of the cortex of the occipital lobe to be buried in deep fissures, which makes it appear relatively small. The brains of monkeys and apes simply do not show this organization. Rather, they show relatively small temporal and parietal lobes and a larger occipital lobe.

Ralph Holloway (1970) has made measurements of the endocasts of various hominid brains. (Endocasts are models made from the interior surface of the fossilized skull.) With a reasonably well preserved fossil

Figure 15-11
Sagittal section of the brain showing the extensive cortical surface of the occipital lobe. It is thought that the expansion of the temporal and parietal lobes in humanlike brains caused much of the occipital lobe to be buried in deep fissures.

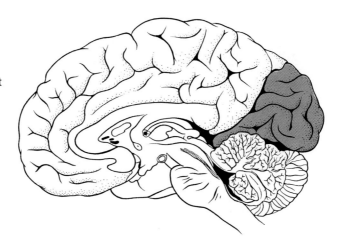

skull it is possible to make some judgments about the general proportions of the ancient brain. A remarkable finding from Holloway's work is that *all* of the hominid skulls going back 3 million years or more show that the hominid brains were more humanlike than they were apelike in their organization.

As noted later in this chapter, the brain mechanisms for the control of speech and language in humans have become lateralized in that the left hemisphere (in right-handed people) is more dominant for the control of this behavior. There is actually an enlargement in the left hemisphere, the so-called **language lump**, which is physical evidence for this lateralization of function. Holloway (as reported in Leakey and Lewin, 1977) found evidence of the language lump in hominid skulls that are more than 2 million years old.

What these findings mean is that whatever evolutionary pressures molded the human brain in its present form began more than 3 million years ago. It also means that the evolution of the neural mechanisms and organization required to produce and interpret complex language and speech had a very early start.

THE RECEDING LARYNX

Earlier in this chapter we noted that the chimpanzee was incapable of producing many of the phonemes required in human language, because the position of its larynx is much higher in the throat than it is in humans. Fossil evidence shows that the position of the larynx recedes progressively in the line of hominids.

Figure 15-12a shows the position of the larynx in humans and its likely position in *Homo erectus*. Note that the elongated tongue and the elevated larynx in *Homo erectus* limit the size and the variability of the pharyngeal space in a fashion similar to that seen in the chimpanzee (refer to Figure 15-9). On the right of Figure 15-12a is the morphology of the vocal tract in the human infant. Note that the baby's tongue rests mostly in the mouth, and the larynx is in a similar position to that seen in *Homo erectus*. The human infant, *Homo erectus*, and chimpanzee configurations more closely approximate the more primitive, two-tube system seen in more primitive vertebrates that allows those species to breathe and swallow simultaneously. The large common tube pharynx is evidently a necessary adaptation to facilitate more complex speech sounds (see Figure 15-12b).

None of what we have discussed here can tell us when language actually began. Part of the problem inherent in this issue in that language, like other forms of behavior, didn't just suddenly begin. It evolved slowly, and there is probably no single point in time that we can point to as the origin of language. There is no sharp boundary between language and nonlanguage. Additionally, the fossil record is too weak for us to make anything more than some general statements concerning the

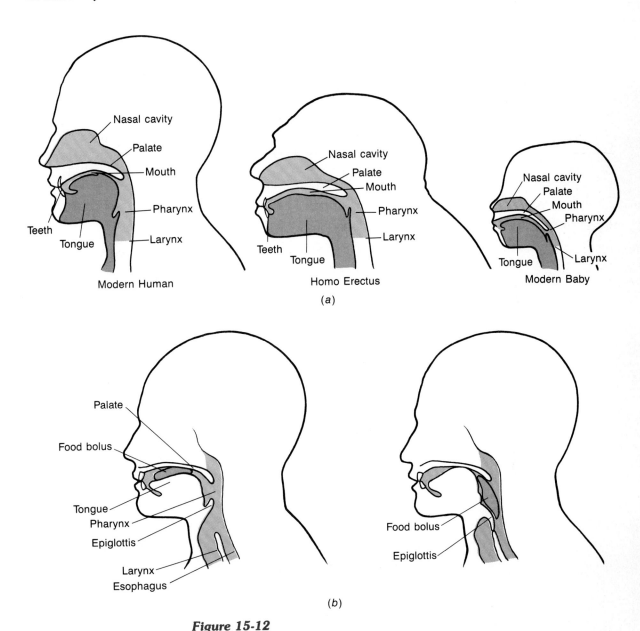

Figure 15-12
a. The vocal machinery of modern humans, *Homo erectus*, and the modern human baby. (See text for explanation.) *b.* The opening of the human breathing and swallowing apparatus is formed by a single tube. To swallow, the epiglottis must close off the larynx to prevent food or water from entering the lungs. Many animals, including the human infant, are able to swallow and breath at the same time because the larynx is positioned higher in the throat.

physical mechanisms associated with language comprehension and speech production. Some researchers feel that true language could not be more than 50,000 years old, because the modern human vocal system evolved at about that time (Lieberman, 1984). Others maintain that the early hominids must have had a form of communication that was far more complex than that seen in any contemporary nonhuman primate and that some form of language may have evolved much before the dawn of mankind (Jerison, 1973; Leakey & Lewin, 1979). We may never know for sure.

Neural Mechanisms in Language and Speech

Our earliest evidence concerning the neural mechanisms that control speech and language come from accidental lesions to the brain. You will recall from Chapter 1 that some of the first evidence suggesting that local areas of the brain were specific in function came from the clinical observation of individuals who had lost some aspect of speech or language following injury to the brain.

Lateralization of Language in the Brain

In 1861, Broca made a postmortem examination of the brain of a patient who had lost the ability to speak. The patient had been normal in all other respects. Broca found a small lesion in the frontal lobe on the left hemisphere. Later Broca had occasion to examine other patients who had experienced similar symptoms. In almost every instance (95% of the cases) he found damage in the same location, and almost always the lesion was located on the left side of the brain. Some years later Wernicke discovered that damage to more posterior areas of the brain caused a different kind of language impairment; however, the same left-side dominance for language was apparent.

Subsequently, the examination of many brain-injured individuals has confirmed that there is a clear statistical difference in behavioral deficits following left and right brain lesions. Lesions to the left side of the brain are far more likely to induce language deficits than lesions to the right side. Right brain lesions are more likely to produce deficits in tasks that require the interpretation of spatial or temporal relationships (e.g., Lansdell, 1970; Luria, 1973b.) (We will see later that these relationships vary depending on other factors such as gender and handedness.) What adaptive advantage(s) can there be for this division of function?

WHY IS THERE LATERALIZATION?

Why do we have a division of function in the left and right brain? Following the discovery of lateralization of function in humans, most researchers assumed that this was a uniquely human condition. Further, because lateralization was first found in language behavior, it was assumed that the development of language was somehow responsible for the phenomenon. More recently it has been shown that lateralization of function is not a uniquely human characteristic. There is evidence that the control of bird song is lateralized in some species (Nottebohm, 1970, 1980) and that the ability to discriminate between various calls is lateralized in some monkeys (e.g., Heffner & Heffner, 1984; Petersen et al., 1978). Interestingly, it is the left side of the brain that appears to be most important for communication in these species.

One theory proposes that it was necessary for speech and language to become lateralized in one side of the brain because speech requires such rapid serial processing of information. The rate of phoneme production in normal speech is 10 phonemes per second, and it may reach 25 to 30 phonemes per second in short bursts (Liberman, 1982). The theory suggests that both the auditory processing of speech input and the motor sequencing of speech production must be accomplished so rapidly that cooperation between the two hemispheres is simply not possible. Further, if cooperation between the two hemispheres were to be necessary, it would impede the process.

There is some evidence to support this notion. For example, it has been shown that stuttering is more common in individuals who have mixed dominance (strong representation for language in both hemispheres) (Pinksy & McAdam, 1980; Quinn, 1972). The implication is that two speech centers may be the cause of the stuttering. Stutterers who are mixed dominant for language do not stutter if they sing the words. Apparently this is due to the fact that singing slows the rate of flow of the words and also utilizes the timing functions of the right hemisphere. (Mel Tillis, the well-known country and western singer, has a rather severe stuttering impediment that does not affect his singing.) A recent discovery has shown that the corpus callosum is about 11% thicker in left-handers than in right-handers (Witelson, 1985). It is possible that the enlarged band of fibers facilitates the additional interhemispheric communication required for individuals who have bilateral representation for the same language functions.

Other theories suggest that brain lateralization for language is somehow related to handedness (e.g., Levy, 1969). No species, other than humans, evidences a preference for one hand (or paw) over the other. Individual animals may show a consistent preference for using one limb to accomplish fine motor tasks; however, there is a 50–50 split in preference for the right or the left limb. Only in humans do we see a statistically clear preference for the use of the right hand.

Cross-cultural studies have shown that only 10% of the people studied are left-handers or ambidextrous. Handedness runs in families, and it is doubtlessly genetically determined. The probability that two right-handed parents will have a left-handed infant is less than 2%. The probability rises to 17% if one parent is a left-hander and to 46% if both parents are left-handers.

Looking at It from Another Angle

When you look at the brain, it appears to be symmetrical. However, we have already noted that for most people there is "language lump" on the left side of the brain. The physical differences between the left and right brain become much more evident if we look at them in a rather unorthodox way.

Throughout this book, whenever we have examined the internal anatomy of the brain, we have followed conventional techniques of dissection. That is, we have made either coronal, sagittal, or horizontal sections of the tissue. Some years ago Geschwind and Levitsky (1968) discovered that if you cut the brain as pictured in the top of Spotlight Figure 15-1, you expose a large surface area of the cortex just above the temporal lobe called the **planum temporale**. This structure is situated quite close to the primary projection area for audition, and it is critical for the comprehension of speech.

The researchers found that the planum temporale was considerably larger in the left hemisphere in 65% of the brains they examined. The difference was by no means subtle and could be seen quite readily with the naked eye. In about 24% of the cases they found no clear difference, and the planum temporale was larger in the right brain in 11% of the cases.

Apparently, the enlarged planum temporale is present long before language develops. Witelson and Pallie (1973) examined the brains of infants who died before they were 3 months old. Of the 14 brains examined, the planum temporale was larger on the left side for 12. These data lend support to the notion that the left side of the brain is more active in language and that the predisposition for this lateralized effect exists at birth.

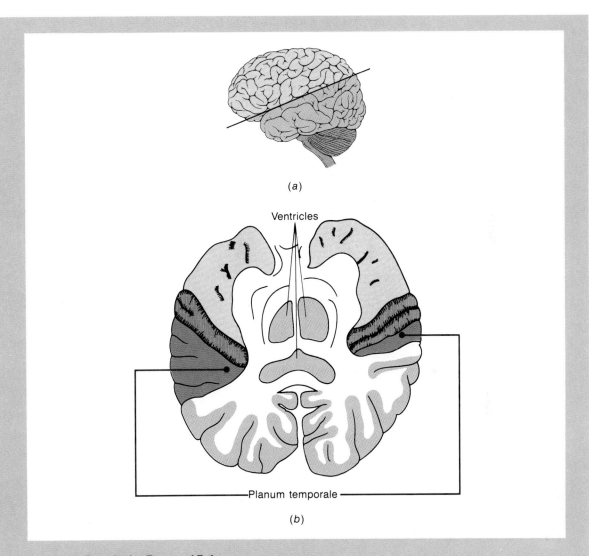

(a)

(b)

Spotlight Figure 15-1
a. Section through the brain that exposes the planum temporale. *b*. Colored area shows the planum temporale on the left and right sides of the brain. In most cases this structure is larger on the left side. (Redrawn from Geschwind & Levitsky, 1968.)

Theories that relate handedness to language laterality suggest the following scenario. As the hominids became tool makers it was adaptive for one hand to steady the work while the other performed the fine motor skills. This preferred hand then became the dominant hand for signaling. Because the left side of the brain controls the right hand, the left brain evolved to be dominant for language. (Why the right hand should have evolved to be the dominant hand in the first place is not known, nor is it clear why some primates show a lateralization for language but no lateralization for handedness. Additionally, the existence of lateralization for vocalization in other species suggests that lateralization predates tool use.)

There is indirect evidence that right-handedness has been a human characteristic for a very long time. Early Egyptian drawings show people engaged in a variety of activities utilizing the right hand rather than the left. Studies of the hand tracings made by *Cro-Magnon* on the walls of caves show that 80% of the tracings are of the left hand. This has been interpreted to mean that the artist used his preferred right hand to make the tracing (Dennis, 1958). There is even some evidence that *Australopithecus*, who lived approximately 4 million years ago, was right-handed. Examination of the fossilized skulls of baboons that had been killed by *Australopithecus* show damage on the left side more often than the right, suggesting that the blow was administered by a right-handed attacker (Dart, 1949).

There is much evidence to support the notion that a relationship exists between handedness and lateralization for language. People who are right-handers tend to use the right hand expressively during speech. Left-handers show no clear pattern of hand movement while speaking (Kimura, 1973). Ninety-nine percent of the people who are right-handers are strongly dominant for language in the left brain. Approximately 60 to 70% of the left-handers are dominant for speech in the left brain; the remainder are either mixed dominant or right brain dominant for speech (Levy, 1982). Satz (1969) has shown that all left-handers—those who are left brain dominant and those who are right brain dominant for speech— have at least some representation for language in both hemispheres.

An Observation: The Sinister Left Hand

It is awkward to be a left-hander. If you are a left-hander, you know this to be true. Most tools and machines are designed to meet the needs of the majority of people who are right-handed. A common example is a simple pair of scissors. If you are a right-hander, as 90% of you are, try to use a pair of scissors with your left hand. You will find that they simply do not fit. Most left-handers are forced to use their nonpreferred hand when cutting unless they have access to a pair of scissors that are specifically designed for use by left-handers. Interestingly, there are many companies now that specialize in objects made for left-handed people.

Left-handers have been the object of discrimination in other ways. Our history and language reflect a long-term bias against the minority of people who are left-handers. There are biblical references to the chosen or preferred people being placed on the right side, whereas those in disfavor are placed on the left side. (e.g., "Then shall he say also unto them on the left hand, Depart from me, ye cursed, into everlasting fire," Matthew.) The technical term for left-handedness is *sinistrality*, which comes from the word *sinister*. Think of what it means when someone pays you a "left-handed" compliment. In French, when you want to say that someone has very clumsy behavior, the term is *très gauche*, which literally means "very left." This has been incorporated into English, and the word *gauche* has come to mean "lacking social grace; awkward or tactless." In Italian the word for left is *mancino*, which also means deceitful.

Years ago it was not uncommon for parents and teachers to try to "correct" left-handers so they too could be "normal." Interestingly, when we became enlightened enough to realize how traumatic that was for children, the number of left-handers in the population increased. This, of course, had nothing to do with biology. It simply reflected the fact that many natural left-handers were no longer being forced to use their genetically determined nonpreferred hand.

THE ONTOGENY OF LATERALIZATION

If the lateralization of language function is truly genetically determined, we should be able to see some evidence of it in human infants. Unfortunately, it is very difficult to test language function in infants because they are not able to speak (although, at times, some parents may complain that they learn to speak all too quickly).

To get around this problem, Dennis Molfese and his colleagues examined the evoked potentials of very young infants to speech sounds (Molfese et al., 1975). In one of their studies the subjects ranged in age from 1 week to 10 months of age. Speech sounds such as "ba" and "ki" were played, and the evoked potential activity of the left and right hemispheres was recorded. Their data showed that 90% of the infants tested showed more left hemisphere involvement to the speech sounds. Significantly, the age of the infants was not a factor. That is, they had the same results for 1-week-old infants who had very limited previous exposure to speech sounds as they did for the older infants. When Molfese presented the infants with nonspeech sounds such as random noise or notes produced by a piano, opposite results were obtained. All of the infants showed evoked potential of higher amplitude in the right hemisphere.

Molfese's work is very exciting because it suggests that although newborn infants are unable to understand or produce language, the brain is organized and "prewired" in an appropriate fashion to process language sounds differently from other sounds. Research done in other laboratories (e.g., Wada & Davis, 1977) support this interpretation.

GENDER AND LATERALITY

There is a considerable amount of evidence indicating that women's brains are less strongly lateralized than are men's. Compared to women, men tend to have more language function concentrated in the left hemisphere and more visuospatial functioning concentrated in the right hemisphere. Additionally, there is a considerable body of evidence that women generally have somewhat superior verbal skills whereas men tend to have superior spatial abilities (Maccoby & Jacklin, 1974). Why this should be, however, is poorly understood.

Jerre Levy has proposed an evolutionary basis for this gender difference. She argues that there must have been positive selection pressures for hominid males to have highly developed spatial skills because they were the hunters and the leaders of migrations. Conversely, females had selective pressures for skills involved in child rearing, such as the use of language. Levy proposes that the greater bilateral function may have somehow facilitated the skills needed for females, whereas a greater separation of function was necessary for males (Levy, 1978). This line of reasoning is interesting but must be considered highly speculative.

Although the function and purpose of gender differences in brain lateralization are not understood, there can be little doubt that the differences do exist. For example, men are three times more likely to have symptoms of aphasia following left brain damage than are women (McGlone, 1978). We noted earlier that the planum temporale is larger in the left hemisphere in most people. On rare occassions this structure is larger on the right side, and this reversal occurs much more frequently in women (Wada, Clark, & Hamm, 1975). Furthermore, a large number of behavioral studies have shown small, but consistent, gender differences for auditory and visual tasks presented selectively to the left or right brain.

Brain Mechanisms in Speech

Whether the lateralization of language behavior in the brain is due to evolutionary pressures associated with handedness, to the need to have rapid processing of sequential information, or to some other yet to be identified causes is not yet known. What is known is that language function *is* lateralized in the brain and that this lateralization is genetically determined. We now examine what is known of the brain mechanisms that control speech and language.

We have already seen that Broca's area, a small part of the frontal cortex located dorsal of the Sylvian fissure at the anteroventral end of the primary motor cortex, has an important role in speech. Broca's area lies adjacent to the part of the primary motor cortex that controls the face and the lips. Lesions to this part of the brain produce what has been termed **Broca's aphasia**. **Aphasia**, which literally means "without speaking," refers to any form of speech or language dysfunction that results from damage to the brain. Broca's aphasia is a form of **expressive aphasia** in that the loss is centered on problems with speech production. The actual symptoms are dependent on the exact size and location of the lesion, the age and sex of the individual, and handedness. Generally, Broca's aphasia is characterized by the following symptoms.

1. Although some people with Broca's aphasia are unable to speak at all, most are able to speak slowly and have poor articulation. The problem is not restricted to motor control of the muscles in the head, because these people also have some difficulty in writing as well.

2. People with Broca's aphasia who can speak tend to use a telegraphic form of speech. Their speech is meaningful, but many connective and qualifying words are omitted.

3. Invariably, Broca's aphasics understand language, both written and spoken, much better than they are able to produce it. They understand what is said to them, and they know what they want to say. The problem is centered on the expression of language.

The following exerpt is an example of expressive aphasia in a woman who had a stroke that caused damage to Broca's area:

EXAMINER: How are you feeling?
PATIENT: I—I'm fine.
E: Have I ever tested you before?
P: No—two, three.
E: What is your full name?
P: Oh dear—Henry—oh—
E: And your full address?
P: Oh dear. Um. Aah. Oh! No—oh. Oh dear. Very-there-were-there ave. Ave-derversher avenyer. (Correct address. Devonshire.)
E: What kind of work did you do before you became ill?
P: Oh. I—I—um. Um—oh dear. I—I—dun know. I don't—want—to.
E: Can you tell me what you did for a living? Did you work? Did you have a job?
P: Oh   yes—I—I—um—um.   The-the-say-si-selum-dum-nogglewife. Oh dear.
E: Look at the picture and tell me what you see going on in the picture.

P: Oh dear. Um—oh dear. That—oh good—um. Oh isn't that good i. There and there and there and there and there.

E: Can you tell me what they're called?

P: Waving and uh—the—oh dear—and the kite and boy and—and eeth. Uh—barking and a-a lil boy and a bigs thing in uh—in the—Oh dear he's dreeging in the uh. Oh dear—I can't say it but he's—ray. And a man and-woman-do no-no-uh-uh sawst all a people-one-two-three and four and—and oh-the-oh boy-good and-oh waitingull but no I-oh. (Condensed from Kertesz, 1982; p. 32)

Electrical stimulation to Broca's area causes the arrest of ongoing speech. The stimulation done during neurosurgery causes a momentary functional lesion to the cortex in the immediate vicinity of the electrodes (see Spotlight 15-2). The actual areas of the brain that appear to produce the same result are not limited to Broca's speech area (see Figure 15-13). In the left hemisphere the arrest of speech can be produced with stimulation to Broca's area, the primary motor cortex, and a wide area of the parietotemporal region. In the right hemisphere the effect is found primarily in the motor cortex, which controls the muscles in the mouth, tongue, and throat (Roberts, 1961).

These data lead to two conclusions. First, the data confirm that there is much more left hemisphere involvement with speech than there is

Figure 15-13
Regions of the cortex where arrest, hesitation, slurring, distortion, or repetition of speech are obtained during electrical stimulation. The mesial surface is shown inverted in the top of the figure. (Redrawn from Roberts, 1961.)

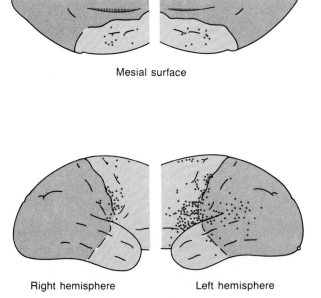

Mesial surface

Right hemisphere   Left hemisphere

right hemisphere involvement. Second, the data show that much more of the brain is involved in speech production than Broca's speech area.

Brain Mechanisms in Language

We have seen that lesions to Broca's area appear mostly to affect expressive language. Lesions to the more posterior part of the left brain, the area named after Wernicke, cause **receptive aphasia**. Unlike individuals with Broca's aphasia people with **Wernicke's aphasia** have difficulty understanding the meaning and the sequencing of words. They are unable to follow simple commands and have great difficulty making any sense out of written material (**dyslexia**) (Vallutino, 1987). The specific symptoms vary to some degree with the size and the specific location of the lesion. Generally, Wernicke's aphasia can be characterized by the following.

1. People with Wernicke's aphasia have little or no difficulty articulating words. They are able to repeat words spoken to them. This is true even for difficult words such as *aluminum* and *Connecticut*. They are able to speak at a normal pace unless they are having difficulty recalling a specific word.

2. Wernicke's aphasics have considerable difficulty comprehending both spoken and written language. For this reason their responses to questions may be totally inappropriate. Although their speech production is usually grammatically correct, it often makes no sense. There is also a tendency to insert nonsense words.

3. People suffering from Wernicke's aphasia evidence **anomia**, or difficulty in finding the right word or in naming common objects. Their speech is frequently interrupted because they have difficulty remembering names.

The following exerpt is an example of receptive aphasia in a woman 2 weeks after a stroke in Wernicke's area:

EXAMINER: How are you today, Mrs. A.?
PATIENT: Yes.
E: Have I ever tested you before?
P: No, I mean I haven't.
E: Can you tell me what your name is?
P: No, I don't I—right I'm right now here.
E: What is your address?
P: I cud if I can help these this like you know—to make it. We are seeing for him. That is my father.
E: What kind of work did you do before you came into the hospital?
P: Never, now Mista Oyge I wanna tell you this happened when happened when he rent. His—his kell come down here and is—he got ren something. It happened. In these ropiers were with him for hi—is friend—like was. And it just happened so I don't know, he did not

Here We Speak English, but Aquí Se Habla Español

Try to imagine the following experiment. The subject is a patient who is undergoing neurosurgery to remove a tumor or to repair a vascular accident. The subject is looking at a back-projection screen that presents stimuli that are being controlled by a research team located in an adjoining room. There is a microphone and a closed-circuit television camera in the surgical suite that allow the researchers to monitor the action in the room. Both the surgeon and the subject have small speakers in one ear so they can receive verbal instructions from the members of the research team.

After the skull of the patient has been opened and the meninges cut to expose the surface of the brain, the experiment is ready to begin. At the direction of the research team the surgeon places a bipolar stimulating electrode gently on the surface of the cortex. The subject is told that the first tiral is about to begin. The stimulus is shown momentarily onto the screen. The patient responds, and the surgeon places a small plastic marker for future reference on the cortex at the site where the electrode stimulated the cortex.

On some of the trials a weak electric current is passed across the poles of the electrode, causing the small area of cortex between the two exposed tips to be functionally lesioned. The power to the electrode is actually controlled by the researchers in the adjoining room, and neither the surgeon nor the subject knows on which trials the electrode is active.

Using this technique, Ojemann and his colleagues have identified a variety of language-related functions that may be affected by electrical stimulation to various sites on the left side of the brain (Ojemann, 1983; Ojemann & Mateer, 1979). Stimulation in some areas blocks repetition of words, other locations interfere with language production, other areas block the ability to name common objects, and still others affect memory for verbal material (see Spotlight Figure 15-2).

One particularly interesting finding from this research was noted when stimulating the brains of people who had been bilingual since childhood. The researchers found that stimulation to some areas would block naming in one language but not the other. For example, if the person spoke both English and Greek, a specific spot on the cortex might block naming in English but not in Greek, whereas another spot on the cortex would have the opposite effect.

It is important to note here that when the surgeon returned the electrode to a given site, the result was always the same. It seems that little islands of cortex became reserved to function in one language but not the other. This finding did not hold true for people who acquired a second language later in life. Evidently, when young children are exposed to two languages early in life, parts of the brain become partitioned to function in just one of the languages. This may explain why young children seem to pick up a second language so rapidly when compared to adults. It is possible that past a certain age we must learn a second language using a different neural mechanism than that used to learn the first language. This may also explain why people who learn a second language as adults are never quite capable of speaking without an accent.

There are some clear problems with the interpretation of the data in this line of research. First, all of the subjects were having neurosurgery for a reason; that is, we are dealing with diseased brains. Second, the number of cases in this research is very small, and it is always somewhat risky to generalize to the general population from so few subjects. Nevertheless, the research is exciting and may lead to a better understanding of brain mechanisms in language.

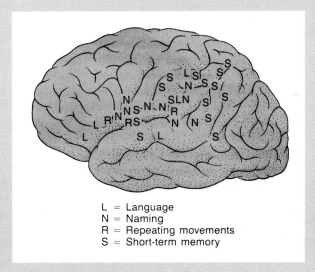

L = Language
N = Naming
R = Repeating movements
S = Short-term memory

Spotlight Figure 15-2
Areas of the brain that arrest language (L), block naming (N), induce speech repetition (R), and affect short-term memory for verbal material (S). (Redrawn from Ojemann & Mateer, 1979.)

bring around anything. And he did not pay it. And he roden all o these arranjen from the pedis on from iss pescid. In these floors now and so. He hasn't had em round here.

    E: Can you tell me a little bit about why you are in the hospital?

    P: No, I don't think I have ... No, I haven't. (Condensed from Kertesz, 1982, p. 38)

DISCONNECTION THEORY OF APHASIA:

The fact that lesions to different areas of the brain produce distinctly different deficits in language suggests that various characteristics of language function are controlled by separate areas of the brain. A theory first proposed by Wernicke, and later updated by Norman Geschwind, suggests that linguistic competence requires the cooperation and coordination of many areas of the brain (Geschwind, 1965a, 1965b).

Geschwind's theory proposes that the *underlying structure* of language (the syntax and grammatical rules necessary for language comprehension) is dealt with by Wernicke's area. The theory proposes that auditory information from the auditory cortex (speech sounds) and visual information from the occipital cortex (written symbols) are sent to Wernicke's area, where they are processed into cognitively meaningful sensations. The neural circuitry for the expression of speech is under control of Broca's area. When a word is to be spoken, some representation of that word is sent from Wernicke's area to Broca's area through a bundle of fibers called the **arcuate fasciculus**. The neural circuitry in Broca's area then sends programmed information to the primary motor cortex, which, in turn, drives the muscles of the face, lips, tongue, and larynx. Figure 15-14 depicts the hypothesized sequence of events for speaking a word that is heard or a word that is written.

According to Geschwind's theory, damage to any part of these interconnected language areas of the brain causes them to be "disconnected" and thus results in some form of aphasia. For this reason the theory is sometimes referred to as the **disconnection theory of aphasia**. The specific loss observed depends on which parts of the brain are disconnected. More anterior lesions would tend to produce larger expressive effects, whereas more posterior lesions would have greater effects on receptive processes. Because accidental lesions to the brain are rarely confined neatly to just one of these brain regions, most individuals will have a mixture of expressive and receptive aphasia.

Support for the disconnection theory can be found in a form of aphasia called **conduction aphasia**. People with conduction aphasia have speech that is similar to receptive aphasics' speech in that it is fluent but meaningless. However, their comprehension of language is quite good—more like that seen in expressive aphasics.

There is evidencce that damage to the arcuate fasciculus causes conduction aphasia (Damasio & Damasio, 1980). This would explain the symptoms. Damage that is restricted to the arcuate fasciculus would

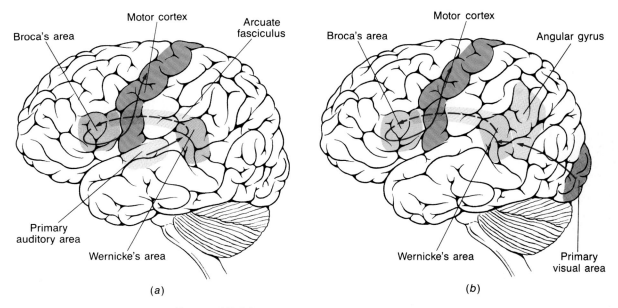

Figure 15-14
Schematic representation of the sequence of neural events required (a) to
speak a word that is heard or (b) to speak a word that is written. (Adapted
from Geschwind, 1979.)

leave both Wernicke's and Broca's areas intact. Therefore, although the
individual is able to comprehend speech (intact Broca's area), the connections between the two brain regions are not complete. Therefore, the
person is unable to send meaningful language information to Broca's
area, resulting in well-articulated, but meaningless, speech (Damasio &
Geschwind, 1984). Table 15-1 provides a summary of the symptoms
associated with the three forms of aphasia.

Table 15-1 Characteristics of Three Kinds of Aphasia

Area Lesioned	Articulation	Speech Meaningfulness	Comprehension
Broca's area (expressive)	Very poor	Fair; omits connectives	Good
Wernicke's area (receptive)	Very good	Grammatically correct but meaningless; trouble finding right words	Very poor
Arcuate fasciculus (connective)	Very good	Poor; unable to repeat what others say	Fair to good

CHAPTER SUMMARY

1. Language, like most other forms of human behavior, is influenced by genetics and the environment. There is evidence to support the notion that the neural mechanisms for language are genetically determined and that environmental influences act on the genetic predisposition for language.

2. *Discrete signals* are those that are universal in all members of the species and that are given in a simple "no" or "off" fashion. *Graded signals* have evolved in a way that increases variability. Communication signals that are invariant and stereotypical are said to have signal specificity.

3. Human language is made up of a very limited number of *phonemes*. The complexity of human language results from the many possible combinations of phonemes. The complexity of human language is increased further because the order of words (*syntax*) determines their meaning. All true languages have *grammar*, a set of rules by which words may be combined.

4. It is difficult to demonstrate the existence of syntax and grammar in nonhuman forms of communication. Researchers have attempted to teach language to other primates using American Sign Language, various shapes and symbols, and interactive computers. A great debate over this research continues. Some researchers believe that they have demonstrated elements of true language in chimpanzees and gorillas. Others maintain that the animals do little more than imitate the behavior of their trainers without understanding the symbols they manipulate.

5. It is extremely difficult to trace the evolution of language development in hominids and humans because the fossil record does not provide much useful evidence. Factors such as social structure, cooperative hunting and gathering, and tool making all placed significant pressures on language development. Endocasts made from hominid skulls indicate that the brains of all hominids were more humanlike than they were apelike. This has been interpreted to mean that the structural organization in the brain needed to support language behavior was present millions of years before humans evolved.

6. The structure of the mouth, tongue, larynx, and pharyngeal cavity has evolved over time in a manner that facilitates complex human speech. The larynx has receded over time to allow for more variance in the size and shape of the pharyngeal space. The fossil record indicates that the mouth parts of *Homo erectus* would have permitted much more complex oral signs than possible in any modern ape.

7. Language function is lateralized in the left side of the brain, and the right side of the brain seems to be superior for tasks requiring spatial skills. One theory concerning the lateralization of function suggests that both the auditory processing of speech input and the motor sequencing of speech production is so rapid that cooperation between the two sides of the brain is not possible. Other theories attribute lateralization to handedness and tool making in early hominids.

8. There is strong evidence that handedness is genetically determined and that handedness and the lateralization of language function are related. The predisposition for lateralization of language in the left brain is present at birth. The brains of women tend to be less lateralized than the brains of men.

9. *Broca's aphasia*, also known as *expressive aphasia*, is characterized by poor articulation, telegraphic speech, and good comprehension. *Wernicke's aphasia*, or *receptive aphasia*, is characterized by good articulation, poor auditory and written comprehension, and *anomia*.

10. The *disconnection theory of aphasia* proposes that linguistic competence requires the cooperation and coordination of many area of the brain. *Conduction aphasia*, which is caused by lesions to the *arcuate fasciculus*, provides support for the disconnection theory of aphasia. The arcuate fasciculus is a band of fibers that connects Wernicke's and Broca's areas. People with conduction aphasia have speech that is similar to receptive aphasics, but their comprehension of language is good, like that seen in expressive aphasics.

SUGGESTED READINGS

Damasio, A. R., & Geschwind, N. (1984). The neural basis of language. *Annual Review of Neuroscience, 7*, 127–148.

Geshwind, N. (1979). Specialization of the human brain. In *The brain* (a *Scientific American* book) ed. San Francisco: Freeman.

Hayes, C. (1951). *The ape in our house.* New York: Harper & Bros.

Savage-Rumbaugh, S. (1986). *Ape language: From conditioned response to symbol.* New York: Columbia University Press.

Schiller, F. (1979). *Paul Broca.* Berkeley: University of California Press.

Springer, S. P., & Deutsch, G. (1981). *Left brain, right brain.* San Francisco: Freeman. *Science, 226*, 75–76.

KEY TERMS

Anomia Language difficulty characterized by problems in naming objects or finding the correct word.

Aphasia Difficulty with speech or language resulting from damage to the brain.

Arcuate fasciculus Band of neural fibers that connect the posterior and anterior brain centers for language and speech.

Broca's aphasia A form of aphasia resulting from lesions to Broca's area of the brain. Characterized primarily by deficits in speech production; *see* Expressive aphasia.

Conduction aphasia Form of aphasia characterized by fluent, but meaningless, speech and good language comprehension.

Disconnection theory of aphasia Theory proposing that aphasia is the result of interruptions between various speech and language areas of the brain.

Discrete signals Forms of communication that are invariant within the species.

Dyslexia Language problem characterized by difficulty in understanding written material.

Expressive aphasia Language difficulty centered

on the production of speech; *see* Broca's aphasia.

Graded signals Forms of communication that vary in intensity and duration.

Language lump Enlarged area on the left side of the brain associated with language.

Phoneme Smallest units of sound that may be combined to produce words.

Planum temporale Cortical area above the tempporal lobe that is essential for the interpretation of speech. This structure tends to be larger on the left side of the brain.

Receptive aphasia Language deficits characterized by the inability to understand spoken or written language; *see* Wernicke's aphasia.

Signal specificity Given signals in a particular communication system elicit one or a few characteristic responses.

Syntax The grammatical pattern or order of words.

Wernicke's aphasia A form of receptive language disorder characterized by the inability to understand spoken or written language.

Knowing

After reading this chapter, you should

1. Be able to discuss the various ways of defining the concept of mind.

2. Be able to compare and contrast the dualist and monist theories of the mind–body problem.

3. Be able to discuss the relationship between language and conscious awareness.

4. Be able to describe the modular column model of cortical organization and be able to relate the model to conscious awareness.

5. Understand the role of the prefrontal cortex in complex human behavior.

6. Know how split-brain surgery isolates the two hemispheres of the brain and be able to discuss how this surgical preparation has added to our understanding of mental processes in each hemisphere.

7. Be able to compare and contrast the mental functions in left and right brain as evidenced in split-brain patients.

I have purposely left an explanation of the biological bases of knowing and mind to the end of this book. I have done this for two reasons. First, from a philosophical and intellectual basis, this is the most difficult issue confronting brain scientists. Second, I felt that this topic could only be dealt with after the reader had a substantial exposure to the functional anatomy of the brain and the physiological factors that influence behavior. I hope the foundation provided by reading and studying the earlier chapters of this text will better equip the reader to deal with this fascinating, but difficult, topic.

Defining Our Terms

What does it mean when I say that you or I *know* something? Is knowing a distinctly human phenomenon that is dependent on uniquely human mental abilities? Is knowing the same thing as mind, or is it a process that takes place in the mind? Is it possible to know something without resorting to the use of language, or is language ability an inherent part of the knowing process? Is it possible for animals, other than humans, to know anything, or are they "mindless"? If animals have minds, how would I go about demonstrating that they in fact know something? Is there some physical event or structure within the brain that represents what is known? If so, where should I look in the brain to find the physical substrate of mind? Is it localized in one or a few areas of the brain, or is mind distributed diffusely throughout the brain? These are some of the most difficult questions that face researchers of brain function, and they are closely tied to the mind–body question.

You will recall from Chapter 1 that one of the most central questions in the study of the biological bases of behavior is concerned with the nature of mind and its relationship to the body, most notably the brain. I indicated in Chapter 1 that the word *mind* is an unfortunate term because it is so poorly defined and means many different things to different people in different contexts. Before we can address the issue of knowing from a physiological perspective, we first need to define our terms.

The Confusing "Mind" The term *mind* has many different meanings. A casual look at your dictionary will give you a feel for the enormity of the problem. My desk dictionary offers the following definitions (among others) for the word *mind* (the emphases are mine):

1. The agency or part in a *human* that reasons, [defined as an acting thing found only in humans]
2. The totality of *conscious and unconscious processes* of the organism, [defined as a process]
3. Reason and/or sanity, [a capacity or state]

4. Psychic or *spiritual being*, as *opposed to matter*, [defined as meta-physical rather than physical]
5. A conscious or *intelligent being*, [defined as a person or entity] (Random House College Dictionary, 1972)

To further confuse the picture, think of the following colloquial uses for the word *mind*:

1. I gave her a piece of my mind. (expression of anger or disapproval)
2. I have a good mind to forget the whole thing. (an intention)
3. Are you out of your mind? (state of being insane or greatly distracted)
4. Bear in mind that tomorrow is a holiday. (remember)
5. He is one of the top 10 minds in the country. (an intelligent person)
6. Never mind. (forget or disregard)
7. Would you mind passing the salt? (feel disturbed)

The most confusing aspect of the term *mind* from a psychobiologist's point of view is that it is sometimes defined as a thing (which it is not) and sometimes as a process (which it is). It is this dichotomous historical view of the concept of mind that has fueled the long-lasting controversy known as the mind–body problem.

What Does the "Minding"? The Mind–Body Problem Revisited

You will recall from Chapter 1 that the mind–body problem centers on the nature of mind and the relationship between mind and body. Traditionally, the philosophical theories concerning the mind–body problem have been divided into two general categories: (1) monist theories, which maintain that brain and mind are not separable entities, and (2) dualist theories, which support the notion that mind and body have a separate status and that they may or may not interact with each other. Let us review the dualist theories first. (You may find it helpful to refer to Figure 16-1.)

DUALIST THEORIES OF MIND AND BODY

The most simplistic forms of dualism, *autonomism* and *parallelism*, suggest that a separate brain and mind exist, that they are independent, and that they do not interact. The theories differ only in that parallelism suggests that brain and mind somehow run in synchrony like two clocks started at the same time—they keep the same time but are totally independent of each other. Autonomism makes no such claim of synchronous action. I know of no contemporary scholar of brain science who takes either of these theories seriously.

Figure 16-1
Pictorial representations of
the various theories con-
cerning the mind–body
problem. The dotted cir-
cle represents mind, and
the little brain represents
the physical brain. The
monist theories are
grouped together on the
left, and the dualist
theories are represented
on the right. (Redrawn
from Bunge, 1980.)

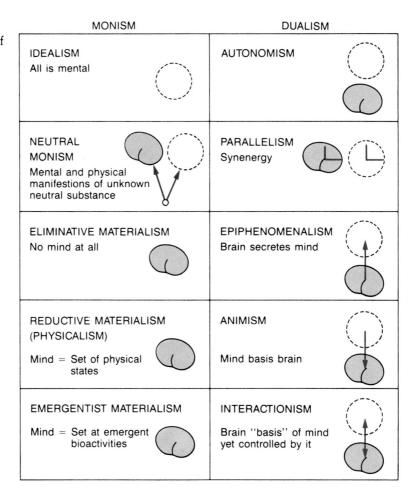

Other forms of dualism suggest that brain and mind are separate
but in some fashion dependent on each other. *Epiphenomenalists* suggest
that mind is a separate, materially different, distinct *product* of the brain.
Animists take an almost opposite position and propose that an independent mind somehow controls or directs the activity of the brain. A third
theory, *interactionism*, takes the position that there is a sort of "give and
take" between brain and mind—that brain is the basis of mind, yet brain
is somehow controlled by mind.

From my perspective a common flaw in all of the dualist theories is
that they give mind the status of a thing, an entity that exists either
totally separate from brain or at best separate from, but interdependent
with, brain. Additionally, although each of these theories suggests that
mind is a separate entity, they fail to provide a precise characterization of
mind or to explain adequately by what process a metaphysical (or
nonphysical) mind interacts with a physical brain and vice versa.

MONIST THEORIES

The monist theories of mind and body are quite varied. What ties them together by the thinnest of threads is the common idea that there is only one psychophysical entity. The more simple forms of monism either reject the existence of mind (*materialism*) or body (*idealism*). The rather egocentric idealist view would suggest that only my (the thinker's) mind exists, and all else is a "figment of my imagination," so to speak. This notion is totally nonscientific and is not accessible to empirical examination. (If the monists are correct, I have wasted a good deal of time and energy writing this book for all of you nonexistent readers!)

Materialism takes a "black box" approach to behavior and proposes that mind does not exist at all. That is, there is only the material body. The most radical forms of behaviorism that viewed behavior as mindless linkages between stimuli and responses are representative of this philosophy. This view quite simply begs the question. You and I know that we have consciousness; it is a fact of our daily experiences. Denying this reality is simply not productive. Neither materialism nor idealism can be taken seriously.

Neutral monism is a poorly elaborated theory which generally states that mind and body are nothing more than different manifestations of the same entity. This relatively obscure theory proposes that both mind and body are the product of some unknowable "neutral substance or energy." I include it here only for the sake of completeness.

The last two monist theories depicted in Figure 16-1, *reductive materialism* and *emergent materialism*, are very similar. Both theories propose that what we call "mind" is physical and a direct consequence of the active processes of the CNS. The two theories differ only in the way that they perceive the CNS. Reductive materialism views the CNS as a very complex biological system that differs from all other biological systems only in the enormity of its complexity. Additionally, reductive materialism proposes that mental activity can be explained (or at least it will eventually be explained) in physical terms that are consistent with the physical laws relevant to the other physical sciences, such as chemistry, physics, and biology.

Emergent materialism views the CNS as a complex biosystem endowed with properties and governed by laws that may be unique to very complex living things. Consciousness and mental activity are unique properties of this system and may not be subject to the same physical laws that govern other physical entities. Although the physical laws that apply to chemistry and physics are necessary to explain CNS function, they are insufficient. Emergent materialism holds that the properties of mental activity are not to be found in the cellular components of the brain. Rather, they are *systemic properties* of the activity of large networks of cells. Further, the theory proposes that these systemic properties *emerged* at some point in time in the course of the evolution of nervous systems.

Those who support an emergent materialist philosophy note that the human brain (and perhaps other very complex brains) has remarkable self-regulatory functions that are rarely encountered in the physical world. Most notably, the active brain is able to anticipate future events and direct its action accordingly. (This brief review of the main views of the mind–body relationship is based largely on Bunge, 1980; Churchland, 1986; and Young, 1987.)

Which Theory Is Correct?

By definition, no theory is known to be correct. If one were known to be so, we would have a law and not a theory. Clearly, reductive materialism and emergent materialism are the two theories of mental activity that are the most consistent with the content of this text. For both of these theories the mind–body problem exists only as an abstraction. Mind and brain are viewed as one. From the perspective of these theories the "problem" of the mind–body problem should not be concerned with understanding the character or nature of a mind entity. Rather, it is a problem of understanding the brain mechanisms that represent mental processes.

I suggested in Chapter 1 that the term *mind* is not useful in a scientific context. For our purposes the term *mind* should be replaced by a more appropriate term such as **mentation**. This term emphasizes the processes of thinking and knowing. On this point we must be absolutely clear. Perceiving, feeling, remembering, imagining, thinking, knowing, and anticipating are different qualities of mental activity. They are *not* concrete things. They are processes of the brain.

When mind is mistakenly characterized as though it were a thing, it becomes possible, and indeed it is likely, for us to apply inappropriate thinglike attributes to mind. We may look for it in a place or ask how mind may impact on other physical things. Things have characteristics and identities of their own. Things can exist in the absence of other things in the world, and one thing may influence other things, just as a hammer may strike a nail.

It is my contention and the theme of this entire book that what we refer to as mind is a process of the working brain. It is as nonsensical to speak of a separate mind and brain as it is to attempt to divorce mass from matter or speed from time. One has no meaning without the other.

There is a human brain in a museum jar in my laboratory. Is that remarkable mass of nonliving tissue also a mind? Of course it is not! Mind isn't the tissue itself. Mind is the work or action of the brain tissues.

We have seen numerous examples throughout this book demonstrating that physical events which affect the normal functioning of the brain may also affect the conscious experience of the individual. Lesions to different areas of the brain can affect changes in memory, produce perceptual distortions, and affect changes in emotions and alterations in personality (see Spotlight 16-1). Anyone who has had too much alcohol to drink, has taken a powerful antihistamine, or has experimented with psychoactive drugs knows that altering the biochemistry of the brain may also alter conscious experience. Treating Parkinson's disease with L-dopa, which in turn elevates the levels of dopamine in the brain, may also induce delusions, hallucinations, and disorganized thoughts that mimic the symptoms of schizophrenia.

Is Mentation Unique to Humans?

At least one of the definitions of *mind* we found in my desk dictionary implies that the faculties of mind are unique to humans. Is this true? Some philosophers and brain scientists believe that mental activity is so closely tied to human language that it is not possible to discuss consciousness and mental activity in the absence of the structure supplied by complex languages (e.g., Langer, 1951; Pribram, 1976). Others profess that nonhuman organisms may indeed have mental faculties but that we must be "agnostic" about this question because it is not possible for us to "know" what other species know (e.g., Eccles, 1973, 1976).

Is there a dichotomy between knowing and not-knowing organisms? Is there a fine line that distinguishes "true" mentation from other brain–behavior processes? Or has mentation evolved slowly so that there are levels or degrees of the phenomenon apparent in various contemporary species? Clearly, the answer to these questions hinges to some degree on just how rigidly we define our terms. If we define *mentation* as a uniquely human characteristic, then, by definition, it is not to be found in other organisms. However, this egocentric philosophy may not be warranted. Let us examine this issue for a moment.

SELF-AWARENESS

One rather obvious characteristic of a knowing organism is its ability to differentiate between self and nonself. That is, the organism possesses **self-awareness**. When a cat or a dog looks into a mirror, does the animal recognize that the image is actually itself? How could you test what the animal "thinks" about the image? In 1970, Gallup placed a bright red spot on the forehead of an anesthetized chimpanzee. When the animal subsequently examined its image in a mirror, it reached up and touched the mark on its own forehead rather than the mark in the mirror image. Gallup interpreted this finding to mean that the chimpanzee has a concept of "self." Similar results have been found for other great apes,

The Famous and "Wonderful" Case of Phineas Gage

On September 13, 1848, a construction accident permanently altered the "mind" of Phineus Gage. Gage was a 25-year-old mild-mannered railroad construction foreman. While tamping explosives into a hole, the explosives accidentally ignited, blowing the 3-ft-long 13-lb tamping iron through his skull. The metal rod entered just below the orbit of the right eye and passed cleanly through the top of the skull. (Refer to Spotlight Figure 16.1.)

Remarkably, Gage recovered consciousness soon after the accident. He was placed on a horse-drawn cart and taken three fourths of a mile to his hotel. With some help he was able to climb the stairs to his room. Two hours after the accident he was seen by a physician, John Harlow. Harlow reported in his notes on the "wonderful" case of Phineas Gage that the patient was quite conscious and alert but that he was exhausted from the hemorrhage from the top of the head.

Two days following the accident, the hemorrhage had ceased, but Gage was delirious. There was an infectious discharge from his mouth, and particles of bone and brain oozed from the opening in the top of his head. By September 27, the discharge from the top of the head had been greatly reduced, but a large fungus growth had to be excised from the top of the mouth. By November 8, he was showing signs of an excellent recovery. On November 14, he was able to walk half a mile, and on the 25th of the same month he returned home, although the wound in the top of his head did not completely close until January 1.

Before the accident Gage had been dependable, industrious, well mannered, and well liked. After the accident he was like a different person. The changes in his behavior were so great that he could not continue in his former work.

He is fitful, irreverent, indulging at times in the grossest profanity (which was not previously his custom), manifesting but little deference for his fellows, impatient of restraint or advice when it conflicts with his desires, at times pertinaciously obstinate, yet capricious and vacillating, devising many plans of future operations, which are no sooner arranged than they are abandoned in turn for others appearing more feasible. A child in his intellectual capacity and manifestations, he has the animal passions of a strong man. Previous to his injury, though untrained in the schools, he possessed a well-balanced mind, and was looked upon by those who knew him as a shrewd, smart business man, very energetic and persistent in executing all his plans of operation. In this regard his mind is radically changed, so decidedly that his friends and acquaintances said he was "no longer Gage." (Harlow, 1868, p. 340)

It is not possible to reconstruct the complete clinical picture that underlies the changes evident in Gage's personality. Part of his personality change may be attributed to the notoriety following the accident. Additionally, his behavior may reflect reactions to the changes in his physical appearance. He did, in fact, travel around for a while with P. T. Barnum displaying himself as a freak. His family left him, and he turned to drink.

Knowing what we now know concerning the function of the prefrontal cortex in the expression and experience of emotion, it seems reasonable that some of

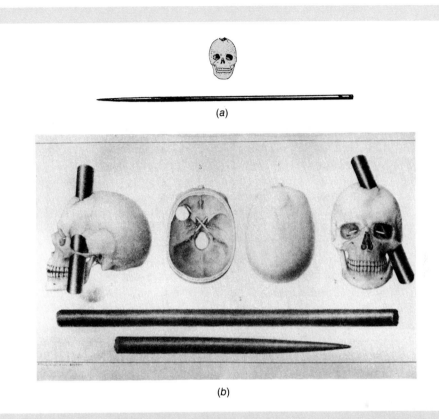

(a)

(b)

Spotlight Figure 16-1
The skull injury of Phineas Gage. *a*. The relative size of the skull and the tamping iron that penetrated Gage's head. *b*. The lateral (*far left*) and frontal (*far right*) aspects of the skull showing the tamping iron, in place, as it passed through the skull. Also shown is the dorsal aspect showing the point of entry below the orbit of the left eye (*center left*) and the fractured surface of the skull (*center right*). (From the National Library of Medicine.)

the changes in Gage's behavior were due to the focal damage to this part of his brain. Also, the frontal cortex has an important function in planning future actions (see the following section on "Planning Ahead"), and this too is consistent with the changes in Gage's behavior.

It is not possible to know what other parts of Gage's brain were affected by the intracranial infection that followed the accident; therefore, brain structures other than the prefrontal cortex most likely contributed to the changes in his personality. Nevertheless, it is clear that the lesion to Gage's brain forever changed his mental processes.

but not in the lesser apes (gibbons) and monkeys (Patterson & Pribram, reported in Pribram 1976; Gallup, 1977; 1979; Red Shaw, 1978; Suarez & Gallup, 1981). Pribram (1976) interprets these findings to mean that self-consciousness is not universal among organisms but has evolved recently and is, therefore, only evident in the most advanced primates.

LANGUAGE, MIND, AND COGNITION

Look at Figure 16-2 for a moment. I am sure that you had no difficulty at all filling in the blank. In fact, it is likely that the correct response came to you almost spontaneously, without the need to resort to language. If I were now to ask you to "think" about *why* you chose the response you did, you would be forced to resort to language to do so. You might say, "Well, the first symbol is upright, and the second is inverted. They alternate. Therefore, the last symbol must also be inverted." Notice that the initial solution of the problem and the verbal explanation of that solution may call on very different brain resources and structures.

Some researchers would propose that the mental process you used to solve the problem, without resorting to language, is not really representative of mind. For example, Sir John Eccles, winner of the Nobel Prize in physiology, contends that the mental task used to complete the sequence is "mere consciousness," a form of behavior we share with some other animals. For Eccles, language, thought, and culture are essential for any idea of mind.

Eccles's position makes two assumptions that may not be warranted. First, it excludes all non-language-based mentation from consideration. Think for a moment of the artist who backs away from the canvas in order to get a global impression of the balance, dynamics, and color of the work; or the conductor striving for the exact balance between the woodwinds and the strings; or the pilot rapidly scanning the flight instruments to ascertain the orientation of the aircraft. Can this be

Figure 16-2
Can you fill in the blank?

? ¿ ? ¿ ?

"mindless" behavior? Or, do these examples represent several qualitatively different forms of mentation?

Second, Eccles assumes that no other species is capable of language. Recall from Chapter 15 that chimpanzees and gorillas that have been specially trained to use sign language or other laboratory devices to enhance communication with humans show some evidence of self-awareness. They learned unique symbols to refer to self and others, and they apparently learned to apply adjectives and qualifiers to their own behavior and the behavior of other individuals. Koko, the gorilla, frequently used the hand signal for "Koko bad" or "Koko dirty" when she was admonished for her behavior. She also used these signs combined with the appropriate name or noun to indicate her displeasure with the behaviors of others.

Although there are alternate interpretations of the research (e.g., Terrace et al., 1979; Rosenbaum, 1983), the matter of language ability in other species cannot be discarded without further investigation. In fact, recent studies of the pigmy chimpanzee by Sue Savage-Rumbaugh and her colleagues at the Yerkes Regional Primate Center suggest that this rare species may be the most facile of all the great apes in the use of arbitrary symbols for communication (Savage-Rumbaugh, et al., 1986). Other research under way at Yerkes is providing some evidence that the chimpanzee can understand concepts such as relative size and number at a rudimentary level.

Brain and Consciousness

If we assume that mental processes are founded in the complex interaction of neural networks, we may also assume that mental processes have evolved just as the complexity of neural networks evolved. What we know of the evolution of the brain directs our attention to the rapidly evolving neocortex. Most brain researchers are in general agreement that thinking and consciousness depend on the processes of the thin cortex of the cerebral hemispheres. We turn now to a tentative model of brain and consciousness.

A Model for Brain and Consciousness

Brain scientists are actively searching for an organizing principle of brain structure and function that will provide testable hypotheses about the relationship between brain structure, action, and conscious experience. One of the most difficult issues concerning the brain mechanisms underlying conscious experience is related to the self-regulatory nature of mental processes. For example, how is the brain able to control itself when you anticipate and then execute the required eye movements to read this sentence? How does the brain formulate an image of the outside world, correlate that image with past experiences, and then plan appropriate actions? A neuronal model of the functional organization of the cortex that may provide some answers to these questions is beginning to emerge.

THE VERTICAL ORGANIZATION OF THE CORTEX

Vernon Mountcastle was the first researcher to note that the cortex is organized in vertical columns of cells (Mountcastle, 1956). Each cellular column extends through the full depth of the cortex and contains approximately 100 cells. Each column appears to function as a basic operational unit. Interestingly, the cellular organization of these columnar arrays is comprised of a small number of different cell types, and the cellular organization remains remarkably similar throughout the neocortex (Szentágothai, 1972). Each module appears to contain the following : (1) an input channel that brings neuronal messages to the unit from subcortical structures and from other regions of the cortex; (2) a local circuit that is actually a complex network of intramodular connections; and (3) an output channel that is largely comprised of the axons of pyramidal cells and that sends information to subcortical structures, the limbic system, and other regions of the cortex (see Figure 16-3).

Mountcastle has proposed that several vertical columns may be organized into an information-processing module he refers to as a **modular column** (Mountcastle, 1975; Mountcastle & Edelman, 1978). Although the modular columns differ slightly in size and organization in various parts of the cortex, the overall structure and function of the modular columns remain essentially the same. The major differences between modules lies in the specific regions of the brain that provide their input and the target of their output. (More recent data suggest that all areas of the cortex may not contain the columnar organization suggested by Mountcastle. (See Kaas, 1987, for a review.)

Finally, Mountcastle proposes that large numbers of modular columns work together and form massive looping circuits through the brain. These loops bring neural information from local cortical areas to other regions of the cortex as well as to subcortical structures and back again to the cortical origin. These information loops are a key feature of the model because they provide an orderly *"reentry"* of information to the cortical arrays.

Keep in mind that each module of vertical columns acts as an information-processing unit. The modules are grouped into much larger entities such as the primary visual cortex, the motor cortex, and the language areas of the brain, which have a primary function. Each of these entities, although dedicated to a primary function, has subsets of modules that are linked to subsets of modules in other entities. (For example, modules in the visual cortex communicate with modules in the somato-

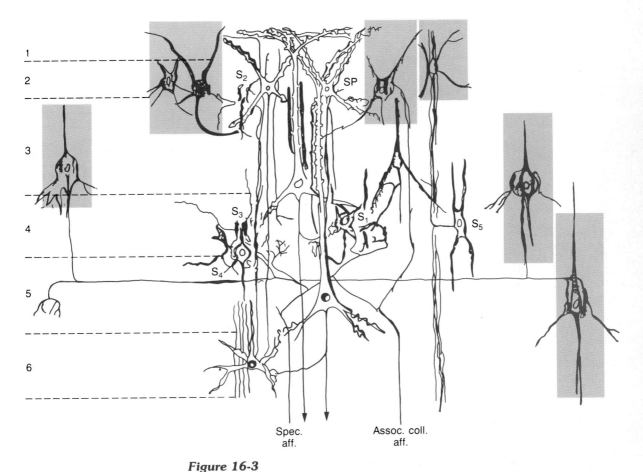

Figure 16-3

Semidiagrammatic drawing of some cell types of the cerebral cortex showing their interconnections. The numbers on the left side of the figure refer to the six cortical layers. Information enters the unit from subcortical structures (Spec. aff.) and other regions of the cortex (Assoc. call. aff.). Information leaves the column via the axons of the pyramidal cells. Other cells within the column (labelled S) provide intracellar communication and interact with pyramidal cells that are in immediately adjacent columns. (Redrawn from Szentágothai, 1969.)

sensory cortex that have similar characteristics.) These interconnected subsets from a distributed network spread over very large areas of the cortex.

According to Mountcastle, distributed neural systems such as this provide two important features. First, any subset of modules can participate in different distributed systems. What systems they interact with at any given moment would depend on what information reaches them at any point in time. For example, suppose there is a hypothetical subset of modules in the association cortex that processes information about the concept of the letter A. The subset may interact with modules in the visual cortex that perform the visual recognition task for the letter A, or modules in the auditory cortex that analyze the speech sounds representing A, or somatosensory modules that could make a tactile discrimination of a solid letter A. Second, distributed systems are less susceptible to lesions. Because the functional system is distributed over large areas of the brain, small lesions never abolish a particular function; they only degrade it.

In an excellent review article, Goldman-Rakic (1988) has outlined the evidence for a "topography of cognition" in the association cortex of primates. She notes that the association cortex (particularly the prefrontal cortex) appears to be organized into functional subdivisions (modules) that appear to have identical operations. That is, each subdivision is structurally organized in a similar way, and each carries out the same processing function. The various subdivisions seem to differ only in the nature of the information on which the operation is performed. This finding is quite consistent with the model proposed by Mountcastle.

THE STRUCTURE OF CONSCIOUSNESS

Let us see how the model may account for conscious experience. Recall that the information-processing units handle reentrant input and output as well as primary input. Therefore, the cortex has available to it at any given moment internally generated (reentrant) information as well as current information. This feature permits constant updating of perceptual images and matching functions that give the cortex the ability to link an image formed in the immediate past with the current information of the outside world being processed by sensory systems. (It may be helpful to think of this matching process as a form of reality testing.) Mountcastle proposes that it is this matching between the internal readout and the external world that *is* the mechanism of consciousness (Mountcastle & Edelman, 1978).

There is now some physical evidence concerning the visual system that tends to support the notion of the reentrant hypothesis. For example, there is clear evidence that visual suppression occurs during saccadic movement of the eyes. This suppression accounts for the fact that we do not see blurred images as the eyes move from one point of fixation to another. Researchers have wondered how we are able to integrate the flow of visual information between saccadic eye movements. That is, how do you make sense out of what you see in one point of fixation compared to the last point of fixation? There is now some evidence for an internal memory matching process that integrates the visual information from the current image with reentrant information (Irwin & Brown, 1989). Additionally, it has been shown that the nature of ongoing mental imaging modifies the processing of visual information. If subjects are instructed to create images in the "mind's eye," the nature of the image modifies the evoked EEG responses to visual stimuli (Farah, Péronnet, Gonon, & Giard, 1989). The researchers believe that this finding implies that perception and active imaging interact at some common locus in the brain. This could be due to the effect of imaging on the reentrant neural mechanism.

The model also helps us understand how different parts of the brain are able to substitute for the conscious functions of lesioned structures. For example, a person who loses hearing and must learn sign language or who is blinded and must learn to use Braille may build on existing "language subsets," merely subsituting the pattern of information input and output. That is, there are visual, auditory, and tactile representations of language that share similar coding strategies and interconnections with the language areas of the brain.

The theory is admittedly sketchy, but you must remember that we are dealing with an extremely complex problem. The human cortex is probably the most intricate and complex system known to us, and our knowledge of the intricate web of interconnections within the cortex is still very limited. Nevertheless, the modular concept is an exciting one that holds much promise. However, much more research is required before we can unravel this Gordian knot.

The Prefrontal Cortex

If you were asked to looked for the areas of the cortex most likely to be associated with "humanlike" behavior it makes sense to look at those parts of the cortex that are relatively exaggerated in the human brain. For this reason researchers have directed much attention at the association cortex. You will recall from Chapter 3 that one of the clearest indicators of the encephalization process is the increase in the amount of association cortex relative to sensory and motor cortex.

We have already seen that the posterior portion of the frontal cortex (Broca's area) and the association areas of the temporal and parietal lobes (Wernicke's area) are critical for speech production and the comprehension of language. The evolutionary expansion of association neocortex is particularly clear in the development of the **prefrontal cortex** (Figure 16-4). The term *prefrontal* is somewhat misleading in that it refers to the part of the frontal lobe that is anterior to the motor cortex.

ORIENTATION IN TIME

In humans, lesions to the prefrontal cortex may produce a variety of changes in behavior, including changes in emotions (recall the case of Phineas Gage), loss of inhibition in social situations, deficits in the

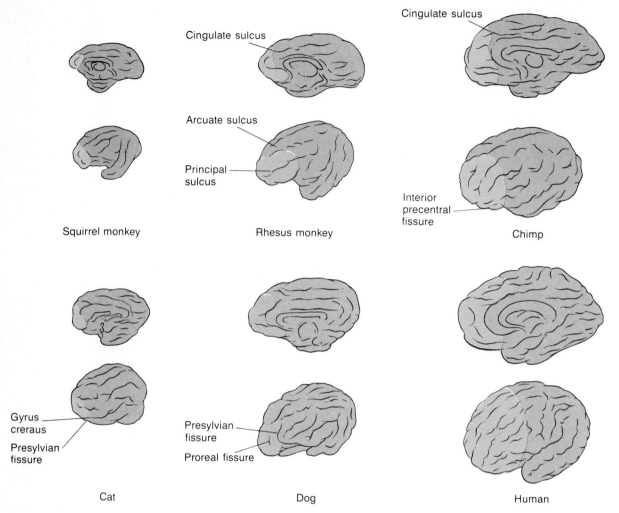

Figure 16-4
The prefrontal cortex of several representative species of mammals.

coordinated movement of the eyes, and problems with tasks requiring inhibition such as delayed response tasks (Golden, 1978). Lesions to the prefrontal cortex may also produce problems with intentions, planning, and orientation in regard to time and place (Benton, 1968).

It appears that the prefrontal cortex has an important function in behaviors that are necessary for planning goals and anticipating future events (Fuster, 1980; Luria, 1966). People with lesions to the prefrontal cortex appear to be easily distracted from carrying out an intended task.

They may set out to accomplish one task and be found moments later doing something quite different from what they originally intended to do. For example, a person with a prefrontal lesion who sets out for the store may be found a few minutes later reading in the living room because the newspaper happened to be on the front steps. Studies with animal models have shed some light on this phenomenon.

LESION STUDIES

Lesion studies using a variety of animals have shown quite clearly that the prefrontal cortex is important in delayed response tasks (Harlow & Settlage, 1948; Jacobsen, 1936; Pribram, 1967). (See Figure 16.5.) The following is a typical example: (1) Show a monkey that a raisin is placed under one of three stimuli, (2) place a curtain in front of the stimuli for 30 seconds to prevent the animal from making a choice, (3) lift the curtain and let the monkey choose the stimulus that covers the raisin. Compared to normal animals, monkeys with prefrontal lesions have considerable difficulty with this task.

Contrary to the way it appears, careful study of these prefrontal lesioned animals shows that their poor performance is not related to

Figure 16-5
The Wisconsin General Test Apparatus (WGTA), used to test animals on delayed response tasks.

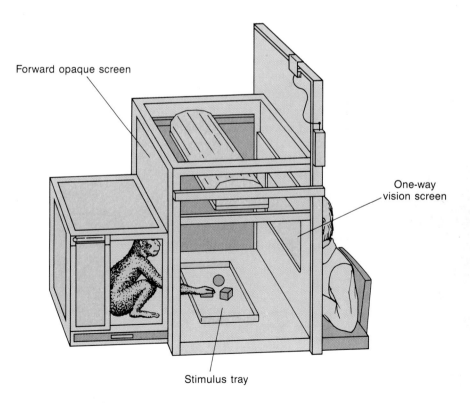

Forward opaque screen

One-way vision screen

Stimulus tray

learning or memory. Rather, their difficulty with this task is due to the animal's inability to integrate events that take place at different times (Pribram, 1967; Pribram & Tubbs, 1967). That is, the frontal cortex lesions appear to produce deficits in programming and coding time-related tasks rather than deficits in memory. Additionally, some of the performance deficit on any visual task following lesions to the prefrontal cortex may be due in part to problems with coordinating visual search (Luria, 1973b).

SINGLE-CELL CHARACTERISTICS

Studies made of the response characteristics of cells in the prefrontal cortex during delayed response tasks provide some clues concerning the role of the prefrontal cortex in this type of task. To perform a delayed response task successfully, the subject really must accomplish three things: (1) maintain attention on the task during the period of the delay, (2) hold the correct stimulus in short-term memory, and (3) maintain a readiness to make the necessary motor response. The data show that given cells in the prefrontal cortex are active in each of these functions (Niki & Wanatabe, 1976).

Figure 16-6 shows the response characteristics of five classes of cells in the prefrontal cortex of monkeys. Note that cell A responds with a brief burst of activity at the onset of the stimulus cue, the delay period, and the motor response. Cell B is activated only at the onset of the stimulus cue and the motor response. Cell C is activated from the onset of the cue throughout the entire task. Cell D is inhibited during stimulus presentation and the motor response but is activated during the period of the delay. Cell I is inhibited during the cue and motor response phase. Trace O is the control condition when no cue is present and no response is made. Clearly, the various cell types are concerned with different aspects of the delayed response task.

Brain Dysfunction and Conscious Experience

We noted earlier, in the case of Phineas Gage, that lesions to the brain can produce remarkable changes in the behavior and the personal characteristics of the afflicted individual. The contemporary clinical literature is full of individual case histories that relate lesions to the brain with a wide spectrum of specific behavioral changes. These clinical reports may also be instructive concerning the relationship between brain function, brain organization, and conscious experience. To make this point, I want to review two examples of cognitive changes resulting from brain trauma.

NEGLECT SYNDROME

As a graduate student, I saw a patient who had a remarkable change in his cognitive experiences following surgery to remove a large

Figure 16-6
Response characteristics of five types of cells in the prefrontal cortex of monkeys. The data show the pattern of firing for each cell during the various stages of a delayed response task trial. The first arrow marked "up" indicates the point where the screen is raised to display the stimuli. At the second arrow the screen is lowered to start the delay period. The third arrow indicates the point where the screen is raised to allow the animal to respond. See the text for more detail. (Redrawn from Fuster, 1973.)

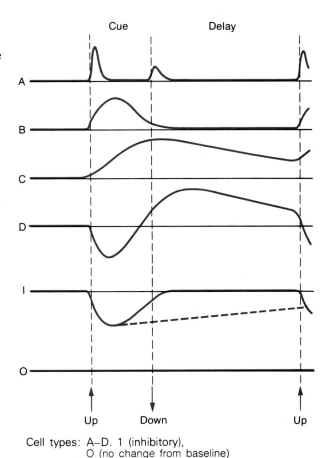

Cell types: A–D. 1 (inhibitory),
O (no change from baseline)

tumor from the right parietal area of his brain. In most regards his intellectual and social behavior was quite normal. He was quite lucid and conversed freely and meaningfully with the staff and patients on his ward. However, his cognitive experiences of space and spatial relationships were quite unusual. For example, he would eat the food on the right side of his plate but not touch the food on the left side. If the plate was rotated 180°, he would finish the remainder of his meal. When walking down the hall, he would tend to recognize and interact with people who passed on his right side, but he seemed to be unaware of the people on his left. When dressing himself, he might put only his right arm in his shirt or his right leg in his pants. At that point he would stop, unable to figure out what was wrong or understand what needed to be done next. Often he was found to be wearing just one slipper (always on the right foot). He would shave the right side of his face but leave the beard on the left side untouched.

It was quite apparent that this young patient was having great difficulty attending to the left side of his world. Tests showed that he had experienced some loss of vision in the left half-field, but this condition alone did not seem sufficient to explain the almost complete lack of attention to the left side of the environment.

One of the most surprising aspects of this patient's **neglect syndrome** became apparent to the nurses on his ward when he began to complain about the overcrowded conditions in the hospital. He was particularly irked by the "fact" that the nurses were apparently slipping another patient into his bed at night while he was asleep and then "sneaking" him back out again in the morning. He became particularly agitated when the night nurses denied that there was anyone in the bed with him and treated him "as though I am crazy." No amount of reasoning from the hospital staff could convince him that (1) there were no overcrowded conditions on the ward (there were in fact empty beds); (2) it was against hospital policy to place two patients in a single bed; and (3) the single hospital bed, with it's side rails up, was simply too narrow to accommodate two adults.

He was having none of this. He had to admit that it didn't seem possible to put two people in that narrow bed. Nevertheless, he was absolutely convinced that there *was* someone else in the bed with him during the night. As you may have guessed by now, the patient was mistaking the left side of his own body as that belonging to someone else! He quite literally did not realize that the left side of his own body belonged to him. (For other examples of neglect syndrome see Muselam, 1985, & Sacks, 1987.)

How is it possible for an otherwise intelligent and reasonable person to fail to attend to one half of his world? Even more bewildering, how is it possible for him not to recognize parts of his own body as being a part of himself? It seems almost too ridiculous to you or me, with our intact brains, to comprehend how any lesion to the brain could result in such a bizarre warping of conscious experience.

We noted earlier in this chapter that one characteristic of a knowing individual is a sense of self-awareness—being able to differentiate between self and others in the environment. Here we have a case of an individual who, at times, experiences (for lack of a better term) "hemi-self-awareness." Clearly, this is not just a visual acuity problem. The patient recognizes his left leg and arm as being a leg and an arm. Not only that, he has motor control over these limbs. Yet, at times, he does not and cannot accept them as his own!

Apparently, the lesioned area in the right parietal cortex of this patient is important for making the connection between those areas of the brain that encode and interpret visual information and other areas of the brain which relate that information with decisions concerning self and nonself. It appears that it may require more or different brain interactions to know "my leg" than it does to recognize "a leg." The lesion to this patient's brain must have in some fashion interrupted the orderly flow of information between those areas of the brain that integrate perceptions of body parts and the concept of self.

MEANING IS MORE THAN THE WORDS

In his wonderful book *The Man Who Mistook His Wife for a Hat and Other Clinical Tales*, Oliver Sacks makes an important point about the nature and complexity of language. He notes that the meaning of words is not only dependent on their order but also on the tone, timing, and expressiveness with which the words are spoken. Additionally, gestures, facial expressions, and various forms of "body language" add to the meaningfulness of what people say.

Sacks notes that aphasic patients, who are unable to understand the meaning of words, are frequently very attuned to the emotion and feeling in the speech of others. Sacks reminds us that Hughlings Jackson, the great British neurologist, compared aphasic patients to dogs in that dogs are unable to understand the meaning of the words in human speech, but they are very sensitive to the emotions and feelings that are communicated by the tone and expressiveness of the speech and the body language of the speaker.

Sacks maintains that it is difficult (if not impossible) to deceive aphasic patients. Because the aphasic person cannot understand the content of the words in your speech, he or she cannot be deceived by them. However, the aphasic person is particularly aware of the emotions of the speaker and is, therefore, able to interpret the true intent of what is being communicated.

Sacks also notes that individuals who have right temporal lobe damage may also experience problems with language processsing. The right temporal area of the brain seems to process information concerning the perception of pitch and the timing of auditory events (e.g., Fedio & Mirsky, 1969). These patients are able to understand the meaning of words quite well but loose their ability to process the tonal and timing characteristics of speech production. (This condition is sometimes referred to as **tonal agnosia**.) Because of this, people with right temporal lesions may have considerable difficulty sensing the *feeling* in the speech of others. Unlike aphasic individuals, these patients are insensitive to the emotion and expression in speech and must depend on the rigid, literal meaning of the order of the words themselves. Jokes and facetious comments, which depend on inflection and timing, are lost on these people. Clearly, the full color and meaning of language are both right and left brain functions. The perception of language is dependent on the orderly flow and integration of information from many areas of the brain.

The clinical data show us that brain function is best understood in holistic terms. This is particularly true when we refer to complex experiences such as self-awareness and language comprehension. These complex forms of conscious experience are the result of the dynamic interaction of *brain systems*, and not the action of specific brain centers. The more complex the behavior becomes, the greater the number of brain structures involved. From this perspective a lesion to the brain is seen to disrupt an ordered sequence of information processing more than it destroys the function of a brain center.

Split Brains and Split Minds?

Consider the following laboratory study for a moment. The corpus callosum and the minor commissures connecting the left and right hemispheres of the brain and the optic chiasma are all severed. The animal (in this case a cat) recovers from the surgery and is brought into the laboratory for testing. When we examine the animal for a variety of behaviors, we find that, quite remarkably, its behavior seems essentially unaltered. Millions of axons have been severed, yet the behavior appears not to be affected!

This surgical preparation literally separates the two large cerebral hemispheres so they are isolated from each other (with the exception of what little information may be transferred through brain stem structures). Cutting through the optic chiasma also severs all of the decussating optic fibers. This prevents any visual information entering the eyes from reaching the contralateral hemisphere. This surgical preparation also produces a loss of one half of the visual field in each eye, a condition known as **hemianopia** (see Figure 16-7).

If one of the cat's eyes is covered with a patch, the animal will only receive visual information in the half-brain that is on the same side as the uncovered eye. With the right eye covered, the animal is taught a visual discrimination task. Pressing a lever marked by a $\triangle$ symbol will provide a food reinforcement. Pressing a lever marked by a $\square$ goes unrewarded. The animal learns to make this discrimination at approximately the same rate as would an intact animal.

Now we switch the patch and test the animal again. The left brain knows nothing of what the right brain has learned! Now we reverse the valence of the visual cues so that the lever marked by the $\square$ is rewarded, and the previously reinforced $\triangle$ goes unrewarded. The cat's left brain learns this task at a normal rate. Following this second period of training, the cat's behavior on the task will be totally determined by which eye (brain) is experiencing the outside world. The left brain responds positively to the lever marked by the $\square$, whereas the right brain responds to the $\triangle$. The information remains isolated in the hemisphere where the learning occured. This study was done by Roger Sperry and his colleagues in the mid 1950s (Sperry, Stamm, & Nimer, 1956). This study, and others that followed, gave rise to the notion that it is possible to have not one, but two minds functioning in one head.

Figure 16-7
Surgical preparation that
separates the two cerebral
hemispheres by cutting
the commissures between
the left and right brain.
The sagittal section of the
optic chiasm restricts
visual information from
each eye to the ipsilateral
side of the brain.

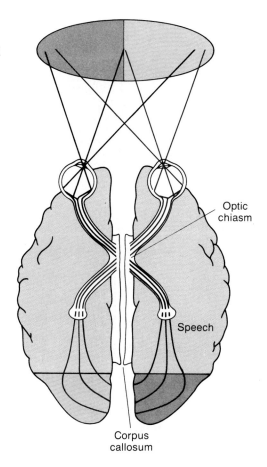

Optic
chiasm

Speech

Corpus
callosum

SPLIT-BRAIN HUMANS

For obvious reasons, one does not go about splitting the brains of
people to study the effect on human brain function and consciousness.
However, some years ago Joseph Bogen, a neurosurgeon, severed the
corpus callosum of patients who were suffering from severe grand mal
epileptic seizures.

EEG recordings had shown that epileptic seizures tend to originate
in a focal area and then spread to mirror areas on the contralateral side of
the brain. The massive and uncontrolled firing of neurons across the
corpus callosum seemed to trigger the very dangerous grand mal seizures. Earlier attempts to sever parts of the corpus callosum to treat
epilepsy had resulted in mixed results (Van Wagenen & Herren, 1940).
However, Bogen reasoned that the less than acceptable results of the
earlier attempts could have been due to the incompleteness of the surgical disconnection. Additionally, new data from surgery on animals

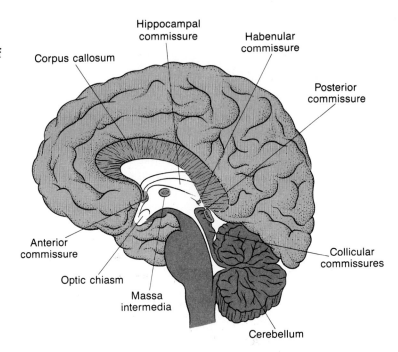

indicated that complete sectioning of the callosum and the minor commissures (**commissurotomy**) seemed to have little effect on most forms
of behavior. Bogen predicted that cutting the callosal fibers and the fibers
of the minor commissures would prevent the spread of the seizures and
limit their severity without seriously affecting the normal functioning of
his patients (refer to Figure 16-8).

Bogen's predictions concerning the outcome of the commissurotomy were generally borne out. The frequency and severity of the epileptic seizures were greatly reduced, and the general behavior, intellect, and
conscious experiences of the patients remained essentially unchanged. As
you might imagine, the behavior of the patients who underwent a commissurotomy has been studied in great depth. It soon became apparent
that the disconnection of the two hemispheres provided a unique opportunity to examine the difference in conscious awareness between the two
sides of the brain.

WHAT THE RIGHT BRAIN KNOWS

In the intact brain the functional differences between the two
hemispheres is often masked because the two sides of the brain interact so
effectively. In the split-brain patients the lateralization of brain function
can be much more apparent. We have seen in previous chapters that the
left brain tends to be superior for language, and the right brain appears
to be superior for tasks concerned with orientation in space and time.

Figure 16-9
The block-design task.
The subject arranges the
small blocks to form the
sample pattern.

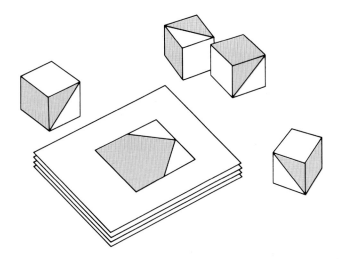

The right brain's superiority (and the left brain's inferiority) for visuospatial tasks became markedly apparent when Gazzaniga and Sperry tested Bogen's first split-brain patient on a blocks-design task. The task requires the subject to match a sample pattern by combining a number of small blocks. Each block has two red sides, two white sides and two sides that are split diagonally, half red and half white. By turning and arranging the blocks appropriately, the subject matches the more complex sample pattern (see Figure 16-9).

At first the patient had great difficulty with the task. It appeared to the researchers that the left hand made some progress on the task, but the right hand seemed to undo what the left hand completed! The subject was then tested using only the left hand, which is controlled by the right brain. In this situation he matched the sample pattern with little difficulty. When tested with the right hand, however, he was at a loss. Films made of the testing session show that during the right-hand trials the subject's left hand "sneaked" in to assist the right hand. The investigators literally had to hold back the subject's left hand to keep it from assisting in the task.

Another clear example of the right brain visuospatial superiority can be seen in the drawings of split-brain patients. Drawings made with the left (nonpreferred) hand consistently evidence better spatial relationships than do drawings made with the right hand (Gazzaniga & LeDoux, 1978).

The right brain advantage for visuospatial tasks is likely to be attributable to two factors. First, the right brain appears to be perceptually superior at understanding spatial relationships (Levy-Agresti & Sperry, 1968). Also, the right brain may be more skilled at executing the motor components of spatial tasks (LeDoux, Wilson, & Gazzaniga,

1977a). Other researchers maintain that the right brain may process information with a different strategy than does the left. That is, the two sides of the brain may have different information-processing styles. Examination of split-brain patients by Jerre Levy led her to conclude that the left hemisphere processes information in a serial and analytic fashion consistent with the left brain's superior language ability. The right brain, conversely, may process information in a more holistic manner that would be consistent with a spatial orientation (Levy, 1974). There is considerable evidence to support the notion that these relationships hold for people with normal, intact brains as well (e.g., Kinsbourne, 1974; Kinsbourne & Hicks, 1978; Moscovitch, 1979).

An Observation: Déjà Vu

Have you ever walked into a room where you have never been before and felt that you have had the very same experience before? Everything, even in the smallest detail, seemed remarkably familiar to you? The situation is so familiar, yet you know that you have never been there before. This is the **déjà vu** phenomenon. If you have had this sort of experience, you are not alone, as many people have reported similar experiences. Can there be a logical explanation for this strange, albeit common, occurrence?

I was at a conference of neuropsychologists in Minneapolis some years ago where I heard a theoretical paper concerned with brain mechanisms in visual information processing. I must confess that I do not recall much of that paper, but I do remember the lively discussion that followed the formal paper presentation. Someone in the audience drew a parallel between mental imaging as when you try to "picture" someone's face in your mind and the déjà vu phenomenon. At that point another member of the audience offered the following theory for this relatively common experience.

Apparently, he had been doing some tachistoscopic research that indicated that the right hemisphere of the brain processes visual information in a holistic manner. Additionally, his research showed that the right brain seemed to process visual information slightly faster than does the left brain. The left/right differences he found, which he attributed to the different processing strategies, were small but consistent. He noted that other researchers had shown rather clearly that the right hemisphere is noted for its poor analytical and language skills. He wondered if it were not possible that the déjà vu experience simply represents the analytical and verbal left brain consciously dealing with what the more rapid, but less verbal, right brain had just processed. The reason why the room looks so familiar to you is that you just saw it a few milliseconds earlier in the mute side of your brain!

WHAT THE LEFT BRAIN KNOWS

As investigators studied the behavior of split-brain patients in depth, they dramatically confirmed that the left brain was the dominant hemisphere for speech. In a typical experiment the subject sits in front of a back projection screen. The investigator instructs the subject to look at a central fixation dot on the screen, and then a word is projected tachistoscopically to the left or right visual field.

The rapid presentation prevents the possibility that the subjects can move their eyes to look directly at the stimulus. Recall from Chapters 4 and 5 that the visual pathways bring information from the right retina of both eyes to the right visual cortex, and the fibers from the left retina of each eye project to the left side of the brain. (In terms of visual fields, the left field is projected to the right brain, and the right field is projected to the left brain.)

If a word is projected to the right visual field (left brain), the subject has no difficulty identifying the word and reporting it orally. If a word is projected to the left visual field, the subject is most likely to report not seeing anything at all. Similarly, if a picture of a cup or a key or some other common object is flashed onto the right visual field, the subject has no difficulty reporting orally what he or she saw. However, when these same common objects are projected onto the left visual field, (right brain) the subject is likely to report having seen nothing.

Now let us see what happens when a word like *hatband* or *rattlesnake* is projected onto the screen (as in Figure 16-10) so that part of the word is projected to the right brain and part to the left brain. The subject will report seeing only the part of the word that was projected to the left brain and will deny that there was anything else in the left visual field.

Quite clearly, the left brain is the verbal brain. It understands language, and it is essential for the production of speech. But how do we

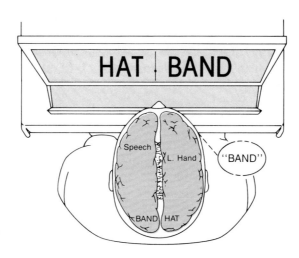

Figure 16-10
In this condition only the part of the word to the right of the fixation dot is reported by the subject. The subject sees and reports the word BAND, which was registered in the left side of the brain. The word HAT is not consciously seen nor is it even subconsciously associated with the word BAND seen in the right visual field. (From Sperry, 1970b.)

interpret the apparent inability of the right brain to deal with language? Is the right brain completely devoid of language ability? Does the right brain understand language but lack access to the speech centers located in the left brain? There is some evidence that the right brain is unable to express itself through speech.

On one occassion while testing a female patient, N. G., Gazzaniga and Sperry flashed a photograph of a nude female onto the left visual field. The patient visibly blushed and giggled. When asked what she saw, she replied, "Nothing, just a flash of light," and giggled again, covering her mouth with her hand in obvious embarrassment. When the investigators questioned her concerning why she was laughing, she replied, "Oh, doctor, you have some machine!"

Evidently, the left brain was made aware of the emotional reaction to the photograph that N. G. experienced at subcortical levels. The actual source of the emotional response, however, was not available to the left (vocal) brain, and the right brain was not able to communicate orally with the investigators.

DOES THE RIGHT BRAIN HAVE LANGUAGE?

At first it appeared that the right brain was without language ability, but more careful examination showed that this was far from accurate. The following is a clear example of this fact.

The name of an object is flashed in the left visual field, and the subject reports seeing only a flash of light. When pressed by the investigator to try to report the name, the subject can only guess. Now the subject is asked to reach under the screen and with the left hand (which is controlled by the right brain) find the object that is hidden from sight among a group of other objects (see Figure 16-11). After picking up the appropriate object, the subject is asked to name what he holds in his hand. Again, he can only guess! Clearly, the right hemisphere knows the meaning of the word; it did guide the left hand to the appropriate object. The right brain just as clearly cannot communicate what it knows to the left hemisphere, which controls speech.

Further study has shown that the right brain is capable of following very simple commands. For example, if the word *scratch* is flashed to the right brain, the subject will scratch himself or herself. Interestingly, if asked what was shown on the screen, the subject might guess "itch." Note that the left brain having seen the action makes a guess that is relevant to what it has seen. The right brain's ability to deal with verbs is extremely limited, and it will often fail to respond to such simple commands as wink, nod, and smile (Gazzaniga, 1983).

Another example of the language ability found in the right hemisphere can be seen in Figure 16-12. In this instance the subject is shown a word in the left visual field. As was true earlier, the subject is unable to speak the word, and the left brain can only guess at what it was. The subject is then asked to write the word using the left hand. The subject

Figure 16-11
Names of objects flashed to the right brain can be read and understood but not spoken. The subject is able to find the named object behind the screen using the left hand but is unable to name the object after it is located. (From Sperry, 1970b.)

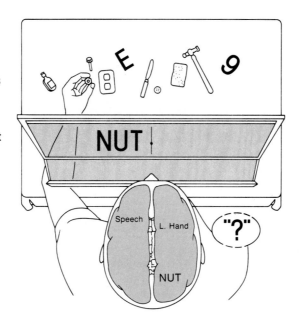

Figure 16-12
An example of left-hand writing of a word flashed to the right side of the brain. After successfully writing the word, the subject is still unable to verbalize the word. (From Nebes & Sperry, 1971.)

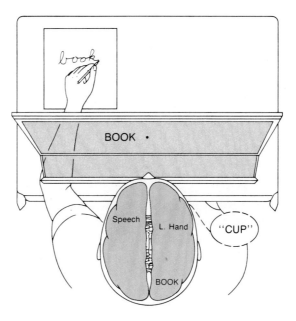

writes the word in script, indicating that this is not simply a pattern-matching task. When asked what is written, the left brain, although aware from the movement of the body that something has been written, can only guess at the word. Left-handed writing in split-brain patients is quite limited, and often the subject will stop after jotting down the first

The Special Case of P. S.

Most people have language localized in the left side of the brain, and this is true for all of the people who have had a commissurotomy to control epilepsy—all, that is, except one. Joseph LeDoux and Michael Gazzaniga have reported on one of their split-brain patients who, although dominant for language in the left hemisphere, had shown in preoperative tests that he possessed a significant amount of right brain language ability. The patient had a history of damage to the left brain as a child, which may explain why the right brain acquired its language skills (Gazzaniga & LeDoux, 1978; LeDoux, Wilson, & Gazzaniga, 1977b).

The patient, known as P. S., was 16 years old at the time of his surgery, and he was studied extensively by LeDoux, Gazzaniga, and their research team for several years. The researchers discovered that P. S. was able to "write" with his left hand using the letters from a Scrabble game. Using this technique, the researchers found that they were able to communicate with the usually mute right brain. They would frame a question orally such as "Who are _____?" and then flash the remainder of the question (e.g., "you") in the left or right visual field. When the last portion of the question was directed to the left brain, P. S. responded verbally. He responded with the Scrabble letters using his left hand when the information was flashed to the right brain (see Spotlight Figure 16-2).

In one group of studies LeDoux and Gazzaniga asked P. S. to rate how he felt about various things. He was to respond on a scale of 1 (like very much) to 5 (dislike very much). The same verbal/visual paradigm was used. The questions were posed verbally except for the key word, which was flashed to either the right or left brain. For example, "How much do you like _____?"

The results showed that P. S.'s right brain could respond to this type of question. What is most interesting is that the responses of the right brain were at times discordant with the responses of the left brain. Another indication that P. S.'s left and right brains were not always in agreement is evident in his response to a question concerning what job he would like to have. The left brain responded "draftsman." The right brain spelled out "automobile race."

The investigators summed up their assessment of P. S. in the following manner:

Each hemisphere in P. S. has a sense of self and each possesses its own system for subjectively evaluating current events, planning for further events, setting response priorities, and generating personal responses. Consequently, it becomes useful now to consider the practical and theoretical implication of the fact that double consciousness mechanisms can exist (LeDoux, Wilson, & Gazzaniga, 1977b).

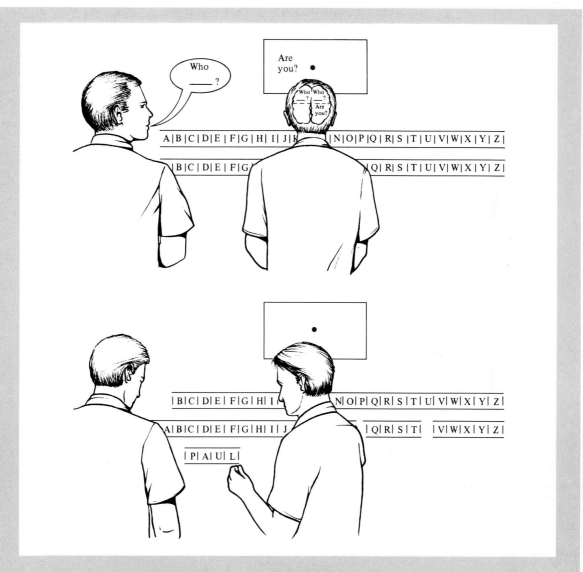

Spotlight Figure 16-2
The patient P. S. can answer questions flashed to the right hemisphere by arranging letters with his left hand. (From Gazzaniga & LeDoux, 1978.)

two or three letters. Nevertheless, this phenomenon is a clear indication that the right brain is able to read, understand, and reproduce words (Nebes & Sperry, 1971).

Eran Zaidel devised a way to limit visual input to one side of the brain while allowing the split-brain patients freedom of eye movement. The device, which is called a **Z lens**, allows the patient to look at a stimulus for as long as he or she wishes while at the same time ensuring that the visual information is restricted to one half of the brain (Zaidel, 1975).

Using this technique, Zaidel has shown that the right side of the brain possesses much greater language skills than previously thought. The right hemisphere appears to understand relationships, and it can follow verbal instructions such as "place the yellow square over the green circle." Zaidel's work would suggest that the right hemisphere has a vocabulary that is equivalent to that of a normal 10-year-old child; however, the right brain cannot produce speech (Zaidel, 1978). Clearly, speech production has been specialized in Broca's and Werniche's areas on the left side of the brain (see Figure 16-13).

Zaidel's work shows that when the right brain has time to process verbal information, it does considerably better than under tachistoscopic

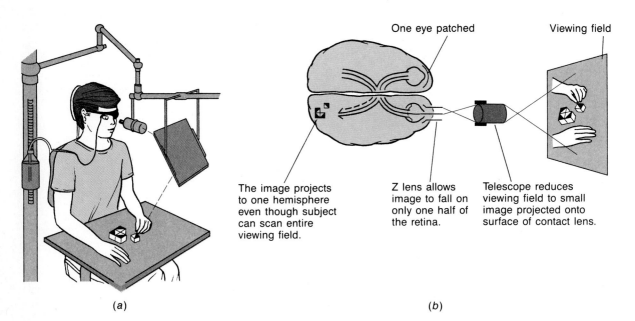

(a) (b)

Figure 16-13
a. The laboratory conditions used to evaluate the language capabilities of split-brain subjects wearing the full-contact Z lens. *b.* The Z lens allows freedom of eye movement while insuring that the visual information is restricted to one half of the retina. The patient's other eye is patched to occlude all visual input. (Redrawn from Zaidel, 1978.)

conditions. The debate over language in the right hemisphere is far from over. The examination of split-brain patients has shown that the right side of the brain is certainly not devoid of language. No one, however, who has examined split-brain patients would suggest that the language ability of the right brain rivals that of the left.

An Observation: Kana versus Kanji

English, and most other written forms of language, are serial in nature. That is, the order of the symbols greatly influences their meaning. The letters represent phonemes, and the order of the phonemes determines the words. The Japanese culture has two types of written language. One is Kana, which is similar to our own language in that it uses symbols to represent sounds. The order of the symbols determines the words. Kanji, the other written form, uses ideographs. Each symbol represents a thing or an idea rather than a sound. See samples of Kanji and Kana in Observation Figure 16-2.

Kana, being similar to other forms of written language, is likely to be processed in the left hemisphere. It may be possible that Kanji ideographs are processed with a visuospatial strategy. If so, we might expect Kanji to be processed in the right brain rather than the left. Evidence from stroke victims suggests that this may indeed be the case. Japanese with stroke damage localized in the left hemisphere show deficits in their ability to read Kana, but their ability to read Kanji is not appreciably affected. Conversely, lesions in the visual cortex associated with pattern recognition interfere with the ability to read and produce Kanji symbols (Sasanuma, 1975; Tanaka, Yamadori, & Murata, 1987).

Observation Figure 16-1

Samples of Kanji and Kana.

Kanji		Kana
木	tree	キ
林	woods	はやし
森	forest	もり
白	white	しろ
鳥	bird	とり
白鳥	swan	はくちょう

Point and Counterpoint

Let us now return to the issue of the mind–body problem. Certainly, the research on patients with split brains has shown us that mind (mentation) is not independent of the physical activity of the brain. Most researchers would agree that interruption of communication between the two cerebral hemispheres produces two conscious entities having separate, but different, cognitive characteristics.

The argument concerning whether or not the conscious characteristics of the right hemisphere can be viewed as "mind" goes on unabated. As we noted earlier, the controversy is highly confounded by varying subjective definitions of *consciousness* and *mind*. For those researchers who inexorably link consciousness and mind to human language, the evidence for the presence of "mind" in the right hemisphere is tenuous at best. For others, the split-brain subjects provide clear evidence that the two sides of the brain contain independent, but qualitatively different, mental identities.

Why Two Brains in One?

The evidence for the existence of two independent conscious entities in the split-brain patient can be seen most clearly in the following experiment. The patient is shown slides of **chimeric** faces. (The term *chimeric* comes from the mythical monster Chimera, who was made up of parts of different animals.) Each face is actually a composite of two half-faces. In previous training the subject has learned to identify the intact photographs of the faces by name. Now she will be shown the chimerics tachistoscopically so that one side of the chimeric is in each visual half-field.

On some trials the subject is told that she will be required to identify the face by name. On other trials the instructions to the subject are that she will be required to identify the face she saw by pointing to the same face from an array of different faces. In one such study the researchers found that when required to report verbally, the subject indicated that she saw the face that was projected to the left brain. However, when required to point to the face in a group of sample faces, the patient pointed to the face that was projected to the right hemisphere (Levy, Trevarthen, & Sperry, 1972). (See Figure 16-14.)

Two conclusions may be drawn from this remarkable study. First, the subject's behavior is determined by the nature of the task. If the intended response requires a verbal strategy, the subject solves the problem with the mental processes of the left brain. However, if the response requires a spatial strategy, the subject engages the mental processes inherent in the right side of the brain. One is tempted to say that the subject "selects" which half-brain ("mind") she will use depending on the anticipated problem requirements.

Second, the patient reports seeing normal, complete faces. In nei-

Figure 16-14
The chimeric face test of split brain patients. *a.* and *b.* The original faces used in the study and representative chimeric stimuli composed of the left and right halves of two different faces. *c.* The chimeric face is presented tachistoscopically so that each half-face is projected very briefly to different sides of the brain. When the instructions require the subject to point to the person she saw, as shown in *c.*, she reports seeing the face that was projected to the right side of the brain. Under conditions where the subject is asked to identify the face by name, she reports seeing the face that was projected to the left side of the brain. (Redrawn from Levy, Trevarthen, & Sperry, 1972.)

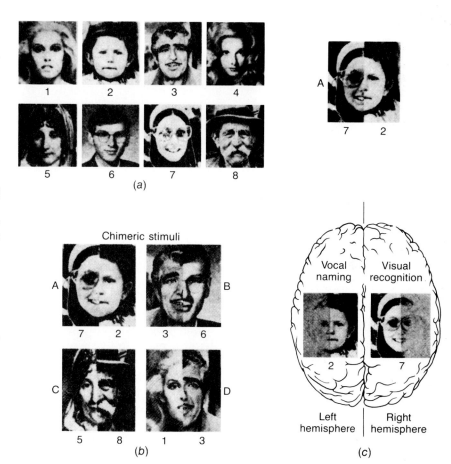

ther response condition does the subject see just a half-face. Nor does the subject see a chimeric face; she only responds to one side. She literally "fills in" the missing half-face. Similar results have been found for chimeric figures other than faces (Levy & Trevarthen, 1977). This **completion phenomenon** is sometimes experienced by patients who have unilateral lesions to the visual area of the brain. Completion is poorly understood, but it is likely one of the reasons that split-brain patients report that the world looks normal to them.

In Chapter 3 we noted that our bilateral CNS, which is built on the same plan as that found in *planaria*, is a natural development of bilaterally symmetrical bodies. In Chapter 15 we traced the evolution of language development, and we discussed some of the theories for the lateralization of language function in the brain. Abilities that are unique to the right hemisphere remain elusive. This fact is due, at least in part, to the pervasiveness of language in so much of what we call intelligent behavior. Nevertheless, the data from lesioned brains, laboratory studies of

lateralized auditory and visual information processing in intact subjects, and the examination of the split-brain patients all indicate that the
mental processes in the right brain are not the same as those found in
the left brain. It is even possible to measure differences in brain metabolism when subjects perform operations with varying task requirements.
For example, by measuring blood flow patterns in the brain, it can be
shown that the right brain is more metabolically active when the individual is performing spatial tasks, and the converse is true for verbal tasks
(Deutsch, Bourbon, Papanicolaou, & Eisenberg, 1988).

Our abilities to generate mental maps, rotate mental images in our
heads, think in terms of three dimensions, and perform other forms of
abstract spatial tasks are likely the functions of the right brain. Did these
right hemisphere skills evolve in concert with the left hemisphere's language skills? Do the unique mental strategies of the two brains complement each other? Is it possible that spatial mental abilities were at one
time common to both hemispheres but later concentrated in the right
hemisphere when language skills developed in the left side of the brain?

Roger Sperry believes that the two hemispheres evolved complementary functions. This adaptation increased the brain's efficiency to
deal with a wider range of behaviors. The division of function permits
each hemisphere to exercise its own unique mental processes independently (Levy-Agresti & Sperry, 1968). Sperry's notion is an attractive
one, and further study should add to what we currently know about the
mental abilities of each side of the brain. It does seem clear, however,
that each hemisphere possesses somewhat unique strategies for dealing
with the environment. Perhaps we would spend our time more meaningfully trying to understand the nature of mentation in the two sides of the
brain rather than concerning ourselves over what truly constitutes
"mind" and whether or not it is found in one side of the brain or the
other.

An Observation:

***The Corpus
Connection***

It is interesting to note that there are gender differences in the size and
shape of the corpus callosum. The degree of these differences varies
widely from one species to another. It appears that the degree of the
gender difference in the corpus callosum is related to the general
sexual dimorphism in a given species. For example, in many species of
prosimians and monkeys the males and females are very similar in
appearance. In these animals the corpus callosum appears to be identical in males and females. In other species such as the baboon and
gorilla, where sexual dimorphism is quite evident, we find clear differences in the corpus callosum of males and females.

Lacoste and Woodward (1988) have noted a trend in that the
more sexually dimorphic species evidence greater gender differences in

the corpus callosum. They have also noted that those species which are more closely related to humans seem to have the greatest degree of gender differences in the shape and size of the hemispheric commissures. Lacoste and Woodward suggest that the morphological differences in the corpus callosum can be related to functional differences in the two hemispheres in males and females and may reflect an evolutionary trend toward greater specialization of function in the left and right brain.

Free Will—Fact or Fiction?

Ramanand Yogi is about to be put to a most rigorous test of "mind over matter." It has been claimed that in the past he has been buried alive for as long as 3 days. The yogi attributes his special abilities to his faith in God and his rigorous lifetime of training in meditation. The researchers want to document his claims. They have placed electrodes on his scalp to monitor his EEG, there are electrodes to monitor his heart rate, and a pneumatic device will monitor his breathing. The yogi is placed in a sealed metal chamber where he will spend the next several hours surviving on less and less oxygen. The researchers will monitor very closely his brain wave activity, his respiration and heart rate, and the dwindling amount of oxygen in his airtight chamber.

As the time passes the researchers are impressed by the yogi's slow, steady heart rate and his steady respiration. The brain wave activity is dominated by α rhythms, and there is no sign of tension. He appears to be in a state of quiet rest. After several hours the yogi is still resting quietly, even though the air samples show reduced levels of oxygen and increased levels of carbon dioxide that would make you or me struggle for each breath. Finally, the yogi presses a button to signal the researchers that he wishes to be released. Although this test hardly supports the claim that Ramanand Yogi could survive after being buried for 3 days, it certainly does show that he has remarkable control over his phsiological processes (Wegner, Bagchi, & Anand, 1961).

One of the most difficult issues concerning the relationship between brain and consciousness relates to how the brain is apparently able to regulate its own activity and control the flow of consciousness. How does the yogi will that his brain wave activity remain quiescent under conditions of oxygen deprivation? How can some people undergo painless dental surgery using hypnotic suggestion? How is it that I am able to move my index finger to press a given key on my computer *when I choose to do so*?

These questions are concerned with the notion of free will. **Free will** refers to our ability to plan our actions, anticipate the possible outcomes of our intended actions, and make conscious decisions concerning when and how to act.

Some brain researchers dismiss free will as a mirage. They maintain that what we think of as free will is nothing more than a reflection of the fact that we are conscious of our own behavior. We are, therefore, able to monitor what we are doing: and this provides the illusion that our mind controls our body, rather than the reverse. Others profess that the existence of free will is patently obvious. Our ability to plan ahead, think through the consequences of our intended actions, and decide to act or not to act is a fact of our everyday experience. The fact that brain scientists can be so far apart on this issue is a clear indication of how little we know and how far we need to go before we can explain, in physical terms, the most complex of human experiences.

We are just beginning to understand the complex and intricate linkage between brain activity, overt behavior, and conscious experience. We have only a shadowy image of the physical substrate of memory, thought, and will. But we should not be discouraged. In the fourteenth century the prevailing view was that the earth was flat. In the eleventh century people believed that life was formed through spontaneous generation. The Egyptians buried their dead with their physical possessions because they believed the possesions could be brought to another life in another world.

There is much we do not know of the workings of the brain, but these things are knowable. The most wonderful thing about our brain is that it can wonder and ponder about the answers yet to come. Perhaps many of these questions will be answered in our lifetime.

Looking Ahead   Fifty thousand years ago men and women walked the face of this planet in small bands as hunters and gatherers. Their technology was limited to creating stone tools. Yet, all the evidence would suggest that their brains were essentially the same as yours or mine. Why is it that brains capable of creating a symphony or building a space station or unlocking the mysteries of subatomic particles evolved just to survive in a Stone Age culture?

If we could transport a contemporary human infant into the Stone Age, he or she could do nothing to advance that culture, because the infant would only bring its genetic potential—a potential that differs little from that of his ancient relatives. However, a Stone Age child transported to our time has the potential to be a mathematical genius, a computer hacker, or a skilled neurosurgeon because he or she would have had the benefit of a cultural history. Our meteoric advances in knowledge in the past few thousand years have been the result of a cultural revolution, not genetic evolution. Evidently, the critical brain mass that was necessary for early humans to develop a primitive hunter—gatherer society is somehow sufficient to deal with the accumulated wisdom of recorded history.

The cultural revolution was ignited by recorded language and fueled by mechanisms for storing and retrieving information. That revolution continues unabated. In fact, it is accelerating at an exponential rate. In the decades to come we may understand and learn to correct the genetic mechanisms that cause schizophrenia and other mental disorders. New knowledge concerning the biochemistry of the brain may allow us to eliminate certain forms of retardation, identify chemical interventions for drug dependency, and develop safer and more effective drugs for the treatment of mental dysfunction. Advances in artificial intelligence may provide new, revolutionary models of brain and behavior that may provide new insights concerning the relationships between brain activity and conscious experience. We may even find ways to teach the brain and body to control the immune system so we may be able to fight cancer and other diseases without the aid of drugs.

We have made enormous advances in our understanding of the biological bases of behavior. We are, however, on the first rung of a very long ladder.

CHAPTER SUMMARY

1. A central question in the study of the biological basis of behavior concerns the relationship between mind and body. This problem is confounded by the many and varied ways of defining the term *mind*.

2. The mind–body problem centers on the nature of mind and the relationship between mind and body. Philosophical theories concerning the mind–body problem generally fall into two categories: *monist* theories, which maintain that brain and mind are not separable entities, and *dualist* theories, which support the notion that mind and body have a separate status. Emergent materialism and reductive materialism are the two monist theories most consistent with the orientation of this text.

3. For the purposes of this book the term *mind* is not particularly helpful. What we refer to as mind is best thought of as mental processes that are in fact inseparable from the active processes of the brain.

4. Self-awareness, the ability to distinguish between self and the environment, has been demonstrated in some nonhuman primates. This quality of cognitive awareness appears to be limited to the great apes that are most closely related to humans.

5. Mountcastle has proposed a model to account for conscious awareness. He proposes that large numbers of *modular columns* in the cortex of the brain form loops of neural circuits. The modular columns are organized in a fashion that processes both current information and *reentry* information. This feature permits constant updating of perceptual images and matching of functions that allow the cortex to link an image formed in the immediate past with the current information of the outside world.

The model proposes that it is this matching of the internal readout and the external world that is the mechanism of conscious awareness.

6. Clinical data from brain-injured patients suggests that lesions to the brain interrupt the organized flow of information from one area of the brain to another. The behavioral effects of brain damage suggest that many parts of the brain are involved in conscious mental activity such as self-awareness and language comprehension.

7. The *prefrontal cortex* is associated with many higher levels of conscious behavior. Lesions to the prefrontal cortex may result in loss of inhibition, problems with intentions and planning, and alterations in emotional behavior. Laboratory studies show that lesions to the prefrontal cortex produce deficits in delayed response tasks. These deficits appear to be related to problems with programming and coding time-related tasks. The response characteristics of single cells in the prefrontal cortex show that various cells are concerned with different aspects of delayed response tasks.

8. The *commissurotomy* surgically separates the two cerebral hemispheres by cutting the corpus callosum and the minor commissures. The surgical procedure allows sensory input exclusively to one hemisphere. Laboratory studies have shown that commissurotomy produces two separate, but functioning, brains in one skull.

9. The commissurotomy has been performed on a number of individuals to control epilepsy. The unique functional qualities of the left and right sides of the brain can be demonstrated dramatically with these split-brain patients. There is still considerable controversy concerning the data from split-brain patients. Generally, it appears that the left brain functions in an analytic manner, is superior for language skills, and has full control over the production of speech. The right brain appears to have a more holistic information-processing style. The right brain has limited language ability but is superior for visuospatial tasks.

10. There is considerable debate concerning whether or not the split-brain subjects have two independent conscious entities in one skull. The argument is confounded by the many and varied interpretations of consciousness and mind. The split-brain data suggest that the two sides of the brain have evolved complementary functions. The adaptive advantage for this may be related to lateralization of language in the left brain.

11. Some researchers believe that *free will* is a fiction. They maintain that what we think of as free will is nothing more than a reflection of our conscious awareness of our own behavior. Others profess that free will is self-evident in our daily experience. These contradictory views suggest that we are far from understanding the biological mechanisms that underlie complex human experience.

SUGGESTED READINGS

Bunge, M. (1980). *The mind–body problem: A psychobiological approach.* New York: Pergamon.

Churchland, P. S. (1986). *Neurophilosophy: Toward a unified science of the mind–brain.* Cambridge, MA: MIT Press.

Mountcastle, V. B., & Edelman, G. M. (1978). *The mindful brain: Cortical organization and the group-selective theory of higher brain function.* Cambridge, MA: MIT Press.

Oakley, D. A. (1985). *Brain and mind.* London: Methuen.

Sacks, O. (1987). *The man who mistook his wife for a hat and other clinical tales.* New York: Harper & Row.

Sperry, R. W. (1976). Mental phenomena as causal determinants in brain function. In G. G. Globus, G. Maxwell, & I. Savodnic, (Eds.), *Consciousness and the brain.* New York: Plenum.

Young, J. Z. (1987). *Philosophy and the brain.* New York: Oxford University Press.

KEY TERMS

Chimeric   Stimulus made up of parts of other stimuli.

Cognition   The act or process of knowing, perceiving, and thinking.

Commissurotomy   Surgical separation of the two cerebral hemispheres by sectioning the corpus callosum.

Completion phenomenon   Visual phenomenon in which the brain "fills in" missing portions in the visual field.

Dualism   Theories of mind and body which propose that mind and body are separate entities.

Free will   The real or apparent control of mind over the actions of the body.

Hemianopia   Vision that is limited to one half of the visual field.

Mentation   The active mental processes of the brain.

Modular column   Several vertical columns of cells in the cortex that are organized as an information-processing local circuit.

Monism   Theories of mind and body that do not consider mind and body as separate entities.

Neglect syndrome   Rarely observed behavior that follows damage to the brain, characterized by attentional neglect of one side of the body.

Prefrontal cortex   Part of the frontal lobe that is anterior to the motor cortex.

Self-awareness   The mental ability to distinguish between self and nonself.

Tonal agnosia   The inability to interpret the timing characteristics of auditory signals.

Z lens   A device that isolates visual information to one half of the retina while allowing free movement of the eyes.

Bibliography

Adams, D. B. (1986). Ventromedial tegmental lesions abolish offense without disturbing predation or defense. *Physiology & Behavior, 38,* 165–168.

Adams, D. B., Gold, A. R., & Burt, A. D. (1978). Rise in female-initiated sexual activity at ovulation and its suppression by oral contraceptives. *New England Journal of Medicine, 299,* 1145–1150.

Agranoff, B. W. (1980). Biochemical events mediating the formation of short-term and long-term memory. In Y. Tsukada & B. W. Agranoff (Eds.), *Neurobiological basis of learning and memory.* New York: Wiley.

Aigner, T. G., & Mishkin, M. (1986). The effects of physostigmine and scopolamine on recognition memory in monkeys. *Behavioral and Neural Biology, 45,* 81–87.

Akert, K. (1961). Diencephalon. In D. E. Sheer (Ed.), *Electrical stimulation of the brain.* Austin: University of Texas Press.

Akil, H., Watson, S. J., Young, E., Lewis, M. E., Khachaturian, H., & Walker, J. M. (1984). Endogenous opiads: Biology and function. *Annual Review of Neuroscience, 7,* 223–255.

Albert, D. J., Walsh, M. L., Gorzalka, B. B., Siemens, Y., Louie, H. (1986). Testerone removal in rats results in decrease in social aggression and a loss of social dominance. *Physiology and Behavior, 36,* 401–407.

Alkon, D. L. (1984). Calcium-mediated reduction of ionic currents: A biophysical memory trace. *Science, 226,* 1037–1045.

Allt, G. (1979). Electron microscopy of cerebral tumors. *Trends in Neurosciences, 2,* 94.

Altmann, S. A. (1962). A field study of the sociobiology of rhesus monkeys, *Macaca mulatta. Annals of the New York Academy of Sciences, 102,* 338–435.

Alving, B. O. (1968). Spontaneous activity in isolated somata of *Aplysia* pacemaker neurons. *Journal of General Physiology, 51,* 29–45.

American Psychiatric Association. (1979). *Diagnostic and Statistical Manual* (3rd ed.). Washington, D.C.: Author.

Amoore, J. E. (1970). *Molecular basis of odor.* Springfield, IL: Thomas.

Amoore, J. E., Johnston, J. W., Jr., & Rubin, M. (1964). The stereochemical theory of odor. *Scientific American, 210* (2), 42–49.

Anand, B. K., & Brobeck, J. R. (1951). Localization of a "feeding center" in the hypothalamus of the rat. *Proceedings of the Society for Experimental Biology and Medicine, 77,* 323–324.

Angrist, B. J., Rotrosen, J., & Gershon, S. (1980). Positive and negative symptoms in schizophrenia—differential response to amphetamines and neuroleptics. *Psychopharmacology, 72,* 17–19.

Anniko, M., Thornell, L. E., Wróblewski, R. (1988). Recent advances in inner ear cytochemistry microanalytical and immunomorphological investigations. *Progress in Neurobiology, 30,* 209–269.

Appleman, P. (1970). *Darwin.* New York: Norton.

Arendash, G. W., & Gorski, R. A. (1983). Effects of discrete lesions of the sexually dimorphic nucleus of the preoptic area of the medial preoptic regions on the sexual behavior of male rats. *Brain Research, 10,* 147–154.

Ariel, R. N., Golden, D. J., Berg, R. A., Quaife, M. A., & Dirksen, J. W. (1983). Regional cerebral blood flow in schizophrenics. *Archives of General Psychiatry, 40,* 258–263.

Arnsten, A. F. T., & Goldmen-Rakic, P. S. (1985). Alphadrenergic mechanisms in prefrontal cortex associated with cognitive decline in aged nonhuman primates. *Science, 230,* 1273–1276.

Aschoff, J. (1979). Circadian rhythms: General features and endocrinological aspects. In D. T. Kreiger (Ed.), *Endocrine rhythms.* New York: Raven Press.

Aschoff, J., von Goetz, C., Wildgruber, C., & Wever, R. A. (1986). Meal timing in humans during isolation without time cues. *Journal of Biological Rhythms, 1,* 151–162.

Aserinsky, N. E., & Kleitman, N. (1955). Regularly occurring periods of eye motility and concomitant phenomena during sleep. *Science, 118,* 273–274.

Attneave, F., & Olson, R. K. (1971). Pitch as a medium: A new approach to psychophysical scaling. *American Journal of Psychology, 84,* 147–166.

Babich, F. R., Jacobson, A. L., Bubash, S., & Jacobson, A. (1965). Transfer of a response to naive rats by injection of ribonucleic acid extracted from trained rats. *Science, 149,* 646–657.

Bachevalier, J., & Mishkin, M. (1986). Visual recognition impairment follows ventromedial but not dorsolateral prefrontal lesions in monkeys. *Behavioral Brain Research, 20,* 249–261.

Bach-y-Rita, P. (1972). *Brain mechanisms in sensory substitution*. New York: Academic Press.

Bach-y-Rita, P. (1988). Brain plasticity. In J. Goodgold (Ed.), *Rehabilitation medicine* (pp. 113–118). St. Louis: Mosby.

Bach-y-Rita, P., & Hughes, B. (1985). Tactile vision substitution: Some instrumentation and perceptual considerations. In C. Warren & E. Strelow (Eds.), *Electronic spatial sensing for the blind*. The Netherlands: Martin Nijhoff.

Baddeley, A. (1986). *Working memory*. Oxford, England: Clarendon.

Baddeley, A. (1988). Cognitive psychology and human memory. *Trends in Neurosciences, 11*, 176–181.

Bailey, C. H., & Chen, M. (1983). Morphological basis of long-term habituation and sensitization in *Aplysia*. *Science, 220*, 91–93.

Balasubramaniam, V., & Kanaka, T. S. (1976). Hypothalamotomy in the management of aggressive behavior. In T. P. Morley (Ed.), *Current controversies in neurosurgery*. Philadelphia: Saunders.

Banks, M. S. & Ginsburg, A. P. (1985). Early visual preferences: A review and new theoretical treatment. In H. W. Reese (Ed.), *Advances in child development and behavior*. New York: Academic Press.

Bard, P. (1928). A diencephalic mechanism for the expression of rage with special reference to the sympathetic nervous system. *American Journal of Physiology, 84*, 490–515.

Barker, R. A. (1988). The basal ganglia and pain. *International Journal of Neuroscience, 41*, 29–34.

Barnes, C. A. (1988). Spatial learning and memory processes: A search for their neurobiological mechanisms. *Neurosciences, 11*, 163–169.

Barr, G. A., Gibbsons, J. L., & Moyer, K. E. (1976). Male–female differences and the influence of neonatal and adult testosterone on intraspecies aggression in rats. *Journal of Comparative and Physiological Psychology, 90*, 69–83.

Basbaum, A. I., & Fields, H. L. (1978). Endogenous pain control mechanisms: Review and hypothesis. *Annals of Neurology, 4*, 451–462.

Basbaum, A. I., & Fields, H. L. (1984). Endogenous pain control systems: Brainstem spinal pathways and endorphin circuitry. *Annual Review of Neuroscience, 7*, 309–338.

Batini, C., Magni, F., Palestini, M., Rossi, G. F., & Zanchetti, A. (1959). Neural mechanisms underlying EEG and behavioral activation in the midpontine pretrigeminal cat. *Archives Italiennes de Biologie, 97*, 13–25.

Baxter, L. R., Schwartz, J. M., Phelps, M. E., Mazziotta, J. C., Guze, B. H., Selin, C. E., Gerner, R. H., & Sumida, R. M. (1989). Reduction of prefrontal cortex glucose metabolism common to three types of depression. *Archives of General Psychiatry, 46*, 243–250.

Baxter, L. R., Phelps, M. E., Mazziotta, J. C., Schwartz, J. M., Gerner, R. H., Selin, C. E., & Sumida, R. M. (1985). Cerebral metabolic rates for glucose in mood disorders. *Archives of General Psychiatry, 42*, 441–447.

Beach, G., Emmens, M., Kimble, K., & Lickey, M. (1969). Autoradiographic demonstration of biochemical changes in the limbic system during avoidance training. *Proceedings of the National Academy of Sciences* (USA), *62*, 692–696.

Beal, M. F., Kleinman, G. M., Ojemann, R. C., & Hockberg, F. H. (1981). Gangliocytoma of third ventricle: Hyperphagia, somnolence and dementia. *Neurology, 31*, 1224–1227.

Beamer, W., Bermant, G., & Clegg, M. (1969). Copulatory behavior of the ram, *Ovis aries*. II. Factors affecting copulatory satiety. *Animal Behavior, 17*, 795–800.

Beatty, W. W., Butters, N., & Janowsky, D. S. (1986). Patterns of memory failure after scopolamine treatment: Implications for cholinergic hypotheses of dementia. *Behavioral and Neural Biology, 45*, 196–211.

Békésy, G. von. (1960). *Experiments in hearing*. New York: McGraw-Hill.

Bemporad, J. R, Ratey, J. H., O'Driscoll, G., & Daehler, M. L. (1988). Hysteria, anorexia and the culture of self-denial. *Psychiatry, 51*, 96–103.

Benes, F. M., Davidson, J., & Bird, E. D. (1986). Quantitative cytoarchitectural studies of the cerbral cortex of schizophrenics. *Archives of General Psychiatry, 43*, 31–35.

Bennett, E. L., Rosenzweig, M. R., Morimoto, H., & Herbert, M. (1979). Maze training alters brain weights and cortical RNA/DNA. *Behavioral and Neural Biology, 26*, 1–22.

Bennett, M. V. L. (1973). Function of electronic junctions in embryonic and adult tissues. *Federation Proceedings, 32*, 65–75.

Bentley, D. (1971). The neurobiology of the cricket song. *Scientific American, 174*, 1139–1141.

Benton, A. L. (1968). Differential behavioral effects in frontal lobe disease. *Neuropsychologia, 6*, 53.

Berger, T. W., & Thompson, R. F. (1978). Neuronal plasticity in the limbic system during classical conditioning of the rabbit nictitating membrane response: 1. The hippocampus. *Brain Research, 145*, 323–346.

Berkeley, M. A. (1981). Animal models of visual development: Behavioral evaluation of some physiological findings in cat visual development. In R. N. Aslin, J. Alberts, & M. J. Petersen (Eds.). *The development of perception: Psychobiological perspectives*. New York: Academic Press.

Bermant, G., & Davidson, J. M. (1974). *Biological bases of sexual behavior*. New York: Harper & Row.

Besson, J. M., Guilbaud, G., Abdelmoumene, M., & Chaouch, A. (1982). Physiolgie de la nociception. *Journal of Physiology* (Paris), *78*, 7–107.

Bingley, T., Leksell, L., Meyerson, B. A., & Rylander, G.

(1972). Stereotactic anterior capsulotomy in anxiety and obsessive-compulsive states. In L. V. Laitinen and K. E. Livingston (Eds.), *Surgical approaches in psychiatry*. Baltimore, MD: University Park Press.

Bingham, V. P., Ioalè, P., Casini, G., & Bangnoli, P. (1987). Impaired retention of preoperatively acquired spatial memory in homing pigeons following hippocampal ablation. *Behavioral Brain Research, 24,* 147–156.

Binkley, S. (1979). A timekeeping enzyme in the pineal gland. *Scientific American, 240,* 66–71.

Blakemore, C., & Cooper, G. F. (1979). Development of the brain depends on the visual environment. *Nature, 228,* 477–478.

Blanchard, D. C., & Blanchard, R. J. (1988). Ethoexperimental approaches to the biology of emotion. *Annual Review of Psychology, 39,* 43–68.

Blass, E. M., & Epstein, A. N. (1971). A lateral preoptic osmosensitive zone for thirst. *Journal of Comparative and Physiological Psychology, 76,* 378–394.

Blass, E. M., & Kraly, F. S. (1974). Medial forebrain bundle lesions: Specific loss of feeding to decreased glucose utilization in rats. *Journal of Comparative and Physiological Psychology, 86,* 679–692.

Bloch, V., Hennevin, E., & Leconte, P. (1977). Interaction between post-trial reticular stimulation and subsequent paradoxical sleep in memory consolidation processes. In R. R. Drucker-Colin & J. L. McGaugh (Eds.), *Neurobiology of sleep and memory*. New York: Academic Press.

Bogerts, B., Meertz, E., & Schönfeldt-Bausch, R. (1985). Basal ganglia and limbic system pathology in schizophrenia. *Archives of General Psychiatry, 42,* 784–791.

Boklage, C. E. (1977). Schizophrenia, brain asymmetry development, and twinning: Cellular relationship with etiological and possible prognostic implications. *Biological Psychiatry, 12,* 19–35.

Bonds, A. B. (1978). Development of orientation tuning in the visual cortex of kittens. In R. D. Freeman, (Ed.), *Developmental Neurobiology of Vision*. New York: Plenum.

Borradaile, L. A., & Potts, F. A. (1961). *The invertebrata: A manual for the use of students*. Cambridge: Cambridge University Press.

Born, J., Kern, W., Bieber, K., & Fehrn-Wolfsdorf, G. (1986). Night-time plasma cortisol secretion associated with specific sleep stages. *Biological Psychiatry, 21,* 1415–1424.

Boynton, R. M. (1988). Color vision. *Annual Review of Psychology, 39,* 69–100.

Brady, J. V., & Nauta, W. J. H. (1953). Subcortical mechanisms in emotional behavior: Affective changes following septal forebrain lesions in albino rat. *Journal of Comparative and Physiological Psychology, 46,* 339–346.

Brady, J. V., Porter, R. W., Conrad, D. G., & Mason, J. W. (1958). Avoidance behavior and the development of gastroduodenal ulcers. *Journal of the Experimental Analysis of Behavior, 1,* 69–72.

Brauman, H., & Gregoire, F. (1979). Hormonal abnormalities in anorexia nervosa (AN). In J. Ballús Obiols, E. González-Monclús, & J. Pujol (Eds.), *Biological psychiatry today*. Amsterdam: Elsevier/North Holland Biomedical Press.

Bredberg, G., Lindeman, H. H., Ades, H. W., West, R., & Engström, H. (1970). Scanning electron microscopy of the organ of Corti. *Science, 170,* 861–863.

Bremer, F. (1937). L' activité cérébrale au cours du sommeil et de la narcose. Contribution à l'étude du mécanisme du sommeil. *Bulletin de l' Académie Royale de Belgique, 4,* 68–86.

Bronowski, J. (1973). *The ascent of man*. Boston: Little, Brown.

Bronson, F. H., & Whitten, W. (1968). Estrus accelerating pheromone of mice: Assay, androgen-dependency, and presence in bladder urine. *Journal of Reproduction and Fertility, 15,* 131–134.

Brookhart, J. M., Dey, F. L. C., & Ranson, S. W. (1940). Failure of ovarian hormones to cause mating reactions in spayed guinea pigs with hypothalamic lesions. *Proceedings of Society for Experimental Biology, 44,* 61–64.

Brooks, V. B. (1984). Cerebellar functions in motor control. *Human Neurobiology, 2,* 251–260.

Brown, B. H. (1973). Further experience with multiple limbic targets for schizophrenia and aggression. In L. Laitinen & K. E. Livingston (Eds.), *Surgical approaches in psychiatry*. Baltimore: University Park Press.

Brown, E. L., & Deffenbacher, K. A. (1979). *Perception and the senses*. New York: Oxford University Press.

Brown, J. L. (1975). *The evolution of behavior*. New York: Norton.

Brown, P. K., & Wald, G. (1964). Visual pigments in single rods and cones of the human retina. *Science, 144,* 145–151.

Brown, R. (1986). *Social psychology* (2nd ed.). New York: Free Press.

Brown, R., Colter, N., Corsellis, N., Crow, T. J., Frith, C., Jagoe, R., Johnstone, E. C., & Marsh, L. (1986). Postmortem evidence of structural brain changes in schizophrenia. *Archives of General Psychiatry, 43,* 36–42.

Bruce, C., Desimone, R., & Gross, C. G. (1981). Visual properties of neurons in the polysensory area in superior temporal sulcus of macaque. *Journal of Neurophysiology, 46,* 369–384.

Bruce, H. M. (1960). Further observations of pregnancy block in mice caused by proximity of strange males. *Journal of Reproduction and Fertility, 2,* 311–312.

Brush, F. R., Mishkin, M., & Rosvold, H. E. (1961). Effects of object preferences and aversions on discrimination learning in monkeys with frontal lesions. *Journal of Comparative and Physiological Psychology, 54,* 319–325.

Bullock, T. H. (1965). Mechanisms of integration. In T. H. Bullock & G. A. Horridge, (Eds.), *Structure and function of the nervous systems of invertebrates*. San Francisco: Freeman.

Bullock, T. H., & Horridge, G. A. (1965). *Structure and function of the nervous systems of invertebrates*. San Francisco: Freeman.

Bullock, T. H., Orkand, R., & Grinnell, A. (1977). *Introduction to nervous systems*. San Francisco: Freeman.

Bunge, M. (1979). The mind–body problem in an evolutionary perspective. In G. Wolstenholme & M. O'Connor (Eds.), *Brain and mind*. Amsterdam: Elsevier, Exerpta Medica, North Holland.

Bunge, M. (1980). *The mind–body problem: A psychobiological approach*. New York: Pergamon.

Bünning, E. (1967). *The physiological clock: Circadian rhythms and biological chronometry*. New York: Springer-Verlag.

Burkhalter, A., & Van Essen, D. C. (1986). Processing of color, form and disparity information in visual area VP and V2 of ventral extrastriate cortex in the macaque monkey. *Journal of Neuroscience, 6*, 2327–2351.

Caballero, A., & de Andrés, I. (1986). Unilateral lesions in the locus coeruleus area enhance paradoxical sleep. *Electroenchephalography & Clinical Neurophysiology, 64*, 339–346.

Calvo, J. M., Badillo, S., Morales-Ramirez, M., & Palacios-Salas, P. (1987). The role of the temporal lobe amygdala in ponti-geniculo-occipital activity and sleep organization in cats. *Brain Research, 403*, 22–30.

Campbell, F. W., Copper, G. F., & Enroth-Cugell, C. (1969). The spatial selectivity of the visual cells of the cat. *Journal of Physiology, 203*, 223–235.

Cannon, W. B. (1927). The James–Lange theory of emotion: A critical examination and an alternative theory. *American Journal of Psychology, 39*, 106–124.

Cannon, W. B. (1929). *Bodily changes in pain, fear, and rage*. New York: Appleton-Century-Crofts.

Cannon, W. B. (1942). "Voodoo" death. *American Anthropologist, 44*, 169–181.

Cannon, W. B., & Washburn, A. L. (1912). An explanation of hunger. *American Journal of Physiology, 29*, 441–454.

Carew, T. J., Walters, E. T., & Kandel, E. R. (1981). Classical conditioning in a simple withdrawal reflex in *Aplysia californica*. *Journal of Neuroscience, 1*, 1426–1437.

Chang, E. L., & Greenough, W. T. (1984). Lateralized effects of monocular training on dendritic branching in adult split-brain rats. *Brain Research, 232*, 283–292.

Changeux, J-P. (1985). *Neuronal man: The biology of mind*. New York: Pantheon.

Chomsky, N. (1980). *Rules and representations*. New York: Columbia University Press.

Chorover, S., & Schiller, P. (1965). Short-term retrograde amnesia in rats. *Journal of Comparative and Physiological Psychology, 59*, 73–78.

Chrobak, J. J., Hanin, I., & Walsh, T. J. (1987). AF64A (ethylcholine aziridinium ion), a cholinergic neurotoxin selectively impairs working memory in a multiple component T-maze task. *Brain Research, 414*, 15–21.

Churchland, P. S. (1986). *Neurophilosophy: Toward a unified science of the mind-brain*. Cambridge, MA: MIT Press.

Clark, E., & O'Malley, C. D. (1968). *The human brain and spinal cord: A historical study illustrated by writings from antiquity to the twentieth century*. Berkeley: University of California Press.

Cohen, D. B. (1979). *Sleep & dreaming: Origins, nature and functions*. New York: Pergamon.

Cohen, N. J., & Squire, L. R. (1981). Retrograde amnesia and remote memory impairment. *Neuropsychologia, 19*, 337–356.

Coleman, C. C., Butcher, J. N., & Carson, R. C. (1980). *Abnormal psychology and modern life*. Springfield, IL: Scott, Foresman.

Conte, F. A., & Grumbach, M. M. (1978). Abnormalities of sexual differentiation. In D. R. Smith (Ed.), *General urology* (9th ed.). Los Altos, CA: Lange.

Cooper, B. R., Konkol, R., & Breese, G. (1978). Effects of catecholamine depleting drugs and d-amphetamine on self-stimulation of the substantial nigra and locus coeruleus. *Journal of Pharmacology and Experimental Therapeutics, 204*, 592–605.

Cooper, J. R., Bloom, F. E., & Roth, R. H. (1978). *The biochemical basis of neuropharmacology* (3rd ed.). New York: Oxford University Press.

Costa, E. (Ed.). (1983). *The bensodiazepines: From molecular biology to clinical practice*. New York: Raven Press.

Costa, L. (1988). Clinical neuropsychology: Prospects and problems. *Clinical Neuropsychologist, 2*, 3–11.

Costanzo, R. M., & Gardner, E. P. (1980). A quantitative analysis of responses of direction-sensitive neurons in somatosensory cortex of awake monkeys. *Journal of Neurophysiology, 43*, 1319–1341.

Cotman, C., & Nieto-Sampedro, M. (1982). Brain function, synapse renewal, and plasticity. *Annual Review of Psychology, 33*, 371–402.

Cowan, W. M. (1979). The development of the brain. In *The brain* [a *Scientific American* book.] New York: Scientific American.

Crawford, M. L. J., & von Noorden, G. K. (1980). Optically induced concomitant strabismus in monkeys. *Investigative Opthalmology and Visual Science, 19*, 1105–1109.

Cross, A. J., Crow, T. J., & Owen, F. (1981). ^{3}H-flupenthixol binding in postmortem brains of schizophrenics: Evidence for a selective increase in dopamine D-2 receptors. *Psychopharmacology, 74*, 122–124.

Curtis, H. (1979). *Biology* (3rd ed.). New York: Worth.

Damasio, A. R., & Geschwind, N. (1984). The neural basis of language. *Annual Review of Neuroscience, 7*, 127–147.

Damasio, H., & Damasio, A. R. (1980). The anatomical basis of conduction aphasia. *Brain, 103*, 337–350.

D'Amato, M. R. (1974). Derived motives. In M. R. Rosenzweig & L. W. Porter (Eds.), *Annual Review of Psychology* (Vol. 25). Palo Alto, CA: Annual Reviews.

Dannemiller, J. L., & Stephens, B. R. (1988). A critical test of infant pattern preference models. *Child Development, 59*, 210–216.

Dart, R. A. (1949). The predatory implement technique of *Australopithecus. American Journal of Physical Anthropology, 7*, 1–38.

Dartnall, H. J. A., Bowmaker, J. K., & Mollon, J. D. (1983). Human visual pigments: Microspectrophotometric results from the eyes of seven persons. *Proceedings of the Royal Society* (London), *B220*, 115–130.

Davies, P. (1985). A critical review of the role of the cholinergic system in human memory and cognition. *Annals of the New York Academy of Sciences, 444*, 212–217.

Davidson, J. M., Camargo, C. A., & Smith, E. R. (1979). Effects of androgen on sexual behavior in hypogonadal men. *Journal of Clinical Endocrinology and Metabolism, 48*, 955–958.

Davidson, R. J. (1984). Affect, cognition, and hemispheric specialization. In C. E. Izard, J. Kagan, & R. B. Zahonc, (Eds.), *Emotions, cognition, & behavior.* New York: Cambridge University Press.

Davis, D. E. (1964). The physiological analysis of aggressive behavior. In W. Etkin, (Ed.), *Social behavior and organization among vertebrates.* Chicago: University of Chicago Press.

Davis, K. L., Mohs, R. C., Tinklenberg, J. R., Pfefferbaum, A., Hollister, L. E., & Kopell, B. S. (1978). Physostigmine: Improvement of long-term memory processes in normal humans. *Science, 201*, 272–274.

DeBold, J. F., & Miczek, K. A. (1981). Sexual dimorphism in the hormonal control of aggressive behavior in rats. *Pharmacology and Biochemistry of Behavior, 14*, 89–93.

Delahunt, J., & Mellsop, G. (1987). Hormone changes in stress. *Stress Medicine, 3*, 123–134.

Delay, J., & Deniker, P. (1952a). Le traitement des psychoses par une methode neurolytique derivée d'hibernothéraphie; le 4560 RP utilisée seul un cure prolongée et continuée. *Comptes Rendus Congrès des Médicins Aliénistes et Neurologistes de France et des Pays de Lanque Française, 50*, 497–502.

Delay, J., & Deniker, P. (1952b). 38 cas des psychoses traitées par la cure prolongée et continuée de 4560 RP. *Comptes Rendus Congrès des Médecins Aliénistes et Neurologistes de France et des Pays de Lanque Francaise, 50*, 503–515.

Delgado, J. M. R. (1969). *Physical control of mind.* New York: Harper & Row.

DeLong, M. R., Alexander, G. E., Georgopoulos, A. P., Crutcher, M. D., Mitchell, S. J., & Richardson, R. T. (1984). The role of the basal ganglia in limb movements. *Human Neurobiology, 2*, 235–244.

Dement, W. C. (1960). The effect of dream deprivation. *Science, 131*, 1705–1707.

Dement, W. C. (1974). *Some must watch while some must sleep.* San Francisco: Freeman.

Denes, P. B., & Pinson, E. N. (1973). *The speech chain: The physics and biology of spoken language* (2nd ed.). New York: Doubleday.

Dennis, W. (1958). Early graphic evidence of dextrality in man. *Perceptual and Motor Skills, 8*, 147–149.

Desimone, R., Albright, T. D., Gross, C. G., & Bruce, C. (1984). Stimulus-selective properties of inferior temporal neurons in the macaque. *Journal of Neuroscience, 8*, 2051–2062.

Desmedt, J. E. (1960). Neurophysiological mechanisms controlling acoustic input. In G. L. Rasmussen, & W. F. Windle, (Eds.), *Neural mechanisms of the auditory and vestibular systems.* Springfield, IL: Thomas.

Desmedt, J. E. (1962). Auditory-evoked potentials from cochlea to cortex as influenced by activation of the efferent olivo-cochlear bundle. *Journal of the Acoustic Society of America, 34*, 1478–1496.

Dethier, V. G. (1967a). Feeding and drinking behavior of invertebrates. In C. F. Code, (Ed.), *Handbook of Physiology,* (Vol. 1). Washington, DC: American Physiology Society.

Dethier, V. G. (1967b). The hungry fly. *Psychology Today, 1*, 64–72.

Dethier, V. G. (1976). *The hungry fly: A physiological study of the behavior associated with feeding.* Cambridge, MA: Harvard University Press.

Deutsch, J. A. (1973). The cholinergic synapse and the site of memory. In J. A. Deutsch, (Ed.), *The physiological basis of memory.* New York: Academic Press.

Deutsch, G., Bourbon, W. T., Papanicolaou, A., & Eisenberg, H. M. (1988). Visuospatial tasks compared via activation of regional cerebral blood flow. *Neuropsychologia, 26*, 445–452.

Deutsch, J. A., & Hardy, W. T. (1977). Cholecystokinin produces bait shyness in rats. *Nature, 266*, 196.

DeValois, R. L., Albrecht, D. G., & Thorell, L. G. (1982). Spatial frequency selectivity of cells in macaque visual cortex. *Vision Research, 22*(7), 545–559.

DeValois, R. L., & DeValois, K. K. (1975). Neural coding of color. In E. C. Charterette, & M. P. Friedman, (Eds.), *Handbook of perception. V: Seeing.* New York: Academic Press.

DeVore, I. (1965). *Primate behavior: Field studies of monkeys and apes.* New York: Holt, Rinehart & Winston.

Dews, P. B., & Wiesel, T. N. (1970). Consequences of monocular deprivation on visual behavior in kittens. *Journal of Physiology, 206*, 437–455.

Diamond, M. C. (1976). Anatomical brain changes induced by environment. In L. Petrinovich, & J. L.

McGaugh (Eds.), *Knowing, thinking, and believing.* New York: Plenum.

Diamond, M. C., Krech, D., & Rosenzweig, M. R. (1964). The effects of an enriched environment on the histology of the rat cerebral cortex. *Journal of Comparative Neurology, 123,* 111–119.

Diamond, M. P., Lindner, B., Johnson, R., Bennet, E. L., & Rozenzweig, M. R. (1975). Differences in the occipital cortical synapses from environmentally enriched, impoverished, and standard colony rats. *Journal of Neuroscience Research, 1,* 109–119.

Dolan, R. J., Mitchell, J., & Wakeling, A. (1988). Structural brain changes in patients with anorexia nervosa. *Psychological Medicine, 18,* 349–353.

Dowling, J. E. (1970). Organization of vertebrate retinas. *Investigative Ophthalmology, 9,* 655–680.

Dowling, J. E., & Boycott, B. B. (1966). Organization of the primate retina: Electron microscopy. *Proceedings of the Royal Society of London, 166,* 80–111.

Dowling, J. E., & Werblin, F. S. (1969). Organization of retina of the mudpuppy, *Necturus maculosus. Journal of Neurophysiology, 32,* 315–354.

Downs, J. F., & Bleibtreu, H. K. (1972). *Human variation: An introduction to physical anthropology.* Mission Hills, CA: Glencoe Press.

Drucker-Colìn, R. R., & McGaugh, J. L. (Eds.). *Neurobiology of sleep and memory.* New York: Academic Press.

Drucker-Colìn, R. R., & Spanis, C. W. (1976). Is there a sleep transmitter? *Progress in Neurobiology, 6,* 1–22.

Duclaux, R., & Kenshalo, D. R. (1980). Response characteristics of cutaneous warm fibers in the monkey. *Journal of Neurophysiology, 43,* 1–15.

Dunn, A. J. (1980). Neurochemistry of learning and memory: An evaluation of recent data. *Annual Review of Psychology, 31,* 343–390.

Dykes, R. W. (1983). Parallel processing of somatosensory information: A theory. *Brain Research Reviews, 6,* 47–115.

Eakin, R. M. (1968). Evolution of photoreceptors. In T. Dobzhansky, M. K. Hecht, & W. C. Steere, (Eds.), *Evolutionary Biology* (Vol. 2). New York: Appleton-Century-Crofts.

Eccles, J. C. (1973). *The understanding of the brain.* New York: McGraw Hill.

Eccles, J. C. (1976). Brain and free will. In G. G. Globus, G. Maxwell, & I. Savodnic (Eds.), *Consciousness and the brain: A scientific and philosophical inquiry.* New York: Plenum.

Edman, G., Åsberg, M., Levander, S., & Schalling, D. (1986). Skin conductance habituation and cerebrospinal fluid 5-hydroxyindoleacetic acid in suicidal patients. *Archives of General Psychiatry, 43,* 582–586.

Edwards, S. B., & Flynn, J. P. (1972). Corticospinal control of striking in centrally elicited attack behavior. *Brain Research, 41,* 51–65.

Ehrhardt, A. A., & Meyer-Balburg, H. F. L. (1981).

Effects of prenatal sex hormones on gender-related behavior. *Science, 211,* 1312–1318.

Ekman, P. (1973). Cross cultural studies of facial expression. In P. Ekman (Ed.), *Darwin and facial expression,* New York: Academic Press.

Ekman, P., Levenson, R. W., & Freisen W. V. (1983). Autonomic nervous system activity distinguishes among emotions. *Science, 221,* 1208–1210.

Ekman, P., & Oster, H. (1979). Facial expressions of emotion. *Annual Review of Psychology, 30,* 527–554.

Epstein, A. N. (1971). The lateral hypothalamic syndrome: Its implications for the physiological psychology of hunger and thirst. In E. Stellar, & J. M. Sprague, (Eds.), *Progress in physiological psychology* (Vol. 4). Orlando, FL: Academic Press.

Epstein, A. N., Fitzsimons, J. T., & Rolls, B. J. (1970). Drinking induced by injection of angiotensin into the brain of the rat. *Journal of Physiology* (London), *210,* 457–474.

Epstein, V. G., Teitelbaum, P. (1962). Regulation of food intake in the absence of taste, smell, and other oropharyngeal sensations. *Journal of Comparative and Physiological Psychology, 55,* 753–759.

Evarts, E. V. (1968). Relation of pyramidal tract activity to force exerted during voluntary movement. *Journal of Neurophysiology, 31,* 14–28.

Evarts, E. V. (1972). Contrasts between activity of precentral and postcentral neurons of cerebral cortex during movement in the monkey. *Brain Research, 40,* 25–31.

Evarts, E. V. (1974). Sensorimotor cortex activity associated with movements triggered by visual as compared to somesthetic inputs. In F. O. Schmitt & F. G. Worden (Eds.), *The neurosciences: Third study program.* Cambridge, MA: MIT Press.

Evarts, E. V., Shinoda, Y., & Wise, S. P. (1984). *Neurophysiological approaches to higher brain function.* New York: Wiley.

Falkai, P., Bogerts, B., & Rozumek, M. (1988). Limbic pathology in schizophrenics: The entorhinal region— A morphometric study. *Biological Psychiatry, 24,* 515–521.

Farah, M. J., Péronnet, F., Gonon, M. A., & Giard, M. H. (1989). Electrophysiological event for a shared representational medium for visual images and visual percepts. *Journal of Experimental Psychology: General, 117,* 248–257.

Fedio, P., & Mirsky, A. F. (1969). Selective intellectual deficits in children with temporal lobe or centrencephalic epilepsy. *Neuropsychologia, 7,* 287.

Fencl, V., Koski, G., & Pappenheimer, J. R. (1971). Factors in cerebrospinal fluid from goats that affect sleep and activity in rats. *Journal of Physiology* (London), *216,* 565–589.

Fields, H. L., & Besson, J. M. (Eds.) (1988). *Pain modulation.* New York: Elsevier.

Fibiger, H. (1978). Drugs and reinforcement mechanisms:

A critical review of the catecholamine theory. *Annual Review of Pharmacology and Toxicology, 18,* 37–56.

Fieve, R. R. (1979). The clinical effects of lithium treatment. *Trends in Neurosciences, 2,* 66–68.

Fisher, A. (1988a). Human origins (I—Evolution): The more things change... *Mosaic, 19,* 23–33.

Fisher, A. (1988b). Human origins (II—Culture): On the emergence of humanness. *Mosaic, 19,* 34–45.

Fisher, D., Gross, J., & Zuch, J. (1965). Cycle of penile erection synchronous with dreaming (REM) sleep. Preliminary report. *Archives of General Psychiatry, 12,* 29–45.

Fitzsimons, J. T. (1961). Drinking by rats depleted of body fluid without increase in osmotic pressure. *Journal of Physiology* (London), *159,* 297–309.

Fitzsimons, J. T. (1972). Thirst. *Physiological Reviews, 52,* 468–561.

Flock, Å. (1970). Transduction of single hair cells in the lateral line organ. In L. M. Beidler & W. E. Reichardt (Eds.), *Sensory transduction. Neurosciences Research Program Bulletin, 8,* 492–496.

Flood, J. F., Bennett, E. L., Rosenzweig, M. R., & Orme, A. E. (1973). The influence of duration of protein synthesis inhibition on memory. *Physiology and Behavior, 10,* 555–562.

Flynn, J., Vanegas, H., Foote, W., & Edwards, S. (1970). Neural mechanisms involved in a cat's attack on a rat. In R. E. Whalen, R. F. Thompson, M. Verzeano, N. M. Weinberger (Eds.), *The neural control of behavior.* New York: Academic Press.

Foltin, R. W., Fischman, M. W., Emurian, C. S., & Rachlinski, J. J. (1988). Compensation for caloric dilution in humans given unrestricted access to food in a residential laboratory. *Appetite, 10,* 13–24.

Foltz, E. L., & Millett, F. E. (1964). Experimental psychosomatic disease states in monkeys. I. Peptic ulcer—"executive monkeys." *Journal of Surgical Research, 4,* 445–453.

Ford, C. S., & Beach, F. A. (1951). *Patterns of sexual behavior.* New York: Harper & Row.

Fouriezos, G., & Wise, R. A. (1976). Pimozide-induced extinction of intracranial self-stimulation: Response patterns rule out motor or performance deficits. *Brain Research, 103,* 377–380.

Fraiberg, S. (1971). Smiling and stranger reaction in blind infants. In J. Helmuth (Ed.), *Exceptional infant* (Vol. 2). New York: Brunner/Mazel.

Frazier, W. T., Kandel, E. R., Kupferman, I., Waziri, R., & Coggeshall, R. E. (1967). Morphological and functional properties of identified neurons in the abdominal ganglion of *Aplysia californica. Journal of Neurophysiology, 30,* 1288–1351.

Freedman, D. G. (1979). *Human sociobiology.* New York: Free Press.

Frieden, E., & Lipner, H. (1971). *Biochemial endocrinology of the vertebrates.* Englewood Cliffs, NJ: Prentice Hall.

Friedman, H. R., & Goldman-Rakic, P. S. (1988). Activation of the hippocampus and dentate gyrus by working-memory: A 2-deoxyglucose study of behaving rhesus monkeys. *Journal of Neuroscience, 8,* 4693–4706.

Frisch, K., von. (1965). *Tranzsprache und orientierung der bienen.* Berlin: Springer-Verlag.

Frisch, K. von. (1967). *The dance language and orientation of bees.* Cambridge, MA: Belknap.

Fukuda, Y., Hsiao, C. F., & Watanabe, M. (1985). Morphological correlates of Y, X, and W type ganglion cells in the cat's retina. *Vision Research, 25,* 319–327.

Fullerton, G., & Cameron, I. (1985). Nuclear resonance imaging in biological systems. *Biotechniques, 3,* 458–465.

Fuster, J. M. (1973). Unit activity in prefrontal cortex during delayed-response performance: Neuronal correlates of transient memory. *Journal of Neurophysiology, 36,* 61–78.

Fuster, J. M. (1980). *The prefrontal cortex.* New York: Raven Press.

Gallistel, C. R., Gomita, Y., Yandin, E., & Campbell, K. A. (1985). Forebrain origins and terminations of medial forebrain bundle metabolically activated by rewarding stimulation or by reward-blocking doses of pimozide. *Journal of Neuroscience, 5,* 1246–1261.

Gallup, G. G., Jr. (1970). Chimpanzees: Self-recognition. *Science, 167,* 86–87.

Gallup, G. G., Jr. (1977). Self-recognition in primates: A comparative approach to the bi-directional properties of consciousness. *American Psychologist, 32,* 329–338.

Gallup, G. G., Jr. (1979). Self-recognition in chimpanzees and man: A developmental and comparative perspective. In M. Lewis, & L. A. Rosenblum (Eds.), *Genesis of behavior, Vol. 2. The child and its family.* New York: Plenum.

Galluscio, E. H. (1971). Amnesia induced by electroconvulsive shock and carbon dioxide anesthesia in rats: An attempt to stimulate recovery. *Journal of Comparative and Physiological Psychology, 75,* 26–31.

Galluscio, E. H., Eggleston, R. G., Koehn, K., Garland, J. G., Schmid, M. J., & Yasuhara, T. (1974). Changes in rat brain morphology and adrenal size as a function of environmental stress. *Journal of Biological Psychology, 16,* 26–31.

Gardner, B. T., & Gardner, R. A. (1975). Evidence for sentence constituents in the early utterances of child and chimpanzee. *Journal of Experimental Psychology: General, 104,* 244–267.

Gardner, R. A., & Gardner, B. T. (1969). Teaching sign language to a chimpanzee. *Science, 165,* 664–672.

Garfield, E. (1984). Anorexia nervosa: The enigma of self-starvation. *Current Contents: Life Sciences,* 1–13.

Garner, D. M., Garfinkel, P. E., Schwartz, D., & Thompson, M. (1980). Cultural expectations of thinness in women. *Psychological Reports, 47,* 483–491.

Gastpar, M. (1979). L-HTP and the serotonin hypothesis, their meaning for treatment of depression. In J. Obiols, C. Ballús, E. Gonsález Monclús, & J. Pujol (Eds.), *Biological psychiatry today*. Amsterdam: Elsevier/North Holland Biomedical.

Gazzaniga, M. S. (1983). Right hemisphere language following brain bisection: A 20-year perspective. *American Psychologist, 38*, 525–537.

Gazzaniga, M. S., & LeDoux, J. E. (1978). *The integrated mind*. New York: Plenum.

Geen, R. G., Beatty, W. W., & Arkin, R. M. (1984). *Human motivation: Physiological, behavioral, and social approaches*. Boston: Allyn & Bacon.

Geer, J. H., O'Donohue, W. T., & Shorman, R. H. (1986). Sexuality. In M. G. H., Coles, E. Donchin, & S. W. Porges (Eds.), *Psychophysiology: Systems, processes and applications* New York: Guilford.

Gerbrandt, L. K. (1980). *Mind as brain: A neuroscience-kindled view*. Paper presented at the American Psychological Association annual meeting, Montreal.

Geschwind, N. (1965a). Disconnexion syndromes in animals and man: Part 1. *Brain, 88*, 237–294.

Geschwind, N. (1965b). Disconnexion syndromes in animals and man: Part 2. *Brain, 88*, 585–644.

Geschwind, N. (1979). Specialization of the human brain. In *The brain* [a *Scientific American* book]. New York: Scientific American.

Geschwind, N., & Levitsky, W. (1968). Human brain: Left–right asymmetries in temporal speech region. *Science, 161*, 186–187.

Gibson, J. J. (1962). Observations on active touch. *Psychological Review, 69*, 477–491.

Gilman, A. (1937). The relation between blood osmotic pressure, fluid distribution and voluntary water intake. *American Journal of Physiology, 120*, 323–328.

Gladue, B. A., Green, R., & Hellman, R. E. (1984). Neuroendocrine response to estrogen and sexual orientation. *Science, 225*, 1496–1499.

Glickman, S. E. (1977). Comparative psychology. In P. Mussen, & M. Rosenzweig (Eds.), *Psychology: An introduction* (2nd ed.). Lexington, MA: Heath.

Globus, A., Rosenzweig, M. R., Bennett, E. L., & Diamond, M. C. (1973). Effects of differential experience on dendritic spine counts in the rat cerebral cortex. *Journal of Comparative and Physiological Psychology, 82*, 175–181.

Goh, Y., Lederhendler, I., & Alkon, D. L. (1985). Input and output changes of an identified neural pathway are correlated with associative learning in *Hermissenda. Journal of Neuroscience, 5*, 536–543.

Gold, P. W., Gwirtsman, H., Avgerinos, P. C., Nieman, L. K., Gallucci, W. T., Kaye, W., Jimerson, D., Ebert, M., Rittmaster, R., Loriaux, D. L., & Chrousos, G. P. (1986). Abnormal hypothalamic-pituitary-adrenal function in anorexia nervosa. *New England Journal of Medicine, 314*, 1335–1342.

Gold, R. M., Jones, A. P., Sawchenko, P. E., & Kapatos, G. (1977). Paraventricular area: Critical focus of a longitudinal neurocircuitry mediating food intake. *Physiology and Behavior, 18*, 1111–1119.

Golden, C. J. (1978). *Diagnosis and rehabilitation in clinical neuropsychology*. Springfield, IL: Thomas.

Goldman-Rakic, P. S. (1988). Topography of cognition: Parallel distributed networks in primate association cortex. *Annual Review of Neuroscience, 11*, 137–156.

Goldstein, B. C. (1984). *Sensation and perception* (2nd ed.). Belmont, CA: Wadsworth.

Gorenstein, E. E. (1984). Debating mental illness: Implications for science, medicine and social policy. *American Psychologist, 39*, 50–56.

Gorski, R. A., Gordon, H. H., Shryne, J. E., & Southam, A. M. (1978). Evidence for a morphological sex difference within the medial preoptic area of the rat brain. *Brain Research, 148*, 333–346.

Gottesman, I. I., & Shields, J. A. (1976). A critical review of recent adoption, twin, and family studies of schizophrenia: Behavioral genetics perspectives. *Schizophrenia Bulletin, 2*, 360–401.

Gottsmann, C. (1988) What the cerveau isolé preparation tells us nowadays about sleep–wake mechanisms. *Neuroscience and Biobehavioral Reviews, 12*, 39–48.

Gould, S. J. (1980a). Is a new general theory of evolution emerging? *Paleobiology, 6*, 119–130.

Gould, S. J. (1980b). In the midst of life. In S. J. Gould, *The Panda's Thumb*. New York: Norton.

Granit, R. (1955). *Receptors and sensory perception*. New Haven, CT: Yale University Press.

Graziadei, P. P. C. (1977). Functional anatomy of the mammalian chemoreceptor system. In Müller-Schwartze & M. M. Mozell (Eds.), *Chemical signals in vertebrates*. New York: Plenum.

Green, J. D., Clement, C. D., & deGroot, A. (1957). Rhinencephalic lesions and behavior in cats. *Journal of Comparative Neurology, 108*, 505–564.

Greenough, W. T. (1976). Enduring brain effects of differential experience and training. In M. R. Rosenzweig & E. L. Bennet (Eds।)., *Neural mechanisms of learning and memory*. Cambridge, MA: MIT Press.

Greenough, W. T., & Bailey, C. H. (1988). The anatomy of memory: Convergence of results across a diversity of tests. *Trends in Neuroscience, 11*, 142–147.

Greenough, W. T., & Volkmar, F. R. (1973). Pattern of dendritic branching in occipital cortex of rats reared in complex environments. *Experimental Neurology, 40*, 491–504.

Gregory, W. K. (1929). *Our face from fish to man*. New York: Putnam.

Gross, C. G., Rocha-Miranda, C. E., & Bender, D. B. (1972). Visual properties of neurons of the temporal cortex of the macaque. *Journal of Neurophysiology, 35*, 96–111.

Grossman, S. P. (1984). Contemporary problems concerning our understanding of brain mechanisms that regulate food intake and body weight. In A. J. Stunkard & E. Stellar (Eds.), *Eating and its disorders*. New York: Raven Press.

Grüsser, O.-J. (1986). Interaction of efferent and afferent signals in visual perception: A history of ideas and experimental paradigms. *Acta Psychologica, 63*, 3–21.

Grüsser, O.-J., & Grüsser-Cornehls, U. (1972). Comparative physiology of movement-detecting neuronal systems in lower vertebrates. *Bibliotheca Ophthalmologica, 82*, 260–273.

Gulevich, G., Dement, W. C., & Johnson, L. (1966). Psychiatric and EEG observations on a case of prolonged (264 hours) wakefulness. *Archives of General Psychiatry, 15*, 29–35.

Gullotta, F., Rehder, H., & Gropp, A. (1982) Descriptive neuropathology of chromosomal disorders in man. *Human Genetics, 57*, 337–344.

Gur, R. E., Gur, R. C., Skolnick, B. E., Caroff, S., Obrist, W. D., Resnick, S., & Reivich, M. (1985). Brain function in psychiatric disorders. *Archives of General Psychiatry, 42*, 324–329.

Hagbarth, K. E., & Kerr, D. I. B. (1954). Central influences on spinal afferent conduction. *Journal of neurology and physiology, 17*, 295–307.

Halberg, F., Johnson, E. A., Brown, B. W., & Bitter, J. J. (1960). Susceptibility rhythm to *E. Coli* endotoxin and bioassay. *Proceedings of the Society for Experimental Biology and Medicine, 103*, 142–144.

Hall, W. G., & Blass, E. M. (1977). Orogastric determinants of drinking in rats: Interaction between absorptive and peripheral controls. *Journal of Comparative and Physiological Psychology, 91*, 365–376.

Hallett, P. E. (1987). Quantum efficiency of dark-adapted human vision. *Journal of the Optical Society of America, 4*, 2330–2335.

Halliday, T. (1980). *Sexual strategy*. Chicago: University of Chicago Press.

Harlow, J. M. (1948). Passage of an iron rod through the head. *Boston Medical and Surgical Journal, 39*, 389–393.

Harlow, J. M., & Settlage, P. (1948). Effect of extirpation of frontal areas upon learning performance in monkeys. *Research Publication Association for Nervous and Mental Disease, 27*, 446–459.

Hart, B. (1967). Sexual reflexes and mating behavior in the dog. *Journal of Comparative and Physiological Psychology, 66*, 388–399.

Hartline, H. K. (1949). Inhibition of activity of visual receptors by illuminating nearby retinal areas in the *Limulus* eye. *Federation Proceedings, 8*(7), 69.

Hartmann, E. (1967). *The biology of dreaming*. Springfield, IL: Thomas.

Hartry, A. L., Keith-Lee, P., & Morton, W. D. (1964). Planaria: Memory transfer through cannibalism reexamined. *Science, 146*, 274–275.

Haseltine, F. P., & Ohno, S. (1981). Mechanisms of gonadal differentiation. *Science, 211*, 1272–1277.

Hatton, G. I. (1976). Nucleus circularis: Is it an osmoreceptor in the brain? *Brain Research Bulletin, 1*, 123–131.

Haustein, W., Pilcher, J., Klink, J., & Schulz, H. (1986). Automatic analysis overcomes limitations of sleep stage scoring. *Electroencephalography & Clinical Neurophysiology, 64*, 364–374.

Hayes, D. (1951). *The ape in our house*. New York: Harper & Bros.

Heath, R. G. (1963). Electrical stimulation of the brain in man. *American Journal of Psychiatry, 120*, 571–577.

Hebb, D. O., & Thompson, W. R. (1968). The social significance of animal studies. In G. Lindzey (Ed.), *Handbook of social psychology*. Cambridge, MA: Addison-Wesley.

Hécaen, H., & Albert, M. L. (1975). Disorders of mental functioning related to frontal lobe pathology. In D. F. Benson & D. Blumer (Eds.), *Psychiatric aspects of neurologic disease*. New York: Grune & Stratton.

Heffner, H. E., & Heffner, R. S. (1984). Temporal lobe lesions and perception of species-specific vocalizations by macaques. *Science, 226*, 75–76.

Hensel, H., & Kenshalo, D. R. (1969). Warm receptors in the nasal region of cats. *Journal of Physiology, 204*, 99–112.

Herbert, W. (1982). Schizophrenia: From adolescent insanity to dopamine disease. *Science News* (March), 173–175.

Hernandez, L., & Hoebel, B. G. (1980). Basic mechanisms of feeding and weight regulation. In A. J. Stunkard (Ed.), *Obesity*. Philadelphia: Saunders.

Herz, A., Albus, K., Metys, J., Schubert, P., & Teschemacher, H. (1970). On the central sites for the antinociceptive action of morphine and fentanyl. *Neuropharmacology, 9*, 539–551.

Herzog, D. B., Norman, D. K., Gorden, C., & Pepose, M. (1984). Sex conflict and eating disorders in 27 males. *American Journal of Psychiatry, 141*, 989–990.

Hess, J. E. (1965). Attitude and pupil size. *Scientific American, 212*(4), 46–54.

Hess, W. R. (1957). *The functional organization of the diencephalon*. New York: Grune & Stratton.

Heston, L. L. (1966). Psychiatric disorders in foster-home-reared children of schizophrenic mothers. *British Journal of Psychiatry, 112*, 819–825.

Hetherington, A. W., & Ranson, S. W. (1940). Hypothalamic lesions and adiposity in the rat. *Anatomical Record, 78*, 149–172.

Hirsch, H. V. B., & Spinelli, D. N. (1971). Modification of the distribution of receptive field orientations in cats by selective visual exposure during development. *Experimental Brain Research, 12*, 509–527.

Hobson, J. A., & McCarley, R. W. (1977). The brain as a dream state generator: An activation-synthesis hypothesis of the dream process. *American Journal of Psychiatry, 134,* 1335–1348.

Holden, C. (1987). A top priority at NIMH. *Science, 235,* 431.

Holloway, R. L. (1970). The endocranial values for the australopithecines. *Nature, 227,* 199–200.

Hooff, J., A., R., A., M., van. (1962). Facial expressions in higher primates. *Symposium of the Zoological Society* (London), *8,* 97–125.

Hoof, J., A., R., A., M., van (1967). The facial displays of catarrhine monkeys and apes. In D. Morris (Ed.) *Primate ethology.* Chicago: Aldine.

Horn, G., Rose, S. P. R., & Bateson, P. P. G. (1973). Experience and plasticity in the central nervous system. Is the nervous system modified by experience? Are such modifications involved in learning? *Science, 181,* 506–514.

Horridge, G. A. (1962). Learning of leg position by the ventral nerve cord in headless insects. *Proceedings of the Royal Society of London, 157*(B), 33–52.

Howells, W. W. (1966). Homo erectus. *Scientific American* (May), 46.

Howells, W. W. (1973). *The evolution of the genus Homo.* Reading, MA: Addison-Wesley.

Hubbard, S. J. (1958). A study of rapid mechanical events in a mechanoreceptor. *Journal of Physiology, 141,* 198–218.

Hubbel, W. L., & Bownds, M. D. (1979). Visual transduction in vertebrate photoreceptors. *Annual Review of Neuroscience, 2,* 17–34.

Hubel, D. H. (1979). The brain. In *The brain* [a *Scientific American* Book]. San Francisco: Freeman.

Hubel, D. H., Wiesel, T. N. (1965). Binocular interaction in striate cortex of kittens reared with artificial squint. *Journal of Neurophysiology, 28,* 1041–1059.

Hubel, D. H., & Wiesel, T. N. (1970). The period of susceptibility to the physiological effects of unilateral eye closure in kittens. *Journal of Physiology, 206,* 419–436.

Hubel, D. H., & Wiesel, T. N. (1977). Functional architecture of macaque monkey visual cortex. *Philosophical Transactions of the Royal Society of London, B198,* 1–59.

Hubel, D. H., & Wiesel, T. N. (1979). Brain mechanisms in vision. *Scientific American, 241,* 150–162.

Hubel, D. H., Wiesel, T. N., & LeVay, S. (1977). Plasticity of ocular dominance columns in monkey striate cortex. *Philosophical Transactions of the Royal Society of London, B278,* 377–409.

Hubel, D. H., Wiesel, T. N., & Stryker, M. P. (1978). Anatomical demonstration of orientation columns in macaque monkeys. *Journal of Comparative Neurology, 177,* 361–380.

Hudspeth, A. J. (1983). Mechanoelectrical transduction by hair cells in the acousticolateralis sensory system. *Annual Review of Neuroscience, 6,* 187–215.

Hughes, J., Smith, T. W., Kosterlitz, H. W., Fothergill, L. A., Morgan, B. A., & Morris, B. A. (1975). Identification of two related pentapeptides from the brain with potent opiate agonist activity. *Nature, 258,* 577–599.

Hydén, H. (1967). Biochemical changes accompanying learning. In G. C. Quarton, T. Melnechuk, & F. O. Schmitt (Eds.), *The neurosciences: A study program.* New York: Rockefeller University Press.

Hydén, H., & Egyházi, E. (1962). Nuclear RNA changes of nerve cells during a learning experiment in rats. *Proceedings of the National Academy of Sciences* (USA), *48,* 1366–1373.

Hydén, H., & Egyházi, E. (1963). Glial RNA changes during a learning experiment with rats. *Proceedings of the National Academy of Sciences* (USA), *49,* 618–624.

Hydén, H., & Egyházi, E. (1964). Changes in RNA content and base composition in cortical neurons of rats in a learning experiment involving transfer of handedness. *Proceedings of the National Academy of Sciences* (USA), *52,* 1030–1035.

Hydén, H., & Lange, P. W. (1970). Protein changes in nerve cells related to learning and conditioning. In F. O. Schmitt (Ed.), *The neurosciences: Second study program* (pp. 278–289). New York: Rockefeller University Press.

Hydén, H., & Lange, P. W. (1971). Do specific biochemical correlates to learning processes exist in brain cells? In A. Lajtha (Ed.), *Handbook of neurochemistry* (*Vol. 6*): *Alterations of chemical equilibrium in the nervous system.* New York: Plenum.

Hyvärinin, J. H., & Poranen, A. (1978). Movement sensitive and direction and orientation-selective cutaneous receptive fields in the hand area of the postcentral gyrus in monkeys. *Journal of Physiology, 283,* 523–537.

Iggo, A., & Andres, K. H. (1982). Morphology of cutaneous receptors. *Annual Review of Neuroscience, 5,* 1–32.

Imbert, M. (1979). Maturation of visual cortex with and without visual experience. In R. Freeman (Ed.), *Developmental neurobiology of vision.* New York: Plenum.

Ingvar, D. (1979). Brain activation patterns revealed by measurements of regional blood flow. In J. E. Desment (Ed.), *Cognitive components in cerebral event-related potentials and selective attention.* Basel: Karger.

Ingvar, D. H., & Lassen, N. A. (Eds.). (1974). *Brain work: The coupling of function, metabolism, and blood flow in the brain.* New York: Academic Press.

Inoué, S., Uchizono, K., & Nagasaki, H. (1982). Endogenous sleep-promoting factors. *Trends in Neurosciences, 5,* 218–220.

Inouye, S. T., & Kawamura, H. (1979). Persistence of circadian rhythmicity in mammalian hypothalamic "island" containing the suprachiasmatic nucleus. *Proceedings of the National Academy of Sciences* (USA), *76,* 5961–5966.

Irwin, D., & Brown, J. S. (1988). Visual masking and visual integration across saccadic eye movements. *Journal of Experimental Psychology: General, 117,* 276–287.

Ivarson, C., de Ribauprene, Y., & de Ribauprene, F. (1988). Influence of auditory localization cues on the neuronal activity in the auditory thalamus of the cat. *Journal of Neurophysiology, 59*, 586–606.

Iverson, L. L. (1979). The chemistry of the brain. *Scientific American, 241*, 134–149.

Jacobsen, C. F. (1936). Studies of cerebral function in primates: 1. The functions of the frontal association areas in monkeys. *Comparative Psychology Monographs, 13*, 3–60.

Jakob, H., & Beckmann, H. (1986). Prenatal development disturbances in the limbic allocortex in schizophrenics. *Journal of Neural Transmission, 65*, 154–161.

James, W. (1884). What is emotion? *Mind, 9*, 188–204.

Jarrard, L. E., Okaichi, H., Steward, O. M., & Goldschmidt, R. B. (1984). On the role of hippocampal connections in the performance of place and cue tasks: Comparisons with damage to hippocampus. *Behavioral Neuroscience, 98*, 946–954.

Jensen, C. (1979). Learning performance in mice genetically selected for brain weight: Problems of generality. In M. E. Hahn, C. Jensen, & B. C. Dudek (Eds.), *Development and evolution of brain size.* New York: Academic Press.

Jensen, E. D. (1965). Paramecia, planaria and pseudolearning. Learning and associated phenomena in invertebrates. *Animal Behavior Supplement, 1*, 9–20.

Jerison, H. J. (1973). *Evolution of the brain and intelligence.* New York: Academic Press.

Jerison, H. J. (1985). On the evolution of mind. In D. A. Oakley (Ed.), *Brain & Mind.* London: Methuen.

Jernigan, T. L., & Hesselink, J. (1985). Human brain-imaging: Basic principles and applications. In R. M. Michels & J. O. Cavenar (Eds.), *Psychiatry,* Philadelphia: Lippincott.

John, E. R., & Schwartz, E. L. (1978). The neurophysiology of information processing and cognition. *Annual Review of Psychology, 29*, 1–29.

Jones, B. E., Bobillier, P., & Jouvet, M. (1969). Effects de la destruction des neurones contenant des catécholamines de mésencéphale sur le cycle veille-sommeils du chat. *Comptes Rendus de la Société de Biologie* (Paris), *163*, 176–180.

Jones, B. E., Harper, S. T., & Halaris, A. E. (1977). Effects of locus coeruleus lesions upon cerebral monoamine content, sleep–wakefulness states and the response to amphetamines in the cat. *Brain Research, 124*, 473–496.

Jouvet, M. (1967). The states of sleep. *Scientific American, 216*, 62–72.

Jouvet, M. (1974). Monoaminergic regulation of the sleep-waking cycle in the cat. In F. O. Schmitt & F. G. Wordens (Eds.), *The neurosciences: Third study program.* Cambridge, MA: MIT Press.

Julesz, B. (1964). Binocular depth perception without familiarity cues. *Science, 45*, 352–356.

Julesz, B. (1971). *Foundations of cyclopean vision.* Chicago: University of Chicago Press.

Kaada, B. (1967). Brain mechanisms related to aggressive behavior. In D. Clemente & D. B. Lindsley, (Eds.), *Aggression and defense.* Berkeley: University of California Press.

Kaas, J. H. (1987). The organization of neocortex in mammals: Implications for theories of brain function. *Annual Review of Psychology, 38*, 129–151.

Kahan, B. E., Krigman, M. R., Wilson, J. E., & Glassman, E. (1970). Brain function and macromolecules: VI. Autoradiographic analysis of the effect of a brief training experience on the incorporation of uridine into mouse brain. *Proceedings of the National Academy of Sciences* (USA), *654*, 300–304.

Kandel, E. R. (1976). *Cellular basis of behavior.* San Francisco: Freeman.

Kandel, E. R. (1979). Small systems of neurons. *Scientific American, 24*, 66–76.

Kandel, E. R., & Schwartz, J. H. (1982). Molecular biology of learning: Modulation of transmitter release. *Science, 218*, 433–434.

Kanof, P., & Greengard, P. (1978). Brain histamine receptors as targets for antidepressant drugs. *Nature, 272*, 329–333.

Kartin, K. I., Kilchiff, T. S., & Dement, W. C. (1986). Evidence for excessive sleepiness in canine narcoleptics. *Electroencephalography & Clinical Neurophysiology, 64*, 447–454.

Katsuki, Y. (1961). Neural mechanism of auditory sensation in cats. In W. A. Rosenblith (Ed.), *Sensory communication.* New York & Cambridge: Wiley & MIT Press.

Keesey, R. E., & Powley, T. L. (1986). The regulation of body weight. *American Review of Psychology, 37*, 109–133.

Kelley, D. D. (1981). Disorders of sleep and consciousness. In E. R. Kandel & J. H. Schwartz (Eds.), *Principles of neural science.* New York: Elsevier.

Kelly, D., Richardson, A., & Mitchell-Heggs, N. (1973). Technique and assessment of limbic leucotomy. In L. Laitinen & K. E. Livingston (Eds.), *Surgical approaches in psychiatry.* Baltimore: University Park Press.

Kennedy, G. C. (1966). Food intake energy balance and growth. *British Medical Bulletin, 22*, 216–220.

Kenshalo, D. R. (1976). Correlations of temperature sensitivity in man and monkey, a first approximation. In Y. Zotterman (Ed.), *Sensory functions of the skin in primates with special reference to man.* New York: Plenum.

Kenshalo, D. R., & Scott, H. A., Jr. (1966). Temporal course of thermal adaptation. *Science, 151*, 1095–1096.

Kerr, D. I. B., & Hagbarth, K. E. (1955). An investigation of olfactory centrifugal fiber system. *Journal of Neurophysiology, 18*, 362–374.

Kertesz, A. (1982). Two case studies: Broca's and Wernecke's aphasia. In M. Arbib, D. Caplan, & J. C. Marshall (Eds.), *Neural models of language processes.* New York: Academic Press.

Kesner, R. P. (1985). Correspondence between humans and animals in coding of temporal attributes: Role of hippocampus and prefrontal cortex. *Annals of the New York Academy of Science, 444,* 122–136.

Kesner, R. P., & Novak, J. M. (1982). Serial position curve in rats: Role of the dorsal hippocampus. *Science, 218,* 173–175.

Kessler, S., Guilleminault, C., & Dement, W. C. (1974). A family study of 50 REM narcoleptics. *Acta Neurologica Scandinavica, 50,* 503–512.

Kety, S. S., Rosenthal, D., Wender, P. H., & Schulsinger, K. F. (1968). The types of prevalence of mental illness in the biological and adoptive families of adopted schizophrenics. In C. Rosenthal & S. S. Kety (Eds.), *The transmission of schizophrenia.* New York: Pergamon.

Keverne, E. B. (1982). Chemical senses: Taste. In H. B. Barlow, & J. D. Mollon (Eds.), Cambridge: Cambridge University Press.

Kinsbourne, M. (1974). The mechanisms of hemisphere asymmetry in man. In M. Kinsbourne & W. L. Smith (Eds.), *Hemispheric disconnection and cerebral function.* Springfield, IL: Thomas.

Kinsbourne, M., & Hicks, R. E. (1978). Mapping cerebral functional space: Competition and collaboration in human performance. In M. Kinsbourne (Ed.), *Asymmetrical function of the brain.* Cambridge: Cambridge University Press.

Kimble, D. P. (1968). Hippocampus and internal inhibition. *Psychological Bulletin, 70,* 285–295.

Kimura, D. (1973a). Manual activity during speaking—I. Right handers. *Neuropsychologia, 11,* 45–50.

Kimura, D. (1973b). Manual activity during speaking—II. Left handers. *Neuropsychologia, 11,* 51–55.

King, M. C., & Wilson, A. C. (1975). Evolution at two levels in humans and chimpanzees. *Science, 188,* 107–116.

Kissileff, H. R., Pi-Sunyer, F. X., Thornton, J., & Smith, G. P. (1981). C-terminal octapeptide of cholecystokinin decreases food intake in man. *American Journal of Clinical Nutrition, 34,* 154–160.

Klawans, H. L., Goetz, C. G., Paulson, G. W., & Barbeau, A. (1980). Levodopa and presymptomatic detection of Huntington's disease—eight-year followup. *New England Journal of Medicine, 302,* 1090.

Klein, M., & Kandel, E. R. (1980). Mechanism of calcium modulation underlying presynaptic facilitation and behavioral sensitization in *Aplysia. Proceedings of the National Academy of Science, 77,* 6912.

Kleiner, K. A. (1987). Amplitude and phase spectra as indices of infants' pattern preferences. *Infant Behavior and Development, 10,* 49–59.

Kleitman, N. (1982). Basic rest–activity cycle—22 years later. *Sleep, 4,* 311–317.

Kleitmen, N., & Engelman, T. G. (1953). Sleep characteristics of infants. *Journal of Applied Physiology, 6,* 269–282.

Klüver, H., & Bucy, P. C. (1937). "Psychic blindness" and other symptoms following bilateral temporal lobectomy in rhesus monkeys. *American Journal of Physiology, 119,* 352–353.

Krieger, D. T., & Hughes, J. C. (1980). *Neuroendocrinology.* Sunderland, ME: Singuer Associates.

Krueger, J. M., Pappenheimer, J. R., & Karnovsky, M. L. (1982). The composition of sleep-promoting factor isolated from human urine. *Journal of Biological Chemistry, 257,* 1664–1669.

Kuffler, S. W. (1952). Neurons in the retina: Organization, inhibition and excitation problems. *Cold Spring Harbor Symposium on Quantitative Biology, 17,* 281–292.

Kuffler, S. W. (1953). Discharge patterns and functional organization of mammalian retina. *Journal of Neurophysiology, 16,* 37–68.

Kuffler, S. W., Nicholls, J. G., & Martin, R. (Eds.). (1984). *From neuron to brain: A cellular approach to the function of the nervous system.* Sunderland, ME: Sinauer Associates.

Kühme, W. (1963). Ergänzende Beobachtungen an afrikanischen Elefanten (*Loxodonta africana* Blumenbach 1797) in Freigenege. *Zeitschrift für Tierpsychologie, 20,* 66–79.

Kupferman, I. T., Carew, T. J., & Kandel, E. R. (1974). Local, reflex, and central commands controlling gill and siphon movements in *Aplysia. Journal of Neurophysiology, 37,* 996–1019.

Lacoste de, M. C., & Woodward, D. J. (1988). The corpus callosum in nonhuman primates. *Brain, Behavior and Evolution, 31,* 318–323.

Laitinen, L. V., & Vilkki, J. (1973). Observations on the transcallosal emotional connections. In L. V. Laitinen, & K. E. Livingston (Eds.), *Surgical approaches in psychiatry.* Baltimore, MD: University Park Press.

Lancet, D. (1984). Molecular view of olfactory reception. *Trends in Neurosciences, 7,* 35–36.

Land, M. F. (1969). Structure of the retinae of the principal eyes of jumping spiders. (*Salticidae: Dendryphantinae*) in relation to visual optics. *Journal of Experimental Biology, 51,* 443–470.

Langer, S. K. (1951). *Philosophy in a new key: A study in the symbolism of reason, rite, and art.* New York: Mentor Books.

Lansdell, H., (1970). Relation of extent of temporal removals to closure and visuomotor factor. *Perceptual and Motor Skills, 31,* 491.

Lashley, K. (1929). *Brain mechanisms and intelligence.* Chicago: University of Chicago Press.

Lashley, K. (1950). In search of the engram. In *Physiological mechanisms in animal behavior* (Society for Experimental Biology, Great Britain). New York: Academic Press.

Lavie, P., Pratt, H., Scharf, B., Peled, R., & Brown, J. (1984). Localized pontine lesion: Nearly total absence of REM sleep. *Neurology, 34,* 1118–1120.

Leakey, L. (1966). Homo habilis, Homo erectus and the australopithecines. *Nature, 209,* 1279.

Leakey, R. E., & Lewin, R. (1978). *Origins.* New York: Dutton.

Lederhendler, I. I., Gart, S., & Alkon, D. L. (1986). Classical conditioning of *Hermissenda*; Origin of a new response. *Journal of Neuroscience, 6,* 1325–1331.

LeDoux, J. E., Wilson, D. H., & Gazzaniga, M. S. (1977a). Manipulo-spatial aspects of cerebral lateralization: Clues to the origin of lateralization. *Neuropsychologia, 15,* 743–750.

LeDoux, J. E., Wilson, D. H., & Gazzaniga, M. S. (1977b). A divided mind: Observations on the conscious properties of the separated hemispheres. *Annals of Neurology, 2,* 417–421.

Lee, van der, S., & Boot, L. M. (1955). Spontaneous pseudopregnancy in mice. *Acta Physiologica et Pharmacologica Néerlandica, 4,* 442–444.

Legrende, R., & Piéron, H. (1913). Recherches dur le besoin de sommeil consécutif a une veille prolongé. *Zeitschrift für Allgemeine Physiologie, 14,* 235–362.

Lehrman. D. S. (1964). The reproductive behavior of ring doves. *Scientific American, 211,* 48–54.

Leibowitz, S. F. (1983). Hypothalamic catecholamine systems controlling eating behavior: A potential model for anorexia nervosa. In P. I. Darby, P. E. Garfinkel, D. M. Garner, & D. V. Coscina (Eds.), *Anorexia nervosa: Recent developments in research.* New York: Liss.

Leiman, A. L., & Hafter, E. R. (1972). Responses of inferior colliculus neurons to free stimuli. *Experimental Neurology, 35,* 431–450.

Leshner, A., Walker, W. A., Johnson, A. E., Kelling, J., Kreisler, S., & Svare, B. (1973). Pituitary andrenocortical activity and intermale aggressiveness in isolated mice. *Physiology & Behavior,* 11, 705–711.

Levin, E. D. (1988). Psychopharmacological effects in the radial-arm maze. *Neuroscience & Biobehavioral Reviews, 12,* 169–175.

Levine, J.D., Gordon, N.C., & Fields, H. L. (1979). The role of endorphins in placebo analgesia. In J. C. Bonica, J. C. Liebeskind, & D. Albe-Fessard (Eds.), *Advances in Pain Research and Therapy,* (Vol. 3). New York: Raven Press.

Levine, P. (1986). Stress. In M. G. H. Coles, E. Donchin, & S. W. Porges (Eds.), *Psychophysiology: Systems, processes, and applications.* New York: Guilford Press.

Levy, A. B., Dixon, K. N., & Stern, S. L. (1989). How are depression and bulimia related? *American Journal of Psychiatry, 146,* 162–169.

Levy, J. (1969). Possible basis for the evolution of lateral specialization of the human brain. *Nature, 224,* 614–615.

Levy, J. (1974). Psychobiological implications of bilateral asymmetry. In S. Dimond & G. Beaumont (Eds.), *Hemispheric function in the human brain.* New York: Halsted Press.

Levy, J. (1978). Lateral differences in the human brain in cognition and behavioral control. In P. Buser & A. Rougeul-Buser (Eds.), *Cerebral correlates of conscious experience.* New York: North Holland.

Levy, J. (1982). Handwriting posture and cerebral organization: How are they related? *Psychological Bulletin, 91,* 589–608.

Levy, J., & Trevarthen, C. (1977). Metacontrol of hemispheric function in human split-brain patients. *Journal of Experimental Psychology: Human Perception and Performance, 2,* 299–312.

Levy, J., Trevarthen, C., & Sperry, R. W. (1972). Perception of bilateral chimeric figures following hemispheric disconnexion. *Brain, 95,* 61–78.

Levy-Agresti, J., & Sperry, R. W. (1968). Differential perceptual capacities in major and minor hemispheres. *Proceedings of the National Academy of Science USA, 61,* 1151.

Lewis, D. M., Misanin, J. R., & Miller, R. R. (1968). Recovery of memory following amnesia. *Nature, 220,* 704–705.

Lewis, V.G., & Money, J. (1983). Gender-identity/role: G-I/R Part A: XY (androgen-insensitivity) syndrome and XX (Rokitansky) syndrome of vaginal atresia compared. In L. Dennersten & G. Burrows (Eds.), *Handbook of psychosomatic obstetrics and gynaecology.* Amsterdam: Elsevier Biomedical Press.

Lieberman, A. M. (1984). On finding that speech is special. *American Psychologist, 37,* 148–167.

Lickey, M. E., & Gordon, B. (1983). *Drugs for mental illness.* New York: Freeman.

Lieberman, P. (1984). The biology and evolution of language. Cambridge, MA: Harvard University Press.

Lind, R. W., & Johnson, A. K. (1982). Central and peripheral mechanisms mediating angiotensin-induced thirst. In D. Ganten, M. I. Phillips, & B. A. Schölkens. The renin angiotensin system in the brain. Berlin: Springer-Verlag.

Lindahl, O. (1974). Pain—A general chemical explanation. In J. J. Bonica (Ed.), *Advances in neurology: International symposium on pain* (Vol. 4). New York: Raven.

Lindsay, P. H., & Norman, D. A. (1972). *Human information processing.* New York: Academic Press.

Lindsley, D. B., Schriener, L. H., Knowles, W. B., & Magoun, H. W. (1950). Behavioral and EEG changes following chronic brain stem lesions in the cat. *Electroencephalography Journal, 2,* 489–498.

Livingstone, M., & Hubel, D. (1988). Segregation of form, color, movement and depth: Anatomy, physiology, and perception. *Science, 240,* 740–749.

Ljungberg. T., & Ungerstedt, U. (1976). Sensory inattention produced by 6-hydroxydopamine-induced degeneration of ascending dopamine neurons in the brain. *Experimental Neurology, 53,* 585–600.

Loehlin, J. C., Willerman, L., & Horn, J. M. (1988). Human behavior genetics. *Annual Review of Psychology, 39,* 101–133.

Loewenstein, W. R., & Rathkamp, R. (1958). The sites for mechano-electric conversion in a Pacinian corpuscle. *Journal of General Physiology, 41,* 1245–1265.

Loewenstein, W. R., & Skalak, R. (1966). Mechanical transmission in a Pacinian corpuscle. An analysis and a theory. *Journal of Physiology, 182,* 346–378.

Logue, C. M., Crowe, R. R., & Bean, J. A. (1989). A family study of anorexia nervosa and bulimia. *Comprehensive Psychiatry, 30,* 179–188.

Loyd, J. E. (1966). Studies on the flash communication system in Photinus fireflies. *Miscellaneous Publications, Museum of Zoology, University of Michigan* (Ann Arbor), *130,* 95.

Lumia, A. R., Zebrowski, A. F., & McGinnis, M. Y. (1987). Olfactory bulb removal decreases androgen receptor binding in amygdala and hypothalamus and disrupts masculine sexual behavior. *Brain Research, 404,* 121–126.

Luria, A. R. (1966). *Higher cortical functions in man.* London: Tavistock.

Luria, A. R. (1973a). *The working brain.* New York: Basic Books.

Luria, A. R. (1937b). The frontal lobes and the regulation of behavior. In K. H. Pribram & A. R. Luria (Eds.), *The Psychophysiology of the frontal lobes.* New York: Academic Press.

Luria, A. R., Karpov, B. A., & Yarbuss, A. L. (1966). Disturbances of active visual perception with lesions of the frontal lobes. *Cortex, 2,* 202–212.

Lynch, G., & Baudry, M. (1984). The biochemical intermediates in memory formation: A new and specific hypothesis. *Science, 224,* 1057–1063.

Maayani, S., Hough, L. B., Weinstein, H., & Green, J. P. (1982). Response of histamine H_2-receptor in brain to antidepressant drugs. In E. Consta & G. Racagni (Eds.), *Typical and atypical antidepressants: Molecular mechanisms.* New York: Raven Press.

Maccoby, E., & Jacklin, C. (1974). *The psychology of sex differences.* Stanford, CA: Stanford University Press.

MacLean, P. D. (1949). Psychosomatic disease and the "visceral brain": Recent developments bearing on the Papez theory of emotion. *Psychosomatic Medicine, 11,* 338–353.

MacLean, P. D. (1954). Studies on the limbic system ("visceral brain") and their bearing on psychosomatic medicine. In E. D. Wittkower & R. A. Cleghorn (Eds.), *Recent developments in psychosomatic medicine.* Philadelphia: Lippincott.

MacLean, P. D. (1970). The limbic brain in relation to the psychoses. In P. Black (Ed.), *Physiological correlates of emotion.* New York: Academic Press.

MacLean, P. D. (1977). The triune brain in conflict. *Psychotherapy and Psychosomatics, 28,* 207–220.

Maddison, S., Rolls, B. J., Rolls, E. T., & Wood, R. J., (1980). The role of gastric factors in drinking termination in the monkey. *Journal of Physiology* (London), *305,* 55–56.

Maffei, L., & Fiorentini, A. (1973). The visual cortex as a spatial frequency analyser. *Vision Research, 13,* 1255–1267.

Mair, W. G. P., Warrington, E. K., & Wieskrantz, L. (1979). Memory disorder in Korsakoff's psychosis. *Brain, 102,* 749–783.

Maki, W. S. (1986). Distinction between new and used traces: Different effects of electroconvulsive shock on memories for places present and places past. *Quarterly Journal of Experimental Psychology: Comparative and Physiological Psychology, 38,* 397–423.

Malsbury, C. W. (1971). Facilitation of male rat copulatory behavior by electrical stimulation of the medial preoptic area. *Physiology and Behavior, 7,* 797–805.

Marks, W. B., Dobelle, W. H., & MacNichol, E. F. (1964). Visual pigments of single primate cones. *Science, 143,* 1181–1183.

Marler, P. R., & Peters, S. (1981). Sparrows learn adult song and more from memory. *Science, 213,* 780–782.

Marler, P., & Tamura, M. (1964). Culturally transmitted patterns of vocal behavior in sparrows. *Science, 146,* 1483–1486.

Marthens, van, E., Grauel, L., & Zamenhof, S. (1974). Enhancement of prenatal development in the rat by operative restriction of litter size. *Biology of the Neonate, 25,* 53–56.

Masserman, J. H., (1941). Is the hypothalamus a center of emotion? *Psychosomatic Medicine, 5,* 3–25.

Mast, S. O., & Pusch, L. C. (1924). Modifications of response in the amoeba. *Biological Bulletin, 46,* 55–59.

Maturana, H. R., Lettvin, J. Y., McCulloch, W. S., & Pitts, W. H. (1960). Anatomy and physiology of vision in the frog (*Rana pipiens*). *Journal of General Physiology, 43,* 129–175.

Mauk, M. D., & Thompson, R. F. (1987). Retention of classically conditioned eyelid response following acute decerebration. *Brain Research, 403,* 89–95.

Mayer, D. J., & Liebeskind, J. C. (1974). Pain reduction by focal electrical stimulation of the brain: An anatomical and behavioral analysis. *Brain Research, 68,* 73–93.

Mayer, J. (1955). Regulation of energy, intake and body weight: The glucostatic theory and the lipostatic hypothesis. *Annals of the New York Academy of Sciences, 63,* 15–43.

Mazure, A. (1983). Hormones, aggression, and dominance in humans. In B. B. Svare (Ed.), *Hormones and aggressive behavior*. New York: Plenum.

McClintock, M. K. (1971). Menstrual synchrony and suppression. *Nature, 229*, 244–245.

McClone, J. (1978). Sex differences in functional brain asymmetry. *Cortex, 14*, 122–128.

McConnel, P. S., Boer, G. J., Romijn, H. J., van de Poll, N. E., & Corner, M. A. (1980). *Adaptive capabilities of the nervous system*. Amsterdam: Elsevier.

McConnell, J. V. (1962). Memory transfer through cannibalism in planaria. *Journal of Neuropsychiatry, 3*, 45.

McConnell, J. V., Jacobson, A. L., & Kimble, D. P. (1959). The effects of regeneration upon retention of a conditioned response in the planarian. *Journal of Comparative and Physiological Psychology, 52*, 1–5.

McCormick, D. A., & Thompson, R. F. (1984). Cerebellum: Essential involvement in the classically conditioned eyelid response. *Science, 223*, 296–299.

McGaugh, J. L. (1968). A multi-trace view of memory storage processes. In D. Bovet (Ed.), *Attuali orientamenti della ricerca sull' apprendimento e la memoria*. Academia Nazionale dei Lincei, Quaderno N. 109.

Meddis, R. (1975). On the function of sleep. *Animal Behavior, 23*, 676–691.

Meddis, R. (1979). The evolution and function of sleep. In D. A. Oakley & H. C. Plotkin (Eds.), *Brain, Behavior and evolution*. Methuen, London.

Melzack, R. (1980). The psychological aspects of pain. In J. J. Bonica (Ed.), *Pain*. New York: Raven.

Menaker, M. (1974). Aspects of the physiology of circadian rhythmicity in the vertebrate central nervous system. In F. O. Schmitt & F. G. Worden (Eds.), *The neurosciences: Third study program*. Cambridge, MA: MIT Press.

Merzenich, M. M., & Kaas, J. H. (1980). Principles of organization of sensory-perceptual systems in mammals. In J. M. Sprague & A. N. Epstein (Eds.), *Progress in psychobiology and physiological psychology* (Vol. 9). New York: Academic Press.

Mesulam, M. M. (1985). *Principles of behavioral neurology*. Philadelphia: Davis.

Miller, N. E., Sampliner, R. I., & Woodrow, P. (1957). Thirst reducing effects of water by stomach fistula versus water by mouth, measured by both a consummatory and an instrumental response. *Journal of Comparative and Physiological Psychology, 50*, 1–5.

Miller, R. R., & Springer, A. D. (1972). Induced recovery of memory in rats following electroconvulsive shock. *Physiology & Behavior, 8*, 645–651.

Milner, B. (1959). The memory defect in bilateral hippocampal lesions. *Psychiatric Research Reports, 11*, 43–58.

Milner, B. (1965). Memory disturbance after bilateral hippocampal lesions. In P. M. Milner & S. E. Glickman (Eds.), *Cognitive processes and the brain*. Princeton, NJ: Van Nostrand.

Milner, B. (1970). Memory and the medial temporal regions of the brain. In D. H. Pribram & D. E. Broadbent (Eds.), *Biology of memory*. New York: Academic Press.

Milner, B. (1972). Disorders of learning and memory after temporal lobe lesions in man. *Clinical Neurosurgery, 19*, 421–446.

Mirsky, A. F., & Duncan, C. C. (1986). Etiology and expression of schizophrenia: Neurobiological and psychosocial factors. *Annual Review of Psychology, 37*, 291–319.

Mishkin, M. (1964). Perseveration of central sets after frontal lesions in monkeys. In J. M. Warren & K. Akert (Eds.), *The frontal granular cortex and behavior*. New York: McGraw-Hill.

Mishkin, M. (1978). Memory in monkeys severely impaired by combined but not separate removal of amygdala and hippocampus. *Nature, 273*, 297–298.

Mishkind, M. E., Rodin, J., Silberstein, L. R., & Striegel-Moore, R. H. (1986). The embodiment of masculinity: Cultural, psychological, and behavioral dimensions. *American Behavioral Scientist, 29*, 545–562.

Mitchell, D. E. (1981). Sensitive periods in visual development. In R. N. Aslin, J. R. Alberts, & M. R. Petersen (Eds.), *Development of perception* (Vol. 2). New York: Academic Press.

Molfese, D. L., Freeman, R. B., Jr., & Palermo, D. S. (1975). The ontogeny of brain lateralization for speech and nonspeech stimuli. *Brain and Language, 2*, 171–185.

Moncrieff, R. W. (1967). *The chemical senses* (3rd ed.). Cleveland, OH: CRC Press.

Money, J. (1968). *Sex errors of the body: Dilemmas, education, counseling*. Baltimore: Johns Hopkins Press.

Money, J. (1974). Prenatal hormones and postnatal socialization in gender identity differentiation. *Nebraska Symposium on Motivation* (Vol. 12, pp. 221–295). Lincoln: University of Nebraska Press.

Money, J. (1987). Sin, sickness, or status? Homosexual gender identity and psychoneuroendocrinology. *American Psychologist, 42*, 384–399.

Moniz, E. (1936). *Tentatives operatoires dans le traitement de certaines psychoses*. Paris: Masson.

Monod, J., Wyman, J., & Changeux, J. P. (1965). On the nature of allosteric transitions: A plausible model. *Journal of Molecular Biology, 12*, 88–118.

Montague, M. F. (1968). The new litany of "innate depravity," or original sin revisited. In M. F. Montague (Ed.), *Man and aggression*. Oxford: Oxford University Press.

Morgane, P. J. (1981). Serotonin: Twenty-five years later. *Psychopharmacology Bulletin, 17*, 13–17.

Morris, D. (1957). "Typical intensity" and its relation to the problem of ritualization. *Behavior, 11*, 1–12.

Moruzzi, G. & Magoun, H. W. (1949). Brain stem

reticular formation and activation of the EEG. *Electroencephalography and Clinical Neurophysiology, 1,* 455–473.

Moscovitch, M. (1979). Information processing. In M. S. Gazzaniga (Ed.), *Handbook of Neurobiology-neuropsychology.* New York: Plenum.

Mountcastle, V. B. (1957). Modality and topographic properties of single neurons of cat's somatic sensory cortex. *Journal of Neurophysiology, 20,* 408–434.

Mountcastle, V. B. (1967). The problem of sensing and the neural code of sensory events. In G. C. Quarton, T. Melnechek, & F. O. Schmitt (Eds.), *The neurosciences; A study program.* New York: Rockefeller University Press.

Mountcastle, V. B. (1975). The view from within: Pathways to the study of perception. *Johns Hopkins Medical Journal, 136,* 109–131.

Mountcastle, V. B., & Edelman, G. M. (1978). *The mindful brain: Cortical organization and the group-selective theory of higher brain function.* Cambridge, MA: MIT Press.

Mountcastle, V. B., & Powell, T. P. (1959). Neural mechanisms subserving cutaneous sensibility, with special reference to the role of afferent inhibition in sensory perception and discrimination. *Bulletin of the Johns Hopkins Hospital, 105,* 201–232.

Moynihan, M. H. (1970). Control, suppression, decay, disappearance and replacement of displays. *Journal of Theoretical Biology, 29,* 85–112.

Müller, G. E., & Pilzecker, A. (1900). Experimentale Beiträge zur Lehre vom Gedächtnis. *Zeitschrift für Psychologie* (Supp.), 1–288.

Murphy, J. M. (1976). Psychiatric labeling in cross-cultural perspective. *Science, 191,* 1019–1028.

Murray, C. L., & Fibiger, H. C. (1986). Pilocarpine and physostigmine attenuate spatial memory impairments produced by lesions of the nucleus basalis magnocellularis. *Behavioral Neuroscience, 100,* 23–32.

Myers, R. D. (1970). An improved push–pull cannula system for perfusing an isolated region of the brain. *Physiology and Behavior, 5,* 243–246.

Nafe, J. P. (1968). Neural correlates of sensation. In D. R. Kenshalo (Ed.), *The skin senses.* Springfield, IL: Thomas.

Naitoh, Y., & Eckert, R. (1969). Ionic mechanisms controlling behavioral responses of *paramecium* to mechanical stimulation. *Science, 164,* 963–965.

Nebes, R., & Sperry, R. W. (1971). Hemispheric disconnection with cerebral birth injury in dominant arm area. *Neuropsychologia, 9,* 247.

Nicol, S. E., & Gottesman, I. I. (1983). Clues to the genetics and neurobiology of schizophrenia. *American Scientist, 71,* 398–404.

Nieuwenhuys, R. (1969). *The cerebellum.* Amsterdam: Elsevier.

Niijima, A. (1969). Afferent impulse discharge from glucoreceptors in the liver of the guinea pig. *Annals of the New York Academy of Science, 157,* 690–700.

Niijima, A. (1982). Glucose-sensitive afferent nerve fibers in the haptic branch of the vagus nerve of the guinea pig. *Journal of Physiology, 332,* 315–323.

Niki, H., & Wanatabe, M. (1976). Prefrontal unit activity and delayed response: Relation to cue location versus direction of response. *Brain Research, 105,* 79–88.

Noback, D. R. (1967). *The human nervous system: Basic elements of structure and function.* New York: McGraw-Hill.

Norgren, R., & Grill, H. (1982). Brain-stem control of ingestive behavior. In D. W. Pfaff (Ed.), *The physiological mechanisms of motivation.* New York: Springer-Verlag.

Nottebohm, F. (1970). Ontogeny of bird song. *Science, 167,* 950–956.

Nottebohm, F. (1980). Brain pathways for vocal learning in birds: A review of the first 10 years. In M. Sprague & A. N. Epstein (Eds.), *Progress in psychology and physiological psychology* (Vol. 9). New York: Academic Press.

Novick, A. (1963). Echolocation of flying insects by the bat, *Chilonycteris parnellii. Biological Bulletin, 128,* 297–314.

Novin, D. (1979). Some expected and unexpected effects of glucose on food intake. In G. A. Bray (Ed.), *Recent advances in obesity research:* II. Westport, CT: Food & Nutrition Press.

Novin, D., Robinson, B. A., Culbreth, L. A., & Tordoff, M. G. (1983). Is there a role for the liver in the control of food intake? *American Journal of Clinical Nutrition, 9,* 233, 246.

Numan, M. (1988). Neuronal bases of maternal behavior in the rat. *Psychoneuroendocrinology, 13,* 47–62.

Oakley, D. A. (1985). Animal awareness, consciousness and self-image. In D. A. Oakley (Ed.), *Brain & mind.* London: Methuen.

Ohno, S. (1979). Major sex-determining genes. *Monograph of Endocrinology, 11,* 1–140.

Ojemann, G. (1983). The intrahemispheric organization of human language, derived with electrical stimulation techniques. *Trends in Neurosciences, 6,* 184–189.

Ojemann, G., & Mateer, C. (1979). Human language cortex: Localization of memory, syntax and sequential motor-phoneme identification systems. *Science, 205,* 1401–1403.

Olds, H., & Fobes, J. L. (1981). The central basis of motivation: Intracranial self-stimulation studies. *Annual Review of Psychology, 32,* 523–574.

Olds, J. (1956). A preliminary mapping of electrical reinforcing effects in the rat brain. *Journal of Comparative and Physiological Psychology, 49,* 281–285.

Olds, J. (1973). Commentary. In E. S. Valenstein (Ed.), *Brain stimulation and motivation.* Glenview, IL: Scott Foresman.

Olds, J., & Milner, P. (1954). Positive reinforcement produced by electrical stimulation of septal area and other regions of rat brain. *Journal of Comparative and Physiological Psychology, 47,* 419–427.

Olson, C. R., & Freeman, R. D. (1975). Progressive changes in kitten striate cortex during monocular vision. *Journal of Neurophysiology, 38*, 26–32.

Olton, D. S. (1983). Memory functions and the hippocampus. In W. Seifert (Ed.), *Neurobiology of the hippocampus.* New York: Academic Press.

Olton, D. S., & Papas, B. C. (1979). Spatial memory and radial arm maze performance of rats. *Learning and Motivation, 8*, 289–314.

Oomura, R., Ohta, M., Ishibashi, S., Kita, H., Okajima, T., & Ono, T. (1979). Activity of chemosensitive neurons related to the neurophysiological mechanisms of feeding. In G. A. Bray (Ed.), *Recent advances in obesity research:* II. Westport, CT: Food and Nutrition Press.

Osborne, N. N. (1979). Is Dale's principle valid? *Trends in Neurosciences, 2*, 73–75.

Oswald, I. (1980). Sleep as a restorative process: Human clues. In P. S. McConnel, G. J. Boer, H. H. Romijn, N. E. van de Poll, & M. A. Corner, *Adaptive capabilities of the nervous system.* Amsterdam: Elsevier.

Palay, S. L., & Chan-Palay, V. (1977). General morphology of neurons and neuroglia. In J. M. Brookhart & V. M. Mountcastle (Eds.), *Handbook of physiology, section I: The nervous system.* Bethesda, MD: American Physiological Society.

Palmer, J. D. (1975). Biological clocks of the tidal zone. *Scientific American, 232*, 70–79.

Papez, J. W. (1937). A proposed mechanism of emotion. *Archives of Neurology and Psychiatry, 38*, 725–744.

Parrett, D. I., Smith, P. A. J., Potter, D. D., Mistlin, A. J., Head, A. S., Milner, A. D., & Jeeves, M. A. (1985). Visual cells in the temporal cortex sensitive to face view and gaze direction. *Proceedings of the Royal Society of London. Series B: Biological Sciences, 223*, 293–317.

Panksepp, J. (1986). The neurochemistry of behavior. *Annual Review of Psychology, 37*, 77–107.

Paul, S. M., Extein, I., Calil, H. M., Potter, W. Z., Chodoff, P., & Goodwin, F. K. (1981). Use of ECT with treatment-resistent depressed patients at the National Institutes of Health. *American Journal of Psychiatry, 138*, 486–489.

Peck, J. W., & Blass, E. M. (1975). Localization of thirst and antidiuretic osmoreceptors by intracranial injections in rats. *American Journal of Physiology, 5*, 1501–1509.

Penfield, W. (1975). *The mystery of the mind.* Princeton, NJ: Princeton University Press.

Penfield, W., & Rasmussen, T. (1950). *The cerebral cortex of man: A clinical study of localization of function.* New York: Macmillan.

Pengelley, E. T., & Asmundson, S. J. (1971). Annual biological clocks. *Scientific American, 224*, 72–79.

Petersen, M. R., Beecher, M. D., Zoloth, S. R., Moody, D. B., & Stebbins, W. C. (1978). Neural lateralization of species-specific vocalizations by Japanese macaques. *Science, 202*, 324–326.

Pfaff, D. W., & Sakuma, Y. (1979). Deficit in the lordosis reflex of female rats caused by lesions in the ventromedial nucleus of the hypothalamus. *Journal of Physiology, 288*, 203–210.

Phillips, A., Van der Kooy, D., & Fibiger, H. (1977). Maintenance of intracranial self-stimulation in hippocampus and olfactory bulb following regional depletion of noradrenalin. *Neuroscience Letters, 4*, 77–84.

Phillips, M. I., & Felix, D. (1976). Specific angiotensin II receptive neurons in the cat subfornical organ. *Brain Research, 109*, 531–540.

Phoenix, C. W., Goy, R. W., Gerald, A. A., & Young, W. C. (1959). Organizing action of prenatally administered testosterone proprionate on the tissue mediating mating behavior in the female guinea pig. *Endocrinology, 65*, 369–382.

Pianka. E. R. (1970). On r- and K-selection. *American Naturalist, 104*(940), 592–597.

Pick, J. (1970). *The autonomic nervous system.* Philadelphia: Lippincott.

Pickar, D., Labarca, R., Doran, A. R., Wolkowitz, O. M., Roy, A., Breier, A., Linnoila, M., & Paul, S. M. (1986). Longitudinal measurement of plasma homovanillic acid levels in schizophrenic patients. *Archives of General Psychiatry, 43*, 669–676.

Pinsky, S. D., & McAdam, D. W. (1980). Electroencephalographic and dichotic indices of cerebral laterality in stutterers. *Brain and Language, 11*, 374–397.

Pi-Sunyer, F. X., Kissileff, H. R., Thornton, J., & Smith, G. P. (1982). C-terminal octapeptide of cholecystokinin decreases food intake in obese men. *Physiology and Behavior, 29*, 627–630.

Pivicki, D. (1988) On dreams. *Psychiatric Forum, 14*, 22–28.

Pivik, R. T. (1986). Sleep: Physiology and psychophysiology. In M. G. H. Coles, E. Donchin, & S. W. Porges (Eds.), *Psychophysiology: Systems, processes, and applications.* New York: Guilford.

Pleim, E. T., & Barfield, R. J. (1988). Progesterone versus estrogen facilitation of female sexual behavior by intracranial administration to female rats. *Hormones & Behavior, 22*, 150–159.

Poggio, G. F. (1984). Processing of stereoscopic information in monkey visual cortex. In G. M. Edelman, W. E. Gall, & W. M. Cowan (Eds.), *Dynamic aspects of neocortical function.* New York: Wiley.

Poggio, G. F., Gonzalez, F., & Krause, F. (1988). Stereoscopic mechanisms in monkey visual cortex: Binocular correlation and disparity selectivity. *Journal of Neuroscience, 8*, 4531–4550.

Poggio, G. F., & Poggio, T. (1984). The analysis of stereopsis. *Annual Review of Neuroscience, 7*, 379–412.

Poirier, F. E. (1977). *In search of ourselves: An introduction to physical anthropology* (2nd ed.) Minneapolis: Burgess.

Pollen, D. A., Gaska, J. P., & Jacobson, L. D. (1988). Response of simple and complex cells to compound sine-wave gratings. *Vision Research, 28*, 25–39.

Porth, C. (1982). *Pathophysiology: Concepts of altered health states*. Philadelphia: Lippincott.

Premack, A. J., & Premack, D. (1972). Teaching language to an ape. *Scientific American*, Oct., 92–99.

Preti, G. Cutler, W. B., Garcia, C. R., & Huggins, G. R. (1986). Human axillary secretions influence women's menstrual cycles: The role of donor extract of females. *Hormones & Behavior, 20*, 474–482.

Pribram, K. H. (1962). Interrelations of psychology and neurological disciplines. In S. Koch (Ed.), *Psychology: A study of a science* (Vol. 4). New York: McGraw-Hill.

Pribram, K. H. (1967). The limbic systems, efferent control of neural inhibition and behavior. In W. Adey & T. Tokizane (Eds.), *Progress in brain research* (Vol. 27). Amsterdam: Elsevier/North Holland.

Pribram, K. H. (1976). The structure of consciousness. In G. G. Globus, G. Maxwell, & I. Savodnik (Eds.), *Consciousness and the brain: A scientific and philosophical inquiry*. New York: Plenum.

Pribram, K. H., & Tubbs, W. E. (1967). Short-term memory, parsing and the primate frontal cortex. *Science, 156*, 1765–1767.

Quinn, P.T. (1972). Stuttering: Cerebral dominance and the dichotic word test. *Medical Journal of Australia, 2*, 639–643.

Rada, R .T., Laws, D. R., & Kellner, R. (1976). Plasma testosterone in the rapist. *Psychosomatic Medicine, 38*, 257–268.

Radinsky, L. (1975). Primate brain evolution. *American Scientist, 63*, 656–663.

Rainbow, R. C., Parsons, B., & McEwen, B. S. (1982). Sex differences in rat brain oestrogen and progestin receptors. *Nature, 300*, 648–649.

Ramm, P. (1979). The locus coeruleus, catecholamines, & REM sleep: A critical review. *Behavioral and Neural Biology, 25*, 415–448.

Ramsay, D. J., Rolls, B. J., & Wood, R. J. (1977). Thirst following water deprivation in dogs. *American Journal of Physiology, 232*, 93–100.

Rechtschaffen, A., Gilliland, M. A., Bergmann, B. M., & Winter, J. B. (1983). Physiological correlates of prolonged sleep deprivation in rats. *Science, 221*, 182–184.

Redshaw, M. (1978). Cognitive development in human and gorilla infants. *Journal of Human Evolution, 7*, 133–141.

Reeves, A. G., & Plum, F. (1969). Hyperphagia, rage, and dementia accompanying a ventromedial hypothalamic neoplasm. *Archives of Neurology, 20*, 616–624.

Richter, C. P. (1957). On the phenomenon of sudden death in animals and man. *Psychomatic Medicine, 19*, 191–198.

Richter, C. P. (1967). Sleep and activity: Their relation to the 24-hour clock. *Proceedings of the Association for Research on Nervous and Mental Disorders, 45*, 8–27.

Riddell, W. I. (1979). Cerebral indices and behavioral differences. In E. Hahn, C. Jensen, & B. C. Dudek (Eds.), *Development and evolution of brain size*. New York: Academic Press.

Riddell, W. I., & Corl, K. G. (1977). Comparative investigation of the relationship between cerebral indices and learning abilities. *Brain, Behavior, and Evolution, 14*, 385–398.

Roberts, L. (1961). Activation and interference of cortical functions. In D. Sheer (Ed.), *Electrical stimulation of the brain*. Austin: University of Texas Press.

Rodieck, R. W. (1979). Visual pathways. *Annual Review of Neuroscience, 2*, 193–226.

Rodin, J. (1976). The relationship between external responsiveness and the development and maintenance of obesity. In D. Novin, W. Wyrwicka, & G. Bray (Eds.), *Hunger, basic mechanisms and clinical implications*. New York: Raven Press.

Rodin, J. (1978). Has the distinction between internal versus external control of feeding outlived its usefulness? In G. Bray (Ed.), *Recent advances in obesity research: II*. Westport, CT: Food and Nutrition Press.

Roeder, K. D., & Treat, A. E. (1962). The reception of bat cries by the tympanic organ of noctuid moths. In W. A. Rosenblith (Ed.), *Sensory communication*. Cambridge, MA: MIT Press.

Roffwarg, H. P., Muzio, J. N., & Dement, W. C. (1966). Ontogenesis development of human sleep–dream cycle. *Science, 152*, 604–619.

Rojas-Ramírez, J. A., & Drucker-Colín, R. R. (1977). Phylogenetic correlates between sleep and memory. In R. R. Drucker-Colín & J. L. McGaugh (Eds.), *Neurobiology of sleep and memory*. New York: Academic Press.

Rolls, E. T. (1984). Neurons in the cortex of the temporal lobe and in the amygdala of the monkey with responses selective for faces. *Human Neurobiology, 3*, 209–222.

Romer, A. S. (1955). *The vertebrate body*. Philadelphia: Saunders.

Rose, J. E., Brugge, J. F., Anderson, D. J., & Hind, J. E. (1967). Phase locked response to low frequency tones in single auditory nerve fibers of the squirrel monkey. *Journal of Neurophysiology, 30*, 769–793.

Rose, R. M. (1978). Neuroendocrine correlates of sexual and aggressive behavior in humans. In M. A. Lipton, A. DiMascio, & K. F. Killam (Eds.), *Psychopharmacology: A generation of progress*. New York: Raven Press.

Rose, S. P. R., Hambley, J., & Haywood, J. (1976). Neurochemical approaches to developmental plasticity and learning. In M. R. Rosenzweig & E. L. Bennet (Eds.), *Neural mechanisms of learning and memory*. Cambridge, MA: MIT Press.

Rosenbaum, S. (1983). Can a chimpanzee make a statement? *Journal of Experimental Psychology: General, 112*, 457–492.

Rosenthal, D. A. (1971). A program of research on heredity in schizophrenia. *Behavioral Science, 16*, 191–201.

Rosenzweig, M. R., & Bennett, E. L (Eds.). (1976). *Neural mechanisms of learning and memory*. Cambridge, MA: MIT Press.

Rosenzweig, M. R., Bennett, E. L., & Diamond, M. C. (1967). Effects of differential environments on brain anatomy and brain chemistry. In J. Zubin & C. Jervis (Eds.), *Psychopathology of mental development*. New York: Grune & Stratton.

Rosenzweig, M. R., Bennett, E. E., & Diamond, M. C. (1972). Brain changes in response to experience. *Scientific American, 226*, 22–29.

Rosenzweig, M. R., Krech, D., & Bennett, E. L. (1961). Heredity, environment, brain biochemistry, and learning. In *Current trends in psychological theory*. Pittsburg: University of Pittsburg Press.

Rosenzweig, M. R., Krech, D., Bennett, E. L., & Diamond, M. (1962). Effects of environmental complexity and training on brain chemistry and anatomy: A replication and extension. *Journal of Comparative and Physiological Psychology, 55*, 429–437.

Ross, H. H. (1965). *A textbook of entomology* (3rd ed.). New York: Wiley.

Rossi, A., Stratta, P., DeCataldo, S., DiMichele, V., Organelli, G., Serio, A., Petruzzi, C., & Casacchia, M. (1988). Cortical and subcortical computed tomographic study in schizophrenia. *Journal of Psychiatric Research, 22*, 99–105.

Rosvold, H., Mirsky, A., & Pribram, K. H. (1954). Influence of amygdalectomy on social behavior in monkeys. *Journal of Comparative and Physiological Psychology, 47*, 173–178.

Rozin, P. (1976). The psychobiological approach to human memory. In M. R. Rosenzweig & F. L. Bennett (Eds.), *Neural mechanisms of learning and memory*. Cambridge, MA: MIT Press.

Rubin, R. T. (1982). Testosterone and aggression in men. In J. V. Beaumont & G. D. Burrows (Eds.) *Handbook of psychiatry and endocrinology*. New York: Elsevier Biomedical Press.

Rumbaugh, D. (1977). *Language learning by a chimpanzee: The Lana project*. New York: Academic Press.

Russek, M. (1971). Haptic controlling feeding behavior. In S. Ehrenpreis (Ed.), *Neurosciences research* (Vol. 4). New York: Academic Press.

Russell, F. V. (1961). Interrelationship within the limbic and centrencephalic systems. In D. E. Sheer (Ed.), *Electrical stimulation of the brain*. Austin: University of Texas Press.

Russell, M. J., Switz, G. M., & Thompson, K. (1977). Olfactory influences on the human menstrual cycle. Paper presented at the American Association for the Advancement of Science annual meeting, San Francisco, June.

Sacks, O. (1987). *The man who mistook his wife for a hat and other clinical tales*. New York: Harper & Row.

Sahebarao, P., Mahadik, H. L., Korenovsky, A., & Karpiak, S. E. (1988). Haloperidol alters rats' CNS cholinergic system: Enzymatic and morphological analyses. *Biological Psychiatry, 24*, 199–217.

Sakata, H., & Iwamura, Y. (1978). Cortical processing of tactile information in the first somatosensory and parietal association areas in the monkey. In G. Gordon (Ed.), *Active touch*. New York: Pergamon.

Salmon, D. P., Zola-Morgan, S., Squire, L. R. (1987). Retrograde amnesia following combined hippocampus-amygdala lesions in monkeys. *Psychobiology, 15*, 37–47.

Salthe, S. (1972). *Evolutionary biology*. New York: Holt, Rinehart & Winston.

Sandberg, P. R., & Coyle, J. T. (1984). Scientific approaches to Huntington's disease. *CRC Critical Reviews in Clinical Neurobiology, 1*, 1–44.

Sandberg, K., Sandberg, P. R., Hanin, I., Fisher, A., & Coyle, J. T. (1984). Cholinergic lesion of the striatum impairs acquisition and retention of a passive avoidance response. *Behavioral Neuroscience, 92*, 162–165.

Sanders, R. J. (1985). Teaching apes to ape language: Explaining the imitative and nonimitative signing of a chimpanzee (*Pan troglodytes*). *Journal of Comparative Psychology, 99*, 197–210.

Sasanuma, S. (1975). Kana and Kanji processing in Japanese aphasics. *Brain and Language, 2*, 369–383.

Sato, M., Ogawa, H., & Yamashita, S. (1975). Response properties of macaque monkey chorda tympani fibers. *Journal of General Physiology, 66*, 78–810.

Satz, P., Levy, M. C., Tyson, M. (1969). Comments on: A model of the inheritance of handedness and cerebral dominance. *Neuropsychologia, 7*, 101–103.

Savage-Rumbaugh, E. S., Pate, J. L., Lawson, J., Smith, S. T., & Schneider, D. (1969). Insect olfaction: Deciphering system for chemical messages. *Science, 163*, 1031–1037.

Savage-Rumbaugh, S. (1986). *Ape language: From conditioned response to symbol*. New York: Columbia University Press.

Savage-Rumbaugh, S., McDonald, K., Sevcik, R., A., Hopkins, W. D., & Rupert, E. (1986). Spontaneous symbol acquisition and communicative use by pygmy chimpanzees (*Pan paniscus*). *Journal of Experimental Psychology: General, 115*, 211–235.

Schachter, S. (1971). Some extraordinary facts about obese humans and rats. *American Psychologist, 26*, 129–144.

Schaefer, G. J. (1988). Opiate antagonists and rewarding brain stimulation. *Neuroscience & Biobehavioral Reviews, 12*, 1–17.

Scharf, B. (1975). Audition. In B. Scharf (Ed.), *Experimental sensory psychology*. Glenview, IL: Scott-Foresman.

Schiffman, S. S., Simon, S. A., Gill, J. M., & Beeker, T. G. (1986). Bretylium tosylate enhances salt taste. *Physiology and Behavior, 36*, 1129–1137.

Schildkraut, J. J., & Kety, S. S. (1967). Biogenic amines and emotion. *Science, 156*, 21–30.

Schnapf, J. L., & Baylor, D. A. (1987). How photoreceptor cells respond to light. *Scientific American, 256*, 40–47.

Schneider, D. (1969). Insect olfaction; Deciphering system for chemical messages. *Science, 163,* 1031–1037.

Schneider-Helmert, D., & Spinweber, C. L. (1986). Evaluation of L-tryptophan for treatment of insomnia: A review. *Psychopharmacology, 89,* 1–7.

Schreiner, L., & Kling, A. (1953). Behavioral changes following rhinencephalic injury in the cat. *Journal of Neurophysiology, 16,* 634–659.

Schwabe, A. D. (1981). Anorexia nervosa. *Annals of Internal Medicine, 94,* 371–381.

Schwartz, A. S., Perez, A. J., & Azulaz, A. (1975). Further analysis of active and passive touch in pattern discrimination. *Bulletin of the Psychonomic Society, 6,* 7–9.

Schwartz, W. J., & Gainer, H. (1977). Suprachiasmatic nucleus: Use of 14C-labelled deoxyglucose uptake as a functional marker. *Science, 197,* 1089–1091.

Scoville, W. B., & Milner, B. (1957). Loss of recent memory after bilateral hippocampal lesions. *Journal of Neurology, Neurosurgery, and Psychiatry, 20,* 11–21.

Seeman, P., Lee, T., Chau-Wong, M., & Wong, K. (1976). Antipsychotic drug doses and neuroleptic/dopamine receptors. *Nature, 261,* 717–719.

Selye, H. (1956). *The stress of life.* New York: McGraw Hill.

Selye, H. (1974). *Stress without distress.* Philadelphia: Lippincott.

Shallice, T. (1982). Specific impairments of planning. In D. E. Broadbent & L. Weiskrantz (Eds.), *The neuropsychology of cognitive function.* London: The Royal Society.

Sheard, M. H. (1983). Aggressive behavior: Effects of neural modulation by serotonin. In E. C. Simmel, M. E. Hahn, & J. K. Walters, (Eds.), *Aggressive behavior: Genetic and neural approaches.* Hillsdale, NJ: Erlbaum.

Sheer, D. E. (1961). *Electrical stimulation of the brain.* Austin: University of Texas Press.

Shepherd, G. M. (1983). *Neurobiology.* New York: Oxford University Press.

Sherman, S. M., & Spear, P. D. (1982). Organization of visual pathways in normal and visually deprived cats. *Physiological Reviews, 62,* 738–855.

Sherrington, C. S. (1906). *Integrative action of the nervous system.* London: Constable.

Shrager, E. E., & Johnson, A. K. (1980). Contributions of periventricular structures of the rostral third ventricle to the maintenance of drinking responses to humoral dipsogens and body fluid homeostasis. *Neuroscience Abstracts, 6,* 128.

Simpson, J. B., Epstein, A. N., & Camardo, J. S., Jr. (1978). The localization of dipsogenic receptors for angiotensin II in the subfornical organ. *Journal of Comparative and Physiological Psychology, 92,* 581–608.

Sinclair, D. (1967). *Cutaneous sensation.* Oxford, England: Oxford University Press.

Sinclair, D. (1981). *Mechanisms of cutaneous sensation.* Oxford, England: Oxford University Press.

Sinz, R., Grenchenko, T. N., & Sokolov, Y. N. (1982). The memory neuron concept: A psychophysiological approach. In R. Sinz & M. R. Rosenzweig (Eds.), *Psychophysiology 1980.* Amsterdam: North Holland.

Sitaram, N. M., Weingartner, H., & Gillin, J. C. (1978). Human serial learning: Enhancement with arecholine and choline and impairment with scopolamine. *Science, 201,* 274–276.

Slater, E., & Cowie, V. (1971). *The genetics of mental disorders.* London: Oxford University Press.

Sloan, W. R., & Walsh, P. C. (1976). Familial persistent Müllerian duct syndrome. *Journal of Urology, 115,* 459–461.

Smeraldi, E., Kidd, K. K., Negri, R., Heimbuch, R., & Melica, A. M. (1979). Genetic studies of affective disorders. In C. Obiols, C. Ballús, E. González Monclús & J. Pujol (Eds.), *Biological psychiatry today.* Amsterdam: Elsevier/North Holland Biomedical.

Smith, G. P., Gibbs, J., & Kulkosky, P. J. (1982). Relationships between brain-gut peptides and neurons in the control of food intake. In B. G. Hoebel & D. Novin (Eds.), *The neural basis of feeding and reward.* Brunswick, MA: Haer Institute.

Smith, K. R. (1947). The problem of stimulation deafness. II. Histological changes in the cochlea as a function of tonal frequency. *Journal of Experimental Psychology, 37,* 304–317.

Smith, L. T. (1975). The interanimal transfer phenomenon: A review. *Psychological Bulletin, 81,* 1078–1095.

Smith, W. (1969). Messages of vertebrate communication. *Science, 165,* 145–150.

Snyder, S. H. (1974). *Madness and the brain.* New York: McGraw-Hill.

Sobal, J., & Stunkard, A. J. (1989). Socioeconomic status and obesity: A review of the literature. *Psychological Bulletin, 105,* 260–275.

Somjen, G. (1972). *Sensory coding in the mammalian nervous system.* New York: Appleton-Century-Crofts.

Sperry, R. W. (1970a). An objective approach to subjective experience. *Psychological Review, 77,* 585–590.

Sperry, R. W. (1970b). Perception in the absence of the neocortical commissures. In *Perception and its disorders,* Research Publication ARNMD (Vol. 48). Association for Research in Nervous and Mental Disease.

Sperry, R. W., Stamm, J., & Nimer, N. (1956). Relearning tests for interocular transfer following division of optic chiasma and corpus callosum in cats. *Journal of Comparative and Physiological Psychology, 49,* 529–533.

Spies, G. (1965). Food versus intracranial self-stimulation reinforcement in food-deprived rats. *Journal of Comparative and Physiological Psychology, 60,* 153–157.

Spinelli, D. H., Jensen, F. E., & DiPrisco, G. V. (1980). Early experience effect on dendritic branching in normally reared kittens. *Experimental Neurology, 62,* 1–11.

Spoendlin, H. (1969). Structural basis of peripheral frequency analysis. In R. Plomp & A. Smoorenberg

(Eds.), *Frequency analysis and periodicity detection in hearing*. Leiden, Netherlands: Sijthoff.

Spoendlin, H. (1973). The innervation of the cochlear receptor. In A. R. Moeller (Ed.), *Basic mechanisms in hearing*. New York: Academic Press.

Squire, L., & Moore, R. (1979). Dorsal thalamic lesion in a noted case of chronic memory dysfunction. *Annals of Neurology, 6,* 503–506.

Squire, L. R., Amaral, D. G., Zola-Morgan, S., Kritchevsky, M., & Press, G. (1989). Description of brain injury in the amnesic patient N. A. based on magnetic resonance imaging. *Experimental Neurology, 105,* 23–35.

Stanus, E., Lacroix, B., Kerkhofs, M., & Mendlewicz, J. (1987). Automated sleep scoring: A comparative reliability study of two algorhythms. *Electroencephalography & Clinical Neurophysiology, 66,* 448–456.

Starr, A., & Phillips, L. (1970). Verbal and motor memory in the amnesic syndrome. *Neurophysiologia, 8,* 75–88.

Staubli, U., Fraser, D., Kessler, M., & Lynch, G. (1986). Studies of retrograde and anterograde amnesia of olfactory memory after denervation of the hippocampus by entorhinal cortex lesions. *Behavioral and Neural Biology, 46,* 432–444.

Stein, L., & Ray, O. (1960). Brain stimulation reward "thresholds" self-determined in the rat. *Psychopharmacologia, 1,* 251–256.

Stephan, F. K., & Nuñez, A. A. (1977). Elimination of circadian rhythms in drinking activity, sleep, and temperature by isolation of the suprachiasmatic nuclei. *Behavioral Biology, 20,* 1–16.

Stephens, B. R., & Banks, M. S. (1987). Contrast discrimination in human infants. *Journal of Experimental Psychology: Human Perception and Performance, 13,* 1–7.

Sternbach, R. A. (1968). *Pain: A psychophysiological analysis.* New York: Academic Press.

Stevens, C. F. (1979). The neuron. In *The brain* [a *Scientific American* book]. New York: Scientific American.

Stevens, J. R. (1982). Neuropathology of schizophrenia. *Archives of General Psychiatry, 39,* 1131–1139.

Stini, W. (1975). *Ecology and human adaptation.* Dubuque, IA: Brown.

Stone, J., & Fukuda, Y. (1974). Properties of cat retinal ganglion cells: A comparison of W- cells with X- and Y- cells. *Journal of Neurophysiology, 37,* 722–748.

Stratta, P., Rossi, A., Gallucci, M., Amicarelli, I., Passariello, R., & Casacchia, M. (1989). Hemispheric asymmetries and schizophrenia: A preliminary magnetic resonance imaging study. *Biological Psychiatry, 25,* 275–284.

Stricker, E. M. (1973). Thirst, sodium appetite, and complementary physiological contributions to the regulation of intravascular fluid volume. In A. N. Epstein, H. R. Kisseleff, & E. Stellar (Eds.), *The neuropsychology of thirst: New findings and advances in concepts.* Washington, DC: Winston.

Stricker, E. M. (1982). The central control of food intake: A role for insulin. In B. G. Hoebel & D. Novin (Eds.), *The neural basis of feeding and reward.* Brunswick, MA: Haer Institute.

Stricker, E. M., & Verbalis, J. C. (1987). Biological bases of hunger and satiety. *Annals of Behavioral Medicine, 9,* 3–8.

Strohmayer, A. J., & Smith, G. P. (1986). Obese male mice (ob/ob) are normally sensitive to the satiating effect of CCK-8. *Brain Research Bulletin, 17,* 571–573.

Strumwasser, F., Schlechte, F. R., & Bower, S. (1972). Distributed circadian oscillators in the nervous system of *Aplysia. Federation Proceedings, 31,* 405.

Stuss, D. T., & Benson, F. D. (1984). Neuropsychological studies of the frontal lobes. *Psychological Bulletin, 95,* 2–28.

Suarez, S. D., & Gallup, G. G., Jr. (1981). Self-recognition in chimpanzees and orangutans, but not gorillas. *Journal of Human Evolution, 10,* 175–188.

Suinn, R. M. (1970). *Fundamentals of behavior pathology.* New York: Wiley.

Svare, B. B. (Ed.). (1983). *Hormones and aggressive behavior.* New York: Plenum.

Swanson, L. W. (1982). Normal hippocampal circuitry: Anatomy. *Neurosciences Research Program Bulletin, 20,* 624–634.

Swanson, L. W., & Sawchenko, P. E. (1983). Hypothalamic integration: Organization of the paraventricular and supraoptic nuclei. *Annual Review of Neuroscience, 6,* 269–324.

Swiercinsky, D. (1978). *Manual for the adult neuropsychological evaluation.* Springfield, IL: Thomas.

Szentágothai, J. (1969). Architecture of the cerebral cortex. In H. H. Jasper, A. A. Ward, & A. Pope (Eds.), *Basic mechanisms of epilepsies.* Boston: Little Brown.

Szentágothai, J. (1972). The basic neuron circuit of the neocortex. In *Symposium on synchronization mechanisms.* Vienna: Springer-Verlag.

Takahashi, Y. (1979). Growth hormone secretion related to the sleep–waking rhythm. In R. Drucker-Colìn, M. Shkurovich, & M. B. Sterman (Eds.), *The functions of sleep.* New York: Academic Press.

Tanabe, T., Iino, M., Oshima, Y., & Takagi, S. F. (1974). An olfactory area in the prefrontal lobe. *Brain Research, 80,* 127–130.

Tanabe, T., Iino, M., & Takagi, S. F. (1975). Discrimination of odors in olfactrory bulb, pyriform-amygdaloid areas and orbito-frontal cortex of the monkey. *Journal of Neurophysiology, 38,* 1284–1296.

Tanaka, Y, Yamadori, A., & Murata, S. (1987). Selective Kana agraphia: A case report. *Cortex, 23,* 679–684.

Tattersall, I. (1975). *The evolutionary significance of Ramapithecus.* Minneapolis, MN: Burgess.

Teitelbaum, P., & Epstein, A. N. (1962). The lateral hypothalamic syndrome: Recovery of feeding and drinking after lateral hypothalamic lesions. *Psychological Review, 69,* 74–94.

Teitelbaum, P., & Stellar, E. (1954). Recovery from failure to eat produced by hypothalamic lesions. *Science, 120*, 894–895.

Terrace, H. (1979). *Nim.* New York: Knopf.

Terrace, H., Petitto, L. A., Sanders, R. J., & Bever, T. G. (1979). Can an ape create a sentence? *Science, 206*, 891–902.

Terzian, H., & Dalle Ore, G. (1955). Syndrome of Klüver and Bucy reproduced in man with bilateral removal of the temporal lobe. *Neurology, 5*, 373–380.

Teuber, H.L., Milner, B., & Vaughan, H. G. (1968). Persistent anterograde amnesia after stab wound of the basal brain. *Neuropsychologia, 6*, 267–282.

Thompson, R. F. (1985). *The brain* [a *Scientific American* book]. New York: Freeman.

Thompson, R. F., Mamounas, L. A., Lynch, G., & Baudry, M. (1983). Increased glutamate receptor binding in hippocampus following classical conditioning of the rabbit eyelid response. *Society for Neuroscience Abstracts, 9*, 830.

Thompson, R. (1981). Rapid forgetting of a spatial habit in rats with hippocampal lesions. *Science, 212*, 959–960.

Thompson, R., & McConnell, J. V. (1955). Classical conditioning in the Planarian, *Dugesia Dorotocephala. Journal of Comparative and Physiological Psychology, 48*, 65–68.

Thurm, U. (1969). General organization of sensory receptors. *Rendiconti della Scuola Internazionale di Fisica "E. Fermi", XLIII Corso* (pp. 64–68).

Tobias, P. (1971). *The brain in hominid evolution.* New York: Columbia University Press.

Tomita, T., Kaneko, A., Murakami, M., & Pautler, E. L. (1967). Spectral response curves of single cones in the carp. *Vision Research, 7*, 519–531.

Tootell, R. B., Silverman, M. S., & DeValois, R. L. (1981). Spatial frequency columns in primary visual cortex. *Science, 214*, 813–815.

Towe, A. (1973). Relative numbers of pyramidal tract neurons in mammals of different sizes. *Brain, Behavior and Evolution, 7*, 1–17.

Tryon, R. C. (1940). Genetic differences in maze learning ability in rats. *Yearbook of the National Society for Studies in Education, 39*, 111–119.

Tunturi, A. R. (1953). A difference in representation of auditory signals for the left and right ears in the isofrequency contours of right middle ectosylvian auditory cortex in the dog. *American Journal of Physiology, 168*, 712–727.

Turner, C. D., & Bagnara, J. T. (1976). *General endocrinology* (6th Ed.). Philadelphia: Saunders.

Tuttle, R. (Ed.). (1972). *The functional and evolutionary biology of primates.* Chicago: Aldine-Atherton.

Ukai, M., & Holtzman, S. C. (1987). Suppression of deprivation-induced water intake in the rat by opioid antagonists: Central sites of action. *Psychopharmacology, 91*, 279–284.

Ungerstedt, U. (1971). Stereotaxic mapping of the monoamine pathways in the rat brain. *Acta Physiologica Scandinavica,* Supplementum, *367*, 1–48.

Uttal, W. R. (1973). *The psychobiology of sensory coding.* New York: Harper & Row.

Valenstein, E. S., & Beer, B. (1962). Reinforcing brain stimulation in competition with water reward and shock avoidance. *Science, 137*, 1052–1054.

Valenstein, E. S., Cox, V. C., & Kakolewski, J. W. (1970). Re-examination of the role of the hypothalamus in motivation. *Psychological Review, 77*, 16–31.

Vallbo, A. B., & Johansson, R. S. (1976). Skin mechanoreceptors in the human hand: Neural and psychophysical thresholds. In Y. Zotterman (Ed.), *Sensory functions of the skin in primates, with special reference to man.* New York: Plenum.

Valli, P., Zucca, G., & Casella, C. (1979). Ionic composition of the endolymph and sensory transduction in labyrinthine organs. *Acta Otolaryngologica, 87*, 466–471.

Valzelli, L., & Garattini, S. (1972). Biochemical and behavioral changes induced by isolation in rats. *Neuropharmacology, 11*, 17–22.

Van Valen, L. (1974). Two modes of evolution. *Nature, 252*, 298–300.

Van Wagenen, W., & Herren, R. (1940). Surgical division of commissural pathways in the corpus callosum. *Archives of Neurology and Psychiatry, 44*, 740–759.

Vaughan, T. A. (1978). *Mammalogy* (2nd ed.) Philadelphia: Saunders.

Vellutino, F. R. (1987). Dyslexia. *Scientific American, 256*, 34–41.

Venter, J. C., DiPorzio, U., Robinson, D. A., Shreeve, S. M., Lai, J., Kerlavage, A. R., Fracek, S. P., Jr., Lentes, K. U., & Fraser, C. M. (1988). Evolution of neurotransmitter receptor systems. *Progress in Neurobiology, 30*, 105–169.

Vergnes, M. (1975). Déclenchment de réactions d'aggression interspécifique après lèsion amygdalienne chez le rat. *Physiology and Behavior, 14*, 271–276.

Vergnes, M. (1976). Contrôle amygdalien de comportements d'aggression chez le rat. *Physiology and Behavior, 17*, 439–444.

Victor, M., Adams, R. D., & Collins, G. H. (1971). *The Wernicke-Korsakoff syndrome.* Philadelphia: Davis.

Wada, J. A., Clark, R., & Hamm, A. (1975). Cerebral hemisphere asymmetry in humans. *Archives of Neurology, 32*, 239–246.

Wada, J. A., & Davis, A. (1977). Fundamental nature of human infants' brain asymmetry. *Canadian Journal of Neurological Sciences, 4*, 203–207.

Wagner, G., Beauving, L., & Hutchinson, R. (1980). The effects of gonadal hormone manipulations on aggressive target-biting in mice. *Aggressive Behavior, 6*, 1–7.

Walls, G. (1942). *The vertebrate eye and its adaptive radiation.*

Bloomfield Hills, MI: Cranbrook Institute of Science. [Reprinted by Hafner Co., New York, 1963]

Washburn, S. L., & DeVore, I. (1961). The social life of baboons. *Scientific American, 204,* 62–71.

Webb, W. B. (1975). *Sleep: The gentle tyrant.* Englewood Cliffs, NJ: Prentice-Hall.

Webb, W. B. (1982). Some theories about sleep and their clinical implications. *Psychiatric Annals, 11,* 415–422.

Weddell, G., & Verrillo, R. T. (1972). Common sensibility. In M. Critchley, J. L. O'Leary, & B. Jennett (Eds.), *Scientific foundations of neurology.* Philadelphia: Davis.

Wegner, M., Bagchi, B., & Anand, B. (1961). Experiments in India on "voluntary" control of the heart and pulse. *Circulation, 24,* 1319–1325.

Weigner, W. A., & Bear, D. M. (1988). An approach to the neurology of aggression. *Journal of Psychiatric Research, 22,* 85–98.

Weinberger, D. R., Bigelow, L. B., Kleinman, J. E., Klein, S. T., Rosenblatt, J. E., & Wyatt, R. J. (1980). Cerebral ventricular enlargement in chronic schizophrenia: An association with poor response to treatment. *Archives of General Psychiatry, 37,* 11–13.

Weinberger, D. R., & Wyatt, R. J. (1982). Brain morphology in schizophrenia: *In vivo* studies. In F. A. Henn, & H. A. Nasrallah (Eds.), *Schizophrenia as a brain disease.* New York: Oxford University Press.

Weinstein, S. (1968). Intensive and extensive aspects of tactile sensitivity as a function of body part, sex, and laterality. In D. R. Kenshalo (Ed.), *The skin senses.* Springfield, IL: Thomas.

Weiss, J. M. (1968). Effects of coping responses on stress. *Journal of Comparative and Physiological Psychology, 65,* 251–260.

Weiss, J. M. (1971). Effects of coping behavior in different warning signal conditions on stress pathology in rats. *Journal of Comparative and Physiological Psychology, 77,* 1–13.

Weiss, J. M. (1972). Psychological factors in stress and disease. *Scientific American, 226,* 104–113.

Weissman, M. M., Gershon, E. S., Kidd, K. K., Prusoff, B. A., Leckman, J. F., Dibble, E., Hamovit, J., Thompson, D., Pauls, D. L., & Guroff, J. J. (1984). Psychiatric disorders in the relatives of probands with affective disorders. *Archives of General Psychiatry, 41,* 14–21.

Weisz, K., Solomin, P. R., & Thompson, R. F. (1980). The hippocampus appears necessary for trace conditioning. *Bulletin of the Psychononic Society, 16,* 164.

Weitzmann, E. D. (1981). Sleep and its disorders. *Annual Review of Neurosciences, 4,* 381–417.

Welker, W. I. (1973). Principles of organization of the ventrobasal complex in mammals. *Brain, Behavior and Evolution, 1,* 253–336.

Welty, J. C. (1975). *The life of birds.* Philadelphia: Saunders.

Wender, P. H., Kety, S. S., Rosenthal, D., Schulsinger, F., Ortmann, J., & Lunde, I. (1986). Psychiatric disorders in the biological and adoptive families of adopted individuals with affective disorders. *Archives of General Psychiatry, 43,* 923–929.

West, R. W., & Greenough, W. T. (1972). Effect of environmental complexity on cortical synapses of rats: Preliminary results. *Behavioral Biology, 7,* 279–284.

Wetterberg, L. (1982). The genetic control of catecholamines and its possible implication in schizophrenia. In G. Hemmings (Ed.), *Biological aspects of schizophrenia and addiction.* New York: Wiley.

Wiesendanger, M. (1984). Pyramidal tract function and the clinical "pyramidal syndrome." *Human Neurobiology, 2,* 227–234.

Williams, J. A., O'Tuama, L. A., Snyder, S. H., Kuhar, M. J., & Gjedde, A. (1986). Positron emission tomography reveals elevated D_2 dopamine receptors in drug-naive schizophrenics. *Science, 234,* 1558–1563.

Wilson, E. O. (1975). *Sociobiology: The new synthesis.* Cambridge, MA: Harvard University Press.

Wilson, E. O., & Bossert, W. H. (1963). Chemical communication among animals. *Recent Progress in Hormone Research, 19,* 673–716.

Wise, R. A. (1974). Lateral hypothalamic electrical stimulation: Does it make animals "hungry"? *Brain Research, 67,* 187–209.

Witelson, S. F. (1985). The brain connection: The corpus callosum is larger in left-handers. *Science, 229,* 665–668.

Witelson, S. F., & Pallie, W. (1973). Left hemisphere specialization for language in the newborn: Neuroanatomical evidence of asymmetry. *Brain, 96,* 641–646.

Whishaw, I. Q. (1987). Hippocampal granule cell and CA3-4 lesions impair formation of a place learning set in the rat and induced reflex epilepsy. *Behavioral Brain Research, 24,* 59–72.

White, F. J., & Wang, R. Y. (1983). Differential effects of classical and atypical antipsychotic drugs on A9 and A10 dopamine neurons. *Science, 221,* 1054–1057.

Wong, D. F. P., Wagner, H. N., Jr., Tune, L. E., Dannals, R. F., Pearlson, G. D. Links, H. M., Tamminga, C. A., Broussolle, E. P., Ravert, H. T., Wilson, A. A., Toung, J. K. T., Malat, J., Weissman, M. M., Merikangas, K. R., Wickramaratne, P., Kidd, K. K., Prusoff, B. A., Leckman, J. F., & Pauls, D. L. (1986). Understanding the clinical heterogeneity of major depression using family data. *Archives of General Psychiatry, 43,* 430–434.

Wurtman, R. J., & Lieberman, H. (1987). Melatonin secretion as a mediator of circadian variations in sleep and sleepiness. *Integrative Psychiatry, 5,* 13–14.

Yaryura-Tobias, J. A., & Neziroglu, F. A. (1981). Aggressive behavior, clinical interfaces. In L. Valzelli & L. Morgese (Eds.), *Aggression and violence: A psycho/biological and clinical approach.* Italy: Edisioni Saint Vincent.

Young, J. Z. (1987). *Philosophy and the brain.* New York: Oxford University Press.

Young, R. (1970). *Mind, brain, and adaptation in the 19th century.* Oxford: Clarendon Press.

Young, R. W. (1970). Visual cells. *Scientific American, 223,* 80–91.

Young, W. C., Goy, R. W., & Phoenix, C. W. (1965). Hormones and sexual behavior. In J. Money (Ed.), *Sex research: New developments.* New York: Holt, Rinehart & Winston.

Yunis, J. J., & Prakash, O. (1982). The origin of man: A chromosomal pictorial legacy. *Science, 215,* 1525–1530.

Zaidel, E. (1975). A technique for presenting lateralized visual input with prolonged exposure. *Vision Research, 15,* 283–289.

Zaidel, E. (1978). Auditory language comprehension in the right hemisphere following cerebral commissurotomy and hemispherectomy: A comparison with child language and aphasia. In A. Caramazza & E. Zurif

(Eds.), *Language acquisition and language breakdown.* Baltimore, MD: Johns Hopkins University Press.

Zeki, S. (1980). The representation of colours in the visual cortex. *Nature, 284,* 412–418.

Zeki, S. (1983). Colour coding in the cerebral cortex: The responses of wavelength-selective and colour-coded cells in monkey visual cortex to changes in wavelength composition. *Neuroscience, 9,* 767–781.

Zola-Morgan, S., Squire, L. R., & Mishkin, M. (1981). The anatomy of amnesia: Amygdala-hippocampus vs. temporal stem. *Society for Neuroscience Abstracts, 7,* 236.

Zornetzer, S. F. (1985). Catecholamine system involvement in age-related memory dysfunction. *Annals of the New York Academy of Sciences, 444,* 242–254.

Zuger, D. (1976). Monozygotic twins discordant for homosexuality: Report of a pair and significance of the phenomenon. *Comprehensive Psychiatry, 17,* 661–669.

ure 2-3: Illustration by Albert Miller in Stevens, C. F. (1979), The neuron. In *The brain*, a Scientific American Book. Copyright 1979 by *Scientific American*, Inc. All rights reserved. Figure 2-13: Thompson, R. F. (1985). *The brain*. Copyright © 1985 W. H. Freeman and Company. Reprinted with permission.

Chapter 3 Figure 3-8a: Adapted from an illustration by Albert Miller from Cowan, W. M. (1979) The Development of the brain. In *The brain*, a *Scientific American* book. Copyright © 1979 by *Scientific American*, Inc. All rights reserved. Figure 3-8b: Adapted from an illustration by Patricia J. Wynne in Hubel, D. H. (1979), in *The brain*, a *Scientific American* book. Copyright © 1979 by *Scientific American*, Inc. All rights reserved. Figure 3-10: Figure 418 from "The Nervous System" in *The vertebrate body*, Fifth Edition, by Alfred Sherwood Romer and Thomas S. Parsons, copyright © 1977 by Saunders College Publishing, a division of Holt, Rinehart and Winston, Inc., adapted by permission of the publisher.

Chapter 4 Figure 4-10a & b: Money, J., & Ehrhardt, A. A. (1973). *Man and woman, boy and girl: Differentiation and dimorphism of gender identity from conception to maturity*. Baltimore/London: The Johns Hopkins University Press. Spotlight Figure 4-1: From Lehrman, D. S. (1964). The reproductive behavior of the ring doves. *Scientific American, 211*, 48-54. Copyright © 1964 by *Scientific American*, Inc. All rights reserved. Figure 4-12: Beamer, W., Bermant, G., & Clegg, M. (1969). Copulatory behavior of the ram, *Ovis aries*. II. Factors affecting copulatory satiety. *Animal Behavior, 17*, 795-800. Reprinted by permission of Academic Press, Inc. (London) Ltd.

Chapter 5 Spotlight Figure 5-1: Kenshalo, D. R., & Scott, R. A., Jr. (1966). Temporal lobe course of thermal adaptation. *Science, 151*, 1095-1096. Copyright 1966 by the AAAS. Figure 5-6a: Frazier, W. T., Kandel, E. R., Kupferman, I., Waziri, R., & Coggeshall, R. E. (1967). Morphological and functional properties of identified neurons in the abdominal ganglion of *Aplysia californica*. *Journal of Neurophysiology, 30*, 1288-1351. Copyright © 1967 by W. H. Freeman and Company. Figure 5-6b: Alving, B. O. (1968). Spontaneous activity in isolated somata of *Aplysia* pacemaker neurons. *Journal of General Physiology*, 51, 29-45, by copyright permission of the Rockefeller University Press. Figure 5-8: Maturana, H. R., Lettvin, J. Y., McCullough, W. S., & Pitts, W. H. (1960). Anatomy and physiology of vision in the frog (*Rana pipiens*). *Journal of General Physiology, 43*, 129-175. Reproduced by copyright permission of the Rockefeller University Press.

Chapter 6 Spotlight Figure 6-1: From Brown, E. L., & Deffenbacher, K. A. (1979). *Perception and the senses*. New York: Oxford University Press. Used by permission of the authors.

Chapter 7 Figure 7-13: Tomita, T., Kaneko, A., Murakami, M., & Pautler, E. L. (1967). Spectral response curves of single cones in the carp. *Vision Research, 7*, 519-537. Copyright 1967 Pergamon Press PLC. Spotlight Figure 7-3: Livingstone, M., & Hubel, D. (1988). Segregation of form, color, movement, and depth: Anatomy, physiology, and perception. *Science, 240*, 740-749. Copyright 1988 by the AAAS.

Chapter 8 Figure 8-7: Spoendlin, H. (1969). Structural basis of peripheral frequency analysis. In Plump, R., & Smoorenberg, A. (Eds.), *Frequency analysis and periodicity detection in hearing*. Sijthoff, Leider Netherlands. Adapted by permission of Kluwer Academic Publishers. Figure 8-8: Norman, D., & Lindsay, P. H., *Human information processing*. Copyright © 1972 by Harcourt Brace Jovanovich, Inc. Adapted by permission of the publisher. Figure 8-22: Amoore, J. E. (1970). *Molecular basis of odor*. Courtesy of Charles C Thomas, Publisher, Springfield, Illinois. Figure 8-25: Sato, M., Ogawa, H., & Yamashita, S., (1975). Response properties of macaque monkey chorda tympani fibers. *Journal of General Physiology, 66*, 781-810. Reproduced by copyright permission of the Rockefeller University Press.

Chapter 9 Figure 9-4: Weinstein, S. (1968). Intensive and extensive aspects of tactile sensitivity as a function of body part, sex, and laterality. In Kenshalo, D. R. (Ed.), *The skin senses*. Courtesy of Charles C Thomas, Publisher, Springfield, Illinois. Figure 9-6: Mountcastle, V. B., & Powell, T. P. S. (1959). Neural mechanisms subserving cutaneous sensibility, with special reference to the role of afferent inhibition in sensory perception and discrimination. Originally published in *Bulletin of the Johns Hopkins Hospital, 105* (1959), 201-232. Reprinted by permission of the Johns Hopkins University Press. Figure 9-8: Sakata, H., & Iwamore, Y. (1978). Adapted with permission from Cortical processing of tactile information in the first somatosensory and parietal association areas in the monkey. In Gordon, G. (Ed.), *Active touch*. Copyright © 1978 Pergamon Press PLC. Figures 9-10 & 9-16: Penfield, W., & Rasmussen, T. (1950). The cerebral cortex of man. Copyright © 1950 by Macmillan Publishing Company, renewed 1978 by Theodore Rasmussen. Adapted with permission of Macmillan Publishing Company.

Chapter 10 Figure 10-4: Adapted with permission from Hatton, G. I. (1976). Nucleus circularis: Is it an osmoreceptor in the brain? *Brain Research Bulletin, 1*, 123-131. Copyright 1976 Pergamon Press PLC. Spotlight Figure 10-3a: Figures 12-7, 12-5A, and 14-12 from *Mammalogy*, Second Edition, by Terry A. Vaughan, copyright © 1978 by Saunders College Publishing, a division of Holt, Rinehart and Winston, Inc., adapted by permission of the publisher. Spotlight Figure b & c: Poirier, F. E. (1977). *In search of ourselves: An introduction to physical anthropology*, 2nd ed. Copyright © 1977 by Burgess Publishing Company, Minneapolis, Minnesota. Figure 10-11: Hetherington, A. W., & Ranson, S. W. (1940). Hypothalamic lesions and adiposity in the rat. *Anatomical Record, 78*, 149-172. Alan R. Liss, Inc., publisher and copyright holder. Figure 10-13: Teitelbaum, P., & Epstein, A. N. (1962). The lateral hypothalamic syndrome: Recovery of feeding and drinking after lateral hypothalamic lesions. *Psychological Review, 69*, 74-84. Copyright 1962 by the American Psychological Association. Adapted by permission. Figure 10-15: Epstein, A. N., & Teitelbaum, P. (1962). Regulation of food intake in the absence of taste, smell, and other oropharyngeal sensations. *Journal of Comparative and Physiological Psychology, 55*, 753-759. Copyright 1962 by the American Psychological Association. Adapted by permission.

Chapter 11 Figure 11-2: Illustration by Bunji Tagawa in Rosenzweig, M. R., Bennett, E. L., & Diamond, M. C.

(1972). Brain changes in response to experience. *Scientific American*, February 1972, p. 23. Copyright © 1972 by *Scientific American*, Inc. All rights reserved. Spotlight Figure 11-2: Weitzmann, E. D. (1981). Sleep and its disorders. Adapted with permission from the *Annual Review of Neuroscience*, Vol. 4, © 1981 by Annual Reviews, Inc. Figure 11-4: Cohen, C. B. (1979). Sleep & dreaming: Origins, nature, and functions. Copyright © 1979. Reproduced with permission of Pergamon Press PLC. Figure 11-5: Hartmann, E. (1967). *The biology of dreaming*, Courtesy of Charles C Thomas, Springfield, Illinois. Figure 11-7: Roffwarg, H. P., Muzio, J. N., & Dement, W. C. (1966). Ontogenesis development of human sleep-dream cycle. *Science, 152,* 604-619. Copyright 1966 by the AAAS. Figure 11-8: Schwartz, W. J., & Gainer, H. (1977). Suprachiasmatic nucleus: Use of 14C-labeled deoxyglucose uptake as a functional market. *Science, 197,* 1089-1091. Copyright 1977 by the AAAS. Spotlight Figure 11-4: Drucker-Colìn, R. R., & Spanis, C. W. (1976). Is there a sleep transmitter? *Progress in Neurophysiology, 6,* 1-22. Reprinted with permission of Pergamon Press PLC.

Chapter 12 Figure 12-8: Kandel, E. R., & Schwartz, J. H. (1982). Molecular biology of learning: Modulation of transmitter release. *Science, 218,* 433–434. Copyright 1982 by the AAAS. Figure 12-11: Alcon, D. L. (1984). Calcium-mediated reduction of ionic currents: A biophysical memory trace. *Science, 226,* 1037–1045. Copyright 1984 by the AAAS. Spotlight Figure 12-2: Norman, D. A., & Lindsay, P. H. (1972). Figure 8-7 from *Human information processing*. Copyright © 1972 by Harcourt Brace Jovanovich, Inc., adapted by permission of the publisher. Figure 12-12: Adapted from Flood, J. F., Bennet, E. L., Rosenzweig, M. R., & Orme, A. E. (1973). The influence of protein synthesis inhibition of memory. *Physiology and Behavior, 10,* 555–562. Copyright 1973 Pergamon Press PLC. Figure 12-13: Illustration by Bunji Tagawa in Rosenzweig, M. R., Bennett, E. L., & Diamond, M. C. Brain changes in response to experience, *Scientific American*, February 1972, p. 23. Copyright © 1972 by *Scientific American*, Inc. All rights reserved. Figure 12-14: Greenough, W. T. (1976). Enduring brain effects of differential experience and training. In Rosenzweig, M. R., & Bennett, E. L., *Neural mechanisms of learning and memory*. Cambridge, MA: MIT Press. Copyright © 1976 by MIT Press. Spotlight Figure 12-3: Milner, P. M., & Glickman, S. E. (Eds.) (1965). *Cognitive processes and the brain*. Copyright © 1965 by D. Van Nostrand Company, Inc. Adapted by permission of Wadsworth, Inc. Figure 12-21: Riddell, W. I., & Corl, K. G. (1977). Comparative investigation of the relationship between cerebral indices and learning abilities. *Brain, behavior, and evolution, 14,* 385–398. Copyright 1977 by S. Karger AG, Basel, Switzerland. Figure 12-25: Chorover, S., & Schiller, P. (1965). Short-term retrograde amnesia in rats. *Journal of comparative and physiological psychology, 59,* 73–78. Copyright 1965 by the American Psychological Association. Adapted by permission.

Chapter 13 Figure 13-4: Adapted from Gregory, W. K. (1929). *Our face from fish to man*. Copyright © 1929 by G. P. Putnam's Sons. Figure 13-10: Brady, J. V., Porter, R. W., Conrad, D. G., & Mason, J. W. (1958). Avoidance behavior and the development of gastroduodenal ulcers. *Journal of the experimental analysis of behavior, 1,* 69–72. Copyright 1958 by the Society for the Experimental Analysis of Behavior, Inc.

Figure 13-14: Adapted from Wagner, G., Beauving, L., & Hutchinson, R. (1980). The effects of gonadal hormone manipulation on aggressive target-biting in mice. *Aggressive Behavior, 6,* 1–7. Alan R. Liss, Inc., publisher & copyright holder.

Chapter 14 Spotlight Figure 14-1: Ingvar, D. (1979). Brain activation patterns revealed by measurements of regional blood flow. In Desment, J. E., Ed., *Cognitive components in cerebral event-related potentials and selective attention*. Copyright 1979 by S. Karger AG, Basel, Switzerland. Figure 14-8: Bogerts, B., Meertz, E., & Schamfeldt-Bausch, R. (1985). Basal ganglia and limbic system pathology in schizophrenia. *Archives of General Psychiatry, 42,* 784–791. Copyright 1985, American Medical Association. Figure 14-10: Seeman, P., Lee, T., Chau-Wong, M., & Wong, K. (1976). Antipsychotic drug doses and neuroleptic/dopamine receptors. Adapted by permission from *Nature, 261,* 717–719. Copyright © 1976 Macmillan Magazines Ltd. Figure 14-11: Adapted from Iversen, L. L. (1979). The chemistry of the brain. *Scientific American, 241,* 134–149. Copyright © 1979 by *Scientific American*, Inc. All rights reserved.

Chapter 15 Figure 15-5: Adapted from Brown, J. L. (1975). *The evolution of behavior* by permission of W. W. Norton & Company, Inc. Copyright © 1975 by W. W. Norton & Company, Inc. Redrawn from Kühme, W. (1963). Ergänzende beobachtung an afrikanischen elefanten (*Loxodonta africana* Blumenbach 1797) in freigehege. *Zeitschrift für Tierpsychologie, 20,* 66–79. Figure 15-6: Marler, P., & Tamura, H. (1964). Culturally transmitted patterns of vocal behavior in sparrows. *Science, 146,* 1483–1486. Copyright 1964 by the AAAS. Figure 15-7: Marler, P., & Peters, S. (1981). Sparrows learn adult song and more from memory. *Science, 213,* 780–782. Copyright 1981 by the AAAS. Figure 15-9: Redrawn from Howells, W. W. (1973). *The evolution of the genus Homo*. Reading, MA: Addison-Wesley. Adapted by permission of The Benjamin/Cummings Publishing Company, Menlo Park, CA 94025. Excerpts from Denes, P. D., & Pinson, E. N. (1963), *The speech chain*. Copyright © 1963 by Bell Telephone Laboratories, Inc. Used by permission of Doubleday, a division of Bantam, Doubleday, Dell Publishing Group, Inc. Spotlight Figure 15-1: Geschwind, N., & Levitsky, W. (1968). Human brain: Left-right asymmetries in temporal speech region. *Science, 161,* 186–187. Copyright 1968 by the AAAS. Figure 15-13: Roberts, L. (1961). Activation and interference of cortical functions. Adapted from Sheer, D. E. (Ed.), (1961). *Electrical Stimulation of the brain: An interdisciplinary survey of neurobehavioral integrative systems,* (Austin: University of Texas Press) by permission of the University of Texas Press. Spotlight Figure 15-2: Ojemann, G., & Mateer, C. (1979). Human language cortex: Localization of memory, syntax, and sequential motor-phoneme identification systems. *Science, 205,* 1401–1403. Copyright 1979 by the AAAS. Figure 15-14: Illustration by Carol Donner from Geschwind, N. (1979). Specializations of the human brain, *Scientific American*, September 1979. Copyright 1979 by *Scientific American*, Inc. All rights reserved.

Chapter 16 Figure 16-12: Nebes, R., & Sperry, R. W. (1971). Hemispheric disconnection with cerebral birth injury in dominant arm area. *Neuropsychologia, 9,* 247. Copyright 1971, Pergamon Press PLC.

Author Index

Subject Index